Design Integration
Using Autodesk Revit

Daniel John Stine

ISBN: 978-1-58503-678-3

SDC
PUBLICATIONS

Schroff Development Corporation

www.SDCpublications.com

Schroff Development Corporation
P.O. Box 1334
Mission KS 66222
(913) 262-2664
www.SDCpublications.com

Publisher: Stephen Schroff

Autodesk Revit is a registered trademark of Autodesk, Inc.
Windows Vista & Windows 7 are trademarks of Microsoft.
Mac and Boot Camp are trademarks of Apple.
Parallels Desktop is a trademark of Parallels.

All other trademarks are trademarks of their respective holders.

Examination Copies:
Books received as examination copies are for review purposes only and may not be made available for student use. Resale of examination copies is prohibited.

Electronic Files:
Any electronic files associated with this book are licensed to the original user only. These files may not be transferred to any other party.

Foreword

The intent of this book is to provide the student with a well-rounded knowledge of Autodesk Revit tools and techniques for use in both academia and industry.

As an instructor, the author understands that many students in a classroom setting have varying degrees of computer experience. To help level the "playing felid" the first chapter is devoted to an introduction to computers. Much of the basics are covered, from computer hardware and software to file management procedures; including step-by-step instruction on using a flash drive!

Chapters 2 through 5 cover many of the Revit basics needed to successfully and efficiently work in the software. Once the fundamentals are covered, the remaining chapters walk the reader through a building project which is started from scratch so nothing is taken for granted by the reader or the author.

This book was designed for the building design industry. All three "flavors" of the Revit platform are introduced in this textbook. This approach gives the reader a broad overview of the Building Information Modeling (BIM) process. The topics cover the design integration of most of the building disciplines: Architectural, Interior Design, Structural, Mechanical, Plumbing and Electrical. Civil is not covered, but adding topography to your model is.

Throughout the book the student develops a two story law office. The drawings start with the floor plans and develop all the way to photo-realistic renderings similar to the one on the cover of this book. Along the way, the building's structure, ductwork, plumbing and electrical (power and lighting) are modeled.

The reader will have a thorough knowledge of many of the Revit basics needed to be productive in a classroom or office environment. Even if you will only be working with one "flavor" of *Revit* in your chosen profession, this book will give you important knowledge on how the other discipline will be doing their work and valuable insight on the overall process.

DVD:
An introduction to creating custom Revit content (families) is presented in chapter 16 and an introduction to Google SketchUp is offered in chapter 17, two bonus chapters provided on the DVD that comes with this book.

The DVD also contains chapter-starter files; these are models of the law office project completed up to the point of the current chapter. This allows instructors/students to jump around in the text, or to skip chapters. For example, an Interior Design class might model the building (walls, doors, windows, ceilings) and skip the structural chapter in order to focus on space layout.

Finally, a draft copy of *Roof Study Workbook* is also provided for use by the owner of the book. This document includes some information on controlling the top surface of the roof in Revit.

Software required:
To successfully complete the exercises in this book you will need to have access to Autodesk's *Revit Architecture 2012*, *Revit Structure 2012* and *Revit MEP 2012*. A 30-day trial of all three "flavors" may be downloaded from Autodesk's website. Additionally, qualifying students may download the free 13-month student version of the software from students.autodesk.com. Both versions are fully functional versions of the software.

The reader will also need access to the free *Autodesk Design Review 2012* DWFx viewer and markup application.

Instructors:
An Instructor's resource guide is available with this book. It contains:
- Answers to the questions at the end of each chapter
- Outline of tools and topics to be covered in each lesson's lecture
- Images of suggested student printouts to use for grading
- Suggestions for additional student work (for each lesson)

About the Author:
Dan Stine is a registered Architect with twenty years of experience in the architectural field. He currently works at LHB (a 160 person multidiscipline firm; www.LHBcorp.com) in Duluth, Minnesota as the CAD Administrator, providing training, customization and support for two regional offices. Mr. Stine has presented at Autodesk University (au.autodesk.com) and will also be presenting two sessions at the first ever Revit Technology Conference (revitconference.com.au/rtc2011us) this June in California.

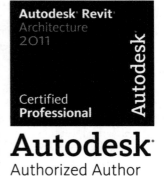

Dan has worked in a total of four firms. While at these firms, he has participated in collaborative projects with several other firms on various projects (including Cesar Pelli, Weber Music Hall – University of Minnesota - Duluth). Dan is a member of the *Construction Specification Institute* (CSI) and the *Autodesk Developer Network* (ADN) and also teaches *AutoCAD* and *Autodesk Revit* classes at Lake Superior College, for the Architectural Technology program; additionally, he is a Certified Construction Document Technician (CDT). Mr. Stine has also written the following textbooks (published by SDC Publications):
- *Commercial Design using Revit Architecture 2012*
- *Design Integration using Revit 2012 (Architecture, Structure and MEP)*
- *Residential Design using AutoCAD 2012*
- *Commercial Design using AutoCAD 2012*
- *Chapters in Architectural Drawing (with co-author Steven H. McNeill, AIA, LEED AP)*
- *Interior Design using Hand Sketching, SketchUp and Photoshop (also with Steven H. McNeill)*

Mr. Stine is the Assistant Cub Master for *Boy Scouts of America* Pack 3043 in Duluth, MN. He likes to spend time with his family, camping, watching movies, fishing and much more! Dan also enjoys riding his bicycle, along the shoreline of Lake Superior, to work when there is no snow on the ground. The total ride distance is only 4 miles but the elevation gain is over 500 feet. Luckily the uphill part is after work!

You can contact the publisher with comments or suggestions at **schroff@schroff.com**.
Please do not email with Revit questions unless they relate to a problem with this book.

Thanks:

Thanks to the following individuals who helped with technical edits and proofing.
Adam Lilyquist, CDT
Brad Anderson
Charles Bouschor II
Joel Aili
Kurt Jankofsky, LEED AP, CDT
Nauman Mysorewala, LEED AP; *College of Mount St. Joseph, Interior Design*

I could not have done this with out the support from my family; Cheri, Kayla & Carter.

Many thanks go out to Stephen Schroff and Schroff Development Corporation for making this book possible!

Table of Contents

DVD Contents

Videos

1. User Interface
2. Walls
3. Doors and Windows
4. Stairs
5. Roofs
6. Floors
7. Ceilings
8. Elevations
9. Sections
10. Schedules
11. Rendering
12. Design Options
13. Sheets and Sheet Lists
14. Worksharing Introduction
15. Phases
16. Sweeps and Reveals
17. Revit Structure
18. Revit MEP - Mechanical
19. Revit MEP - Electrical

Notes:

Lesson 1
Introduction to Computers

Although many design students have some experience using computers, many do not have a good working knowledge of the parts of a computer and what they do. The goal of this chapter is to provide a solid foundation in basic computer terms and functions. This study will help ensure students are able to hit the ground running when working through the sections in this book. The last part of this chapter will cover the essentials of file management, including saving and backing up your files.

Exercise 1-1:
Computer Basics: Terms and Functions

What you need to know
This study is not interested in the history or philosophy related to computers, but rather a more concise introduction will be presented. A person just starting to use a computer or learn a program, such as SketchUp AutoCAD, Revit or Photoshop, does not need to know everything about computers before being productive. This exercise will begin by presenting several computer terms and their functions. Many readers will be familiar with much of this information, but one will likely learn a few new things along the way.

Hardware

The next few pages will introduce various pieces of computer hardware, the portion of the computing experience on which a person can place their hands. This is in contrast to software and documents (covered later) which live electronically "within" the computer's hardware.

Computer
Some use the term "computer" in the all-inclusive sense – including the monitor, computer chassis, mouse, etc. Other times, the term "computer" is used to just describe the box to which the monitor and mouse connect. Either usage is valid. Finally, a laptop (see "Laptop" below) can be called a computer as well.

Computer: **Desktop Computer**

A desktop computer is most commonly used in the design profession due to the lower cost and additional "horsepower" when compared to a laptop. A desktop computer is modular; meaning the monitor, mouse, keyboard and speakers are separate components connected by wires (can be wireless). This allows for different hardware combinations depending on the needs of the user. CAD/BIM users typically need a larger, high resolution, monitor due to the large, complex drawings and amount of time spent looking at the screen in a given day.

Desktop computers are easier to enhance and upgrade than laptops as well. This is because of the large chassis (or box) in which the internal computer components are housed. An end user can easily add an additional hard drive, video card or RAM, for which most new computers allow room and connections. Depending on the age of the computer, however, it is often better to simply buy a new computer than it is to upgrade. For example, if a two year old computer were to be upgraded to a 64bit Operating System (OS), plus additional RAM, Video Card and a second hard drive installed to manage virtual memory, one might find that a brand new computer costs just a little more money and also has a better motherboard.

What kind of computer should a student buy?

When asking the question "what kind of a computer does a student need?" one might first consider if one is needed at all. Certainly a student may benefit from having access to their own personal computer but it may not be required. Some schools do require students to buy their own computer and software. Autodesk allows students to use their software for free (see website students.autodesk.com for more information), and Google offers a free version of SketchUp to everyone. But others do not, for example, there is no free version of Photoshop or Microsoft Office. Most schools provide computer labs that are accessible during class and at other times as well. Once the typical student is finished with school, their employer usually provides a computer to use while at work.

Most students who buy a computer get a laptop for its portability. It is very convenient to use your computer in class. Many schools provide wireless network access and internet connections throughout the school, and some also allow access to the printers via the wireless connection. Being able to work on CAD/BIM assignments and other homework can be especially convenient when students have jobs.

Although certain designs (i.e., CAD/BIM drawings) can become huge and extremely taxing on the computer and the software, most drawings done within the context of school do not demand the most powerful and expensive computers. Take a look at the manufacturer's recommendations for computers for the software you wish to use. Many, such as Autodesk, provide "minimum" and "preferred" system specifications. The minimum specifications will likely be sufficient in a classroom environment. Of course, if you can afford it, you will have a better overall experience with the "preferred" system.

When considering options for a new computer, in addition to the minimum system requirements, you may want to prioritize as follows:

- CPU (and bus speed)
- RAM (total amount and speed)
- Graphics Card (including its amount of RAM)
- Size of high resolution monitor/screen
- Warranty (especially for laptops which are more prone to damage as they are mobile and easily dropped)

Computer: **Laptop Computer**

Laptop computers are becoming more powerful and less expensive every year. The once clear line between desktop computers and laptops is beginning to become not so clear (laptops used to be very expensive and slower). However, as stated in the previous section, a desktop computer is often a better overall value in terms of computing power. With that being said, the student would likely give up a little computing horsepower for the convenience of portability. Most projects worked on in school do not consume the kind of resources needed in a professional design firm.

As with most things, you get what you pay for. Extremely inexpensive laptops have low quality displays, low end graphics cards, minimal RAM and may not even have a CD/DVD drive. On the opposite end of the spectrum are high end desktop-grade laptops that have large, high quality displays, a fast CPU, the ability to house two hard drives and more.

Due to the compact nature of laptops, they are more difficult to upgrade. It is not too hard to add more RAM or replace the hard drive with a higher capacity unit, but rarely is a graphics card or display upgraded.

An extended warranty is a good idea for laptops given they are portable and more prone to damage. Some extended warranties will only cover parts that have stopped working under otherwise normal conditions, while better (and likely more expensive) ones will cover everything except it being lost or stolen, including the laptop being dropped or a soda spilled on the keyboard!

Computer: **Central Processing Unit (CPU)**

The CPU (aka *processor*) is the "heart" of the computer; this is where all the work is done. The speed and number of processors is a key factor in how a computer performs overall.

The speeds are measured in Gigahertz (GHz) and a higher number is better (i.e., faster). Dealing with the heat these things produce is an ongoing challenge for computer manufacturers – especially in laptops.

Until recently, the average computer on the market only had one CPU. But newer technology is shifting that trend toward multiple processors packed into one unit. These *Dual, Quad* and *six core* processors are becoming very popular; multiple cores cast into one die (i.e., CPU).

Multiple processors are useful for a couple of reasons.

1. When multiple applications (i.e., programs) are running, each can use a different processor and thus keep the overall system robust and working faster. One application might be AutoCAD or Revit *Architecture* doing a rendering, while the user is working in a spreadsheet or a word-processor with minimal delays.

2. A few applications, like Autodesk's 3DS Max have the ability to utilize multiple processors in order to complete a task sooner. Many applications can only use one processor at a time.

3. In the case of most software, multi-threading is accomplished by the computer spreading out work over multiple processors. The processors can run in parallel to shorten computing time.

Computer: **RAM**

The formal name, which nobody really uses, is Random Access Memory (RAM) – also called Temporary Memory (or just Memory). RAM is extremely fast memory that is only available and can only hold information when it has power, in contrast to hard drives (aka permanent memory).

When a computer is turned on, the operating system (e.g., Windows Vista) is loaded into RAM from the hard drive. Then, when a user starts a program (e.g., Photoshop), that program is loaded into RAM. While using an *application* (program), the user opens a *document* (e.g., an image file), the file is then also loaded into RAM. In short, RAM allows multiple configurations to take place. For example, memory might hold an application one minute and then a video file, and then finally a Photoshop file. It is truly multi-dimensional.

Bits and pieces of the information in RAM are sent over to the CPU as needed to perform the additions and edits you are making to the *document* via the *application*.

> **WARNING:**
> *When working on a* document *(in any application, e.g., AutoCAD, Word, etc.) the user should* Save *regularly to avoid losing work due to a computer "crash" (i.e., software failure) or power failure. Any information in RAM is immediately lost when power is lost or the computer is restarted. Therefore, committing/writing the information in RAM to the hard drive (aka, permanent storage) using the* Save *command is very important. Some programs, like Word and AutoCAD, have an "autosave" feature that helps avoid losing large amounts of work. In most programs, pressing the* **Ctrl** *key followed by the* **S** *key causes the application to perform a* Save, *writing the information from RAM to the computer's hard drive.*

As one can guess, if too many *applications* and *documents* are opened at once, the space in RAM can reach maximum capacity. MS Windows has a backup plan in that event; the *operating system* begins to write information from RAM to the hard drive as *virtual memory*. This is good in that it keeps the computer from "crashing", but bad in the sense that the hard drive is significantly slower than fast-reacting RAM when sending data to the CPU. This slowness (or better, *slow access memory*) becomes a virtual bottleneck and the entire computing experience is degraded.

The cost of RAM continues to decline, but it still is far from free. A computer should meet the minimum RAM requirement stated by the software manufacturer, for both the OS and the application, keeping in mind these minimums are not likely taking into account additional applications being used concurrently. RAM is fairly easy to add for most computers. A student should buy as much as they can afford for a better computing experience.

One final note about RAM: a computer typically only has 4-6 slots for RAM and they usually have to be used in pairs. Thus, if all the slots are full, the existing memory may have to be discarded in order to upgrade. Generally, when it is time to upgrade, the cost of the on-board memory is so inexpensive, completely removing the old RAM and replacing it with all new RAM makes the most sense.

Computer: **Motherboard**

The *motherboard* is essentially a large circuit board within the computer. All the computer hardware connects directly to it: the CPU, RAM, graphics card (which then connects to the monitor), hard drive, mouse, keyboard, etc. There is a lot more that could be said about the motherboard, but we will save that for the computer science and engineering students!

Computer: **Graphics Card**

When the computer needs to display something on the screen, it does so through the *graphics card*. A graphics card has its own CPU (which is actually called a GPU, *graphics processing unit*) and RAM which are dedicated to displaying complex graphics. Some graphics cards are built into the computer's motherboard on less expensive computers and are not well suited for intense CAD/BIM programs (the RAM needed for the graphics card is usually taken from the computer's main RAM). A high quality graphics card consists of a separate card that inserts into a special slot on the computer's motherboard. One side of the card is exposed on the back of the computer so the monitor cable can be plugged into it. High end graphics cards can be made more powerfully by "teaming" multiple graphics cards.

Some programs are designed to take more advantage of the power of graphics cards than are others. An application such as Autodesk's 3DS Max can use many of the features on a high end graphics card; the graphics card's software will even have special settings in it for 3DS Max (as well as other popular applications with which they have partnered). However, other applications do not use some of these special features.

AutoCAD has a special optimization utility that automatically runs when the program is first launched (and manually from the *Options* dialog). Autodesk Revit has a special setting within its *Options* dialog in which the graphics card's "hardware acceleration" can be used, as does SketchUp and Photoshop.

As one can see, the graphics card is an important part of the computer in the CAD/BIM world. When selecting a graphics card consider the following:
- Does the manufacturer's website offer regular software updates that can be downloaded?
- Does the manufacturer mention the CAD/BIM software you use in any of its literature or on its website? They are likely to mention widely used programs such as AutoCAD and 3DS Max, but may not mention other programs such as Revit or SketchUp.
- Does the CAD/BIM software manufacturer recommend a specific graphics card or manufacturer? Most will not "play favorites" and recommend one over another, but they may list minimum specifications (e.g., RAM) or list several cards that have been tested and found compatible with the software.
- What are the connection options to the monitor? See the discussion on monitors for more information.

Computer: **Drives**

Hard Drive

The computer *hard drive* is where all the software is stored: the operating system (OS), the applications (e.g., Photoshop, MS Word, AutoCAD, Revit) and the documents (e.g., drawings, letters, photos, music files, etc.). Most computers come with an adequately sized hard drive, especially in an office setting where all documents are stored on the server so they can be automatically backed up each night.

Given the fact that hard drives have moving parts, they are susceptible to failure. It is vital that important files are backed up. Several options are available for backing up data: tape drives (used on servers and some desktops), external hard drives (see the next topic on this), disc (CD, DVD, Blu-ray – these would be a manual process), and flash drives. Several internet backup companies have recently entered the market, offering both manual and automatic backup of data files over the internet; this has the added benefit of residing at a remote location in case of fire, theft or natural disaster.

Desktop computers and some laptops have the ability to house two (or more) internal hard drives. A high end CAD/BIM station might have a second hard drive dedicated solely to Window's virtual memory.

Again, due to the moving parts in a hard drive, they tend to be the bottleneck in speed, especially when opening and saving a file. Server hard drives are usually faster but much more expensive.

External Hard Drive

External hard drives come in all shapes and sizes. They typically plug into a USB port and sit near the computer. It is possible to carry one around but caution must be used so as not to damage it. A flash drive has no moving parts, which makes it better suited for portability. An external hard drive can have terabytes (2,000,000MB) of space, whereas, at the time of this writing, a flash drive can have up to 64GB (64,000MB) of space.

Some external hard drives come with software that can be installed on a computer which automatically backs up data from the main hard drive (e.g., emails, documents, photos, etc.).

Flash Drive

A *flash drive* is a "must have" for a student. It is a small portable data storage unit that plugs into any computer's USB port. Once plugged in, after a few seconds of configuration, a new drive letter shows up on the computer and one will have access to the data and any free storage space on it. Flash drives, which are solid state, are fast and tend to last a long time, compared to the moving parts of hard drives. These devices continue to get cheaper and hold more data. The larger flash drives, 64GB capacity, are larger than most students would need for school work; a 4 to 8GB unit would likely suffice.

A flash drive should be used to back up all school work, whether it is done on a school computer or at home. It is important to protect your data (i.e., documents) from loss or corruption. One does not need to back up software, just one's drawings, papers and photos for example.

> **TIP:**
> *AutoCAD, Revit and SketchUp create backup files that do not need to be backed up, they are the same size file as the primary file and would quickly use up all your available space. AutoCAD's backup files have a .BAK extension and Revit files have the same file name and extension, but have a suffix added to the file name, like "001", "002" and "003". SketchUp backup files have a .SKB file extension.*

Online Storage

It is now possible to save data to the internet (aka, *"cloud"*). Several companies are now providing "cloud" data storage space to which you upload files to a user account and can then download them from anywhere in the world, as long as you remember your user name and password. Some offer this service for a fee, offering perks such as guaranteed backup, redundant servers/locations, 24/7/365 access and software that will automatically backup user data files. Others offer free storage space with various limitations and may display advertising. Simply search the internet for "free online storage" to learn more.

Online storage is a great benefit to a student as it allows files to be safely backed up away from home and school, protected from fire, theft, etc. Also, as just mentioned, the files are accessible from any computer connected to the internet. When this process is used, the files are copied to the "internet" once the CAD/BIM program is closed. It would not be advisable, or even possible in most instances, to work directly in the file stored online.

Compact Disk (CD)

A CD is the original "disk" format that holds about 650MB of data. Most computers come with a drive that can read these, and many have the ability to write data to blank disks.

DVD

A DVD was initially created to store feature-length movies and then became a data storage option. A DVD can hold 4.7GB (4,700MB) of data (and more in some cases). Double-sided DVD's can stretch the storage to 8.5GB of data and are readable by most DVD equipped computers. Many computers come with a drive that can read these, and many have the ability to write data to blank DVD disks.

Blu-ray Disk (BD)

A Blu-ray Disk (aka, BD) was designed to store HD movies. This format can store 25-50GB of data (single layer vs. double layer). The most amazing thing is that the disk is the same size for a CD, DVD and BD. Most computers do not yet have the ability to read or write to a Blu-ray disk.

Computer: **Monitor**

Monitors come in many shapes and sizes. The older style monitor is the CRT; this is the deep, heavy monitor with a glass tube. The new monitors are typically LCD; they are approximately 1″ thick and are very lightweight.

In the world of CAD/BIM it is ideal to have a large monitor given the fact that the designer spends a large amount of time looking at the screen. A 20″-24″ widescreen LCD monitor capable of high resolutions is commonplace in the design industry. Note that computer monitors are capable of higher resolutions than 1080p HD televisions, so don't get confused. A widescreen 24″ monitor can have a resolution of 2560x1600, which is the number of pixels in each direction. 1600 pixels is a lot more than an HDTV's 1080 pixels.

Monitors can also come with built-in *card readers* (e.g., to download photos from a digital camera's memory card), USB hubs and speakers. All of these increase cost but the added convenience and reduced clutter on the desktop may be worth it.

Monitor Cable/Connection types: HDMI, Display Port, DVI, S-Video, VGA.

HDMI is typically for HDTV's and Blu-ray players. They have a digital video signal which also includes the audio, thus requiring fewer cables. The newest computer to monitor cable is the **Display Port** (make sure your graphics card and monitor both support it, or that you have the proper adaptors). **DVI** is a digital cable that has been around for a few years as has **S-Video** (S-Video is found on some laptops and not commonly used). Finally, **VGA** is the age-old analog cable, which is best to avoid as it is desirable to have the best picture possible due to the time spent looking at the screen.

Computer: **Speakers**

Speakers are not necessary for CAD software directly. However, many training videos and webcasts over the internet make speakers a highly recommended option.

Computer: **Mouse**

The main thing to know about a mouse is that it should have a decent scroll wheel. In AutoCAD, and Revit, the scroll wheel is used to quickly **zoom** in and out as well as **pan** around the current drawing. ***FYI:*** *Panning is moving the part of the drawing seen on the screen, not actually moving the drawing.* Try to avoid scroll wheels that tilt left and right to scroll horizontally in MS *Word* and *Excel* as they make the button action of the wheel more difficult to operate accurately.

A wireless mouse is nice but more of a convenience than a necessity.

Computer: **Input/Output**

Printer

Most school and business printers are capable of printing on 8 ½" x 11" and 11" x 17" paper. Toner based printers are usually faster than ink based (aka, inkjet) printers; they are also less susceptible to smudging than ink.

In workgroup environments, the printer may be built into the copier, which can also have a scanner and fax machine built in. They are connected to a network and located in a central area in the office or class lab.

This image shows an office printer. This class of printer typically also has a built-in scanner and fax machine. Scans can be directed to a shared folder on the network; as a PDF or JPG formatted file.

Plotter

A plotter is only different from a printer in the size of paper on which it prints. A plotter prints on large paper, such as 22" x 34" or 36" x 48". The paper is typically on a roll; when the plotter is done printing it cuts the paper off the roll at the required length. An example of a plotter can be seen in the image below.

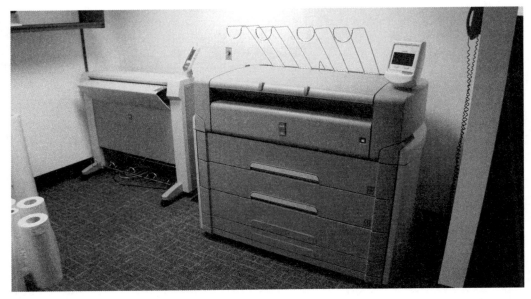

This image shows a large format plotter (right) and scanner (left). Scans can be sent directly to the plotter as a copy or to a file for use in various software programs such as Photoshop.

Scanner

Most design firms have the ability to scan paper (i.e., hardcopy) documents to a digital file. Many multi-function printers can scan 8 ½″ x 11″ (i.e., letter) and 11″x17″ (i.e., tabloid) sized paper. Scanners often have something called an automatic document feeder on top which allows several pages to be loaded and scanned automatically. The final file can even be a single, multi-page PDF (PDF = Portable Document Format), a highly shareable file format.

Another standard option in most design firms is a large format scanner. Oftentimes the drawings of an original building need to be scanned and saved to a file because the originals must to be returned to the client or building owner. These scanned files can be used to reference dimensions when drawing the existing building on the computer. The digital files can even be linked into the CAD/BIM program and traced over if the quality and accuracy is good enough.

TIP:

Scanned images can be very large files depending on the scanner settings. Factors such as resolution (dpi) and color can make a big difference. When scanned images need to be printed at a large size, the resolution needs to be increased to keep the printout from looking pixilated (i.e., like little boxes). Also, scanning a drawing with redlines would likely require a color scanner, all of which can significantly increase the file size. Finding the right balance takes practice, trial and error.

Finally, linking large scanned images into a CAD/BIM program can seriously slow down the program, e.g., Open, Zoom, Pan, Save, etc. Oftentimes it would be better to redraw a building rather than rely on a scanned image. It might be acceptable to link the image in temporarily to trace over it and then remove it when complete.

Software

Once the computer hardware is in place, it is necessary to have the appropriate software to utilize it. Software is the part of a computing experience that cannot be touched *per se*; it is possible to touch a hard drive, but it does not feel any different if it is empty or totally full of software or data.

Software may come preloaded on a computer, be downloaded from the internet or come on a CD/DVD, or be written by the computer user.

Software: **Operating System**

When the computer is first turned on the *Operating System (OS)*, stored on the hard drive, is loaded into RAM and displayed on the screen.

Most computers are sold with an OS, so the only time someone usually buys an OS apart from a computer is when they are upgrading. For example, if a two year old computer has Microsoft Windows Vista, it may be upgraded to Windows 7 (the newest OS from Microsoft at the time of this printing).

Microsoft Windows 7 is the newest operating system from Microsoft. This is the box provided when purchasing the software apart from a computer.

This image shows the Graphical User Interface (GUI) for a typical PC Operating System; this loads automatically every time the computer is turned on.

Most of the CAD world is standardized on the PC versus the Apple Macintosh (Mac). There are some CAD applications that run on the Mac such as AutoCAD; SketchUp and Photoshop also have Mac versions. Revit and 3DS Max are only designed to run on a PC along with Microsoft's OS. It is possible to run Revit on a Mac using an add-on program for the Mac (e.g., Apple Boot Camp, Parallels Desktop, etc.).

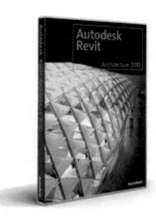

Also, it is possible to install a Microsoft OS on a Mac. When the computer is started you select which OS you want to launch. You have to purchase a full version of the Microsoft OS in addition to the Mac computer (which comes with a proprietary OS). Additionally, if you have a program such as Adobe Photoshop, it would have to be installed twice. Once for each OS, in order to use it in both OS environments.

The student will likely get a better value sticking with a PC and will gain experience and learn workflows that are more likely encountered in the workplace than if a Mac were used.

Software: **Applications**

Once a person has a computer with an *operating system* they can then begin to purchase and install *applications*. The only limit on the number of applications you can have installed on a computer is your budget and available space on your hard drive.

Applications (i.e., software) can cost anywhere from nothing to thousands of dollars. Think of applications as tools, much like your desk chair, lights, stapler, pens, etc., used to get your work done accurately and efficiently. The cost of software often relates to:

1. How sophisticated it is (e.g., it was time consuming and challenging to write the software).
2. The amount of work it can help you to do compared to other programs or doing it manually (i.e., drawing with pencils or using a calculator).
3. Competition. Do other programs exist that help keep the price competitive?

Most professional applications have hundreds of employees that write the software, test it to make sure it works correctly, write user manuals and tutorials, market the product and the list goes on. All this and regular updates cost a lot of money. Autodesk updates their design software yearly.

Application costs (approximately):
- Autodesk Revit Architecture: $5,495
- Autodesk AutoCAD: $3,995
- Adobe Photoshop CS5: $699
- SketchUp Pro 8 $495
- Microsoft Office Home & Student: $149

Each application has its own set of system requirements that should be compared to your computer system before buying any software. Some programs require a lot of horsepower to make the program run smoothly. This information can be found on the packaging, if shopping in a store, or on the manufacturer's website.

> **NOTE:** *Some programs such as AutoCAD and Revit cannot be purchased in a store; they must be obtained through authorized resellers.*

Applications can come on CD, DVD or be downloaded from the internet.

> **TIP:** *Beware of buying "used" software. Some software is pirated, which is illegal, and updates and upgrades are therefore not available. Also, the software license agreement which you accept before you can use the software often forbids resale of the software; this is the case with Autodesk software. Really cheap software online typically IS too good to be true and should be avoided.*

Autodesk provides free software to students. If you are a student with a valid EDU email address, you should be able to register and download Autodesk design software for free. Autodesk allows students to download and install a student version of their design software (e.g., Revit and AutoCAD) for use in the education process. The software is usable for 13 months from the day it is activated. The student version is the same as the full version with few exceptions. The student version cannot be used in any way to make money (i.e., you cannot draw up someone's house plans for a few hundred dollars). Also, a student stamp appears on the four edges of any page that is printed.

Visit the following website to learn more: **students.autodesk.com**

> **WARNING:** *If you are working in a design office while going to school, do not open and edit your employer's CAD files. The student stamp will be permanently added to the file. Even when printed from a full version of AutoCAD, not the student version, the "student version" stamp will appear at the perimeter of the page.*

An application's size on the hard drive can vary greatly. The list below compares five applications (note that 1GB is equal to 1000MB).

- AutoCAD: 812mb
- Autodesk Revit Architecture: 1.56gb
- Adobe Photoshop: 416mb (64bit pro version)
- Microsoft Office: 419mb (professional version)
- SketchUp   131mb

Software: **32bit versus 64bit**

Virtually all computer CPUs and motherboards (aka, computer architecture) have been 64bit for a number of years now. However, software has mainly been 32bit, thus not taking full advantage of the additional power, bandwidth and memory available. Software needs to be significantly re-written to support 64bit operating systems and hardware.

A lot of 32bit applications will run on a 64bit operating system. This is because the operating system has a "compatibility" mode built into it. This helps sell customers on 64bit OS, knowing that they will not have to immediately buy all new application software.

One of the major benefits of the 64bit OS and applications in the CAD world is the access gained to more RAM. Programs such as Revit can require a significant amount of RAM when working on large multi-million dollar projects. A 32bit OS can only access about 3.5mb of Ram, whereas a 64bit OS does not have a practical limit. Technically speaking, a 64bit OS could have a little over **17 billion GB of RAM**. However, not too many computer manufacturers are providing this configuration yet! A computer with 8 – 16GB of RAM is considered pretty high at the moment.

Most of Autodesk's products come in both 32bit and 64bit versions. If you buy AutoCAD, the DVD will have both versions on it. Other than the size of file/project that can be worked on, there is usually no discernable difference to the user when working with the software.

> *TIP: Some older hardware, such as printers, scanners, palm pilots, digital cameras, etc., may not work at all in a 64bit OS environment. Manufacturers of some of these products may have discontinued support for outdated technology in order to focus on new and future technology.*

Software: **Updates and Upgrades**

Advanced applications, such as AutoCAD, Revit and Photoshop, are always changing to meet the demands of the design industry. Every year or two a software company will come out with an update to their application(s). This provides new features with the goal of creating better designs more efficiently. Updates also help keep the software companies in business! Operating systems are updated less frequent due to their large impact on hardware and applications. However, security patches or bug fixes are done on a monthly basis to keep systems safe and stable.

Upgrades cost a fraction of the original cost of the software.

Application upgrade costs (approximately):
- Autodesk Revit Architecture: $895
- Autodesk AutoCAD: $595
- Adobe Photoshop CS5 $199
- SketchUp Pro 8 $95

With Autodesk software, a subscription option exists which allows you to budget a specific amount each year for the applications you have. Then, when a new version is released you have automatic access to the software and any extras that are only available on the subscription website. Over time, this works out to be the cheapest way to go. It is not less expensive to skip every other release either because the cost goes up when the program you are upgrading from is older. For example, the AutoCAD upgrade price above is for upgrading from release 2010 to 2011. To go from release 2009 to 2011 is $1,995, not $595.

Also, given the complexity of the software and its ability to be customized, the inevitably of "bugs" (i.e., errors in the programs code) are found in the software. When "bugs" are found, software manufacturers release "service packs" (or web updates, hot fixes, patches, etc.). These "fixes" are typically downloaded from the internet for free. You may have to periodically check for these updates as some software manufacturers do not inform you that an update is available.

Some software can automatically check for updates and let you know when they are available. For example, Microsoft's operating systems and the Office suites are able to do this. This can be very important when it comes to the OS as some of the updates deal with viruses and security issues.

Software: **Documents**

Once you have a computer, with an OS, and one or more applications, you can start creating *documents*. Whenever you save your work within an application, you are creating a "document" file on the computer's hard drive.

Here are a few examples of documents and their extensions: MS Word letter (DOCx), MS Excel spreadsheet (XLSx), AutoCAD drawing (DWG), Revit project (RVT), SketchUp (SKP), and Photoshop (PSD).

The OS and application files tend to take up more space on your hard drive than do document files. However, document backups, archives and copies can take up a significant amount of space. Therefore, it is good practice to occasionally check the amount of free space on your hard drive. Running out of disk space while saving can corrupt your document.

Enough cannot be said about backing up your document files. The document files, for the most part, are the only files that need to be backed up. If your computer crashes and you replace it or the hard drive, it is better to reinstall the OS and the applications from the original CD/DVD's than restore them from a backup. Also, backing up the OS and applications would take a lot more time to complete.

Most organizations require that all document files be saved on a server so everyone has access to them and they automatically get backed up every night by the IT department, or in a smaller office where the architect, interior designer or engineer wears multiple hats.

Software: **Viruses and Hackers**

It seems there is always somebody in the world looking to make a dishonest buck or make another person's life more complicated. In the computer world, these come in the form of *viruses* and *hackers*.

A *virus* is a program that somehow becomes installed on your computer and does something you have not authorized. Sometimes the virus causes great harm to your computer's data (i.e., files on the hard drive) and other times they send personal information over the internet without your knowledge.

Several *anti-virus software applications* exist to help protect your computer from viruses and hackers. It is absolutely critical that a high quality anti-virus application be installed on your computer. If you are using a computer in a school lab, it will have likely have an anti-virus program running. Additionally, the entire institution will usually be behind a *Firewall* (which detects viruses and hackers before they even get close to the end user's computers).

Software: **Piracy**

As the saying goes "nothing in life is free"; this is mostly true for software. Unfortunately, it is a challenge to get everyone who uses the software to pay for it. This is not a problem for hardware manufacturers; if someone wants a new hard drive they have to pay for it before one is given to them. With software, things are a little different. It is possible to illegally share software with others and download bootlegged software from the internet. Most software manufacturers develop ways to prevent this by requiring software to be activated online using a unique serial number before the software becomes fully functional.

Most software licenses only allow installation onto one computer. It does not matter if a person owns three computers and would only ever use one at a time. However, some programs have what is called a network license, in which case it can be installed on every computer. This is when a user opens a program (e.g., AutoCAD), a license is "pulled" from the pool of available licenses.

Installing software that has not been paid for is called *piracy*. The software company has intellectual rights to the software and its usage. When it is discovered that a business or person is illegally using software (i.e., pirating), a lawsuit is filed in order to get compensated.

Oftentimes students have access to cheap or free software. Student software usually has a built-in time limit (e.g., Autodesk software is 13 months); at the end of that time period, if still a student, the new version may be downloaded and used for another 13 months.

For more information on software piracy, visit Business Software Alliance: **www.bsa.org**.

Network

A typical network involves one or more servers and several clients (i.e., your computer). Each client computer, network printer/copier and VoIP phone (Voice Over IP – i.e., network cables) has a physical wire that runs to the server room. There the unit connects to a large panel called a switch, which then connects to the server.

A server can be a regular computer or a room with modular computer components installed on racks. A server does the following:

- centralizes hard drives
- performs the scheduled backups
- manages network enabled printers
- runs the email system
- provides a connection to the internet
- controls security (who has access to what)
- ties into the VoIP (voice over IP) telephone system
- allows external access to office recourses

The main things a student needs to know about a network are that it provides access to your files from multiple computers on the system and it is where all documents are backed up.

Wireless Network

A wireless network allows access to the network via radio waves and thus does not require a wire. This technology has advanced in recent years by improving speed and security. However, a wired connection is still faster and more secure, although wireless networks allow computers to be placed where it would be difficult to run wires.

Many places now provide wireless network connectivity to their patrons. For example, coffee shops, hotels, public libraries, schools, etc. This can be handy if you have a laptop and need to access the internet while studying away from home or school. Of course, this can be a distraction as well. Spending too much time browsing the web or checking out social networking sites can burn up valuable study time!

Make sure your internet security suite [which includes firewall, malware, antivirus, and antispyware] is up-to-date prior to using any public/un-secured wireless network. A computer infection can happen within minutes when your internet security suite is out of date; always update your internet security suite prior to surfing the web on a new wireless network.

Exercise 1-2:
Overview of the Windows User Interface

Introduction:

Every program or software application has a ***user interface*** (UI). This is the way in which you, the "user", tell the computer what you want it to do. The UI can also be referred to as a *graphical user interface* (GUI) due to the graphical icons and dialog boxes, as compared to the mainly text interface that was once common several years ago.

The image below shows the UI for Microsoft's **Windows 7** operating system (OS). This, or something very similar, is what is seen when the computer first starts. The text following this image and on the next few pages describes each of the main components of the UI.

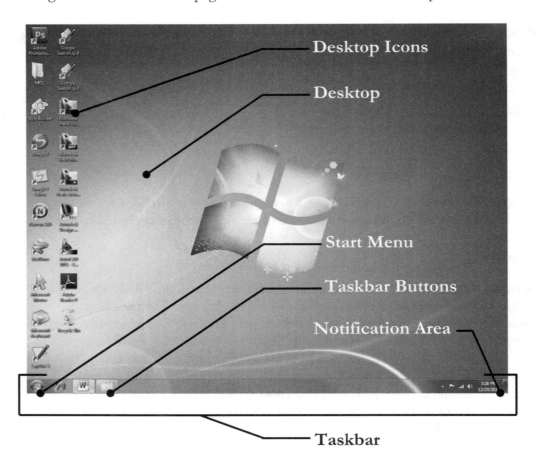

Microsoft's *Windows XP* and *Windows Vista* are very similar to what is shown above for *Windows 7*. You should be able to follow with any of these operating system versions.

Desktop:

The desktop serves two main purposes:

1) To hold *desktop icons* (see next section), and

2) As an area on which one or more *application window(s)* is open

Application windows can be "<u>maximized</u>" (i.e., "full screen") to fill the entire screen or they can be "<u>sized</u>" on the *desktop* in order to view two or more applications at once. Also, applications can be "<u>minimized</u>" to the *Taskbar* so they are not visible on the *desktop*, but are still open and quickly accessible.

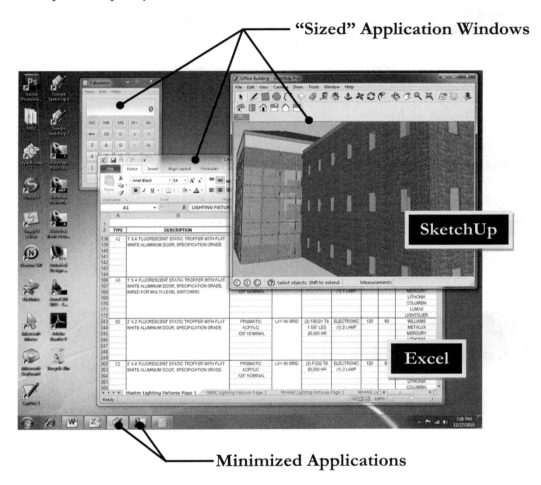

"Sized" Application Windows

Minimized Applications

This notion of "windows" on the *desktop* is where the name of the OS comes from; i.e., Microsoft's *Windows 7*.

> ***FYI:*** Microsoft *is the name of the company that makes the software, and* 7 *is the specific version of Windows OS.*

In the upper right corner of each application window are three buttons. The middle one changes depending on the current state of the window size. When the application window is "maximized", that is, it fills the entire *desktop*, the middle button shows a graphic in the button that represents "sized" windows. Thus, clicking it changes the window from being "maximized" to being "sized" (see the first image below). Conversely, if the middle button shows a "maximize" icon, then the window is currently "sized" (see second image below).

The far left icon (in both images below) will "minimize" the application down to the *taskbar* so it is not visible on the *desktop*. On the far right is the "**Close** application" icon. When clicking the red "x" to close an application, it will prompt you to save any changes that have not already been saved before closing.

Window Icons while maximized   *Window Icons while sized*

Some applications, such as AutoCAD, have a second set of these icons (see image below). The upper set is for the application, and the lower set is for the current *active* document.

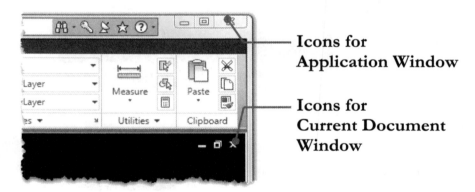

Icons for Application Window

Icons for Current Document Window

When the document windows are "sized", each document window has its own set of icons, as seen in the image below.

One document window is always "active"; the title bar is darker to indicate this.

Title Bar

TIP: *Double-clicking on the Title Bar for an application or document will "maximize" or "tile" it – the setting will be opposite of whatever the current state is.*

Desktop Icons:

The *desktop* may contain the following types of files in general:

- Documents
- Folders
- Shortcuts (for folders, documents and programs on your computer).

The image to the right shows a sampling of *desktop icons* presented in the same order as the list above (i.e., in the top row are documents, next folders and then shortcuts).

02157LIGH...   CFB Shed.rvt   _02157LIGH...

Misc   Kitchen   temp

AutoCAD 2010 - E...   Autodesk Revit Arch...   Adobe Acrobat 9 Standard

Another icon found on the *desktop* is the **Recycle Bin**. Anytime a file is deleted from your computer's hard drive, it is moved into the *Recycle Bin*. This is good information for the student learning to use computers and/or CAD. On occasion you may need to double-click on the *Recycle Bin* icon and retrieve a file or two. Consequently, a deleted file is not really deleted and still takes up space on your computer's hard drive. There are settings to control how space is used. Once this limit is reached, the oldest files in the *Recycle Bin* are deleted to make room for newer files. If space is at a premium on your hard drive, you may want to occasionally empty out the *Recycle Bin*. To do this, simply right-click on the *Recycle Bin* icon and select *Empty Recycle Bin*. If you have plenty of disk space, it is better to leave the files in the *Recycle Bin* so they are accessible if needed at a later time.

Recycle Bin   Recycle Bin
empty   *filled*

> **NOTE:** *Files deleted off of a network drive or flash drive are* **not** *copied to your computer's hard drive and placed in the* Recycle Bin. *The image above shows the empty versus filled (not necessarily full) icon.*

The *desktop* icons can be manually dragged around to reposition them on the *desktop*. It is also possible to **right-click on the *desktop*** and select from a few options related to *Desktop* icon organization and visibility. Those right-click options are shown in the two images below:

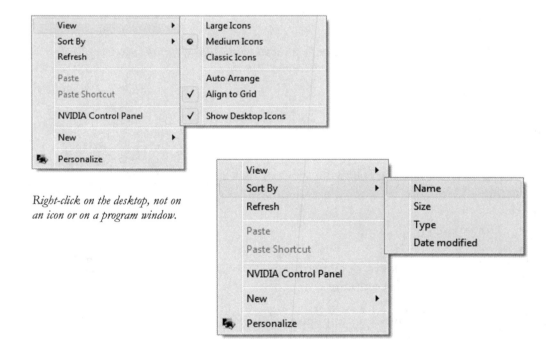

Right-click on the desktop, not on an icon or on a program window.

Start Menu:

The *Start* menu is a pivotal tool in the UI. The *Start* menu allows quick, convenient access to several tasks. Below is a brief overview followed by a more detailed description:

- Start installed programs
- Access icons for recently used programs
- Search for files, folders, and programs
- Adjust computer settings
- Turn off the computer

Click here to access the Windows *Start* menu

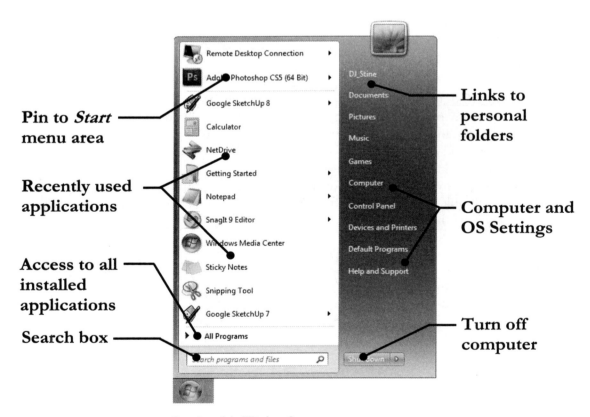

Overview of the Windows Start menu

Recently used applications

This area shows a list of recently used applications. This is convenient as it takes less time to get to the icons for programs you use frequently (note that the terms *application* and *program* are synonymous). Single-clicking on one of these files starts the program. Right-clicking on one of these files shows a handful of options, including "Remove from this list" and "Pin to Start Menu" so it always shows.

All Programs

When clicking on the *All Programs* link in the image on the previous page, the "recently used applications" list is replaced with the *All Programs* list.

The image to the right shows the *All Programs* list and the number of clicks required to start AutoCAD 2011. Note that the first click is on the *All Programs* list (seen in the image above), which then changes to the "Back" link shown in the image to the right.

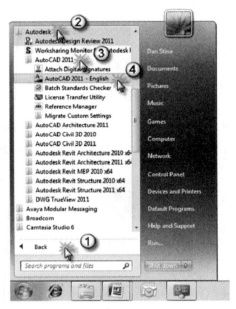

> *TIP: Dragging an icon from this list to the desktop, while holding the **Ctrl** key, will add a copy of the icon to the desktop.*

Computer and OS Settings

A computer has many options and settings to control how it operates and looks; the two groups of links in the lower right are for this. The *Computer* link opens a window that allows you to copy, move and delete files and folders.

The *Control Panel* gives you access to hardware settings; for example, you can specify how fast you have to double-click an icon before Windows will run it. You can also add and remove programs via the *Control Panel*.

Search Box

Rather than browsing through the *Start* menu looking for a specific tool, icon, or *application*, you can just start typing its name in the *Search Box*. As soon as you start typing, Windows begins to search for items; you do <u>not</u> need to press **Enter**.

A sample search for Revit is shown in the image to the right. Notice the search box only has the first three letters entered and the Revit application has already been located. Windows searches for *Programs, Favorites and History, Files* and *Communications* (i.e., emails).

Clicking the "**X**" to the right of the *Search Box* will restore the *Start Menu*. Closing the *Start* menu (by clicking off of it somewhere, or pressing the **Esc** key, will also restore the *Start* menu to its original hidden condition.

Start menu: using the Search Box to locate programs, files and emails.

Links to personal folders

The links in the upper right of the *Start* menu are shortcuts to your personal folders, which are tied into the login name used to access the computer; this mainly applies to computers in an office or at school. If multiple people use the same computer, Windows will make a set of folders for each user; each user's icons will be mapped accordingly, based on login name.

> **WARNING:** *The files in your "personal" folders are still accessible by others; they are just not "connected" to the links in the Start menu. This is another reason to backup often!*

Taskbar:

The *taskbar* can generally be thought of as the entire bar across the bottom of the *desktop* as shown in the image below.

The *Start* menu, on the far left, was covered in the previous section. The remaining elements of the Window's *taskbar* will now be covered.

Quick Launch Toolbar (only for Windows XP and Vista)

The *Quick Launch Toolbar* is shown in the image below. It is the series of icons directly to the right of the *Start* menu. These icons are always visible, unlike the *desktop* icons, and only require a single-click. It is typically not turned on by default on most computers. However, it is a very handy feature and easy to enable.

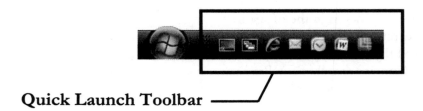

Quick Launch Toolbar ——

To enable the *Quick Access Toolbar* do the following:
1. Right-click on the *taskbar*.
2. Select *Properties* (see image below).
3. On the *taskbar*, check "Show Quick Launch."
4. Uncheck "Lock the taskbar" (see image on next page).

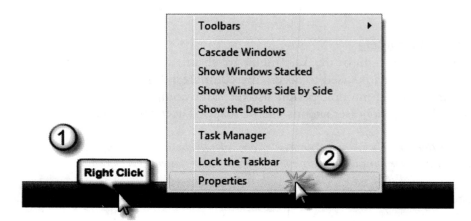

Right-clicking on the Windows taskbar

TIP: *In Windows 7 you can right click on any button within the Start menu and select "Pin to Taskbar". This will add a button to the taskbar; it is always there, even when the program is closed. So, the Quick Launch Toolbar is essentially built into the taskbar in Windows 7.*

Taskbar Properties (pre Windows 7)

Application icons may be dragged from the *desktop* or the *Start* menu onto the *Quick Launch Toolbar*. It is also possible to right-click on any icon (on the *Start* menu or *desktop*) and select "Add to *Quick Launch*" from the pop-up menu. Also, by unlocking the *taskbar*, it is possible to adjust the width of the space used on the *taskbar* by the *Quick Launch* bar. Setting the *taskbar* to *Auto-hide* will provide additional height for your applications.

It is also possible to remove an icon by right-clicking on the icon in the *Quick Launch Toolbar* and selecting *Delete*.

> **TIP:** *Take a few moments to explore the other tabs and options on the* Taskbar and Start Menu Properties *dialog shown above.*

Taskbar Buttons

When an application is opened, a "button" is added to the *taskbar*. This provides a quick way to switch between each application that is open. Also, when an application is minimized, the "button" is all that is visible; left-clicking it restores the window to its previous state.

Taskbar buttons (Windows XP and Vista)

When several applications are open and the *taskbar* becomes full, the "buttons" will begin to "stack" for similar items (such as Internet Explorer, email, etc.). Otherwise, the "buttons" get narrower and thus become harder to read because less of the application name is visible.

> **FYI:** *The* taskbar *can be dragged to any edge of the* desktop. *It is also possible to drag the inside edge of the* taskbar *to make it taller, displaying more application "buttons". It is not usually necessary to enlarge the* taskbar *because the number of open applications should be kept to a minimum to avoid slowing the computer down.*

In Windows 7, notice the graphic preview one receives when hovering their cursor over the "stack" of *Internet Explorer* buttons (image below). Moving your cursor over the previews presents a larger preview (the application window temporarily restored) and an "x" to close the window with the need to restore it first.

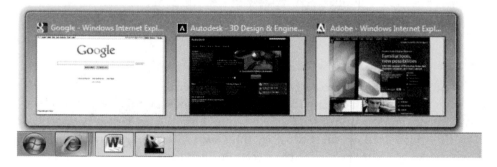

Taskbar buttons (Windows 7)

Notification Area

The most obvious aspect everyone notices about the *notification area* is that it displays the current time (and date in Windows 7).

Hovering your cursor over the "clock" will display the date as shown in the image to the right.

Notification Area (Windows Vista)

Notification Area (Windows 7)

The various icons to the left (of the clock) show various "background" tools and features that are running. These icons are automatically added by Windows or when applications are installed on your computer. When printing, for example, a small printer icon will appear until the print job has completely left your computer. Hovering over the icon will display additional information via a tooltip.

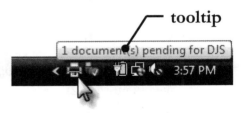

Double-clicking and right-clicking on these icons will open a program, a dialog box or a pop-up menu.

Some icons are hidden, which is good because the number of icons that appear here can get quite large at times. Clicking the "arrow" icon at the far left will temporarily expand this area to show all icons. It will automatically reset itself after a few moments.

If the time or date is incorrect, simply right-click on the "clock" and select "Adjust Date/ Time" in the pop-up menu.

Exercise 1-3:
File Management Introduction

Introduction:

It is primarily important to keep track of document files created using an application. This starts from the very first time you save; where you specify the name and location of the file. Then you need to know where the file is located and what it is called the next time you want to work in it. It is also important to backup your document files to help prevent losing files.

It is not necessary to know where the program files are or files related to the operating system. In fact it is better that you don't until you become more proficient using the software and come across a need to delve deeper into the computers file structure.

In AutoCAD (an application), each drawing (e.g., floors plans, elevations, sections, details, etc.) is an individual file that ends with the file extension (.DWG). With Revit and SketchUp (also applications), each project (.RVT or .SKP) is a single file which can become quite large: 100-300mb or more.

It is important to understand where these files are on your computer and how to back them up. This is what you will begin to study now.

Windows Explorer (aka, *My Computer*, or simply *Computer*) allows you to manage the files on your computer's hard drive as well as on a network, flash drive, digital camera and CD/DVD drives. This is a feature that is built into the Microsoft Windows operating system (OS). There are a number of different ways in which to open *Windows Explorer*:

- Click the **Start** icon and then **Computer** (see Figure 1-3.1).

- Right-click on the **Start** icon and select **Explore** (see Figure 1-3.2).

- Press the "**Windows key**" and then the letter "**E**", the quickest and most efficient method.

Windows key, as found in the lower left corner of most PC-based keyboards.

FIGURE 1-3.1 Accessing Windows Explorer via the Start menu

FIGURE 1-3.2 Accessing Windows Explorer via the Start menu

The image below shows an example of the interface (Windows 7 shown):

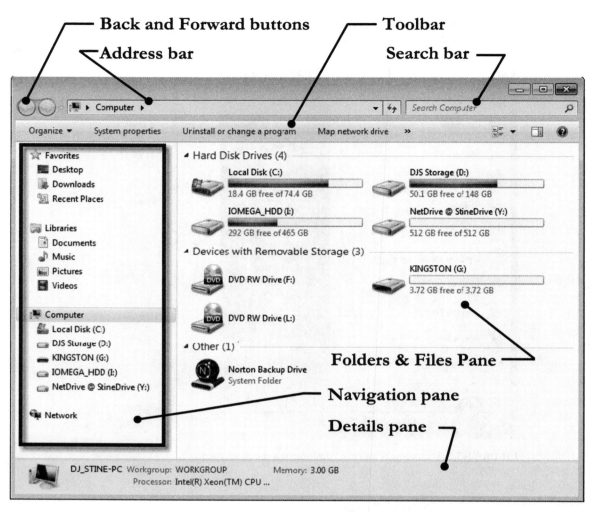

FIGURE 1-3.3 *Windows Explorer – the file management interface for Microsoft Windows*

The following provides details about each area identified in Figure 1-3.3:

Navigation Pane

The *Navigation Pane* is typically where you start when using *Windows Explorer*. This interface provides access to all **drives** and **folders** on your computer. You cannot see any **files** in this pane.

NOTE: A drive could be:
- **Hard drive** (in the computer)
- **External hard drive**
- **Network drives** (when on a network)
- **Cloud Drive** (storage on the internet – see Y drive in Figure 1-3.3)
- **Flash drive** (via USB connection)
- **Floppy drive** (obsolete)
- **CD/DVD/BD Drive**
- **Memory card reader**
- **Camera** (via cable connection)

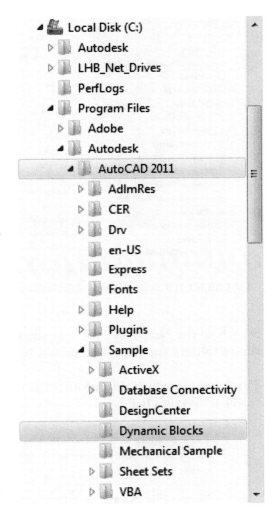

Figure 1-3.3 shows how *Windows Explorer* looks when first opened (by pressing the "Windows" key + "E" key). The image to the right shows an example of the *Navigation Pane* with a few folders opened. The *Address Bar* shows the exact path to the current location.

When your cursor is within the *Navigation Pane* you can see little icons appear next to *drives* and *folders* that may be expanded, meaning they have at least one sub-folder which can be viewed. Solid right-triangles indicate folders which have been expanded.

Clicking an open triangle icon will expand the adjacent folder, and clicking a solid icon will collapse a folder to hide its content and "clean up" the pane.

Any folder within another folder is called a ***subfolder***. Any *file* or *folder* at the highest level, or directly under the drive letter, is said to be at the "root" level of that drive.

Folders and Files Pane

Once you have expanded and selected a folder in the *Navigation Pane*, you can then see the selected folder's contents directly to the right in the *Folders and Files Pane*.

In Figure 1-3.4 below, the **subfolder** "Adobe Photoshop CS5 (64 Bit)" is selected in the *Navigation Bar*, and its contents are shown in the pane to the right, which includes several **folders** and **files**.

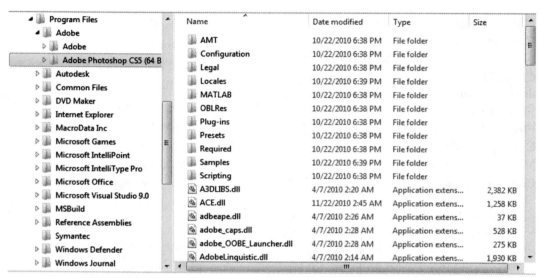

FIGURE 1-3.4 *Windows Explorer – "Folders and Files pane" on the right*

So, where the *Navigation Pane* only shows **drives** and **folders**, the *Folders and Files Pane* only shows **folders** and **files** – no drives. Notice that both areas show folders.

The format in which this information is displayed can vary. This will be covered in the "toolbar" section below.

> **TIP:** Folders *and* subfolders *always have a small yellow "folder" icon next to them. Files usually have an icon provided by the software manufacturer which helps describe, graphically, the various types of files.*
>
> *Notice a* **File Name** *has descriptive text indicating what the file is and is then followed by a* **dot** *(i.e., a period) and then three to four characters. The portion after the dot is called the file's* **Extension**. *Like the icon, this too helps to identify the file type.*
>
> *The file extension may not be visible by default but can be turned on if desired.*

Navigation Pane: *Favorites and Libraries*

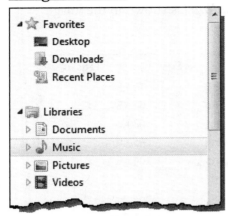

If you find yourself browsing to the same folder often, that folder should be added to your **Favorites** section to save time. A single click on a link here will instantly update the *Navigation Pane* and the *Folders and Files Pane* to show the contents of the "favorites" folder.

Simply drag a folder from the *Folders and Files Pane* onto the *Favorites Link* area to add a new item. When you want an item to go away, right-click and select "Remove".

The **Libraries** section of the *Navigation Pane* provides quick access to the default location in which to save your documents. The location you are taken to is tied to your login if working on a network or in a school lab. Most applications will automatically bring you to the *Documents* folder when you select **Save** or **Open**.

Address Bar

This area gives you a reference as to where you are in the file structure. The information shown is mostly a duplication of information shown in the *Navigation Pane*.

Clicking on a folder listed here will redirect the *Panes* to the selected folder's location.

If you click within the *Address Bar*, the more formal **path** is displayed (see image below). Notice the path always starts with the drive letter and then the folders separated by a backslash.

This path can be copied to the *Windows Clipboard* by highlighting it and pressing **Ctrl+C** on the keyboard. This information could then be pasted (**Ctrl+V**) into an email to inform someone of a specific file's location.

Folders and Files Panel: *File List Headings*

Each column in the *Folders and Files Pane* has a ***file list heading*** (as shown in the image below); the example below is set to the "Details" view type.

Name	Date modified	Type	Size	Tags
DJS55803ADB..wg	2/22/2008 1:36 PM	AutoCAD Drawing	79 KB	
DJS55803ADE03.dwg	2/22/2008 1:37 PM	AutoCAD Drawing	68 KB	
DJS55803ADE04.dwg	2/22/2008 1:37 PM	AutoCAD Drawing	68 KB	
DJS55803ADE05.dwg	2/22/2008 1:38 PM	AutoCAD Drawing	95 KB	
DJS55803ADE06.dwg	2/22/2008 1:39 PM	AutoCAD Drawing	104 KB	

Each header/column can have its width adjusted by dragging the vertical line between two header labels. A small icon, pointed out in the image above, indicates how the files are being sorted. In the example above, the files are being sorted by the file ***Name*** in **ascending order**. If you click on the *Name* header, the files will be sorted in descending order. Also, notice the icon in the header changes direction for ascending versus descending (see image below).

Name	Date modified	Type	Size	Tags
DJS55803AIE05.dwg	2/22/2008 1:42 PM	AutoCAD Drawing	163 KB	
DJS55803AIE04.dwg	2/22/2008 1:41 PM	AutoCAD Drawing	151 KB	
DJS55803AIE03.dwg	2/22/2008 1:41 PM	AutoCAD Drawing	148 KB	
DJS55803AIE02.dwg	2/22/2008 1:40 PM	AutoCAD Drawing	142 KB	
DJS55803AIE01.dwg	2/22/2008 2:59 PM	AutoCAD Drawing	175 KB	
DJS55803AGD01.dwg		AutoCAD Drawing	84 KB	

Clicking on another header, such as *Size*, will then sort the files by size.

Name	Date modified	Type	Size	Tags
DJS55803AIE05.dwg	2/22/2008 1:42 PM	AutoCAD Drawing	163 KB	
DJS55803AIE04.dwg	2/22/2008 1:41 PM	AutoCAD Drawing	151 KB	
DJS55803AIE03.dwg	2/22/2008 1:41 PM	AutoCAD Drawing	148 KB	
DJS55803AIE02.dwg	2/22/2008 1:40 PM	AutoCAD Drawing	142 KB	
Room Finish Schedule....	2/22/2008 1:43 PM	AutoCAD Drawing	116 KB	
DJS55803ADE06.dwg	2/22/2008 1:39 PM	AutoCAD Drawing	104 KB	

Be careful not to click and drag on the headers as it is possible to rearrange them. If you right-click on the headers, you may also turn on additional columns of information. This information is called *Meta Data*, which is data about the file and not really part of the primary use of the file.

Search Bar

Windows 7 (and Vista) has a very efficient search feature in *Windows Explorer*. Simply click in the *search box* and begin typing a word and before you finish typing, Windows will start searching for any files with that name.

In the example below, "autocad" was entered into the search box. The results are then listed below. Now you can select a file listed to copy it or open it. Right-clicking on a file, listed in the search results, provides an option to "open file location" which makes that location current in the *Navigation Pane*. Or, you can click the **Back** button to return to where you were.

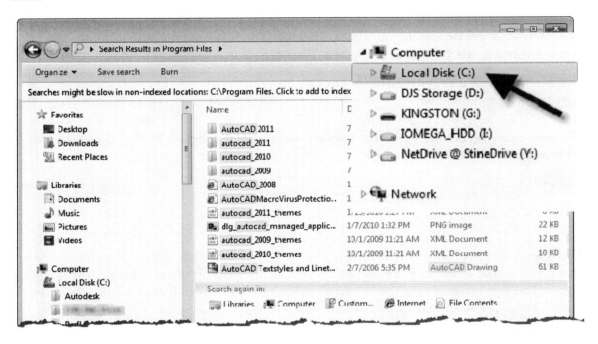

For best results and the most thorough search, click the **C:** drive in the *Navigation Pane* first (as shown in the image to the right). If you know the file is in a general location on your hard drive, you should select that folder before typing the search. Windows will begin looking in the selected folder and any of its sub-folders. This could save a lot of time on a large drive which is close to capacity.

Details Pane

The *Details Pane* shows information about the selected file. In some cases, as in the example below, a preview image is shown (on the left).

Toolbar

The *toolbar* changes depending on what is selected. The first example below shows the options available when a folder is selected. The options may vary depending on programs installed on your computer.

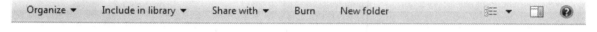

The next example, below, shows the options when a file is selected. Here you can quickly print or email the selected file(s).

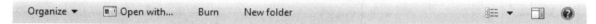

The **Views** option changes the format of the *Folders and Files Pane*. When you click the down arrow next to the *Views* icon, on the *toolbar*, you see the pop-up menu shown in the image below. The first image shows the "Details" mode, while the next image (on the left) shows "Large Icons." You should try each and decide which one you prefer.

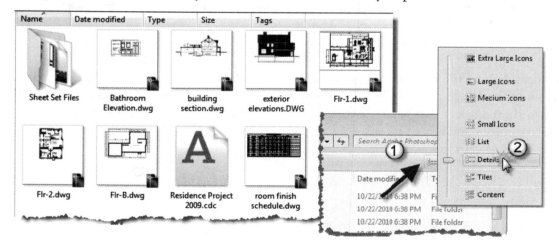

This concludes the overview of the *Windows Explorer* user interface.

Now that you are generally familiar with the *Windows Explorer* user interface, you will be given instruction on a few specific and important tasks. Namely:

- Creating new folders and sub-folders
- Creating new files
- Copying files
- Moving Files
- Deleting files and folders
- Copying files to a flash drive
- Recovering files from the *Recycle Bin*

Creating new folders and subfolders

It is important to create *folders* in order to organize your files. This is the same concept as putting printed pages in folders within a file cabinet; if all files were placed in a single folder, it would be hard to find specific files.

This example will show how to create a folder and a few *subfolders* in the *Documents* folder (aka, *My Documents* folder in Windows XP). These files will be located on your computer's hard drive. Any files saved here should be backed up in another location other than the same hard drive. If the hard drive crashes, all files could be lost.

The following steps describe how to create a folder (Figure 1-3.5):

- Open *Windows Explorer* per the methods previously mentioned (e.g., "Windows" key + "E" key).
- In the *Favorites* list, click **Documents**.
- For Windows 7
    - Select **New Folder** on the *toolbar*
- For Windows XP and Vista:
    - In the *Folders and Files Pane*, **right-click in the white space** (not on a folder or file).
    - Hover over the **New** fly-out menu.
    - In the *New* fly-out, select **Folder**.
- Begin typing the folder name: **CAD Class**; press **Enter** when done.

The following steps describe how to create a subfolder (Figure 1-3.6):

1. Double-click on the **CAD Class** folder within the *Folders and Files Pane* (or expand *Documents* and select *CAD Class* within the *Navigation Pane*).

2. Right-click in the white space of the *Folders and Files Pane*.

3. Create a new folder as outlined above named **Exercise 1**.

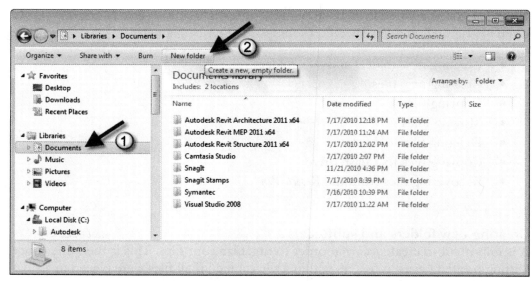

FIGURE 1-3.5 *Creating a folder*

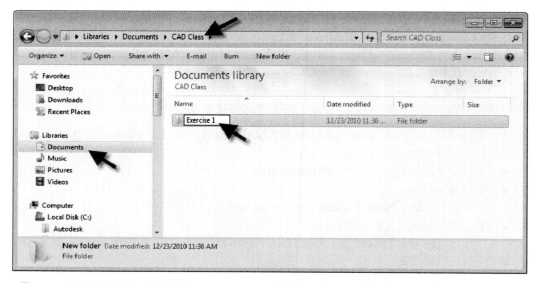

FIGURE 1-3.6 *Creating a Subfolder*

Creating folders and subfolders on other drives and locations is the same. Just navigate to the desired location. When you click the **New Folder** button on the *toolbar*, a new folder will be created in the location listed in the *Address Bar*.

If you don't provide a name, the folder will be called "New Folder". At any time you can right-click on a folder and select "rename" to change the folder name. You should never change the name of a folder in the *Program Files* or *Windows* folders as this could seriously mess up your computer.

Creating new files

Creating a file is typically done within an application. That is, you start a new drawing file (using SketchUp, AutoCAD or Revit) or a new word-processing file (using MS Word) and then **Save**. The first time you save a file, the application will prompt you for a name and location.

The **Shortcut Pane** on the left (See Figure 1-3.7 – #1) provides a quick link to the *Documents* folder; remember this is the *Documents* folder for the person currently logged into the computer. You can then double-click on the folders within the *Folders and Files Pane* on the right; in this example we double-click on *CAD Class* and then *Exercise 1*. Once you have established the location, you enter a descriptive name at the bottom (Step #3 in the image below), and click **Save**.

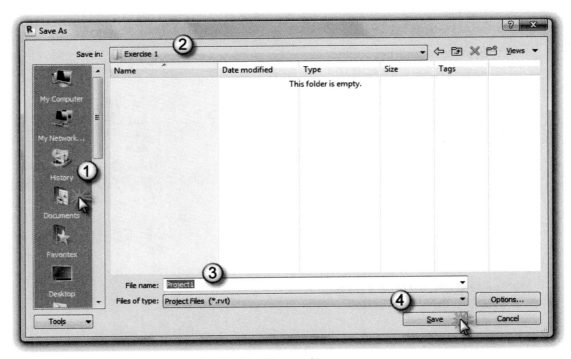

FIGURE 1-3.7 *Creating a file (saving from Revit in this example)*

It is important to pay close attention to the locations and names of your files so you can find them in the future when necessary.

In addition to creating files within an application, you can create an empty "place holder" file for a few file types. In *Windows Explorer*, simply right-click in the white space within the *Files and Folders Pane* (see image to the right).

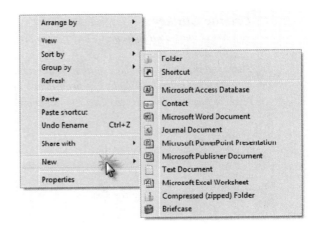

Copying files

Knowing how to copy a file is important. You mainly do this when backing up files. However, whenever you are experimenting with a drawing or document, it is a good idea to make a copy first and then edit that file.

There are two main ways in which to copy a file:

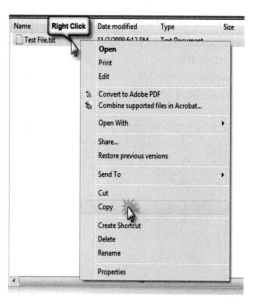

1. Right-click method

   a. Select a file (or files) to be copied.

   b. Right-click on the file (cursor must be over one of the selected files when right-clicking).

   c. Select **Copy**.

   d. Browse to another folder.

   e. Right-click in the white space and select **Paste**.

2. Keyboard shortcuts method

   a. Select a file (or files) to be copied.

   b. Press **Ctrl+C** on the keyboard (for Copy).

   c. Browse to another folder.

   d. Press **Ctrl+V** on the keyboard (for Paste).

SELECTING MULTIPLE FILES:
Here are a few tips for selecting multiple files:
Drag a window –
   Start clicking in "white space" and then move the cursor, while holding down the left mouse button, over the desired files.
Use the Shift key to select blocks of files –
   Click the first file and then, while pressing the Shift key, click the last file. All files in between are selected.
Use the Ctrl key –
   Select individual files in any order while pressing the Ctrl key. Clicking on an already selected file unselects it.
Any combination of the above options also works. For example, you have a large group of files you want to select with the exception of two random ones in the middle. Use the Shift key to select the block of files and then use the Ctrl key to remove two from the current selection.

Copying files to a flash drive

This section will walk you through the steps required to copy files to and from a *USB flash drive* (aka, *jump drive*). A flash drive is one of the most convenient ways to back up files and transport them between work, school and home. A 2 to 4 gigabyte flash drive will likely be sufficient for a student in a CAD/BIM program; if more space is needed, you could move the older files to a CD/DVD.

Flash Drive connected to a laptop computer

Flash drives are small which makes them easy to carry around. They plug into any open **USB port** on a computer. USB ports have now been standard on computers for several years; most things that plug into a computer do so via a USB connection, e.g., printers, digital cameras, mice, keyboards, external hard drives, high speed modems, etc. Because everything uses the USB port, you may find that a computer does not have a port available. In this case you can purchase a **USB hub**, which expands one port into several more; a hub usually has three to six additional ports. Some higher end monitors have a USB port built into them allowing you to connect flash drives and the like to ports on its side.

Connecting a flash drive to a computer:

1. Turn computer on.

2. Insert the flash drive into an open USB port.

    a. Do not force it; the flash drive only goes in one way. You may have to flip it over and try again.

3. The first time your flash drive is connected to a computer, the computer will automatically install software which allows the computer to work with the specific type of flash drive. You will see a "balloon" message similar to the one shown in the image below.

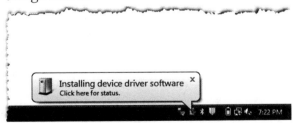

Flash Drive installing automatically

4. Finally, a message will appear, depending on how your computer is configured, asking you what you want to do (see image to the right). Select **Open folder to view files**.

At this point you are in *Windows Explorer* which has been covered in the last several pages. The steps are identical, with the exception that you are using a different *drive letter* (i.e., other than **C:**, the computer's primary hard drive).

The drive letter can vary from computer to computer depending on the number of things installed or connected to the computer that require a drive letter; such as:

- Hard drive
- Second hard drive
- CD/DVD
- Second CD/DVD (maybe a burner)
- Floppy drive (rare)
- Memory card drive (for digital cameras and cell phones)

Copying a file(s) to the flash drive:

1. Select a file (or files) to be copied.
2. Press **Ctrl+C** on the keyboard (for Copy).
3. Locate the newly added drive letter (see image on next page).
   a. Click on the drive in the *Navigation Pane* to make it active.
4. *Optional:* Browse to a subfolder (or create one).
5. Press **Ctrl+V** on the keyboard (for Paste).

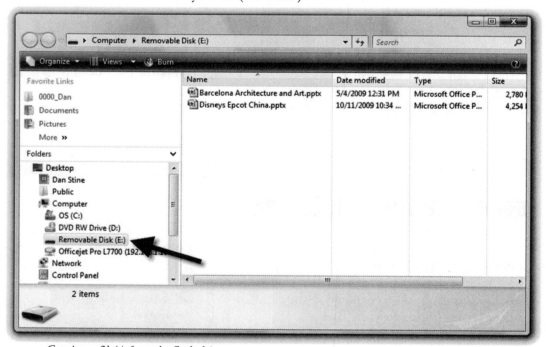

Copying a file(s) from the flash drive

The steps are simply reversed from the ones outlined on the previous page.

Verifying free space:
It is a good idea to keep track of the amount of space available on your flash drive. You should know the selected files will fit on the flash drive before trying to copy them so you minimize the chance for problems. You may need to free up space on a flash drive before trying to back up several files in an office or classroom setting. It is easy to verify free space.

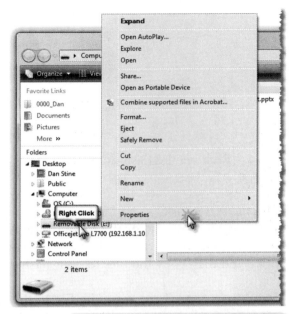

1. Open *Windows Explorer.*

2. Right-click on the flash drive letter in the *Navigation Pane* (see arrow added to image above).

3. Select *Properties* (see image to right).

The image to the right shows the status of the selected drive; note this technique can be used on the C: drive as well.

The flash drive in this example only has 283MB free of 2GB (nominal). This is not considered very much free space, especially if working with Revit files or large CAD files.

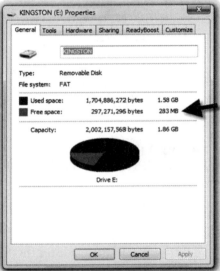

"Safely removing" the flash drive:
It is important to follow the proper procedure when removing a flash drive from a computer. Files sometimes continue to copy in the background, so removing a flash drive suddenly may cause files to be incomplete and thus corrupt.

1. Click on the **Safely Remove *Hardware*** icon in the *Notification Area.*

    a. You may have to fully expand the *Notification Area* to see all the icons located there.

2. Select **Safely remove USB Mass Storage Device – Drive(E:)**; see image below.

    NOTE: *The drive letter may vary.*

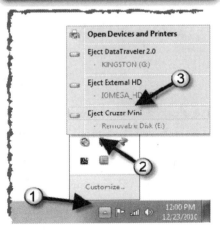

3. Click **OK** to the prompt that it is safe to remove the device.

4. Remove the flash drive.

A couple of warnings:

Don't work directly off the flash drive! Although it is possible, you can run into problems if the flash drive becomes full or is suddenly removed from the computer. Work off the **C:** drive and then copy the files to your flash drive via *Windows Explorer.*

Don't use *Save As* to copy the file to the flash drive! When finished working on a file, close the application (e.g., Revit, AutoCAD, Excel, Word, etc.). Then use *Windows Explorer* to copy the file. New students often get the current file mixed up between the flash drive and the C: drive.

> ***FYI:*** *If you open a file, do some work in it and then just do a Save-As, the original file is unchanged and only the new file will have the current changes. This works well in some cases, but not when you think you are making a duplicate backup.*

Moving Files

The steps to move a file are similar to copying a file:

1. Right-click method:

   a. Select a file (or files) to be moved.

   b. Right-click on the file (cursor must be over one of the selected files when right-clicking).

   c. Select **Cut**.

   d. Browse to another folder.

   e. Right-click in the white space and select **Paste**.

2. Keyboard shortcuts method:

   a. Select a file (or files) to be copied.

   b. Press **Ctrl+X** on the keyboard (for Cut).

   c. Browse to another folder.

   d. Press **Ctrl+V** on the keyboard (for Paste).

A file will not be deleted from its original location until it has been pasted somewhere else. So, if you select **Cut** and then never **Paste** the file(s) anywhere, you will not lose the files.

Deleting files and folders

It is important to remove unnecessary files to keep your hard drive clean and get rid of incorrect data. However, you should never delete files unless you know for sure what they are for. **Deleting certain files from your computer could render it inoperable!**

To delete a file simply:

1. Right-click

    a. Select a file(s).

    b. Right-click (directly on the file).

    c. Select **Delete** from the pop-up menu.

2. Keyboard shortcuts

    a. Select a file(s).

    b. Press the **Delete** key on the keyboard.

Recovering files from the *Recycle Bin*

One last important item to cover concerning file management is the *Recycle Bin*. This feature can really save you at times. Whenever you delete a file from your computer it is actually moved to the *Recycle Bin* rather than being totally deleted. The file will remain in the *Recycle Bin* until the space is needed, then the oldest files are permanently deleted. Simply select the *Recycle Bin* icon in the *Navigation Pane* to see its contents; and then copy any needed files to another location.

Exercise 1-4:
File Management Exercise

Browse to a folder on the "C:" drive.

1. Use the *Folders* pane, on the left, to browse to the following location:
   C:\Program Files\Internet Explorer\en-US

   TIP: Click the plus sign next to C:, *and then the plus next to* Program File, *etc.*

   How many files are in this folder? _____

   What is the size of the smallest file? _____

Search for a file.

1. In the *Folders* pane, click the **C:** drive to select it.
2. Click in the **Search** box near the top-right of the Windows Explorer window.
3. Type **Arial.ttf** (you do not need to press **Enter**).

   What is the full path to this file, including the drive letter?

   _____

Create a folder.

1. Browse to the *Documents* folder using the shortcut link on the left.
2. On the right, right-click in the white space and select **New → Folder**.
3. Type "Learning Revit" and then press **Enter**.
4. Double-click on the folder to open it.

Copy files.

1. Browse to the files provided for this text (on the DVD).
2. Select the first file (single-click; do not double-click).
3. While pressing the **Shift** key, click the last file.
4. With all the files selected, right-click on one of the selected files.
5. Select **Copy** from the pop-up menu.
6. Browse to the "Learning Revit" folder and open it.
7. Right click in the white space.
8. Select **Paste** from the pop-up menu.

   How many files did you copy? _____

Delete a file.

1. In your "Learning Revit" folder, click to select file **Text File A2-02**.
2. Right-click on it and select **Delete**.

Open and Edit a file.
1. Open the "Learning Revit" folder (if needed).
2. Double-click on file **Text File A2-00** to open it.
3. Place your cursor at the end of the last sentence on the last line.
4. Press **Enter** twice.
5. Type your name.
6. Click the "X" in the upper right corner of the screen; click **Yes** to save the changes.

Write the text that was in the file before you added your name:

_____

_____

Rename a file.
1. Right-click on file **A4-01** and select **Rename**.
2. Use the arrow keys and the **Backspace** key to change the file name to **A5-00**.
3. Click away, in any white space, to complete the action.

Move files.
1. Create a new folder, in the "Learning Revit" folder, called "Misc".
2. In the "Learning Revit" folder, press and hold the **Ctrl** key.
3. Select the following files:
   a. Text File A1-00
   b. Text File A2-00
   c. Text File A3-00
4. Right-click on one of the selected files.
5. Select **Cut**.
6. Open the "Misc" subfolder.
7. Right-click in the white space and select **Paste**.

How many files remain in the "Learning Revit" folder? _____

Self-Exam:

The following questions can be used as a way to check your knowledge of this lesson. The answers can be found at the bottom of this page.

1. RAM is a type of software. (T/F)

2. A printer can make larger printouts than a plotter. (T/F)

3. Software is updated every year or two. (T/F)

4. The _____ _____ holds deleted files.

5. It is a good idea to keep track of the amount of space available on your Flash Drive. (T/F)

Review Questions:

The following questions may be assigned by your instructor as a way to assess your knowledge of this section. Your instructor has the answers to the review questions.

1. The Central Processing Unit (CPU) is the "heart" of the computer. (T/F)

2. Most computers can read Blu-ray discs. (T/F)

3. The latest software takes advantage of the new 32bit technology. (T/F)

4. When an application is only visible on the *taskbar* it is considered "minimized". (T/F)

5. The *Quick Launch Toolbar* shows the current time. (T/F)

6. The Windows file management utility: _____ _____.

7. This book recommends working off your Flash Drive rather than the computer's (or server's) hard drive. (T/F)

8. Backing up your files regularly is vital to ensure data is not lost. (T/F)

9. A Graphics Card is not that important to CAD/BIM applications. (T/F)

10. Autodesk makes much of its software available free to students. (T/F)

Lesson 2
Getting Started with Autodesk Revit Architecture 2012:

This chapter will introduce you to Autodesk Revit Architecture 2012. You will study the User Interface and learn how to open and exit a project and adjust the view of the drawing on the screen. It is recommended that you spend an ample amount of time learning this material, as it will greatly enhance your ability to progress smoothly through subsequent chapters.

Exercise 2-1:
What is Revit Architecture 2012?

What is Autodesk Revit used for?

Autodesk Revit (Architecture, Structure and MEP) is the world's first fully parametric building design software. This revolutionary software, for the first time, truly takes architectural computer aided design beyond simply being a high tech pencil. Revit is a product of Autodesk, makers of AutoCAD, 3DS Max, Maya and many other popular design programs.

What is a parametric building modeler?

Revit is a relatively new program designed from the ground up using state-of-the-art technology. The term parametric describes a process by which an element is modified and an adjacent element(s) is automatically modified to maintain a previously established relationship. For example, if a wall is moved, perpendicular walls will grow, or shrink, in length to remain attached to the related wall. Additionally, elements attached to the wall will move, such as wall cabinets, doors, windows, air grilles, etc.

Revit stands for **Rev**ise **I**nstantly; a change made in one view is automatically updated in all other views and schedules. For example, if you move a door in an interior elevation view, the floor plan will automatically update. Or, if you delete a door, it will be deleted from all other views and schedules. You can even delete a door from the door schedule and the drawings will instantly be revised to reflect the change.

A major goal of Revit is to eliminate much of the repetitive and mundane tasks traditionally associated with CAD programs allowing more time for design, coordination and visualization. For example: all sheet numbers, elevation tags and reference bubbles are updated automatically when changed anywhere in the project. Therefore it is difficult to find a miss-referenced detail tag.

The best way to understand how a parametric model works is to describe the Revit project file. A single Revit file contains your entire building project. Even though you mostly draw in 2D views, you are actually drawing in 3D. In fact, the entire building project is a 3D model.

From this 3D model you can generate 2D elevations, 2D sections and perspective views. Therefore, when you delete a door in an elevation view you are actually deleting the door from the 3D model from which all 2D views are generated and automatically updated.

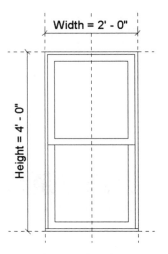

Another way in which Revit is a parametric building modeler is that **parameters** can be used to control the size and shape of geometry. For example, a window model can have two *parameters* set up which control the size of the window. Thus, from a window's properties it is possible to control the size of the window without using any of the drawing modify tools such as *Scale* or *Move*. Furthermore, the *parameter* settings (i.e., width and height in this example) can be saved within the window model (called a *Family*). You could have the 2′ x 4′ settings saved as "Type A" and the 2′ x 6′ as "Type B". Each saved list of values is called a *Type* within the *Family*. Thus, this one double-hung window *Family* could represent an unlimited number of window sizes! You will learn more about this later in the book.

Window model size controlled by parameters Width *and* Height

What about the different "flavors" of Revit?

Revit comes in three different "flavors": Architecture, Structure and MEP (which stands for Mechanical, Electrical and Plumbing). Any "flavor" of Revit can open and edit the same Revit Project file or content (aka, *Families*). The only requirement is that each "flavor" of Revit be the same version, for example, Autodesk Revit Architecture 2012, Autodesk Revit Structure 2012 and Autodesk Revit MEP 2012.

The tutorials in this textbook require all three "flavors" Revit. You can download the free 30-day trial from autodesk.com. Students may download a free 13-month version of all three "flavors" of Revit at www.students.autodesk.com.

Revit model of an existing building, with architecture, structural, mechanical, plumbing and electrical all modeled.

Image courteous of LHB, Inc.   www.LHBcorp.com

Now is as good a time as any to make sure the reader understands that Revit is not, nor has it ever been, backwards compatible. This means there is no *Save-As* back to a previous version of Revit. Also, an older version of Revit cannot open a file, project or content, saved in a newer format. So make sure you consider what version your school or employer is currently standardized on before upgrading any projects or content.

Why use Revit?

Many people ask the question, why use Revit versus other programs? The answer can certainly vary depending on the situation and particular needs of an individual or organization.

Generally speaking, this is why most companies use Revit:

- Many designers and drafters are using Revit to streamline repetitive drafting tasks and focus more on designing and detailing a project.
- Revit is a very progressive program and offers many features for designing buildings. Revit is constantly being developed and Autodesk provides incremental upgrades and patches on a regular basis; Revit 2012 was released about a year after the previous version.
- Revit was designed specifically for architectural design and includes features like:
  - Mental Ray's photorealistic renderer
  - Phasing (which makes Revit a 4D tool)
  - Pantone digital color
  - Vectoral Shadows (real-time shadows)
  - Design Options
  - Conceptual Energy Analysis

32bit versus 64bit?

Starting in the 2009 version of Revit, a 64bit version of the software is available. This allows the software to take full advantage of hardware that, for the most part, has now been 64bit for a few years. One of the biggest advantages is access to more than 3GB of RAM. Many BIM stations have 8GB of RAM to handle large projects. It should be pointed out that most computers come with a 32bit operating system (e.g., MS Windows XP, MS Windows Vista or MS Windows 7); however, each has a 64bit version which costs a little more. The 64bit version of Revit looks the same and creates a model identical to one created in the 32bit version of Revit. Either version of Revit will work fine for this textbook.

A few basic Revit concepts:

The following is meant to be a brief overview of the basic organization of Revit as a software application. You should not get too hung up on these concepts and terms as they will make more sense as you work through the tutorials in this book. This discussion is simply laying the groundwork so you have a general frame of reference on how Revit works.

The Revit platform has three fundamental types of elements:
* Model Elements
* Datum Elements
* View-Specific Elements

Model Elements

Think of *Model Elements* as things you can put your hands on once the building has been constructed. They are typically 3D, but can sometimes be 2D. There are two types of *Model Elements*:

* **Host Elements** (walls, floors, slabs, roofs, ceilings) – Tools vary depending on the "flavor" of Revit (e.g., Revit Architecture has a *Ceiling* tool whereas Revit Structure does not).

* **Model Component** (Stairs, Doors, Furniture, Beams, Columns, Pipes, Ducts, Light Fixtures, Model Lines) – Options vary depending on the "flavor" of Revit (e.g., Revit MEP has a *Duct* tool whereas Revit Architecture and Revit Structure do not).

   o Some *Model Components* require a host before they can be placed within a project. For example, a window can only be placed in a host, which could be a wall, roof or floor depending on how the element was created. If the host is deleted, all hosted or dependent elements are automatically deleted.

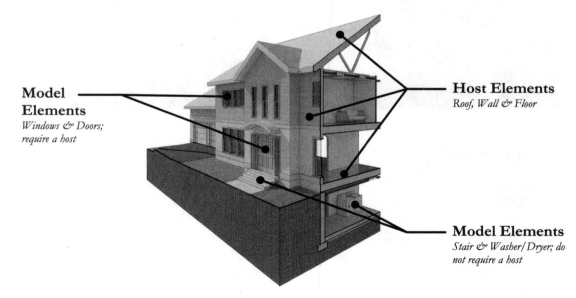

Model Elements
Windows & Doors; require a host

Host Elements
Roof, Wall & Floor

Model Elements
Stair & Washer/Dryer; do not require a host

Datum Elements

Datum Elements are reference planes within the building that graphically and parametrically define the location of various elements within the model. These features are available in all "flavors" of Revit. These are the three types of *Datum Elements*:

- **Grids**
  - ○ Typically laid out in a plan view to locate structural elements such as columns and beams, as well as walls. Grids show up in plan, elevation and section views. Moving a grid in one view moves it in all other views as it is the same element. (See the next page for an example of a grid in plan view.)

- **Levels**
  - ○ Used to define vertical relationships, mainly surfaces that you walk on. They only show up in elevation and section views. Many elements are placed relative to a *Level*; when the *Level* is moved those elements move with it (e.g., doors, windows, casework, ceilings). ***WARNING:*** *If a* Level *is deleted, those same "dependent" elements will also be deleted from the project!*

- **Reference Planes**
  - ○ These are similar to grids in that they show up in plan and elevation or sections. They do not have reference bubbles at the end like grids. Revit breaks many tasks down into simple 2D tasks which result in 3D geometry. *Reference Planes* are used to define 2D surfaces on which to work within the 3D model. They can be placed in any view, either horizontally or vertically.

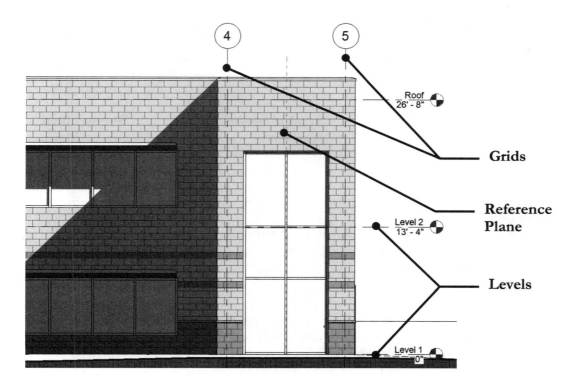

View-Specific Elements

As the name implies, the items about to be discussed only show up in the specific view in which they are created. For example, notes and dimensions added in the architectural floor plans will not show up in the structural floor plans. These elements are all 2D and are mainly communication tools used to accurately document the building for construction or presentations.

- **Annotation elements** (text, tags, symbols, dimensions)
  - o Size automatically set and changed based on selected drawing scale

- **Details** (detail lines, filled regions, 2D detail components)

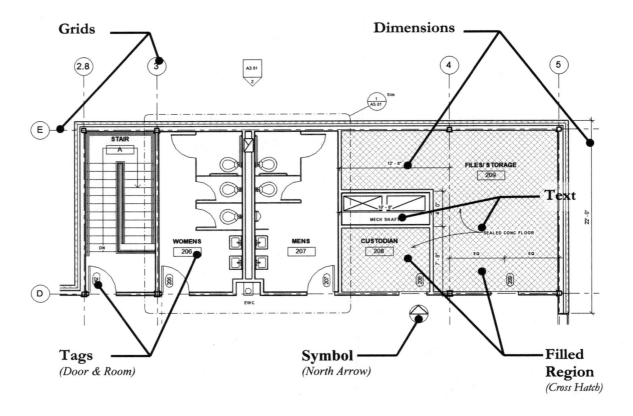

Grids

Dimensions

Text

Tags
(Door & Room)

Symbol
(North Arrow)

Filled
Region
(Cross Hatch)

File Types (and extensions):
Revit has four primary types of files that you will work with as a Revit user. Each file type, as with any Microsoft Windows based program, has a specific three letter file name extension; that is, after the name of the file on your hard drive you will see a period and three letters. They are:

.RVT	Revit project files; the file most used (also for backup files)
.RFA	Revit family file; loadable content for your project
.RTE	Revit template; a project starter file with office standards preset
.RFT	Revit family template; a family starter file with parameters

The Revit platform has three fundamental ways in which to work with the elements (for display and manipulation):

- Views
- Schedules
- Sheets

The following is a cursory overview of the main ideas you need to know. This is not an exhaustive study on views, schedules and sheets.

Views

Views, accessible from the *Project Browser* (see Page 5-4), is where most of the work is done while using Revit. Think of views as slices through the building, both horizontal (plans) and vertical (elevations and sections).

- **Plans**
    - o A *Plan View* is a horizontal slice through the building. You can specify the location of the cut plane, which determines if certain windows show up or how much of the stair is seen. A few examples are: architectural floor plan, reflected ceiling plan, site plan, structural framing plan, HVAC floor plan, electrical floor plan, lighting [ceiling] plan, etc. The images below show this concept; the image on the left is the 3D BIM. The middle image shows the portion of building above the cut plane removed. Finally, the last image on the right shows the plan view in which you work and place on a sheet.

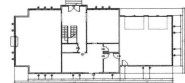

- **Elevations**
    - o Elevations are vertical slices, but where the slice lies outside the floor plan as in the middle image below. Each elevation created is listed in the *Project Browser*. The image on the right is an example of a South exterior elevation view, which is a "live" view of the 3D model. If you select a window here and delete it, the floor plans will update instantly.

- **Sections**
  - Similar to elevations, sections are also vertical slices. However, these slices cut through the building. A section view can be cropped down to become a wall section or even look just like an elevation. The images below show the slice, the portion of building in the foreground removed, and then the actual view created by the slice. A setting exists, for each section view, to control how far into that view you can see. The example on the right is "seeing" deep enough to show the doors on the interior walls.

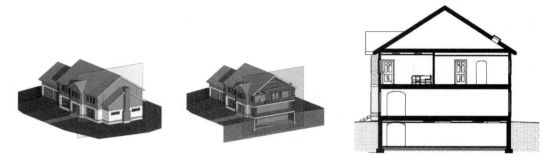

- **3D and Camera**
  - In addition to the traditional "flattened" 2D views that you will typically work in, you are able to see your designs more naturally via 3D and Camera views. A 3D view is simply a non-perspective 3D view of the project viewed from the exterior. A Camera view is a true perspective view; cameras can be created both in and outside of the building. Like the 2D views, these 3D/Camera views can be placed on a sheet to be printed. Revit provides a number of tools to help explore the 3D view, such as Section Box, Steering Wheel, Temporary Hide and Isolate, and Render.

    The image on the left is a 3D view set to "shade mode" and has shadows turned on. The image on the right is a camera view set up inside the building; the view is set to "hidden line" rather than shaded, and the camera is at eyelevel.

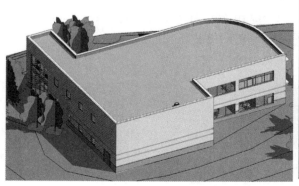

Schedules

Schedules are lists of information generated based on content that has been placed, or modeled, within the project. A schedule can be created, such as the door schedule example shown below, that lists any of the data associated with each door that exists in the project. Revit allows you to work directly in the schedule views. Any change within a schedule view, is a change directly to the element being scheduled. Again, if a door were to be deleted from this schedule, that door would be instantly deleted from the project.

DOOR AND FRAME SCHEDULE												
DOOR NUMBER	DOOR				FRAME		DETAIL			GLAZING	FIRE RATING	HDWR GROUP
	WIDTH	HEIGHT	MATL	TYPE	MATL	TYPE	HEAD	JAMB	SILL			
1000A	3' - 8"	7' - 2"	WD		HM		11/A8.01	11/A8.01					
1046	3' - 0"	7' - 2"	WD	D10	HM	F10	11/A8.01	11/A8.01 SIM				34	
1047A	6' - 0"	7' - 10"	ALUM	D15	ALUM	SF4	6/A8.01	6/A8.01	1/A8.01 SIM	1" INSUL		2	CARD READER N. LEAF
1047B	6' - 0"	7' - 2"	WD	D10	HM	F13	12/A8.01	11/A8.01 SIM		60 MIN	85	MAG HOLD OPENS
1050	3' - 0"	7' - 2"	WD	D10	HM	F21	8/A8.01	11/A8.01		1/4" TEMP		33	
1051	3' - 0"	7' - 2"	WD	D10	HM	F21	8/A8.01	11/A8.01		1/4" TEMP		33	
1052	3' - 0"	7' - 2"	WD	D10	HM	F21	8/A8.01	11/A8.01		1/4" TEMP		33	
1053	3' - 0"	7' - 2"	WD	D10	HM	F21	8/A8.01	11/A8.01		1/4" TEMP		33	
1054A	3' - 0"	7' - 2"	WD	D10	HM	F10	8/A8.01	11/A8.01		1/4" TEMP	-	34	
1054B	3' - 0"	7' - 2"	WD	D10	HM	F21	8/A8.01	11/A8.01		1/4" TEMP	-	33	
1055	3' - 0"	7' - 2"	WD	D10	HM	F21	8/A8.01	11/A8.01		1/4" TEMP		33	
1056A	3' - 0"	7' - 2"	WD	D10	HM	F10	9/A8.01	9/A8.01			20 MIN	33	
1056B	3' - 0"	7' - 2"	WD	D10	HM	F10	11/A8.01	11/A8.01			20 MIN	34	
1056C	3' - 0"	7' - 2"	WD	D10	HM	F10	20/A8.01	20/A8.01			20 MIN	33	
1057A	3' - 0"	7' - 2"	WD	D10	HM	F10	8/A8.01	11/A8.01			20 MIN	34	
1057B	3' - 0"	7' - 2"	WD	D10	HM	F30	9/A8.01	9/A8.01		1/4" TEMP	20 MIN	33	
1058A	3' - 0"	7' - 2"	WD	D10	HM	F10	9/A8.01	9/A8.01			-	33	

Sheets

You can think of sheets as the pieces of paper on which your views and schedules will be printed. Views and schedules are placed on sheets and then arranged. Once a view has been placed on a sheet, its reference bubble is automatically filled out and that view cannot be placed on any other sheet. The settings for each view, called "view scale," control the size of the drawing on each sheet; view scale also controls the size of the text and dimensions.

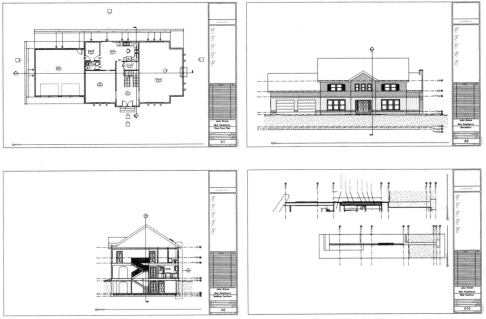

Exercise 2-2:
Overview of the Revit User Interface

Revit is a powerful and sophisticated program. Because of its powerful feature set, it has a measurable learning curve, though its intuitive design makes it easier to learn than other CAD programs. However, like anything, when broken down into smaller pieces, we can easily learn to harness the power of Revit. That is the goal of this book.

This section will walk through the different aspects of the User Interface (UI). As with any program, understanding the user interface is the key to using the program's features.

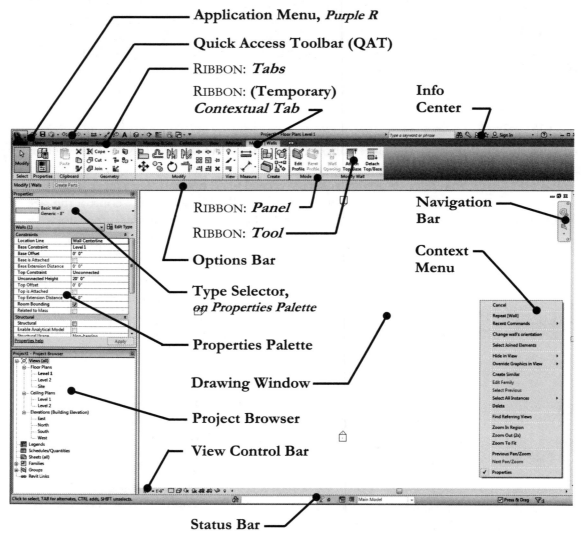

FIGURE 2-2.1 Revit User Interface

The Revit User Interface:

TIP: See the DVD for a more in-depth look at the User Interface.

Application Menu:

Access to *File* tools such as *Save, Plot, Export* and *Print* (both hardcopy and electronic printing). You also have access to tools which control the Revit application as a whole, not just the current project, such as *Licensing* and *Options*.

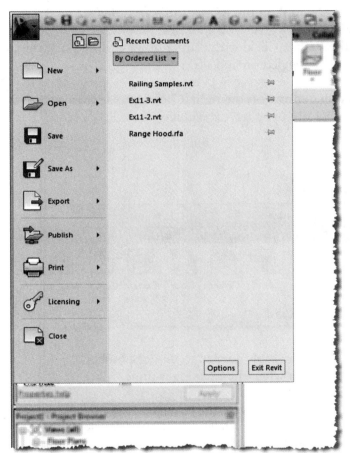

Recent and Open Documents:

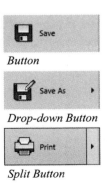

These two icons (from the *Application* menu) toggle the entire area on the right to show either the recent documents you have been in (icon on the left) or a list of the documents you currently have open.

In the *Recent Documents* list you click a listed document to open it. This saves time as you do not have to click *Open → Project* and browse for the document (*Document* and *Project* mean the same thing here). Finally, clicking the "Pin" keeps that project from getting bumped off the list as additional projects are opened.

In the *Open Documents* list the "active" project you are working in is listed first, clicking another project switches you to that open project.

The list on the left, in the *Application Menu* shown above, represents three different types of buttons: *button, drop-down button* and *split button*. Save and Close are simply **buttons**. *Save-As* and *Export* are **drop-down buttons**, which means they reveal a group of related tools. If you click or hover your cursor over one of these buttons, you will get a list of tools on the right. Finally, **split buttons** have two actions depending on what part of the button you click on; hovering over the button reveals the two parts (see bottom image to the right). The main area is the most used tool; the arrow reveals additional related options.

Button

Drop-down Button

Split Button

Quick Access Toolbar:

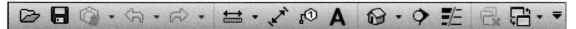

Referred to as *QAT* in this book, this single toolbar provides access to often used tools (*Open, Save, Undo, Redo, Measure, Tag*, etc.). It is always visible regardless of what part of the *Ribbon* is active.

The *QAT* can be positioned above or below the *Ribbon* and any command from the *Ribbon* can be placed on it; simply right-click on any tool on the *Ribbon* and select *Add to Quick Access Toolbar*. Moving the *QAT* below the *Ribbon* gives you a lot more room for your favorite commands to be added from the *Ribbon*. Clicking the larger down-arrow to the right reveals a list of common tools which can be toggled on and off.

Some of the icons on the *QAT* have a down-arrow on the right. Clicking this arrow reveals a list of related tools. In the case of *Undo* and *Redo*, you have the ability to undo (or redo) several actions at once.

Ribbon – Home Tab:

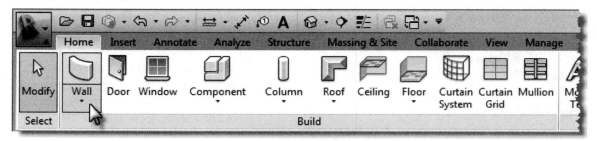

The *Home* tab on the *Ribbon* contains most of the tools needed to model a building, essentially the things you can put your hands on when the building is done.

Each tab starts with the *Modify* tool, i.e., the first button on the left. This tool puts you into "selection mode" so you can select elements to modify. Clicking this tool cancels the current tool and unselects elements. With the *Modify* tool selected you may select elements to view their properties or edit them.

The *Ribbon* has three types of buttons, *button, drop-down button* and *split*, as covered on the previous page. In the image above you can see the *Wall* tool is a **split button**. Most of the time you would simply click the top part of the button to draw a wall. Clicking the down-arrow part of the button, for the *Wall* tool example, gives you the option to draw a *Wall, Structural Wall, Wall by Face, Wall Sweep*, and a *Reveal*.

> ***TIP:*** *The Model Text tool is only for placing 3D text in your model, not for adding notes!*

Ribbon – Annotate Tab:

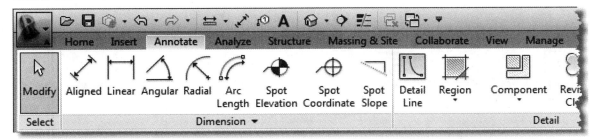

To view this tab, simply click the label "Annotate" near the top of the *Ribbon*. This tab presents a series of tools which allow you to add notes, dimensions and 2D "embellishments" to your model in a specific view, such as a floor plan, elevation, or section. All of these tools are **view specific**, meaning a note added in the first floor plan will not show up anywhere else, not even another first floor plan, for instance, a first floor electrical plan.

Notice, in the image above, that the *Dimension* panel label has a down-arrow next to it. Clicking the down-arrow will reveal an **extended panel** with additional related tools.

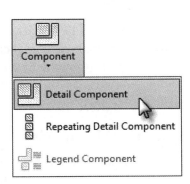

Finally, notice the *Component* tool in the image above; it is a **split button** rather than a *drop-down button*. Clicking the top part of this button will initiate the *Detail Component* tool. Clicking the bottom part of the button opens the fly-out menu revealing related tools. Once you select an option from the fly-out, that tool becomes the default for the top part of the split button for the current session of Revit (see image to right).

Ribbon – Modify Tab:

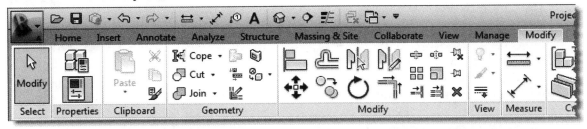

Several tools which manipulate and derive information from the current model are available on the *Modify* tab. Additional *Modify* tools are automatically appended to this tab when elements are selected in the model (see *Modify* contextual tab on the next page).

> ***TIP:*** *Do not confuse the Modify tab with the Modify tool when following instructions in this book.*

Ribbon – View Tab:

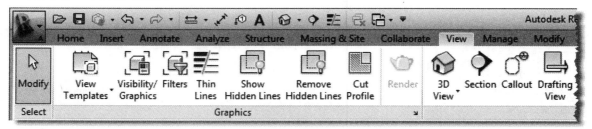

The tools on the *View* tab allow you to create new views of your 3D model; this includes views that look 2D (e.g., floor plans, elevations and sections) as well as 3D views (e.g., isometric and perspective views).

The *View* tab also gives you tools to control how views look, everything from what types of elements are seen (e.g., Plumbing Fixture, Furniture or Section Marks) as well as line weights.

> **NOTE:** *Line weights can be controlled on a view-by-view basis or at a project wide level.*

Finally, notice the little arrow in the lower-right corner of the *Graphics* panel. When you see an arrow like this, you can click on it to open a dialog box with settings that relate to the panel's tool set (*Graphics* in this example). Hovering over the arrow reveals a tooltip which will tell you what dialog box will be opened.

Ribbon – Modify Contextual Tab:

The *Modify* tab is appended when certain tools are active or elements are selected in the model; this is referred to as a *contextual tab*. The first image, below, shows the *Place Wall* tab which presents various options while adding walls. The next example shows the *Modify Walls* contextual tab which is accessible when one or more walls are selected.

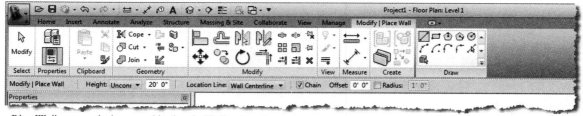

Place Wall contextual tab – accessible when the Wall tool is active.

Modify Walls contextual tab – accessible when a wall is selected.

Ribbon – Customization:

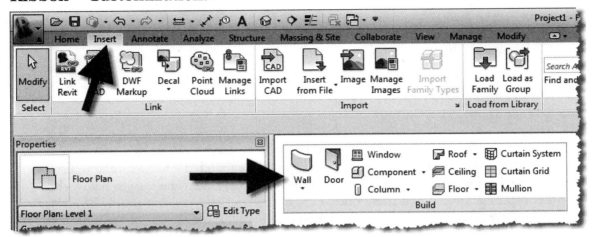

There is not too much customization that can be done to the *Ribbon*. One of the only things you can do is pull a panel off the *Ribbon* by clicking and holding down the left mouse button. This panel can be placed within the *drawing window* or on another screen if you have a dual monitor setup.

The image above shows the *Build* panel, from the *Home* tab, detached from the *Ribbon* and floating within the drawing window. Notice that the *Insert* tab is active. Thus, you have constant access to the *Build* tools while accessing other tools. Note that the *Build* panel is not available on the *Home* tab as it was literally moved, not just copied.

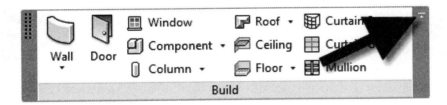

When you need to move a detached panel back to the *Ribbon* you do the following: hover over the detached panel until the sidebars show up and then click the "Return panels to *Ribbon*" icon in the upper right (identified in the image above).

> **FYI:** *Whenever the resolution of your monitor is too low or you don't have the Revit application maximized on the screen, the buttons may be modified to take up less room on the Ribbon; typically the words are removed. Compare the image to the right with the Build panel above.*

Ribbon – States:

The *Ribbon* can be displayed in one of four states:

- Full Ribbon (default)
- Minimize to Tabs
- Minimize to Panel Tiles
- Minimize to Panel Buttons

The intent of this feature is to increase the size of the available drawing window. It is recommended, however, that you leave the *Ribbon* fully expanded while learning to use the program. The images in this book show the fully expanded state. The images below show the other three options. When using one of the minimized options, you simply hover (or click) your cursor over the tab or panel to temporarily reveal the tools.

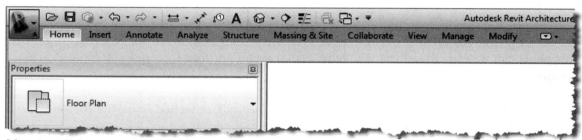

Minimize to Tabs

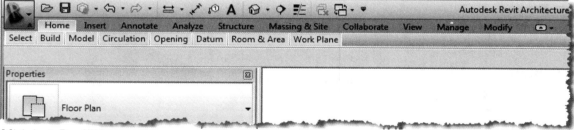

Minimize to Panel Tiles

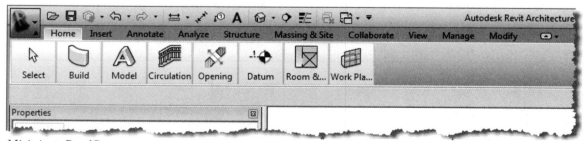

Minimize to Panel Buttons

Ribbon – References in this Book:

When the exercises make reference to the tools in the *Ribbon*, a consistent method is used to eliminate excessive wording and save space. Take a moment to understand this so that things go smoothly for you later.

Throughout the textbook you will see an instruction similar to the following:

> 23. Select **Home → Build → Wall**.

This means, click the ***Home*** tab, and within the ***Build*** panel, select the ***Wall*** tool. Note that the *Wall* tool is actually a split button, but a subsequent tool was not listed so you are to click on the primary part of the button. Compare the above example to the one below:

> 23. Select **Home → Build → Wall → Structural Wall**.

The above example indicates that you should click the down-arrow part of the *Wall* tool in order to select the *Structural Wall* option.

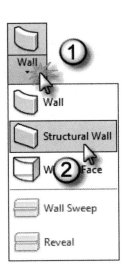

Thus the general pattern is this:

Tab → Panel → Tool → drop-down list item

Tab: This will get you to the correct area within the *Ribbon*.

Panel: This will narrow down your search for the desired tool.

Tool: Specific tool to select and use.

Drop-down list item: This will only be specified for drop-down buttons and sometimes for split buttons.

The image below shows the order in which the instructions are given to select a tool; note that you do not actually click the panel title.

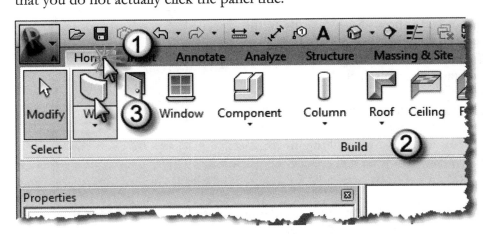

Options Bar:

This area dynamically changes to show options that compliment the current operation. The *Options Bar* is located directly below the *Ribbon*. When you are learning to use Revit you should keep your eye on this area and watch for features and options appearing at specific times. The image below shows the *Options Bar* example with the *Wall* tool active.

Properties Palette – Element Type Selector:

Properties Palette; nothing selected

The *Properties Palette* provides instant access to settings related to the element selected or about to be created. When nothing is selected, it shows information about the current view. When multiple elements are selected, the common parameters are displayed.

The *Element Type Selector* is an important part of the *Properties Palette*. Whenever you are adding elements or have them selected, you can select from this list to determine how a wall to be drawn will look, or how a wall previously drawn should look (see image to right). If a wall type needs to change, you never delete it and redraw it; you simply select it and pick a new type from the *Type Selector*.

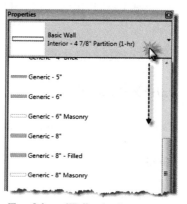

Type Selector; Wall tool active or a Wall is selected

The **Selection Filter** drop-down list below the *Type Selector* lets you know the type and quantity of the elements currently selected. When multiple elements are selected, you can narrow down the properties for just one element type, such as *wall*. Notice the image to the right shows four walls are in the current selection set. Selecting **Walls (4)** will cause the *Palette* to only show *Wall* properties even though many other elements are selected (and remain selected).

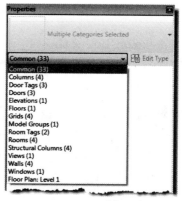

Selection Filter; multiple elements selected

The width of the *Properties Palette* and the center column position can be adjusted by dragging the cursor over that area. You may need to do this at times to see all the information. However, making the *Palette* too wide will reduce the useable drawing area.

The *Properties Palette* should be left open; if you accidentally close it you can reopen it by **View → Window → User Interface → Properties**.

Project Browser:

The *Project Browser* is the "Grand Central Station" of the Revit project database. All the views, schedules, sheets and content are accessible through this hierarchical list. The image to the left shows the seven major categories; any item with a "plus" next to it contains sub-categories or items.

Double-clicking on a *View*, *Legend*, *Schedule* or *Sheet* will open it for editing. Right-clicking will display a pop-up menu with a few options such as *Delete* and *Copy*.

Like the *Properties Palette*, the width of the *Project Browser* can be adjusted. When the two are stacked above each other, they both move together.

The *Project Browser* should be left open; if you accidentally close it, by clicking the "X" in the upper right, you can reopen it by:
View → Window → User Interface → Project Browser.

The *Project Browser* and *Properties Palette* can be repositioned on a second monitor, if you have one, when you want more room to work in the drawing window.

Status Bar:

This area will display information about the current command or list information about a selected element. The right hand side of the *Status Bar* shows the number of elements selected. The small funnel icon to the left of the selection number can be clicked to open the *Filter* dialog box, which allows you to reduce your current selection to a specific category. For example, select the entire floor plan, and then filter it down to just the doors. This is different than the *Selection Filter* in the *Properties Palette* which keeps everything selected.

Unchecking **Press & Drag** prohibits Revit from automatically starting to move an element directly below your cursor when you click and drag the mouse.

The two drop-down lists towards the center of the *Status Bar* control **Design Options** and **Worksets**. The latter is not covered in this book but *Design Options* are. *Worksets* relate to the ability for more than one designer to be in the model at a time.

Drawing Window:

This is where you manipulate the Building Information Model (BIM). Here you will see the current view (plan, elevation or section), schedule or sheet. Any changes made are instantly propagated to the entire database.

View Control Bar:

This is a feature which gives you convenient access to tools which control each view's display settings (i.e., scale, shadows, detail level and graphics style). The important thing to know is that these settings only affect the current view, the one listed on the *Application Title Bar*. All of these settings are available in the *Properties Palette*, but this toolbar cannot be turned off like the *Properties Palette* can.

Context Menu:

The *context menu* appears near the cursor whenever you right-click on the mouse. The options on that menu will vary depending on what tool is active or what element is selected.

Elevation Marker:

This item is not really part of the Revit UI, but is visible in the drawing window by default via the various templates you can start with, so it is worth mentioning at this point. The four elevation markers point at each side of your project and ultimately indicate the drawing sheet on which you would find an elevation drawing of each side of the building. All you need to know right now is that you should draw your floor plan generally in the middle of the four elevation markers that you will see in each plan view; DO NOT delete them as this will remove the related view from the *Project Browser*.

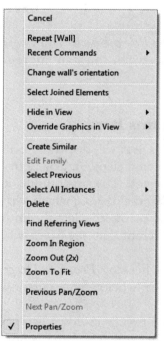

Context menu example with a wall selected

This concludes your brief overview of the Revit user interface. Many of these tools and operations will be covered in more detail throughout the book.

Exercise 2-3:
Open, Save and Close an Existing Project

To *Open* **Revit Architecture 2012**:

Start → All Programs → Autodesk → Autodesk Revit Architecture 2012

FYI: Your icon may not say "x64"; this is not a problem.

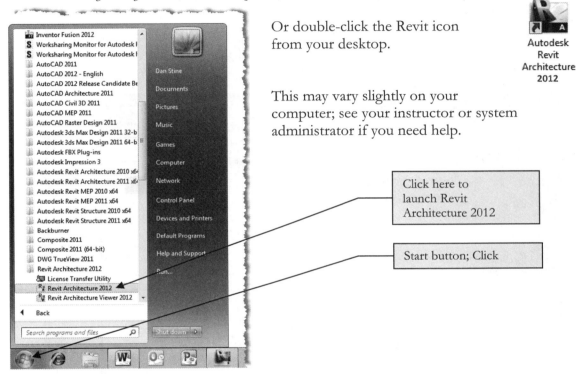

Or double-click the Revit icon from your desktop.

This may vary slightly on your computer; see your instructor or system administrator if you need help.

Autodesk Revit Architecture 2012

Click here to launch Revit Architecture 2012

Start button; Click

FIGURE 2-3.1 Starting Revit

Open an Existing Revit Project:

By default, Revit will open in the *Recent Files* window, which will display thumbnails of recent projects you have worked on. Clicking on the preview will open the project.

1. Click the **Open** link (see the image to the right).

You may click **Open** under *Project* or on the *Quick Access Toolbar*.

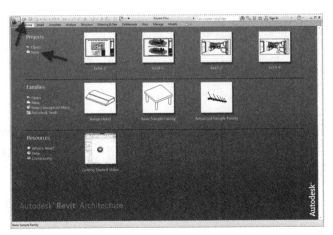

Recent Files startup screen

Next you will open an existing Revit project file. You will select a sample file provided on the DVD that came with this book.

2. Click the drop-down box at the top of the *Open* dialog (Figure 2-3.2). Browse to your DVD drive; the drive letter will vary from computer to computer.

> ***TIP:*** *If you cannot locate the DVD that came with this textbook, you can substitute any Revit file you can find; try clicking on the Training Files shortcut on the left if needed.*

> ***TIP:*** *The training folder may not contain any files depending on how Revit was installed on your computer. You can access the files on Autodesk's website (www.autodesk.com).*

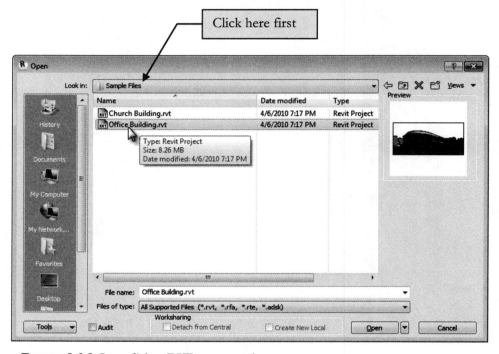

FIGURE 2-3.2 Open dialog; DVD contents shown

3. Select the file named **Office Building.rvt** and click **Open**.

> ***FYI:*** *Notice the preview of the selected file. This will help you select the correct file before taking the time to open it.*

The *Office Building.rvt* file is now open and the last saved view is displayed in the drawing window (Figure 2-3.3). This is the project shown on page 2-3 displaying Revit's photo-realistic rendering capabilities.

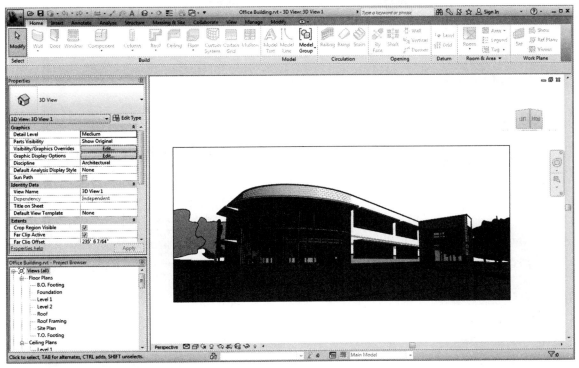

FIGURE 2-3.3 Sample file "Office Building.rvt"

The *Application Menu* lists the projects and views currently open on your computer (Figure 2-3.4).

4. Click **Application Menu →
   Open Documents (icon)**
   (Figure 2-3.4).

Notice that the *Office Building.rvt* project file is listed. Next to the project name is the name of a view open on your computer (e.g., floor plan, elevation).

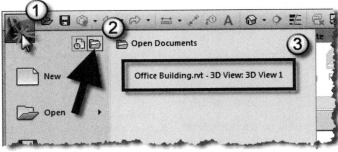

Figure 2-3.4 Application Menu: Open Documents view

Additional views will be added to the list as you open them. Each view has the project name as a prefix. The current view, the view you are working in, is always at the top of the list. You can quickly toggle between opened views from this menu by clicking on them.

You can also use the *Switch Windows* tool on the *View* tab; both do essentially the same thing.

Switch
Windows

Open another Revit Project:

Revit lets you open more than one project at a time.

5. Click **Open** from the *Quick Access Toolbar*.

6. Per the instructions previously covered, browse to the **DVD**.

7. Select the file named **Church Building.rvt** and click **Open** (Figure 2-3.5).

> *TIP: If you cannot locate the DVD that came with this textbook, substitute one of the training files.*

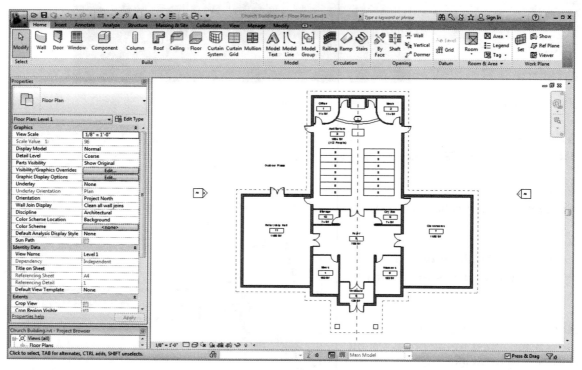

FIGURE 2-3.5 Sample file "Church Building.rvt"

8. Click **Open Documents** from the *Application* menu (Figure 2-3.6).

Notice that the *Church Building.rvt* project is now listed along with a view: *Floor Plan: Level 1.*

Try toggling between projects by clicking on *Office Building.rvt – 3D View: 3D View 1.*

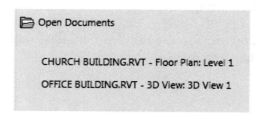

FIGURE 2-3.6 Open Documents

Close a Revit Project:

9. Select **Application menu → Close**; click **No** if prompted to save.

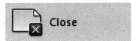

This will close the current project/view. If more than one view is open for a project, only the current view will close. The project and the other opened views will not close until you get to the last open view.

10. Repeat Step 9 to close the other project file.

If you have not saved your project yet, you will be prompted to do so before Revit closes the view. **Do not save at this time.** When all open project files are closed, you find yourself back in the *Recent Files* screen – which is where you started.

Saving a Revit Project:

At this time we will not actually save a project.

To save a project file, simply select *Save* from the *Quick Access Toolbar.* You can also select *Save* from the *Application* menu or press *Ctrl + S* on the keyboard.

You should get in the habit of saving often to avoid losing work due to a power outage or program crash.

You can also save a copy of the current project by selecting **Save As** from the *Application* menu. Once you have used the *Save As* command you are in the new project file and the file you started in is then closed.

Closing the Revit Program:

Finally, from the *Application* menu select **Exit Revit**. This will close any open projects/views and shut down Revit. Again you will be prompted to save, if needed, before Revit closes the view. **Do not save at this time**.

You can also click the "X" in the upper right corner of the *Revit Application* window.

Exercise 2-4:
Creating a New Project

Open **Autodesk Revit Architecture**.

Creating a New Project File:

The steps required to set up a new Revit Architecture model project file are very simple. As mentioned earlier, simply opening the Revit program starts you in the *Recent Files* window.

To manually create a new project (maybe you just finished working on a previous assignment and want to start the next one):

1. Select **Application menu → New → Project**.

   NOTE: *If you select the* New *link in the* Recent Files *startup screen, a new project is quickly setup using the default template. This is not recommended as this template is lacking content, views and sheets.*

After clicking *New → Project* you will get the ***New Project*** dialog box (Figure 2-4.1).

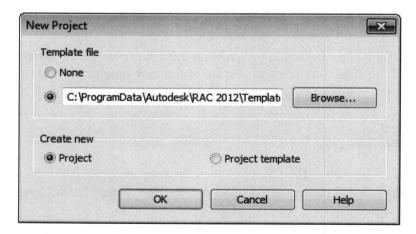

FIGURE 2-4.1 New Project dialog box

The *New Project* dialog box lets you specify the template file you want to use, or to not use a template at all. You can also specify whether you want to create a new project or template file.

2. Leave the **default.rte** *template file* selected. You need to click in the textbox and "arrow key" to the right to see the template file name, and leave *Create new* set to **Project** (Figure 2-4.1).

3. Click **OK.** You now have a new unnamed project file.

To name an unnamed project file, you simply *Save.* The first time an unnamed project file is saved, you will be prompted to specify the name and location for the project file.

4. Select **Application menu → Save** from the *Menu Bar.*

5. Specify a **name** and **location** for your new project file.
   Your instructor may specify a location or folder for your files if in a classroom setting.

What is a Template File?

A template file allows you to start your project with specific content and certain settings preset the way you like or need them.

For example, you can have the units set to Imperial or Metric. You can have the door, window and wall families you use most loaded and eliminate other less often used content. Also, you can have your company's title block preloaded and even have all the sheets for a project set up.

A custom template is a must for design firms using Revit and will prove useful to the student as he or she becomes more proficient with the program.

> **Be Aware:**
> It will be assumed from this point forward that the reader understands how to create, open and save project files. Please refer back to this section as needed. If you still need further assistance, ask your instructor for help.

Exercise 2-5:
Using Zoom and Pan to View Your Drawings

Learning to *Pan* and *Zoom* in and out of a drawing is essential to accurate and efficient drafting and visualization. We will review these commands now so you are ready to use them with the first design exercise.

Open **Revit Architecture**.

You will select a sample file from the DVD that came with this textbook.

1. Select **Open** from the *Quick Access Toolbar*.

2. Browse to the **DVD** (usually the D drive, but this can vary).

3. Select the file named **Church Building.rvt** and click **Open** (Figure 2-5.1).

   TIP: *If you cannot locate the DVD that came with this textbook, substitute any of the training files that come with Revit.*

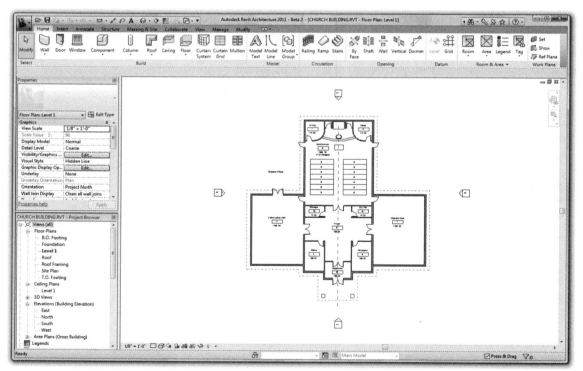

FIGURE 2-5.1 Church Building.rvt project

If the default view that is loaded is not **Floor Plan: Level 1**, double-click on **Level 1** under **Views\Floor Plans** in the *Project Browser*. Level 1 will be bold when it is the active or current view in the drawing window.

Using Zoom and Pan Tools:

You can access the zoom tools from the ***Navigation Bar***, or the *scroll wheel* on your mouse.

The *Zoom* icon contains several *Zoom* related tools:
- The default (i.e., visible) icon is *Zoom in Region*, which allows you to window an area to zoom into.
- The *Zoom* icon is a **split button**.
- Clicking the down-arrow part of the button reveals a list of related *Zoom* tools.
- You will see the drop-down list on the next page.

Zoom In

4. Select the top portion of the *Zoom* icon (see image to right).

5. Drag a window over your plan view (Figure 2-5.2).

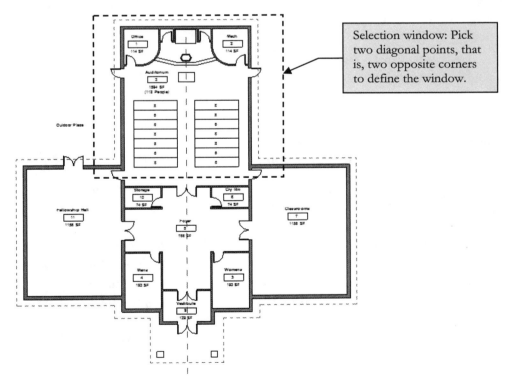

Selection window: Pick two diagonal points, that is, two opposite corners to define the window.

FIGURE 2-5.2 Zoom In window

You should now be zoomed in to the specified area (Figure 2-5.3).

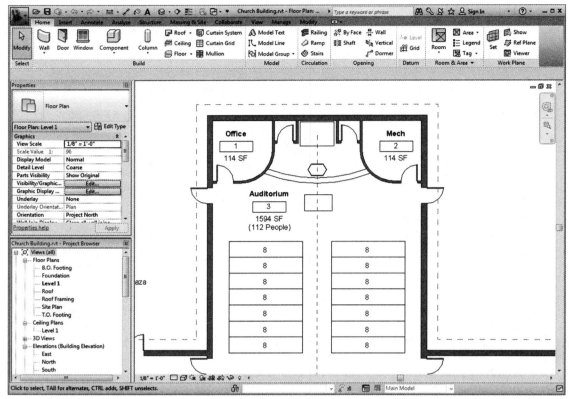

FIGURE 2-5.3 Zoom In results

Zoom Out

6.   Click the down-arrow next to the zoom icon (Figure 2-5.4). Select **Previous Pan/Zoom**.

You should now be back where you started. Each time you select this icon you are resorting a previous view state. Sometimes you have to select this option multiple times if you did some panning and multiple zooms.

Take a minute and try the other *Zoom* tools to see how they work. When finished, click **Zoom to Fit** before moving on.

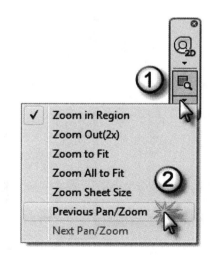

FIGURE 2-5.4 Zoom Icon drop-down

Default 3D View

Clicking on the *Default 3D View* icon, on the *QAT*, loads a 3D View. This allows you to quickly switch to a 3D view.

7. Click on the **Default 3D View** icon.

8. Go to the **Open Documents** listing in the *Application Menu* and notice the *3D View* and the *Floor Plan* view are both listed at the bottom.

   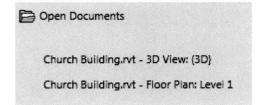

   REMEMBER: You can toggle between views here.

9. Click the **Esc** key to close the *Application* menu.

ViewCube

The *ViewCube* gives you convenient view control over the 3D view. This technology has been implemented in many of Autodesk's programs to make the process seamless for the user.

10. You should notice the ***ViewCube*** in the upper right corner of the drawing window (Figure 2-5.5). If not, you can turn it on by clicking *View → Windows → User Interface → ViewCube*.

    TIP: The ViewCube only shows up in 3D views.

Hovering your cursor over the *ViewCube* activates it. As you move about the *Cube* you see various areas highlight. If you click, you will be taken to that highlighted area in the drawing window. You can also click and drag your cursor on the *Cube* to "roll" the model in an unconstrained fashion. Clicking and dragging the mouse on the disk below the *Cube* allows you to spin the model without rolling. Finally, you have a few options in a right-click menu, and the **Home** icon, just above the *Cube*, gets you back to where you started if things get disoriented!

FIGURE 2-5.5 ViewCube

11. Give the *ViewCube* a try, then click the **Home** icon when you are done.

    REMEMBER: The Home icon only shows up when your cursor is over the ViewCube.

Navigation Wheel

Similar to the *ViewCube*, the *Navigation Wheel* aids in navigating your model. With the *Navigation Wheel* you can walk through your model, going down hallways and turning into rooms. Revit has not advanced to the point where the doors will open for you; thus, you walk through closed doors or walls as if you were a ghost!

The *Navigation Wheel* is activated by clicking the upper icon on the *Navigation Bar*.

Unfortunately, it is way too early in your Revit endeavors to learn to use the *Navigation Wheel*. You can try this in the chapter on creating photorealistic renderings and camera views. You would typically use this tool in a camera view.

Figure 2-5.6 Navigation Wheel

12. **Close** the *Church Building* project **without** saving.

Using the Scroll Wheel on the Mouse

The scroll wheel on the mouse is a must for those using BIM software. In Revit you can *Pan* and *Zoom* without even clicking a *Zoom* icon. You simply **scroll the wheel to *Zoom*** and **hold the wheel button down to *Pan***. This can be done while in another command (e.g., while drawing walls). Another nice feature is that the drawing zooms into the area near your cursor, rather than zooming only at the center of the drawing window. Give this a try before moving on. Once you get the hang of it, you will not want to use the icons. The only thing you cannot do is *Zoom to Fit* so everything is visible on the screen.

Exercise 2-6:
Using Revit's Help System

This last section of your introductory chapter will provide a quick overview of Revit Architecture's *Help System*. This will allow you to study topics in more detail if you want to know how something works beyond the introductory scope of this textbook.

1. Click the **round question mark** icon in the upper-right corner of the screen.

You are now in Revit's *WikiHelp* site (Figure 2-6.1). This is a website which opened in your web browser. This window can be positioned side by side with Revit, which is especially nice if you have a dual-screen computer system. This interface required a connection to the internet. As a website, Autodesk has the ability to add and revise information at any time, unlike files stored on your hard drive. This also means that the site can change quite a bit, potentially making the following overview out of date. If the site changes, just follow along as best you can for the next three pages.

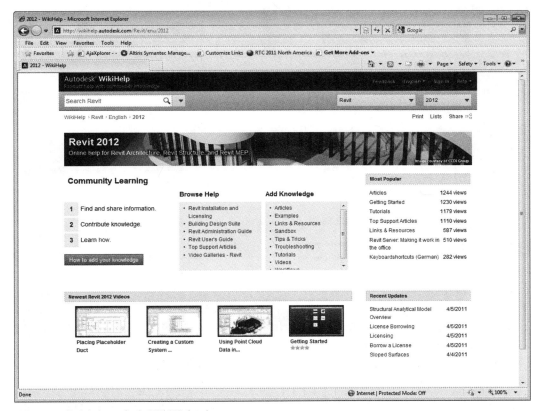

FIGURE 2-6.1 Autodesk WikiHelp site

In the upper left you can search the *Help System* for a word or phrase. You may also click any one of the links to learn more about the topic listed. The next few steps will show you how to access the *Help System's* content on the Revit user interface, a topic you have just studied.

2. In the *Browse Help* section, select **Revit User's Guide**.

3. Click the first link in the search results list; it should be **User Interface**.

Notice the tree structure on the left. You can use this to quickly navigate the user's guide.

4. On the left, click the plus symbols for: **Revit User's Guide** → **Introduction to Revit** → **User Interface** and then click directly on **Ribbon**.

You now see information about the *Ribbon* as shown in the image below. Notice additional links are provided below on the current topic. You can use the browser's *Back* and *Forward* buttons to move around in the *Help System*.

FIGURE 2-6.2 Help window; Ribbon overview

Next you will try searching the Revit *Help System* for a specific Revit feature. This is a quick way to find information if you have an idea of what it is you are looking for.

5. In the upper left corner of the current *Help System* web page, click in the *Search* textbox and enter **gutter**.

6. Press **Enter** on the keyboard.

The search results are shown in Figure 2-6.3. Each item is a link which will take you to information on that topic.

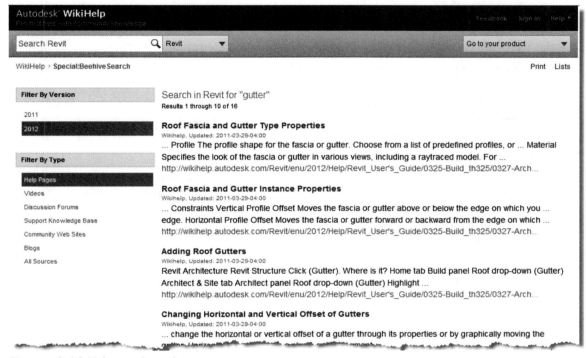

FIGURE 2-6.3 Help search results

The *Help System* can be used to complement this textbook. It is a reference resource, not a tutorial. As you are working though the tutorials in this book, you may want to use the *Help System* to fill in the blanks if you are having trouble or want more information on a topic.

What is a Wiki

A Wiki site is a special type of website where anyone can add information to the site. This makes the potential knowledgebase very large. Anyone who sees a mistake in the steps or instructions provided can make a change. Additionally, a person with specific expertise can add additional information which will help other users. This is similar to the popular information website *Wikipedia*. For more information about Autodesk's *WikiHelp* site and how users such as you may add to and edit the content, visit: http://wikihelp.autodesk.com/training/enu/wiki_guidelines.

Self-Exam:

The following questions can be used as a way to check your knowledge of this lesson. The answers can be found at the bottom of this page.

1. The *View* tab allows you to save your project file. (T/F)

2. You can zoom in and out using the wheel on a wheel mouse. (T/F)

3. Revit is a parametric architectural design program. (T/F)

4. A _____ file allows you to start your project with specific content and certain settings preset the way you like or need them.

5. In the Revit user interface, projects are viewed in the _____ window.

Review Questions:

The following questions may be assigned by your instructor as a way to assess your knowledge of this section. Your instructor has the answers to the review questions.

1. The *Options Bar* dynamically changes to show options that complement the current operation. (T/F)

2. Revit is strictly a 2D drafting program. (T/F)

3. The Projects/Views listed in the *Open Documents* list allow you to see which Projects/Views are currently open. (T/F)

4. When you use the *Pan* tool, you are actually moving the drawing, not just changing what part of the drawing you can see on the screen. (T/F)

5. Revit was not originally created for architecture. (T/F)

6. The icon with the floppy disk picture ( ) allows you to _____ a project file.

7. Clicking on the _____ next to the *Zoom* icon will list additional *Zoom* tools not currently shown in the *View* toolbar.

8. You do not see the *ViewCube* unless you are in a _____ view.

Lesson 3
Quick Start: Small Office::

In this lesson you will get a "down and dirty" overview of the functionality of Revit Architecture. The very basics of creating the primary components of a floor plan – Walls, Doors, Windows, Roof, Annotation and Dimensioning – will be covered. This lesson will show you the amazing "out-of-the-box" powerful, yet easy to use, features in Revit. It should get you very excited about learning this software program. Future lessons will cover these features in more detail while learning other editing tools and such along the way.

Exercise 3-1:
Walls, Grids and Dimensions

In this exercise you will draw the walls, starting with the exterior. Read the directions carefully; everything you need to do is clearly listed.

Exterior Walls:

1. Start a new project named **Small Office** per the following instructions:

    a. **Application Menu → New → Project**

    b. Click **Browse...** (Figure 3-1.1).

    c. Select the template file named **Commercial-Default.rte**. *(You should be brought to the correct folder automatically.)*

    d. Click **Open**.

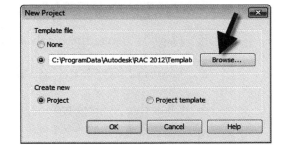

FIGURE 3-1.1 New Project

    e. With the template file just selected and *Create new* "Project" selected, click **OK** (Figure 3-1.1).

    See Lesson 1 for more information on creating a new project.

2. Select **Home → Build → Wall** on the *Ribbon*. (See Figure 3-1.2.)

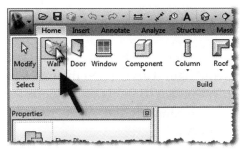

FIGURE 3-1.2 Wall tool

Notice that the *Ribbon, Options Bar* and *Properties Palette* have changed to show settings related to walls. Next you will modify those settings.

> ***FYI:*** *By default, the bottoms of new walls will be at the current floor level and the tops of the walls are set via the Options Bar as shown in the next step.*

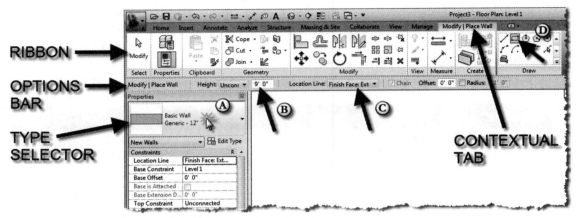

FIGURE 3-1.3 Ribbon and Options Bar

3. Modify the *Ribbon, Options Bar* and *Type Selector* to the following (Figure 3-1.3):

    a. *Element Type Selector:* Click the down-arrow and select <u>*Basic Wall:*</u> **Generic – 12″**.

    b. *Height:* Change the height from 14′-0″ to **9′-0″**.

    c. *Location Line:* Set this to **Finish Face : Exterior**.

    d. Click the *Rectangle* icon. *(This allows you to draw four walls at once [i.e., a rectangle], rather than one wall at a time.)*

You are now ready to draw the exterior walls.

4. In the drawing window, click in the upper left corner.

    > ***TIP:*** *Make sure to draw within the four elevation markers (see image to right).*

5. Start moving the mouse down and to the right. **Click** when the two temporary on-screen listening dimensions are approximately **100′** (wide) and **60′** (deep).

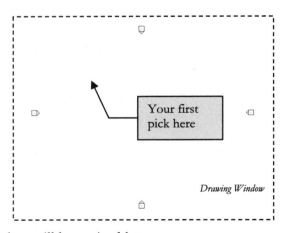

Getting the dimensions exact is not important as they will be revised later on.

Your drawing should look similar to Figure 3-1.4, similar in that the dimensions do not have to be exact right now and the building's location relative to the four elevation tags may vary slightly.

The *temporary dimensions* are displayed until the next action is invoked by the user. While the dimensions are displayed, you can click on the dimension text and adjust the wall dimensions. Also, by default the *temporary dimensions* reference the center of the wall. You can change this by simply clicking on the grips located on each *witness line*; each click toggles the witness line location between center, exterior face and interior face.

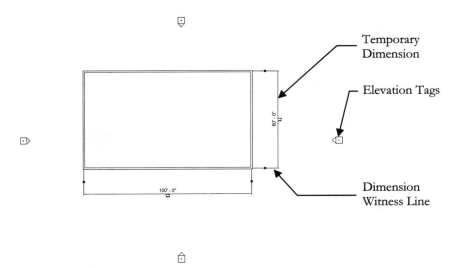

Temporary Dimension

Elevation Tags

Dimension Witness Line

FIGURE 3-1.4 Exterior walls

In the next few steps you will create grid lines and establish a relationship between the walls and the grids, such that moving a grid causes the wall to move with it.

Grids:

Grids are used to position structural columns and beams in a building. Adding a grid involves selecting the *Grid* tool and then picking two points in the drawing window.

6. Click **Modify** on the *Ribbon* (to finish using the *Wall* tool) and then select **Home → Datum → Grid**.

Grid

Next, you will draw a vertical grid off to the left of your building. Once you have drawn all the grids, you will use a special tool to align the grid with the walls and lock that relationship.

7. [*First pick*] **Click** down and to the left of your building as shown in Figure 2.1-5.

    FYI: 'Click' always means left-click, unless a right-click is specifically called for.

8. [*Second pick*] Move the cursor straight up (i.e., vertically) making sure you see a dashed cyan line, which indicates you are snapped to the vertical plane, and the angle dimension reads 90 degrees. Just past the North edge of the building (as shown in Figure 2.1-5), click.

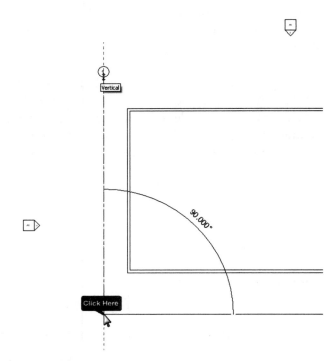

FIGURE 3-1.5 Drawing a grid

You have now drawn your first grid line. Next you will quickly draw four more grid lines;: two horizontal and two vertical.

> *NOTE: The Grid tool will remain active until you select another tool or select Modify. (Selecting Modify allows you to select other elements in the drawing window.)*

9. Draw another vertical grid approximately centered on your building. BEFORE YOU PICK THE FIRST POINT, make sure you see a dashed cyan reference line indicating the grid line will align with the previous grid line. (You will see this before clicking the mouse at each end of the grid line.) Then go ahead and pick both points (Figure 3-1.6).

10. Draw the remaining grid lines shown in Figure 3-1.6. Again, do not worry about the exact location of the grid lines; just make sure the ends align with each other.

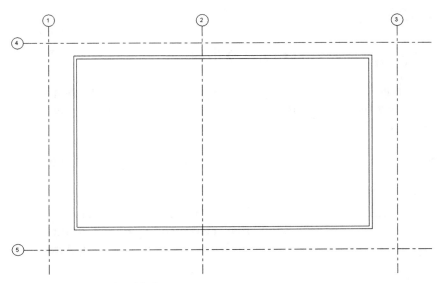

FIGURE 3-1.6 Grids added

Next you will change the two horizontal grid lines to have letters instead of numbers.

11. Zoom in on the grid bubble for the upper horizontal grid line.

12. Click *Modify* and then click on the grid line to select it.

13. With the grid line selected, click on the dark blue text within the bubble.

14. Type **A** and press **Enter** on the keyboard (Figure 3-1.7).

15. Click **Modify** again.

16. Change the other horizontal grid to **B**.

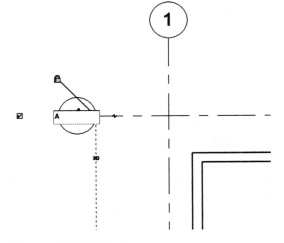

FIGURE 3-1.7 Grid edit

Align:

Next you will use the *Align* tool to reposition the grid lines so they "align" with the exterior face of the adjacent walls. The steps are simple: select the *Align* tool from the *Ribbon*; pick the reference line (i.e., the exterior wall face); and then you select the item to move (i.e., the grid line). This tool works on many Revit objects!

17. Select **Modify** → **Modify** → **Align** from the *Ribbon*.

REMINDER: *Ribbon instructions are* Tab → Panel → Tool.

18. [*Align: first pick*] With the *Align* tool active notice the prompt on the *Status Bar*; select **Wall faces** on the *Options Bar*, next to **Prefer**, and then select the exterior face of the wall adjacent to Grid Line 1.

19. [*Align: second pick*] Select **Grid Line 1**. Be sure to see the next step before doing anything else!

The grid line should now be aligned with the exterior face of the wall. Immediately after using the *Align* tool, you have the option of "locking" that relationship; you will do that next. The ability to lock this relationship is only available until the next tool is activated. After that, you would need to use the *Align* tool again.

20. Click the unlocked **padlock** symbol to "lock" the relationship between the grid line and the wall (see Figure 3-1.8).

21. Use the steps just outlined to **Align** and **Lock** the remaining grid lines with their adjacent walls. Do not worry about the location of Grid Line 2 (i.e., the vertical grid in the center).

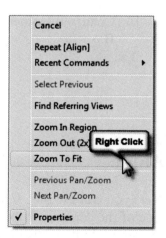

FIGURE 3-1.8 Align "lock"

Dimensions:

Next you will add dimensions to the grid lines and use them to drive the location of the walls and grids and learn how to lock them.

22. Select **Modify** and then **right-click** anywhere within the drawing window; click **Zoom To Fit**.

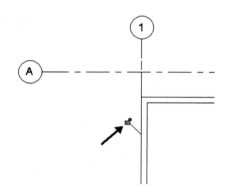

23. Select **Annotate → Dimensions → Aligned** tool.

Aligned

At this point you are in the *Dimension* tool. Notice the various controls available on the *Ribbon* and *Options Bar*. You can set things like the dimension style (via the *Element Type Selector*) and the kind of dimension (linear, angle, radius, etc.) and which portion of the wall to *Prefer* (e.g., face, center, core face).

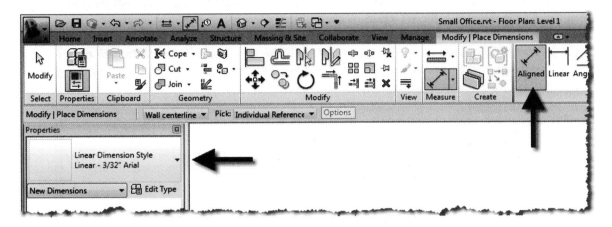

24. With the *Ribbon, Options Bar* and *Properties Palette* as shown above, which should have been the default settings, **select** Grid Line **1**.

   FYI: *The grid line will pre-highlight before you select it, which helps make sure you select the correct item (e.g., the grid line versus the wall).*

25. Now **select Grid Line 2** and then **select** Grid Line **3**.

Your last pick point is to decide where the dimension line should be.

26. Click in the location shown in Figure 3-1.9 to position the dimension line.

   TIP: *Do not click near any other objects or Revit will continue the dimension string to that item.*

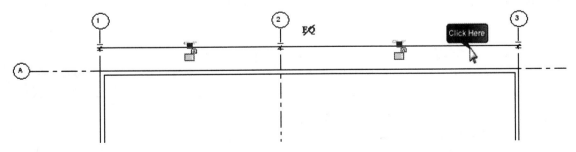

FIGURE 3-1.9 Adding dimensions

Notice that while the dimension string is selected, you see an **EQ** symbol with a slash through it. This symbol indicates that the individual components of the dimension string are not equal in length. The next step will show you how easy it is to make these dimensions equal!

27. With the dimension string selected, click the EQ symbol located near the middle of the dimension.

The grid lines are now equally spaced (Figure 3-1.10) and this relationship will be maintained until the EQ symbol is selected again to toggle the "dimension equality" feature off.

> *NOTE: When dimension equality is turned off or the dimension is deleted, the grid line **will not** move back to its original location; Revit does not remember where the grid was.*

Typically, you would not want to click the padlock icons here because that would lock the current dimension and make it so the grid lines could not be moved at all.

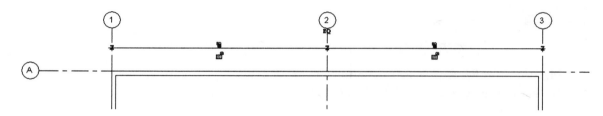

FIGURE 3-1.10 Toggling dimension equality

Next you will add an "overall building" dimension from Grid Line 1 to Grid Line 3. This dimension can be used to drive the overall size of your building (all the time, keeping Grid Line 2 equally spaced).

28. Using the **Aligned** dimension tool, add a dimension from Grid Line **1** to Grid Line **3** and then pick to position the dimension line (Figure 3-1.11).

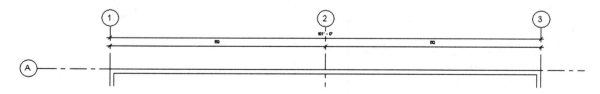

FIGURE 3-1.11 Overall building dimension added

When using a dimension to drive the location of geometry, you need to select the item you want to move and then select the dimension text to enter the new value. You cannot just select the dimension because Revit does not know whether you want the left, right or both grid lines to move. The only thing you can do, graphically, by selecting the dimension directly is "lock" that dimension by clicking on the padlock symbol and then clicking the blue dimension text to add a suffix if desired. Next, you will adjust the overall building size.

29. Click **Modify** (or press the **Esc** key twice) to make sure you cancel or finish the *Dimension* tool and that nothing is selected.

30. **Select** Grid Line **3**.

31. With Grid Line **3** selected, click the dimension text; type **101** and then press **Enter**.

    FYI: Notice that Revit assumes feet if you do not provide a foot or inch symbol.

32. Repeating the previous steps, add a dimension between Grid Lines A and B, and then adjust the model so the dimension reads **68′-0″**.

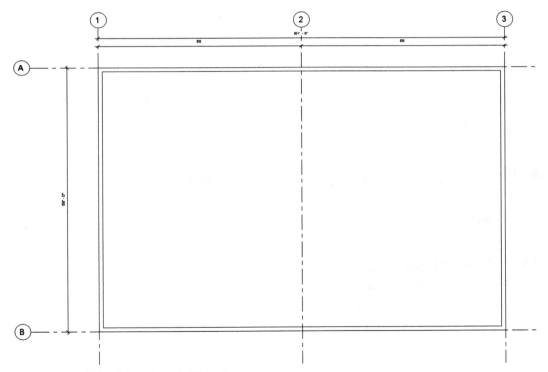

FIGURE 3-1.12 Building size established

Your project should now look similar to Figure 3-1.12. You should notice that dimensions must "touch" two or more items (the grid lines in this case). Also, because the walls were aligned and locked to the grids, moving the grids caused the walls to move.

The last thing you will do before moving on to the interior walls is to swap out the generic walls with a more specific wall. This would be a common situation in a design firm; a generic wall is added as a "place holder" until the design is refined to the point where the exterior wall system is selected.

The process for swapping a wall is very simple: select the wall and pick a different type from the *Type Selector*. The next steps will do this, but will also show you how to quickly select all the exterior walls so you can change them all at once!

33. Click **Modify** and then hover your cursor over one of the exterior walls so it pre-highlights. (Do not click yet.)

34. *With an exterior wall pre-highlighted,* take your hand off the mouse and press the **Tab** key until all four walls pre-highlight.

   FYI: The Tab *key cycles through the various items below your cursor. The current options should include: one wall, a chain of walls, and a grid line.*

35. *With all four walls pre-highlighted:* **click** to select them.

36. *With all four walls selected:* pick *Basic Wall:* **Exterior – Brick on CMU** from the *Type Selector* on the *Properties Palette*.

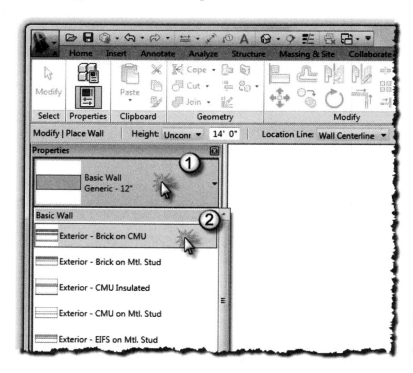

Type Selector with the four exterior walls selected.

Detail Level:

Revit allows you to control how much detail is shown in the walls.

37. On the *View Control Bar*, located in the lower left corner of the drawing window on the *View Control Bar*, set the *Detail Level* to **Fine**.

As you can see in the two images below, *Coarse* simply shows the outline of a wall type and *Fine* shows the individual components of the wall (i.e., brick, insulation, concrete block, etc.).

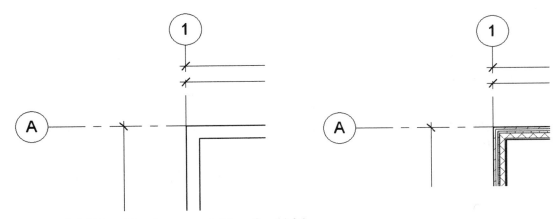

FIGURE 3-1.13 Detail level – coarse (left) vs. fine (right)

Now that you have the exterior walls established, the grid lines properly placed, and their relationships locked in the project, you can now proceed with the layout of the interior spaces.

Interior Walls:

38. With the **Wall** tool selected, modify the *Ribbon, Options Bar* and *Properties Palette* to the following (also, see image on the following page):

    a. *Type Selector:*   Click the down-arrow and select *Basic Wall:* **Interior – 4 7/8″ Partition (1-hr)**.

    b. *Height:*   **Roof**

    c. *Location Line:*   Set this to **Wall Centerline**.

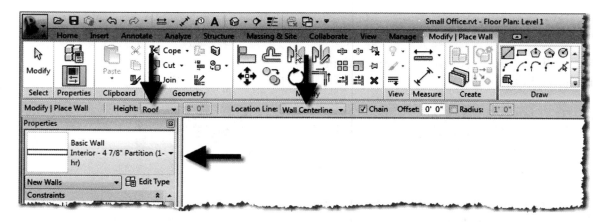

39. Draw a wall from the West wall (i.e., "vertical" wall on the left) to the East wall (on the right). See Figure 3-1.14.

a. Make sure your cursor "snaps" to the wall before clicking.

b. Before clicking the second point of the wall, make sure the dashed cyan line is visible so you know the wall will be truly horizontal.

c. The exact position of the wall is not important at this point as you will adjust it in the next step.

d. With the temporary dimensions still active, proceed to the next step.

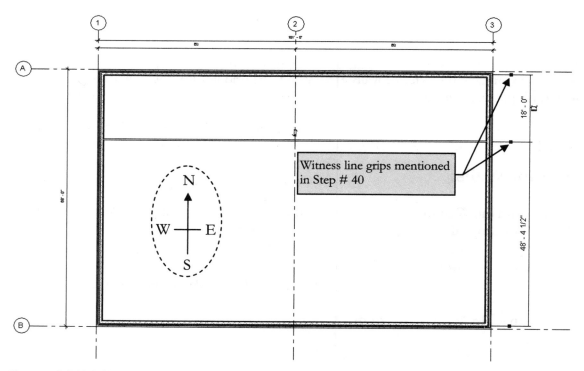

Witness line grips mentioned in Step # 40

FIGURE 3-1.14 Adding interior walls – North indicator added for reference only

40. Click the **witness line grips** (see Figure 3-1.14) until the "clear" space of the room is listed. (See Figure 3-1.15.)

41. Now click the blue text of the temporary dimension, type **22**, and then press **Enter** (Figure 3-1.15).

42. Click **Modify** to finish the current task.

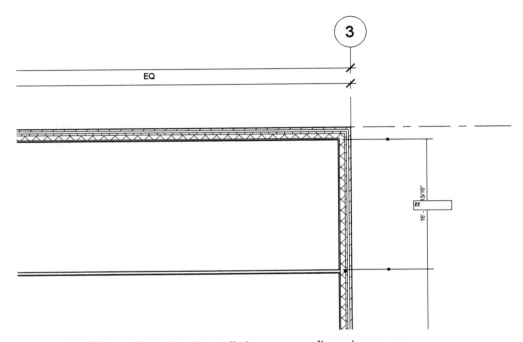

FIGURE 3-1.15 Repositioning interior wall via temporary dimensions

The clear space between the interior wall and the North wall is now 22'-0". Next, you will add additional interior walls to create equally spaced rooms in this area.

43. Using the same settings as the interior wall just added, draw five (5) vertical walls as shown in Figure 3-1.16.
    a. Make sure they are orthogonal (i.e., the dashed cyan line is visible before picking the walls' endpoints).
    b. Make sure you "snap" to the perpendicular walls (at the start and endpoints of the walls you are adding).
    c. Do not worry about the exact position of the walls.

    TIP: Uncheck Chain on the Options Bar.

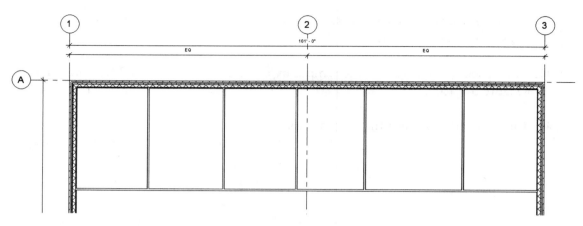

FIGURE 3-1.16 Adding additional interior walls

In the next step you will use a dimension string to reposition the walls so they are equally spaced. This process is similar to what you did to reposition Grid Line 2. However, you have to specify which part of the wall you want to dimension to (center, face, core center, core face).

> **FYI:** *The "core" portion of a wall system typically consists of the structural element(s) such as the concrete block (in your exterior walls) or the metal studs (in your interior walls).*

44. Select **Annotate → Dimension → Aligned** tool on the *Ribbon*.

45. On the *Options Bar*, select **Wall Faces**.

This setting will force Revit to only look for the face of a wall system. You can select either face depending on which side of the wall you favor with your cursor. This feature lets you confidently pick specific references without needing to continually zoom in and out all over the floor plan.

46. Select the interior face of the West wall to start your dimension string.

The next several picks will need to reference the wall centerlines. Revit allows you to toggle the wall position option on the fly via the *Options Bar*.

47. Change the setting to **Wall Centerlines**.

48. The next five picks will be on the five "vertical" interior walls. Make sure you see the dashed reference line centered on the wall to let you know you are about to select the correct reference plane.

49. Change the wall location setting back to **Wall Faces** and select the interior face of the East wall (the wall at Grid Line 3).

50. Your last pick should be away from any elements to position the dimension string somewhere within the rooms (Figure 3-1.17).

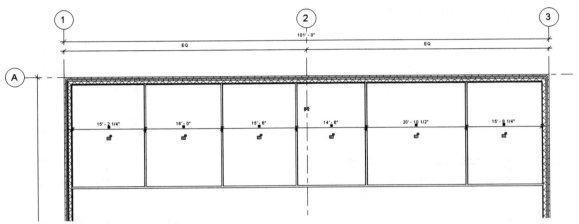

FIGURE 3-1.17 Adding a dimension string

51. Click the **EQ** symbol to reposition the interior walls.

52. Click **Modify**.

The interior walls are now equally spaced (Figure 3-1.18)!

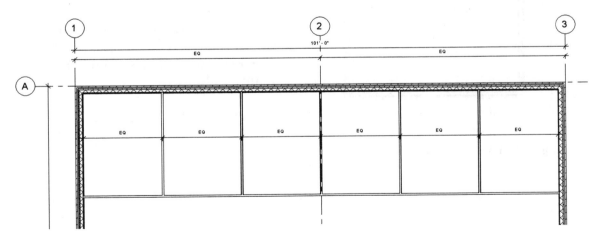

FIGURE 3-1.18 Enabling dimension equality

53. Add a vertical "clear" dimension to indicate the depth of the rooms. Set *Prefer* to **Wall Faces** for both ends of the dimension line. See Figure 3-1.19.

54. Click the **padlock** symbol (🔒) to tell Revit this dimension should not change (Figure 3-1.19).

55. Click **Modify**.

Next you will adjust the overall building dimensions and notice how the various parametric relationships you established cause the model to update!

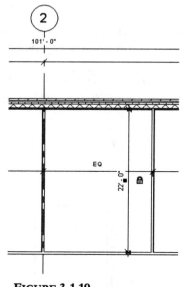

FIGURE 3-1.19
Locking dimensions

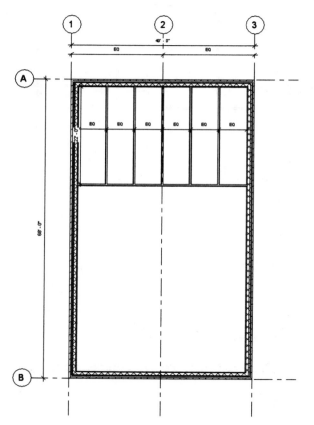

FIGURE 3-1.20 Adjusting dimensions

56. Click Grid Line 3 and change the overall dimension from 101 to **40**, by clicking on the dimension text and then press **Enter**.

> *TIP: When adjusting the building footprint via the dimensions, you need to select the grid line, not the East wall, because the dimension references the grid line.*

Notice the interior walls have adjusted to remain equal, and Grid Line 2 is still centered between Grids 1 and 3 (Figure 3-1.20).

57. Change the 40'-0" dimension to **110'-0"**.

58. Select Grid Line A and change the 68'-0" dimension to **38'-0"**.

Your model should now look similar to Figure 3-1.21. Notice the interior wall maintained its 22'-0" clear dimension because the interior wall has a dimension which is locked to the exterior wall, and the exterior wall has an alignment which is locked to Grid Line A.

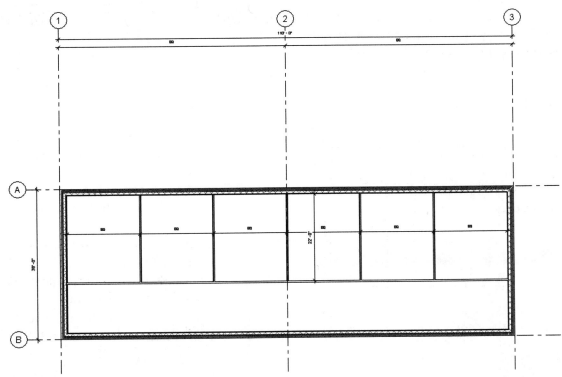

FIGURE 3-1.21 Adjusting dimensions

59. Click **Undo** icon on the *QAT* to restore the 68' dimension.

Your building should now be 110'-0" x 68'-0".

60. **Save** your project (*Small Office.rvt*).

> **TIP:** *You can use the* Measure *tool to list the distance between two points. This is helpful when you want to quickly verify the clear dimension between walls. Simply click the icon and snap to two points and Revit will temporarily display the distance. You can also click "chain" on the Options Bar and have Revit add up the total length of several picks.*

Exercise 3-2:
Doors

In this exercise you will add doors to your small office building.

1. Open **Small Office.rvt** created in Exercise 3-1.

Placing Doors:

2. Select **Home → Build → Door** tool on the *Ribbon* (Figure 3-2.1).

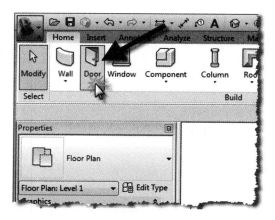

Notice that the *Ribbon, Options Bar* and *Properties Palette* have changed to show options related to doors. Next you will modify those settings.

The *Type Selector* indicates the door style, width and height. Clicking the down arrow to the right lists all the doors pre-loaded into the current project.

FIGURE 3-2.1 Door tool

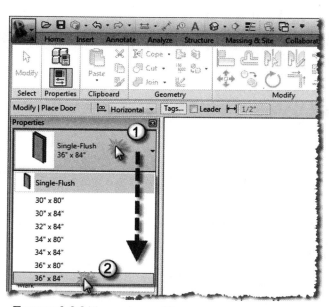

FIGURE 3-2.2 Type selector: Doors

The default template project that you started from has several sizes for a single flush door. Notice, in Figure 3-2.2, that there are two standard heights in the list. The 80″ (6′-8″) doors are the standard residential height and the 84″ (7′-0″) doors are the standard commercial door height.

3. Change the *Element Type Selector* to:
   Single-Flush: **36″ x 84″**.

4. Move your cursor over a wall and position the door as shown in **Figure 3-2.3**. (Do <u>not</u> click yet.)

Notice that the swing of the door changes depending on what side of the wall your cursor is favoring.

Also, notice Revit displays *listening dimensions* to help you place the door in the correct location.

5. Click to place the door. Revit automatically trims the wall and adds a *door tag*.

    TIP: Press the spacebar *before clicking to flip the door swing if needed.*

6. While the door is still selected, click on the *change swing (control arrows)* symbol to make the door swing against the wall if it does not already (Figure 3-2.4).

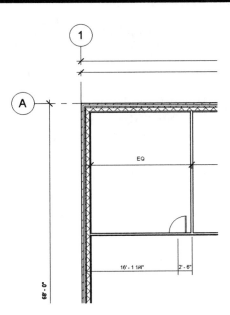

FIGURE 3-2.3 Adding door

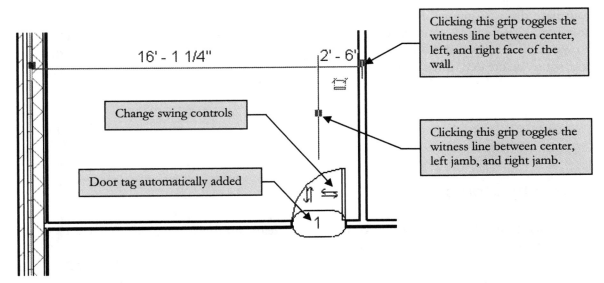

FIGURE 3-2.4 Door just placed

Next you will reposition the door relative to the adjacent wall.

7. Click **Modify** to finish the *Door* tool.

8. Click the door, (not the door tag) you just placed, to select it.

9. Click the **witness line grips** so the temporary dimension references the right door jamb and the wall face as shown in Figure 3-2.5.

TIP: You can also click and drag the witness line grip to another wall or line if the default location was not what you are concerned with.

10. Click on the dimension text, type **4″** and press **Enter**. Make sure you add the inch symbol or you will get feet rather than inches (Figure 3-2.5).

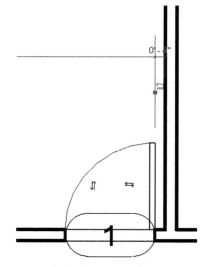

FIGURE 3-2.5 Edit door location

Unfortunately, the door *Families* loaded in the commercial template do not have frames. So the 4″ dimension just entered provides for a 2″ frame and 2″ of wall. The library installed on your hard drive, along with the Revit "web library", do provide some doors with frames. It is possible to create just about any door and frame combination via the *Family Editor*. The *Family Editor* is a special mode within Revit Architecture that allows custom parametric content to be created, including doors with sidelights, transoms and more!

Mirroring Doors:

The *Mirror* command will now be used to quickly create another door opposite the adjacent perpendicular wall.

11. With the door selected, click the **Mirror → Pick Mirror Axis** on the *contextual* tab.

12. On the *Options Bar*, click **Copy**. If Copy was not selected, then the door would be relocated rather than copied.

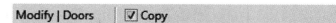

13. With the door selected and the *Mirror* command active, hover the cursor over the adjacent wall until the dashed reference line appears centered on the wall. Keep moving the mouse until you see this, and then click (Figure 3-2.6).

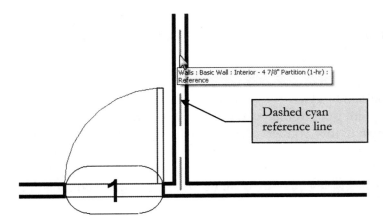

FIGURE 3-2.6 Mirroring a door

As you can see in Figure 3-2.7, the door has been mirrored into the correct location.

Revit does not automatically add door tags to mirrored or copied doors. These will be added later.

> *TIP: The size of the door tag is controlled by the view's scale.*

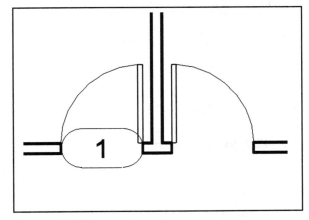

FIGURE 3-2.7 Door mirrored

Copying Doors:

Now you will copy the two doors so the other rooms have access.

14. Click to select the first door (not the door tag) and then press and hold the **Ctrl** key. *While holding the **Ctrl** key,* click to add the second door to the selection set.

15. With the two doors selected, click the **Copy** tool.

16. On the *Options Bar*, select **Multiple**.

At this point you need to pick two points: a "copy from here" point and a "copy to there" point. The first point does not have to be directly on the elements(s) to be copied. The next step will demonstrate this; you will pick the midpoint of the wall adjacent to the two doors (first pick) and then you will pick the midpoint of the wall where you want a set of doors (second pick). With "multiple" checked, you can continue picking "second points" until you are finished making copies (pressing **Esc** or *Modify* to end the command).

17. Pick three points:

    a. *First pick:* midpoint/centerline of wall (see Figure 3-2.8);

    b. *Second pick:* midpoint/centerline of wall shown in Figure 3-2.9;

    c. *Third pick:* midpoint/centerline of wall shown in Figure 3-2.9.

18. Pick **Modify** to end *Copy.*

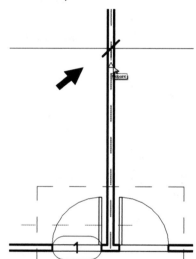

The doors are now copied.

FIGURE 3-2.8 Copy – first point with midpoint symbol visible

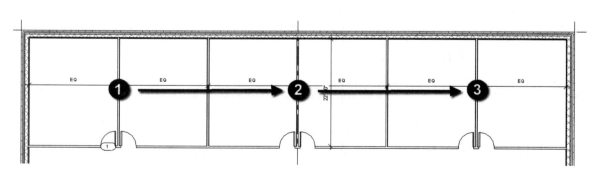

FIGURE 3-2.9 Numbers indicate pick-points listed in Step #17

You will now add two exterior doors using the same door type.

19. Using the **Door** tool, add two exterior doors approximately located per Figure 3-2.10. Match the swing and hand shown.

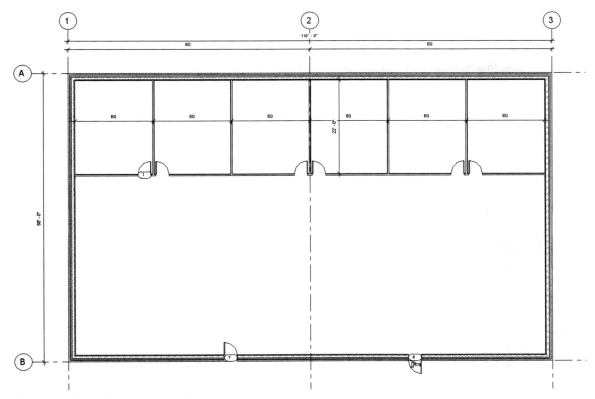

FIGURE 3-2.10 Adding exterior doors

Tag All (Not Tagged):

Revit provides a command to quickly add a tag (e.g., a door tag) to any door that does not currently have one in the current view. The tag might have to be moved or rotated once placed, but this still saves time and the possibility of missing a door tag.

20. Select **Annotate → Tag → Tag All**.

21. In the *Tag All Not Tagged* dialog box, select **Door Tags** under *Category* and set *Orientation* to **Vertical**. Click **OK**. (See image on next page.)

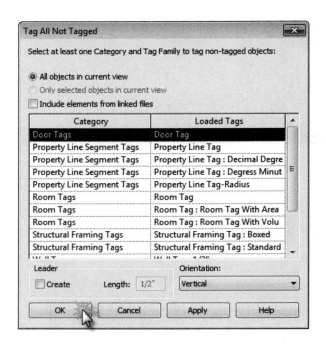

All the doors should now be tagged in your floor plan.

FYI: Door tags can be deleted at any time and added again later at any time. Tags simply display information about the element being tagged, thus, no information about the element is being deleted; the building information integrity remains intact.

Deleting Doors:

Next you will learn how to delete a door when needed. This process will work for most elements (i.e., walls, windows, text, etc.) in Revit.

22. Click **Modify**.

23. Click on door number 7 (the door on the left, not the door tag) and press the **Delete** key on your keyboard.

As you can see, the door is deleted and the wall is automatically filled back in. Also, a door tag can only exist by being attached to a door; therefore the door tag was also deleted.

One last thing to observe: Revit numbers the doors in the order in which they have been placed (regardless of level). Doors are not automatically renumbered when one is deleted. Also, doors can be renumbered to just about anything you want.

24. **Save** your project *(Small Office.rvt)*.

Exercise 3-3:
Windows

In this exercise you will add windows to your small office building.

1. Open **Small Office.rvt** created in Exercise 3-2.

Placing Windows:

2. Select **Home → Build → Window**.

Notice that the *Ribbon, Options Bar* and *Properties Palette* have changed to show options related to windows. Next you will modify those settings.

The *Type Selector* indicates the window style, width and height. Clicking the down arrow to the right lists all the windows loaded in the current project.

3. Change the *Type Selector* to *Fixed:* **36″ x 48″** and toggle off *Tag on Placement* (Figure 3-3.1).

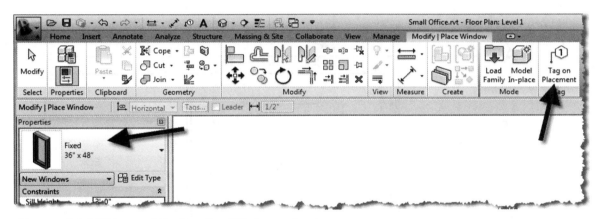

FIGURE 3-3.1 Ribbon and Options Bar: Window tool active

4. Move your cursor over a wall and place **two windows** as shown in **Figure 3-3.2**. *Notice that the position of the window changes depending on what side of the wall your cursor favors.*

   FYI: *The window sill height is controlled by the Properties Palette which you will study later in this book. For now, the default dimension is used.*

5. Adjust the **temporary dimensions** per the following:

   a. Dimensions per Figure 3-3.2.

   b. Use the witness line grip to adjust the witness line position.

   REMEMBER: *The selected item moves when temporary dimensions are adjusted. Pick the left window to set the 6'-0" dimension and the right for the 8'-0" dimension.*

6. Using the **Copy** command, in a way similar to copying the doors in the previous exercise, copy the two windows into each office as shown in Figure 3-3.3. (Do not worry about exact dimensions.)

7. **Save** your project *(Small Office.rvt).*

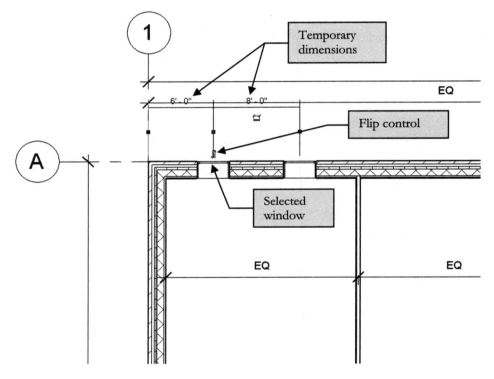

FIGURE 3-3.2 Adding windows – temporary dimensions still active

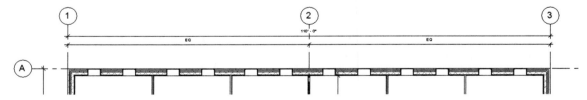

FIGURE 3-3.3 Windows added to North wall

The windows will not adjust with the grid lines and interior walls; it is possible to add dimensions and get this to work. If you tried to change the overall dimension from 110′ to 40′ again, Revit would let you know it needed to delete some windows before the change could be made. Like doors, windows need their host to exist.

The windows can all be adjusted via the temporary dimensions. The window selected is the largest width available in the project (based on the template file from which the project was started), but it is not a masonry dimension. However, additional window sizes can be added on the fly at any time. Additionally, you can create your own template file that has the doors, windows, walls, etc. that you typically need for the kind of design work you do.

In addition to the preloaded windows, several window styles are available via the family library loaded on your hard drive and the *Autodesk Web Library* (e.g., dbl-hung, casement, etc.). It is also possible to create just about any window design in the *Family Editor*.

Object Snap Symbols:
By now you should be well aware of the snaps that Revit suggests as you move your cursor about the drawing window.

If you hold your cursor still for a moment while a snap symbol is displayed, a tooltip will appear on the screen. However, when you become familiar with the snap symbols you can pick sooner (Figure 3-3.4).

The **Tab** key cycles through the available snaps near your cursor.

The keyboard shortcut turns off the other snaps for one pick. For example, if you type **SE** on the keyboard while in the Wall command, Revit will only look for an endpoint for the next pick.

Finally, typing **SO** (snaps off) turns all snaps off for one pick.

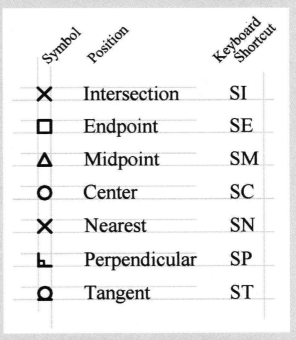

FIGURE 3-3.4 Snap Reference Chart

Exercise 3-4:
Roof

You will now add a simple roof to your building.

1. Open **Small Office.rvt** created in Exercise 3-3.

The first thing you will do is take a quick look at a 3D view of your building and notice an adjustment that needs to be made to the exterior walls.

2. Click the **Default 3D View** icon on the *QAT*.

The *3D* icon switches you to the *Default 3D View* in the current project. Your view should look similar to Figure 3-4.1. Notice the exterior walls are not high enough, which is due to a previous decision to set the wall height to 9'-0". Next you will change this, which can be done in plan view or the current 3D view.

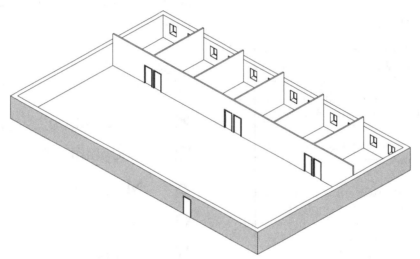

FIGURE 3-4.1 3D view of small office

3. In the 3D view, hover your cursor over one of the exterior walls to pre-highlight it, then (before clicking) press the **Tab** key to pre-highlight a "chain of walls" (i.e., all the exterior walls), and then click to select them.

Next you will access the properties of the selected walls so you can adjust the wall height. In Revit, most any design decisions that are made can be adjusted at any time.

4. Change the following in the *Properties Palette*:

    a. *Top Constraint:*   **Up to level: Roof**

    b. *Top Offset:*   **2'-0"**

    c. Click **OK** (Figure 3-4.2B).

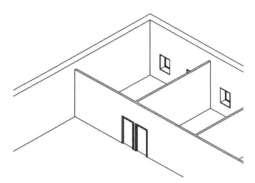

FIGURE 3-4.2A Exterior wall heights adjusted

Setting the top of wall to be associated with a *Level* establishes a parametric relationship that causes the wall height to automatically adjust if the level datum is adjusted (e.g., from 12'-0" to 14'-0").

Plus, the *Top Offset* at 2'-0" creates a 2'-0" parapet, which will always be 2'-0" high no matter what the roof elevation is set to. There are instances when you would want the height to be fixed.

All of the settings related to the selected wall show up here; these are called instance parameters.

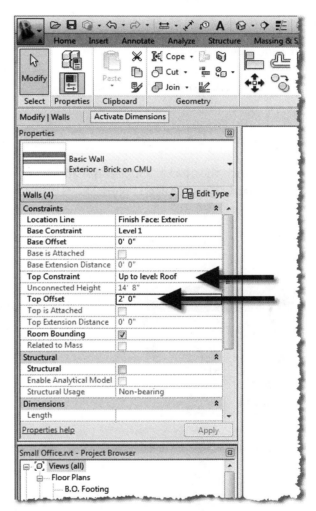

Figure 3-4.2B Selected wall properties

Sketching a Roof:

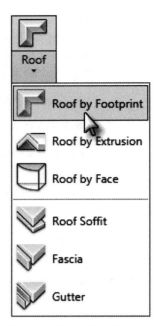

Now that the exterior walls are the correct height, you will now add the roof. This building will have a flat roof located at the roof level.

5. Double-click **Level 1** in the *Project Browser* to switch back to that view.

6. Click **Home → Build → Roof** (Figure 3-4.3).

The fly-out prompts you to choose the method you want to use to create the roof.

7. Click **Roof by Footprint**.

At this point you have entered *Sketch Mode* where the Revit model is grayed out so the perimeter you are about to sketch stands out.

FIGURE 3-4.3 Roof tool

Also notice the *Ribbon, Options Bar* and *Properties Palette* have temporarily been replaced with *Sketch* options relative to the roof (Figure 3-4.4).

8. Click **Extend to Core** on the *Options Bar* and make sure **Defines Slope** is not checked (Figure 3-4.4).

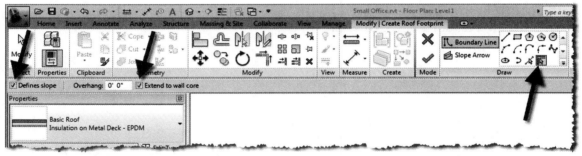

FIGURE 3-4.4 Roof sketch tools

9. Select all the exterior walls:

    a. Hover your cursor over one of the exterior walls to pre-highlight the wall.

    b. Press **Tab** to select a "chain of walls" (i.e., all the exterior walls).

    c. **Click** to select the exterior walls.

At this point you should have four magenta lines, one on each wall, which represent the perimeter of the roof you are creating. When sketching a roof footprint, you need to make sure that lines do not overlap and corners are cleaned up with the *Trim* command, if required. Your sketch lines require no additional edits because of the way you added them (i.e., pick *Walls* and **Tab** select).

Before you finish the roof sketch, you need to adjust the level on which the roof will be created. By default, the top surface of the roof element will be parametrically aligned with the current level (i.e., Level 1 in this case). You will change this to the *Roof* level.

FIGURE 3-4.5 Roof instance properties

10. In the *Properties Palette*, set *Base Level* to **Roof** (Figure 3-4.5).

Now you are ready to finish the roof and exit sketch mode.

11. Click the **green check mark** on the *Ribbon*.

12. Click **Yes** to the join geometry prompt (Figure 3-4.6).

The join geometry option will make the line work look correct in sections. If you clicked "No," the wall and floor lines would just overlap each other and look messy.

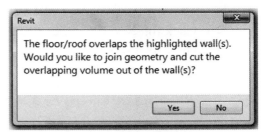

FIGURE 3-4.6 Join geometry prompt

The roof is now created and, in section, will extend through the finishes to the concrete block because "extend to core" was selected when the sketch lines were added. Also, because you used the "Pick Walls" option on the *Ribbon* (which was the default), the roof edge will move with the exterior walls.

13. To see the roof, click the ***Default 3D View*** icon.

14. To adjust the 3D view, press and hold the **Shift** key while pressing the **wheel button** and dragging the mouse around.

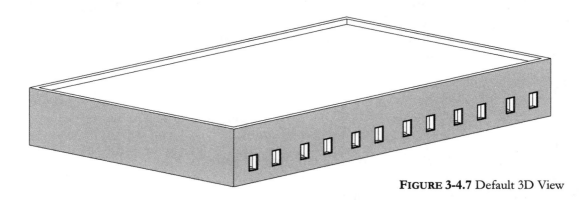

FIGURE 3-4.7 Default 3D View

15. Click the **X** in the upper right corner of the drawing window to close the current view (*3D*). This will close the *3D* view but not the project or the *Level 1* view.

    REMEMBER: *Clicking the **X** in the upper right of the application title bar will close Revit, but it will prompt you to save first, if needed.*

16. **Save** your project.

Exercise 3-5:
Annotation, Room Tags & Schedules

Adding text is very simple in Revit. In this exercise you will add a title below the floor plan. You will also place room tags.

Placing Text:

1. Open **Small Office.rvt** created in Exercise 3-4.

2. Make sure your current view is **Level 1**. The text "Level 1" will be bold under the *Floor Plans* heading in your *Project Browser*. If *Level 1* is not current, simply double-click on the "Level 1" text in the *Project Browser*.

3. Select **Annotate** → **Text** → **Text** tool on the *Ribbon*.

Once again, notice the *Ribbon* has changed to display some options related to the active tool (Figure 3-5.1).

FIGURE 3-5.1 Ribbon with Text tool active

The *Type Selector* indicates the text style (which determines the font style, height and more); users can create additional text styles. From this contextual tab, on the *Ribbon*, your alignment (i.e., *Left justified*, *Centered* or *Right justified*) can also be set.

4. Set the *Ribbon* settings to match those shown above. **Click** below the floor plan to place the text (Figure 3-5.2).

5. Type **OFFICE BUILDING – Option A**, then click somewhere in the plan view to finish the text (do not press **Enter**).

The text height, in the *Type Selector*, refers to the size of the text on a printed piece of paper. For example, if you print your plan you should be able to place a ruler on the text and read ¼″ when the text is set to ¼″ in the *Type Selector*.

Text size can be a complicated process in CAD programs; Revit makes it very simple. All you need to do is change the **View Scale** for **Level 1** and Revit automatically adjusts the text and annotation to match that scale – so it always prints ¼″ tall on the paper.

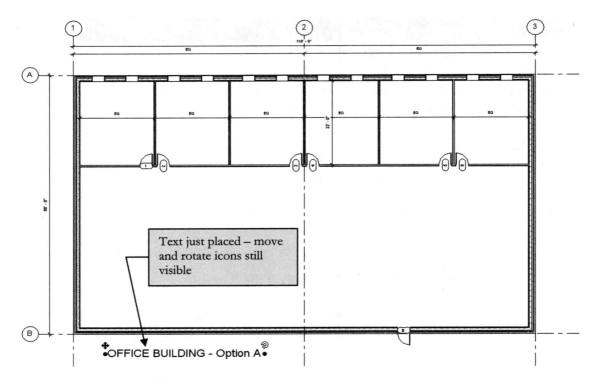

FIGURE 3-5.2 Placing text

You will not change the scale now, but it can be done via the *View Control Bar* (Figure 3-5.3). If you want to try changing it, just make sure it is set back to ⅛″ = 1′-0″ when done.

You should now notice that your text and even your door and window symbols are half the size they used to be when changing from ⅛″ to ¼″.

You should understand that this scale adjustment will only affect the current view (i.e., *Level 1*). If you switched to *Level 2* (if you had one), you would notice it is still set to ⅛″ = 1′-0″. This is nice because you may, on occasion, want one plan at a larger scale to show more detail.

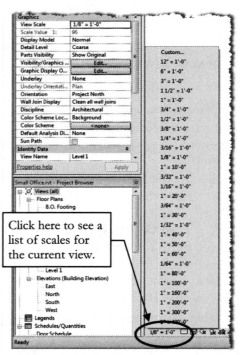

FIGURE 3-5.3 Set View Scale

Placing Room Tags:

Placing *Room Tags* must be preceded by placing a *Room*. A *Room* element is used to define a space and hold information about that space (e.g., floor finish, area, department, etc.). See this author's article in the *AUGI AEC-Edge* magazine for a detailed discussion on this topic (www.AUGI.com). Like a *Door Tag*, a *Room Tag* simply lists information contained within the element being tagged.

The *Room* tool searches for areas enclosed by walls; a valid area is pre-highlighted before you click to create it.

By default, Revit will automatically place a *Room Tag* at the cursor location when you click to add the *Room* element.

6. Select **Home → Room & Area → Room**.

7. Set the *Type Selector* to **Room Tag: Room Tag With Area** and make sure **Tag on placement** is selected on the *Ribbon*.

8. Click within each room in the order shown in Figure 3-5.4; watch for the dashed reference line to align the tags.

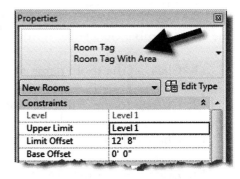

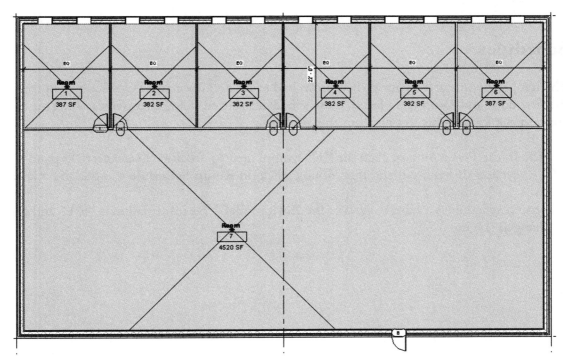

FIGURE 3-5.4 Placing rooms and room tags

While the *Room* tool is active, the placed rooms in the model are shaded light blue so you can see which spaces already have rooms placed. The large "X" is also part of the room. When the *Room* tool is not active, you can hover the cursor over the approximate location of the "X" until it pre-highlights, then you can click to select the room. With the *Room* object selected you can add information or delete it via the *Properties Palette*.

9. Click **Modify** to end the current tool.

Notice the rooms are not visible and the "X" is gone. Also notice, the *Room Tag* selected shows the following information stored within the *Room* object: Name, Number and Area.

> *FYI:* The area updates automatically when the walls move. Next you will change the room names.

10. Click on the *Room Tag* for **room number 1** to select it.

When a *Room Tag* is selected the "dark blue" text is editable and the "lighter blue" text is not. An example of text that cannot be edited would be the actual text "Sheet Number" next to the sheet number on a sheet border.

11. Click on the room name text, type **OFFICE**, and then press **Enter** on the keyboard.

12. Change rooms 3-4 to also be named **OFFICE**.

13. Change the large room name to **LOBBY**.

14. Leave two rooms (5 and 6) as "Room" for now.

Schedules:

The template you started your project from had room and door schedules set up,. so from the first door and room you placed, these schedules started filling themselves out! You will take a quick look at this to finish out this section.

15. In the *Project Browser*, click the "**+**" symbol next to *Schedules/Quantities* to expand that section (if required) and then double-click on **Room Schedule** to open that view.

The room schedule is a tabular view of the Revit model. This information is "live" and can be changed (Figure 3-5.5).

Room Schedule							
Room Number	Room Name	Floor Finish	Base Finish	Wall Finish	Ceiling Finish	Ceiling Height	Comments
1	OFFICE						
2	OFFICE						
3	OFFICE						
4	OFFICE						
5	Room						
6	Room						
7	LOBBY						

FIGURE 3-5.5 Room Schedule

Next, you will change the two rooms named "Room", and see that the floor plan is automatically updated!

16. Click in the *Room Name* column for room number 5 and change the text to read **MEN'S TOILET RM**.

17. Click in the *Room Name* column for room number 6 and change the text to read **WOMEN'S TOILET RM**.

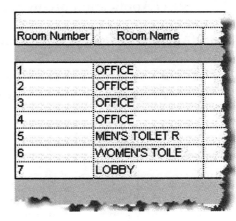

18. Click the lower "X" in the upper right of the drawing window to close the *Room Schedule* view.

19. Switch to *Level 1* (if required) and **zoom in** on rooms 5 and 6 (Figure 3-5.6).

Notice that the room names have been updated because the two views (*Floor Plan* and *Schedule*) are listing information from the same "parameter value" in the project database.

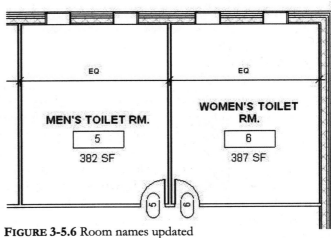

FIGURE 3-5.6 Room names updated

20. **Open** and **Close** the *Door Schedule* to view its current status.

21. **Save** your project.

Exercise 3-6:
Printing

The last thing you need to know to round off your basic knowledge of Revit is how to print the current view.

Printing the current view:

1. In *Level 1* view, right-click anywhere and select **Zoom to Fit**.

2. Select **Application Menu → Print**.

3. Adjust your settings to match those shown in **Figure 3-6.1**.

    • Select a printer from the list that you have access to.
    • Set *Print Range* to: **Visible portion of current window**.

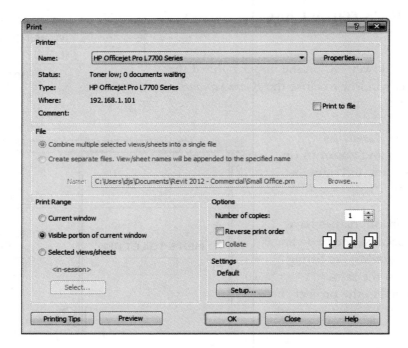

FIGURE 3-6.1 Print dialog

4. Click on the **Setup** button to adjust additional print settings.

5. Adjust your settings to match those shown in **Figure 3-6.2**.

    • Set *Zoom* to: **Fit to page**

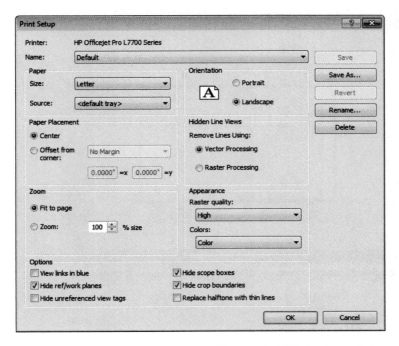

FIGURE 3-6.2 Print Setup dialog

6. Click **OK** to close the *Print Setup* dialog and return to *Print*.

7. Click the **Preview** button in the lower left corner. This will save paper and time by verifying the drawing will be correctly positioned on the page (Figure 3-6.3).

8. Click the **Print** button at the top of the preview window.

9. Click **OK** to print to the selected printer.

> ***FYI:*** *Notice you do not have the option to set the scale (i.e., ⅛″ = 1′-0″). If you recall from our previous exercise, the scale is set in the properties for each view. If you want a quick half-scale print you can change the zoom factor to 50%. You could also select "Fit to page" to get the largest image possible but not to scale.*

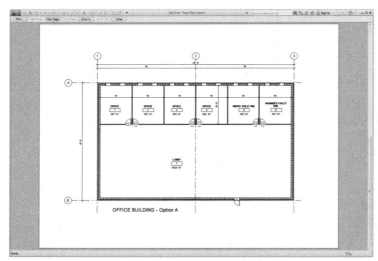

FIGURE 3-6.3 Print Preview

Printer versus Plotter?

Revit can print to any printer or plotter installed on your computer.

A <u>Printer</u> is an output device that uses smaller paper (e.g., 8½″x11″ or 11″x17″). A <u>Plotter</u> is an output device that uses larger paper; plotters typically have one or more rolls of paper ranging in size from 18″ wide to 36″ wide. A roll feed plotter has a built-in cutter that can – for example – cut paper from a 36″ wide roll to make a 24″x36″ sheet.

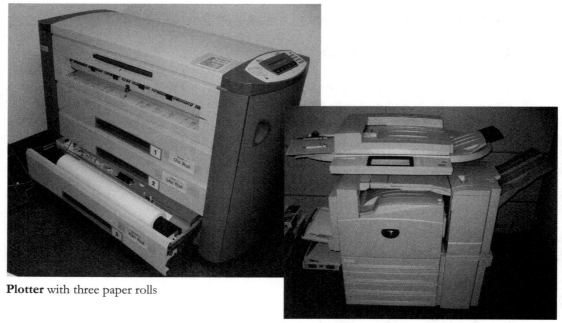

Plotter with three paper rolls

Color **printer** / copier

Self-Exam:

The following questions can be used as a way to check your knowledge of this lesson. The answers can be found at the bottom of this page.

1. The *Measure* tool is used to dimension drawings. (T/F)

2. Revit will automatically trim the wall lines when you place a door. (T/F)

3. Snap will help you to draw faster and more accurately. (T/F)

4. A 6'-8" door is a standard door height in _____ construction.

5. While using the *Wall* tool, the height can be quickly adjusted on the

   _____ *Bar.*

Review Questions:

The following questions may be assigned by your instructor as a way to assess your knowledge of this section. Your instructor has the answers to the review questions.

1. The *View Scale* for a view is set by clicking the scale listed on the *View Control Bar.* (T/F)

2. Dimensions are placed with only two clicks of the mouse. (T/F)

3. The relative size of text in a drawing is controlled by the *View Scale.* (T/F)

4. You can quickly switch to a different view by double-clicking on that view's label in the *Project Browser.* (T/F)

5. You cannot select which side of the wall a window is offset to. (T/F)

6. The _____ key cycles through the available snaps near your cursor.

7. The _____ tool can be used to list the distance between two walls without drawing a dimension.

8. While in the *Door* tool you can change the door style and size via the

   _____ _____ within the *Properties Palette.*

Notes:

Lesson 4
Overview of Linework and Modify Tools:

It may seem odd to you that, in a revolutionary 3D design program, you will begin by learning to draw and edit 2D lines and shapes. However, any 3D object requires, at a minimum, detailed information in at least two of the three dimensions. Once two dimensions are defined, Autodesk® Revit® Architecture can begin to automate much of the third dimension for you. Many building components and features will require you to draw the perimeter using 2D lines.

Many of the edit tools that are covered in this lesson are the same tools that are used to edit the 3D building components.

Exercise 4-1:
Lines and Shapes

Drawing Lines

You will draw many 2D lines in Autodesk Revit Architecture, typically in what is called *Sketch* mode. Two dimensional lines in Autodesk Revit Architecture are extremely precise drawing elements. This means you can create very accurate drawings. Lines, or any drawn object, can be as precise as 8 decimal places (i.e., 24.999999999) or 1/256.

Autodesk Revit Architecture is a vector based program. That means each drawn object is stored in a numerical database. When geometry needs to be displayed on the screen, Autodesk Revit Architecture reads from the project database to determine what to display on the screen. This ensures that the line will be very accurate at any scale or zoom magnification.

A raster based program, in contrast to vector based, is comprised of dots that infill a grid. The grid can vary in density, and is typically referred to as resolution (e.g., 600 x 800, 1600 x 1200, etc.). This file type is used by graphics programs that typically deal with photographs, such as Adobe Photoshop. There are two reasons this type of file is not appropriate for computer aided design (CAD) programs:

- A raster based line, for example, is composed of many dots on a grid, representing the line's width. When you zoom in, magnifying the line, it starts to become pixilated, meaning you actually start to see each dot on the grid. In a vector file you can "infinitely" zoom in on a line and it will never become pixilated because the program recalculates the line each time you zoom in.

- A CAD program, such as Revit, only needs to store the starting point and end point coordinates for each wall, for example; the dots needed to draw the wall are calculated on-the-fly for the current screen resolution. Whereas a raster file has to store each dot that represents the full length and width of the line, or lines in the wall example. This can vary from a few hundred dots to several thousand dots, depending on the resolution, for the same line.

The following graphic illustrates this point:

Vector vs. Raster Lines

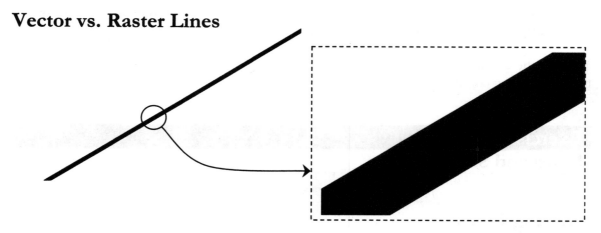

FIGURE 4-1.1 Vector Line Example
File Size: approx. 33kb

FIGURE 4-1.1A Vector Line Enlarged 1600%

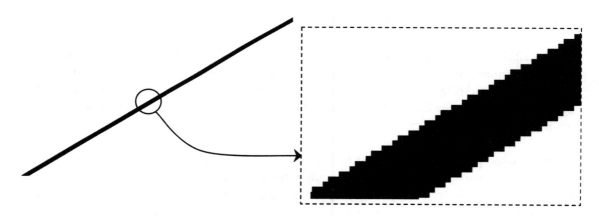

FIGURE 4-1.2 Raster Line Example
File Size: approx. 4.4MB

FIGURE 4-1.2A Raster Line Enlarged 1600%

The Detail Lines Tool:

You will now study the *Detail Lines* tool.

1. **Open** Revit.

Each time you start Revit, you are in the *Recent Files* view. This view is closed automatically when a new or existing project is opened.

2. Start a new project: select **Application Menu → New → Project** and then click **OK** to start a new project based on the default template.

The drawing window is set to the *Level 1 Floor Plan* view. The 2D drafting will be done in a drafting view. Next you will learn how to create one of these views.

3. Select **View → Create → Drafting View**
   (***REMEMBER:*** *This means* Tab → Panel → Icon *on the Ribbon.*)

   Drafting
   View

4. In the *New Drafting View* dialog box, type **Ex 4-1** for the *Name* and set the *Scale* to **3/4″ = 1′-0″** by clicking the down-arrow at the right (Figure 4-1.3).

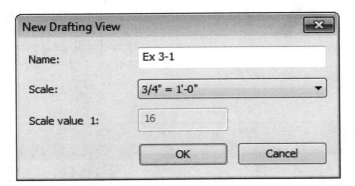

FIGURE 4-1.3 New Drafting View dialog

You are now in the new view and the *Project Browser* will contain a category labeled *Drafting Views (Detail)*. Here, each *Drafting View* created will be listed.

5. In the *Project Browser*, click the plus symbol next to the label **Drafting Views (Detail)**; this will display the *Drafting Views* that exist in the current project (Figure 4-1.4).

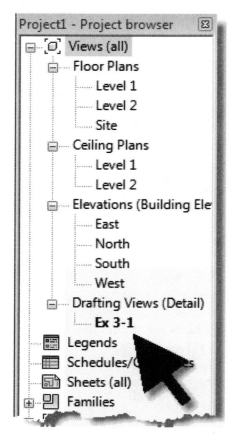

FIGURE 4-1.4 Project Browser: Drafting Views

You are now ready to start looking at the *Detail Line* tool:

6. Select the **Annotate** tab on the *Ribbon*.

7. On the *Detail* panel, select **Detail Line** (Figure 4-1.5).

   Detail Line

   TIP: *Do not use the "Model Line" tool on the Home tab.*

8. **Draw a line** from the lower left corner of the screen to the upper right corner of the screen, by simply clicking two points on the screen within the drawing window.

   NOTE: *Do not drag or hold your mouse button down; just click (Figure 4-1.6).*

After clicking your second point, you should notice the length and the angle of the line are graphically displayed; this information is temporary and will disappear when you move your cursor.

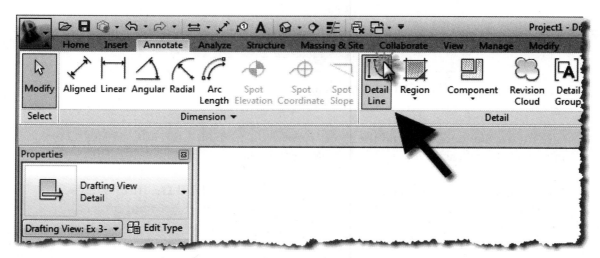

FIGURE 4-1.5 Annotate tab

You should also notice that the *Detail Line* tool is still active, which means you could continue to draw additional lines on the screen.

9. After clicking your second point, select the **Modify** tool from the left side of the *Ribbon*.

Selecting *Modify* cancels the current tool and allows you to select portions of your drawing for information or editing. Revit conveniently places the *Modify* tool in the same location on each tab so it is always available no matter which tab on the *Ribbon* is active.

> **TIP:** *Pressing the* Esc *key twice reverts Revit back to* Modify *mode.*

Did You Make a Mistake?

Whenever you make a mistake in Revit you can use the **UNDO** command, via the *QAT*, to revert to a previous drawing state. You can perform multiple UNDO's all the way to your previous *Save*.

Similarly, if you press Undo a few too many times, you can use **REDO**.

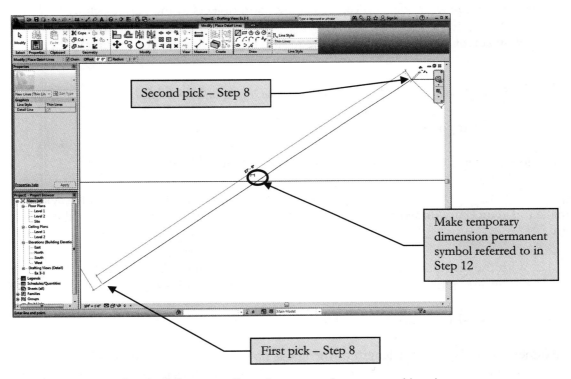

FIGURE 4-1.6 Your first detail line; exact dimensions are not important at this point.

Notice in the image above, that while the *Detail Line* tool is active, the *Modify | Place Detail Line* contextual tab is shown. As soon as you click the *Modify* button or press **Esc**, the tab reverts back to the basic *Modify* tab.

This constitutes your first line! However, as you are probably aware, it is not a very accurate line as far as length and angle are concerned. Your line will likely be a different length due to where you picked your points and the size and resolution of your monitor.

Typically you need to provide information such as length and angle when drawing a line; you rarely pick arbitrary points on the screen as you did in the previous steps. Revit allows you to get close with the on-screen dimension and angle information. Most of the time you also need to accurately pick your starting point. For example, how far one line is from another or picking the exact middle point on another line.

Having said that, however, the line you just drew still has precise numbers associated with its length and angle; this information is displayed after the line is drawn. The dimension and angle information is displayed until you begin to draw another line or select another tool. You can also select the line. While the dimensions are still visible, they can be used to modify the length and angle of the line; you will try that later.

10. If not already selected, click the **Modify** tool from the *Ribbon*.

Notice that the temporary dimensions have disappeared.

While you are in *Modify* mode, you can select lines and objects in the current view.

11. Now **select the line** by clicking the mouse button with the cursor directly over the line.

> *FYI: Always use the left button unless the right button is specifically mentioned.*

Notice that the temporary dimensions have returned.

The following step shows how to make a temporary dimension permanent:

If, at any point, you want to make a temporary dimension permanent, you simply click the "make this temporary dimension permanent" symbol near the dimension. You will try this now.

12. With the diagonal line still selected, click the "make this temporary dimension permanent" symbol near the dimension (Figure 4-1.6).

13. Select **Modify** to unselect the line.

The dimension indicating the length of the line is now permanent (Figure 4-1.7). The value of your dimension will not be the same as the one in this book as the size of your monitor and the exact points picked can vary greatly.

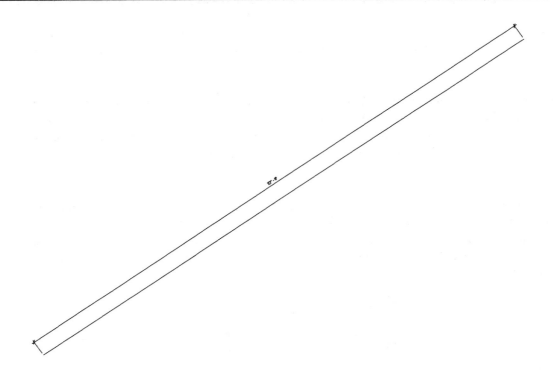

FIGURE 4-1.7 Temp dimension converted to permanent dimension

The following shows how to change the length of the line:

Currently, the line is approximately 20 - 30' long (27'-6" in Figure 4-1.7). If you want to change the length of the line to 22'-6", you select the line and then change the dimension text, which in turn changes the line length. This can also be done with the temporary dimensions; the key is that the line has to be selected. You will try this next.

> *FYI: Your detail line length will vary slightly depending on the size and resolution of your computer monitor. This also assumes you have not performed any zooming, including spinning the wheel button on your mouse. If your line is way off, you should Undo or start over so the next several steps work out as intended.*

14. In *Modify* mode, select the diagonal line.

15. With the line currently selected, click on the dimension-text.

A dimension-text edit box appears directly over the dimension, within the drawing window. Whatever you type as a dimension changes the line to match.

16. Type **22 6** (i.e., 22 *space* 6) and press **Enter** (Figure 4-1.8).

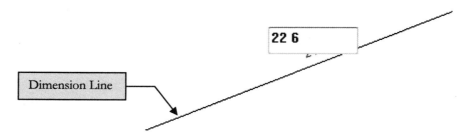

FIGURE 4-1.8 Editing dimension to change line length

You should have noticed the line changed length. Revit assumes that you want the line to change length equally at each end, so the midpoint does not move. Try changing the dimension to 100′ and then **Undo**.

Locking Dimensions:

Revit allows you to *Lock* a dimension, which prevents the dimension and line length from changing. You will investigate this now to help avoid problems later.

17. Make sure the line is *not* selected; to do this press **Esc** or click **Modify**.

18. Select the dimension, not the line, and note the following about the selected dimension (Figure 4-1.9).

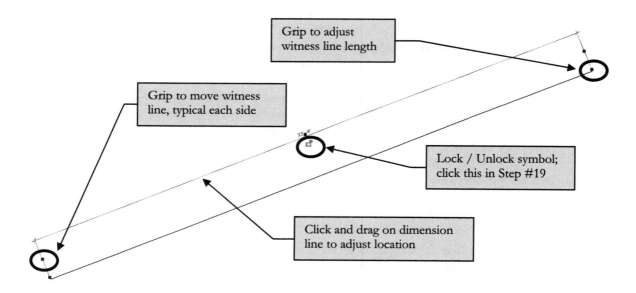

FIGURE 4-1.9 Selected dimension

19. Click on the **lock/unlock** padlock symbol to lock the dimension (Figure 4-1.9).

The dimension is now locked. Again, this means that you cannot change the dimension OR the line, though you can move it. The dimension is attached to the line in such a way that changing one affects the other. Next you will see what happens when you try to modify the dimension while it is locked.

Any time the line or dimension is selected, you will see the *lock* or *unlock* symbol in the locked position.

> *FYI: Clicking the dimension's padlock icon anytime it is visible will toggle the setting between locked and unlocked.*

20. Select **Modify** to unselect the *Dimension*.

21. Select the line (not the dimension).

22. Click on the dimension text and attempt to modify the line length to **21'**.

As you can see, Revit will not let you edit the text.

Even though your current view is showing a relatively small area, i.e., your *Drafting View*, it is actually an infinite drawing board.

In architectural CAD drafting, everything is drawn true to life size, or full-scale, ALWAYS! If you are drawing a building, you might draw an exterior wall that is 600'-0" long. If you are drawing a window detail, you might draw a line that is 8" long. In either case you are entering that line's actual length.

You could, of course, have an 8" line and a 600'-0" line in the same *Drafting View*. Either line would be difficult to see at the current drawing magnification (i.e., approximately 22' x 16' area; also recall that your diagonal line is 22'-6" long). So, you would have to zoom in to see the 8" line and zoom out to see the 600'-0" line. Next you will get to try this.

When the diagonal line is selected, notice the *Properties Palette* lists the type of entity selected (i.e., Lines), the *Style* (i.e., Thin Lines) and the *Length* (i.e., 22'-6"). See Lesson 2 for more information on the *Properties Palette* and how to open it if you accidentally closed it.

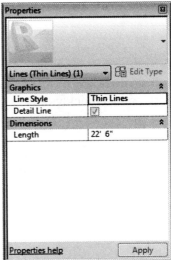

FIGURE 4-1.10 Properties Palette with diagonal line selected

Draw an 8″ Line:

The next steps will walk you through drawing an 8″ horizontal line. Revit provides more than one way to do this. You will try one of them now.

23. Select **Annotate → Detail → Detail Line**.

24. Pick a point somewhere in the upper left corner of the drawing window.

25. Start moving the mouse towards the right, and generally horizontal, until you see a dashed reference line extending in each direction of your line appear on the screen, as in Figure 4-1.11.

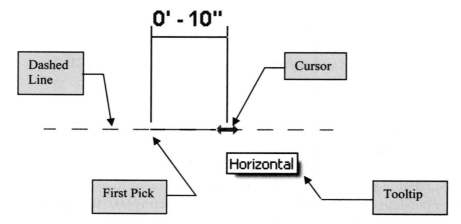

FIGURE 4-1.11 Drawing a line with the help of Revit

> *TIP: You will see a dashed horizontal line and a tooltip when the line is horizontal.*

As you move the mouse left and right, you will notice Revit displays various dimensions that allow you to quickly draw your line at these often used increments. See the next exercise to learn more about how to control the increments shown.

26. With the dashed line and *tooltip* visible on the screen, take your hand off the mouse, so you do not accidentally move it, and type: **8″** and then press **Enter**.

> *TIP: Remember, you have to type the inch symbol; Revit always assumes you mean feet unless you specify otherwise. A future lesson will review the input options in more detail.*

You have just drawn a line with a precise length and angle!

27. Use the *Measure* tool to verify it was drawn correctly. Click **Modify →
Measure → Measure (down arrow)→ Measure Between Two References**.

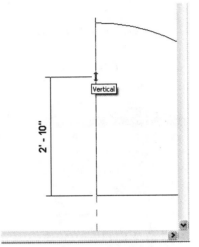

28. Use the *Zoom In Region* tool to enlarge the view of the 8″ line via the *Navigation Bar* (image to right).

29. Now use the *Zoom to Fit* or *Previous Pan/Zoom* tools so that both lines are visible again.

Draw a 600′ Line:

30. Select the **Detail Line** tool and pick a point in the lower right corner of the drawing window.

31. Move the cursor straight up from your first point so that the line snaps to the vertical and the dashed line appears (Figure 4-1.12).

32. With the dashed line and *tooltip* visible on the screen, take your hand off the mouse so you do not accidentally move it; type: **600** and then press **Enter**.

> *TIP #1: Notice this time you did not have to type the foot symbol (′).*

> *TIP #2: You do not need to get the temporary dimension close to reading 600′; the temporary dimension is ignored when you type in a value.*

FIGURE 4-1.12 Drawing another Detail Line; 600′-0″ vertical line – lower right

33. Press the **Esc** key twice to exit the *Detail Line* tool and return to the *Modify* mode.

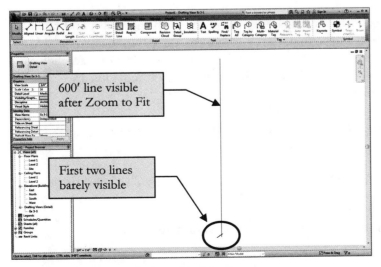

600′ line visible after Zoom to Fit

First two lines barely visible

FIGURE 4-1.13 Detail view with three lines

Because the visible portion of the drawing area is only about 16′ tall, you obviously would not expect to see a 600′ line. You need to change the drawing's magnification by zooming out to see it.

34. Use *Zoom to Fit* to see the entire drawing (Figure 4-1.13).

Drawing Shapes:

Revit provides several tools to draw common shapes like squares, rectangles, circles and ellipses. These tools can be found on the *Ribbon* while the *Detail Line* tool is active. You will take a look at *Rectangle* and *Circle* now.

Creating a Rectangle:

35. Use **Previous Pan/Zoom**, or **Zoom Region**, to get back to the original view where the diagonal line spans the screen.

36. Select the **Detail Line** tool.

Notice the *Ribbon, Options Bar* and *Properties Palette* have changed to show various options related to *Detail Lines* (Figure 4-1.14).

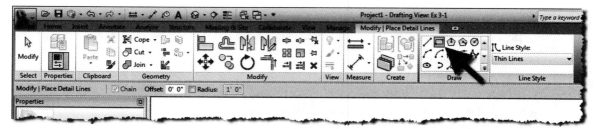

FIGURE 4-1.14 Place Detail Lines tab on Ribbon

37. Select the **Rectangle** tool from the *Ribbon*.

   TIP: Hover your cursor over the icon to see the tooltip until you learn what tools the icons represent.

38. Pick the "**first corner point**" somewhere near the lower center of the drawing window (Figure 4-1.15).

Notice the temporary dimensions are displaying a dimension for both the width and height. At this point you can pick a point on the screen, trying to get the dimensions correct before clicking the mouse button. If you do not get the rectangle drawn correctly, you can click on each dimension text and change the dimension while the temporary dimensions are displayed; see the next two steps for the rectangle dimensions.

39. Draw a 2'-8" x 4'-4" rectangle using the temporary dimensions displayed on the screen; if you do not draw it correctly, do the following:

   a. Click the dimension text for the horizontal line, then type **2'-8"** and press **Enter**.

   b. Type **4'-4"** and then press **Enter** for the vertical dimension.

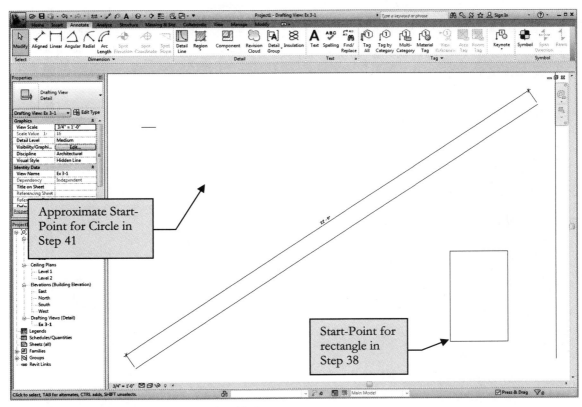

FIGURE 4-1.15 Drawing with Rectangle added

Creating a Circle:

40. With the *Detail Line* tool active, select **Circle** from the *Ribbon* (Figure 4-1.16).

41. You are now prompted to pick the center point for the circle; pick a point approximately as shown in Figure 4-1.15.

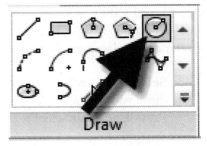

FIGURE 4-1.16 Detail Line shapes

You should now see a dynamic circle and a temporary dimension attached to your cursor, which allows you to visually specify the circle's size. Move your mouse around to see that you could arbitrarily pick a point on the screen to create a quick circle if needed, then proceed to Step 42 where you will draw a circle with a radius of 1'-6⅝".

42. Type **1 6 5/8** and then press **Enter** (Figure 4-1.17).

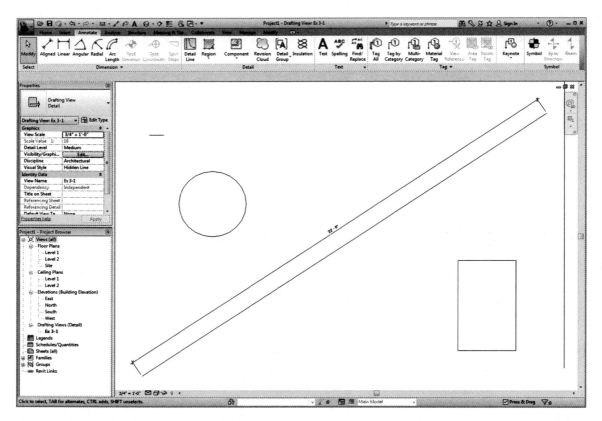

FIGURE 4-1.17 Drawing with Circle added

Notice in the image above the *Detail Line* is still active because the *contextual tab*, **Modify | Place Detail Lines**, is visible and the *Status Bar* is prompting to "Click to enter circle center". You need to press **Esc** or click **Modify** to cancel the command; clicking another command will also cancel the current command.

43. **Select the circle** and notice a temporary dimension appears, indicating the circle's radius. Press **Esc** to unselect it (Figure 4-1.18).

    TIP: This temporary dimension can be used to change the radius of the circle while the circle is selected.

44. **Save** your project as "**ex4-1.rvt**".

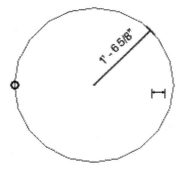

FIGURE 4-1.18
Circle selected

Exercise 4-2:
Snaps

Snaps are tools that allow you to accurately pick a point on an element. For example: when drawing a line you can use *Object Snap* to select, as the start-point, the endpoint or midpoint of another line or wall.

This feature is absolutely critical to drawing accurate technical drawings. Using this feature allows you to be confident you are creating perfect intersections, corners, etc. (Figure 4-2.1).

Object Snaps Options:

You can use *Object Snaps* in one of two ways.

o "Normal" mode
o "Temporary Override" mode

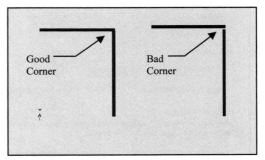

FIGURE 4-2.1 Typical problem when *Snaps* are not used

"Normal" *OSNAP* mode is a feature that constantly scans the area near your cursor when Revit is looking for user input. You can configure which types of points to look for.

> **NOTE:** *The term "normal" is not a Revit term; rather it is simply a description used in this book to differentiate this portion of the Snaps feature from the Temporary Override portion discussed next.*

Using a "temporary override" *Object Snap* for individual pick-points allows you to quickly select a particular point on an element. This option will temporarily disable the other *Object Snap* settings, which means you tell Revit to just look for the endpoint on an object, for the next pick-point only, rather than the three or four types being scanned for by the "normal" *Object Snaps* feature.

Overview of the Snaps Dialog Box:

Revit provides a *Snaps* dialog box where you specify which *Object Snaps* you want enabled. Next you will take a look at it.

1. Open project **Ex4-1** and select **Manage → Settings → Snaps**.

Snaps

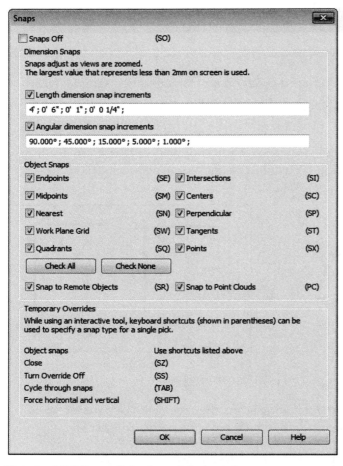

FIGURE 4-2.2 Snaps dialog box; default settings

You should now see the *Snaps* dialog box (Figure 4-2.2). Take a minute to study the various settings that you can control with this dialog box. Notice the check box at the top that allows you to turn this feature off completely.

Dimension Snaps
This controls the automatic dimensions that Revit suggests when you are drawing. Following the given format, you could add or remove increments. If you are zoomed in close, only the smaller increments are used.

Object Snaps
This controls the "normal" *Object Snaps* that Revit scans for while you are drawing. Unchecking an item tells Revit not to scan for it anymore. Currently, all *Object Snaps* are enabled (Figure 4-2.2).

Temporary Overrides
This area is really just information on how to use temporary overrides.

While drawing, you will occasionally want to tell Revit you only want to *Snap* to an Endpoint for the next pick. Instead of opening the *Snaps* dialog and un-checking every *Object Snap* except for Endpoint, you can specify a *temporary override* for the next pick. You do this by typing the two letters, in parentheses, in the *Object Snaps* area of the *Snaps* dialog (Figure 4-2.2).

2. Make sure the *Snaps Off* option is unchecked in the upper left corner of the dialog box; this turns Snaps completely off.

3. Click on the **Check All** button to make sure all *Snaps* are checked.

4. Click **OK** to close the *Snaps* dialog box.

Understanding Snap Symbols:

Again, you should be well aware of the *Object Snap* symbols that Revit displays as you move your cursor about the drawing window, while you are in a tool like *Wall* and Revit is awaiting your input or pick-point.

If you hold your cursor still for a moment, while a snap symbol is displayed, a tooltip will appear on the screen. However, when you become familiar with the snap symbols you can pick sooner, rather than waiting for the tooltip to display (Figure 4-2.3).

The **Tab** key cycles through the available snaps near your cursor.

Finally, typing **SO** turns all snaps off for one pick.

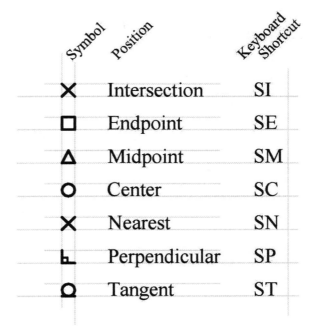

Symbol	Position	Keyboard Shortcut
✕	Intersection	SI
☐	Endpoint	SE
△	Midpoint	SM
○	Center	SC
✕	Nearest	SN
⌐	Perpendicular	SP
◌	Tangent	ST

FIGURE 4-2.3 Snap symbols

FYI: The Snaps shown in Figure 4-2.2 are for Revit in general, not just the current project. This is convenient; you don't have to adjust to your favorite settings for each Project or View, existing or new.

Setting Object Snaps:

You can set Revit to have just one or all Snaps running at the same time. Let us say you have Endpoint and Midpoint set to be running. While using the *Wall* tool, you move your cursor near an existing wall. When the cursor is near the end of the wall you will see the Endpoint symbol show up; when you move the cursor towards the middle of the line you will see the Midpoint symbol show up.

The next step shows you how to tell Revit which Object Snaps you want it to look for.

5. First you will save a new copy of your project.

6. Select **Application Menu → Save-As → Project** and name the project **ex4-2.rvt**.

7. As discussed previously, open the ***Snaps*** dialog box.

8. Make sure only the following *Snaps* are checked:
   a. Endpoints
   b. Midpoints
   c. Centers
   d. Intersections
   e. Perpendicular

9. Click **OK** to close the dialog box.

For More Information:

For more on using Snaps, search Revit's *Help System* for **Snaps**. Then double-click **Snap Points** or any other items found by the search.

Now that you have the *Snaps* adjusted, you will give this feature a try.

10. Using the ***Detail Line*** tool, move your cursor to the lower left portion of the diagonal line (Figure 4-2.4).

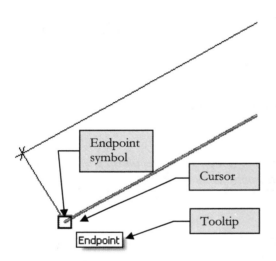

11. Hover the cursor over the line's endpoint (without picking); when you see the *Endpoint* symbol you can click to select that point.

Just So You Know

It is important that you see the *OSNAP* symbol before clicking. Also, once you see the symbol you should be careful not to move the mouse too much.

These steps will help to ensure accurate selections.

Endpoint symbol

Cursor

Tooltip

Endpoint

FIGURE 4-2.4 Endpoint SNAP symbol visible

While still in the Detail Line tool you will draw lines using *Snaps* to sketch accurately.

12. Draw the additional lines shown in **Figure 4-2.5** using the appropriate *Object Snap*, changing the selected Snaps as required to select the required points.

TIP #1: At any point, while the Line *tool is active, you can open the* Snap *dialog box and adjust its settings. This will not cancel the* Line *command.*

*TIP #2: Also, remember you can press **Tab** to cycle through the various snap options below or near your cursor.*

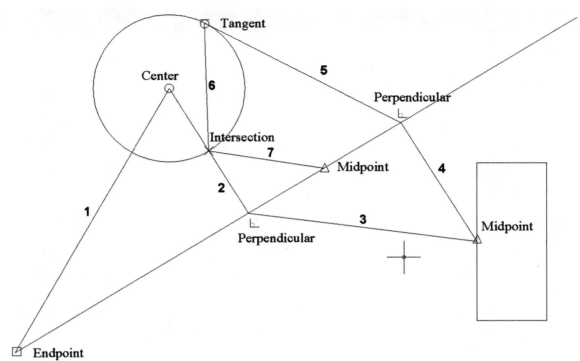

FIGURE 4-2.5 Lines to draw and Snaps to use

13. **Save** your project.

Your drawing might look slightly different depending on where you drew the rectangle and circle in the previous steps.

This is a Residential Example?

OK, this is not really an architectural example yet. However, the point here is to focus on the fundamental concepts and not architecture just yet.

Save Reminders:

Revit is configured to remind you to save every 30 minutes so you do not lose any work (Figure 4-2.6).

It is recommended that you do not simply click *Cancel*, but do click the **Save the project** option.

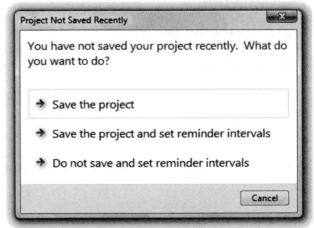

FIGURE 4-2.6 Save reminder

Exercise 4-3:
Edit Tools

The *edit tools* are used often in Revit. A lot of time is spent tweaking designs and making code and client related revisions.

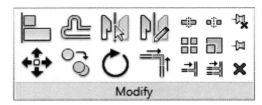

Example: you use the *design tools* (e.g., *Walls*, *Doors*, *Windows*) to initially draw the project. Then you use the *edit tools* to *Move* a wall so a room becomes larger, *Mirror* a cabinet so it faces in a different direction, or *Rotate* the furniture per the owner's instructions.

FIGURE 4-3.1 Modify panel

You will usually access the various edit tools from the *Modify* menu or *Modify* contextual tab on the *Ribbon*. You can probably visualize what most of the commands do by the graphics on the icons; see Figure 4-3.1. When you hover over an icon, the tool name will appear. The two letters shown to the right are its keyboard shortcut; pressing those two keys, one at a time, activates that tool.

In this exercise you will get a brief overview of a few of the edit tools by manipulating the tangled web of lines you have previously drawn.

1. **Open** project **ex4-2.rvt** from the previous lesson.

2. **Save-As** "**ex4-3.rvt**".

> *FYI: You will notice that instructions or tools that have already been covered in this book will have less "step-by-step" instruction.*

Delete Tool:

It is no surprise that the *Delete* tool is a necessity; things change and mistakes are made. You can *Delete* one element at a time or several. Deleting elements is very easy; you select the elements, and then pick the *Delete* icon. You will try this on two lines in your drawing.

3. While holding the **Ctrl** key, select the lines identified in **Figure 4-3.2**.

> *TIP: See the section below Figure 4-3.2 on Selecting Entities.*

4. Select **Delete** from the *Ribbon* (or press the **Delete** key on the keyboard).

The lines are now deleted from the project.

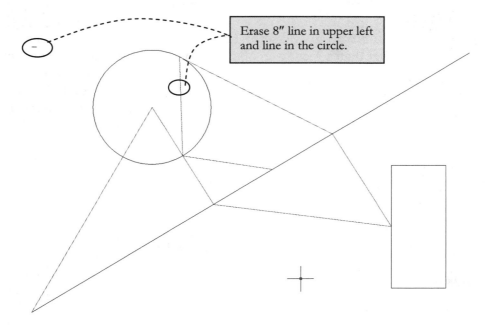

Erase 8″ line in upper left and line in the circle.

FIGURE 4-3.2 Lines to be erased

Selecting Objects:

At this time we will digress and take a quick look at the various techniques for selecting entities in Revit. Most tools work the same when it comes to selecting elements.

When selecting entities, you have two primary ways to select them:
- o Individually select entities one at a time
- o Select several entities at a time with a window

You can use one or a combination of both methods to select elements when using the *Copy* tool.

<u>Individual Selections:</u>
When prompted to select entities to *Copy* or *Delete*, for example, you simplly move the cursor over the element and click; holding the **Ctrl** key, you can select multiple objects. Then you typically click the tool you wish to use on the selected items. Press **Shift** and click on an item to subtract it from the current selection set.

Continued on next page

<u>Window Selections:</u>

Similarly, you can pick a *window* around several elements to select them all at once. To select a *window*, rather than selecting an object as previously described, you select one corner of the *window* you wish to define. That is, you pick a point in "space" and hold the mouse button down. Now, as you move the mouse you will see a rectangle on the screen that represents the windowed area you are selecting; when the *window* encompasses the elements you wish to select, release the mouse.

You actually have two types of windows you can select. One is called a **window** and the other is called a **crossing window**.

Window:

This option allows you to select only the objects that are completely within the *window*. Any lines that extend out of the *window* are not selected.

Crossing Window:

This option allows you to select all the entities that are completely within the *window* and any that extend outside the *window*.

Using Window versus Crossing Window:

To select a *window* you simply pick and drag from left to right to form a rectangle (Figure 4-3.3a).

Conversely, to select a *crossing window*, you pick and drag from right to left to define the two diagonal points of the window (Figure 4-3.3b).

Selecting a chain of lines (hover, tab, click):

Revit provides a quick and easy way to select a chain of lines, that is, a series of lines (or walls) whose endpoints are perfectly aligned. You simply hover your cursor over one line so it highlights, then press the **Tab** key once, and then click the mouse button. This trick can be used to quickly select all the exterior walls on a building, for example.

Turning off **Press & Drag** on the *Status Bar* helps to avoid accidentally clicking directly on an element and moving it rather than starting the intended first corner of a selection window.

Remember, all these draw, modify and select tools have direct application to working with Revit's 3D building components, not just the 2D geometry being covered in this chapter.

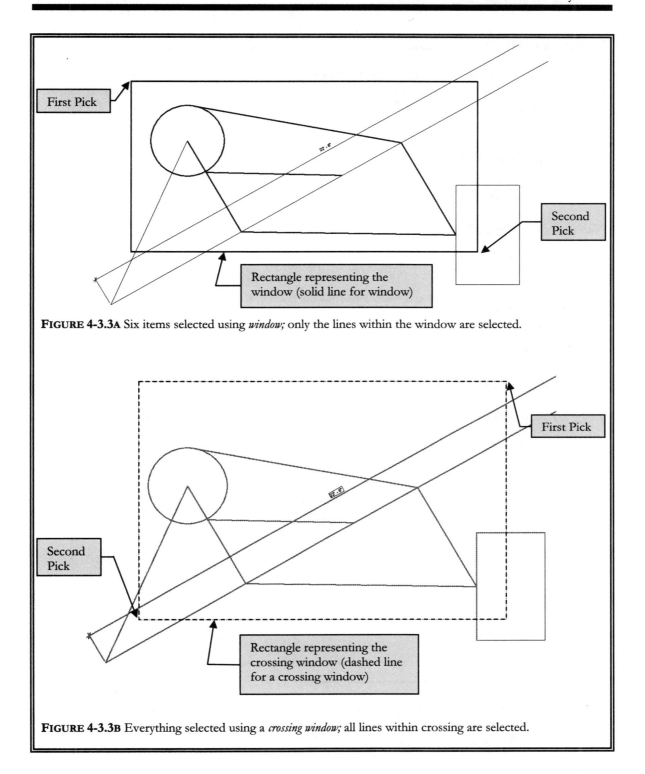

FIGURE 4-3.3A Six items selected using *window;* only the lines within the window are selected.

FIGURE 4-3.3B Everything selected using a *crossing window;* all lines within crossing are selected.

Copy Tool:

The *Copy* tool allows you to accurately duplicate an element(s). You select the items you want to copy and then pick two points that represent an imaginary vector, which provides both length and angle, defining the path used to copy the object. You can also type in the length if there are no convenient points to pick in the drawing. You will try both methods next.

5. **Select the circle.**

6. Select **Copy** from the *Ribbon*.

Notice the prompt at the bottom: Click to enter move start point.

7. Pick the **center** of the **circle** (Figure 4-3.4).

> ***FYI:*** *You actually have three different Snaps you can use here: Center, Endpoint and Intersection. All occur at the exact same point.*

Notice the prompt at the bottom: Click to enter move end point.

8. Pick the **endpoint** of the angled line in the lower left corner (Figure 4-3.4).

> ***FYI:*** *If you want to make several copies of the circle, select Multiple on the Options Bar.*

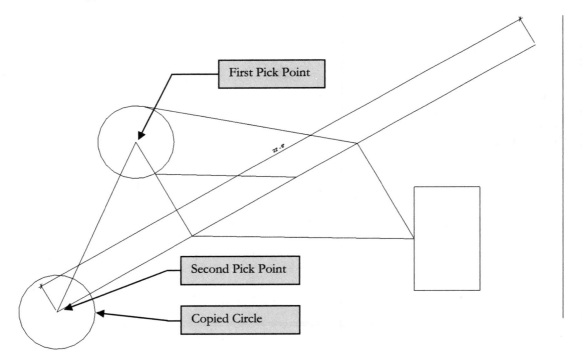

FIGURE 4-3.4 Copied circle; also indicates points selected

9. **Select the rectangle** *(all four lines)*.

   TIP: Try the "hover, tab, click" method discussed on page 4-22.

10. Select **Copy**.

11. Pick an arbitrary point on the screen. In this scenario it makes no difference where you pick; you will see why in a moment.

At this point you will move the mouse in the direction you want to copy the rectangle, until the correct angle is displayed, and then type in the distance, rather than picking a second point on the screen.

12. Move the mouse towards the upper right until 45 degrees displays, then type **6′** and then press **Enter** (Figure 4-3.5).

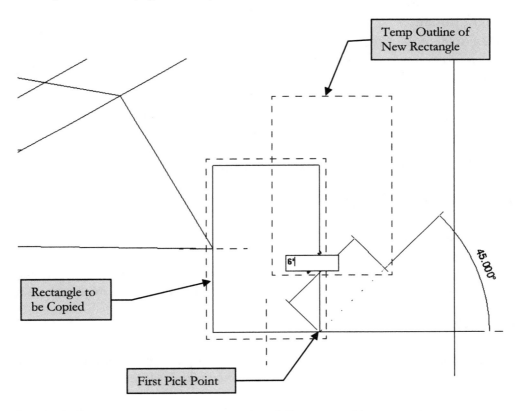

FIGURE 4-3.5 Copying rectangle; angle set visually and distance typed in

NOTE: Your drawing may look a little different than this one because your drawing is not completely to scale.

Move Tool:

The *Move* tool works exactly like the *Copy* tool except, of course, you move the element(s) rather than copy it. Given the similarity to the previous tool covered, the *Move* tool will not be covered now. You are encouraged to try it yourself; just **Undo** your experiments before proceeding.

Rotate Tool:

With the *Rotate* tool, you can arbitrarily or accurately rotate one or more objects in your drawing. When you need to rotate accurately, you can pick points that define the angle, assuming points exist in the drawing to pick, or you can type a specific angle.

Rotate involves the following steps:
- Select element(s) to be rotated.
- Select **Rotate**.
- Determine if the *Center of Rotation* symbol is where you want it.
  - If you want to move it:
    - Simply drag it, or
    - Click *Place* on the *Options Bar*
- Select a point to define a reference line and begin rotation.
- Pick a second point using one of the following methods:
  - By selecting other objects or using the graphic angle display *or*
  - You can type an angle and press **Enter**.

13. **Select the new rectangle** you just copied *(all four lines)*.

14. Select **Rotate** on the *Ribbon*.

Notice that the *Center of Rotation* grip, by default, is located in the center of the selected elements. This is the point about which the rotation will occur. See Figure 4-3.6.

You will not change the *Center of Rotation* at this time.

15. Pick a point directly to the right of the *Center of Rotation* grip; this tells Revit you want to rotate the rectangle relative to the horizontal plane (Figure 4-3.6).

Now, as you move your mouse up or down, you will see the temporary angle dimension displayed. You can move the mouse until the desired angle is displayed and then click to complete the rotation, or you can type the desired angle and then press **Enter**. If you recall, the *Snaps* dialog box controls the increments of the angles that Revit displays. They are all whole numbers, so if you need to rotate something 22.45 degrees, you must type it as Revit will never display that number as an option.

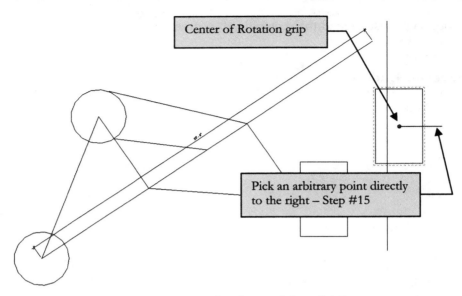

FIGURE 4-3.6 Rotate tool; first step – select lines and then click Rotate

16. Move the mouse up and to the left until 90 degrees is displayed and then click to complete the rotation (Figure 4-3.7).

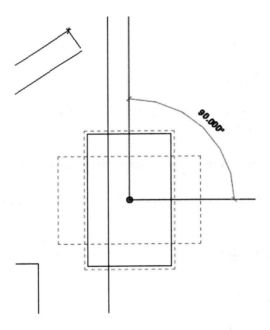

FIGURE 4-3.7 Rotate tool; last step – select angle visually or type angle

The previous steps just rotated the rectangle 90 degrees counter-clockwise about its center point (Figure 4-3.8).

17. Select the **Undo** icon.

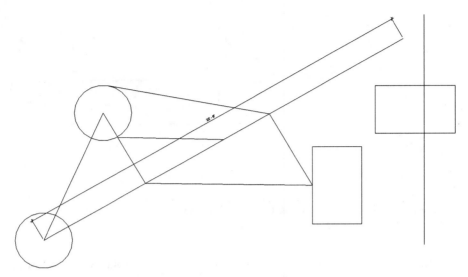

FIGURE 4-3.8 Rotate tool; rectangle rotated about its center point

Now you will do the same thing, except with a different angle and center of rotation.

18. **Select the rectangle** and then pick **Rotate**.

19. Click and drag the *Center or Rotation* grip to the left and *Snap* to the midpoint of the vertical line (Figure 4-3.9).

20. Pick a point to the right, creating a horizontal reference line.

21. Start moving your mouse downward, then type **22.5** and then press **Enter** (Figure 4-3.10).

The rectangle is now rotated 22.5 degrees in the clockwise direction (Figure 4-3.11).

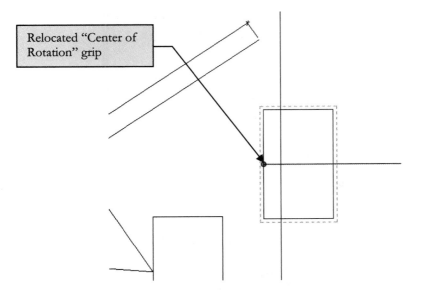

Relocated "Center of Rotation" grip

FIGURE 4-3.9 Rotate tool; relocated Center of Rotation grip

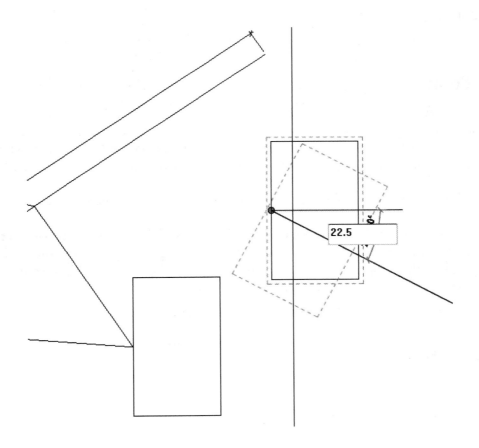

22.5

FIGURE 4-3.10 Rotate tool; typing in exact angle

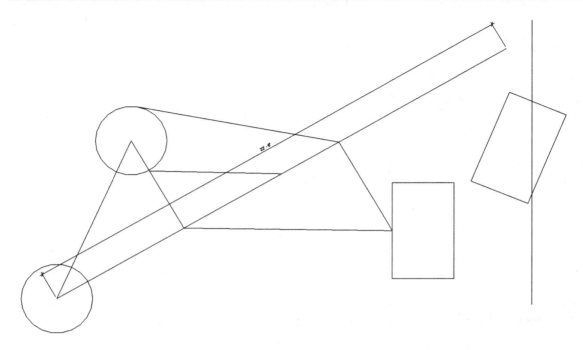

FIGURE 4-3.11 Rotate tool; rectangle rotated 22.5 degrees

Scale Tool:

The *Scale* tool has steps similar to the *Rotate* tool. First, you select what you want to scale or resize, specify a scale factor and then you pick the base point. The scale factor can be provided by picks on the screen or entering a numerical scale factor (e.g., 2 or .5, where 2 would be twice the original size and .5 would be half the original size).

Next, you will use the *Scale* tool to adjust the size of the circle near the bottom.

Before you resize the circle, you should use the *Modify* tool/mode to note the **diameter** of the circle. Select the circle and view its temporary dimensions. After resizing the circle, you will refer back to the temporary dimensions to note the change. This step is meant to teach you how to verify the accuracy and dimensions of entities in Revit.

22. Select the bottom circle.

23. Select the **Scale** icon from the *Ribbon*.

On the *Options Bar* you will specify a numeric scale factor of .5 to resize the circle to half its original size.

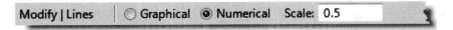

24. Click **Numerical** and then type **.5** in the textbox *(see the Options Bar above)*.

You are now prompted: **Click to enter origin** on the *Status Bar*. This is the base point about which the circle will be scaled; see examples in Figure 4-3.13 on the next page.

25. Click the center of the circle.

You just used the *Scale* tool to change in the size of the circle from 1'-6 5/8" to 9 5/16" radius. A *Scale Factor* of .5 reduces the entities to half their original scale (Figure 4-3.12).

Selecting the Correct Center of Rotation *(Base Point)*:

You need to select the appropriate *Center of Rotation*, or Base Point, for both the *Scale* and *Rotate* commands to get the results desired. A few examples are shown in Figure 4-3.13. The dashed line indicates the original position of the entity being modified. The black dot indicates the base point selected.

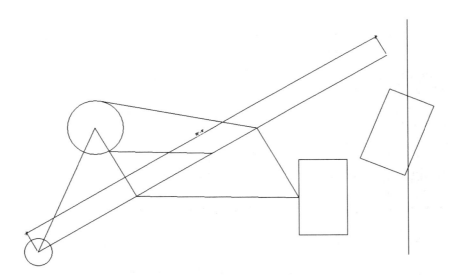

FIGURE 4-3.12 Resize circle; notice it is half the size of the other circle

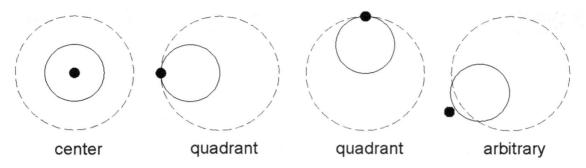

Center of Rotation Options: Scale Command

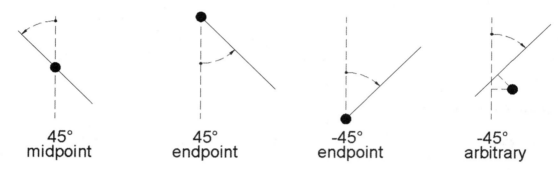

Center of Rotation Options: Rotate Command

FIGURE 4-3.13 Center of Rotation options and the various results

This will conclude the brief tour of the *edit* tools. Do not forget, even though you are editing 2D lines, the edit tools work the same way on 3D elements such as walls, floors, roofs, etc. Exception: you cannot *Scale* walls, doors, etc.; these objects have to be modified by other methods. You would not typically change the door thickness when changing its width and height as would happen if you could use the *Scale* tool on it.

As you surely noticed, the *Modify* panel on the *Ribbon* has a few other tools that have not been investigated yet. Many of these will be covered later in this book.

26. **Save** the project. Your project should already be named "ex4-3.rvt" per Step 2 above.

Carter Residence

Images courtesy of LHB
www.LHBcorp.com

Exercise 4-4:
Annotations

Annotations, or text and notes, allow the designer and technician to accurately describe the drawing. Here you will take a quick look at this feature set.

Annotations:

Adding annotations to a drawing can be as essential as the drawing itself. Often the notes describe a part of the drawing that would be difficult to discern from the drawing alone.

For example: a wall framing drawing showing a bolt may not indicate, graphically, how many bolts are needed or at what spacing. The note might say *"5/8" anchor bolt at 24" O.C."*

Next you will add text to your drawing.

1. **Open** project **ex4-3.rvt** from the previous lesson.

2. **Save-As "ex4-4.rvt"**.

3. Use **Zoom** if required to see the entire drawing, except for the 600' line which can run off the screen.

4. Select **Annotate → Text → Text**.

   Note that the *Model Text* tool on the *Home* tab is only for drawing 3D text; *Drafting Views* are only 2D so that command is not even an option currently.

From the *Text* icon tooltip (see image to the right), you can see that the keyboard shortcut for the *Text* tool is **TX**. Thus, at any time you can type T and then X to activate the *Text* tool; if you have another command active, Revit will cancel it.

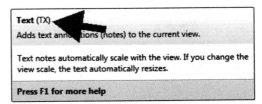

Text icon's tooltip (hover cursor over icon)

Experienced and efficient designers use a combination of keyboard shortcuts and mouse clicks to save time. For example, while your left hand is typing TX, your right hand can be moving toward the location where you want to insert the text. This process is generally more efficient than switching between tabs on the *Ribbon* and clicking icons, or fly-out icons which require yet another click of the mouse.

Notice the current *prompt* on the *Status Bar* at the bottom of the screen; you are asked to "Click to start text or click and drag rectangle to create text wrapping text". By clicking on the screen you create one line of text, starting at the point picked, and press **Enter** to create additional lines. By clicking and dragging a rectangle you specify a window, primarily for the width, which causes Revit to automatically move text to the next line. When the text no longer fits within the window it is pushed below, or what is called "text wrapping" (Figure 4-4.1).

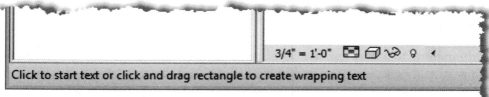

FIGURE 4-4.1 Status Bar while Text tool is active

You should also notice the various text options available on the *Ribbon* while the *Text* tool is active (Figure 4-4.2). You have two text heights loaded from the template file you started with, text justification icons (Left, Center, Right) and the option to attach leaders, or pointing arrows, to your drawings. The *Text* tool will be covered in more detail later in this book.

> **FYI:** *The text heights shown (i.e., 1/4", 3/32" via Type Selector) are heights the text will be when printed on paper, regardless of the View Scale.*

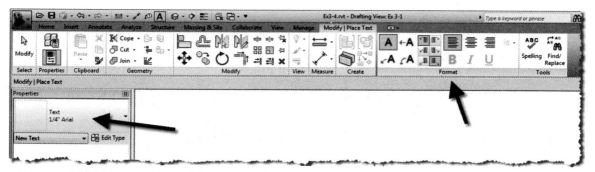

FIGURE 4-4.2 Ribbon and Properties Palette with the Text tool active

5.   Pick a point in the upper left portion of the view as shown in Figure 4-4.3.

6.   Type "**Learning Revit Architecture is fun!**"

7.   Click anywhere in the view, except on the active text, to finish the *Text* command; pressing **Enter** will only add new lines.

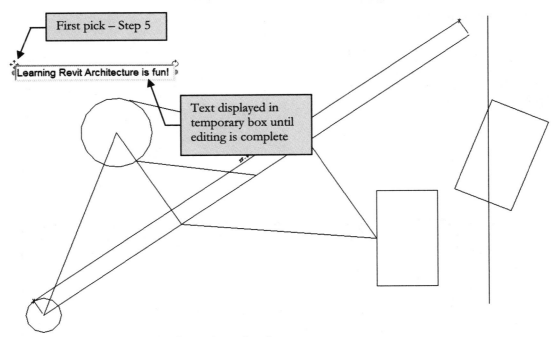

FIGURE 4-4.3 Text tool; picking first point and typing text.

As soon as you complete the text edit, the text will still be selected and the *Move* and *Rotate* symbols will be displayed near the text; this allows you to more quickly *Move* or *Rotate* the text after it is typed (Figure 4-4.4).

FIGURE 4-4.4 Text tool; text typed with Move and Rotate symbols showing.

8. Finish the *Text* tool completely by pressing **Modify** or clicking in the drawing.

> **TIP:** *Notice that the text is no longer selected and the symbols are gone; the contextual tab also disappears on the Ribbon.*

Your text should generally look similar to Figure 4-4.5.

9. Print your drawing; refer back to page 3-38 for basic printing information. Your print should fit the page and look similar to Figure 4-4.5.

10. **Save** your project.

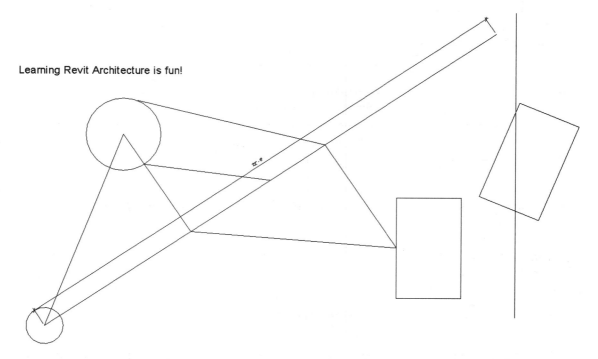

Learning Revit Architecture is fun!

FIGURE 4-4.5 Text tool; text added to current view

Carter Residence

Images courtesy of LHB
www.LHBcorp.com

Self-Exam:

The following questions can be used as a way to check your knowledge of this lesson. The answers can be found at the bottom of the page.

1.   Revit is only accurate to three decimal places. (T/F)

2.   The triangular shaped *Snap* symbol represents the *Midpoint* snap. (T/F)

3.   You can move or rotate text via its modify symbols when the text is selected. (T/F)

4.   Use the _____ tool to duplicate objects.

5.   When selecting objects, use the _____ _____ to select all the objects in the selection window and all objects that extend through it.

Review Questions:

The following questions may be assigned by your instructor as a way to assess your knowledge of this section. Your instructor has the answers to the review questions.

1.   Revit is a raster based program. (T/F)

2.   The *Center of Rotation* you select for the *Rotate* and *Scale* commands is not important. (T/F)

3.   Entering 16 for a distance actually means 16'-0" to Revit. (T/F)

4.   Use the *Detail Line* tool, with _____ selected on the *Ribbon*, to create squares.

5.   You can change the height of the text from the *Type Selector*. (T/F)

6.   Pressing the _____ key cycles you through the snap options.

7.   Where do the two predefined text heights come from? _____

8.   Specifying degrees with the *Rotate* tool, you must type the number when Revit does not display the number you want, the increments shown on-screen are set in the

     _____ dialog box.

9.   List all the Snap points available on a circle (ex. Line: endpoint, midpoint,

     nearest) _____.

10. The *Snaps Off* option must not be checked in the *Snaps* dialog box to automatically and accurately select snap points while drawing. (T/F)

SELF-EXAM ANSWERS:
1 – F, 2 – T, 3 – T, 4 – Copy, 5 – Crossing Window

Notes:

Lesson 5
Revit Basics: Drawing 2D Architectural Content:

This lesson is meant to give you practice "sketching" in Revit. The term "sketching" is a process of drawing two-dimensionally. Revit breaks many 3D tasks down into simple 2D tasks. For example, when creating a floor you sketch the perimeter of the floor and any opening within it; the third dimension is created automatically by Revit based on the floor type selected.

Even though this chapter is entirely 2D sketching, every bit of it is applicable to the 3D tasks. This chapter focuses on the fundamental aspects of the *Modify* tools and 2D sketches, which will make the 3D tasks done later easier to grasp.

If you have used other design programs, like AutoCAD or MicroStation, these lessons will help you understand the different way to draw using Revit, or specifically, a more visual or graphic based input system.

The steps provided in this chapter show you how to create 2D content *Families* that can be used in your Revit building projects. The final chapter in this book (on the DVD) will provide a more in-depth introduction to creating *Families*. You are encouraged to revisit this chapter once you are done with the book and see if you can create this same content in 3D. Some firms that work on super large projects will actually use 2D content to reduce the size of the project file and increase day to day computer system performance. However, most firms typically use 3D content to aid in visualization and coordination.

For some of the symbols to be drawn, you will have step-by-step instruction and a study on a particular tool that would be useful in the creation of that object. Other symbols to be drawn are for practice by way of repetition and do not provide step-by-step instruction.

Exercise 5-1:
Sketching Rectilinear Objects

Overview:

All the content you will draw in this exercise consists entirely of straight lines, either orthogonal or angular.

All the objects MUST BE drawn in SEPERATE files. Each object will have a specific name provided, which is to be used to name the file. All files should be saved in your personal folder created for this course.

Getting started:

The first thing you need to do is start from the proper **family template** file. These initial instructions will not give you much background on why or what you are doing, but more will come later in the book.

Follow these steps for each object to be created in this chapter:

- Open Revit.
- From the *Application* menu, select **New → Family**.
- Select **Generic Model.rft**.

Now that the file has been created...

- Select **Category and Parameters** from the *Ribbon*.

- Select the appropriate category for the object you are drawing:

  o Bookcase = Furniture
  o Sink = Plumbing Fixture
  o Tree = Planting
  o Clg. Fan = Lighting Fixtures

- Sketch the 2D linework per the instructions provided with each object using the **Model Line** tool.

  TIP: The intersection of the two reference planes determines the insertion point when the object is being placed in a project.

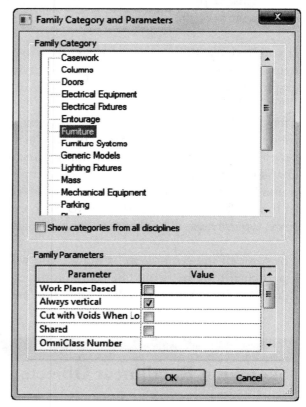

Now that the family is complete...

- Select **Save** from the *Quick Access Toolbar*.

  o The file name should match the object name (e.g., Bookcase – 2D).

file name: **Bookcase – 2D**

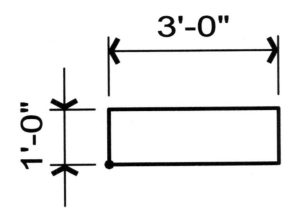

This is a simple rectangle that represents the size of a bookcase.

1. **Open** a new *family file* per the instructions on the previous page; follow the first five steps.

2. Make sure the current view is **Ref. Level** in the *Project Browser*.

3. Select **Model Line** from the *Home* tab.

By default, the current line style is set to *Furniture* (which matches the Category selected). You can see this on the *Ribbon* when the *Model Line* tool is active.

4. Set the line style to **Furniture** (Figure 5-1.1 to the right).

5. Click the **Rectangle** button on the *Ribbon* (Figure 5-1.2).

6. **Draw a rectangle**, per the dimensions shown above.

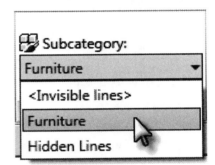

FIGURE 5-1.1 Line Style options

a. The black dot, in the lower left, indicates the insertion point of the object in a project, which coincides with the intersection of the two reference planes. Do not draw the black dot.

TIP: You should be able to accurately draw the rectangle using the temporary dimensions; if not, click on the dimension text to change it.

FIGURE 5-1.2 Ribbon; Model Lines (Furniture) and Rectangle selected

file name: **Coffee Table – 2D**

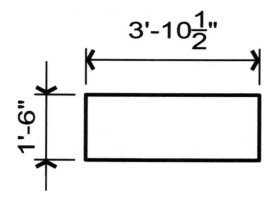

3'-10½"

1'-6"

7. Create a new *family file.*

   NOTE: *This step will be assumed for the rest of the drawings in this exercise.*

8. Similar to the steps listed above, plus the suggestions mentioned below, create the coffee table shown to the left.

Draw the rectangle as close as possible using the visual aids; you should be able to get the 1'-6" dimension correct. Then click on the text for the temporary horizontal dimension and type in 3'-10 1/2".

Entering fractions: the 3'-10½" can be entered in one of four ways.

o 3 10.5   *Notice there is a space between the feet and inches.*
o 3 10 1/2   *Note the two spaces; they separate the feet, inches and fractions.*
o 0 46.5   *This is all in inches; that is, 3'-10½" = 46.5".*
o 46.5"   *Omit the feet and use the inches symbol.*

---

file name: **Small Desk – 2D**

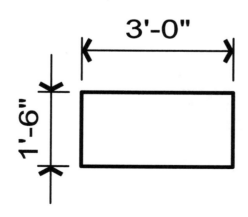

3'-0"

1'-6"

9. Draw the *Small Desk* in its own file, similar to the steps outlined above.

   TIP: *You should double-check your drawing's dimensions using the Measure tool. Pick the icon from the Modify tab and then pick two points. A temporary dimension will display.*

file name: **Night Table – 2D**

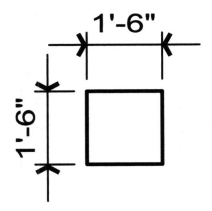

Obviously you could draw this quickly per the previous examples. However, you will take a look at copying a *family file* and then modifying an existing drawing.

You will use the *Move* tool to stretch the 3'-0" wide desk down to a 1'-6" wide night table.

10. Make sure **Small Desk** is saved and open. Click **Save** on the *Quick Access Toolbar.*

11. Select **Application Menu** → **Save As** → **Family**.

12. For the new family file name, enter: **Night Table – 2D**.

You are now ready to modify the copy of the *Desk-1* linework. You will use the *Move* tool to change the location of one of the vertical lines, which will cause the two horizontal lines to stretch with it. Revit's *Model Lines* automatically have a parametric relationship to adjacent lines when their endpoints touch each other.

13. Select the vertical line on the <u>right</u> and then click the **Move** icon on the *Ribbon*.

14. Pick the mid-point of the vertical line, move the mouse **1'-6"** to the left and then click again (Figure 5-1.3).

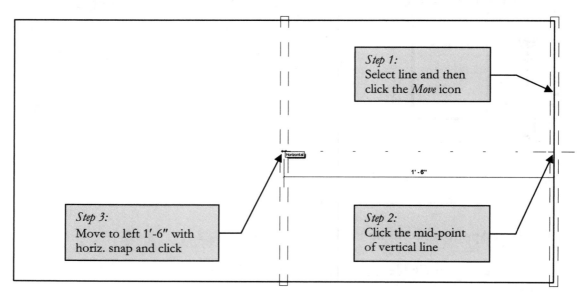

FIGURE 5-1.3 Move tool used to stretch a rectangle

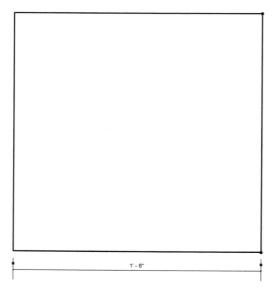

FIGURE 5-1.4 Stretch rectangle (using Move tool)

The rectangle is now resized, or stretched, to be half its original width.

You will notice that the horizontal lines automatically adjusted.

Revit assumes a special relationship between a line being edited and any line whose endpoint is directly touching it.

TIP: You can select "disjoin" on the Options Bar while in the Move command if you don't want other lines to move or stretch with it. You will not do that here though.

15. **Save** your project.

file name: **Large Dresser – 2D**

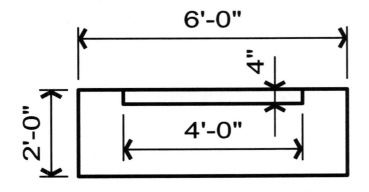

16. Draw the dresser using the following tip:

    TIP: *Simply draw two rectangles. Move the smaller rectangle into place using the Move tool and Snaps.*

file name: **Small Dresser – 2D**

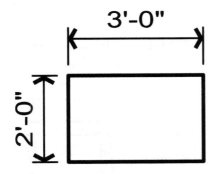

17. Draw this smaller dresser.

file name: **Medium Desk – 2D**

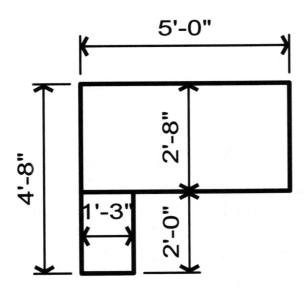

18. Draw this desk in the same way you drew *Large Dresser.*

file name: **File Cabinet – 2D**

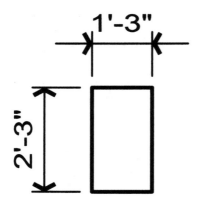

19. Draw this file cabinet.

file name: **Square Chair – 2D**

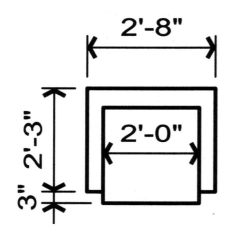

20. Draw this chair per the following tips:

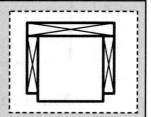

Draw the 2'x2' square first, and then draw three separate rectangles as shown to the right. Move them into place with Move and Snaps. Next, delete the extra lines so your drawing looks like the one shown on the left. Pay close attention to the dimensions!

file name: **Square Sofa – 2D**

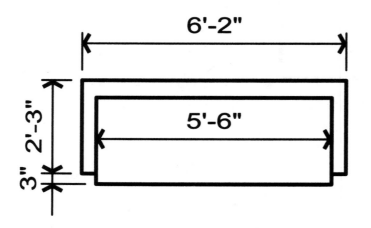

21. *Save As* and *Rename* the *Square Chair* file to start this drawing.

TIP: *See the next page for more information on creating this drawing.*

You can create the *Sofa* in a similar way to how you created the *Night Table*. That is, you will use the *Move* tool. Rather than selecting one vertical line, however, you will select all the lines on one side of the copied chair.

You can select all the lines on one side in a single step rather than clicking each one individually while holding the **Ctrl** key. You will select using a *Window*, not a *Crossing Window*, selection.

22. **Select** all the lines on the right side (Figure 5-1.5).

> *TIP: Pick from left to right for a window selection.*

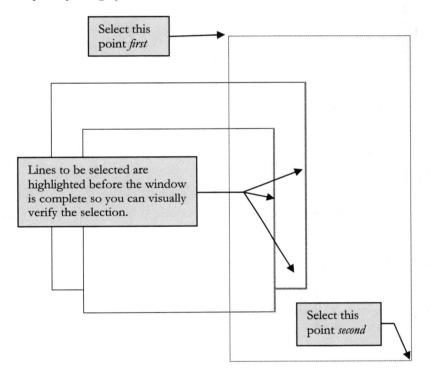

FIGURE 5-1.5 Stretch *Chair* using the Move tool

23. Use the *Move* tool to extend the chair into a sofa.

> *TIP: The difference between the chair width and the sofa width is the distance the lines are to be moved.*

You have just successfully transformed the chair into a sofa! Do not forget to *Save* often to avoid losing work. Also, use the *Measure* tool to verify your drawing's accuracy.

file name: **Double Bed – 2D**

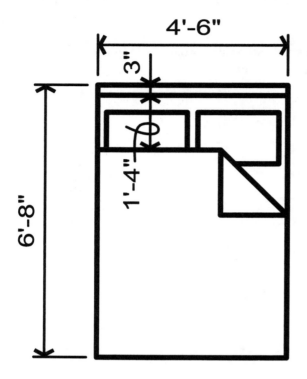

24. Draw this bed using lines and rectangles; the exact size of items not dimensioned is not important.

   TIP: Starting the family name with the word "bed" would make all the other bed sizes (e.g., queen, king, etc.) show up next to each other in any lists because Revit sorts most lists alphabetically.

Exercise 5-2:
Sketching Objects with Curves

Similar to the previous exercise, you will draw several objects; this time they will have curves in them.

You will look at the various commands that allow you to create curves, like *Arc*, *Circle* and *Fillet*.

You may draw the dimensions if you want as they will not appear when placed into a project; each drawing should be drawn in its own family file. Name the file with the label provided.

Finally, the **black dot** represents the location from which the symbol would typically be inserted or placed, align this part of the object drawing with the intersection of the *Reference Planes* provided in plan view.

file name: Laundry Sink – 2D

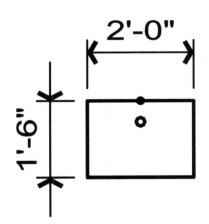

This is a simple rectangle that represents the size of a laundry sink, with a circle that represents the drain.

1. **Open** a new Revit family file per page 5-2; steps typical for each object.

2. Draw the rectangle shown; refer to Exercise 5-1 for more information.

3. Use the *Measure* tool to verify the size of your rectangle.

Next, you will draw a circle for the drain. The drain needs to be centered left and right, and 5" from the top edge. The following steps will show you one way in which to do this.

4. Select the *Model Line* tool from the *Home* tab.

5. Select the *Circle* icon from the *Ribbon* (Figure 5-2.1).

FIGURE 5-2.1 Sketch Options for detail lines

6. Pick the midpoint of the top line (Figure 5-2.2).

    FYI: *This is the center of the circle.*

7. Type **0 1** for the radius and press **Enter** (0 1 = 0'-1").

    FYI: *This creates a 2" Dia. Circle.*

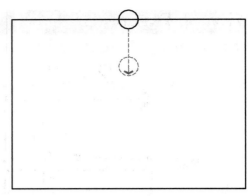

FIGURE 5-2.2 Creating a circle and moving it into place.

At this point you may get an error indicating the "Line is too short" (Figure 5-2.3) or "Element is too small on screen". This is supposed to prevent a user, like yourself, from accidentally drawing a very small line when you click the mouse twice right next to each other or trying to change the dimension to a previously drawn line to something less than 1/32". If you get this error, you simply zoom in on your drawing more so the circle is more prominently visible on the screen. However, the 2012 version of Revit has improved this issue and lines can easily be adjusted smaller and not always drawn from scratch given the current zoom factor.

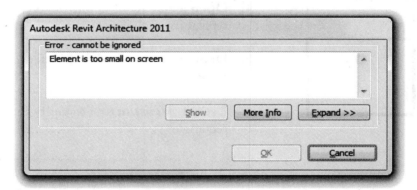

FIGURE 5-2.3 Revit error message when creating the circle IF you are zoomed out too far

8. If you did get the error message just described, click *Cancel, Zoom In* and then draw the *Circle* again.

9. Select the circle and then the ***Move*** tool.

10. **Move** the circle straight down 5" (Figure 5-2.2).

That's it! Do not forget to save your files often.

file name: **Dryer – 2D**

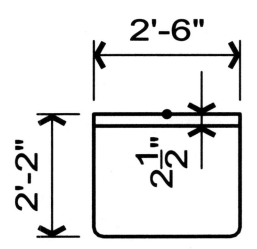

Here you will draw a dryer with rounded front corners. This, like all the other symbols in this lesson, is a plan view symbol, as in viewed from the top.

11.   Draw a 30"x26" rectangle.

12.   Use the ***Measure*** tool to verify your dimensions.

Next you will draw the line that is 2½" from the back of the dryer. You will draw the line in approximately the correct position and then use the temporary dimensions to correct the location.

13.   Select the ***Model Line*** tool and then pick a point approximately 3" down from the upper-left corner; a temporary dimension will be displayed before clicking your mouse button (Figure 5-2.4).

14.   Complete the horizontal line by picking a point perpendicular to the vertical line on the right (Figure 5-2.4).

15.   With the temporary dimensions still displayed, click the text for the 0'-3" dimension, type **0 2.5** and then press **Enter** (Figure 5-2.5).

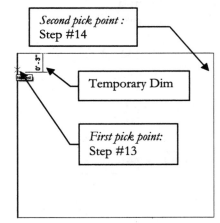

FIGURE 5-2.4 Drawing a line

16.   Click **Modify** to clear the selection and make the *Temporary Dimensions* go away.

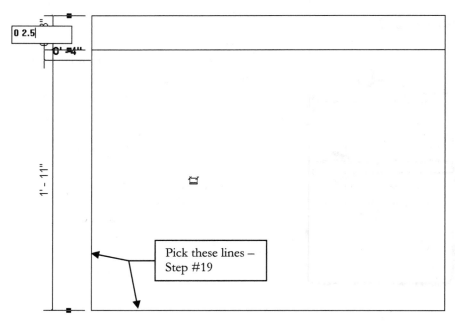

FIGURE 5-2.5 Adjusting new lines position via temporary dimensions

Next you will round the corners. You still use the *Model Line* tool, but use a *Sketch Option* called *Fillet Arc* (pronounced "*Fill*-it"). You will try this next.

17. With the ***Model Line*** tool active, select the **Fillet Arc** *Draw* option on the *Ribbon* (Figure 5-2.6).

18. Check **Radius** and enter **0′ 2″** in the text box on the *Options Bar* (Figure 5-2.6).

FIGURE 5-2.6 Ribbon and Options Bar: options for Model Lines in Fillet Arc mode

19. Pick the two lines identified in Figure 5-2.5.

The intersection of the two lines is where the arc is placed, notice the two lines you picked have been trimmed back to the new *Fillet* (arc).

20. Repeat the previous step to **Fillet** the other corner.

file name: **Washer – 2D**

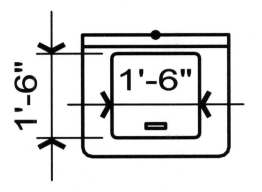

This drawing is identical to the dryer except for the door added to the top. You can copy the dryer file to get a jump start on this drawing.

To draw the door you will use the **Offset** option, which is part of the *Model Line* tool.

The **Offset** tool is easy to use; to use it you:
- o Select the *Model Line* tool.
- o Select the *Pick Lines* icon on the *Ribbon*.
- o Enter the *Offset* distance on the *Options Bar*.
- o Select near a line, and on the side to offset.

21. Select the **Model Line** tool.

22. Select the **Pick Lines** icon on the *Ribbon* (Figure 5-2.7).

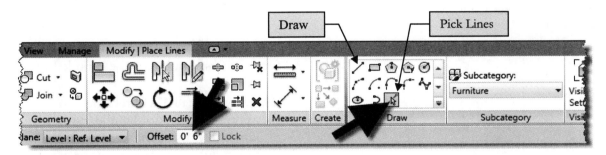

FIGURE 5-2.7 Options Bar: options for Model Lines in Pick Lines mode

Note that the *Pick Lines* icon toggles you from *Draw* mode to *Pick Lines* mode. The *Pick Lines* mode allows you to use existing linework to quickly create new linework. You should notice the available options on the *Options Bar* have changed after selecting *Pick Lines;* you can switch back by selecting any of the other *Draw* icons on the *Ribbon* (Figure 5-2.7).

23. Enter **0' 6"** for the *Offset* distance (Figure 5-2.7).

Next you will need to select a line to offset. Which side of the line you click on will indicate the direction the line is offset. Revit provides a visual reference line indicating which side the line will be offset to and its location based on the offset distance entered.

Without clicking the mouse button, move your cursor around the drawing and notice the visual reference line. Move your mouse from side-to-side on a line to see the reference line move to correspond to the cursor location.

24. **Offset** the left vertical line towards the right.

TIP: Make sure you entered the correct offset distance in the previous step (Figure 5-2.7).

You will need to look at the *Washer* drawing and the *Dryer* drawing dimensions to figure out the door size (i.e., the offset amount).

25. Offset the other three sides; your sketch should look like Figure 5-2.9.

26. Use the **Fillet Arc** sketch mode, in the *Model Line* tool, to create a 1″ radius on the four corners.

27. Click **Modify** to finish the current command.

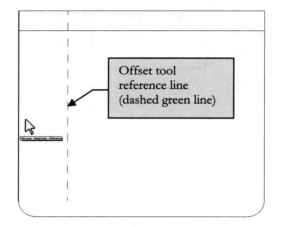

FIGURE 5-2.8 Offset left vertical line towards the right 6″

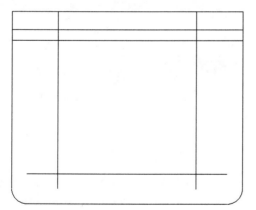

FIGURE 5-2.9 All four lines offset inward to create outline for washer door

All four corners should now be rounded off.

28. Draw a small 4″x1″ rectangle to represent the door handle. Draw it anywhere; using *Snaps*, move it to the midpoint of the bottom door edge, and then move the handle 2″ up.

29. **Save** your file and make sure it is named "*Washer – 2D*".

file name: **Range – 2D**

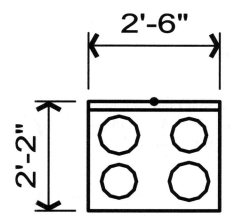

Now you will draw a kitchen range with four circles that represent the burners.

In this exercise you will have to draw temporary lines, called reference planes, to create reference points needed to accurately locate the circles. Once the circles have been drawn the temporary lines can be erased.

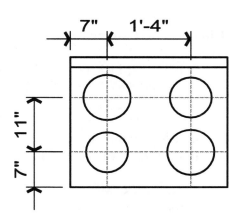

30. **Draw** the range with a 2″ deep control panel at the back; refer to the steps described to draw the *Dryer* if necessary.

31. Draw the four temporary lines shown in Figure 5-2.10. Use the **Reference Plane** tool on the *Home* tab.

32. **Draw** two 9½″ Dia. circles and two 7½″ Dia. circles using the intersections of the construction lines to locate the centers of the circles (Figure 5-2.10).

   TIP: Refer back to the Laundry Sink – 2D for sketching circles.

FIGURE 5-2.10 Range with four temporary lines (i.e., reference planes)

33. **Erase** the four **reference plane** lines.

34. **Save** your project.

TIP:
When using the Measure tool, you can select Chain on the Options Bar to have Revit calculate the total length of several picks. For example, you can quickly get the perimeter of a rectangle by picking each corner. Notice, as you pick points, the Total Length is listed on the Options Bar.

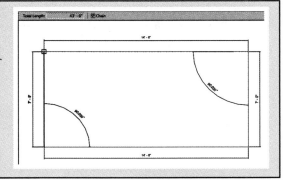

file name: **Rounded Chair – 2D**

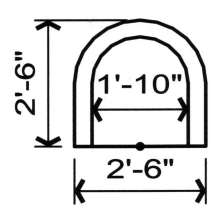

Now you will sketch another chair. You will use *Model Line* with *Offset* and the *Arc* settings.

First you will draw the arc at the perimeter.

35. Select **Model Line** and then **Center – Ends Arc** from the *Ribbon* (Figure 5-2.1).

Notice on the *Status Bar* you are prompted to **"Click to enter arc center"**.

36. *First pick:* Pick a point somewhere in the middle of a new family file (Figure 5-2.11).

You are now prompted, on the *Status Bar* **"Drag arc radius to desired location"**.

37. *Second pick:* Move the cursor towards the left, while snapped to the horizontal, until the temporary dimension reads **1'-3"** (Figure 5-2.11).

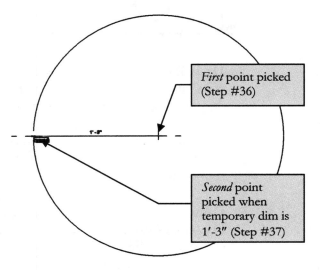

First point picked (Step #36)

Second point picked when temporary dim is 1'-3" (Step #37)

FIGURE 5-2.11 Sketching an arc; picking second point

NOTE: *As you can see, Revit temporarily displays a full circle (Figure 5-2.11) until you pick the second point. This is because Revit does not know which direction the arc will go or what the arc length will be. The full circle allows you to visualize where your arc will be.*

38. *Third pick:* Move the cursor to the right until the arc is 180 degrees and snapped to the horizontal again (Figure 5-2.12).

TIP: *Notice that your cursor location determines which direction or side the arc is created; move the cursor around before picking the third endpoint to see how the preview arc changes on screen.*

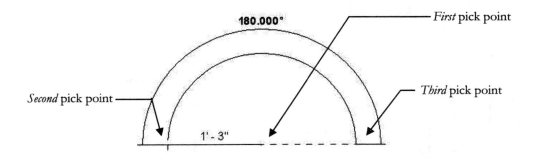

FIGURE 5-2.12 Pick points for Arc command

Next you will draw the three *Model Lines* to complete the perimeter of the chair.

39. **Draw** two vertical lines **1'-3"** long.

> *TIP: Don't forget to use the "Furniture" line style when sketching Model Lines. If you forgot, you can select the lines, while in Modify mode, and select "Furniture" from the Element Type Selector on the Ribbon, or whichever line style is appropriate for the object being drawn.*

40. **Draw** the **2'-6"** line across the bottom.

Notice the radius is 1'-3". You did not have to enter that number because the three points you picked was enough information for Revit to determine it automatically.

If you had drawn the three lines in Steps 39 and 40 before the arc, you would not have had the required center point to pick while creating the arc. However, you could have drawn a temporary horizontal line across the top to set up a center pick that would allow you to draw the circle in its final location; or even better, use the **Start-End-Radius** *Model Line* option.

You have now completed the perimeter of the chair.

41. Use the **Offset** tool to offset the arc and two vertical lines the required distance to complete the sketch.

42. **Save** your file.

file name: **Love Seat – 2D**

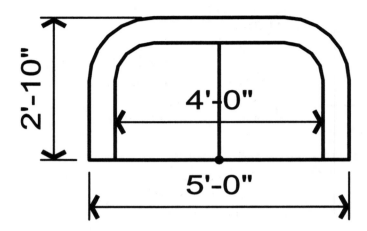

You should be able to draw this Love Seat without any further instruction; use the same radius as the *Rounded Chair - 2D*.

You can do so using a combination of the following tools:
- o Detail Line
- o Fillet Arc
- o Offset
- o Move

file name: **Tub – 2D**

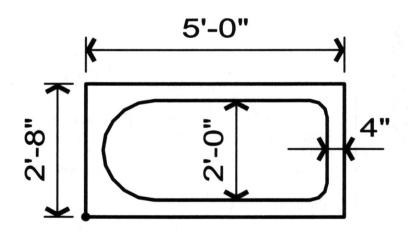

Now you will draw a bathtub using several commands previously covered.

You will use the following tools:
- o Model Line
- o Fillet Arc
- o Offset
- o Move

You may also wish to draw one or more *reference planes* to help locate things like the large radius, although it can be drawn without any. Reference planes are also helpful when using the *Mirror* tool, as it can be selected as the axis of reflection.

file name: **Rectangular Lav – 2D**

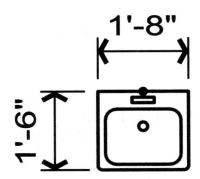

Draw this lavatory per the following specifications:

o Larger arcs shown shall have a 2½″ radius.

o Smaller arcs shown shall have a 1″ radius, outside corners.

o Sides and Front of sink to have 1½″ space, offset.

o Back to have 4″ space, offset.

o Small rectangle to be 4½″x1″ and 1½″ away from the back.

o 2″ Dia. Drain, 8″ from back.

file name: **Oval Lav – 2D**

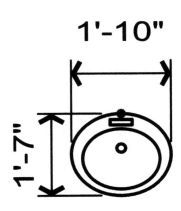

Next you will draw another lavatory. This time you will use the *Ellipse* tool.

43. Create a new file.

44. Select *Model Lines* and then **Ellipse** from the *Ribbon* (Figure 5-2.1).

Notice the *Status Bar* prompt: **"Click to enter ellipse center."**

45. Pick at the intersection of the two reference planes.

46. With the cursor snapped to the vertical, point the cursor straight down and then type **0 9.5**; press **Enter**.

NOTE: 9½″ is half the HEIGHT: 1′-7″.

Now you need to specify the horizontal axis of the ellipse.

47. Again, snapping to the horizontal plane, position the cursor towards the right, type **0 11** and then press the **Enter** key.

NOTE: 11″ is half the width: 1′-10″.

That's all it takes to draw an ellipse!

48. **Copy** the ellipse vertically downward **3½″** (Figure 5-2.13).

Next you will use the *Scale* tool to decrease the size of the second ellipse. To summarize the steps involved: select the ellipse to be resized, select the *Scale* icon, pick the origin, pick the opposite side of the ellipse, and then enter a new value for the ellipse.

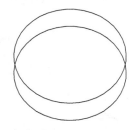

FIGURE 5-2.13
Ellipse copied downward 3½″

49. Select the lower second ellipse.

50. Select the **Scale** icon on the *Ribbon*; the ellipse must be selected first.

Notice the *Status Bar* prompt: "**Pick to enter origin.**" The origin, or base point, is a point on or relative to the object that does not move.

51. *First pick:* Pick the top edge, midpoint, of the selected ellipse (Figure 5-2.14).

52. *Second pick:* Pick the bottom edge, midpoint, of the same ellipse (Figure 5-2.14).

53. Type **1 2** (i.e., 1′-2″) and press **Enter**; this will be the new distance between the two points picked.

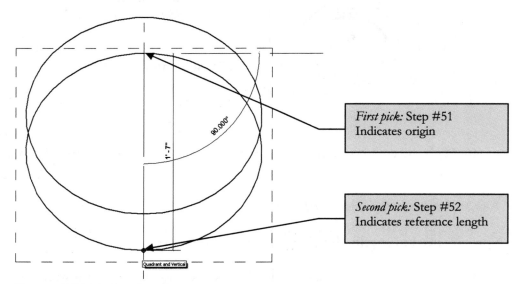

First pick: Step #51
Indicates origin

Second pick: Step #52
Indicates reference length

FIGURE 5-2.14 Scaling the ellipse

Next you need to draw the faucet and drain. As it turns out, the faucet and drain for *Lav-1* are in the same position relative to the middle/back (black dot). So to save time, you will *Copy/Paste* these items from the *Rectangular Lav – 2D* file into the **Oval Lav – 2D** view.

54. Open the **Rectangular Lav – 2D** family file.

55. Select the entire *Rectangular Lav – 2D* sketch.

56. Pick **Modify | Lines** → **Clipboard** → **Copy** while the *Rectangular Lav – 2D* linework is selected.

57. Switch back to the **Oval Lav – 2D** view and press **Ctrl + V** on the keyboard (press both keys at the same time).

58. Pick a point to the side of the *Oval Lav – 2D* sketch (Figure 5-2.15).

59. Select the faucet, the small rectangle, and the drain, the circle.

   TIP: *Use a Window selection, picking from left to right.*

60. Select the **Move** tool; pick the middle/back of the *Rectangular Lav – 2D* sketch and then pick the middle/back of the *Oval Lav – 2D* sketch.

   NOTE: *These two points represent the angle and distance to move the selected items.*

61. **Erase** the extra *Rectangular Lav – 2D* linework.

You should now have the faucet and drain correctly positioned in your *Oval Lav – 2D* family file.

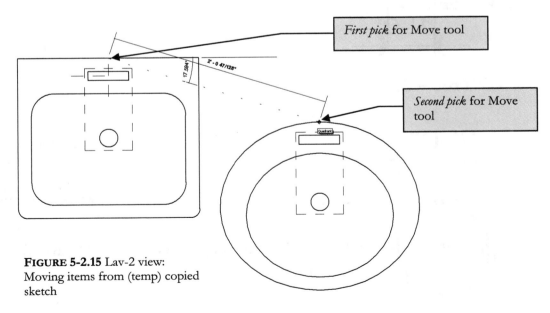

FIGURE 5-2.15 Lav-2 view: Moving items from (temp) copied sketch

file name: **Double Sink – 2D**

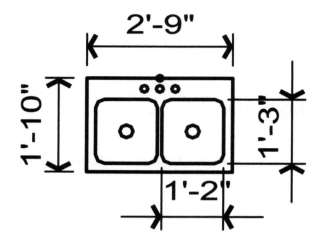

Draw this sink per the following specifications:

- o 2″ space, offset at sides and front
- o 3″ Dia. Circles centered in sinks
- o 2″ rad. for Fillets
- o 1½″ Dia. at faucet spaces, 3½″ apart

file name: **Water Closet – 2D**

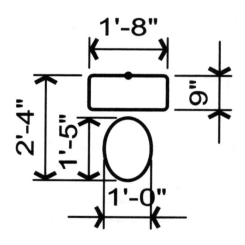

You should be able to draw this symbol without any help.

TIP: Draw a reference plane from the Origin (i.e., black dot) straight down 11″ (2'-4″ - 1'-5″ = 11″). This will give you a point to pick when drawing the ellipse.

file name: **Tree – 2D**

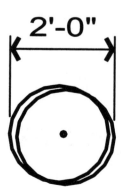

62. Draw one large circle and then copy it, similar to this drawing.

63. Draw one small 1″ diameter circle at the approximate center.

64. Set the **Category** to *Planting* and then **Save** your project.

file name: **Door 36 – 2D**

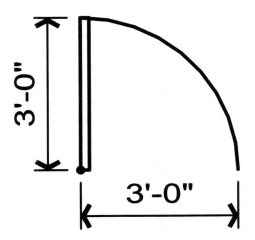

This symbol is used to show a door in a floor plan. The arc represents the path of the door as it opens and shuts.

A symbol like this, 90 degrees open, helps to avoid the door conflicting with something in the building like cabinets or a toilet. Existing doors are typically show open 45 degrees so it is easier to visually discern new from existing.

Revit has an advanced *Door* tool, so you would not actually draw this symbol very often. However, you may decide to draw one in plan that represents a gate in a reception counter or one in elevation to show a floor hatch. These same techniques can be used in a 3D family to show 2D geometry in certain views, via the *Symbolic Lines* tool.

65. Draw a **2″ x 3′-0″ rectangle**.

66. Draw an Arc using **Center – Ends Arc**; select the three points in the order shown in Figure 5-2.16.

TIP: Be sure your third pick shows the cursor snapped to the horizontal plane.

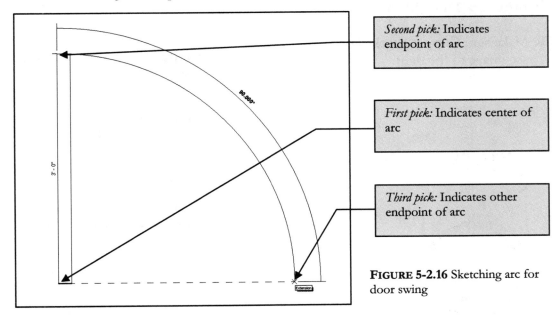

FIGURE 5-2.16 Sketching arc for door swing

file name: **Door2-36 – 2D**

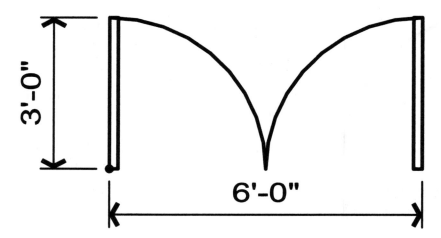

Here you will use a previous drawing and the *Mirror* tool to quickly create this drawing showing a pair of doors in a single opening.

67. Do a **Save As** of *Door 36 – 2D* file.

68. **Name** the new file ***Door2-36 – 2D***.

Next you will mirror both the rectangle and the arc.

69. Select the rectangle and the arc using a *Crossing Window* by picking from right to left, and then pick the **Modify | Lines → Modify → Mirror → Draw Mirror Axis** tool from the *Ribbon*.

70. Make sure **Copy** is checked on the *Options Bar*, see image to the right.

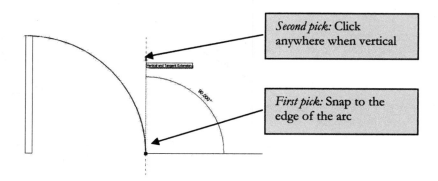

Second pick: Click anywhere when vertical

First pick: Snap to the edge of the arc

FIGURE 5-2.17 "Drawing" axis of reflection

Notice the *Status Bar* is prompting you to "**Pick Start Point for Axis of Reflection.**"

71. Pick the two points shown in **Figure 5-2.17**.

At this point the door symbol, the rectangle and arc, is mirrored and the *Mirror* tool is done.

72. Select **Modify**, via *QAT*, to end the command and unselect everything.

73. **Save** your file as "**Door2-36 – 2D**".

file name: **clg-fan-1 – 2D**

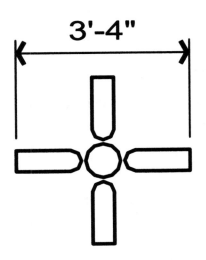

You will use the *Array* command while drawing this ceiling fan.

The *Array* command can be used to array entities in a rectangular pattern (e.g., columns on a grid) or in a polar pattern (i.e., in a circular pattern).

You will use the polar array to rotate and copy the fan blade all in one step!

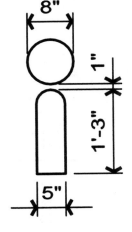

74. Start a new file and create the portion of drawing shown in the figure to the right.

75. Select the fan blade (i.e., one arc and three lines) and then select **Array** from the *Ribbon*.

Similar to the *Rotate* tool, you will relocate the *Center of Rotation* symbol to the center of the 8″ circle. This will cause the fan blade to array around the circle rather than the center of the first fan blade.

76. Click **Radial** on the *Options Bar* and then click and *drag* the ***Rotation*** icon to the center of the 8″ circle; make sure Revit snaps to the center point before clicking (see Figure 5-2.19).

> *FYI: In addition to dragging the* Rotation *icon, you may also click the* "Place" *button on the Options Bar. This is helpful when the extents of the elements being rotated is large and the icon may not be visible on the screen (without zooming way out).*

77. Make the following changes to the *Options Bar* (Figure 5-2.18).

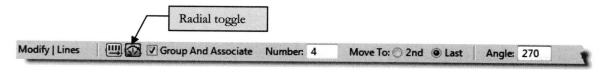

FIGURE 5-2.18 Array options on the Options Bar

78. After typing the angle in the *Options Bar*, press **Enter**.

You should now see the three additional fan blades and a temporary array number. This gives you the option to change the array number if desired.

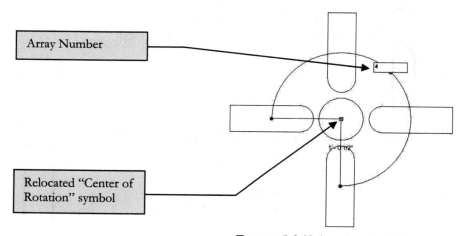

FIGURE 5-2.19 Arraying fan blades

79. Click **Modify** to complete the array and finish the ceiling fan.

Because you left "Group and Associate" checked when you created the array on the *Options Bar*, you can select any part of a fan blade and the array number will appear like a temporary dimension and allow you to change the number. You can select *Ungroup* from the *Ribbon* to make each item individually editable as if you had drawn everything from scratch.

80. **Save** your file.

Self-Exam:

The following questions can be used as a way to check your knowledge of this lesson. The answers can be found at the bottom of the page.

1. Revit does not allow you to copy linework between views. (T/F)

2. Entering 4 3.25 in Revit means 4'-3¼". (T/F)

3. Reference planes (aka, construction lines) are useful drawing aids. (T/F)

4. Use the _____ tool to sketch an oval shape.

5. When you want to make a previously drawn rectangle wider, you would use the _____ tool.

Review Questions:

The following questions may be assigned by your instructor as a way to assess your knowledge of this section. Your instructor has the answers to the review questions.

1. Use the *Offset* option to quickly create a parallel line(s). (T/F)

2. If Revit displays an error message indicating a line is too small to be drawn, you simply zoom in more and try again. (T/F)

3. Use the _____ command to create a reverse image.

4. With the *Move* tool, lines completely within the selection window are actually only moved, not stretched. (T/F)

5. You can relocate the *Center of Rotation* when using *Radial Array*. (T/F)

6. Occasionally, you need to draw an object and then move it into place to accurately locate it. (T/F)

7. The _____ (which is an option within the *Model Line* tool) allows you to create a rounded corner where two lines intersect.

8. When using the *Mirror* tool, you occasionally need to draw a temporary line that represents the *Axis of Reflection*. (T/F)

9. What is content called in Revit terminology? _____

10. In the *Model Line* tool, how many options allow you to draw arcs? _____

Notes:

Lesson 6
Law Office: FLOOR PLANS:

In this lesson you will draw the architectural floor plans of an office building. The office building will be further developed in subsequent chapters. It is recommended that you spend adequate time on this lesson as later lessons build on this one.

Exercise 6-1:
Project Setup

The Project:

A **program statement** is created in the pre-design phase of a project. Working with the client or user group, the design team gathers as much information as possible about the project before starting to design.

The information gathered includes:
- Rooms: What rooms are required?

- Size: How big the rooms need to be? For example, toilets for a convention center are much bigger than for a dentist's office.

- Adjacencies: This room needs to be next to that room. For example, the public toilets need to be accessible from the public lobby.

Looking at the Program Schedule (Figure 6-1.1), on the next page, the reader can see a simple example of a program statement created in Revit, using its schedule feature. In this example, each room name is being grouped by department: Admin., Exec., Misc., Public, Staff. The actual designed area is then compared to the original programmed, or desired, area.

>   *NOTE: The actual area would really be blank at this point in the project.*

Next, the *Area Check* column is used to identify any rooms that are way too big or small and would affect cost or function. Finally, any required adjacencies are spelled out.

With the project statement in hand, the design team can begin the design process. Although modifications may, and will, need to be made to the program statement, it is used as a goal to meet the client's needs.

This Program Schedule will not actually be created in Revit, though it is possible to do so even before anything has been drawn. The actual *Area* column would say "not enclosed" until the room was placed into the model.

PROGRAM SCHEDULE					
Name	Area	PROGRAM AREA	AREA CHECK	ADJACENCIES	Comments
ADMINISTRATION					
ADMIN ASSIST	385 SF	350 SF	1.099231		
OFFICE MANAGER	139 SF	150 SF	0.925591	ADMIN ASSIST	
	524 SF	500 SF			
EXECUTIVE					
EXEC CONF RM	525 SF	500 SF	1.049186	2ND FLOOR	
EXEC OFFICE	203 SF	200 SF	1.016296	CONF RM	
EXEC OFFICE	241 SF	200 SF	1.205583	CONF RM	
	969 SF	900 SF			
MISC					
CONF ROOM	330 SF	300 SF	1.098994	1ST FLOOR	
CUSTODIAN	70 SF	80 SF	0.870683		
FILES/ STORAGE	316 SF	300 SF	1.053266		
HALL	282 SF				
LAW LIBRARY	1614 SF	1500 SF	1.075987		
MECH & ELEC ROOM	433 SF	400 SF	1.081616		
STAIR	140 SF	150 SF	0.932319		
	3184 SF	2730 SF			
PUBLIC					
COAT CLOSET	36 SF	20 SF	1.806169	LOBBY	
ENTRY VESTIBULE	297 SF	300 SF	0.989502		
LOBBY	1577 SF	1500 SF	1.051604	TOILET RMS	
LOUNGE	297 SF	300 SF	0.989502	2ND FLR	
MENS	165 SF				
MENS	165 SF				
UPPER LOBBY	1101 SF	1000 SF	1.100529		
WAITING	212 SF	200 SF	1.061807		
WOMENS	165 SF				
WOMENS	165 SF				
	4180 SF	3320 SF			
STAFF					
ASSOCIATES OFFICE	294 SF	300 SF	0.980222	EXEC OFFICES	
BREAK RM	143 SF	150 SF	0.955858		
OFFICE	104 SF	120 SF	0.865974		
OFFICE	116 SF	120 SF	0.962979		
OPEN OFFICE	884 SF	1000 SF	0.883816		
PARALEGAL	504 SF	500 SF	1.007133		
WORK ROOM	329 SF	300 SF	1.097483		
	2374 SF	2490 SF			
	11230 SF	9940 SF			

FIGURE 6-1.1 Program Schedule

Project Snap Shot:

Below you will find a preview of the floor plans that will be developed in the text. Compare the room names with those shown in the Program Schedule.

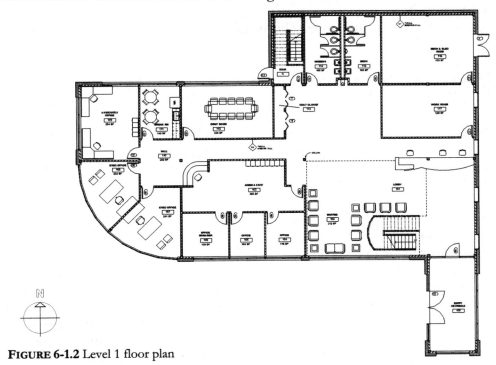

FIGURE 6-1.2 Level 1 floor plan

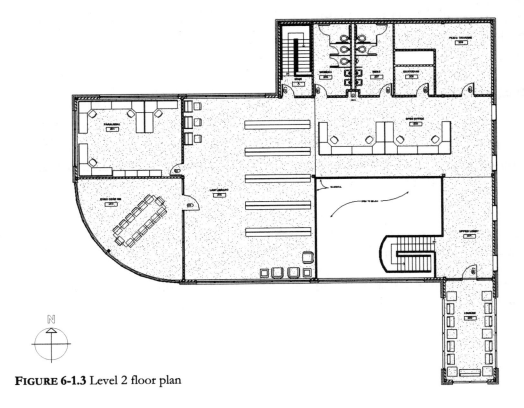

FIGURE 6-1.3 Level 2 floor plan

Project Timeline:

The textbook generally follows the workflow a design firm would take when designing a building. After gathering the programming information, floor plans are first developed that align with the program. Next, the vertical relationships are studied; floors, ceilings and roofs are added along with the beams and joists. This helps to establish the required floor to floor heights.

Once these basic elements have been modeled, the elevations and a few primary sections can be studied. The floor plans are then further refined, developing toilet room layouts, furniture and casework. All these building objects in the model can then be scheduled in order to list information about each, such as manufacturer, model number and cost.

Mechanical and electrical systems are then distributed through the facility. All the while ensuring proper clearances exist while routing ducts and piping.

With the project basically complete, photorealistic renderings are created to present the project to others. Finally, all the drawings (i.e., views of the model) are then placed on sheets to create a set of construction documents.

Each new chapter will instruct the reader to open a partially completed file as a first step. This will help avoid any problems with previous exercises being skipped or not completed properly. Also, in the chapters on structural, mechanical and electrical, the beginning model files will have a portion of the work completed to reduce the amount of work required of the student and result in a more complete project. Additionally, a few custom components will be provided that are not found in the out-of-the-box content that comes with Revit. **Therefore, ensure the DVD is available while working through the textbook so the required files are accessible.**

Creating the Project File:

A Building Information Model (BIM), as previously mentioned, consists of a single file. This file can be quite large. For example, the prestigious architectural design firm SOM used Revit to design the Freedom Tower in New York. As you can imagine, a skyscraper would be a large BIM file, whereas a single family residence would be much smaller.

Large databases are just starting to enter the architectural design realm. However, banks, hospitals, and the like have been using them for years, even with multiple users!

When Revit is launched, the *Recent Files* view is loaded. Template files have several items set up and ready to use (e.g., some wall, door and window types). Starting with the correct template can save you a significant amount of time.

Revit *Architecture* provides a handful of templates with particular project types in mind. They are Commercial, Construction and Residential.

In this exercise you will use the Commercial template. It has several aspects of the project file already set up and ready for use. A few of these items will be discussed momentarily.

As your knowledge in Revit increases, you will be able to start refining a custom template, which probably will originate from a standard template. The custom template will have things like your firm's title block and a cover sheet with abbreviations, symbols and such, all set up and ready to go.

Next you will create a new project file.

1. Select *Application Menu* → *New* → *Project*.

You are now in the *New Project* dialog box. Rather than clicking **OK**, which would use a stripped-down default template, you will select **Browse** so you can select a specialized template (Figure 6-1.4).

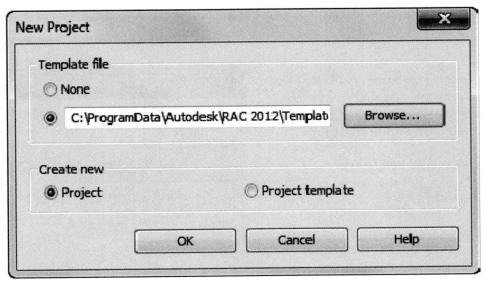

FIGURE 6-1.4 New Project dialog

2. Click the **Browse...** button.

3. Select the template named **Commercial-Default.rte** from the list of available templates (Figure 6-1.5).

4. Click **Open** to select the highlighted template file.

5. Click **OK** to complete the *New Project* dialog.

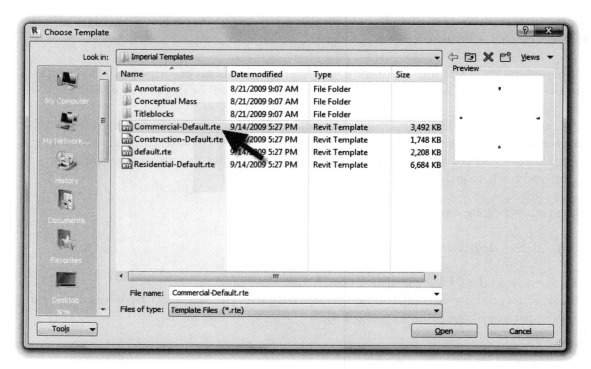

FIGURE 6-1.5 Choose Template dialog

You have just set up a project file that has sheets and schedules created and various building elements preloaded to save time when starting on a commercial project.

Next you will take a look at the predefined wall types that have been loaded.

6. Select **Home → Build → Wall**.

7. Click the *Type Selector* down-arrow on the *Properties Palette* (Figure 6-1.6).

Wall Types:

Notice the wall types that have been preloaded as part of the Commercial template. These wall types are a few of the types of walls one would expect to find on a basic commercial construction project.

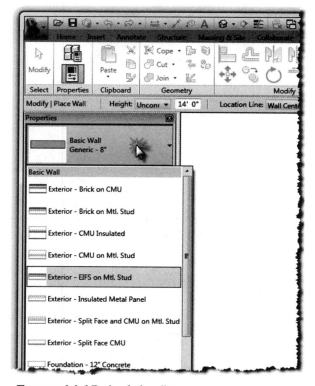

FIGURE 6-1.6 Preloaded wall types

The walls are mostly masonry and metal stud walls, both interior and exterior. If you look at the Residential template, you will see mostly wood stud wall types. Additionally, the thicknesses of materials can vary between Commercial and Residential; this is also accounted for in the templates. For example, gypsum board is typical ⅝″ thick on commercial projects whereas it is usually only ½″ on residential work.

To reiterate the concept, consider the following comparison between a typical commercial interior wall and a typical residential interior wall.

- Typical Commercial Wall
  - + ⅝″ Gypsum Board
  - + 3⅝″ Metal Stud
  - + ⅝″ Gypsum Board
    - = Total thickness: **4⅞″**

- Typical Residential Wall
  - + ½″ Gypsum Board
  - + 2x4 Wood Stud (3 ½″ actual)
  - + ½″ Gypsum Board
    - = Total Thickness: **4½″**

Project Browser:

Take a few minutes to look at the *Project Browser* and notice the views and sheets that have been set up, via the template file selected (Figure 6-1.7).

Many of the views that you need to get started with the design of a commercial project are set up and ready to go (Figure 6-1.7).

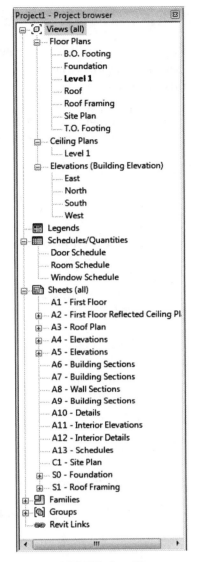

FIGURE 6-1.7 Project Browser: various items preloaded

For the architectural drawings, practically all the sheets typically found on a commercial project have been created; see Figure 6-1.7 under the *"Sheets (all)"* heading of the *Project Browser*. Also, notice the sheets with a "plus" symbol next to them. These are sheets that already have one or more views placed on them. You will study this more later, but a view, such as your East elevation view, is placed on a sheet at a scale you select. This means your title block sheets will have printable information as soon as you start sketching walls in one of your plan views.

You will be creating additional views and sheets for the other disciplines; structural, mechanical and electrical.

Project Information:

Revit provides a dialog to enter the basic project information. You will enter this information next.

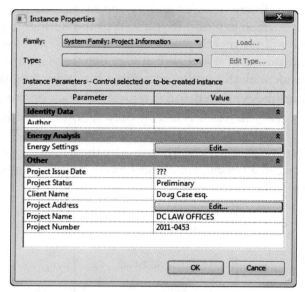

FIGURE 6-1.8 Project Information dialog

8. Select **Manage → Settings → Project Information**.

Project
Information

9. Enter the *Project Information* shown in Figure 6-1.8.

> *FYI: For now you will enter three question marks for the date.*

Project Issue Date:	**???**
Project Status:	**Preliminary**
Client Name:	**DOUG CASE esq.**
Project Name:	**DC LAW OFFICES**
Project Number:	**2011-0453**

10. Click the **Edit** button next to the *Project Address* parameter (Figure 6-1.8).

11. Enter the project address shown in Figure 6-1.9.

> *FYI: This is the address where the law office is going to be built, not the client's current address.*

Enter:
6400 THIRD AVENUE NORTH MINNEAPOLIS, MN 55401

NOTE: You can enter any address you want to at this point; the address suggested is fictional.

12. Click **OK**.

FIGURE 6-1.9 Adding Project Address (partial view)

13. Click the **Edit** button next to the *Energy Settings* parameter. Enter the information shown (Figure 6-1.10).

14. Change the *Project Phase* to **New Construction**. Click **OK**.

15. Click **OK** to close the *Project Information* dialog box.

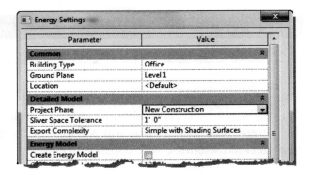

FIGURE 6-1.10 Adding Energy Data (partial view)

The *Location* option, shown in the figure above, will be covered in Chapter 14. This option lets the designer specify where the building is on the Earth.

The project information is now saved in your Revit project database. Revit has already used some of this information to infill in a portion of your title block on each of your sheets. You will verify this next.

Note that the *Energy Settings* information is mainly used by external applications or Revit *MEP* to perform energy analysis like heating and cooling loads. Using Revit in conjunction with programs like *Autodesk Green Building Studio*, *Autodesk Ecotect* or *IES Virtual Environment* (iesve.com – look for their free Revit *Architecture* plug-in) can help create more energy efficient buildings because you can study the design impacts on energy consumption earlier in the project when changes are still possible.

16. Under the **Sheets** heading, in the *Project Browser*, double-click on the sheet **A1 – First Floor**.

17. **Zoom** in to the lower right area of title block (Figure 6-1.11).

Notice that much of the information is automatically filled in, and this is true for every sheet!

Your project database is now setup.

18. **Save** your project as **Law Office.rvt**.

FIGURE 6-1.11 Sheet A1 – First Floor Plan: Title block with Project Information added automatically

Exercise 6-2:
Exterior Walls

You will begin the first floor plan by drawing the exterior walls. Like many projects, early on you might not be certain what the exterior walls are going to be. So, you will start out using the generic wall styles. Then you will change them to a more specific wall style once you have decided what the wall construction is.

Often, a building is designed with a specific site in mind. However, to keep in line with most drafting and design classes, where floor plans are studied before site plans, you will develop the floor plans now.

Adjust Wall Settings:

1. Switch to **Level 1** view; select **Wall** from the *Home* tab.

2. Make the following changes to the wall options within the *Ribbon* and *Options Bar* (Figure 6-2.1):

   a. *Wall style:* **Basic Wall: Generic – 12"**   d. *Location Line:* **Finish Face; Exterior**

   b. *Height:* **Unconnected**   e. *Chain:* **checked**

   c. *Height:* **30' 0"**

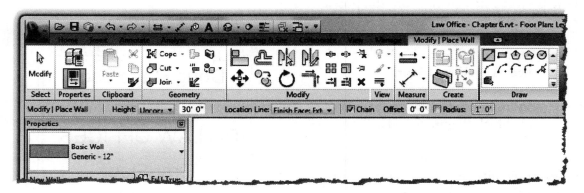

FIGURE 6-2.1 Ribbon and Option Bar – Wall command active

The wall thickness of 12" was selected because the exterior wall will be masonry with insulation, so it is wise to select a wall that is close to what you anticipate it will be. The height is set at 30'-0" based on the design team's experience with this type of project and required space for higher ceilings, beams and ductwork. It can, and will, be changed later in the design process. The "unconnected" setting means the wall is a fixed height and will not adjust when any other floor levels, above the first floor, are adjusted. When drawing masonry walls, the exterior face of the building should be drawn to masonry coursing dimensions to reduce cutting and waste. Setting the *Location Line* to <u>Finish Face; Exterior</u> allows the coursing dimensions to be entered in for the length of the walls.

Draw the Exterior Walls:

3. **Draw** the walls shown in Figure 6-2.2. Do not draw the dimensions. Use the *Measure* tool to double-check your work. Center the building between the elevation tags (see Figure 2-2.1).

    a. <u>Drawing the curved wall</u>: Draw all the walls and leave the curved wall for last. Next, use the ***Fillet Arc*** option within the *Wall* tool and set the Radius to **26'-0"**. Refer back to page 5-14 for a refresher on this process.

    NOTE: If you draw in a clockwise fashion, your walls will have the exterior side of the wall correctly positioned. You can also use the spacebar to toggle which side the exterior face is on.

    TIP: When using the Wall tool, you can click Chain to continuously draw walls. When Chain is not selected you have to pick the same point twice: once where the wall ends and again where the next wall begins.

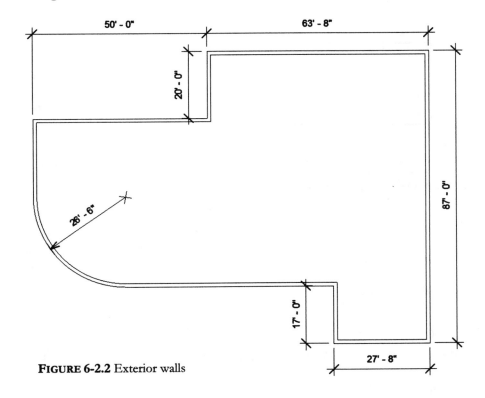

FIGURE 6-2.2 Exterior walls

Modifying Wall Dimensions:

Now that you have the exterior walls drawn, you might decide to adjust the building size for masonry coursing, or subtract square footage to reduce cost.

Editing walls in Revit is very easy. You can select a wall and edit the temporary dimensions that appear, or you can use the *Move* tool to change the position of a wall. Any walls whose endpoints touch the modified wall are also adjusted; they grow or shrink, automatically.

Next you will adjust the dimensions of the walls just drawn.

4. Click **Modify** and then select the <u>far right wall</u> (Figure 6-2.3).

5. Select the temporary dimensions text (26'-8") and then type **14 0** (Figure 6-2.3).

> *FYI: Remember that you do not need to type the foot or inch symbol; the space distinguishes between them.*

> *TIP: Whenever you want to adjust the model via temporary/permanent dimensions, you need to select the object you want to move first and then select the text (i.e., number) of the temporary/permanent dimension.*

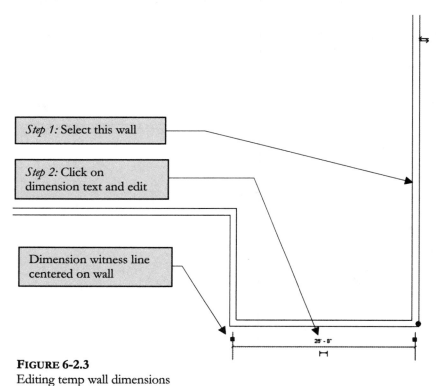

Step 1: Select this wall

Step 2: Click on dimension text and edit

Dimension witness line centered on wall

26' - 8"

FIGURE 6-2.3
Editing temp wall dimensions

6. In the lower right corner of the floor plan, select the wall shown in Figure 6-2.4.

7. Edit the 17'-0" dimension to **26'-0"**.

> *TIP: Just type 26 and press Enter; Revit will assume feet when a single number is entered.*

> *FYI: You can edit the location of the witness lines if desired by going to Manage → Settings → Additional Settings → Temporary Dimensions; here you can set the default to "face" rather than "centerlines". Do not make changes at this time.*

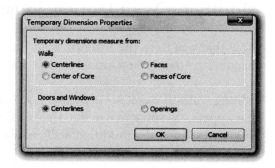

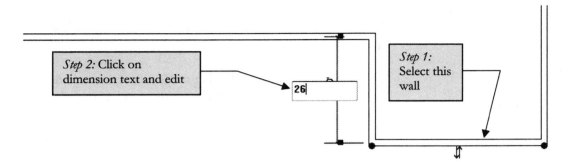

FIGURE 6-2.4 Editing exterior walls; lower right corner of floor plan

Because the temporary dimensions measure to the centerline of the walls, the reported dimension will not always match the original dimension you entered, which was based on the face of the wall rather than the centerline.

> ***TIP:*** *Concrete blocks, or CMU, come in various widths, and most are 16" long and 8" high. With drawing plans, there is a simple rule to keep in mind to make sure you are designing walls to coursing. This applies to wall lengths and openings within CMU walls.*
>
> *Dimension rules for CMU coursing in floor plans:*
> - E' -0" or E' -8"   where E is any even number (e.g., 6'-0" OR 24'-8")
> - O' -4"   where O is any odd number (e.g., 5'-4")

Using the Align tool with walls:

Revit has a tool called *Align* that allows you to quickly make one wall align with another. After they are aligned, you have the option to *Lock* that relationship so the two walls will move together, which is great when you know you want two walls to remain aligned but might accidentally move one, for instance, while zoomed in and you cannot see the other wall.

8. Select the **Modify → Modify → Align** icon.

Notice the *Status Bar* is asking you to select a reference line or point. This is the wall, or linework, that is in the correct location; the other walls will be adjusted to match the reference plane.

9. Set *Prefer* to **Wall Faces** on the *Options Bar*, and then select the exterior face of the vertical wall shown in Figure 6-2.5).

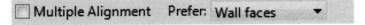

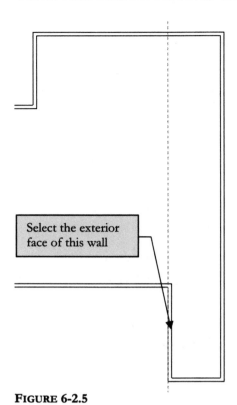

FIGURE 6-2.5
Align tool: wall selected

You should notice a temporary dashed line appear on screen. This will help you to visualize the reference plane.

Notice the *Status Bar* is prompting you to select an entity to align with the temporary reference plane.

10. Now, select the exterior face of the north (top) vertical wall (see Figure 6-2.6).

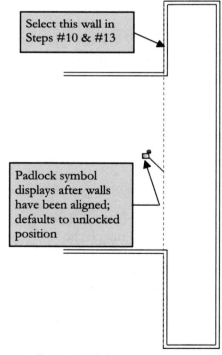

FIGURE 6-2.6
Align tool: select wall to be aligned

Note that if you would have selected the interior face of the wall, that side of the wall would have aligned with the reference plane rather than the exterior, as it is. If you made a mistake, click *Undo* and try it again.

Also, notice that you have a padlock symbol showing. Clicking the padlock symbol will cause the alignment relationship to be maintained (i.e., a parametric relationship). Next you will lock the alignment relationship and experiment with a few edits to see how modifying one wall affects the other.

11. Click on the **padlock** symbol (Figure 6-2.6).

The padlock symbol is now in the locked position.

12. Click **Modify** to unselect the walls.

Modify

13. Select the vertical wall identified in Figure 6-2.6.

Next, you will make a dramatic change so you can clearly see the results of that change on both "locked" walls.

14. Change the 14'-0" dimension to **60'-0"** (Figure 6-2.7).

Notice that both walls moved together (Figure 6-2.7). Also notice that when either wall is selected the padlock is displayed, which helps in identifying "locked" relationships while you are editing the project. Whenever the padlock symbol is visible, you can click on it to unlock it or remove the aligned relationship.

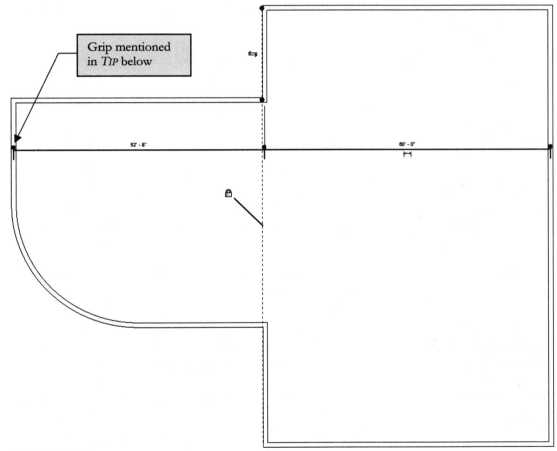

FIGURE 6-2.7
Wall edit: Both walls move together

TIP: Clicking the grip on the witness line of a temporary dimension causes the witness line to toggle locations on the wall (i.e., exterior face, interior face or center). You can also drag the grip to a different wall.

As it turns out, we don't need the two vertical walls aligned. So the next step instructs you to remove the alignment.

15. With one of the two vertical walls (that are locked in alignment with each other) selected; click the **padlock** icon to unlock it.

Next you will make a few more wall modifications, on your own, to get the perimeter of the building in its final configuration and to masonry coursing.

16. Modify wall locations by selecting a wall and modifying the temporary dimensions; the selected wall is the one that moves to match Figure 6-2.8; do not draw the dimensions at this time.

TIP #1: Select the wall to be relocated before editing a dimension.

TIP #2: Make sure you use the Measure tool to verify all dimensions before moving on! Also, do not delete the elevation tags.

TIP #3: Utilize the TIP on the previous page to adjust the witness line location before editing the dimensions.

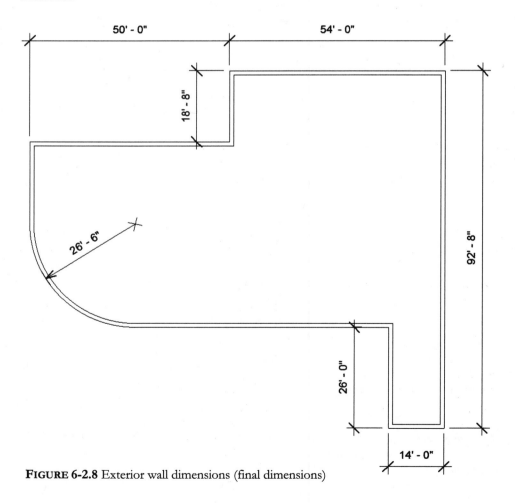

FIGURE 6-2.8 Exterior wall dimensions (final dimensions)

Changing a Wall Type:

In the following steps, you will learn how to change the generic walls into a more refined wall type. Basically, you select the walls you want to change and then pick a different wall type from the *Type Selector* on the *Ribbon*. Remember, the *Ribbon*, *Options Bar* and *Properties Palette* are context sensitive, which means the wall types are only listed in the *Type Selector* when you are using the *Wall* tool or you have a wall selected.

17. Select all the walls in your **First Floor** plan view.

> **TIP:** *You can select all the walls at once: click and drag the cursor to select a Window. Later in the book you will learn about "Filter Selection" which also aids in the selection process.*

18. From the *Type Selector* on the *Properties Palette*, select **Exterior – Split Face and CMU on Mtl. Stud** (Figure 6-2.9).

19. Click **Modify** to unselect the walls.

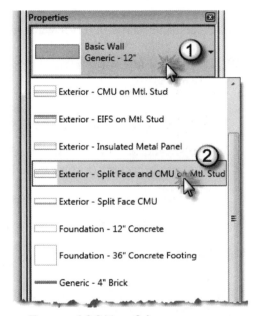

FIGURE 6-2.9 Type Selector

If you zoom in on the walls, you can see their graphic representation has changed a little. It will change more when you adjust the *View's Detail Level* near the end of this exercise. Typically, try to start with a wall closest to the one you think you will end up with; you may never even have to change the wall type.

Even though the wall did not change much graphically in this plan view, it did change quite a bit. In a 3D view, which you will look at in a moment, the wall now has horizontal accent bands and a wall cap or a parapet cap! The image to the right a snapshot of the 30'-0" tall wall you now have in your model.

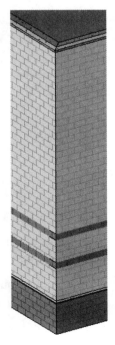

It was important that the *Location Line* be set to "Finish Face: Exterior" when the walls were drawn. When the walls were just changed, the *Location Line* position did not move. Thus, all the exterior dimensions are still accurate. All the walls grew in thickness towards the interior.

Exploring the Exterior Wall Style:

As previously mentioned, Revit provides several predefined wall styles, from metal studs with gypsum board to concrete block and brick cavity walls.

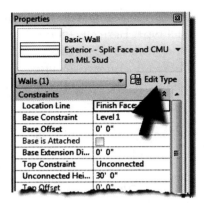

FIGURE 6-2.10
Element Properties icon

Next, you will take a close look at the predefined wall type you are using for the exterior walls.

20. Select one of the exterior walls in your floor plan.

21. Draw your attention to the *Properties Palette*; type **PP** if it is not visible.

22. Select the ***Edit Type*** button (Figure 6-2.10).

23. You should be in the *Type Properties* dialog box. Click the ***Edit*** button next to the *Structure* parameter (Figure 6-2.11).

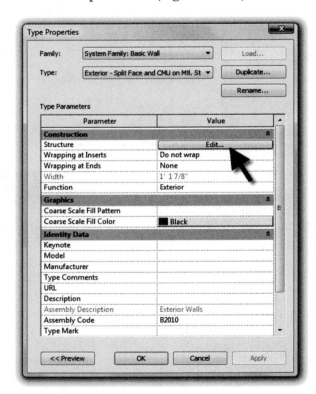

FIGURE 6-2.11 Type Properties

FYI: Revit has two types of properties, **Instance** (shown in the *Properties Palette*) and **Type** (shown to the left):

Instance Properties: This is information that can vary by instance (i.e., individual walls, doors, windows, etc.), for example, the height to the bottom of a window, or the fire rating of a wall or door. These values can vary from instance to instance.

Type Properties: This is information that is the same for every instance of a specific type. For example the width and height of window type "W1" should be the same for all, and the width of wall type "S6" should be the same for all. Any changes to these values changes all previously, and yet to be drawn, objects of that type in the model.

24. Finally, you are in the *Edit Assembly* dialog box. This is where you can modify the construction of a wall type. Click **<<Preview** to display a preview of the selected wall type (Figure 6-2.12).

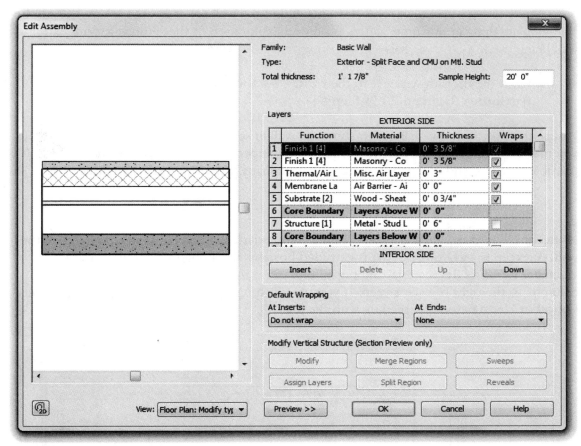

FIGURE 6-2.12 Edit Assembly

Here, the *Edit Assembly* dialog box allows you to change the composition of an existing wall.

Things to notice (Figure 6-2.12):

- Each row is called a *Layer*. By clicking on a *Layer* and picking the **up** or **down** buttons, you can reposition materials within the wall assembly. Clicking **Insert** adds a new material.

- The **exterior** side is labeled at the top and **interior** side at the bottom.

- You will see horizontal lines, or *Layers*, identifying the core material. The core boundary can be used to place walls and dimension walls. For example: the *Wall* tool will let you draw a wall with the interior or exterior core face as the reference line. On an interior wall you might dimension to the face of stud rather than to the finished face of gypsum board; this would give the contractor the information needed for the part of the wall they will build first.

Next, you will see how the vertical elements within the wall are established. You will not be changing anything at this time, as this is only an exploration of the settings for our exterior wall being used.

25. Click the drop-down next to the word *View* and select **Section: Modify Type Attributes** (Figure 6-2.13 - Step #1).

Notice the preview now changes to show the wall in section. The height of this wall is determined by the "sample height" setting in the upper right of the *Edit Assembly* dialog. It is possible to zoom and pan within the preview window; first you must click within it.

26. Next, click the **Sweeps** button (Figure 6-2.13 – Step #2).

Notice the *Wall Sweeps* dialog shows there are four elements that are being imposed on the wall. A sweep is a 2D outline that is extruded horizontally along the length of a wall wherever it occurs. Its material and position in or on the wall can be adjusted via the columns to the right of each sweep. If you try adjusting these values, make sure you select Cancel or Undo before proceeding with the text.

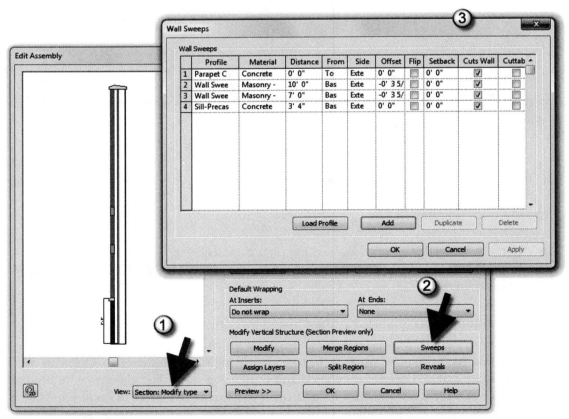

FIGURE 6-2.13 Wall Sweeps

27. Select **Cancel** to close all the open dialog boxes.

For many of the walls, Revit can display more refined linework and hatching within the wall. This is controlled by the *Detail Level* option for each view. You will change the *Detail Level* for the **First Floor** plan view next.

28. Click on the ***Detail Level*** icon in the lower left corner of the drawing window (Figure 6-2.14).

29. Select **Medium**.

> **FYI:** *This view adjustment is only for the current view, as are all changes made via the View Control Bar.*

FIGURE 6-2.14 Detail Level; Set to Medium

The typical commercial project floor plan scale is $\frac{1}{8}'' = 1'\text{-}0''$ – this allows larger buildings to fit on a standard sheet (e.g., 22″ x 34″). However, the law office is a smaller building so the scale can be increased to $\frac{1}{4}'' = 1'\text{-}0''$ to show more detail.

30. Set the View Scale to $\frac{1}{4}'' = \mathbf{1'\text{-}0''}$.

You may need to zoom in, but you should now see additional lines and some hatching for the various *Layers* within the wall. The two images below show the difference between *Coarse* and *Medium* settings. **FYI:** *The* View Scale *changes the size of the hatch pattern.* Give it a try, but set the scale back to $\frac{1}{4}'' = 1'\text{-}0''$ before proceeding.

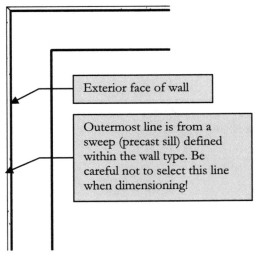

Exterior face of wall

Outermost line is from a sweep (precast sill) defined within the wall type. Be careful not to select this line when dimensioning!

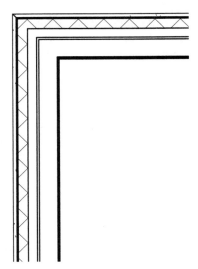

FIGURE 6-2.15A
Detail Level; Set to Coarse

FIGURE 6-2.15B
Detail Level; Set to Medium

If you did not pay close enough attention when drawing the walls originally, some of your walls may show the CMU to the inside of the building.

> *TIP: On the View tab you can select Thin Lines to temporarily turn off the line weights; this has no effect on plotting.*

31. Select **Modify** (or press **Esc**); select a wall. You will see a symbol appear that allows you to flip the wall orientation by clicking on that symbol (Figure 6-2.16).

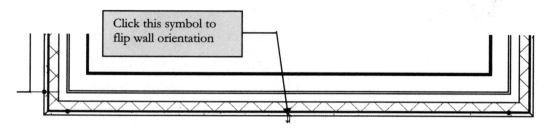

Click this symbol to flip wall orientation

FIGURE 6-2.16 Selected Wall

32. Whether you need to adjust walls or not, click on the flip symbol to experiment with its operation.

> *TIP: The flip symbol is always on the exterior side, or what Revit thinks is the exterior side of the wall.*

33. If some walls do need to be adjusted so the CMU, and flip symbol, are to the exterior, do it now. You may have to select the wall(s) and use the *Move* tool to reposition the walls to match the required dimensions.

> *TIP: Walls are flipped about the Location Line, which can be changed via the Properties Palette when the wall is selected. So changing the Location Line to Wall Centerline before flipping the wall will keep the wall in the same position. Be sure to change the Location Line back to Exterior Face.*

TIP: You can use the *MOVE* tool on the *Ribbon* to accurately move walls. The steps are the same as in the previous chapters!

Follow these steps to move an object:
- Select the wall.
- Click the *Move* icon.
- Pick any point on the wall.
- Start the mouse in the correct direction, don't click.
- Start typing the distance you want to move the wall and press **Enter**.

You can see your progress nicely in a 3D view. Click the
Default 3D View icon on the *Quick Access Toolbar*. The walls
are shaded to make the image read better (Figure 6-2.17).

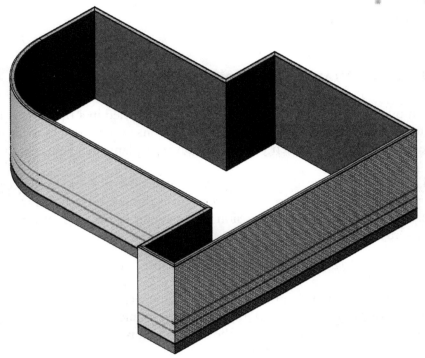

FIGURE 6-2.17 Default 3D View

If you zoom in on the walls, you can see how much detail Revit can store in a wall type. By
picking a few points, you defined the wall's width, height and exterior finish materials!

34. Close the **3D** view and switch back to the **First Floor** plan view.

35. **Save** your project.

> ***TIP:*** *Holding down the* Shift *key while pressing the wheel button on the mouse allows you to fly
> around the building. You will have to experiment with how the mouse movements relate to the
> building's rotation. Selecting an item first causes that item to remain centered on the screen during
> orbit.*

Exercise 6-3:
Interior Walls

In this lesson you will draw the interior walls for the first and second floors. Using the line sketching and editing techniques you have studied in previous lessons, you should be able to draw the interior walls with minimal information.

Overview On How Plans Are Typically Dimensioned:

The following is an overview of how walls are typically dimensioned in a floor plan. This information is intended to help you understand the dimensions you will see in the exercises, as well as prepare you for the point when you dimension your plans (in a later lesson).

Stud walls, wood or metal, are typically dimensioned to the center of the walls; this can vary from region to region and from office to office. Some firms dimensions to the face of stud. Here are a few reasons why you should dimension to the center of the stud rather than to the face of the gypsum board:

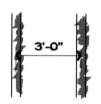

Dimension Example
– Two Stud Walls

    o The contractor is laying out the walls in a large "empty" area. The most useful dimension is to the center of the stud; that is where they will make a mark on the floor. If the dimension was to the face of the gypsum board, the contractor would have to stop and calculate the center of the stud, which is not always the center of the wall thickness, for example, a stud wall with one layer of gypsum board on one side and two layers of gypsum board over resilient channels on the other side of the stud.

    o When creating a continuous string of dimensions, the extra dimensions, text and arrows, indicating the thickness of the walls would take up an excessive amount of room on the floor plans, space that would be better used by notes.

Occasionally you should dimension to the face of a wall rather than the center; here's one example:

    o When indicating design intent or building code requirements, you should reference the exact points and surfaces. For example, if you have uncommonly large trim around a door opening, you may want a dimension from the edge of the door to the face of the adjacent wall. Another example would be the width of a hallway; if you want a particular width you would dimension between the two faces of the wall and add the text "clear" below the dimension to make it known, without question, that the dimension is not to the center of the wall.

Dimensions for masonry and foundation walls:

o Foundation and masonry walls are dimensioned to the nominal face and not the center. These types of walls are modular (e.g., 8″x8″x16″) so it is helpful, for both designer and builder, to have dimensions that relate to the masonry wall's coursing.

Dimension Example
– Two masonry Walls

Dimensions from a stud wall to a masonry wall:

o The rules above apply for each side of the dimension line. For example, a dimension for the exterior CMU wall to an interior stud wall would be from the exterior face of the foundation wall to the center of the stud on the interior wall.

Again, you will not be dimensioning your drawings right away, but Revit makes it easy to comply with the conventions above.

Dimension Example
– Stud to masonry

Drawing the First Floor Interior Walls:

Now that you have the perimeter drawn, you will draw a few interior walls. When drawing floor plans it is good practice to sketch out the various wall systems you think you will be using; this will help you determine what thickness to draw the walls. Drawing the walls at the correct thickness helps later when you are fine-tuning things.

One of the most typical walls on a commercial project consists of $3\frac{5}{8}$″ metal studs (at 16″ O.C.) with one layer of gypsum board on each side, making a wall system that is $4\frac{7}{8}$″ thick.

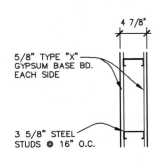

This composition can vary greatly. For example, you may need to add resilient channels to one side of the wall to enhance sound control; they are $\frac{7}{8}$″ thick and are installed on the noisy side of the wall

Finishes: Gypsum board walls can be finished in a variety of ways. The most economical finish is usually one or more colors of paint. Other options include: wall fabrics like high-end wall paper, which are used in executive offices and conference rooms; fiberglass liner panels which are used in janitor rooms and food service areas; veneer plaster which is used for durability, or high-impact gypsum board can also be used; tile, which is used in toilet rooms and showers, to name a few. These finishes are nominal and are not included in the thickness used to draw the wall.

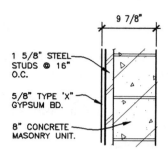

Concrete block, referred to as "CMU", walls are often used to construct stair and elevator shafts, high traffic or high abuse areas, and for security; filling the cores with concrete or sand can increase strength, sound control and even stop bullets. The most used size is 8″ wide CMU; 6″, 10″ and 12″ are also commonly used. Typically, 4″ and 6″ wide is used for aesthetics and 10″ and 12″ CMU for structural reasons.

Finishes: Concrete block can just be painted or it can have special finishes, such as Glazed Block or Burnished Concrete Block, which cost more but are durable and are available in many colors. In offices, conference rooms and other more refined areas, concrete block walls are not desirable so they are covered with metal furring channels and gypsum board; especially in rooms where three walls are metal studs and only one would be CMU. The sooner this is taken into consideration, the better, as this can significantly affect space for furniture in a room. Another major furniture obstacle is fin-tube radiation at the exterior walls.

Walls often have several Life Safety issues related to them. Finishes applied to walls must have a certain flame spread rating, per local building code. Several walls are usually required to be fire rated, protecting one space from another in the event of a fire; these walls have restrictions on the amount of glass (windows + doors), type of door and window frames (wood vs. steel) and the need to extend the wall to the floor or roof deck above.

Revit *Architecture* and Revit *MEP* can help to coordinate many of these things just mentioned. Walls can hold information about fire ratings and sound control. This information can then be presented in a schedule, or a feature called *View Filters* can be used to make the walls stand out.

Drawing the fin-tube radiation or displacement ventilation (i.e., the things that heat the room and take up space) in Revit *MEP* gives the architects and interior designers the information they need to design casework and furniture around those things.

Adjust Wall Settings:

1. Select **Wall** from the *Home* tab on the *Ribbon*.

2. Make the following changes to the wall options in the *Ribbon, Options Bar* and *Properties Palette* (similar to Figure 6-2.1):

   a. *Wall style:*   **Interior – 4 7/8″ partition (1-hr)**

   b. *Height:*   **Roof** (aka, *Top Constraint*)

   c. *Location Line:*   **Wall Centerline**

All your interior walls will be **4 7/8″** for each floor, unless specifically noted otherwise.

3. Draw a horizontal, East to West, wall approximately as shown in Figure 6-3.1. Do not worry about the location; you will adjust its exact position in the next step.

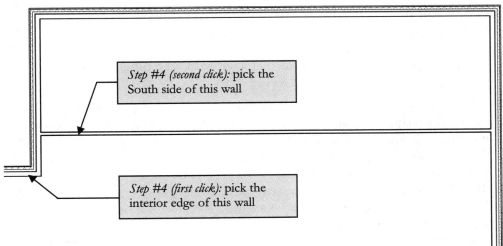

Step #4 (second click): pick the South side of this wall

Step #4 (first click): pick the interior edge of this wall

FIGURE 6-3.1 First interior wall

4. Use the *Align* tool to align the interior wall you just drew with the edge of the exterior wall (Figure 6-3.1). Set *Prefer* to <u>Wall Faces</u> on the *Options Bar*. When you are done, the wall should look like Figure 6-3.2.

FYI: *You do not need to "lock" this alignment.*

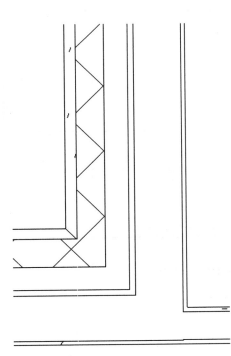

Notice the gypsum board is not the same thickness between the exterior and interior walls. You will adjust the **exterior wall** to the standard ⅝″ thickness for commercial projects.

5. Adjust the gypsum board (row 10) from ½″ to ⅝″; refer back to page 6-18, Steps 20-24.

Because you edited a Type Parameter, all walls of type *Exterior - Split Face and CMU on Mtl. Stud* updated instantly to the new thickness. However, the interior wall now needs to be aligned again because it was not locked after aligning the two walls previously.

6. Use the *Align* tool to align the two walls again; zoom in if needed.

FIGURE 6-3.2 Aligned wall

Next you will draw a handful of walls per the given dimensions. You will use the same partition type: 4⅞″ partition (1-hr).

7. Draw the interior walls shown in Figure 6-3.3a and b; see the *TIPS* on the next two pages which should help you sketch the walls more accurately.

    a. Use **Trim, Copy, Split** and temporary dimensions, as needed.

    b. The centerlines show walls that align with each other. Do not draw the centerlines. ***TIP:*** *Use the Align tool.*

    c. The angled wall is centered on the curved wall and at a 45 degree angle. Start the wall by snapping to the midpoint of the curved wall and then draw the wall an arbitrary length, snapped to the 45 degree plane; then use the *Trim* tool to finish the other side.

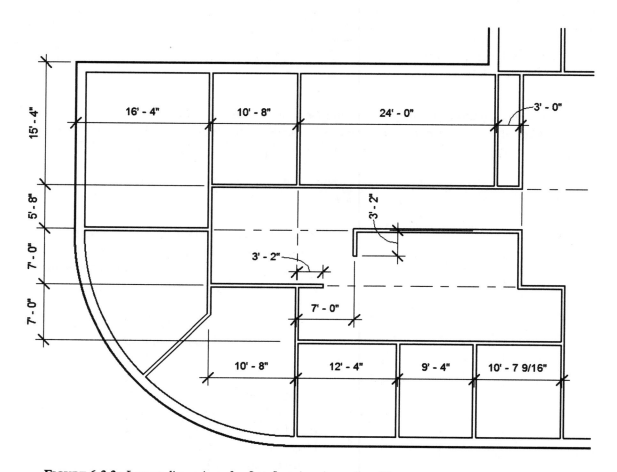

FIGURE 6-3.3A Layout dimensions for first floor interior walls – West

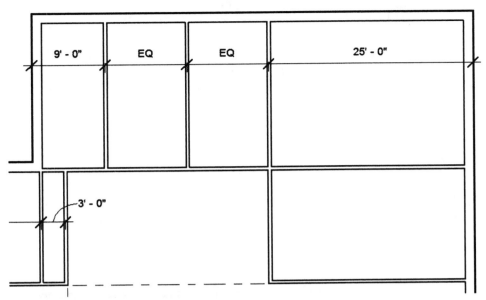

FIGURE 6-3.3B Layout dimensions for first floor interior walls – North-East

TIP – DIMENSION WITNESS LINE CONTROL:

When sketching walls, you can adjust the exact position of the wall after its initial placement. However, the temporary dimensions do not always reference the desired wall location (left face, right face or center). You will see how easy it is to adjust a dimension's *Witness Line* location so you can place the wall exactly where you want it.

First, you will be introduced to some dimension terminology. The two boxed notes below are only for permanent dimensions; the others are for both permanent and temporary.

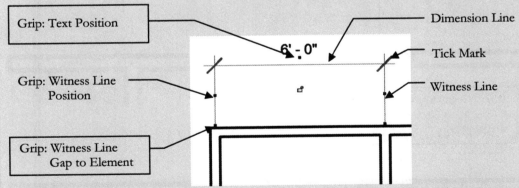

Next, you will adjust the *Witness Lines* so you can modify the inside clear dimension, between the walls, in the above illustration.

Continued on next page

TIP – DIMENSION WITNESS LINE CONTROL... *(Continued from previous page)*

When you select a wall you will see temporary dimensions, similar to the image below.

NOTE: Some elements do not display temporary dimensions; in that case, you can usually click the "Activate Dimensions" button on the Options Bar to see them.

Clicking, not dragging, on the witness line grip causes the witness line to toggle between the location options (left face, right face, center). In the example below, the grip for each witness line has been clicked until both witness lines refer to the "inside" of the room.

Click the *Witness Line Grip* until the *Witness Line* references the element location you prefer; repeat for the other side.

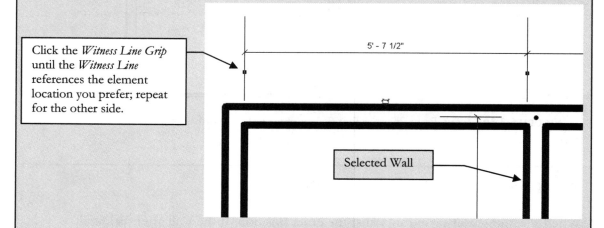

5' - 7 1/2"

Selected Wall

In the above example the temporary dimension could now be modified, which would adjust the location of the wall to a specific inside or clear dimension.

Not only can you adjust the *Witness Line* about a given element, you can also move the *Witness Line* to another element. This is useful because Revit's temporary dimensions for a selected element do not always refer to the desired element. You can relocate a *Witness Line* (temporary or permanent) by clicking and dragging the grip; see example below.

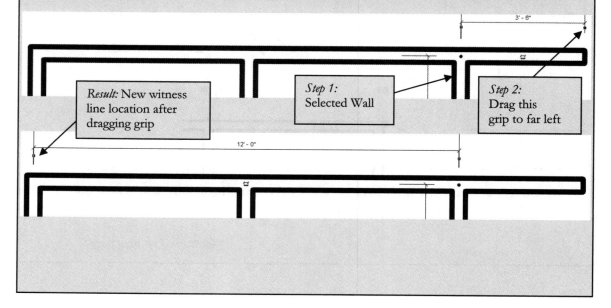

3' - 6"

Result: New witness line location after dragging grip

Step 1: Selected Wall

Step 2: Drag this grip to far left

12' - 0"

8. Use the *Measure* tool to double check all dimensions.

The image below shows what your first floor plan should now look like.

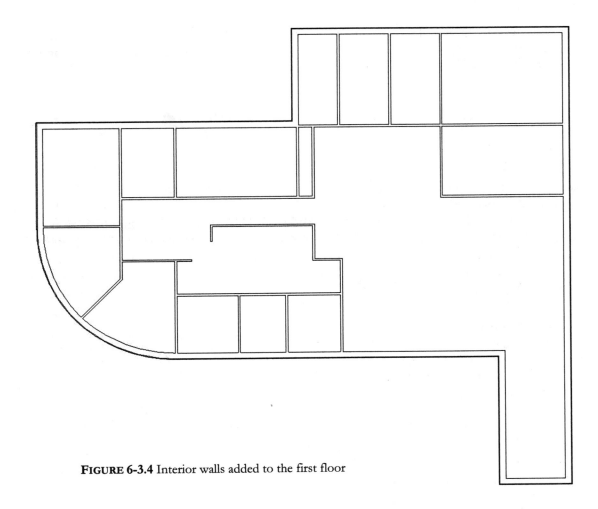

FIGURE 6-3.4 Interior walls added to the first floor

It is important to remember that the "flip control" symbol is displayed on the exterior side of the wall, even for interior walls, when the wall is selected. This corresponds to the Exterior Side and Interior Side designations with the wall type editor, this helps on interior walls that are not symmetrical. If your symbol is on the wrong side, click it to flip the wall and the symbol to the other side. All of your interior walls are symmetrical, so this is not necessary. You may have to move or align the wall so it is flush with the adjacent exterior wall.

Setting Up the Second Floor Plan:

Looking at the *Project Browser*, you should notice a second floor plan view does not exist. Setting one up in involves two steps.

First, you need to create a Level datum in an elevation or section view. This serves as a reference plane which hosts several types of elements in Revit. For example, the bottoms of walls, doors, cabinets, etc. are parametrically assigned to a level. If the Level datum moves, everything attached to the level moves as well.

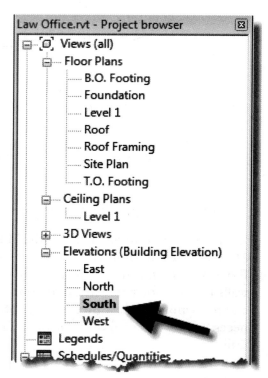

Level datum example

Second, you need to create a floor plan view and ceiling plan view that are associated to the new *Level*. It is possible to have multiple floor plan views based off of the same level; floor plan, code plan, finish plan, power plan, lighting plan, HVAC plan, plumbing plan, and framing plan. Each of these views represents a horizontal slice through the building and each will have its own notes and tags as well as visibility manipulations. For example, the structural framing plan does not need to see the casework and the architectural plan does not need to see the fire dampers.

Because you already have several walls whose tops are associated with the roof *Level* datum, you will simply rename it to be the second floor. After that you can create a floor plan view for that level. Finally, you will create a *Level* datum for the roof.

Typically, you only create *Levels* for surfaces you walk on.

9. Switch to the **South** elevation view via the *Project Browser* (see Figure 6-3.5). Double-click **South**.

You are now viewing the *South* elevation (see Figure 6-3.6). The *Level* datums should extend past the building on each side if you started your floor plan near the center of the elevation tags as originally instructed.

Levels can only be created and edited in elevations and sections.

FIGURE 6-3.5 Opening the South elevation

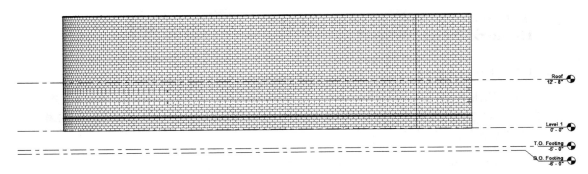

FIGURE 6-3.6 South elevation view showing walls and levels

10. Select the **Roof** *Level* datum.

11. Click on the roof text and enter **Level 2**; press **Enter**.

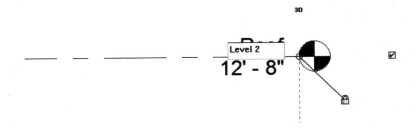

12. Click **Yes** to the prompt shown in the image below.

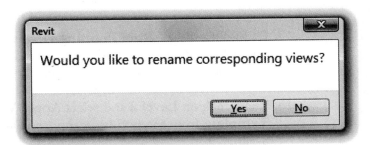

The ***Roof*** view under *Floor Plans*, in the *Project Browser*, has now been changed to **Level 2**.

13. Click on the 12'-8" text, of the ***Level 2*** *datum*, and change it to **13'-4"**, then press **Enter**.

The second floor level is now set properly for our project. This value can be changed at any time during the project, but it is safer to set it as early as possible as some things do not automatically adjust, such as stairs.

Next you will create a new *Level* datum for the roof.

14. While still in the **South** elevation view, select
Home → Datum → Level.

Level

15. Draw a new **Level**.

    a. Pick from left to right.

    b. Align the ends with the ends of the levels below. They will snap into place before you click.

    c. Draw the *Level* datum anywhere above Level 2.

    d. Once drawn, edit the elevation text to be: **26'-8"**

    e. Change the title from *Level 3* to **Roof**.

    f. Click **Yes** to rename corresponding views.

When you select the **Roof** level datum in the **South** elevation, a dashed line and a padlock should appear. This indicates the Levels are locked together. If one moves, they all move.

16. **Close** the **South** elevation view.

There are just two more house cleaning items to do before drawing the Level 2 walls. First, the **Roof Framing** view is tied to the **Level 2** datum, so that will be deleted. You will create structural views later in the text. Second, you will apply a *View Template* to the **Level 2** view to make sure it is set up properly for a floor plan view; a *View Template* is a saved set of view parameters.

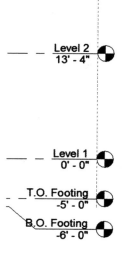

FIGURE 6-3.7
New roof level added

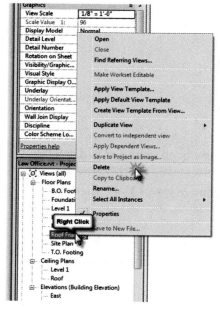

17. Right-click on the **Roof Framing** view listed under *Floor Plans* in the *Project Browser* and select **Delete** from the pop-up menu.

18. Right-click on **Level 2** and select **Apply View Template** from the pop-up menu (see Figure 6-3.8).

You are now in the *Apply View Template* dialog box (Figure 6-3.9). Take a moment to notice the various settings it stores and is thus able to apply to the selected view.

FIGURE 6-3.8
Apply View Template

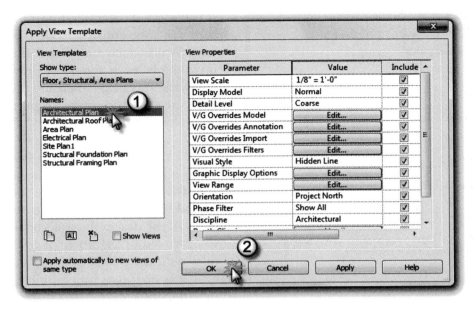

FIGURE 6-3.9 Apply View Template dialog box

19. Make sure **Architectural Plan** is selected on the left, and then click **OK**.

> *FYI: The* View Template *only has a one-time effect on the selected view. That means, if the View Template is changed, the Views that have used it previously will not be updated. You would have to reapply the View Template to any views, if desired, after the View Template has been updated. You may select more than one View in the Project Browser and apply a View Template to all the selected Views at once.*

20. Open the **Level 2** view.

21. Set the *View Scale* to **1/4" = 1'-0"** and the *Detail Level* to **Medium**.

Notice the exterior walls are already shown (Figure 6-3.10). If you recall, the exterior walls drawn on Level 1 were set to be 30'-0" tall. Also, Level 2 is at 13'-4' with a cut plane 4"-0" above that; thus, Level 2 cuts the 30'-0" at 17'-4". This is why the exterior wall is shown and the interior walls are not; the interior walls are set to only extend up to Level 2, which was the Roof level initially. Finally, the Level 2 *view* is set to only look down to the Level 2 *datum* and not beyond. This is why we do not see the interior walls below even though we have not yet drawn a 3D element representing a floor. Next you will quickly explore these settings.

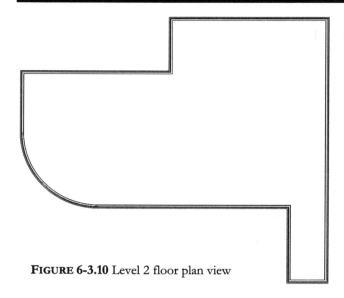

FIGURE 6-3.10 Level 2 floor plan view

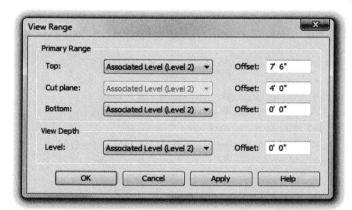

FIGURE 6-3.11 Level 2 floor plan view

It is ideal to draw walls similar to how they would be constructed in the field. Walls which are tall and extend up multiple levels should be drawn as one wall. This helps to ensure the walls are always in proper alignment from floor to floor.

On the other hand, if walls between floors align but are not connected, you would not likely want the wall to extend through the floor. If at some point in the design the walls needed to move out of alignment, it could be difficult if the wall had several hosted elements on it (i.e., wall cabinets, mirrors, urinals, etc.).

22. While in the *Level 2* view, make sure nothing is selected and note the *Properties Palette* is displaying the *Level 2 View Properties*.

23. In the *Properties Palette*, scroll down and click **Edit** next to *View Range*.

Looking at Figure 6-3.11, notice the *Cut Plane* is set at 4'-0", recalling that Level 2 is currently set at 13'-4" and could change if needed. The *View Depth* setting determines how far down Revit looks into your 3D model. Often, the *Bottom* settings and *View Depth* are the same number; if not, anything between the *Bottom* settings and the *View Depth* setting gets an override to a linestyle called *Beyond*. You will learn more about this later.

The image to the right is a graphic representation of the Level 1 and 2 Cut Planes on the Law Office model we are developing.

24. **Cancel** out of the *View Range* dialog box.

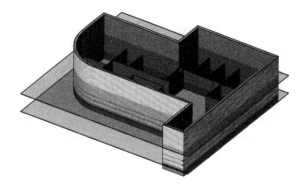

FIGURE 6-3.12 Cut planes

Second Floor Plan Interior Walls:

You are now ready to begin drawing the Level 2 interior walls. The first thing you will do is learn how to copy walls from the first floor to the second floor, as some walls are in the same location on both floors (e.g., the toilet room walls typically align so the plumbing stacks).

25. Open the **Level 1** floor plan view.

26. Holding the **Ctrl** key down allows you to select multiple objects. Select the walls highlighted in Figure 6-3.13.

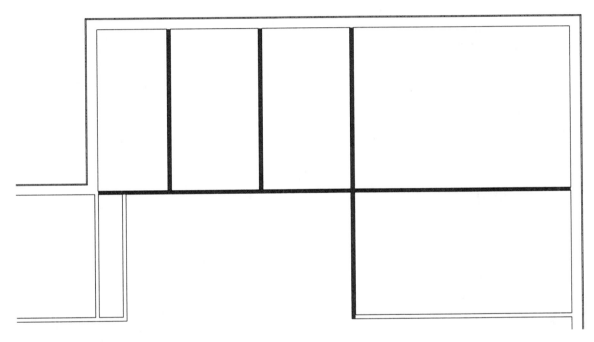

FIGURE 6-3.13 Level 1 walls to be copied to Level 2

27. With the four walls selected, click
Modify | Walls → Clipboard → Copy.

   a. Notice in the lower right corner of the screen, Revit lists the number of elements currently selected (see image to the right).

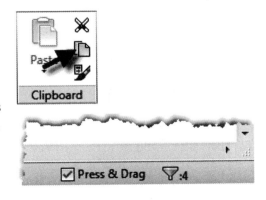

Next you will copy the walls in the clipboard to Level 2.

28. Click **Modify** to clear the current selection.

29. Switch to **Level 2** floor plan view.

30. Click **Modify → Clipboard → Paste → Aligned to Current View** (Figure 6-3.14).

The four walls have now been added to Level 2 in your Revit model (Figure 6-3.15).

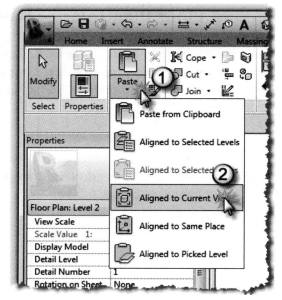

FIGURE 6-3.14 Paste from clipboard

Next you will learn how to trim the longer vertical wall back to the horizontal wall so all three vertical lines are the same length.

31. Click **Modify → Modify → Trim/ Extend Single Element**

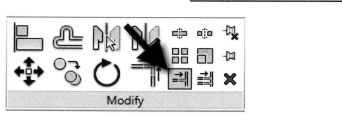

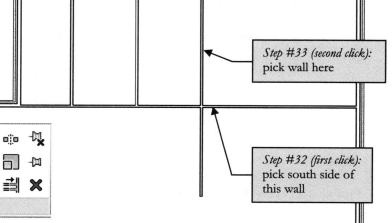

Step #33 (second click): pick wall here

Step #32 (first click): pick south side of this wall

FIGURE 6-3.15
Level 2: Walls pasted from clipboard

32. Click the horizontal wall as the **trim boundary** (Figure 6-3.15).

33. Click the upper portion of the vertical wall (i.e., the portion you wish to keep) as shown in Figure 6-3.15.

The wall should now be trimmed to match the adjacent walls just copied. Another way to achieve the same results is to simply select the vertical wall and drag its end-grip back to the horizontal wall. If you want to try this, click **Undo** and make the same edit using this technique.

34. Select **Wall** from the *Home* tab on the *Ribbon*.

35. Make the following changes via the *Ribbon, Options Bar* and *Properties Palette*:

    a. *Wall style:* **Interior – 4 7/8″ partition (1-hr)**

    b. *Height:* **Roof**

    c. *Location Line:* **Wall Centerline**

36. Draw the five walls shown in Figure 6-3.16. Do not add the dimensions at this time.

REMEMBER: *Dimensions are from the exterior face of the exterior walls and the centerline of all interior walls.*

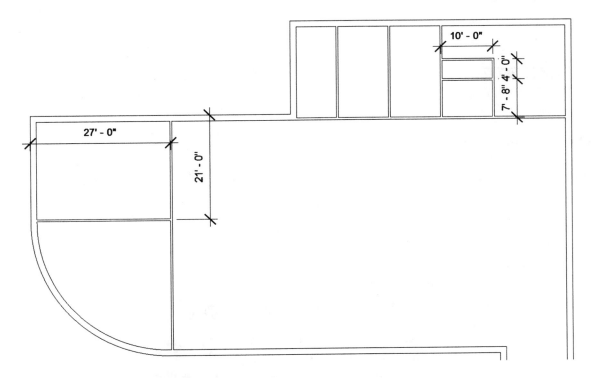

FIGURE 6-3.16 Level 2: Remaining wall to be added (detail level set to Coarse for clarity)

You now have all the major Level 1 and Level 2 walls placed in your Building Information Model (BIM). In the next exercise you will add doors and windows.

37. **Save** your project.

Don't forget to frequently backup your Revit project file. This one file contains all your work; if it becomes corrupt or is accidentally overwritten you will have to start all over again! Well, at least that is what would happen in the real world. In this book you will get a new file to start with at the beginning of each chapter.

Exercise 6-4:
Doors, Windows and Curtain Walls

This lesson will take a closer look at inserting doors and windows.

Now that you have sketched the walls, you will add some doors. A door symbol indicates which side the hinges are on and the direction the door opens.

New doors are typically shown open 90 degrees in floor plans, which helps to avoid conflicts such as the door hitting an adjacent base cabinet. Additionally, to make it clear graphically, existing doors are shown open only 45 degrees.

Door symbol Example – New Door
drawn with 90 degree swing

Door symbol Example – Existing Door
shown with 45 degree swing

One of the most powerful features of any CAD program is its ability to reuse previously drawn content. With Revit you can insert entire door systems (door, frame, trim, etc). You drew a 2D door symbol in Lesson 4; however, you will use Revit's powerful *Door* tool which is fully 3D.

For those new to drafting, you may find this comparison between CAD and hand-drafting interesting: when hand-drafting, one uses straight edges or a plastic template that has doors and other often used symbols to trace.

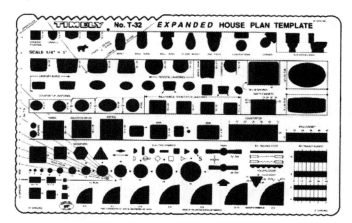

Hand Drafting Template – Plastic template with holes
representing common residential shapes (at ¼" – 1'-0")

Image used by permission, Timely Templates
www.timelytemplates.com

Doors in stud walls are dimensioned to the center of the door opening. On the other hand, and similar to dimensioning masonry walls, doors in masonry walls are dimensioned to the face. See example below.

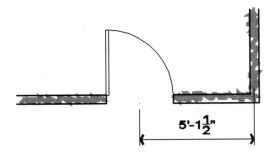

Door Dimension Example – Dimension to the center of the door opening

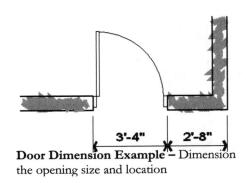

Door Dimension Example – Dimension the opening size and location

Accessible Doors

Most building codes in the US require that a door's clear opening is a minimum of 32″ wide. If you look at a typical commercial door that is open 90 degrees, you will notice that the stops on the door frame, the door thickness and the throw of the hinges all take space from the actual width of the door in the closed position; therefore 36″ wide doors are typically used (see Figure 6-4.1).

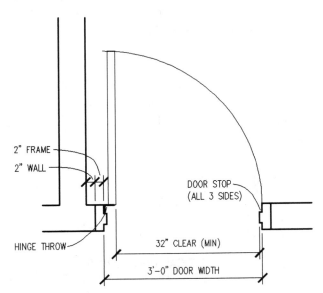

FIGURE 6-4.1
Details to know about accessible doors

Door Stops are usually in integral part of the hollow metal door frame. Their main function is to "stop" the door when being shut. However, they also provide visual privacy and can have sound or weather strips applied. Door stops are NOT typically drawn in floor plans.

Hinge Throw is the distance the door is projected out into the opening as the door is opened, which varies relative to the hinge specified.

The **2″ Wall** dimension is the amount of wall many designers provide between the frame and any adjacent wall. This helps to ensure that the door will open the full 90 degrees regardless of the door hardware selected.

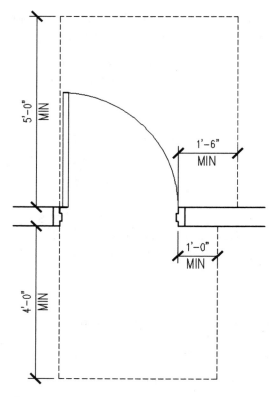

FIGURE 6-4.2
Clear floor space at accessible doors

Building Codes can vary regarding clearances required at a door, but most are pretty similar. Typically, doors that have BOTH a closer and a latch must have sufficient space for a handicapped person to operate the door.

Pull Side of a door that is required to be accessible typically needs to have 18″ clear from the edge of the door, not the outside edge of the frame, to any obstruction. An obstruction could be a wall, a base cabinet or furniture.

Push Side of a door that is required to be accessible typically needs to have 12″ clear from the edge of the door to any obstruction.

Most building codes and the Americans with Disabilities Act (ADA) require slightly different dimensions depending on approach, meaning is the person approaching the door perpendicular or parallel to the wall or door?

In this book, all doors adjacent to a wall will have a 2″ dimension between the wall and the edge of the door frame (per Figure 6-4.3), and all other doors will be dimensioned. A note to this effect is usually found in a set of Construction Documents, which significantly reduces the number of doors that need to be dimensioned.

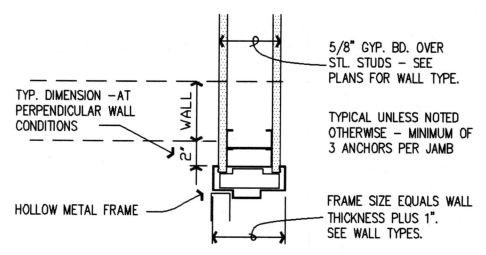

FIGURE 6-4.3 Typical hollow metal door jamb detail

Loading Additional Door Families:

Revit has done an excellent job providing several different door families. This makes sense, seeing as doors are an important part of an architectural project. Some of the provided families include bi-fold, double, pocket, sectional (garage), and vertical rolling, to name a few. In addition to the library groups found on your local hard drive, many more are available via the web library feature (seek.autodesk.com) which requires an internet connection.

The default template you started with, "Commercial-Default.rte", only provides one door family. Each family typically contains multiple door sizes. If you want to insert additional styles, you will need to load additional *Families* from the library. The reason for this step is that, when you load a family, Revit actually copies the data into your project file. If every possible group was loaded into your project at the beginning, not only would it be hard to find what you want in a large list of doors, but the files would also be several megabytes in size before you even drew the first wall.

You will begin this section by loading a few additional *Families* into your project.

Load Family

1. Open your project, if necessary.

2. With the *Door* tool selected, select **Load Family** on the *Ribbon* (Figure 6-4.4).

3. Browse through the **Doors** folder for a moment; the *Doors* folder is a sub-folder of *Imperial Library*; Revit should have taken you there by default. If not you can browse to:

    a. *XP:* C:\Documents and Settings\All Users\Application Data\ Autodesk\ RAC 2012\Libraries\US Imperial\ Doors.

    b. *Vista and Windows 7:* C:\ProgramData\Autodesk\RAC 2012\Libraries\US Imperial\ Doors

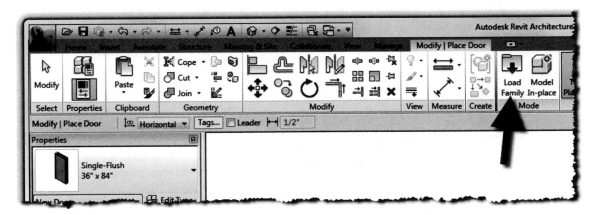

FIGURE 6-4.4 Load content from Library - Door tool active

Each file represents a *Family*, each having one or more *Types* of varying sizes. Next, you will load three door *families* into your project.

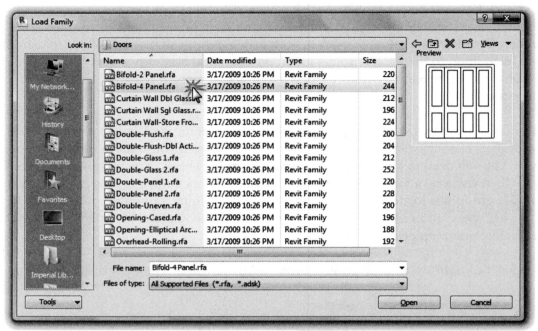

FIGURE 6-4.5 Door Families on hard drive

4. Select **Bifold-4 Panel.rfa**, and then click **Open** (Figure 6-4.5).

As soon as you click *Open*, the selected family is copied into your current project and is available for placement.

5. Repeat Steps 2 – 4 to load the following door groups:

    a. **Double-Flush**

    b. **Curtain Wall Sgl Glass**

    TIP: If you hold the Ctrl key you can select several door files and load them at one time.

6. In the *Project Browser*, expand the *Families* category and then *Doors* to see the loaded door *families* (Figure 6-4.6).

If you expand the *Doors* sub-category itself in the *Project Browser*, you see the predefined door sizes associated with that family. Right-clicking on a door size allows you to rename, delete or duplicate it. <u>To add a door size, you duplicate and then modify properties for the new item</u>.

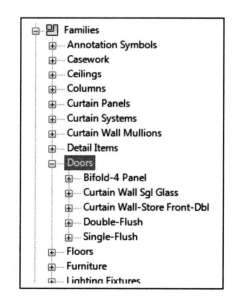

FIGURE 6-4.6 Loaded door families

FYI: The two curtain wall "doors" will not show up when using the Door tool. These doors only work in a wall type that is a curtain wall (more on this later).

Placing Level 1 Doors:

Next, you will start inserting the doors into the first floor plan.

7. With the *Door* tool selected, pick **Single-Flush: 36″ x 84″** from the *Type Selector* on the *Properties Palette*.

8. In the **Level 1** floor plan view, insert one door in the Northeastern-most room as shown in Figure 6-4.7.

   a. Set the distance between the door opening and the adjacent wall to **4″**. Refer back to Exercise 3-2 for a refresher on this. The 4″ dimension accounts for a 2″ portion of wall and 2″ door frame, which the Revit door families unfortunately do not show. See Figure 6-4.3.

FIGURE 6-4.7 First door placed on Level 1, Northeastern room

Immediately after the door is inserted, or when the door is selected, you can click on the horizontal or vertical flip-controls to position the door swing and hand as desired.

Since "Tag on placement" was selected on the *Ribbon*, Revit automatically adds a *Door Tag* near the newly inserted door. The door itself stores information about the door that can then be compiled in a door schedule. The doors are automatically numbered in the order they are placed. The number can be

Tag on
Placement

changed at any time to suit the designer's needs. Most architects and designers use "1x" or "1xx" (i.e., 12 or 120) numbers for the first floor and "2x" or "2xx" numbers for the second floor.

The *Door Tag* can be moved simply by clicking on it to select it, and then clicking and dragging it to a new location. You may need to press the **Tab** key to pre-highlight the tag before you can select it.

Also, with the *Door Tag* selected you can set the vertical or horizontal orientation and if a leader should be displayed when the tag is moved; it is done via the settings on the *Options Bar*. **NOTE:** *The tag must be selected.*

9. With the newly inserted door selected, note the door's *Instance Properties* in the *Properties Palette*.

   TIP: Type PP if the Properties Palette is not visible.

Notice, in Figure 6-4.8, you see the *Instance Parameters* which are options that vary with each door, e.g., Sill Height and Door Number (Mark). These parameters control selected or yet to be created items.

The *Type Parameters* are not visible in this dialog. To be sure you want to make changes that affect all doors of that type, Revit forces you to click the *"Edit Type"* button and make changes in the *Type Properties* dialog. Also, in the *Type Properties* dialog, you can add additional predefined door sizes to the "Single-Flush" door family by clicking the *Duplicate* button; providing a new name and changing the "size" dimensions for that new *Type*.

10. Click *Modify* to unselect the door.

11. Finish inserting the 17 additional doors for Level 1. (Figure 6-4.9) Use the following guidelines:

    a. Use the door styles shown in Figure 6-4.9; doors not labeled are to be **Single-Flush 36" x 84"**.

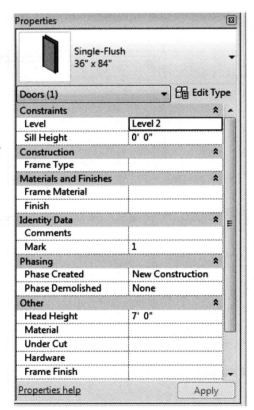

FIGURE 6-4.8 Instance Properties for door

b. While inserting doors, you can control the door swing by moving the cursor to one side of the wall or the other and by pressing the spacebar on the keyboard.

c. The order in which the doors are placed does not matter; this means your doors may be in a random order. You will modify these numbers later in the book.

d. Unless dimensioned, all doors are to be **4"** away from adjacent wall; see Figure 6-4.3. Do not draw dimensions.

e. Note that the image below has the *Detail Level* set to *Coarse*, the *Door Tags* turned off and the scale temporarily modified to make the image more readable. You do not need to make these adjustments. If you do, set them back before proceeding.

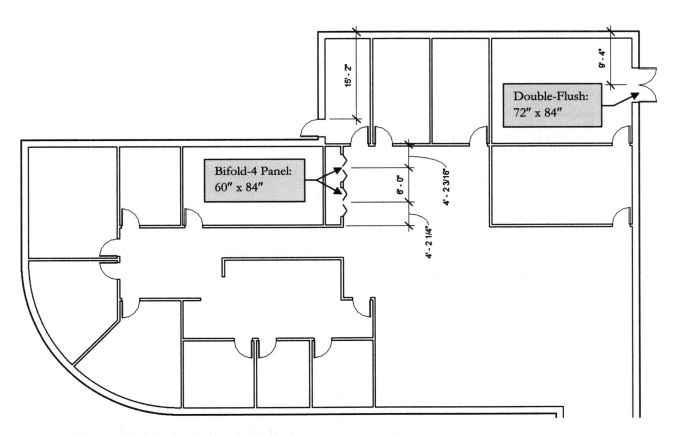

FIGURE 6-4.9 Level 1 doors to be inserted

Placing Level 2 Doors:

Next you will start inserting the doors into the second floor plan.

12. Place the 6 additional doors for Level 2, following the same guidelines as Level 1 (Figure 6-4.10).

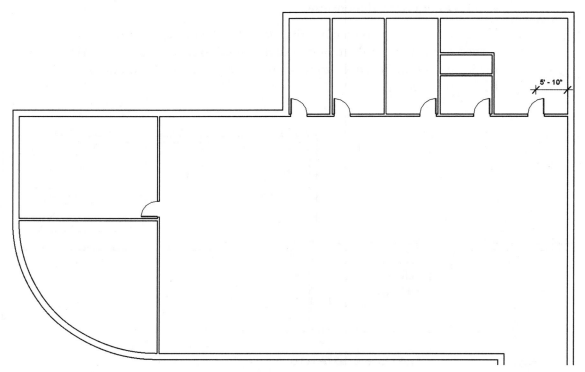

FIGURE 6-4.10 Level 2 doors to be inserted

A few additional doors will be added later. Note that the bottom of a door is automatically attached to the *Level* on which it is inserted. Also, because doors are 7'-0" tall, they pass through the view's 4'-0" *Cut Plane*. Some *Families*, like these doors, are set to show 2D linework, or *symbolic lines* in place of the 3D objects when **cut** in plan view. This allows the arc to appear that represents the swing of the door. In a 3D elevation or section view, the 3D door object is shown, which is in the closed position in this case.

Note on Wall Openings:

Although your building does not contain any openings, you will learn about them before moving on to placing windows. An opening is similar to a door in that, when placed, it removes a portion of wall automatically, creating a circulation route. Also, like doors, openings come in different pre-defined shapes and sizes.

One common mistake is to break a wall so the floor plan appears to have an opening. However, when a section is cut through the opening, there is no wall above the opening. This is also problematic for the room tagging feature and the *Ceiling Placement* tool.

One of the keys to working successfully in Revit is to model the building project just like you would build it, because that is the way Revit is designed to work.

One opening family type can be found in the *Door* folder, called *Opening-Elliptical Arch*. The *Type Properties* dialog for it is shown below (Figure 6-4.11). Notice the various fields that can be filled in. For example, you could enter how much it would cost to construct an opening with an arched top in the *Cost* field.

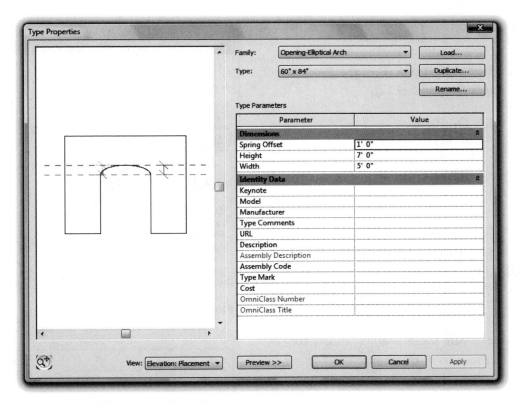

FIGURE 6-4.11 Properties for wall opening

Insert Windows:

Adding windows to your project is very similar to adding doors. The template file you started from has one family preloaded into your project; it is called <u>Fixed</u>. By contrast, the Residential template has three: <u>Casement with Trim</u>, <u>Double Hung with Trim</u> and <u>Fixed with Trim</u>. While in the *Window* tool and looking at the *Element Type Selector* drop-down, you will see the various sizes available for insertion. Additional *Families* can be loaded, similar to how you loaded the doors, although your project will only use the *Fixed* family and *Store Front* walls which are covered directly after the windows.

Most of the exterior fenestrations will be Store Front walls. However a few windows, aka punched openings, will be placed along the east wall.

13. Switch to the **Level 1** floor plan view.

14. Using the ***Window*** tool, on the *Basics* tab, select **Fixed: 24″ x 48″** in the *Element Type Selector.*

We actually want a 48″ x 48″ window, but one does not exist. The next steps will walk you through the process of creating a new *Type* within the *Fixed* window family.

15. Select **Edit Type** from the *Properties Palette* (Figure 6-4.12).

16. Click **Duplicate**.

17. For the name of the new *Type*, enter: **48″x 48″** and then click **OK** (Figure 6-4.13).

You now have a new *Type* named 48″ x 48″ but the parameters are still set for the 24″ x 48″ *Type* that was selected when you clicked *Duplicate*. Next you will adjust those settings.

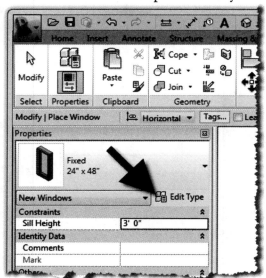

FIGURE 6-4.12 Window type properties

18. Make sure the *Width* and *Height* are both set to **4′-0″** (Figure 6-4.14).

The sill height will be different for each floor, so you will not bother to change that setting.

FIGURE 6-4.13 Name new family type

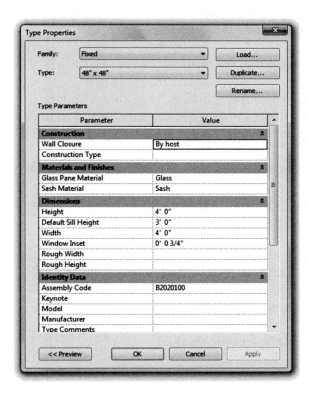

FIGURE 6-4.14 Window type properties

19. Insert the windows as shown in **Figure 6-4.15**; be sure to adjust the window locations to match the dimensions shown. Do not add the dimensions.

20. Be sure to click towards the exterior side of the wall so the glass and window frame are on the exterior side of the wall. Use the flip controls if any correction is needed.

   TIP: *To edit location: Modify → Select window → Adjust temporary dimension witness lines → Edit temporary dimension text, just like repositioning doors.*

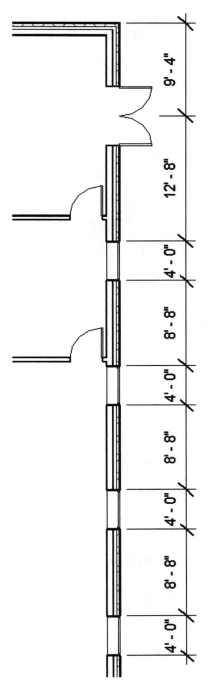

FIGURE 6-4.15
Level 1 windows to be added;
North East corner of plan

With a window *Type*, not only is the window size pre-defined, but the vertical distance off the ground is as well. Next you will see where this setting is stored.

21. Select one of the windows that you just placed in the wall.

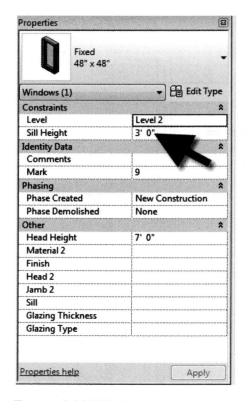

FIGURE 6-4.16 Window instance properties

As previously discussed, this dialog shows you the various settings for the selected item, a window in this case (Figure 6-4.16).

As you might guess, the same size window could have more than one sill height (i.e., distance from the floor to the bottom of the window). So Revit lets you adjust this setting on a window by window basis.

Another setting you might have noticed by now is the *Phase Created*. This is part of what makes Revit a 4D program; the fourth dimension is time. Again, you might have several windows that are existing and two to three new ones in an addition, all the same size window. Revit lets you do that!

22. Set the *Sill Height* to **3'-8"** and click **OK**.

23. Repeat the previous step for the remaining three windows.

Copying Windows from Level 1 to Level 2:

In the next few steps you will copy the windows from Level 1 up to Level 2. You will use a slightly different technique than when you copied the walls.

24. Select the four windows on Level 1.

25. Click **Copy** in the *Clipboard* panel, not the *Modify* panel.

26. Without the need to leave the **Level 1** view, click **Modify → Clipboard → Paste → Aligned to Selected Levels** (Figure 6-4.17).

27. Click **Level 2** and then **OK** (Figure 6-4.18).

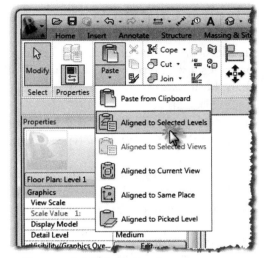

FIGURE 6-4.18 Select levels options

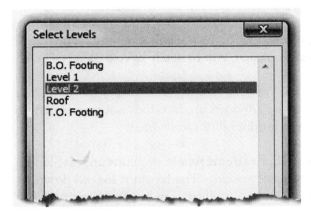

FIGURE 6-4.17 Paste aligned options

TIP: On a high rise building it would be possible to select multiple levels and have the clipboard contents copied to multiple floors at once!

28. Switch to **Level 2** to see the newly added windows.

29. Change the sill height for the **Level 2** windows to **3'-4"**.

CLEANING HOUSE:

As previously mentioned, you can view the various *Families* and *Types* loaded into your project via the *Project Browser*. The more *Families* and *Types* you have loaded the larger your file is, whether or not you are using them in your project. Therefore, it is a good idea to get rid of any door, window, etc., that you know you will not need in the current project. You do not have to delete any at this time, but this is how you do it:

- In the *Project Browser*, navigate to Families → Windows → Fixed. Right-click on **36" x 72"** and select **Delete**.

Another reason to delete types is to avoid mistakes. As you have seen, loading a door family brings in 6'-8" and 7'-0" tall doors. On a commercial project you would rarely use 6'-8" tall doors, so it would be a good idea to delete them from the project so you do not accidentally pick them.

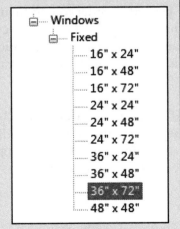

FIGURE: Project Browser

Placing Curtain Walls:

In addition to what are often referred to as punched openings, or the windows, Revit also provides a wall type called **Curtain Wall**. *Curtain Walls* are placed using the *Wall* tool, rather than the *Window* tool, but represent an expanse of glass.

If you select the *Wall* tool, you will see that the commercial template you started with provides three *Curtain Wall* types: <u>Curtain Wall</u>, <u>Exterior Glazing</u> and <u>Storefront</u>.

The first one, <u>Curtain Wall</u>, represents one extreme, that being a blank slate in which you totally design the mullion layout. When the wall is placed, you basically have a panel of glass the entire length and height of the wall.

The second wall type, <u>Exterior Glazing</u>, has the glass divided up, but does not provide any mullions. This would be like a butt-glazed system until mullions are added.

Thirdly, the <u>Storefront</u> wall type represents the other extreme where mullions are placed in both the horizontal and vertical direction at a specific spacing. The layout is locked down, i.e., pinned, and cannot be accidentally modified unless a mullion is manually un-pinned. For simplicity in this tutorial, this will be the system you use.

A Curtain Wall has four primary elements:

- Wall
- Panel
- Grid
- Mullion

Each of these elements must be individually selected in order to edit them. You often have to tap the **Tab** key to cycle through and select something specific; once the item is pre-highlighted, you click to select it.

The blank slate *Curtain Wall* wall type represents the simplest condition: the wall and a single panel that coincides with the wall (see Figure 6-4.19).

FIGURE 6-4.19 Curtain wall

To begin dividing up a curtain wall you need to add *Curtain Grids* (see Figure 6-4.20); Revit has a specific tool for this on the *Home* tab. When a *Curtain Grid* is added, the panel in which it was placed gets split.

The image to the right has:

      8   Curtain Panels
      4   Curtain Wall Grids
      1   Wall

When a **Curtain Grid** is selected, you may adjust its location with the *Move* tool or the temporary dimensions.

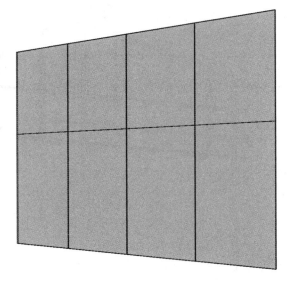

FIGURE 6-4.20 Curtain wall with grids added

When a **Curtain Panel** is selected, you can swap it out with other Revit elements such as walls and special curtain wall doors.

Once *Curtain Grids* have been placed, you may use the **Mullion** tool to place *Mullions* on *Curtain Grids*.

The image to the right shows *Mullions* at each of the four grids and along the perimeter. A portion of a *Mullion* was deleted at the bottom edge and a *Curtain Panel* was swapped out for a door (Figure 6-4.21).

The image to the right has:

      7   Curtain Panels
      4   Curtain Wall Grids
    21   Curtain Wall Mullions
      1   Door
      1   Wall

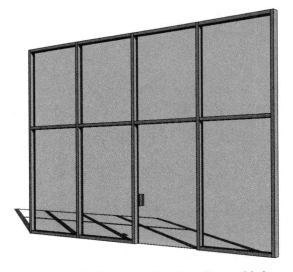

FIGURE 6-4.21 Curtain wall with mullions added

Notice the large number of mullions in the list above. Mullions stop and start at each *Curtain Grid* intersection. This made it easy to select the mullion at the desired door opening location and simply delete it.

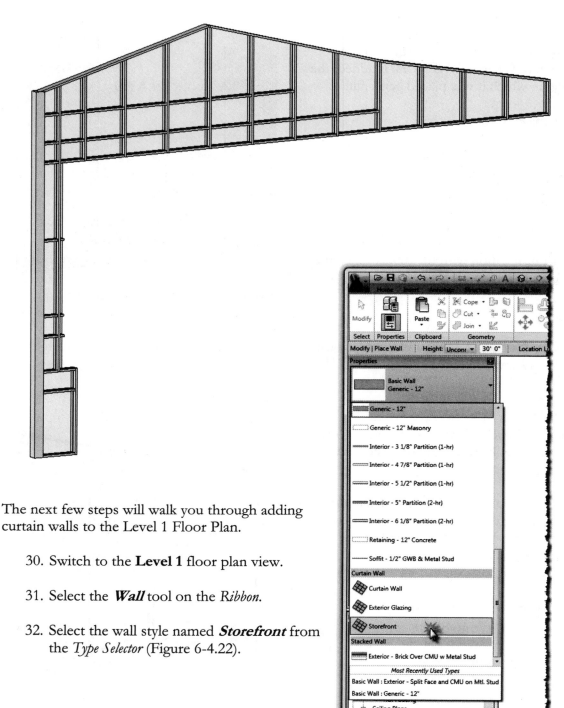

The next few steps will walk you through adding curtain walls to the Level 1 Floor Plan.

30. Switch to the **Level 1** floor plan view.

31. Select the ***Wall*** tool on the *Ribbon*.

32. Select the wall style named ***Storefront*** from the *Type Selector* (Figure 6-4.22).

Before drawing the *Storefront* wall type you will review its properties.

FIGURE 6-4.22
Curtain wall named Storefront

33. Note the *Instance Properties* via the *Properties Palette*.

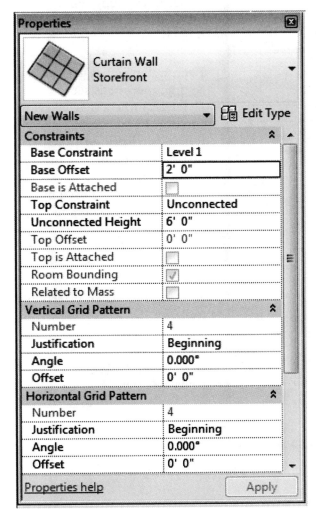

Take a moment to notice a few things about the information presented (Figure 6-4.23).

The *Base Constraint* is equal to the floor plan level you are currently on. Keep in mind **Level 1** refers to the *Level datum* and not the name of the *view* that you are in.

The *Sill Height* is set by the *Base Offset* parameter and the *Head Height* is set by *Top Constraint*.

Because these are *Instance Parameters* they can vary from location to location within the project.

34. Make the following adjustments:

    a. *Base Offset:*   **2'-0"**

    b. *Unconnected Height:* **6'-0"**

35. Click the ***Edit Type*** button to view the *Type Properties*.

FIGURE 6-4.23 Storefront instance properties

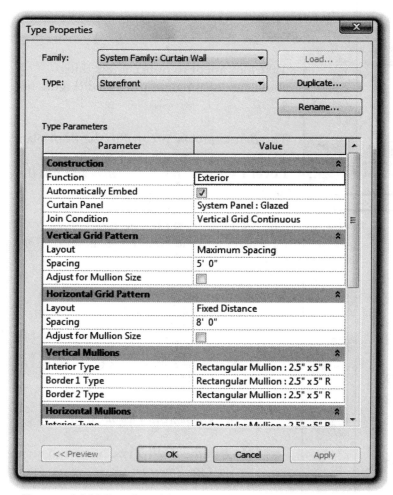

FIGURE 6-4.24 Storefront Type properties

Again, take a moment to notice a few things about the information presented (Figure 6-4.24).

Each wall type has a *Function* setting; this one is set to Exterior. Others may be set to Interior, Foundation, Retaining, Soffit, or Core-Shaft. This setting has an effect on how the wall is drawn and may be used by energy analysis programs.

Automatically Embed allows one wall to cut a hole in another, similar to what a door or window does when placed in a wall.

Various rules on the mullions and their spacing are adjustable here.

36. Press **OK** to close out of the open dialog box.

37. In the Northwest corner of the building, snap to the middle of the wall, **4'-0"** down from the corner and then click. (See Figures 6-4.25a and 6-4.26 for the location.)

38. Move your cursor straight downward, along the wall, and click when the temporary dimension reads **14'-0"** (see Figure 6-4.25b).

The Curtain Wall is now placed in the West wall (Figure 6-4.25c). The flip-control appears on the exterior side of the curtain wall when it is selected, similar to regular walls. If the flip-control is on the interior side of the wall, (as in Figure 6-4.25c), click the control to flip the curtain wall so the glass favors the exterior side of the wall.

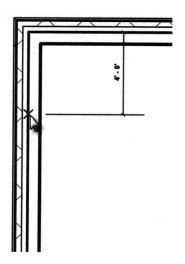

FIGURE 6-4.25A
Storefront – *first pick*

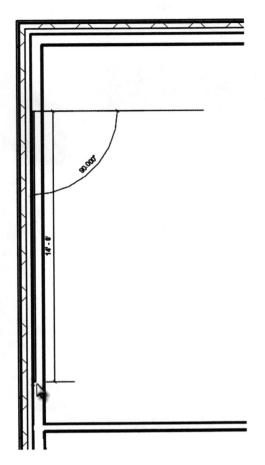

FIGURE 6-4.25B Storefront – *second pick*

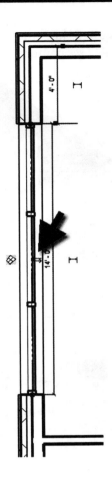

FIGURE 6-4.25C Storefront – selected

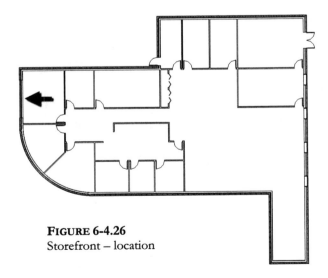

FIGURE 6-4.26
Storefront – location

You have now placed your first curtain wall. The next few steps will instruct you to add the remaining curtain walls. Several will be similar to the first one, with some occurring on each floor. However, at the main entry you will add two-story tall curtain walls that will extend past the second floor, which will then automatically show up in both floor plans.

Notice, in Figure 6-4.27, that the curtain wall already has mullions; this is based on the settings for the *Type* named "Storefront" we used.

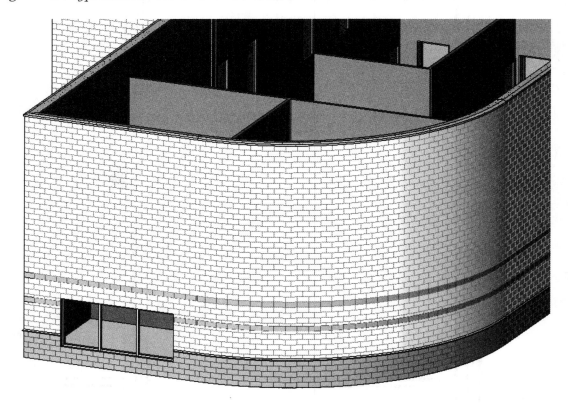

FIGURE 6-4.27 Storefront – shown in 3D view

39. Add four more **Storefront** type curtain walls using the same settings:

a. See Figure 6-4.28 for locations.

b. Do not add the dimensions at this time.

TIP: *Draw Detail Lines first to help position the edges of the curtain wall within the main wall.*

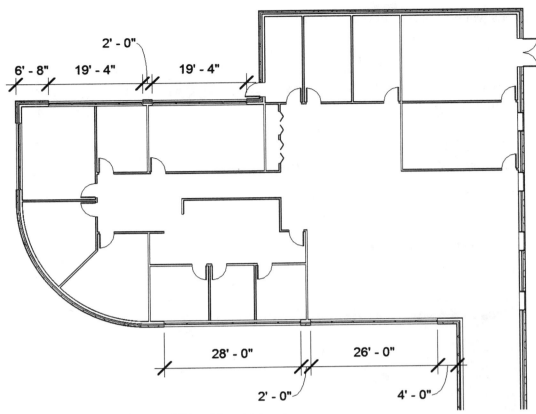

FIGURE 6-4.28 Storefront – additional Level 1 locations

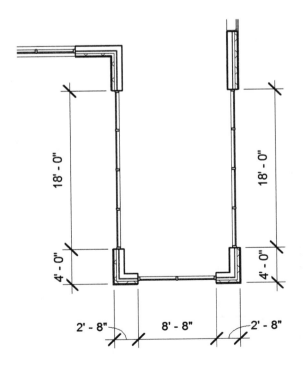

FIGURE 6-4.29 Storefront – additions at main entry

40. Add the three curtain walls at the main entry.

    a. *Base Offset:*   **0'-0"**

    b. *Unconnected Height:*   **21'-4"**

See Figure 6-4.29.

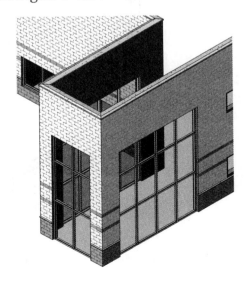

The mullions will be adjusted in the chapter that deals with creating and editing elevations.

Next, you will draw a curtain wall along the curved wall. This will also be a two-story tall wall. You will learn how it is possible to draw walls based on linework that existing within other elements, such as walls. This bypasses the need to pick the points to define the wall length, and angle if curved.

41. Place the curved curtain wall (Figure 6-4.30A):

    a. *Wall type:* Curtain wall: **Storefront**

    b. *Base Offset:*   **0'-0"**

    c. *Unconnected Height:*   **21'-4"**

    d. Select the "pick" tool in the *Draw* panel (Step #1 in image below).

    e. Click the centerline of the curved wall (Figure 6-4.30B).

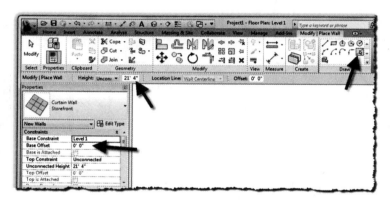

FIGURE 6-4.30A Curved Storefront – UI settings

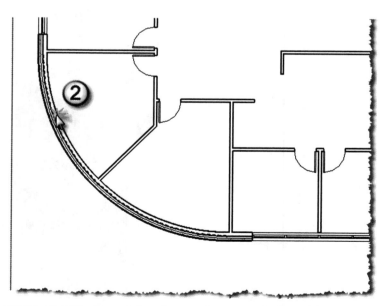

FIGURE 6-4.30B Curved Storefront – placement via the "pick" option

Because the curtain wall is the same length as the solid curved wall, the sweeps in the wall cannot be created; this is not a problem in this case. The curtain wall is not as tall as the solid wall, so some of the wall still exists above the curtain wall as seen in the image to the right.

42. Click the "X" to close the warning.

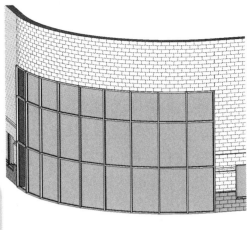

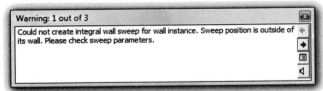

For some reason, the way Revit is programmed, the curtain wall may extend past the curved wall we selected so one quick correction is required *(next three steps)*.

43. Select the curtain wall; be sure to select the dashed line that represents the entire length of wall, not a mullion or curtain grid.

44. A round grip appears at the end of a wall when it is selected; right-click on the grip.

45. Select ***Disallow Join*** (Figure 6-4.32).

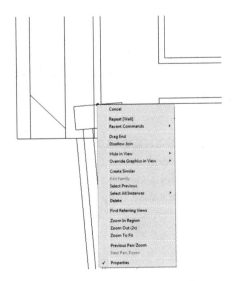

FIGURE 6-4.32
Right-click on wall grip

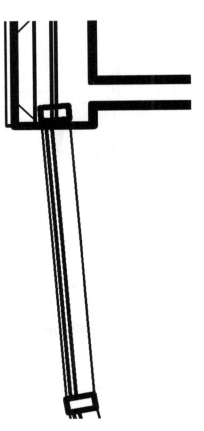

FIGURE 6-4.31
Storefront – problem at jamb

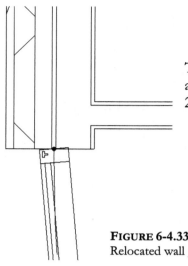

46. Click and drag the grip down and snap to the endpoint of the vertical wall (Figure 6-4.33)

The curtain wall is now adjusted to the correct length. You are now ready to add the remaining curtain walls on Level 2.

FIGURE 6-4.33
Relocated wall grip

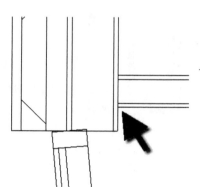

TIP: *The Disallow Join feature works on regular walls. One popular use is when a new wall abuts an existing wall and you do not want them to join. For example, if the exterior wall were existing and the interior partition new, you would want a line to separate them as in Figure 6-4.34. You do not need to make this change to your model.*

FIGURE 6-4.34
Disallow Join example

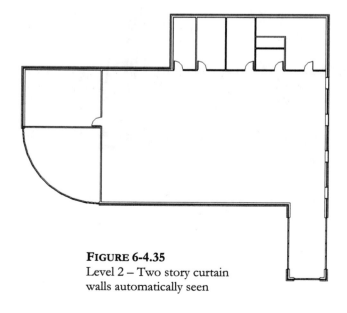

47. Switch to the **Level 2** floor plan view.

Notice the four curtain wall elements drawn 21'-4" tall are visible right away in the **Level 2** view because they pass through this view's *Cut Plane.*

FIGURE 6-4.35
Level 2 – Two story curtain walls automatically seen

48. Using the techniques previously covered, copy and paste the five curtain walls from Level 1 to Level 2.

    a. See Figure 6-4.36.

    b. All dimensions and settings should remain the same as Level 1.

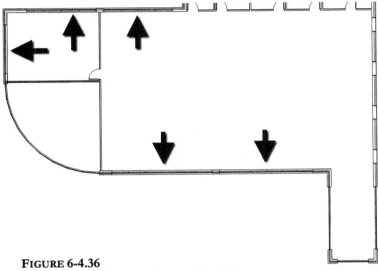

FIGURE 6-4.36
Level 2 – remaining storefront walls added

Your project now has a lot of glass to allow daylight to enter the building! Later in the text you will add sun shades to reduce the amount of hot summer sun that enters the office. Looking at the default **3D** view, you can see your building already starting to take shape.

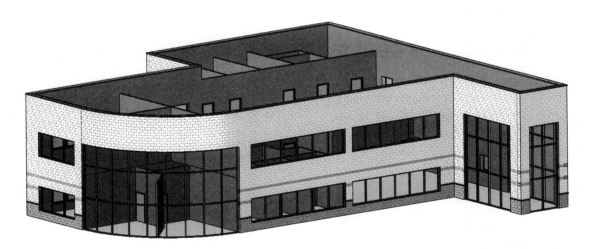

FIGURE 6-4.37
3D view – Showing Storefront added

Exercise 6-5:
Stairs

Next you will add stairs to your stair shafts. Revit provides a powerful *Stairs* tool that allows you to design stairs quickly with various constraints specified in the family (i.e., 7″ maximum riser).

Pre-Defining Parameters:

Before you draw the stair, it will be helpful to review the options available in the *Stair Family*.

1. Open your Revit project.

2. From the *Project Browser*, expand the Families → Stairs → Stair (i.e., click the plus signs next to these labels).

3. Right-click on the stair type: **Steel Pan Stair**, and select the **Type Properties** option from the pop-up menu.

You should now see the options shown in Figure 6-5.1.

Take a couple minutes to see what options are available. You will quickly review a few below.

- Tread: Depth of tread in plan view.

- Nosing Length (Depth): Treads are typically 12″ deep (usually code min.) and 1″ of that depth overlaps the next tread. This overlap is called the nosing.

- Riser: This provides Revit with the maximum dimension allowed (by code, or if you want, less). The actual dimension will depend on the floor to floor height.

- Stringer Dimensions: These dimensions usually vary per stair depending on the stair width, run and materials, to name a few variables. A structural engineer would provide this information after designing the stair.

- Cost: Estimating placeholder.

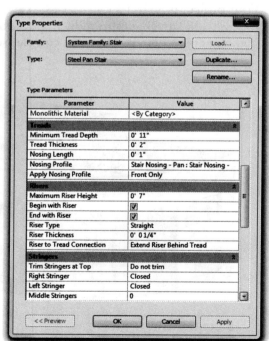

FIGURE 6-5.1 Stair type properties

Calculate Tread/Riser Size:

Although Revit automatically calculates the rise and tread dimensions for you, it is still a good idea to understand what is happening.

The Riser is typically calculated to be as large as building codes will allow. Occasionally, a grand stair will have a smaller riser to create a more elegant stair.

Similarly, the Tread is usually designed to be as small as allowable by building codes.

The largest riser and shortest tread creates the steepest stair allowed. This takes up less floor space; see image below. A stairway that is too steep is uncomfortable and unsafe.

Building codes vary by location; for this exercise, you will use 7″ (max.) for the risers and 12″ (min.) for the treads, 11″ tread plus a 1″ nosing.

Codes usually require that each tread be the same size, likewise with risers.

Calculate the number and size of the risers:

> *Given:*
> Risers: **7″** max.
> Floor to floor height: **13′-4″**.

Stairs

> *Calculate the number of risers:*
> 13′-4″ divided by 7″ (or 160″ divided by 7″) = 22.857

Seeing as each riser has to be the same size we will have to round off to a whole number. You cannot round down because that will make the riser larger than the allowed maximum (13′-4″ / 22 = 7.3″). Therefore, you have to round up to 23. Thus: 13′-4″ divided by 23 = 6.957

So you need **23** risers that are **6 15/16″** each.

Riser: 7″
Tread: 9″
37°

Riser: 4″
Tread: 12″
18°

Drawing the Stairs In Plan:

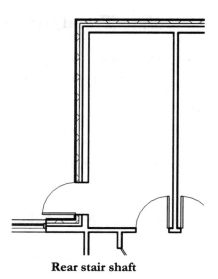

4. Make sure you are in the **Level 1** floor plan view.

5. **Zoom in** to the rear stair shaft.

6. Click on the *Home* tab in the *Ribbon*.

7. Select the *Stairs* tool, in the *Circulation* panel.

8. Make sure the *Type Selector* is set to **Steel Pan Stair**.

9. In the *Properties Palette*, set the *Width* to **3'-6"**, and then select **Apply** (Figure 6-5.3).

Rear stair shaft

10. Position the cursor approximately as shown in **Figure 6-5.4**; you are selecting the start point for the first step. Make sure you are snapping to the wall with *Nearest*.

11. Pick the remaining points as shown in Figures 6-5.5, 6-5.6 and 6-5.7.

12. **Move** everything North (i.e., stair sketch lines) so the landing touches the exterior wall. Click **Finish Stairs** (Figure 6-5.2).

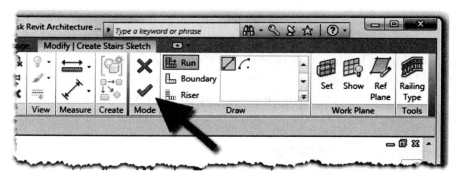

FIGURE 6-5.2 Finish Stair Sketch Button

Notice as you draw the stairs, Revit will display the number of risers drawn and the number of risers remaining to be drawn to reach the next level. If you click Finish Stairs before drawing all the required risers, Revit will display an error message. You can leave the problem to be resolved later.

Notice the **Multistory Top Level** parameter in Figure 6-5.3. If the floor to floor distance is the same for each floor, you can use this feature to have Revit automatically repeat the stair all the way up the stair shaft!

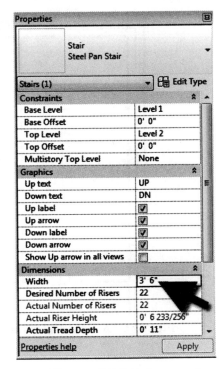

FIGURE 6-5.3 Stair properties

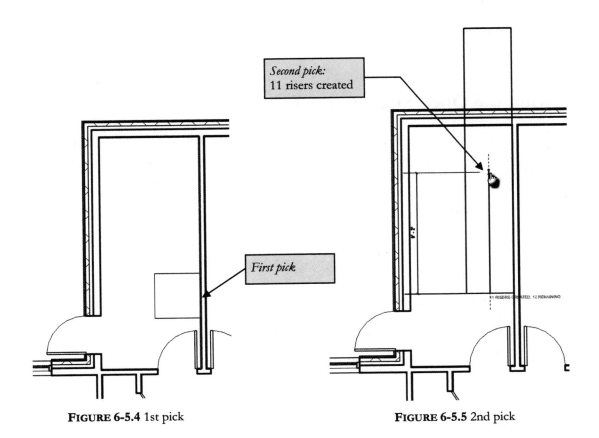

FIGURE 6-5.4 1st pick   **FIGURE 6-5.5** 2nd pick

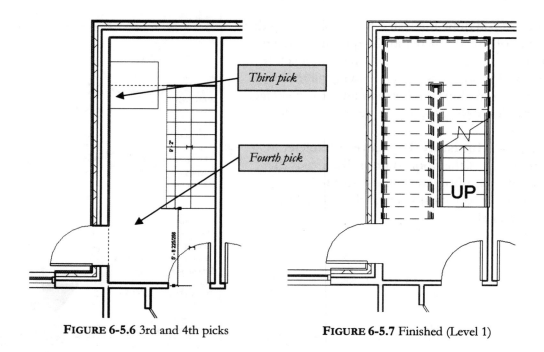

FIGURE 6-5.6 3rd and 4th picks   **FIGURE 6-5.7** Finished (Level 1)

FYI: Revit has drawn the intermediate landings between levels. However, the landings at the main floor levels have not been created. Some projects extend the primary floor structure into the stair shaft to act as the landing for that level and also support the stair. In a later lesson you will draw a floor system that extends into the stair shaft.

Drawing the Open Stairs in the Lobby:

The previous steps just walked you through the basics. This is all you would typically need to do early in a project. As the project is more refined and the walls stop moving, the stairs may be refined for stringer type and location, as well as landing size and shape.

13. Select the **Stair** tool.

14. Set the *Width* to **4'-0"**.

Next you will begin drawing a switchback stair similar to the one in the stair shaft. But, before you finish the stair sketch, you will modify the sketch lines at the landing. You will make it curved as in the image below (Figure 6-5.8).

The exact location of the stair is not important as the next chapter will have you reposition the stair once the floor is drawn.

FIGURE 6-5.8 Landing modified to have curved edge and railing

15. Draw the **4'-0"** wide stair approximately as shown in Figure 6-5.9 (exact location not important at this point).

The sketch lines shown in Figure 6-5.8 can be stretched, rotated and moved to adjust the footprint of the stair. This can be done until the stair sketch is finished. Once the stair is finished, you must select the stair and select *Edit* on the *Ribbon*; this places you back in *Sketch* mode and allows for additional edits.

16. Select the far left vertical line that forms the edge of the landing and delete this line.

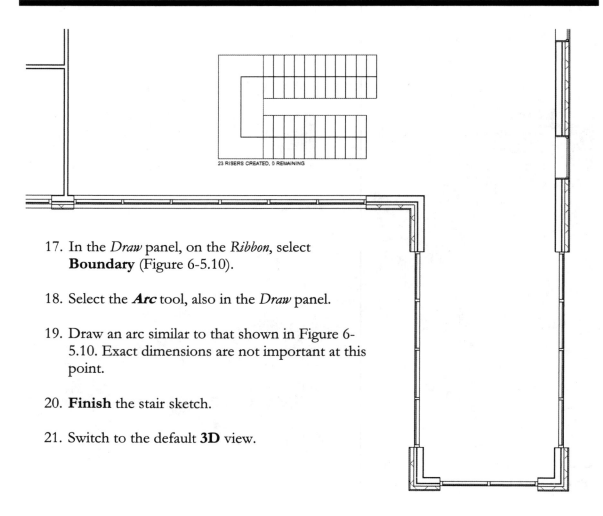

17. In the *Draw* panel, on the *Ribbon*, select **Boundary** (Figure 6-5.10).

18. Select the *Arc* tool, also in the *Draw* panel.

19. Draw an arc similar to that shown in Figure 6-5.10. Exact dimensions are not important at this point.

20. **Finish** the stair sketch.

21. Switch to the default **3D** view.

FIGURE 6-5.9
Stair layout in the lobby

Notice the railing automatically followed the curved landing. In a later lesson you will add railings at the second level which ties into the stair railings.

22. **Save** your project.

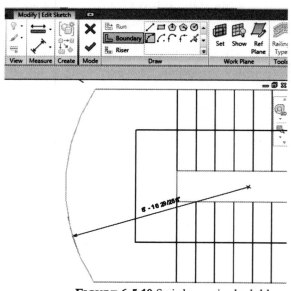

FIGURE 6-5.10 Stair layout in the lobby

Stair Sample File from Revit's Web Site:

Make sure to examine the stair sample file available on Autodesk's online content library (seek.autodesk.com – search for "Revit samples" and select the stair option) You can download this file and see examples of several different stair types side-by-side (see image below). You can select one and view its properties to see how it is done. You can also Copy/Paste one into your project, select your stair, and then select the newly imported type(s) from the *Type Selector*. The partial view of the sample file, shown below, has open riser, single stringer, no stringer, spiral…

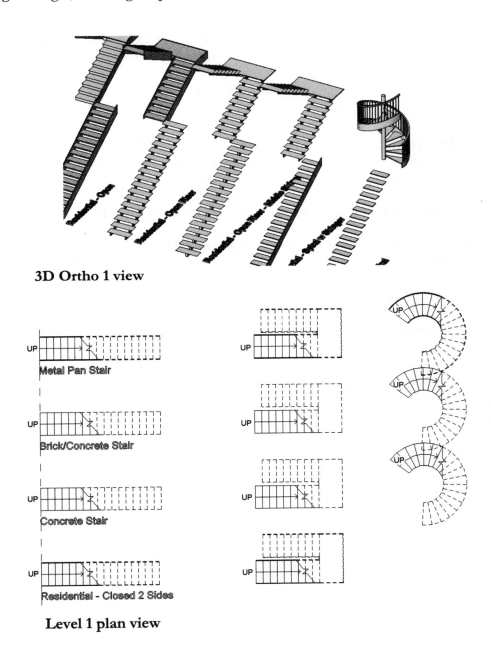

3D Ortho 1 view

Level 1 plan view

Self-Exam:

The following questions can be used as a way to check your knowledge of this lesson. The answers can be found at the bottom of the page.

1. The *Options Bar* allows you to select the height your wall will be drawn at. (T/F)

2. It is not possible to draw a wall with the interior or exterior face of the core as the reference point. (T/F)

3. Objects cannot be moved accurately with the *Move* tool. (T/F)

4. The _____ tool, in the *Quick Access Toolbar*, has to be selected in order to select an object in your project.

5. A wall has to be _____ to see its flip icon.

Review Questions:

The following questions may be assigned by your instructor as a way to assess your knowledge of this section. Your instructor has the answers to the review questions.

1. Revit comes with many predefined doors and windows. (T/F)

2. The *Project Information* dialog allows you to enter data about the project, which is automatically added to sheet borders. (T/F)

3. You can delete unused families and types in the *Project Browser*. (T/F)

4. It is not possible to add a new window type to a window family. (T/F)

5. It is not possible to select which side of the wall a window should be on while you are inserting the window. (T/F)

6. What tool will break a wall into two smaller pieces? _____

7. The _____ tool allows you to match the surface of two adjacent walls.

8. Use the _____ key, on the keyboard, to flip the door swing while placing doors using the *Door* tool.

9. You adjust the location of a dimension's witness line by clicking on (or dragging) its

   _____ .

10. The _____ file has a few doors, windows and walls preloaded in it.

Lesson 7
Law Office: ROOF, FLOORS & CEILINGS:

Now that you have the floor plans developed to a point where only minor changes will occur, you can start thinking about the horizontal planes within the building: roofs, floors and ceilings.

In this text you will start with the roof. This is the first element most often modeled of the three elements covered in this chapter. It is first because, with the roof in place, the exterior of the building begins to take its final shape, specifically in 3D and camera views.

Floors and ceilings are then added so the building sections start to take shape. These elements, plus a consultation with the mechanical engineer on the approximate size of the ductwork, will help to determine the distance required between the floors and the roof.

The depth of the structural system is also an important factor when processing the horizontal conditions of your building. This will be covered in the next chapter, but in reality would be considered parallel with the information covered in this chapter via the structural engineer.

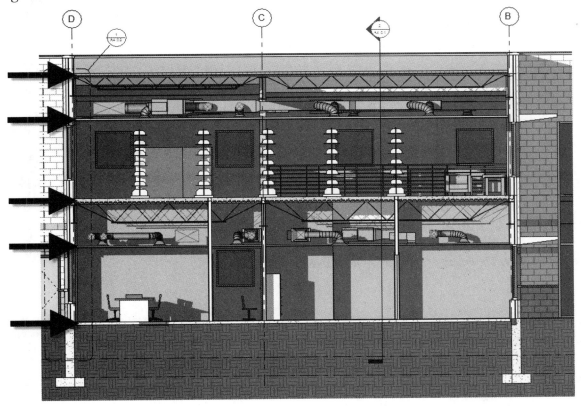

Building section showing floors, ceilings and the roof; notice structural and ductwork as well.

Exercise 7-1:
Introduction to the Roof Tool

In this lesson you will look at the various ways to use the *Roof* tool to draw the more common roof forms used in architecture today.

Start a New Revit Project:

You will start a new project for this lesson so you can quickly compare the results of using the *Roof* tool.

1. Start a new project using the **default.rte** template.

2. Switch to the **North** elevation view and rename the level named *Level 2* to **T.O. Masonry**. This will be the reference point for your roof. Click **Yes** to rename corresponding views automatically.

    TIP: Just select the Level *datum and click on the level datum's text to rename.*

3. Switch to the *Level 1* floor plan view.

Drawing the Buildings:

4. Set the Level 1 *"Detail Level"* to **Medium**, so the material hatching is visible within the walls.

    TIP: Use the View Control Bar *at the bottom.*

5. Using the *Wall* tool with the wall *Type* set to **"Exterior - Brick on Mtl. Stud,"** draw a **40'-0" x 20'-0"** building (Figure 7-1.1).

    FYI: The default Wall height is OK; it should be 20'-0".

Be sure to draw the building
within the elevation tags.

*TIP: You can draw the building
in one step if you use the
Rectangle option on the Ribbon,
while using the Wall tool.*

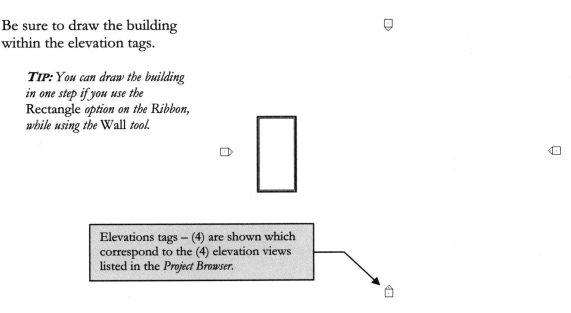

Elevations tags – (4) are shown which
correspond to the (4) elevation views
listed in the *Project Browser.*

FIGURE 7-1.1 Bldg. and Elev. tags

You will copy the building so that you have a total four buildings. You will draw a different
type of roof on each one.

6. Drag a window around the walls to select them. Then use the **Array** command to set
up four buildings **35'-0" O.C.** (Figure 7-1.2). See the *ARRAY TIP* below.

*TIP: Zoom in and make sure
the brick is on the exterior side
of the wall. If not, you can
select each wall and click its
flip icon.*

*ARRAY TIP: Select the first
building; select Array. Just
like the Copy command,
define a copy 35' to the right,
then enter the number of copies.*

FIGURE 7-1.2 Four buildings

7. Select all of the buildings and click **Ungroup**
from the *Ribbon.*

Ungroup

Hip Roof:

The various roof forms are largely defined by the **Defines slope** setting. This is displayed in the *Options Bar* while the *Roof* tool is active. When a wall is selected and the **Defines slope** option is selected, the roof above that portion of wall slopes. You will see this more clearly in the examples below.

8. Switch to the **T.O. Masonry** floor plan view.

9. Select the **Home → Build → Roof** *(down-arrow)* **→ Roof by Footprint** tool.

10. Set the overhang to **2'-0"** and make sure **Defines slope** is selected (checked) on the *Options Bar*.

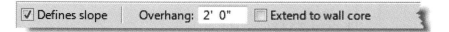

11. Select the four walls of the West building, clicking each wall one at a time.

    TIP: Make sure you select towards the exterior side of the wall; notice the review line before clicking.

12. Click **Finish Edit Mode** (i.e., the green check mark) on the *Ribbon* to finish the *Roof* tool.

13. Click **Yes** to attach the roof to the walls.

14. Switch to the **South** elevation (Figure 7-1.3).

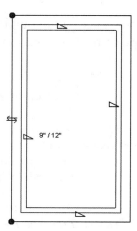

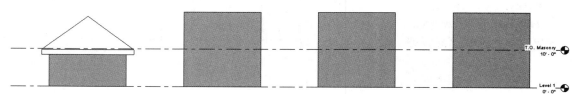

FIGURE 7-1.3 South elevation – Hip roof

You will notice that the default wall height is much higher than what we ultimately want. However, when the roof is drawn at the correct elevation and you attach the walls to the roof, the walls automatically adjust to stop under the roof object. Additionally, if the roof is raised or lowered later, the walls will follow; you can try this in the South elevation view by simply using the *Move* tool. **REMEMBER:** *You can make revisions in any view.*

15. Switch to the **3D** view using the icon on the *QAT* (Figure 7-1.4).

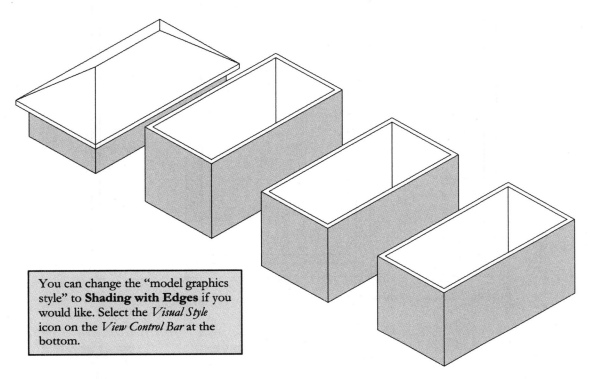

You can change the "model graphics style" to **Shading with Edges** if you would like. Select the *Visual Style* icon on the *View Control Bar* at the bottom.

FIGURE 7-1.4 3D view – hip roof

Gable Roof:

16. Switch back to the **T.O. Masonry** view (not the ceiling plan for this level).

17. Select the **Roof** tool, and then **Roof by Footprint**.

18. Set the overhang to **2'-0"** and make sure **Defines slope** is selected (checked) on the *Options Bar*.

19. Only select the two long (40'-0") walls.

20. **Uncheck** the **Defines slope** option.

21. Select the remaining two walls (Figure 7-1.5).

22. Pick the **green check mark** on the *Ribbon* to finish the roof.

23. Select **Yes** to attach the walls to the roof.

24. Switch to the **South** elevation view (Figure 7-1.6).

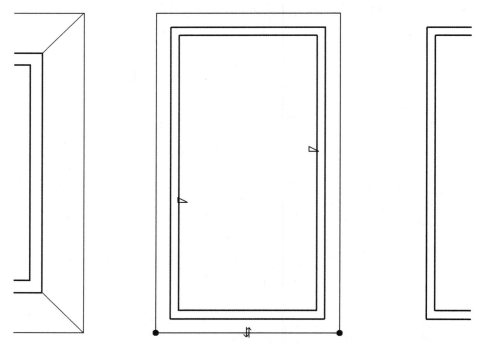

FIGURE 7-1.5 Gable – plan view

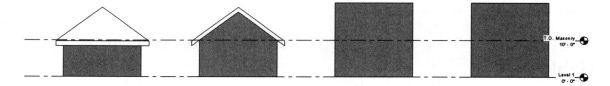

FIGURE 7-1.6 South elevation – gable roof

25. Switch to the **3D** view (Figure 7-1.7).

Notice the wall extends up to conform to the underside of the roof on the gable ends.

> *FYI: You may be wondering why the roofs look odd in the floor plan view. If you remember, each view has its own cut plane. The cut plane happens to be lower than the highest part of the roof – thus, the roof is shown cut at the cut plane. If you go to Properties Palette → View Range (while nothing is selected) and then adjust the cut plane to be higher than the highest point of the roof, then you will see the ridge line.*

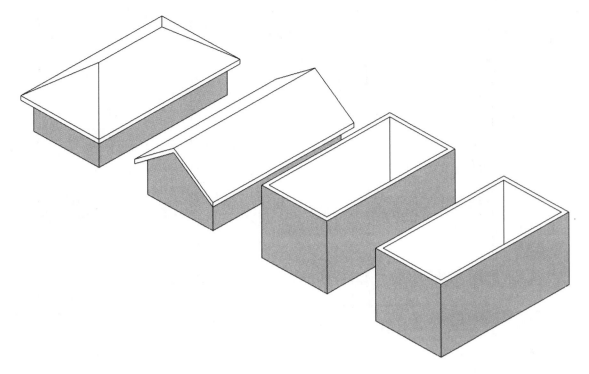

FIGURE 7-1.7 3D view – gable roof

Shed Roof:

26. Switch back to the **T.O. Masonry** view.

27. Select the **Roof** tool, and then **Roof by Footprint**.

28. Check **Defines slope** on the *Options Bar*.

29. Set the overhang to **2'-0"** on the *Options Bar*.

30. Select the East wall (40'-0" wall, right-hand side).

31. Uncheck **Defines slope** in the *Options Bar*.

32. Select the remaining three walls (Figure 7-1.8).

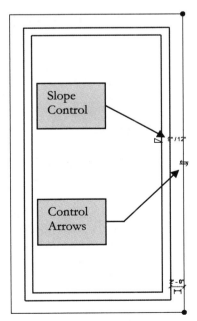

FIGURE 7-1.8 Selected walls

33. Set the **Slope**, or roof pitch, to 3/12 (Figure 7-1.9) on the *Properties Palette*.

34. Click **Apply** on the *Properties Palette*.

35. Pick the **green check mark** on the *Ribbon* to finish the roof.

36. Select **Yes** to attach the walls to the roof.

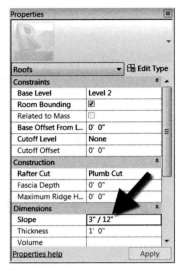

FIGURE 7-1.9
Properties for Roof tool

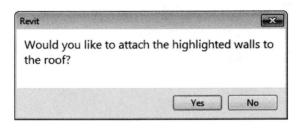

FYI: You can also change the slope of the roof by changing the Slope Control text (see Figure 7-1.8); just select the text and type a new number.

TIP: You can use the control arrows, *while the roof line is still selected, to flip the orientation of the roof overhang if you accidentally selected the wrong side of the wall and the overhang is on the inside of the building.*

37. Switch to the **South** elevation view (Figure 7-1.10).

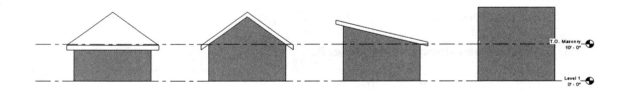

FIGURE 7-1.10 South elevation – shed roof

38. Switch to the *Default 3D* view (Figure 7-1.11).

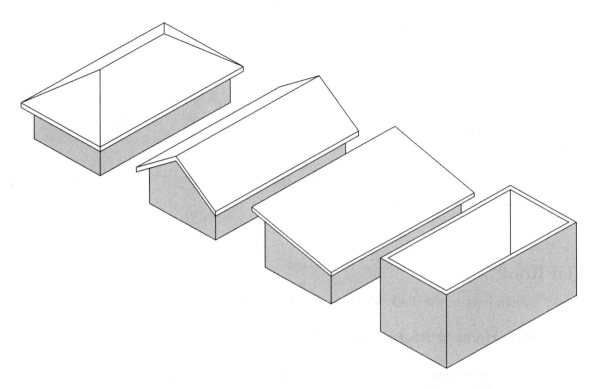

FIGURE 7-1.11 Default 3D view – shed roof

Once the roof is drawn, you can easily change the roof's overhang. You will try this on the shed roof. You will also make the roof slope in the opposite direction.

39. In **T.O. Masonry** view, select **Modify** from the *Ribbon*, and then select the shed roof.

40. Click **Edit Footprint** from the *Ribbon*.

Edit
Footprint

41. Click on the East roof sketch-line to select it.

42. Uncheck **Defines slope** from the *Options Bar*.

43. Now select the West roofline and check **Defines slope**.

If you were to select the green check mark now, the shed roof would be sloping in the opposite direction. But, before you do that, you will adjust the roof overhang at the high side.

44. Click on the East roofline again, to select it.

45. Change the overhang to **6'-0"** in the *Options Bar.*

Changing the overhang only affects the selected roofline.

46. Select the **green check mark.**

47. Switch to the South view to see the change (Figure 7-1.12).

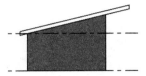

Thus you can see it is easier to edit an object than to delete it and start over. Just remember, you have to be in sketch mode (i.e., *Edit Sketch*) to make changes to the roof. Also, when a sketch line is selected, its properties are displayed in the *Properties Palette.* That concludes the shed roof example.

FIGURE 7-1.12 South elevation – shed roof (revised)

Flat Roof:

48. Switch back to the **T.O. Masonry** floor plan view.

49. Select **Home → Roof → Roof by Footprint.**

50. Set the overhang to **2'-0"** and make sure **Defines slope** is not selected (i.e., unchecked) in the *Options Bar.*

51. Select all four walls.

52. Pick the **green check mark.**

53. Select **Yes** to attach the walls to the roof.

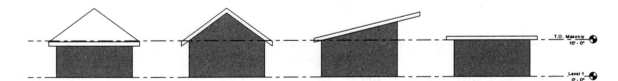

FIGURE 7-1.13 South elevation – flat roof

54. Switch to the South elevation view (Figure 7-1.13).

55. Also, take a look the **Default 3D view** (Figure 7-1.14).

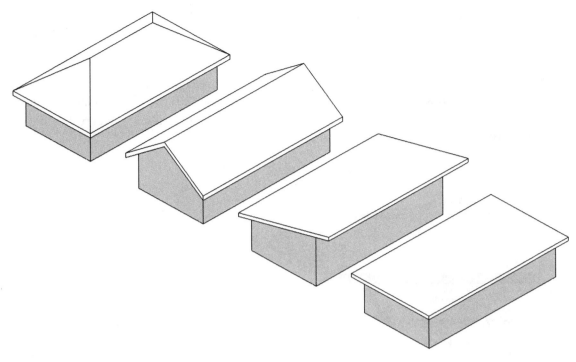

FIGURE 7-1.14 Default 3D view – flat roof

56. Save your project as **ex7-1.rvt**.

Want More?

Revit has additional tools and techniques available for creating more complex roof forms. However, that is beyond the scope of this book. If you want to learn more about roofs, or anything else, take a look at one of the following resources:

- Revit **Web Site** (www.autodesk.com)
- Revit **Newsgroup** (potential answers to specific questions)
    www.augi.com; www.revitcity.com; www.autodesk.com; www.revitforum.org
- Revit **Blogs** information from individuals (some work for Autodesk and some don't)
    www.revitoped.com, insidethefactory.typepad.com

Reference material: Roof position relative to Wall

The remaining pages in this chapter are for reference only and do not need to be done to your model. You are encouraged to study this information so you become more familiar with how the *Roof* tool works.

The following examples use a brick and concrete wall example. The image below shows the *Structure* properties for said wall type. Notice the only item within the *Core Boundary* section is the *Masonry – Concrete Block* (i.e., CMU) which is 7⅝" thick (nominally 8"). Keep this in mind as you read through the remaining material.

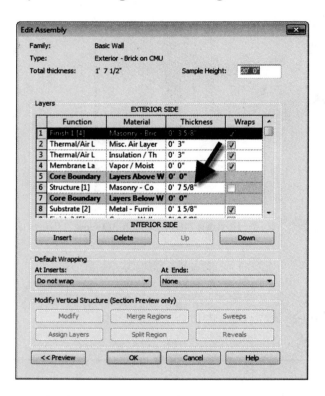

The following examples will show you how to control the position of the roof system relative to the wall below, both vertically and horizontally. The roof properties that dictate its position basically involve relationships between three things: the **Level Datum**, the exterior **Wall System** and the bottom edge of the **Roof System**. There are several other properties (e.g., pitch, construction, fascia, etc.) related to the roof that will not be mentioned at the moment so the reader may focus on a few basic principles.

The examples on this page show a sloped roof sketched with *Extend into wall (to core)* enabled and the *Overhang* set to 2'-0''. Because *Extend into wall (to core)* was selected, the bottom edge of the roof is positioned relative to the *Core Boundary* of the exterior wall rather than the finished face of the wall. See the discussion about the wall's *Core Boundary* on the previous page.

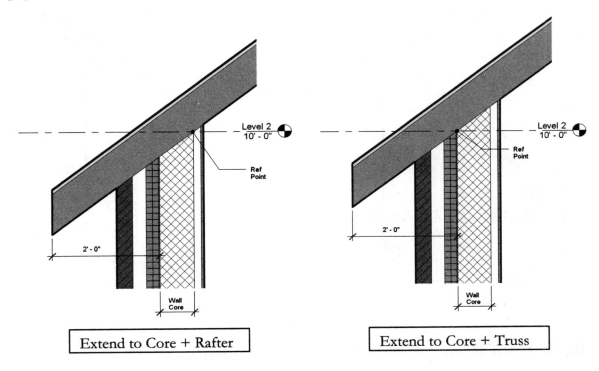

Extend to Core + Rafter   Extend to Core + Truss

Revit Roof Properties under Consideration:

Extend Into Wall:
(To Core)
This option was *checked* on the *Options Bar* while sketching the roof.

Rafter or Truss:
This option is an *Instance Parameter* of the roof object; the example on the above left is set to *Rafter* and the other is set to *Truss*.

NOTE: The Extend into Wall (to core) *option affects the relative relationship between the wall and the roof, as you will see by comparing this example with the one on the next page.*

Base Level:
Set to *Level 2*: By associating various objects to a level, it is possible to adjust the floor elevation (i.e., *Level Datum*) and have doors, windows, floors, furniture, roofs, etc., all move vertically with that level.

Base Offset:
From Level
Set to *0'-0''*. This can be a positive or negative number which will be maintained even if the level moves.

The examples on this page show a sloped roof sketched with *Extend into wall (to core)* NOT enabled and the *Overhang* set to 2'-0". Notice that the roof overhang is derived from the exterior face of the wall (compared to the *Core Boundary* face on the previous example when *Extend into wall* was enabled).

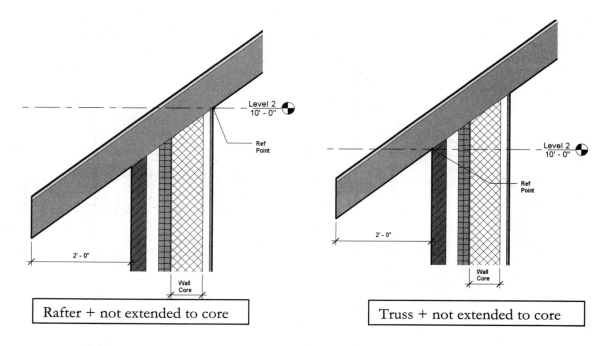

| Rafter + not extended to core | Truss + not extended to core |

Revit Roof Properties under Consideration:

Extend into Wall:
(To Core)
This option was *NOT checked* on the *Options Bar* while sketching the roof.

Rafter or Truss:
This option is an *Instance Parameter* of the roof object; the example on the above left is set to *Rafter* and the other is set to *Truss*.

NOTE: The Extend into wall (to core) *option affects the relative relationship between the wall and the roof, as you will see by comparing this example with the one on the previous page.*

Base Level:
Set to *Level 2*. By associating various objects to a level, it is possible to adjust the floor elevation (i.e., *Level Datum*) and have doors, windows, floors, furniture, roofs, etc., all move vertically with that level.

Base Offset:
From Level
Set to *0'-0"*. This can be a positive or negative number which will be maintained even if the level moves.

As you can see from the previous examples, you would most often want to have *Extend to wall (to core)* selected while sketching a roof because it would not typically make sense to position the roof based on the outside face of brick or the inside face of gypsum board, for commercial construction.

Even though you may prefer to have *Extend to wall (to core)* selected, you might like to have a 2'-0" overhang relative to the face of the brick rather than the exterior face of concrete block. This can be accomplished in one of two ways:

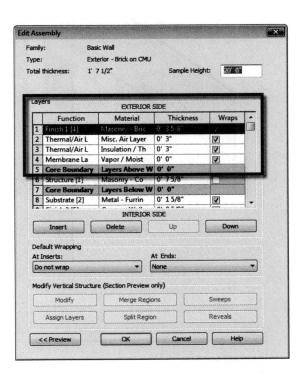

(A) You can modify the overhang, while sketching the roof, to include the wall thickness that occurs between the face of wall and face of core: 2'-0" + 9⅝" = 2'-9⅝". See the image to the right.

(B) The second option is to manually edit the sketch lines. You can add dimensions while in *Sketch* mode, select the sketch line to move, and then edit the dimension. The dimension can also be *Locked* to maintain the roof edge position relative to the wall. When you finish the sketch the dimensions are hidden.

Energy Truss:

In addition to controlling the roof overhang, you might also want to control the roof properties to accommodate an energy truss with what is called an *energy heal*, which allows for more insulation to occur directly above the exterior wall).

To do this you would use the *Extend into wall (to core)* + *Truss* option described above and then set the *Base Offset from Level* to 1'-0" (for a 1'-0" energy heal). See the image and the *Properties Palette* shown on the next page.

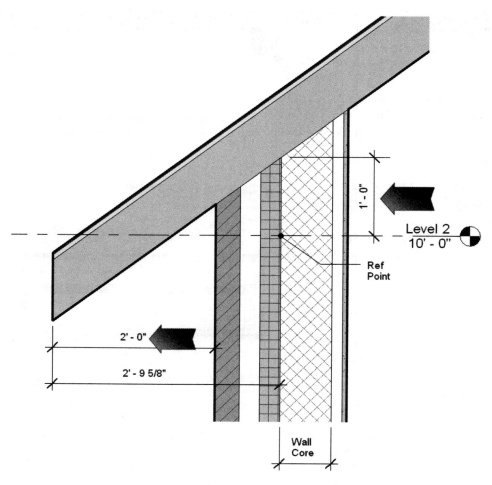

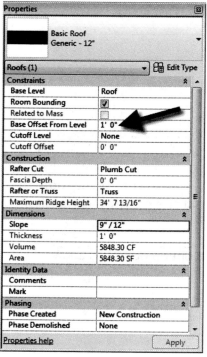

Many other properties and techniques exist which one can use to develop the roof for a project, things like the *Rafter Cut* and *Fascia Depth* which control the fascia design. Also, you can apply a sweep to a roof edge to add a 1x fascia board around the building. These are intermediate to advanced concepts and will not be covered here.

This concludes the study of the *Roof* tool!

Exercise 7-2:
Law Office Roof

The template file you started with already has a **Roof** plan view created. However, you renamed that to Level 2 and then created a new *Roof* datum and corresponding views. If you recall, the *Roof* datum is at 26'-8" (see page 6-34). This Roof plan view creates a working plane for the *Roof* tool; the thickness of your roof sits on top of the reference plane.

Create a Flat Roof:

1. Open your **Law Office** BIM file.

2. Switch to the **Roof** plan view.

Your image should look something like Figure 7-2.1. The exterior walls you can see in the **Roof** plan view were created in Lesson 6; the specified height extends into the Roof's *View Range*. The interior walls and stairs are visible, but are shaded gray (i.e., halftone); this is because of a view setting called **Underlay**. The Underlay feature is used to visually coordinate items between floors. In the roof plan you might want to know where the wall between the two toilet rooms is to discern where the vent pipe will penetrate the roof.

You will be selecting the exterior walls to define the edge of the roof. Before you can finish a roof sketch, you must have the entire perimeter of the roof drawn with line endpoints connected. Revit allows you to sketch additional lines and use tools like *Trim* to complete the perimeter of the roof sketch if needed.

3. Select the ***Roof*** tool from the *Home* tab; click the down-arrow.

4. Select **Roof by Footprint** from the pop-up menu.

5. Make sure **Pick Walls** is selected *Ribbon: Home → Draw (panel)*.

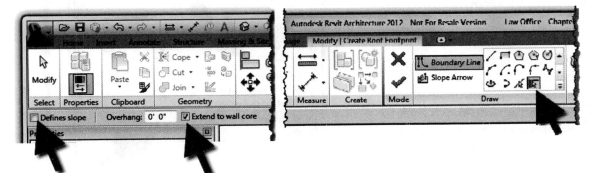

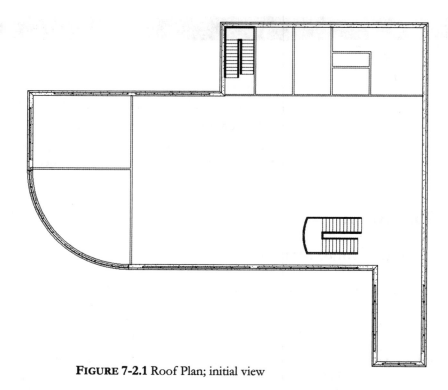

FIGURE 7-2.1 Roof Plan; initial view

6. Uncheck **Defines Slope** on the *Options Bar* to make a flat roof.

7. Change the drop-down selector, on the *Properties Palette*, to **New <Sketch>** (Figure 7-2.2).

These are the properties for the sketch lines, not the roof element (compare *Roof Instance Properties*).

8. Notice if this were a sloped roof, you could change the roof pitch here.

9. Change the drop-down back to **Roof** so you can see the roof element properties.

10. Check **Extend to wall core** on the *Options Bar*.

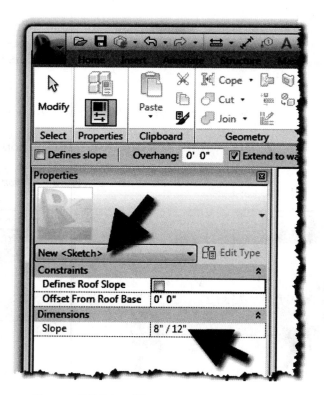

FIGURE 7-2.2 Roof Properties

We will digress for a moment to explain exactly what "extend to wall core" means. This will help ensure you create the roof correctly. First the properties of the wall will be exposed so you understand what constitutes a wall type core. Next, you will learn how this ties into the *Roof* tool. If you want to follow along, you can select *Cancel Roof* on the *Ribbon* and then repeat the previous steps before moving on to the next numbered steps.

Back on page 6-18 and following you explored the exterior wall style. There it pointed out where to view/edit the "structure" of the wall *Layers*, via the *Edit Assembly* dialog. The graphic below shows a variety of wall types with their wall cores highlighted. Within the *Edit Assembly* dialog, the highlighted Layer(s) fall within the *Core Boundary* section.

Generally speaking, the *Wall Core* represents the real-world structural portion of the wall. Walls can be both drawn and dimensioned based on the faces and centerline of the wall core. The *Wall Core* has a higher precedence when walls intersect. Revit automatically cleans up similar *Layers* within other wall types. Additionally, in the case of this exercise, the wall core is used in conjunction with creating the roof element. This is also true for floors as well.

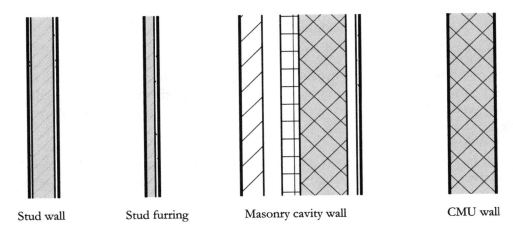

Stud wall   Stud furring   Masonry cavity wall   CMU wall

Notice a few things about the walls above before moving on. The two walls on the left have the metal stud *Layer* within the *Wall Core*, but the masonry cavity wall does not. In the first two, the studs are the structural element holding up the wall, in the latter the CMU holds up the wall and the metal studs are just used to fasten the gypsum board to it. Finally, the fourth wall contains one *Layer* which is the *Wall Core*. Every wall must have at least one *Layer* within the *Core Boundary*. An example of two *Layers* within the *Core Boundary* might be the studs and the sheathing which is used for shear; making both *Layers* part of the structural makeup of the wall. In this case you would never want any intersecting wall to interrupt the sheathing.

When using the *Roof* tool, it is possible to have Revit automatically sketch the roof's edge based on one of the two faces of a *Wall Core*. Therefore, it is important to select towards the side of the wall relating to the core face you want. The two images below show the two options possible when *Extend wall to core* is selected within the *Roof* tool.

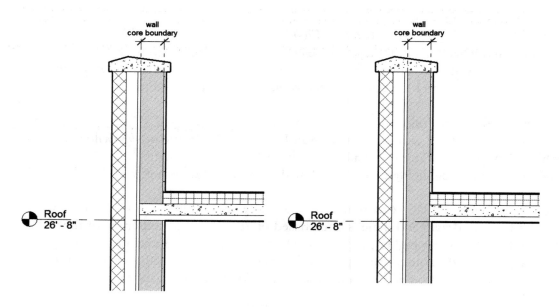

Roof tool: Extend to core options

Notice in both images above, the gypsum board *Layer* within the wall type is interrupted by the roof. You will employ the option on the left. However, either option is perfectly valid depending on how the building is intended to be constructed: a separate parapet or balloon framing.

In either case, due to the use of metal studs, the roof deck will be supported by steel beams at the perimeter. The structural system will be added in the next chapter. Revit does not care if a roof or floor is not properly supported, which is not the case with beams, as you will see in the upcoming structural section.

11. Select each of the exterior walls, favoring the exterior side when clicking the wall. Just before clicking, the dashed reference line should be at the exterior face of the wall core per the example shown in Figure 7-2.3.

   TIP: Use the flip control *icon while the line is still selected if your dashed reference line is on the wrong side (i.e., interior).*

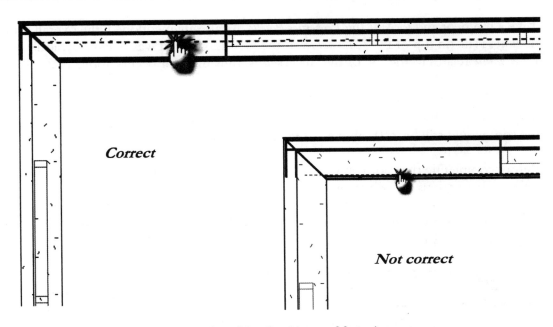

FIGURE 7-2.3 Roof Plan; four walls selected for sketching roof footprint

Note that the exterior walls, just selected, can be selected in any order.

All of the sketch lines should have automatically trimmed at the corners (Figure 7-2.4). If not, you would need to use the *Trim* tool to close the perimeter of the roof footprint. Many of your 2D drafting skills learned earlier in this book can be applied to this type of *Sketch* mode.

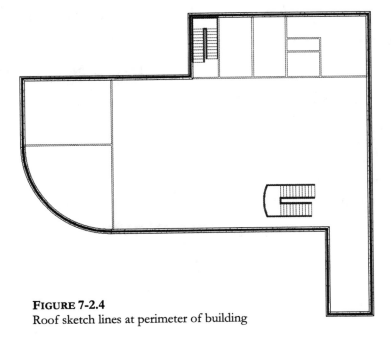

FIGURE 7-2.4
Roof sketch lines at perimeter of building

Take a moment and look at the *Properties Palette*. As already mentioned, the overall roof thickness sits on top of the *Level datum* of the view in which it was drawn. Typically, the *Roof Level datum* relates to the top of the steel beams, thus the roof occurs above that elevation.

Notice the parameter *Base Offset From Level*. This allows you to enter a distance in which to move the roof up from the *Base Level*. If you entered 2'-0" and the roof level datum changed, the roof would still be 2'-0" above the repositioned level datum.

Before completing the roof you will learn how to specify the *Roof Type*. This is similar to walls in that various *Layers* can be defined within the roof element.

12. Select **Edit Type** button on the *Properties Palette* notice the various *Parameters* and *Types* available; click **OK** to close without making any changes.

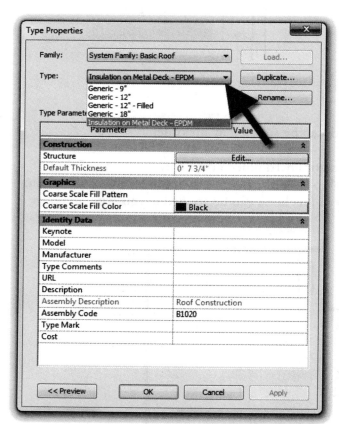

Notice in Figure 7-2.5 that the *Type* drop-down at the top lists five roof types.

13. Make sure the *Type Selector* is set to **Insulation on Metal Deck – EPDM** on the *Properties Palette*.

Now that the roof footprint is complete you can finish the roof.

14. Select **Finish Roof** from the *Ribbon*.

15. Click **No** to attach walls (Figure 7-2.6).

FIGURE 7-2.5 Roof type properties; selecting roof type

FIGURE 7-2.6 Roof Plan; attachment warning

16. Click **Yes** to join the roof and exterior walls.

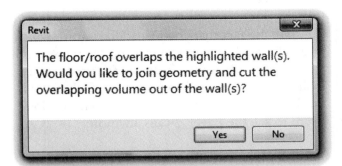

Joining the roof and walls via this prompt is what interrupts the stud *Layer* as shown in the graphic on page 7-20.

FIGURE 7-2.7 Roof Plan; join and cut prompt

17. Switch to your **3D** view via the *Quick Access Toolbar.*

Your project should look like Figure 7-2.8.

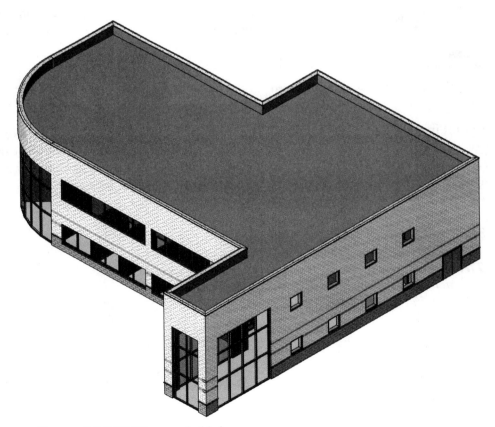

FIGURE 7-2.8 3D View; roof added

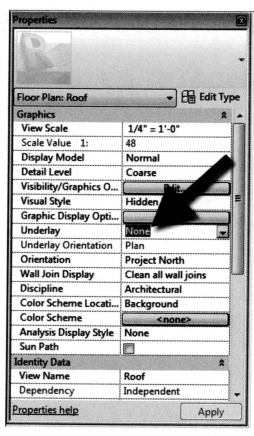

FIGURE 7-2.9 Roof plan view; view propertied

18. Switch back to your **Roof** floor plan view.

Despite the fact that you just added a roof, which is a solid 3D element, you can still see the second floor walls. When the **Underlay** feature is set, it will show the selected level on top of whatever is visible in the current view. At this point we don't want to see the Level 2 walls anymore.

19. Make sure nothing is selected so the *View Properties* are showing in the *Properties Palette*.

20. Set the **Underlay** *Parameter* to **None** (Figure 7-2.9).

21. Click **Apply** to make the adjustment to the view.

The *Level 2* walls are now removed from the **Roof** plan view.

At some point in the project you would edit the roof surface to have the required sloped surfaces to shed rain water towards the roof drains. But those types of edits are best saved for later in the design process. If you spent the time to model that information now and then the client decided to make a big change, you would have to redo all that work.

22. **Save** your project.

> *TIP: You have probably figured this out by now: the last view open when you close the project will be the view that is opened the next time the project is opened.*

Exercise 7-3:
Floor Systems

In this exercise you will add the Level 1 and Level 2 floors. The Level 1 floor is a slab-on-grade example, as the building has no basement, and Level 2 is a composite concrete and metal deck floor. Both of these floors are already defined in the project, which stems from the template from which it was started.

Level 1, Slab on Grade:

Sketching floors is a lot like sketching roofs; you can select walls to define the perimeter and draw lines to fill in the blanks and add holes, or cut outs, in the floor object.

1. **Open** your Revit project (Law Office).

2. Switch to the **Level 1** floor plan view if needed.

3. Select **Home → Build → Floor** (down-arrow) → **Floor**.

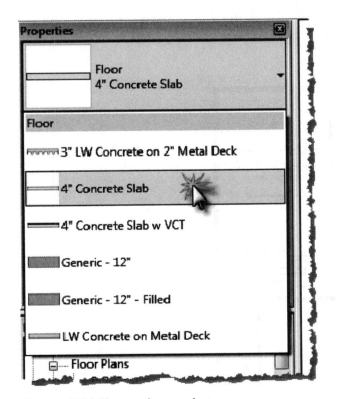

Floor

4. Click the ***Type Selector*** on the *Properties Palette*.

5. Set the *Type* to **4″ Concrete Slab** (if not already); see Figure 7-3.1.

6. Click **Apply** to accept the change.

Notice, in the *Properties Palette*, the *Height Offset From Level* which allows the slab to be moved up or down relative to the *Level* that hosts the slab.

Also, the *Phase Created* allows you to manage which portion of the building is existing and new. The law office project is all new, so you do not have to worry about any *Phase* settings.

FIGURE 7-3.1 Floor tool; type selector

Similar to the *Roof Sketch* mode, you will be drawing the *Boundary Line* for the floor by picking walls. Ultimately your slab will stop at the foundation walls, but they have not been drawn yet so you will draw the slab to the interior face of core. Remember, for the roof you went to the exterior face of core.

7. Make sure the *Ribbon* and *Options Bar* match the settings shown in Figure 7-3.2.

    a. *Boundary Line* selected (*Draw* panel)

    b. *Pick Walls* icon selected (*Draw* panel)

    c. *Extend into wall (to core)* checked (*Options Bar*)

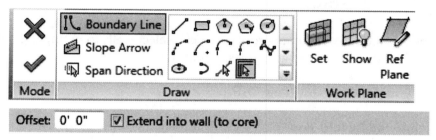

FIGURE 7-3.2 Floor tool; ribbon and options bar settings

8. Select the interior side of each exterior wall, with the exception of the curtain wall (do not select it yet). See Figure 7-3.3.

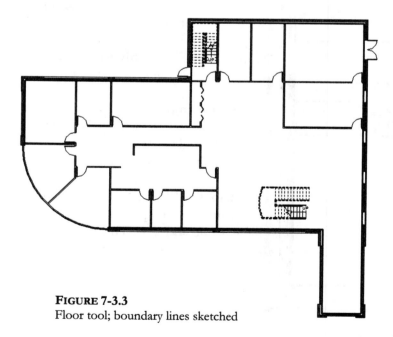

FIGURE 7-3.3
Floor tool; boundary lines sketched

You will select the curtain wall in a moment. However, it is a different thickness and does not have a core like the other walls. So, when you pick the wall, the floor boundary sketch line will be centered on the curtain wall. You will have to manually sketch lines and trim them at each end of the curtain wall in order to properly enclose the floor boundary.

9. Select the curtain wall, which in turn adds a curved boundary line.

10. Zoom in to each end of the curtain wall, and select the *Line* icon from the *Draw* panel on the *Create Floor Boundary* tab.

11. Sketch a line, using snaps, from the end of the arc to the adjacent wall sketch line (Figure 7-3.4).

12. Use the *Trim* tool, while still in the *Floor Sketch* mode, to clean up any corners that are not perfect. This is likely only going to be at the transition from the curved wall to the orthogonal walls.

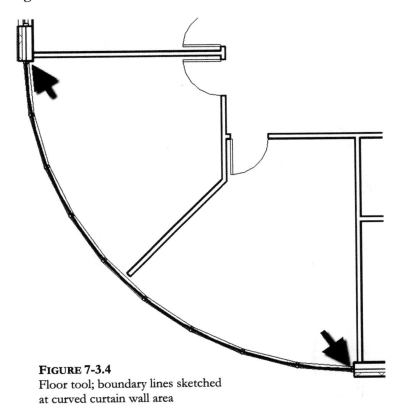

FIGURE 7-3.4
Floor tool; boundary lines sketched
at curved curtain wall area

Now that you have the perimeter of the floor defined, you may finish the creation of the floor element.

13. Click the **green check mark** on the *Ribbon* to finish the floor.

TIP: If you get any errors, see the next page.

COMMON ERRORS FINISHING A FLOOR SKETCH:

If you get an error message when trying to finish a floor sketch, it is probably due to a problem with the sketched perimeter lines. Here are two common problems:

Perimeter not closed:
You cannot finish a floor if there is a gap, large or small, in the perimeter sketch.
Fix: Sketch a line to close the loop.

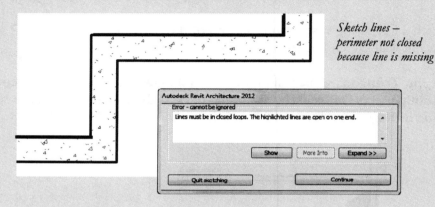

Sketch lines – perimeter not closed because line is missing

Error message after clicking finish sketch

Perimeter lines intersect:
You cannot finish a floor if any of the sketch lines intersect.
Fix: Use Trim to make it so all line endpoints touch.

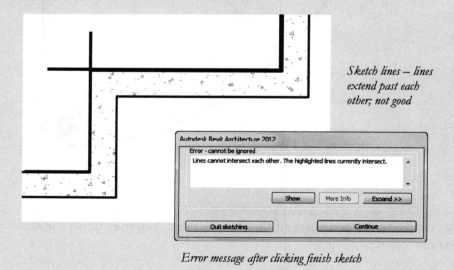

Sketch lines – lines extend past each other; not good

Error message after clicking finish sketch

The floor for Level 1 has now been created. However, because it has no surface pattern assigned to it, you cannot really see it. The only place it is visible is at the two exterior door openings (Figure 7-3.5); this is the best place to select the slab by pressing **Tab** to get past the door and select the slab.

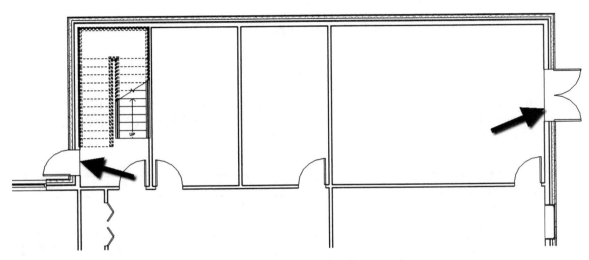

FIGURE 7-3.5 Level 1 floor plan; floor slab visible at exterior door openings

Often a surface pattern is not assigned to the structural slab. Instead, another floor is added in each room to define floor finishes later during the design process once the plan is fixed. A ⅛″ thick *Floor* can be created for each floor finish. The ⅛″ *Floor* is then added to each room, offset ⅛″ from the host level so it is on top of the structural slab. This method allows various surface patterns to be applied. If a surface pattern were added to the structural slab, it would be visible everywhere, such as toilet rooms, the lobby, and the mechanical room. The other benefit is the ability to schedule the floor finishes and get quantities. You can even add **formulas** to the schedules and get total cost for each flooring type!

Level 2, Slab on Grade:

Creating the second and third floors will be a little more involved than the first floor. This is because the upper floors require several openings. For example, you need to define the openings for the stair shaft and the two-story lobby space. However, Revit makes the process very simple.

You will again use a predefined floor type for the Level 2 floor. The floor you will use is 5½″ thick: a 1½″ metal deck and the remaining is concrete. At this early stage in the project it may be helpful to modify the floor to have a *Layer* that represents a placeholder for the structural joists that hold up the floor. In section view, this can help better visualize the required space, before the structural engineers add their elements to the BIM.

14. Switch to the **Level 2** floor plan view.

15. Click to start the **_Floor_** tool on the _Ribbon_.

16. Click **Edit Type** on the _Properties Palette_.

17. Set the _Type_ to **LW Concrete on Metal Deck**.

18. Click **Edit**, next to the _Structure_ parameter.

You are now in the _Edit Assembly_ dialog; here you will temporarily add a _Layer_ to serve as a placeholder for the bar joists (Figure 7-3.6). This process is identical for editing Revit walls and roofs!

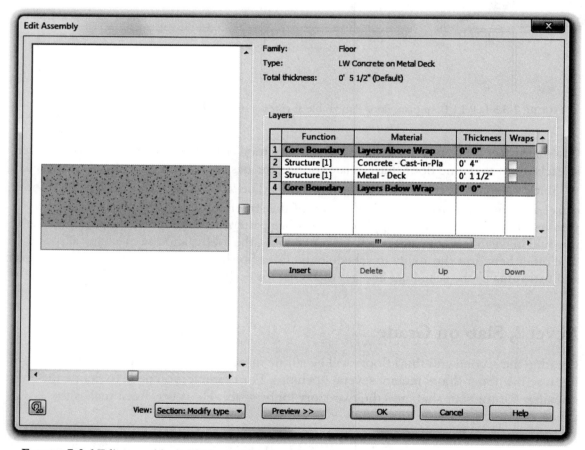

FIGURE 7-3.6 Edit assembly dialog for current floor type.

19. Click the **Insert** button.

The new _Layer_ should have been placed below the bottom _Core Boundary_ placeholder. This is fine for what we are attempting to do. You will also set the _Function_ to "finish" so the walls are not adversely affected by this temporary element in the floor type.

20. Change the new *Layer* as follows (Figure 7-3.7):

    a. *Function:*   **Finish 2 [5]**

    b. *Material:*   **\<By Category\>**

    c. *Thickness:*   **1'-2"**

	Function	Material	Thickness	Wraps	Variable
1	Core Boundary	Layers Above	0' 0"		
2	Structure [1]	Concrete - C	0' 4"	☐	☐
3	Structure [1]	Metal - Deck	0' 1 1/2"	☐	☐
4	Core Boundary	Layers Below	0' 0"		
5	Finish 2 [5]	\<By Categor	1' 2"	☐	☐

FIGURE 7-3.7 Floor properties: layer settings

21. Close the open dialog boxes (i.e., click **OK** two times).

You are now ready to start sketching the boundary of the Level 2 floor.

22. Using the *Pick Wall* icon, select the walls shown in Figure 7-3.8:

    a. Make sure *Extend into wall (to core)* is selected.

    b. Click to the <u>exterior</u> side of the exterior walls, opposite to what you did for Level 1.

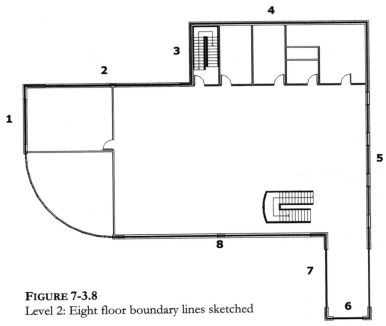

FIGURE 7-3.8
Level 2: Eight floor boundary lines sketched

23. Zoom into the North stair, and make the edits shown in Figure 7-3.9.

    a. Use the *Line* and *Trim* tools from the *Ribbon*. Remember, these are the tools and techniques you mastered in Chapter 5.

    b. The 8'-4" line should align with the top riser, in the North-South direction.

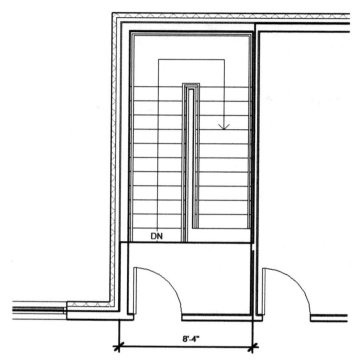

FIGURE 7-3.9
Level 2: Floor boundary at North stair

24. While still in *Sketch* mode for the Level 2 floor, pan to the right to show the area in Figure 7-3.10.

You will now define a hole in the floor for ductwork. On a real project, this may be added later in the project once the mechanical engineer gets involved and suggests the size of supply and return air ducts needed. You will add the hole now regardless.

25. Select the **Pick Walls** icon and with *Extend into wall (to core)* checked, select the shaft side of the four walls.

    a. Use the flip-control arrows for each sketch line if needed because the wrong side of the wall may have been selected.

    b. Use Trim to clean up the corners.

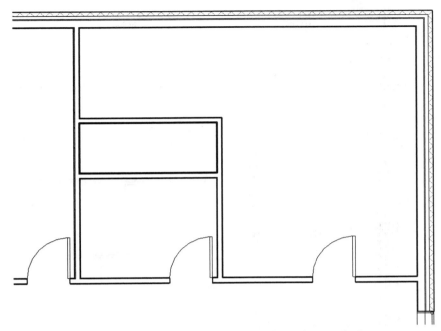

FIGURE 7-3.10 Level 2 (North-East corner): Floor boundary at shaft

Whenever a perimeter is drawn within another, it defines a hole.

Next you will define the floor boundary at the two-story lobby, which starts on Level 1.

26. Sketch the floor opening as shown in Figure 7-3.11:

   a. Use the *Split* tool on the sketch line along the exterior wall.

   b. Use the *Line* tool to sketch the floor opening per the dimensions shown.

   c. Use *Trim* as needed to clean up the corners.

   d. You do not have to add the dimensions, but you can if desired. They will be hidden when the floor is finished.

The last area to define is the curved edge at the curtain wall. On Level 1 the floor went under the curtain wall; on Level 2 the floor edge needs to be held back from the curtain wall, allowing room for it to pass by.

27. Using a similar technique as Level 1, sketch the Level 2 floor edge as shown in Figure 7-3.12.

   a. The curved line is 5″ in (towards the interior of the building) in relation to the adjacent sketch lines.

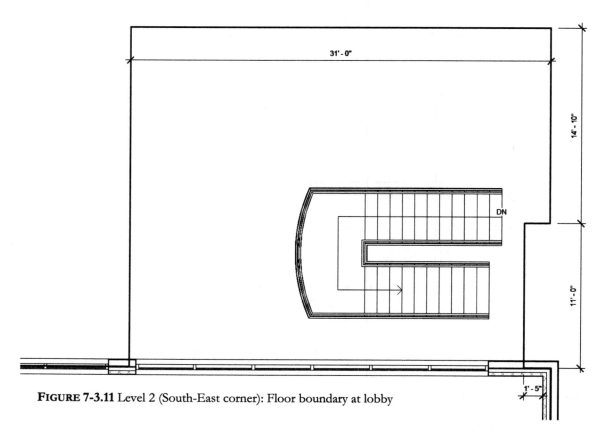

FIGURE 7-3.11 Level 2 (South-East corner): Floor boundary at lobby

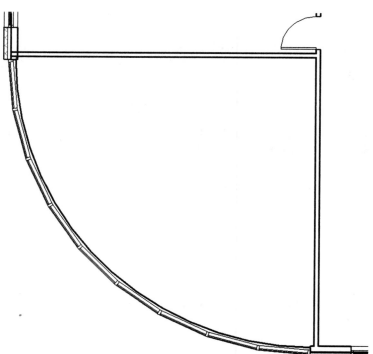

FIGURE 7-3.12 Level 2 (South-West corner):
Floor boundary at curtain wall

You are now ready to finish the floor sketch and let Revit create the 3D floor object in the BIM.

28. Click on the *Ribbon* to finish the floor sketch.

29. Click **Yes** to extending the floor below up to the new floor.

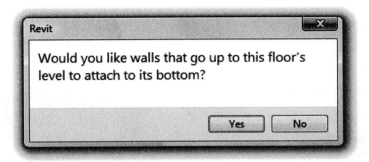

30. Click **Yes** to join and cut walls.

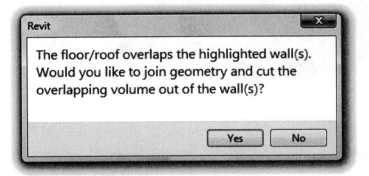

31. Select the lobby stair and use the *Move* tool to reposition it as shown in Figure7-3.13.

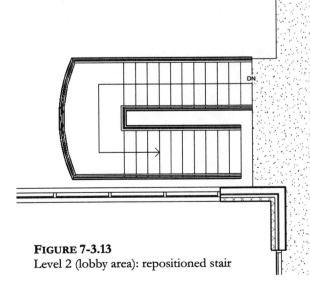

FIGURE 7-3.13
Level 2 (lobby area): repositioned stair

Notice, unlike the Level 1 slab, the <u>LW Concrete on Metal Deck</u> has a surface pattern defined, which shows up everywhere. You will leave this for now as it helps to see the extents of the floor in this early design phase of the project.

32. Switch to the ***Default 3D View***.

33. Use the ***ViewCube*** to move around the exterior of your building.

Notice you can see the Level 1 and Level 2 floors through the curtain wall glazing!

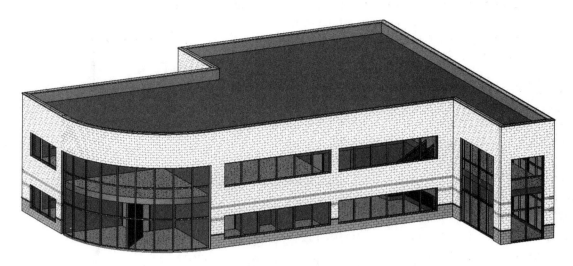

FIGURE 7-3.14 default 3D view: floors visible through glazing

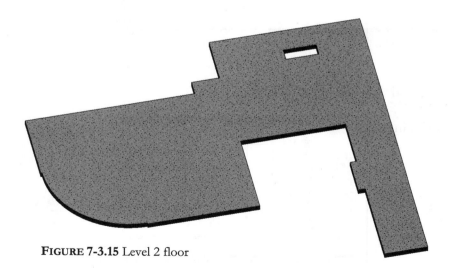

FIGURE 7-3.15 Level 2 floor

The image to the right was generated from the ***3D*** view above. Simply select the floor, click the sunglasses on the *View Control Bar* then select *Isolate Element*.

34. **Save** your project.

Exercise 7-4:
Ceiling Systems

This lesson will explore Revit's tools for modeling ceilings. This will include drawing different types of ceiling systems.

Suspended Acoustical Ceiling Tile System:

1. **Open** your Law Office project.

2. Switch to the *Level 1* ceiling plan view, from the *Project Browser*; ceiling plans are just below the floor plans.

Notice the doors' and windows' visibility are automatically "turned" off in the ceiling plan views (Figure 7-4.2). Actually, the ceiling plan views have a cutting plane similar to floor plans, except they look up rather than down.
You can see this setting by right-clicking on a view name in the *Project Browser* and then selecting **View Range** in the *Properties Palette*. The default value is 7'-6". You might increase this if, for example, you had 10'-0" ceilings and 8'-0" high doors. Otherwise, the doors would show because the 7'-6" cutting plane would be below the door height (Figure 7-4.1).

FIGURE 7-4.1 Properties: View Range settings

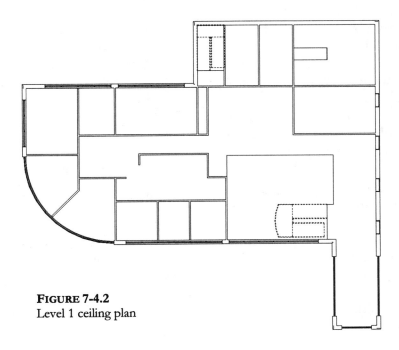

FIGURE 7-4.2
Level 1 ceiling plan

3. Close the open dialog boxes and then select **Home → Build → Ceiling**.

Ceiling

You have four ceiling types, by default, to select from (Figure 7-4.3).

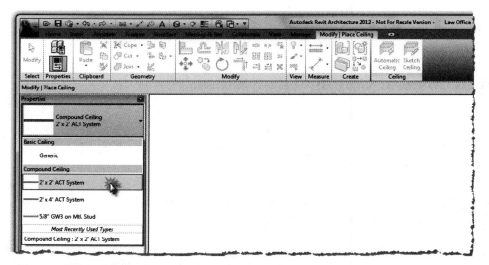

FIGURE 7-4.3 Ceiling: Ribbon options

4. Select *Compound Ceiling:* **2'x2' ACT System**.

Next you will change the ceiling height. The default setting is 10'-0" above the current level. You will change the ceiling height to 8'-0", this will give plenty of space above the ceiling to the bottom of the joists, perhaps for recessed light fixtures and ductwork. This setting can be changed on a room by room basis. Hence, it is an instance parameter.

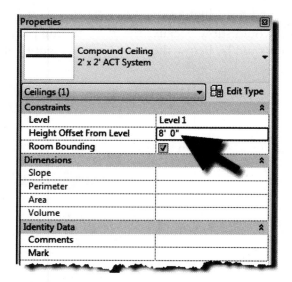

5. Ensure the *Properties Palette* is visible; type **PP** if not.

6. Set the *Height Offset From Level* setting to **8'-0"** (Figure 7-4.4).

FIGURE 7-4.4 Ceiling: Properties

You are now ready to place ceiling grids. This process cannot get much easier, especially compared to other CAD programs.

7. Move your cursor anywhere within the office in the North-West corner of the building. You should see the perimeter of the room highlighted.

8. Pick within that Northwest room; Revit places a grid in the room (Figure 7-4.5).

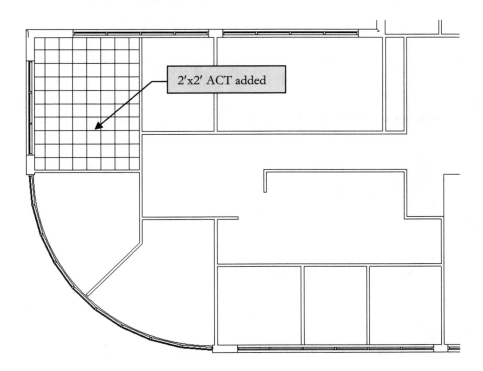

FIGURE 7-4.5: Level 1 Ceiling Plan view: 2'x2' suspended acoustical ceiling tile added to office

You now have a 2'x2' ceiling grid at 8'-0" above the floor, Level 1 in this case. Later in the book, when you get to the exercise on cutting sections, you will see the ceiling with the proper height and thickness.

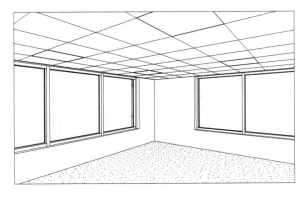

The image to the left is a *camera* view of the room you just added the ceiling to. You will learn how to create camera views in Chapter 14.

Next you will add the same ceiling system to several other Level 1 rooms.

9. Use the **Ceiling** tool to place 2'x 2' acoustic ceiling tile (ACT) at 8'-0" above finished floor (AFF) in the rooms shown (Figure 7-4.6).

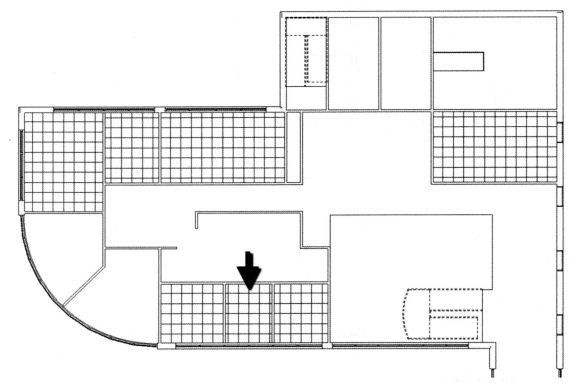

FIGURE 7-4.6: Level 1 Ceiling Plan view: 2′x2′ suspended acoustical ceiling tile added to rooms.

When you place a ceiling grid, Revit centers the grid in the room. The general rule of thumb is you should try to avoid reducing the tile size by more than half of a tile. You can see in Figure 7-4.6 that the East and West sides are small slivers for the center office on the South exterior wall. You will adjust this next.

10. Select **Modify** from the *Ribbon*.

11. **Select** the ceiling grid identified in Figure 7-4.6. Only one line will be highlighted.

12. Use the ***Move*** tool to move the grid 12″ to the East (Figure 7-4.7).

Moving the grid does not move the ceiling element itself; only its surface pattern.

Next, you will look at drawing gypsum board ceiling systems. The process is identical to placing the grid system.

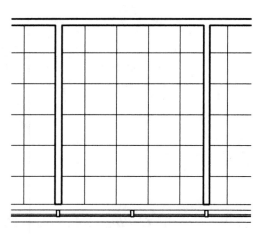

FIGURE 7-4.7
Level 1 Ceiling plan view: ceiling grid relocated.

Gypsum Board Ceiling System:

You will create a new ceiling type for a gypsum board (Gyp. Bd.) ceiling. To better identify the areas that have a Gyp. Bd. ceiling, you will set the ceiling surface to have a stipple pattern. This will provide a nice graphical representation for the Gyp. Bd. ceiling areas. The ceiling you are about to create would lean more towards a commercial application. You will add this ceiling to toilet rooms; as it holds up better in locations with moisture and provides better security. The space above a Gyp. Bd. ceiling is not easily accessible as acoustical ceiling tile (ACT) is, so access panels are often required to access shutoff valves, VAV's, etc.

The first thing you will do is look at the Revit *Materials* which are assigned to elements throughout the model. Materials are used to manage the pattern applied to the surface of an element seen in elevation, and the pattern applied when an element is cut in section. Additionally, a color can be selected for *Shaded with Edges* (Model Graphics Style). Later in the book, you will also learn how a rendering material can be added, which is used when creating a photorealistic rendering.

Several elements can reference the same material. For example, a door, trim, a custom ceiling, furniture, etc., could refer to the same wood material, which could be set to clear maple. If, at any point in the project, the *Material* for wood is changed to stained oak, all elements which reference it are updated. Thus, if several wood finishes or species are required, you would have to create multiple *Materials* in Revit.

13. Select **Manage → *Settings* → Materials**. *This is the list of materials you select from when assigning a material to each layer in a wall system, etc.*

Materials

14. Select *Gypsum Wall Board* in the *Name* list and then click the **Duplicate** button and enter the name: **Gypsum Ceiling Board** (see Figure 7-4.8 and image to right).

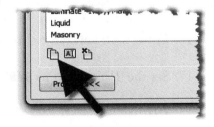

15. In the *Surface Pattern* area, pick the button and select **Gypsum-Plaster** from the list, and then click **OK** (Figure 7-4.8).

The *Surface Pattern* setting is what will add the stipple pattern to the Gyp. Bd. ceiling areas. With this set to *none*, the ceiling has no pattern, like the basic ceiling type. Creating a new material allows you to separately control the surface pattern of Gyp. Bd. walls vs. ceilings. Walls do not have a surface pattern typically, whereas ceilings do.

Thus, if you wanted Carpet 1 finish to never have the stipple hatch pattern, you could change the surface pattern to *none* via the *Materials* dialog and not have to change each view's visibility override.

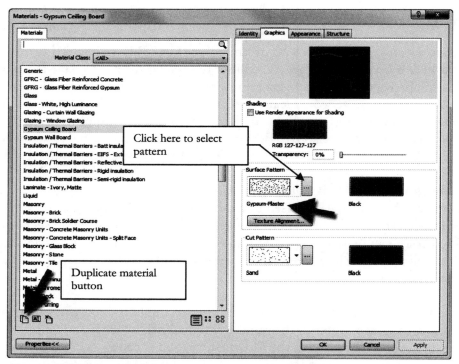

FIGURE 7-4.8 Materials dialog

The template you started from does have one Gyp. Bd. Ceiling, but this is meant for a soffit or a small room where the ceiling is not suspended from the structure above; it has 3⅝″ metal studs. You will use this ceiling as a starting point, and create a ceiling with ¾″ metal furring over 1½″ metal studs/channels. All of this is then suspended by wires from the structure above; these wires are not modeled in Revit.

16. From the *Home* tab on the *Ribbon*, select **Ceiling**.

17. Set the *Type Selector* to **5/8″ GWB on Metal Stud**.

   FYI: You are selecting this because it is most similar to the ceiling you will be creating. GWB = Gypsum Wall Board

18. Click the **Edit Type** button.

19. Click *Duplicate* and type the name **Susp GB on Metal Stud**.

At this point you have a new ceiling type available to be placed in the model. However, it is exactly like the one you copied (i.e., ⅝″ GWB on Metal Stud). Next, you will modify the composition of your new ceiling type system family.

20. Select **Edit** next to the *Structure* parameter.

21. Create a *Layer* and set the values as follows (Figure 7-4.9):

    a. **1½″ Mtl. Stud**

    b. **¾″ Mtl. Stud**

    c. **Gypsum Ceiling Board**
       (This is the material you created in Step 13.)

    TIP: *Use the Insert button to add a new Layer and then, with the new Layer selected, use the up and down buttons to reposition the Layer within the ceiling system.*

22. Click **OK** two times to close the open dialog boxes.

    FYI: *The ceiling assembly you just created represents a typical suspended Gyp. Bd. ceiling system. The Metal Studs are perpendicular to each other and suspended by wires, similar to an ACT system.*

You are now ready to draw a gypsum board ceiling.

23. Make sure **Susp GB on Metal Stud** is selected in the *Type Selector* on the *Properties Palette*.

24. Set the ceiling height to **8′- 0″**.

25. Pick the two toilet rooms as shown in **Figure 7-4.10**.

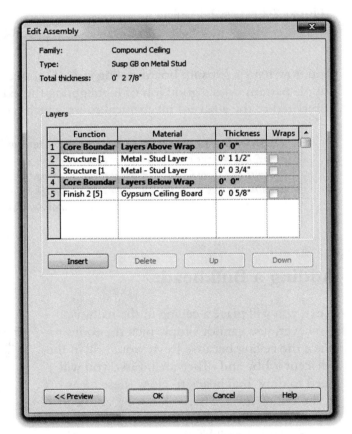

FIGURE 7-4.9 New ceiling – edit assembly

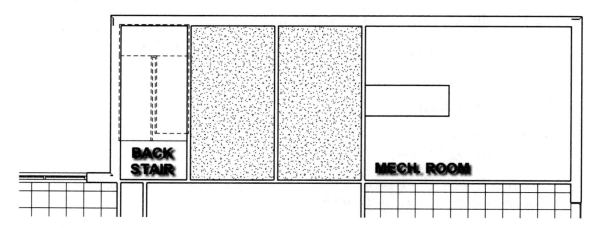

FIGURE 7-4.10 Gyp. Bd. Ceiling

You now have a gypsum board ceiling at 8'-0" above the Level 1 floor slab. Notice the stipple pattern does a good job of highlighting the extents of the Gyp. Bd. Ceiling, as compared to the adjacent mechanical room which will not have a ceiling.

> ***DESIGN INTEGRATION TIP:*** *Once the structure and HVAC (i.e., ductwork) have been added, any ceilings will obscure those elements if they are lower in elevation. However, all those elements will show in the mechanical room. Showing the structure and HVAC is great for coordination and helps the contractor understand the project better. For instance, how difficult would it be to paint the Mechanical Room structure and ductwork.*

Adding a Bulkhead:

Next, you will place a ceiling in the hallway. However, you cannot simply pick the room to place the ceiling because Revit would fill in the adjacent lobby and office area. First, you will need to draw bulkheads to close these areas off at the ceiling level. They will not be visible in the floor plan view as they do not pass through its cut plane. A bulkhead is a portion of wall that hangs from the floor or structure above (see image to right) and creates a closed perimeter for a ceiling system to abut into. The bulkhead will create a perimeter that the *Ceiling* tool will detect for the proper ceiling placement.

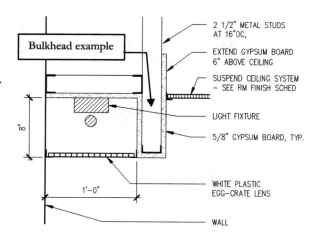

26. While still in the **Level 1** ceiling plan view, select the **Wall** *tool*.

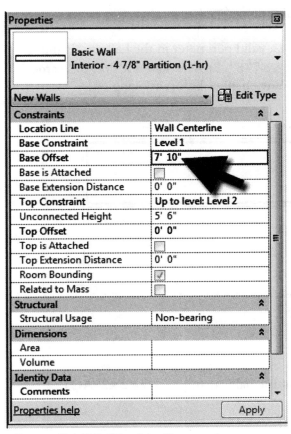

FIGURE 7-4.11 Bulkhead (wall) properties

27. In the *Type Selector*, set the wall type to:
Interior – 4 7/8" Partition (1-hr)

28. In the *Properties Palette*, set and the <u>Base Offset</u> to **7'-10"**. *This will put the bottom of the wall to 7'-10" above the current floor level, Level 1 in this case* (Figure 7-4.12).

29. Set the <u>Top Constraint</u> to: **Up to level: Level 2** (Figure 7-4.11).

   TIP: The next time you draw a wall, you will have to change the Base Offset back to 0'-0" or your wall will be 7'-10" off the floor; this is hard to remember!

30. **Draw the bulkhead**; make sure you snap to the adjacent walls (Figure 7-4.12).

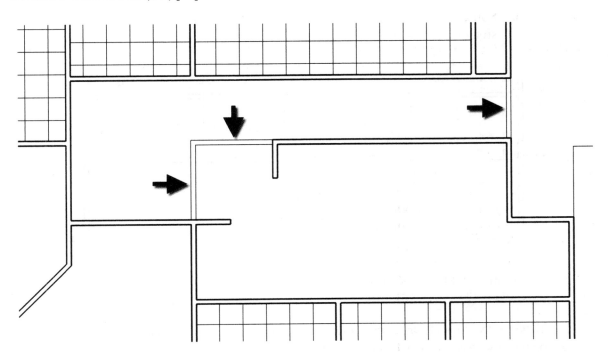

FIGURE 7-4.12 Bulkhead modeled

31. Select the *Ceiling* tool and hover your cursor over the hallway.

Notice, in Figure 7-4.13, how the bulkheads create a valid perimeter in the hallway. If the bulkhead bottom was 8'-2" or the ceiling height were 7'-8", Revit would not find this same perimeter. Take a moment and give it a try. Undo any changes before moving on.

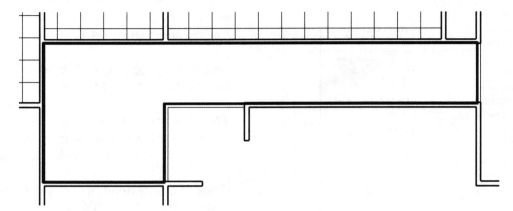

FIGURE 7-4.13 Ceiling perimeter highlighted

32. With the ceiling height set to **8'-0"**, click in the hallway to place the **2'x2' ACT System**.

33. Reposition the grid as shown in Figure 7-4.14.

    a.   Sometimes, with odd shaped rooms like this, it can be impossible not to have small slivers of tiles.

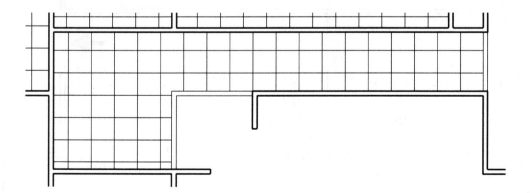

FIGURE 7-4.14 Hallway ceiling placed

DESIGN INTEGRATION TIP: *In addition to laying out the ceiling tile to minimize sliver tiles, the grid needs to accommodate the lighting design. In the hallway, a full tile is provided down the center with this in mind.*

34. Place the remaining bulkheads and 2'x2' ACT ceilings per the image below; note the ceiling and bulkhead heights vary (Figure 7-4.15).

35. Use the **_Align_** tool to make adjacent ceiling grids line up as shown; remember, select the item you do not want to move first.

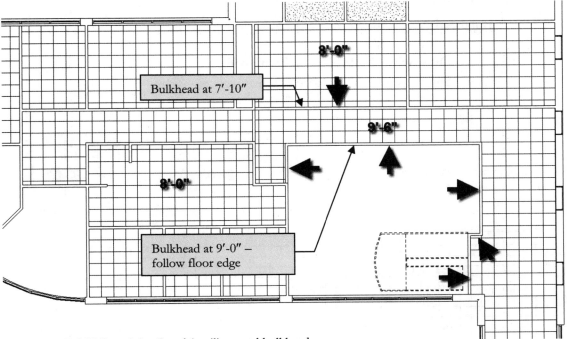

Bulkhead at 7'-10"

8'-0"

9'-6"

8'-0"

Bulkhead at 9'-0" — follow floor edge

FIGURE 7-4.15 Remaining Level 1 ceilings and bulkheads

You are now ready to move on to the Level 2 reflected ceiling plan. First, you need to create a view in which to work.

36. Select **View → Create → Plan Views → Reflected Ceiling Plan**.

37. Do the following:

    a. Select **Level 2**.

    b. Set the scale to **1/4" = 1'-0"**

38. Click **OK**.

Deleting a Ceiling Grid:

When selecting a ceiling grid, Revit only selects one line. This does not allow you to delete the ceiling grid. To delete: hover cursor over a ceiling grid line and press the **Tab** key until you see the ceiling perimeter highlight, then click the mouse. The entire ceiling will be selected. Press Delete.

You now have a Level 2 ceiling plan view in which to work. It is possible to make multiple plan or ceiling views of the same level (e.g., floor plan, finish plan, code plan, etc.)

39. Using the techniques previously covered, add the Level 2 ceilings per the information provided in Figure 7-4.16.

    a. Rotated ceiling:
        i. Select a grid line.
        ii. Use the **Rotate** tool.
        iii. **Move** the grid as shown.

    b. Bulkhead:
        i. Bottom at **8'-0"**
        ii. Draw with **Arc** tool or *Pick* with offset.
        iii. Show approx. **3'-0"** from exterior wall.

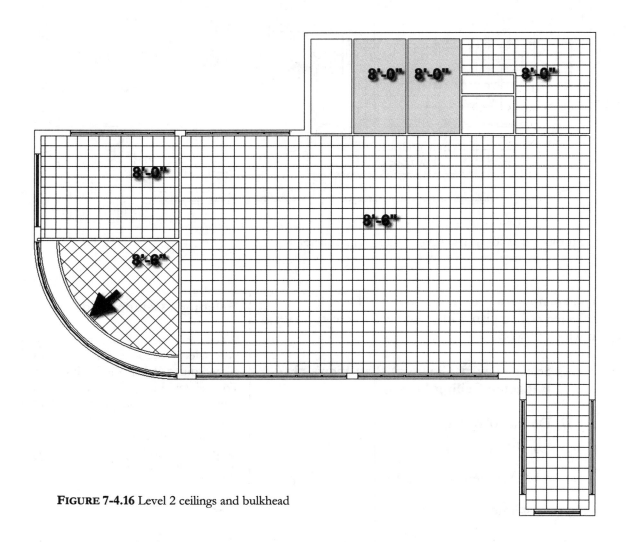

FIGURE 7-4.16 Level 2 ceilings and bulkhead

40. **Save** your project.

Self-Exam:

The following questions can be used as a way to check your knowledge of this lesson. The answers can be found at the bottom of the page.

1. You don't have to click *Finish Roof* when you are done defining a roof. (T/F)

2. The wall below the roof automatically conforms to the underside of the roof when you join the walls to the roof. (T/F)

3. The roof overhang setting is available from the *Options Bar*. (T/F)

4. To create a gable roof on a building with 4 walls, two of the walls should not have the _____ option checked.

5. Is it possible to change the reference point for a temporary dimension that is displayed while an object is selected? (Y/N)

Review Questions:

The following questions may be assigned by your instructor as a way to assess your knowledge of this section. Your instructor has the answers to the review questions.

1. When creating a roof using the "*create roof by footprint*" option, you need to create a closed perimeter. (T/F)

2. The **Defines slope** setting can be changed after the roof is "finished." (T/F)

3. The ceiling grid position cannot be modified. (T/F)

4. To delete a ceiling grid, you must first select the perimeter. (T/F)

5. While using the ***Roof*** tool, you can use the _____ tool from the *Ribbon* to fill in the missing segments to close the perimeter.

6. You use the _____ variable to adjust the vertical position of the roof relative to the current working plane (view).

7. Tool used to draw a bulkhead: _____ .

8. You need to use the _____ _____ to flip the roofline when you pick the wrong side of the wall and the overhang is shown on the inside.

9. A second, internal, perimeter creates a hole in the floor. (T/F)

10. Changing the name of a level tag (in elevation) causes Revit to rename all the corresponding views (plan, ceiling, etc.) if you answer yes to the prompt. (T/F)

SELF-EXAM ANSWERS:
1 - F, **2** – T, 3 – T, **4** – defines slope, **5** – Y

Notes:

Lesson 8
Law Office: STRUCTURAL SYSTEM:

This chapter will introduce you to Autodesk Revit *Structure 2012*. You will study the User Interface (UI) and learn how it is different from Revit *Architecture*. Next, you will develop the structural model for the law office, placing grids, columns, beams joists and footings. Finally, you will learn how to add annotations and tags that report the size of individual structural elements.

Exercise 8-1:
Introduction to Revit Structure

What is Revit Structure 2012 used for?

Revit *Structure 2012* is the companion product to Revit *Architecture 2012* and Revit *MEP 2012*. This is a specialized version of Revit for designing the structural aspects of a building, or bridge.

The image below shows the structural elements you will be adding in this chapter. Keeping in line with the overall intent of this textbook, you will really just be skimming the surface of what Revit *Structure* can do. For example, Revit *Structure* can model concrete beams and columns, precast floors and roof planks, cross bracing and rebar.

> **WARNING:** *This is strictly a fictitious project. Although some effort has been made to make the sizes of structural components realistic, this structure has not been designed by a structural engineer. There are many codes and design considerations that need to be made on a case by case basis.*

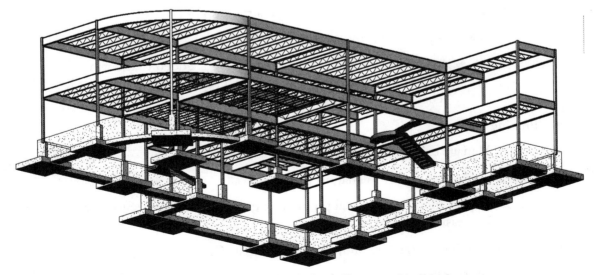

FIGURE 8-1.1 The completed structural model for the law office created in this chapter

Listed below are a few of the highlights of using Revit Structure:

- 3D modeling of the entire structure
- Multi-user environment
  - Several people can be working on the same model when "worksharing" has been enabled (not covered in this book).
- Coordination with *Architecture* and *MEP*
  - Visually via 2D and 3D views
  - Using Interference Check feature
- 2D construction drawings generated in real-time from 3D model
  - Presentation drawings, including photo-realistic renderings
  - Construction Drawings (CD's phase)
    - Views can show true 3D geometry or single line
  - Construction Administration (CA phase)
    - Addendum
    - Architectural Supplemental Information (ASI)
    - Proposal Request (PR)
    - Change Order (CO)
- Schedules
  - Schedules are live lists of elements in the BIM.
- Design Options
  - Used to try different ideas for a structural design in the same area of a project (e.g., exposed cross-bracing vs. rigid structure)
  - Also used to mange bid alternates during CD's.
    - A bid alternate might be an extra 25'-0" added to the wing of a building. The contractor provides a separate price for what it would cost to do that work.
- Phasing
  - Manage existing, new and future construction
- Several options to export to analysis programs
  - Export model to external program (e.g., Autodesk Robot Structural Analysis Professional, RISA, etc.)
- Export to industry standard shop drawing format (CIS/2)
  - Shop drawings are created and used by fabricators and contractors, once the design is done and the project has been bid.

Many of the highlights listed on the previous page are things that can be done in Revit *Architecture* as well. The list was generated with the structural engineer and technician in mind relative to current software and processes used.

The Revit Platform

All three "flavors" of Revit are built on the same basic Revit platform. Much of the programming code is common between the three flavors, which is why the design team can all view each other's models and even share the same BIM file if desired.

Whenever a project involves all three flavors of Revit, the same version <u>must</u> be used. Because Revit is not backwards compatible, it is not possible for the structural design team to use Revit *Structure 2011* and the architects and MEP engineers use Revit *Architecture* and Revit *MEP 2012*. The structural design team would have no way to link or view the architectural or MEP files; an older version of Revit has no way to read a newer file format.

Furthermore, it is not possible to Save-As to an older version of Revit, as can be done with other programs such as AutoCAD or Microsoft Word.

It is perfectly possible to have more than one version of Revit installed on your computer. You just need to make sure you are using the correct version for the project you are working on. If you accidentally open a project in the wrong version, you will get one of two clues:

- *Opening a 2011 file with Revit 2012:* You will see an upgrade message while the file is opened. It will also take longer to open due to the upgrade process. If you see this and did not intend to upgrade the file, simply close the file without saving. The upgraded file is only in your computer's RAM and is not committed to the hard drive until you Save.

- *Opening a 2012 file with Revit 2011:* This is an easy one as it is not possible. Revit will present you with a message indicating the file was created in a later version of Revit and cannot be opened.

Many firms will start new projects in the new version of Revit and finish any existing projects in the version it is currently in; which helps to avoid any potential upgrade issues. Sometimes, a project that is still in its early phases will be upgraded to a new version of Revit.

It should be pointed out that Autodesk releases about one Service Pack (SP) per quarter. This means each version of Revit (i.e., 2011 or 2012) will have approximately 3 SPs. It is best if everyone on the design team is using the same build (i.e., 2012 + SP3) but is not absolutely required.

You will be looking at more specifics about the Revit *MEP* flavor in Chapters 12 and 13 later in the text.

One Model or Linked Models

If the structural engineer is not in the same office, the linked scenario must be used as it is currently not practical to share models live over the internet. Linking does not work over the internet either; a copy of the model needs to be shared with each company at regular intervals.

When all disciplines are in one office, on the same network, they could all work in the same Revit model, where each discipline uses their specific flavor of Revit to manipulate the same Building Information Model (BIM). However, on large projects, the model is still typically split by discipline to improve performance due to software and hardware limitations. When a multi-discipline firm employs links, however, they are live and automatically updated when any one of the model files is opened.

In this book you will employ the one model approach. The process of linking and controlling the visibility of those links in the host file is beyond the scope of this text. Instead, you will focus your energy on the basic Revit tools for each discipline.

Revit *Structure 2012* comparison to Revit *Architecture 2012*:
- Rebar
  - Design and annotation
- *Beam Annotations* feature
  - Places multiple beam tags, annotations and spot elevations
- Analyze
  - Analytical model tools
  - Define load conditions
  - As previously mentioned, Revit *Structure* does not do structural analysis, but it allows you to build a valid model that is ready for use in an external analysis program.
- Selection sets
  - *Save*, *Load* and *Edit* selection sets
- Structural Settings dialog (with more options)
  - Detailed settings for symbolic representation and analytical settings which apply to the entire project

What Revit *Structure* <u>cannot</u> do that Revit *Architecture* can:
- Ceilings
- Rooms and Room tags

Some firms are fortunate to have access to all three flavors of Revit, as do most educational facilities. Students also have free access, for learning purposes only, to each flavor of Revit via **www.students.autodesk.com**.

Based on the list above, it was possible to do everything in this book up to this point, except adding the ceilings, using Revit *Structure*. But the ceiling views could have been set up, and ceilings created in Revit *Architecture* can be edited in Revit *Structure*.

The Revit Structure User Interface:

This section will mainly cover the differences between Revit *Structure* and Revit *Architecture*. You should note that about 90 percent of the material covered in Exercise 2-2, *Overview of the Revit User Interface*, applies to Revit *Structure* as well.

Looking at the image below, you see the Revit *Structure* User Interface is very similar to Revit *Architecture* (Figure 8-1.2). Both have a *Ribbon, Project Browser, Quick Access Toolbar, View Control Bar* and a drawing window; compare to Figure 2-2.1.

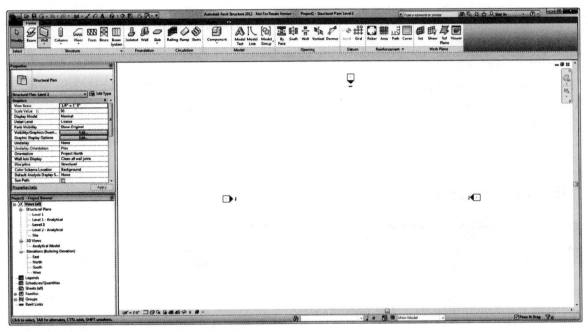

FIGURE 8-1.2 Revit Structure User Interface

Many of the tabs on the *Ribbon* are identical to the same named tabs in Revit *Architecture*. The following are identical to Revit *Architecture*:

- Insert   *exception:* RAC has an additional *Decal* tool
- Collaborate
- View   *exception:* Two icons swapped locations
- Manage   *exception:* Added *Structural Settings* button & *Selection* panel
- Modify

Ribbon – Home tab:

As can be seen from the image above, the *Home* tab is laid out with the structural engineer or technician in mind. The very first tool is *Beam*, whereas *Wall* is the first tool for Revit *Architecture*. Also notice the panel names, *Structure*, *Foundation* and *Reinforcement*, are all discipline oriented.

Many tools are duplicates from those found in Revit *Architecture*; they even have the same icon. Duplicate tools, such as *Stairs*, have the exact same programming code and create the same element which can then be edited by either flavor of Revit.

Notice the <u>*Reinforcement* panel</u> is the only one with a fly-out section. This fly-out contains *Rebar Cover Settings* and *Abbreviations* (see image to the right).

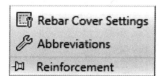

Ribbon – Analyze tab:

The *Analyze* tab reveals several tools which allow the structural designer to specify various loads on the structure, once it has been modeled.

When structural elements are being drawn, Revit *Structure* is creating the analytical model automatically. An example of this is shown to the right by single lines for each element that connect to each other, even though the 3D elements do not because a plate usually connects the beam to the column, so there is a gap in between.

Revit provides tools to check the validity of the analytical model; e.g., Check Supports will notify you if a column does not have a footing under it!

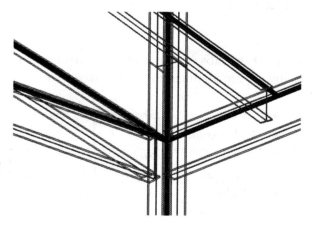

FIGURE 8-1.3 Analytical model lines

Ribbon – Architect & Site tab:

The *Architect & Site* tab provides several tools that are not typically required to be drawn by the structural engineer. However, some "structural only" firms may occasionally have a project that does not involve an architect and needs to show doors and windows; for that these tools are provided.

The *Conceptual Mass* tools can be used to create unusual shapes. These shapes should never be used directly as part of a project. Revit provides *Model by Face* tools which allow walls, curtain walls, floors and roofs to be created based on the surface of a *Conceptual Mass*. This allows certain elements to be created that could not otherwise be done in Revit.

Structural Settings Dialog Box:

From the *Manage* tab, select *Structural Settings*.

Structural Settings

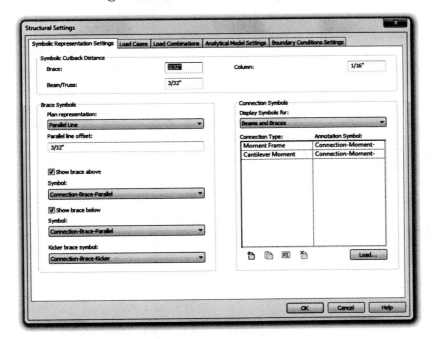

Revit *Structure* provides a *Structural Settings* dialog box that allows changes to be made in how the program works and displays structural elements. These settings only apply to the current project, but apply to all views and schedules for that project.

Do not make any changes in this dialog unless instructed to do so. This will help to ensure your drawings match those presented in the book.

Structural Content:

A vast array of industry standard beams, columns, joists, stiffeners, joists and, more are provided! Even some obsolete shapes are provided to aid in modeling existing structures. What is not provided can typically be modeled in Revit or the *Family Editor* as needed.

Structural Templates:

Revit *Structure* provides only one template from which a new structural project can be started from; compared to the four that Revit *Architecture* provides. This one template has all the basic views and components needed to start modeling a building's structure.

In an office environment multiple templates may be needed if drastically different types of projects are worked on. For example, housing which often is often wood framed and government which has specific annotation and dimensioning requirements.

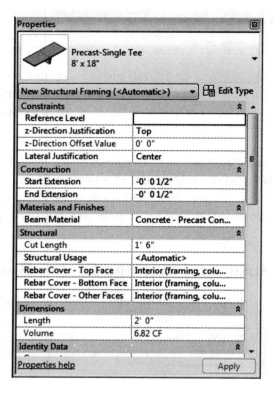

Because you will be starting the structural model within the architectural model, you will not automatically have several important components ready to go. Not to worry, however, as the first thing you will do in the next exercise will be to import several elements from another project file, which will be based on the structural template.

Autodesk Revit Resources:

Autodesk's *Revit Structure Resource Center:*
resources.autodesk.com/adsk/servlet/Revit-Structure

Autodesk's *Revit Extensions Website:*
www.extensions4revit.com

Autodesk's *Revit Structure Blog:*
bimandbeam.typepad.com

Autodesk's *Revit Structure Discussion Group:*
discussion.autodesk.com/forums
(Click the link to Autodesk Revit *Structure*.)

Autodesk's *Subscription Website (for members only):*
subscription.autodesk.com

> **FYI:** *The subscription website provides several bonuses for those who are on subscription with Autodesk, including tutorials and product "advantage packs." Subscription is basically what firms do to be able to budget their yearly design software expenses, a yearly payment with access to all new software the moment is becomes available. The subscription route also saves money.*

Exercise 8-2:
Creating Views and Loading Content

In this lesson you will begin to prepare your BIM file for the structural modeling tasks. One of the challenges with modeling everything in one model, versus separate models linked together, is that Autodesk does not provide a template specifically for this. A good starting template is provided for each discipline (or flavor of Revit), but not for a multi-discipline project.

The first steps in this lesson, therefore, will walk the reader through the process of importing *Project Standards* from another file into your law office project. Once that has been done, you can then set up views in which to model and annotate the structural aspects of the building. These views will be similar to the floor plan views that currently exist for the architectural plans; they are defined by a horizontal slice or section through the building. The main difference is that various *Categories* will be turned off, such as casework, plumbing fixtures, etc., that are not directly relevant to the structure of the building.

Transfer Project Standards:

Revit provides a tool which allows various settings to be copied from one project to another; it is called *Transfer Project Standards*. In order to use this feature, two Revit project files need to be open. One is your law office project file and the other is a file that contains the settings you wish to import. You will start a new Revit structural project from a template file and use this file as the "standards" file; this file will not be used after this step is complete.

1. **Open** Revit *Structure 2012*.

   a. If you do not have this flavor of Revit, you may download it from Autodesk.com and use it in 30-day trial mode for this chapter, which should be plenty of time to complete the tutorials. The free trial version is a fully functional version of the software. Also, students with a valid ".edu" email address may download the free 13-month version from students.autodesk.com.

   > **FYI:** *All three "flavors" of Revit can be installed on the same computer and even be running at the same time. However, you cannot have the same file open unless Worksharing has been enabled. Your law office project does not have this feature enabled; it is beyond the scope of this textbook.*

2. Create a new file from the structural template; select **Application Menu → New → Project**.

Revit *Structure* only comes with one template, unlike Revit *Architecture* and Revit *MEP* which have multiple templates to cater to the broader potential uses of these applications. Thus, the default template listed is the one you will use; you will not have to click *Browse*.

3. Click OK to create a new project.

   a. The file *should be* C:\ProgramData\Autodesk\RST 2012\Imperial Templates\ **Structural Analysis-default.rte**.

You now have a new Revit project with is temporarily named <u>Project 1.rvt</u>. This will be the project from which you import various *Structural Settings* and *Families* into your law office project. Take a moment to notice the template is rather lean; it has no sheets and only a handful of views set up. A structural engineering department would take the time to set up an office standard template with sheets, families and views all ready to go for their most typical project to save time in the initial setup process.

4. **Open** your law office Revit project file.
   You may wish to start this lesson from the data file provided on the DVD that accompanies this book. Make sure you select the file from the correct folder.

Now that you have both files open, you will use the *Transfer Project Standards* tool to import several important things into the law office project file.

5. With the law office project file current (i.e., visible in the maximized drawing window), select **Manage → Project Settings → Transfer Project Standards**.

6. Make sure *Copy from* is set to **Project1**, the file you just created.

7. Click the **Check None** button to clear all the checked boxes.

8. Check only the boxes for the items listed (Figure 8-2.1):

   a. Annotation Family Label Types
   b. Foundation Slab Types
   c. Halftone and Underlay Settings
   d. Line Patterns
   e. Line Styles
   f. Load Types
   g. Pad Types
   h. Material
   i. Rebar Cover Settings
   j. Rebar Types
   k. Slab Edge Settings
   l. Structural Settings

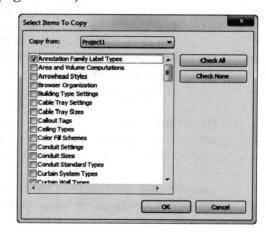

FIGURE 8-2.1 Transfer project settings

9. Click **OK** to import the selected items.

Because some items overlap, Revit prompts you about *Duplicated Types*; you can *Overwrite* or select *New Only*. Selecting "New Only" is safer if you are not sure what will be brought in by the template (or project file in this case). For the law office, you will use *Overwrite* to make sure you get all the structural settings and parameters needed.

10. Scroll down to see all the "duplicate types" so you have an idea what overlap there is; click **Overwrite** (see Figure 8-2.2).

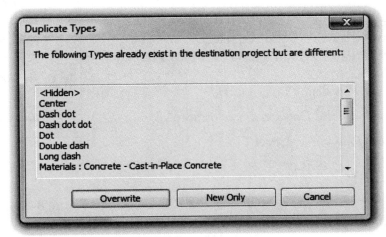

FIGURE 8-2.2 Transfer project settings; duplicate types warning

In the lower right corner of the screen, you may see a *Warning* prompt which can be ignored and will go away on its own. It is letting you know that some types have been renamed rather than overwritten to avoid conflicts (Figure 8-2.3).

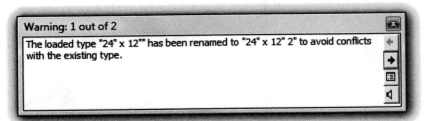

FIGURE 8-2.3 Warning message after transfer of standards

At this point you have many of the key settings loaded into your BIM file, such as *View Templates* and *Structural Settings*. A few items do not come across (e.g., boundary conditions and bracing symbols). However, that will not be a problem for this tutorial. **At this time you may close the temporary Project1 file without saving.**

Creating Structural Plan Views:

Next you will create three structural floor plan views:
- Level 1 – Structural Slab and Foundation Plan
- Level 2 – Structural Framing Plan
- Roof – Structural Framing Plan

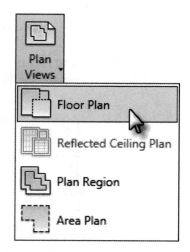

After creating each of these views you will apply a **View Template**, which is a way to quickly adjust all the view-related parameters to a saved standard (i.e., a *View Template*).

11. While in the law office project, select
    View → Create → Plan Views → Floor Plan.

12. In the *New Plan* dialog box, select:

    a. Uncheck the *Duplicate Views* option.

    b. *Floor Plan Views:* **Level 1**

    c. *Scale:* **1/4″ = 1′-0″**

13. Click **OK** (see Figure 8-2.4).

At this point you have a new *View* created in the *Project Browser*. This view is in a new section, under *Views (all)*, called **Structural Plans** (Figure 8-2.5). Each view has separate notes and dimensions which is beneficial, because the structural drawings do not need to show a dimension from a wall to the edge of a countertop or sink.

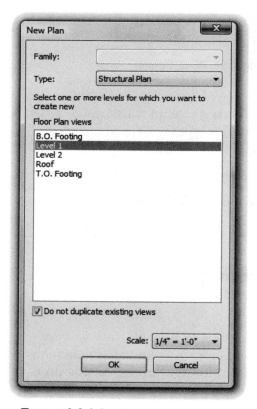

FIGURE 8-2.4 Creating a new plan view

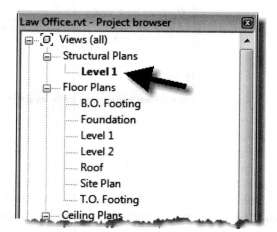

FIGURE 8-2.5 New structural plan created

Next, you will rename the *View* and apply a *View Template*.

14. In the *Project Browser*, right-click on **Level 1 Structural Plans**.

15. Select **Rename** from the pop-up menu.

16. Enter: **Level 1 – Structural Slab and Foundation Plan**.

   FYI: *This is the name that will appear below the drawing when it is placed on a sheet.*

17. Click **OK**.

18. Click **No** to the "Rename corresponding level and views" prompt.

It is best to rename views and levels manually; you do not typically want levels renamed to match the view name. All other disciplines see the same name; it should remain **Level 1**.

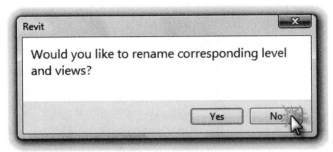

FIGURE 8-2.6 Rename level and views prompt; click No

View Templates:

Next, you will apply a *View Template* to your view so it is closer to what is needed for the design and documentation of a foundation plan. First, you will look at the current settings and how they will be changed by applying a *View Template*.

19. Ensure nothing is selected and no commands are active so the *Properties Palette* is displaying the current view's properties.

Notice the *Discipline* is set to **Architectural** and an *Underlay* is active. The *View Template* will quickly correct these settings.

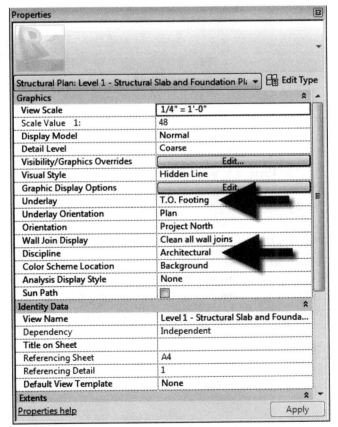

FIGURE 8-2.7 View properties – Structural Level 1

Next, you will look at the *View Range* settings. These control the location of the horizontal slice through the building.

20. With the ***Level 1 – Structural Slab and Foundation Plan*** view active; scroll down and click **Edit** next to *View Range* in the *Properties Palette*.

The ***View Range*** dialog has a significant role in what shows up in a plan view and what does not. In Revit *Structure*, things typically show up only when they fall at or below the *Cut plane*, and are above the *View Depth Level/Offset*. Search Revit's *Help System* for "view range" for a good description and graphics on these settings (Figure 8-2.8).

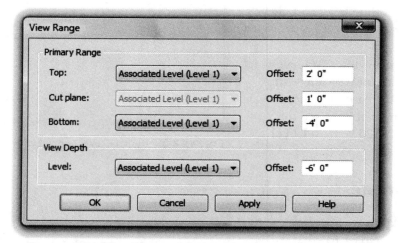

FIGURE 8-2.8 View Range – Structural Level 1

21. Click **Cancel** to close the *View Range* dialog without saving.

22. Type **VV** to open the *Visibility/Graphics Overrides* for the current view.

23. On the *Model Categories* tab, **check** *Show categories from all disciplines*.

The ***Visibility/Graphics Overrides*** dialog (Figure 8-2.9) also has a significant role in what shows up and what does not in a view. The main thing to understand here is that the visibility of the items in these various categories can be controlled here for the current view, and only the current view. Unchecking *Casework* hides all the items that exist within that category, such as base and wall cabinets and custom casework such as reception desks, assuming they have been created with the correct *Category* setting. The *View Template* you are about to apply to this view will uncheck many of these *Categories*.

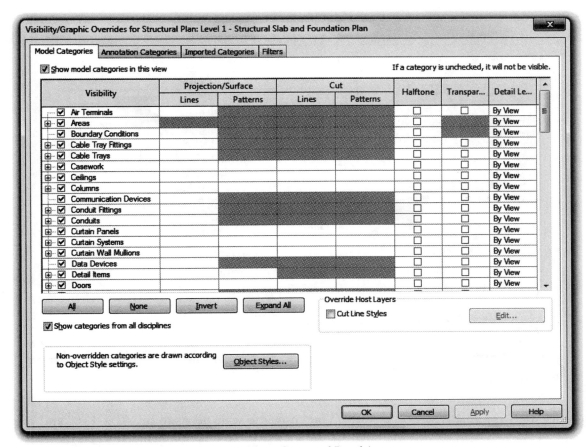

FIGURE 8-2.9 Visibility and Graphic Overrides – Structural Level 1

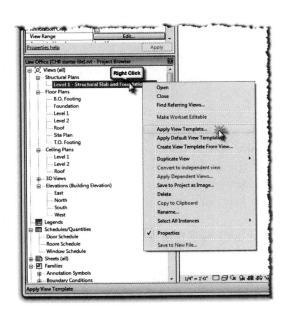

24. Click **Cancel** to close the *Visibility/ Graphic Overrides* dialog without saving.

Now you will apply the *View Template* and then review what it changes.

25. Right-click on ***Level 1 – Structural Slab and Foundation Plan*** in the *Project Browser* (see image to right).

26. Click **Apply View Template** from the pop-up menu.

27. On the left, select **Structural Foundation Plan**.

You are now in the *Apply View Template* dialog (Figure 8-2.10). Take a moment to observe all the settings it has stored and are about to be applied to the selected view, the one you right-clicked on.

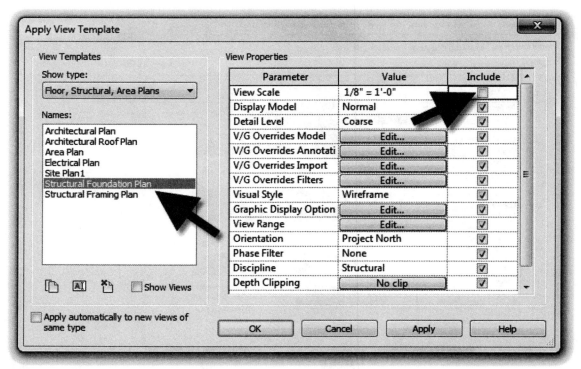

FIGURE 8-2.10 Apply View Template dialog – Structural Level 1

Notice the *View Scale* is set to ⅛″-1′-0″. You know the scale needs to be ¼″ = 1′-0″ and you have already set that, so you will uncheck the *View Scale* so it is not included when the template is applied.

28. **Uncheck** *View Scale* (Figure 8-2.10).

29. Click **OK** to apply the *View Template.*

The model visibility has now changed to mainly show the floor slab and stairs. All the walls, doors, etc., have been hidden in this view; they still exist, but are just not visible in this view.

Go back and repeat Steps 19-24 to compare the changes made to the *View Properties,* *View Range* and the *Visibility settings.*

> *FYI: A* View Template *with the same name, in the default structural template, leaves the door category visible.*

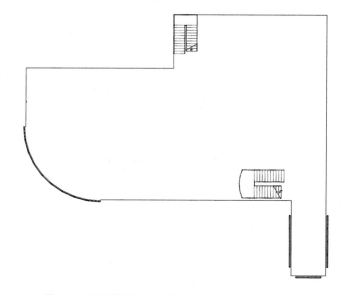

FIGURE 8-2.11 Result of applying view template

Next you will set up the two remaining views. It is expected that you will refer back to the previous steps if you need a review on the process.

    30. Create the following Structural Plans:

        a. Level 2
            i. *Name:*   **Level 2 – Structural Framing Plan**
            ii. *Scale:*   ¼″ = 1′-0″
            iii. *View Template to apply:*   Structural Framing Plan

        b. Roof
            i. *Name:*   **Roof – Structural Framing Plan**
            ii. *Scale:*   ¼″ = 1′-0″
            iii. *View Template to apply:*   Structural Framing Plan

Loading Content:

Now that the structural views are set up and ready to go, you will look at how structural content is loaded into the project. The process is identical to how content is loaded using Revit *Architecture* and Revit *MEP*.

This section will just show you how to load a few elements. As you work through the rest of this chapter, you will have to load additional content; reference this information if needed.

    31. Click **Insert** → **Load Family** from the *Ribbon* (Figure 8-2.12).

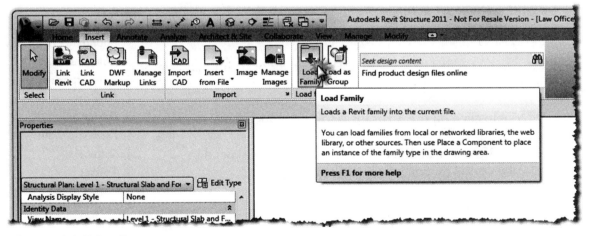

FIGURE 8-2.12 Loading content

Revit *Structure* brings you to the *Imperial Library* content location on your computer's hard drive. This content should have been installed with the Revit *Structure* application. If not, it can be downloaded from Autodesk.com.

> *FYI: Revit provides two major sets of content: Imperial (feet and inches) and Metric.*

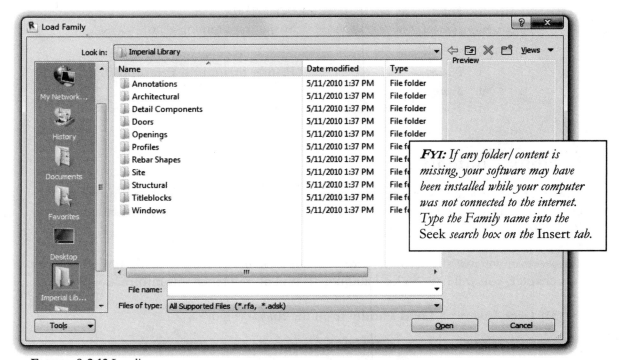

FIGURE 8-2.13 Loading content

Most everything needed by the structural engineer or technician is in the *Structural* folder.

Structural folder

32. Double-click on the **Structural** folder to open it.

Notice the subfolders listed in the *Structural* folder are named to describe each one's contents; see list to right.

First, you will load a steel column.

33. Double-click the **Columns** folder to open it.

Notice the *Columns* folder is also broken down further into types of material; see list to right.

Columns folder

34. Double-click the **Steel** folder to open it.

You now have the choice of several types of steel column *Families* (Figure 8-2.14). Even though there are only eleven *Families* listed here, they represent hundreds of column sizes. Each column has several *Types* defined for the various standard sizes available in the USA.

> ***FYI:*** *A* Type *is a group of parameters with specific values entered for a parametric family. See Chapter 16 for more on Families and Types.*

Most *Families* load all the *Types* associated with them. For example, a table might have three sizes, each defined as a type. When the table is loaded into a project, all three types are loaded and are available for use by the designer.

With steel shapes, however, there are way too many *Types* to have them all loaded into the project. If they were, the file would be bogged down with excess data and it would make finding the sizes you need more difficult.

Revit uses **Type Catalogs** to deal with *Families* that have a large set of *Types*. A *Type Catalog* is simply a list that is provided just below loading the family, from which you can choose one or more *Types* to be loaded from the family. Other *Types* can be added later at any time.

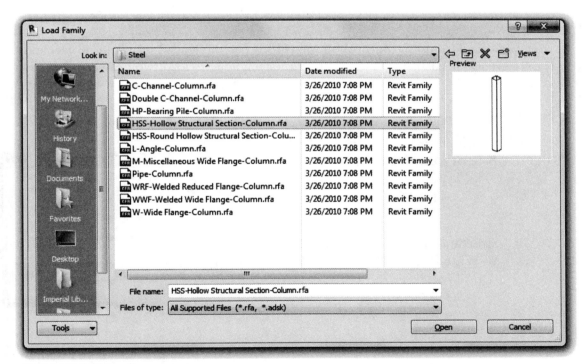

FIGURE 8-2.14 Loading content

35. Double-click the **HSS-Hollow Structural Section-Column.rfa** file.

You should now see the *Type Catalog*.

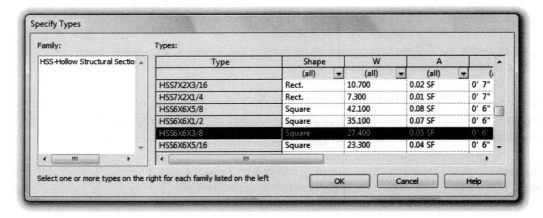

36. Scroll down and select the type name: **HSS6x6x3/8**.

37. Click **OK** to load it.

>   *TIP: Holding the **Ctrl** key allows you to select multiple Type names from the Type Catalog.*

You now have the **Hollow Structural Shape (HSS)** column loaded into your project and ready to be used as needed. You will use the same technique to load two beams and two bar joists.

38. Use the techniques just described load the following content:

> a. Structural → Framing → Steel →
>   **K-Series Bar Joist-Rod Web.rfa**
>   i. Types:
>   - 16k5
>   - 26k9
>
> b. Structural → Framing → Steel →
>   **W-Wide Flange.rfa**
>   i. Types:
>   - W24x55
>   - W30x90

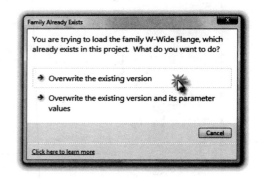

Any time a family already exists in a project, Revit gives you a prompt asking if you want to overwrite the version in the project, which may have been changed.

39. Click **Overwrite the existing version**.

40. **Save** your law office project.

Exercise 8-3:
Grids, Columns and Beams

In this exercise you will finally start placing some structural elements within the law office model. First, you will start with the grid layout; structural engineers do this with several rules-of-thumb in mind and experience. Once the grid is laid out with total spans and maximum depths of structural elements in mind, the columns can be placed. Finally, in this exercise, you will place the beams which span between the columns.

You will wrap this exercise up by creating a 3D view that only shows the building's structural elements. This is handy when the structural designer or technician wants to visualize and validate the structural model without the other building elements obscuring the view.

Location of Grids, Columns and Beams in Exterior Walls:

Placing a grid is simple and has been covered in one of the introductory chapters (see Exercise 3, Lesson 3-1). You will not align and lock these grids to the exterior wall as was done in that chapter because the grid line does not fall directly on any of the lines within the wall. The image below shows the typical location of the grid line relative to the exterior wall. *See the next page for a few comments regarding the image below.*

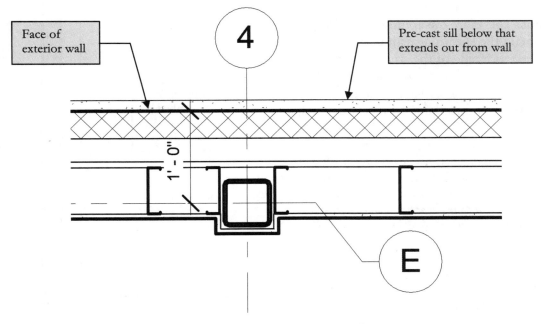

FIGURE 8-3.1 Typical location of column in exterior wall

Notice in Figure 8-3.1 that the wall has an outermost line which represents a precast concrete sill; this can also be seen in Figure 8-3.2. Use caution when dimensioning to this wall, ensuring you do not pick this line rather than the main exterior face. This element within the wall is called a *Sweep*. Unfortunately they cannot be hidden from the floor plan view, so you have to work around them.

Looking at Figure 8-3.2 one more time, notice the beams line up on the grids in addition to the columns. Therefore the columns are also positioned to maintain the sheathing as it passes by the studs on the exterior side of the studs. As you can see, the beam just fits behind the sheathing. If the column were any closer to the exterior, the beams would poke out into the cold, or warm, air space.

> *FYI: In this tutorial you are using a prebuilt wall with several features in order to move things along and make for a nice looking building. However, it would be a good idea to provide rigid insulation on the exterior side of the studs for a more uniform insulation barrier at the floor edges and structural locations.*

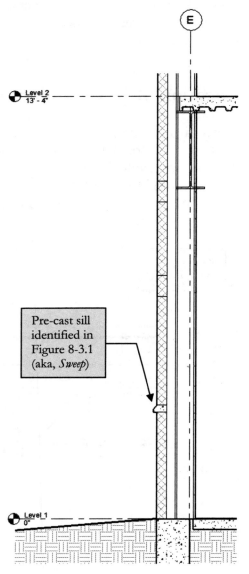

Pre-cast sill identified in Figure 8-3.1 (aka, *Sweep*)

FIGURE 8-3.2
Typical exterior wall – notice profile

Laying Out the Grids:

You are now ready to start laying out the grids.

1. **Open** your law office using Revit *Structure*.

Next, you will temporarily switch to the architectural floor plan view so you can see the architect's exterior walls, which are needed in order to properly place the grids.

2. Switch to the **Architectural Level 1** floor plan view.

3. Use the *Grid* tool. See page 3-3, if needed, for more information.

    a. The *Grid* tool is identical in functionality across the Revit platform.

4. Layout the grid as shown in Figure 8-3.3.

    TIP: Draw a grid using the Align tool to position it along the exterior face of the exterior wall. Do not lock the alignment. Then Move the grid 1'-0" towards the interior to properly position the grid. Do not add the dimensions at this time.

    a. Make sure the grid's start and end points align as you sketch them so they lock. When locked, they will all move together when just one grid bubble or end point is moved.

    b. Use this as an opportunity to double-check the overall dimensions of your building. Many of the grids can be laid out based on the 1'-0" distance from the exterior face of the exterior wall rule we have established. Additionally, Figure 8-3.3 shows dimensions between each grid; this can be used to locate the remaining grids and verify dimensions.

Grids are usually laid out with numbers across the top and letters along one side. A few goals a structural engineer strives for is simplicity, repetition and consistency. If the spans are the same and the loads are the same, the structural members can usually be the same, thus making it more straight-forward to design and build. However, these ideals are not always attainable for various reasons: code issues, dead load and live load variations and the architect's design.

In our project we have a design that does not afford a perfectly consistent and symmetrical grid layout due to the architect's design. This is not necessarily a bad thing, as steel can come in pretty much any length one needs. Also, on the second floor there is a law library which significantly increases the loads in that area, thus requiring deeper beams and joists.

Having various sizes on a project is still preferred over making everything the same, using more materials when not necessary and increasing the cost.

> *FYI:* In the image below (Figure 8-3.3), you can see two dimensions with the word "**TYP.**" below them. First off, this is an abbreviation which should only be used if it has been defined in an abbreviation list somewhere in the set of documents. This abbreviation means "TYPICAL", and when used like this, lets the contractor know that any grid line near an exterior wall should be this same dimension (1'-0" in this case).

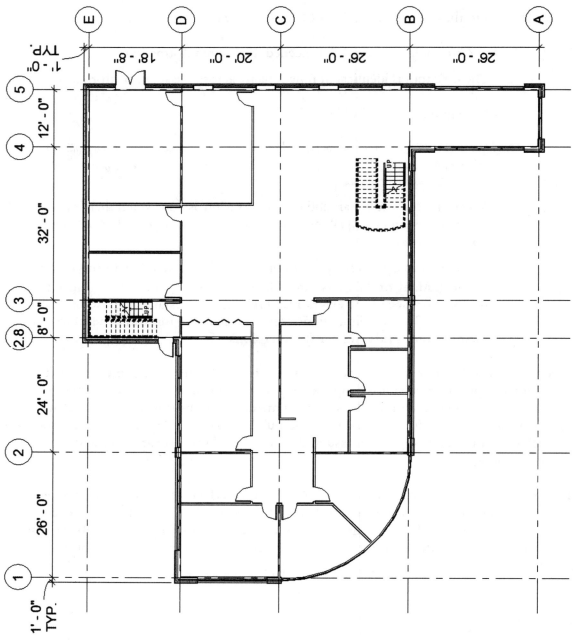

FIGURE 8-3.3
Grid numbers, letters and dimensions; image rotated on page to enlarge detail

The Various Options When a Grid Is Selected:

When a grid is selected, a **small square box** shows up at each end (Figure 8-3.4). When the box is checked, a grid bubble shows up at that end. It is possible to have a grid bubble at both ends of the grid line; it is also possible to have the bubble turned off at each end.

The **padlock** shows that you properly aligned this end of the grid with the adjacent grids while sketching it, per the previous steps. Thus, when one grid end is repositioned, they will all move together. If one needed to move it apart from the others, you simply click on the *Padlock* to unlock it.

The **3D symbol** means, if you reposition the grid, the 3D plane this grid represents will move and possibly affect other views. If you click the 3D symbol, it becomes a 2D symbol and only the current view is adjusted. This only relates to changing the overall length of the grid in a view(s). If the grid is ever moved (in the other direction), the grid will always instantly update in all views; it is not possible for the same grid to be in two contradicting locations.

The small **circle grip** at the end of the grid line is what you click and drag on to reposition the end of the grid, the length. This can be hard to select if you are not zoomed in far enough.

Finally, the small **"break line"** symbol allows the grid head to be offset from the main grid line (see example in Figure 8-3.1). This is helpful when two grids are close to each other and would otherwise overlap. This option is often accidentally selected when trying to reposition the grid when zoomed out too far. If this happens, click *Undo*, zoom in and try again.

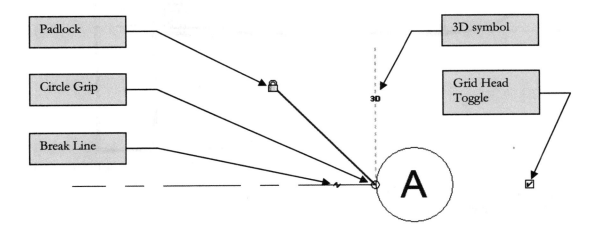

FIGURE 8-3.4
Various options when a grid line is selected

Grids are actually 3D planes that will show up in all views, plan, elevation and section, when a view's *Cut Plane* passes through a grid line plane. This will be covered more later, but for now you will simply explore the results.

5.   Switch to the **Level 2 Architectural Floor Plan** view.

Notice the grids appear (Figure 8-3.5). Later, when you study elevations and sections, you will see grids automatically show up in those views as well.

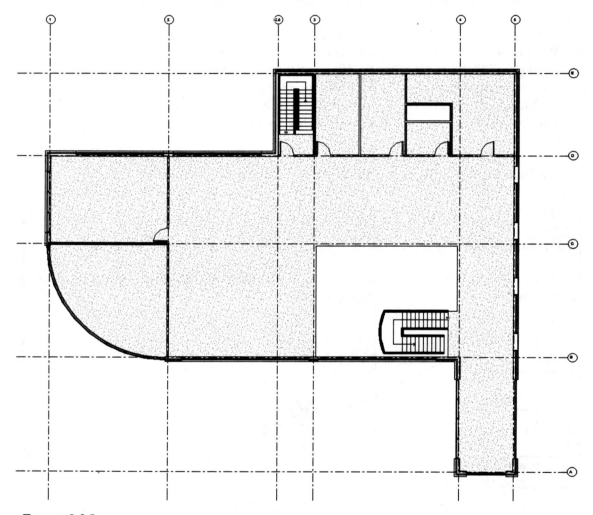

FIGURE 8-3.5
Level 2 Architectural Floor Plan view; grids automatically show up

Adding Columns:

Now that the grids have been placed you can begin to add structural columns; these columns will run from the Level 1 slab up to the roof. When modeling in Revit, you often need to model things the way they would be built. So, if the column size changed, you would need to stop and start a new column where the size change occurred. Say, for example, a tall building might have smaller and smaller columns the closer you get to the top because the load is getting lighter. Another consideration is column heights; they can only be so long before they do not fit on a truck; column splits are usually a few feet above the floor level.

6. Switch to the **Level 2 – Structural Framing Plan.**

7. Zoom in to the *intersection* of Grids **2** and **C**.

8. From the *Ribbon*, select **Home → Structure → Column.**

   a. Select the upper part of the split button, which selects *Structural Column* rather than *Architectural Column.*

9. Set the *Type Selector* to **HSS6x6x3/8** (Figure 8-3.6).

   a. *Under family name:*   HSS-Hollow Structural Section-Column

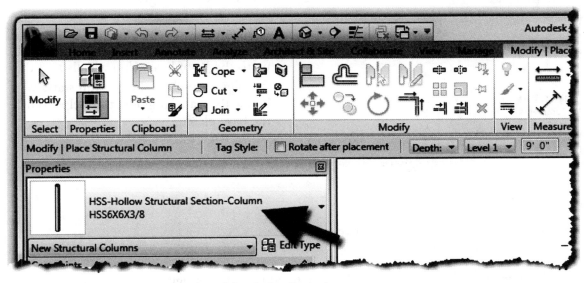

FIGURE 8-3.6 Options selected for placing first column

10. Click, using **Snaps**, at the intersection of Grids **2** and **C**.

You have now added a structural column to the model! This column will show up in all views of the project. Next you will look at a few properties related to the column you just placed, before placing the remaining columns.

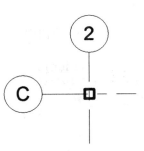

The first thing to note about columns is that they are placed from the top down, rather than the bottom up like walls. This is why you were instructed to switch to Level2, rather than Level 1. Notice, back in Figure 8-3.6, that the depth of the column is listed on the *Options Bar* rather than the height. Next, you will view the new column's properties to see this.

11. **Select** the new column in the **Level 2 Structural Plan** view.

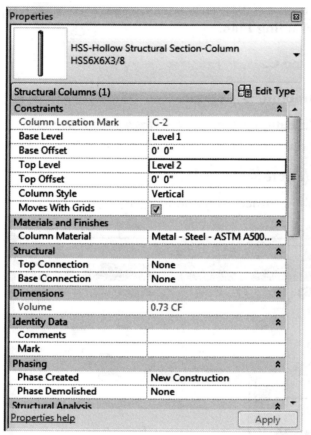

Note the information listed in the *Properties Palette*.

Notice, in Figure 8-3.7, that the *Base Level* is set to <u>Level 1</u>, per the *Options Bar* when placed, and the *Top Level* is set to <u>Level 2</u> per the current view.

Also, Revit is keeping track of the grid lines when the column falls directly on them. When "Moves With Grids" is checked, the columns will automatically follow a relocated grid.

Next you will change the *Top Level* to <u>Roof</u> so the column fully extends from <u>Level 1</u> up to the <u>Roof</u> level. You will also set the *Base Offset* to -8″ so the column starts below the slab-on-grade; this helps to hide the base plate.

FIGURE 8-3.7 Instance properties for selected column

12. Change the *Base Offset* to **-8″**. Be sure to add the minus sign.

13. Change the *Top Level* to **Roof**.

14. Click **Apply** or simply move your cursor back into the drawing window.

This new column will now show up on the **Level 2** architectural plan as well as the **Roof** structural plan. You will now add the remaining columns to the **Level 2 – Structural Framing Plan** view.

15. Place twenty additional columns.

    a. See Figure 8-3.8.

    b. A temporary circle has been added at each column location to help highlight them. Do not add this circle.

    c. Do not change the column height; this will be done later using the *Filter* tool.

    d. Notice not all grid intersections have a column.

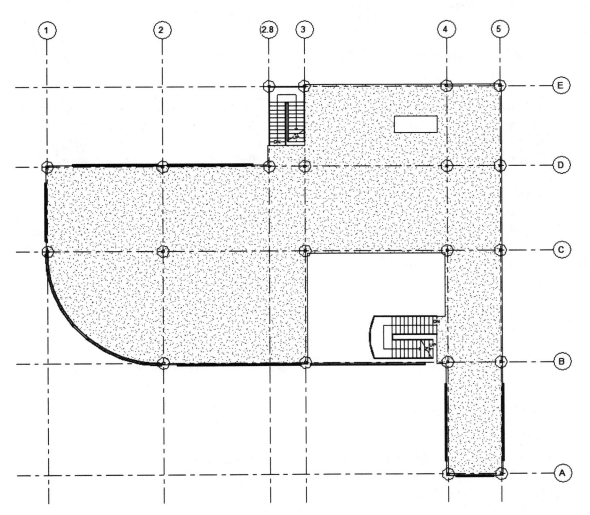

FIGURE 8-3.8 Level 2 – Structural Framing Plan; columns added

16. With all 21 columns placed, drag a selection window around the entire drawing which will select everything in the view.

Notice the total number of items that are currently selected is listed in the lower right. Immediately to the left of that is the *Filter* icon. The *Filter* tool allows you to narrow down your selection to a specific group of elements (i.e., doors, walls, columns, etc.). You will explore this next.

17. Click the ***Filter*** icon at the lower right corner of the window; see Figure 8-3.9.

18. Click the ***Check None*** button; see Figure 8-3.10.

FIGURE 8-3.9
Filter icon and number of elements selected

19. Check the **Structural Columns** category; see Figure 8-3.10.

Clicking *Check None* and then selecting what you want is often faster than individually unchecking all the categories you do not want.

Notice a total count break down is listed to the right of each category. Only categories that have selected elements are listed; as you can see *Doors* is not listed, but would be if any were selected.

20. Click **OK** to close the *Filter* dialog and change what is currently selected.

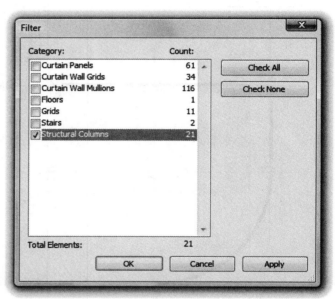

FIGURE 8-3.10
Filter dialog; various elements selected

Note that the lower right corner of the application window indicates that only 21 elements are now selected. Now that you have filtered elements down to just the *Structural Columns*, you can easily change the top and base settings.

21. Per steps 12-14, do the following to the selected columns:

    a. Set the *Base offset* to **-8″**.

    b. Set the *Top Level* to **Roof**.

The columns have been placed, as previously mentioned, based on maximum spans for the beams and joists and the architectural design. Often, the architects will agree to move their walls to accommodate a "cleaner" structural system layout; cleaner meaning whole foot dimensions without inches or fractions, standard bay sizes. A bay here is an area enclosed by four grids.

This tutorial started with the architectural walls on the correct location, so you will not have to move any walls to account for the newly added structural elements.

Controlling Visibility:

In this case, just before placing your first beam, you decide you want to turn off the curtain wall (i.e., glass openings) in the plan view to reduce confusion. These were not turned off by the *View Template* you had previously applied to this view.

22. In the **Level 2 – Structural Framing Plan**, type **VV**.

23. Check **Show categories from all disciplines**. (See Figure 8-3.11.)

24. Uncheck the three "**Curtain**" categories. (See Figure 8-3.11.)

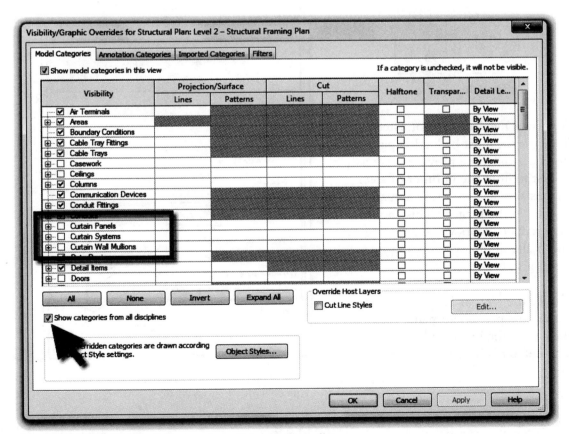

FIGURE 8-3.11 Visibility dialog; turning off the curtain walls

Placing Beams:

Now that the columns are placed, you can start adding beams between them. For now you will place them directly below the floor. However, later the vertical position of the beam will be adjusted downward when a bar joist is bearing on it (more on all this later). The first thing you will do is load a tag which will display the beam size for each member. The tag is added automatically as you model the structural framing members.

25. Per the steps outlined in the previous exercise, load the following family: Annotation\Structural**Structural Framing Tag.rfa**.

26. Zoom in on Grid line **D**, between Grids **1** and **2**.

Beam

27. Select **Home → Structure → Beam**.

28. Select **W24x55** from the *Type Selector*; see Figure 8-3.12.

   a. Make sure **Tag on Placement** is selected on the *Ribbon*.

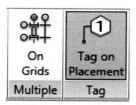

Any sizes needed, but not listed in the *Type Selector*, must be loaded per the instructions in the previous exercise. It is best to limit the number of steel shapes and sizes to those actually needed in the project. This should help reduce errors when selecting sizes and make finding what you want easier and faster.

Notice the *Options Bar* in the image below; the placement plane is where the top of the beam will be placed. The default is based on the current view.

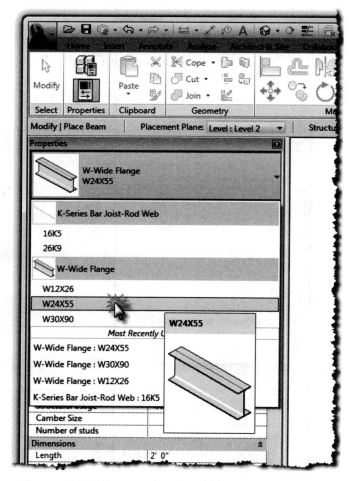

FIGURE 8-3.12 Beam tool active; picking a size via the type selector

Next, you will simply click at the midpoint of each column to place the beam. Because there is not an *Offset* option on the *Options Bar*, you will adjust the vertical position of the beam after it is placed.

29. Click at the midpoint of the columns at Grid intersections **D/1** and **D/2**.

The beam will be created and appear as shown below in Figure 8-3.13. Notice a tag was placed above the beam which indicates its size. This is because "Tag" was selected on the *Ribbon* when the beam was being placed into the model.

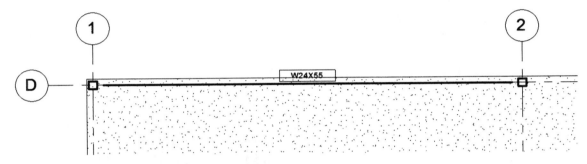

FIGURE 8-3.13 First beam placed

30. Press the **Esc** key twice or click **Modify** to deactivate the *Beam* tool.

It has been decided that the floor will be concrete over metal deck, at a total of 5½″. The floors drawn by the architects, or you in Chapter 7, will be refined in the next chapter. This anticipated thickness will be used to reposition the beam vertically. Currently the top of the beam aligns with the top of the floor.

Additionally, some beams support bar joists, which in turn support the floor. The beams which support bar joists need to be lowered to accommodate the thickness of the bar joist at the bearing location. The beams which do not support bar joists, perhaps for frame rigidity, shear and edge of slab conditions, need to be directly below the slab.

The two typical beam conditions can be seen in the sections shown in Figures 8-3.14 and 8-3.15. Also, a snapshot of the completed structural framing plan shows the direction the joists are spanning (Figure 8-3.16).

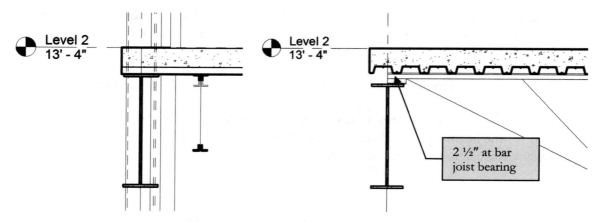

FIGURE 8-3.14 Beam parallel to bar joist   **FIGURE 8-3.15** Beam supporting bar joist

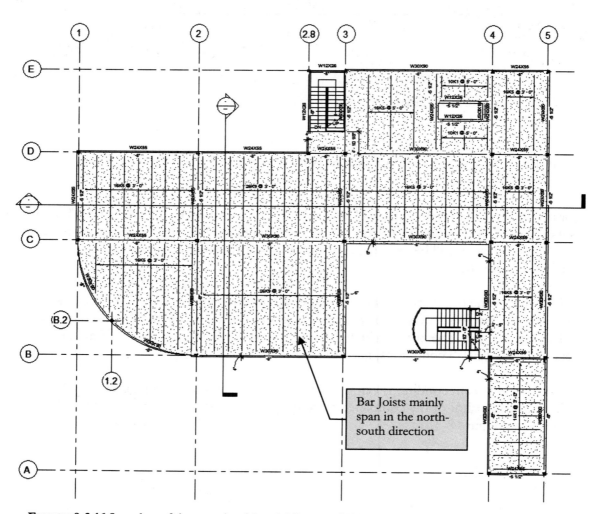

FIGURE 8-3.16 Snapshot of the completed Level 2 Structural Framing Plan, for reference only at this point. Note the direction of the bar joists which support the floor.

The image below shows the column at the intersection of Grid 1 and D; this is typically referred to as Grid 1/D.

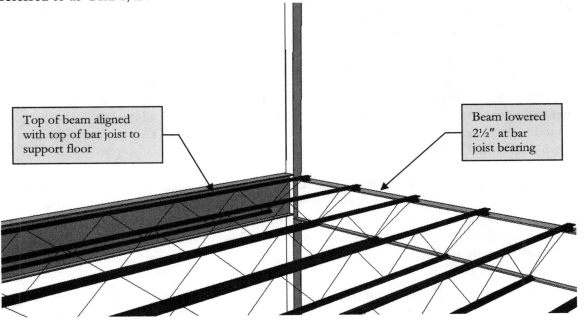

Top of beam aligned with top of bar joist to support floor

Beam lowered 2½" at bar joist bearing

FIGURE 8-3.17 Perspective view of structural framing at Grid 1/D

Now that you know why the beam you just placed needs to be repositioned vertically, you will make that change.

31. Select the **Beam** and view its properties via the *Properties Palette* (Figure 8-3.18).

32. Change...

    a. *Start Level Offset* to **-0' 8"**

    b. *End Level Offset* to **-0' 8"**

33. Click **Apply** to commit the change.

34. With the beam still selected, see the image and comment on the next page.

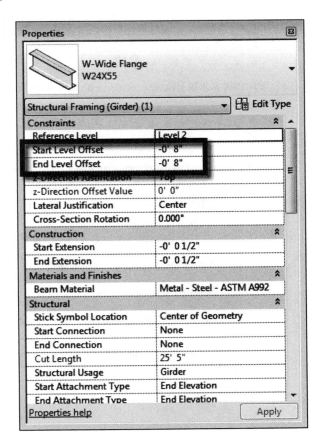

FIGURE 8-3.18 Beam properties

Note the following about the image below (Figure 8-3.19). When the beam is selected you see the elevation of the beam listed at each end. This text is blue, which means you can select it and edit it without needing to open the properties dialog. This is particularly handy for sloped beams.

However, the *Properties Palette* may be the better way to go once the bar joists have been placed. When changed via properties, Revit does not make any changes to the model until you click **Apply**. When you change the on-screen text at one end, it makes the change to that end immediately. Revit may pause as it calculates repositioning all the bar joists along a sloped beam. Then you wait again when the other end is modified. This is great when the beam does slope!

Finally, the triangular grips at each end allow you to manually adjust the one-line beam end location. When the view's *Detail Level* is set to *Coarse*, Revit will show a simplified version of the beam: a single line centered on the beam. At each end, the beam stops short of the column or wall to make the drawing more readable. This conforms to industry standard structural drafting techniques.

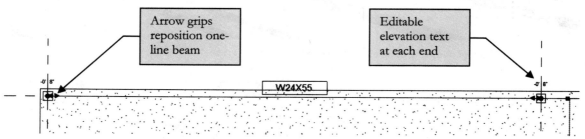

FIGURE 8-3.19 Beam selected in plan view, with "thin lines" toggled on via the *View* tab

The beam is now properly positioned to support the bar joists that will be added later.

Next you will place the remaining beams for this elevation on Level 2.

35. Place all the beams shown in Figure 8-3.20.

   a. All beams shown are at **-8″**.

   b. Select the correct beam size via the *Type Selector*.

   c. Load additional beams sizes as needed per steps previously covered.

   TIP: Place all beams and then select them using the Filter tool and change the vertical positions all at once.

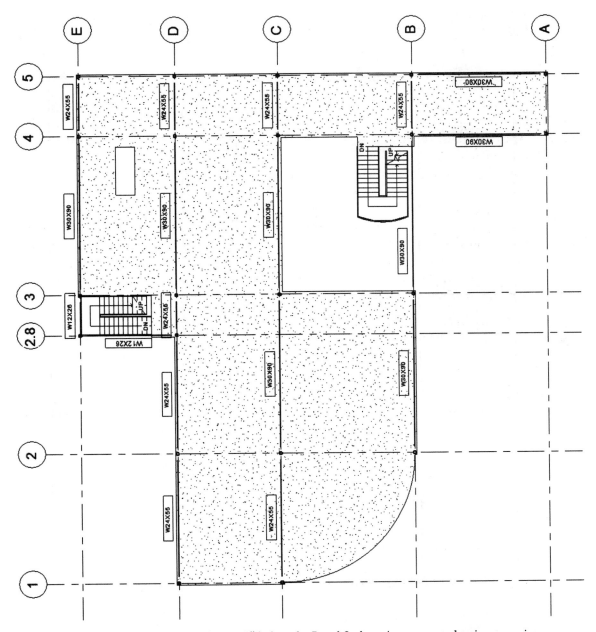

FIGURE 8-3.20 Level 2 beams with tops 8″ below the Level 2 plane; image rotated to increase size

Now that you have the beams that support bar joists placed, except at the curved wall, you will place the remaining beams which directly support the floor. Thus, the vertical offset will be 5½″, the thickness of the floor.

36. Place all the beams shown in Figure 8-3.21.

    a. All beams shown are at **-5½″**.

    b. All steps are similar to the previous step; however, *Filter* will not work because you do not want to change the -8″ beams.

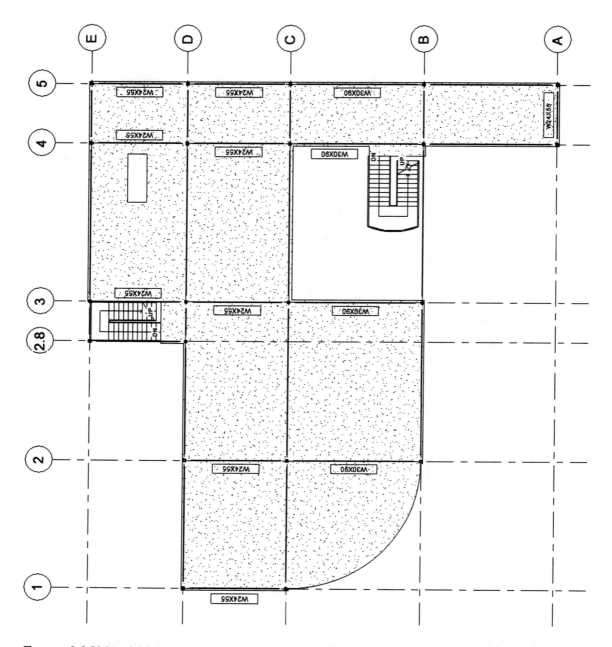

FIGURE 8-3.21 Level 2 beams with tops 5½″ below the Level 2 plane; image rotated to increase size, and the beam tags have been temporarily hidden for the beams placed in the previous step.

Beam tags are typically centered on the beam span in plan view and directly above it or to the left; this is Revit's default. Sometimes things such as notes or dimensions are in the way and the tag is not legible. It is possible to select the tag and move it (via the *Move* tool or by dragging it). The image above has a few such modifications: at both of the stairs and the floor opening in the Northeast corner of the building.

Next, you will add framing for the floor opening.

So far all your beams have been supported by columns. In the next steps you will place a few beams that are supported by other beams. Additionally, walls may support beams; the wall's parameter *Structural Usage* should be set to *Bearing* when supporting a beam; the default is non-bearing. Revit will automatically notify the user of this problem; see image to the right.

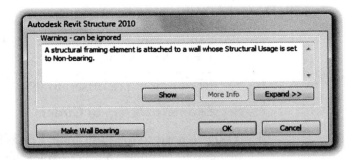

37. Place the W24x55 beam approximately as shown in Figure 8-3.22.

    a. Set the *Structural Usage* to **Girder** on the *Options Bar*.

    b. Snap to each of the previously placed beams.

    c. Revit may give you a prompt like the one shown above; simply click **OK** to ignore the warning.

    d. Move the beam down 5½" via properties. Once lowered, drag the end grip back, and then drag it to the adjacent beam again. This will cause Revit to properly connect to the adjacent beam and clean up the connection graphically.

38. Select the beam and use the temporary dimensions to position it **12'-2"** from Grid 4. Remember, you can drag the grips to reposition the temporary dimensions so it goes from the beam to Grid 4.

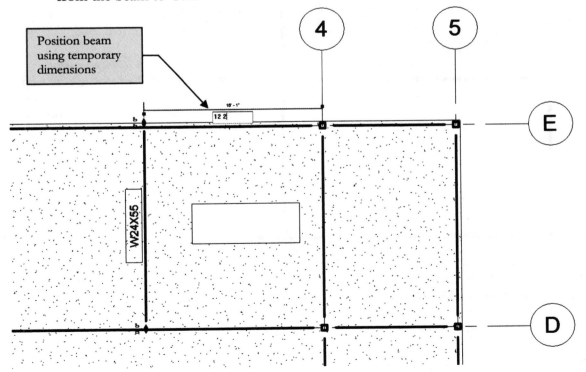

FIGURE 8-3.22 Beam is added near opening in floor and about to be repositioned via temporary dimensions

39. Draw the three remaining beams to support the floor opening:

    a.   Position the center of the beam **5 13/16″** from the floor opening using the temporary dimensions.

    b.   Set the elevation (i.e., offset) to **-5½″**.

    c.   Set the *Structural Usage* to **Girder**.

    d.   You will need to load the angle **L5x3x1/4** before placing it: *Load Family* → Structural\Framing\Steel\L-Angle.rfa

    e.   Once the elevation is set properly, drag the beam endpoint to its support so it snaps to it.

    f.   See Figure 8-3.23.

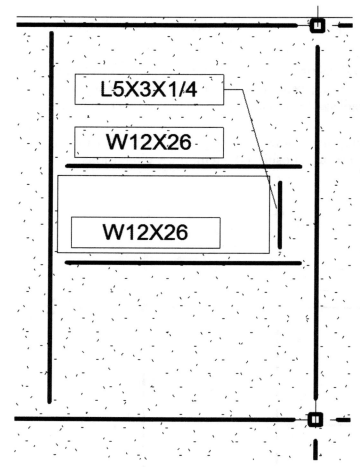

The *Structural Usage* determines the line weight of the line in *Coarse* mode. This setting also relates to structural analysis via the external programs that can import a Revit *Structure* model.

Notice, in this case, an angle is set to be a girder because it is holding up part of the floor, albeit a small portion with minimal load.

FYI: *It is possible to add a permanent dimension from the floor opening to the beam and then load the dimension. This would cause the beam to automatically move with the floor opening.*

FIGURE 8-3.23 Framing at floor opening

You will now add the curved beam, a column and two grids to finish off the Level 2 primary structure. The curved beam is too long, so a column is required at the midpoint. Rather than trying to locate the grids and column first, you will place the beam first. Then you can place the column centered on the beam, and place the grids based on the column location. Finally, you will split the beam at the new column location. This shows that things can typically be modeled in any order. There is not always one correct way to complete tasks.

40. Place the curved beam; see Figure 8-3.24.

    a. Select the **Beam** tool.

    b. On the *Ribbon*, select the **Arc** icon identified.

    c. Set the size to **W30x90**.

    d. Pick the points in the order shown.

    e. Lower the beam to -8″.

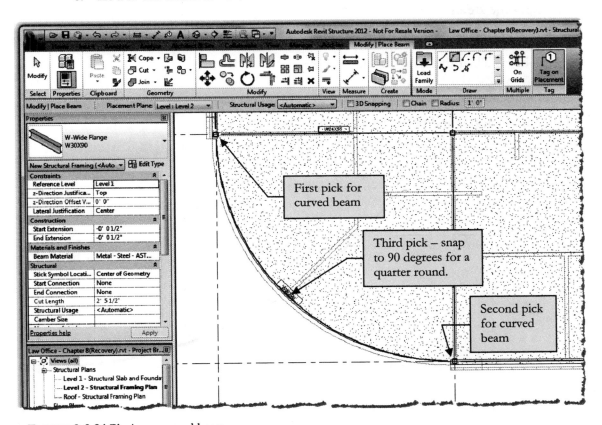

FIGURE 8-3.24 Placing a curved beam

For the next steps, see Figure 8-3.25.

41. Place a **column** at mid-span of the curved beam; use the midpoint snap.

   a. Use the same size HSS6x6x3/8 and top/bottom settings.

   b. *Bottom* at **-8"** and *Top* at **Roof**.

42. Select the column and then use the ***Rotate*** tool to rotate the column **45** degrees.

43. Add two **Grids**:

   a. Snap to the center of the column for the first point.

   b. Draw the grids as shown; adjust the endpoints.

   c. Change the grid number or letter as shown.

44. Split the **Beam**:

   a. Click **Modify → Edit → Split**.

   b. Click at the center of the column.

45. Delete the **beam tag** for the curved beam:

   a. Select it and press the Delete key.

   b. This tag will be added later.

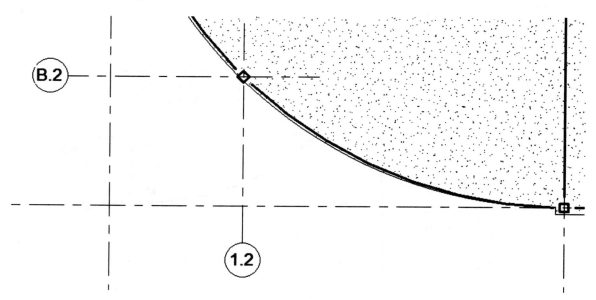

FIGURE 8-3.25 Adding a column and grids at mid-span of the curved beam

The roof is done in the same fashion as the *Level 2* floor framing. This information will be automatically added in the next chapter's file.

Exercise 8-4:
Floors and Bar Joist Layout

With the grids, columns and beams laid out, you can now focus on the floor and the structure that holds it up: the steel bar joists. The structural template has a few floor systems ready to go, and you already imported them into your project. In order for you to better understand how the floors work in Revit, you will modify the architectural floor previously created to have the proper structural representation. This process also illustrates that the architect's Revit geometry, from Schematic Design or Design Development phases, does not have to be discarded.

Level 2 Floor Construction:

Here you will modify the architect's Level 2 floor element to have the correct structural thickness and metal deck which spans the correct direction: perpendicular to the joists. If you recall, a temporary placeholder was added to the floor to represent the anticipated bar joist depth. This placeholder will be removed as the actual bar joists are about to be drawn.

1. **Open** the law office model, if not already open.

2. Load the following family: Profiles\Structural**Form Deck_Composite.rfa**.

3. Switch to **Level 2 – Structural Framing Plan**, if needed.

4. Select the floor element; use the *Filter* tool if needed.

5. View the selected floor's type properties, by clicking **Edit Type** from the *Properties Palette*.

6. Select **Edit**, next to the *Structure* parameter.

7. Make the following changes to the floor types structure (Figure 8-4.1):

    a. Select Row 2 and change the thickness from 4″ to **5½″**.

    b. Select Row 5 and **Delete** the 1′-2″ thick finish layer.

    c. Change the Function of Row 3 to **Structural Deck [1]**.

    d. Once the previous step has been done, you now have access to the *Structural Deck Properties*. Do the following:
        i. *Deck Profile:*   **Form Deck_Composite 1½″ x 6″**
        ii. *Deck Usage:*   **Bound Layer Above**

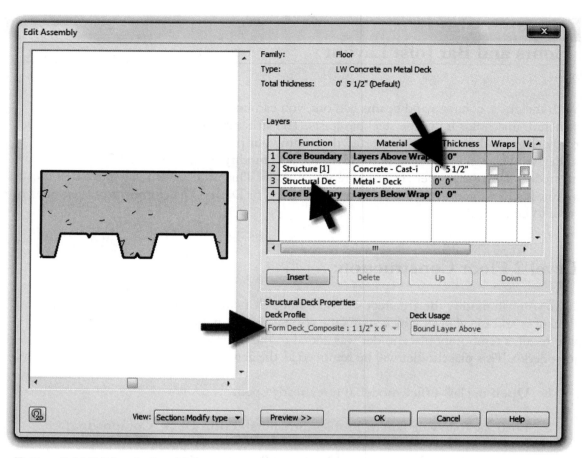

FIGURE 8-4.1 Editing the Level 2 floor construction

Notice in the preview above, the profile of the metal deck is visible in the preview window. It is important to show this profile in sections and details so the contractor knows which way the decking should be installed. The metal decking is only strong in one direction; that is the direction in which the flutes run. In the other direction the metal deck can actually bend to conform to a curved beam or roof. As you will see in a moment, Revit has a way in which you can specify the direction the decking runs.

In addition to selecting a deck profile, you also have a *Deck Usage* option in the lower right. The current setting is "bound layer above" which makes the metal deck exist within the overall thickness of the layer directly above it. (Only one exists in this example; it is concrete). The other option for *Deck Usage* is "standalone deck". This options makes the metal deck exist separately from the layer above; see the image to the right.

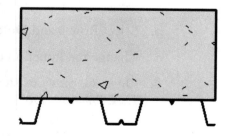

8. Select **OK** twice to close the open dialog boxes.

Next, you will add a *Span Direction* symbol which is used to indicate the direction the metal deck spans. The floor placed by the architects (in Revit *Architecture*) is an *Architectural Floor*. You will need to change it to a *Structural Floor* before it can be tagged. This is done by simply checking a box in the *Instance Properties* dialog box for the floor.

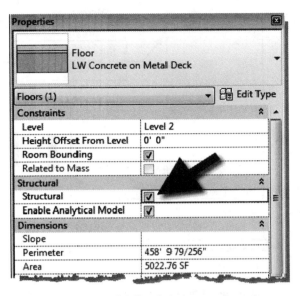

FIGURE 8-4.2 Level 2 floor's instance properties

9. **Select** the *Level 2* floor.

10. View its *Instance Properties* via the ***Properties Palette***.

11. **Check the box** next to the *Structural* parameter (Figure 8-4.2).

12. Click **Apply**.

13. Load the following family: Annotation\Structural**Span Direction.rfa**

14. Select **Annotate → Symbol → Span Direction** from the *Ribbon*; see image to the right.

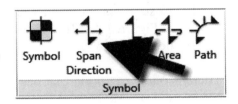

You have to select the edge of the structural floor before Revit can place the symbol.

15. **Click** the edge of the Level 2 floor.

16. **Click** anywhere within the middle of the floor (Figure 8-4.3).

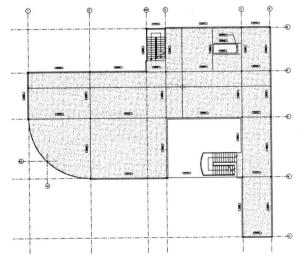

FIGURE 8-4.3 Level 2 span direction tag placed

17. Click **Modify** to finish the *Span Direction* tool.

The filled arrowheads indicate the direction the flutes run, and thus the span direction of the deck. In this example, the filled arrows should be on the left and the right. If not, you simply select the symbol and use the *Rotate* command. Also, when the symbol is selected, it can be moved so it does not obscure any text, tags or dimensions.

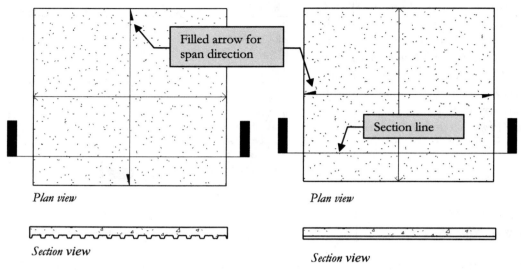

FIGURE 8-4.4 Span direction results

> *FYI:* The Span Direction *can also be adjusted while in* Sketch *mode for the floor. Click the* **Span Direction** *icon and then click a sketch line.*

The image above shows a clear example of the effect the *Span Direction* symbol has on the structural floor.

18. Ensure that the filled arrows are on the left and right, as in the example on the right in Figure 8-4.4. If not, select the symbol and use the *Rotate* tool to rotate it 90 degrees.

There is one more thing that has to be addressed before we can consider the Level 2 floor complete. Looking back at Figure 8-3.16, you can see the primary direction the bar joists span, which you will be drawing soon. This dictated the direction the metal deck should span, perpendicular to the joists. However, in the Southeastern corner of the building at the main entry, the joists turn 90 degrees to span the shorter direction and thus reduce the depth of joist and amount of steel required. In this case, you need to break the floor element into two pieces so you can control the span direction independently for both areas.

19. Select the Level 2 floor element.

20. With the floor selected, click **Edit Boundary** on the *Ribbon*.

Edit
Boundary

21. Modify the floor boundary so it stops at Grid **B**, as shown in Figure 8-4.5.

   a. Use *Trim* and *Delete* to edit the boundary.

   > *TIP:* Copy the linework for the portion of floor to be removed. This can then be pasted into the sketch of the new floor to be created in the next steps.

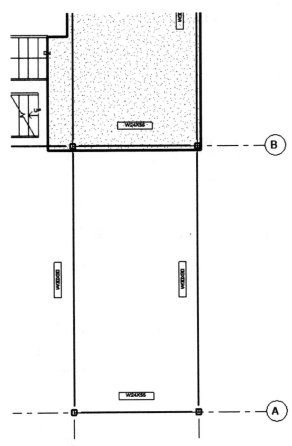

FIGURE 8-4.5 Revised floor boundary

22. Click **Finish Edit Mode** once the boundary has been updated; click **NO** to both prompts.

The area between Grids A and B does not have a floor currently. You will create a new floor element for this area and adjust the Span Direction symbol appropriately.

23. Select **Home → Structure → Floor**.

24. Sketch the boundary of the floor that was just deleted, making it the same 4⅝″ from the grid line to the edge of slab.

    a. If you copied the linework to the clipboard as suggested in Step 21, you can paste it by selecting *Paste → Aligned Current to View* from the *Ribbon*.

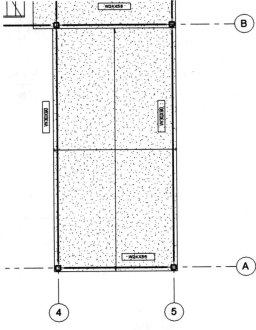

FIGURE 8-4.6 New floor added

25. Once you have an enclosed boundary with no gaps or overlaps, click **Finish Edit Mode** on the *Ribbon*.

26. Click **No** to any prompts.

Notice, when the structural floor is placed, a **Span Direction** symbol is automatically added (Figure 8-4.6).

27. If the filled arrows do not point North-South, opposite of the main floor, select it and *Rotate* it 90 degrees in either direction.

This wraps up the floor editing process. The roof is a similar process and the slab-on-grade, Level 1, is acceptable as-is.

Level 2 Floor Joists Using the Beam System Feature:

Now you will begin to place the bar joists. This is relatively easy as Revit provides a tool called *Beam Systems* that will fill an entire structural bay with bar joists, following predefined rules for spacing.

You will place bar joists in the Northwestern corner near Grids D/1. The joists will be spaced at 3'-0" O.C. (on center) with any extra space being split at each end.

28. In the **Level 2 Structural Plan** view, **zoom in** to the Northwestern corner near Grids D/1.

29. Load the family: Annotation\Structural**Structural Beam System Tag.rfa**.

30. On the *Ribbon*, select **Home → Structure → Beam System**.   ▥ Beam System

The *Ribbon* now displays the *Place Beam System* contextual tab and the *Options Bar* has several options to control what is modeled, joist size and spacing. ***NOTE:** Revit thinks of any horizontal support member as a beam; its* Structural Usage *parameter defines how it is used and* <u>Joist</u> *is one of those options.* You will be placing bar joists in the building to hold up the floor, but the *Beam System* tool will work equally well with I-joists, wide flange beams, dimensional lumber, or anything defined within the *Structural Framing* category.

31. Adjust the *Options Bar* to match Figure 8-4.7.

    a. *Beam Type (drop-down):* **16k5**

    b. *Justification (drop-down):* **Center**

    c. *Layout Rule:* **Fixed Distance**

    d. *Fixed Distance Value:* **3'-0"**

    e. *3D:* **Checked**

    f. *Walls Define Slope:* **Checked**

    g. *Tag type (drop-down):* **System**

    h. *Tag on Placement:* **Selected** (on the *Ribbon*)

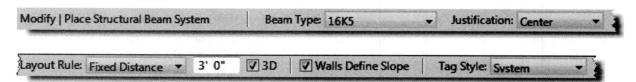

FIGURE 8-4.7 Beam system tool active; Options Bar settings

You loaded the 16k5 joist at the end of Exercise 8-2. Only families, specifically structural framing category families, loaded into the project will appear in the *Beam Type* list. If the structural member needed was not listed, you would have to click *Modify* to cancel the command and load the family.

Next you will adjust the elevation of the top of joist; the reasoning for the number you enter will be provided momentarily.

32. View the ***Instance Properties*** of the *Beam System* you are about to place via the *Properties Palette*.

33. Set the *Elevation* to **2 ½"** and click **Apply** (Figure 8-4.8).

FIGURE 8-4.8 Instance properties for Beam System

Now for the easy part: you simply click one of the perimeter beams that defines a bay. The beam you select needs to be parallel to the span of the joists as you will learn in the next step.

34. DO NOT CLICK THE MOUSE IN THIS STEP: **Hover** your cursor over the beam which runs along Grid 1 and notice the ghosted joist layout that appears; now **hover** your cursor over the Grid D beam to see the joist layout that would be created if you clicked on it.

35. **Click** the beam along Grid 1 as shown in Figure 8-4.9.

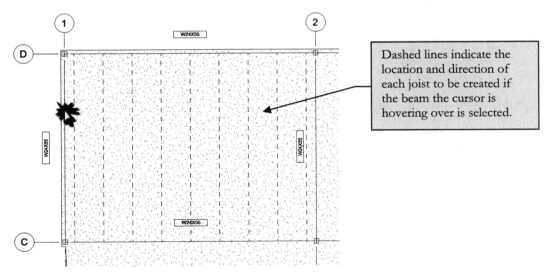

FIGURE 8-4.9 Creating a beam system for the bar joists

The *Beam System* is now created; see Figure 8-4.10. Notice the single-line representation provided for each joist with the ends stopping short of their supports to make things graphically clear; this is due to the *Detail Level* being set to *Coarse*. Also, a tag is provided indicating the joist size and spacing.

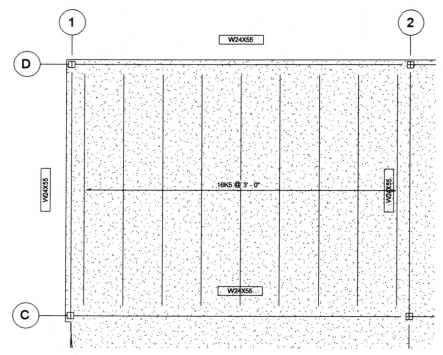

FIGURE 8-4.10 *Beam System* created

The figure below shows what things currently look like in section. You will learn how to create sections in the next chapter.

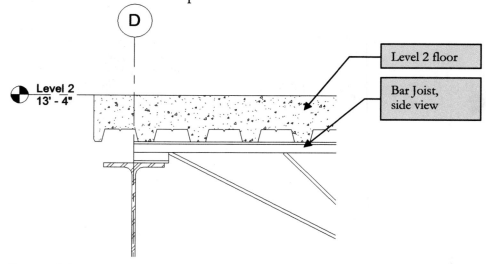

FIGURE 8-4.11 *Beam System* correctly positioned, section view

A bar joist typically only needs a minimal amount of bearing on a steel beam. However, sometimes the joist "seat", the bearing portion of the joist, needs to extend further to support the floor or another structural element. Although you will not do that in this tutorial, here is how it is done.

Each joist in the *Beam System* can be selected; it does not work if the entire *Beam System* itself is selected. Then you can view its *Instance Properties* (via the *Properties Palette*). There you may adjust the "start extension" and the "end extension". The image below has one extension set to 4″. You would have to select each joist to make this change. Having a start and end parameter allows you to individually control each end of the joist.

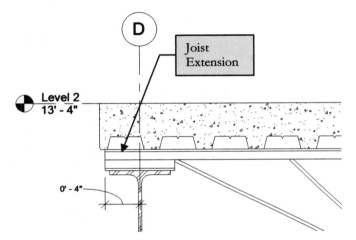

Construction	
Start Offset	0' 0"
Start Extension	0' 0"
End Offset	0' 0"
End Extension	0' 4"

FIGURE 8-4.12 Bar joist with joist extension

Now you will use the same technique to place the remaining *Beam Systems* throughout the second floor.

36. Place the remaining *Beam Systems* for the information shown in Figure 8-4.13.

    a. The bay with the curved beam will take a few minutes for the *Beam System* to be created as each joist is a different size.

    b. You should get a prompt like the one below in the curved bay area; click *Delete Type* to continue (Figure 8-4.14).

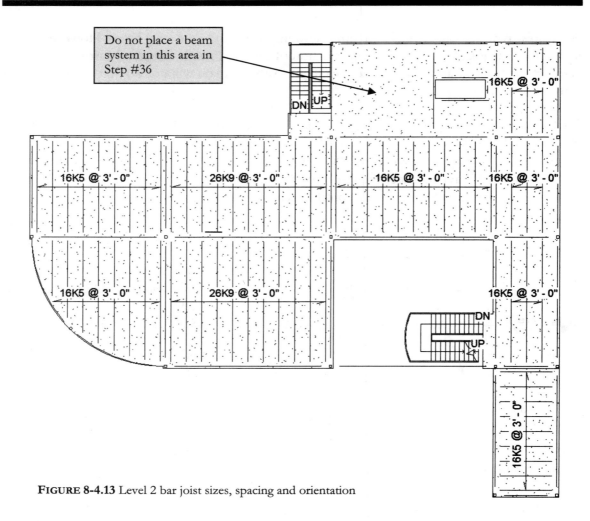

FIGURE 8-4.13 Level 2 bar joist sizes, spacing and orientation

FIGURE 8-4.14 Warning message

Sketching the Perimeter of a Beam System:

The last area you will look at is near the Northeastern corner of the building, by the floor opening. You cannot use the one-click method here, as Revit will fill in the area from Grid 3 all the way past the floor opening to Grid 4. In this case, Revit provides a way in which you can sketch the perimeter of the *Beam System*.

37. Select the **Beam System** tool.

Sketch
Beam System

38. Click the **Sketch Beam System** button from the *Ribbon*.

Rather than sketching new lines from scratch, you will use the *Pick Supports* options which will force you to pick the beams that will define the perimeter of the *Beam System*.

39. Click the **Pick Supports** icon in the *Draw* panel of the *Ribbon* (Figure 8-4.15).

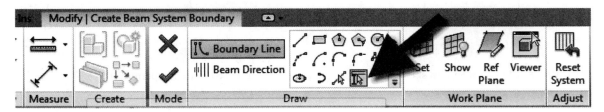

FIGURE 8-4.15 Ribbon: Beam system tool while in Sketch mode

Next, you will pick the four beams that define the perimeter of the area to receive joists.

40. Pick a vertical beam first (see highlighted beam in Figure 8-3.16); this defines the beam span. The beam span is defined by picking a beam parallel to the desired joist span.

41. Pick the other three beams to define the bay (Figure 8-4.17).

42. Use **Trim** to clean up the four corners.

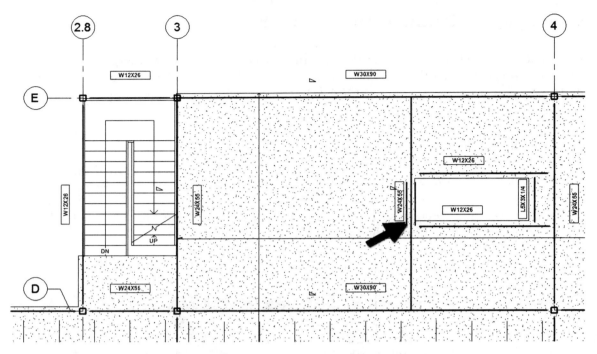

FIGURE 8-4.16 Beam System sketch mode; pick supports and trim used to define perimeter

43. Verify the following settings via the *Properties Palette*:

    a. *Elevation =*   **2 ½"**

    b. *3D =*   **checked**

    c. *Joist size =*   **16k5**

    d. *Layout rule:*   **Fixed Distance**

    e. *Fixed Spacing:* **3'-0"**

    f. See Figure 8-4.8.

44. Click **Apply** if any changes have been made to the *Properties Palette*.

45. Click **Finish Edit Mode** (green check mark) to have Revit place the joists.

The *Beam System* is now placed as desired in your Building Information Model (BIM), as you can see in Figure 8-4.17. You now only have two small areas to the East in which to place joists and Level 2 is then complete.

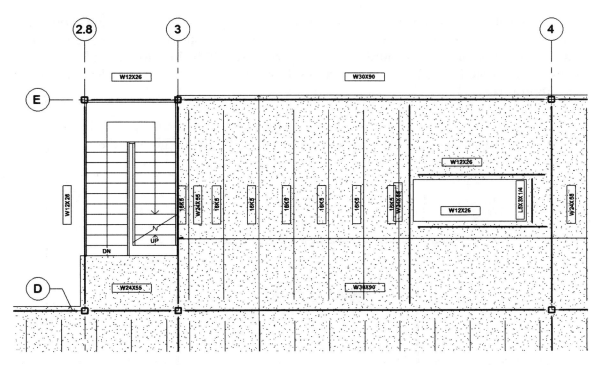

FIGURE 8-4.17 Beam System completed using the manual sketch technique

Revit does not give you the option to tag the *Beam System*. It only tags the individual beams, joists. This makes the plan cluttered, so we will delete them. In the next section you will learn how to manually add beam and beam system tags when needed.

46. Select each joist tag and delete it by pressing the *Delete* key; do not delete the beam tags from the previous exercise.

   a. Select each tag one at a time and delete it, or select them all first, using the *Ctrl* key, and then delete them all at once.

A tag can be deleted at any time without worries. A tag only reports information contained within the element it is tagging; it contains no information itself. The point is, deleting a tag will not cause any information to be eradicated from the BIM. As you will see in the next exercise, tags can be added manually at any time.

Finally, you will place bar joists in the last two areas adjacent to the floor opening. You will need to load a new, smaller, bar joist size. If you tried to place one of the larger joists in this area you would get an error because the snap is too short and the joist too deep; Revit cannot build a valid joist given such conditions. Given the short span, the smaller joists are more appropriate.

47. Using techniques previously discussed, i.e., loading content and creating beam systems via sketching, place the remaining joists shown in Figure 8-4.18.

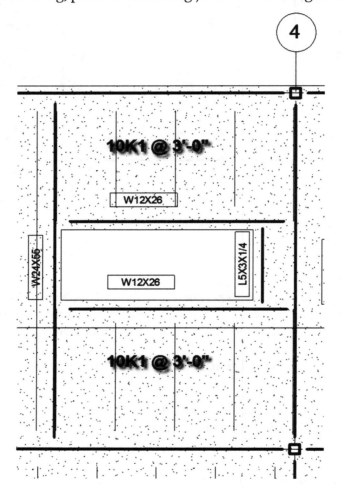

FIGURE 8-4.18 Beam Systems adjacent to the floor opening

The roof layout is pretty much the same process, with different joist sizes and spacing depending on the design requirements. The joists are often smaller and spaced further apart on the roof. This is because the roof can bounce more compared to a floor where people would feel uncomfortable and materials such as ceramic floor tile would crack. Sometimes snow loads, a dead load, would require similarly sized and spaced structural members.

Exercise 8-5:
Foundations and Footings

This exercise will look at developing the building's below-grade structural elements, namely the foundations and footings. This information will be modeled and documented in the **Level 1 Structural Plan** view previously created.

1. **Start** Revit *Structure.*

2. Switch to the **Level 1 – Structural Slab and Foundation** plan view.

Setting Up the View:

The first thing you will do is set up the view; a few things need to be turned off. Plus, you will use a feature called "underlay" which lets you superimpose another plan over your current plan view. One trick here is that you can use the same level to see the architectural walls temporarily. You will use the exterior architectural walls to locate the foundation walls.

3. Type **VV** (do not press *Enter*) to access the *Visibility/Graphic Overrides* dialog for the current view.

4. Make the following changes to the *Model Categories* tab:

    a. **Check** *Show categories from all disciplines*

    b. **Uncheck** (i.e., turn off the visibility of):
       i. Curtain Panels
       ii. Curtain Systems
       iii. Curtain Wall Mullions
       iv. Floor
       v. Stairs

5. Click **OK.**

6. With nothing selected and no commands active, draw your attention to the *Properties Palette*, which is displaying the *View Properties* for the current view.

    a. Type **PP** to display the *Properties Palette* if it is not visible.

7. In the *Properties Palette*, set *Underlay* to **Level 1.**

8. Make sure *Underlay Orientation* is set to **Plan.**

9. Click **Apply** to apply the changes.

The plan should now look like Figure 8-5.1. Notice all the architectural walls for Level 1 are showing plus the Level 2 bar joists.

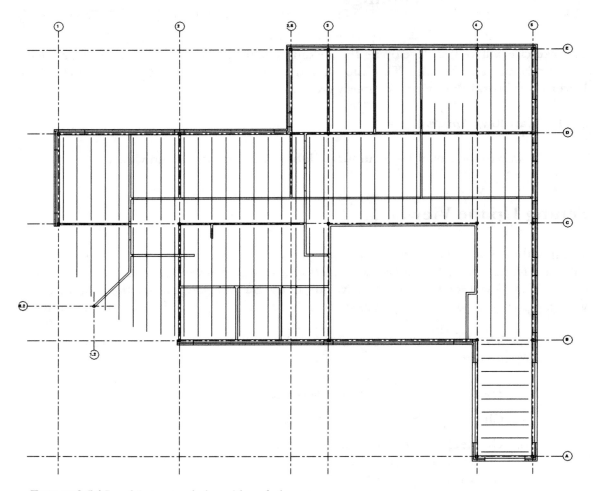

FIGURE 8-5.1 Level 1 structural plan with underlay setup

Foundation Walls:

Now you will draw the foundation walls around the perimeter of the building. Foundation walls are drawn using the *Wall* tool, and are drawn from the top down, like structural columns. The wall knows it is a foundation based on the *Type Parameter* <u>Function</u>, which is set to <u>Foundation</u> for the wall type you will be using.

10. Select **Home → Structure → Wall** from the *Ribbon*.

11. Set the *Type Selector* to **Foundation – 12″ Concrete** (Figure 8-5.2).

12. Set the *Location Line* to **Finish Face: Exterior** on the *Options Bar* (Figure 8-5.2).

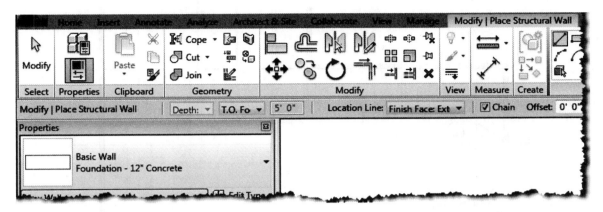

FIGURE 8-5.2 Wall tool – *Ribbon* and *Options Bar* for foundation walls

Note in the image above, the wall *Depth* is being specified. In the next step you will ensure this is set to <u>T.O. Footing</u> (T.O. = top of). This will create a parametric relationship between the bottom of the foundation wall and the *Level Datum* named <u>T.O. Footing</u>. Thus, any change made to the <u>T.O. Footing</u> Level will automatically change the depth of all the foundation walls.

13. Make sure the *Depth* is set to **T.O. Footing** on the *Options Bar* (Figure 8-5.2).

14. Begin drawing the foundation wall around the perimeter of the building (Figure 8-5.3).

  a. Start at the point shown and work in a clockwise direction; if needed, press the spacebar to flip the wall to the correct side.

  b. Use *Snaps* and pick the inside and outside corners along the architectural exterior walls which are shown via the *Underlay*.

  c. When you reach the last straight wall segment, click the arc symbol in the *Draw* panel on the *Ribbon*.

  d. Draw the curved wall to close off the perimeter.

At this point you can turn off the *Underlay* as you only needed it to locate the foundation walls along the perimeter. The remaining foundations can be placed based on the steel column locations, which will remain visible in the view even after the *Underlay* is turned off.

15. Turn off the <u>Level 1</u> *Underlay* by setting the option back to *None* in the view's *Properties*.

Your plan should now look like Figure 8-5.4, which shows the grids, columns and the newly added foundation walls.

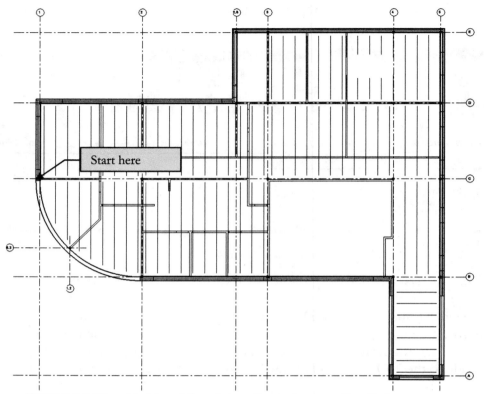

FIGURE 8-5.3 Level 1 slab and foundation plan; perimeter walls added

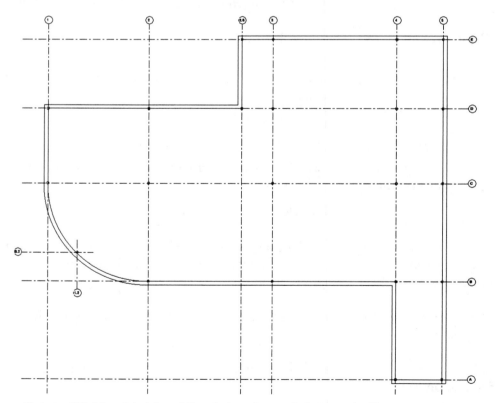

FIGURE 8-5.4 Level 1 slab and foundation plan; underlay turned off

Below Grade Concrete Columns (or Piers):

Next, you will add concrete footings below each steel column. This is done using the *Column* tool, the same one used to place the steel columns. But in this case, you will be placing concrete columns that extend below grade to footings.

Because the steel columns are not completely over the 12″ exterior foundation wall, you will have to add columns below them. These columns will be joined with the wall to properly represent the monolithic concrete pour. However, the column remains a separate element so it can be repositioned as needed.

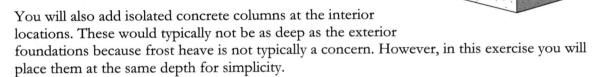

You will also add isolated concrete columns at the interior locations. These would typically not be as deep as the exterior foundations because frost heave is not typically a concern. However, in this exercise you will place them at the same depth for simplicity.

All the concrete columns will be 18″x18″ and the top will be held 8″ below the Level 1 slab. The 8″ recess is to allow the Level 1 slab to wrap around the steel column and accommodate floor finishes.

    16. Select **Home → Structural → Column** to activate the *Structural Column* tool.

After looking at the *Type Selector*, you realize the concrete column family needs to be loaded into the project.

    17. While still in the *Column* command, click the **Load Family** button on the *Ribbon*.

    18. Browse to **Structural\Columns\Concrete**.

    19. Pick **Concrete-Square-Column** from the list, select **Open**.

The family is now loaded with four *Types*: 12″x12″, 18″x18″, 24″x24″ and 30″x30″.

    20. Set the *Type Selector* to **18″x18″** Concrete-Square-Column.

    21. Make sure the *Depth* setting on the *Options Bar* is set to **T.O. Footing**.

    22. Snap to the center point of each steel column, to place a concrete column (Figure 8-5.5).

Your plan should now look like the image below (Figure 8-5.5). Notice how the column and the foundation wall automatically joined. When placing the columns, you did not have an option to lower the top of the column down 8″; you will do that next. This will create an unrealistic condition at the exterior walls that will not be addressed in this tutorial; typically, a notch or reveal would be added to make a consistent bearing area for the column and its bearing plate.

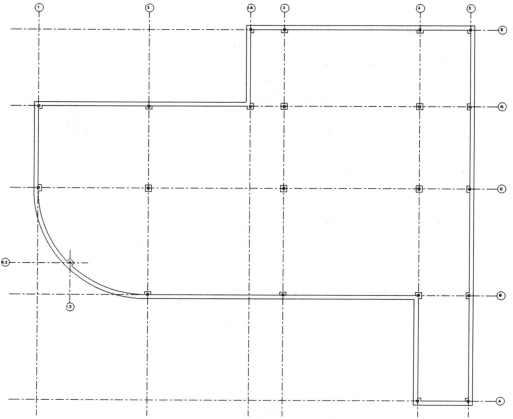

FIGURE 8-5.5 Level 1 slab and foundation plan; concrete columns added

23. Select and **Rotate** the concrete column (45 degrees) at the middle of the curved foundation wall (Figure 8-5.5).

24. Select one of the concrete columns.

25. Right-click and pick **Select all instances > In Entire Project** from the pop-up menu.

You now have all the concrete columns selected; notice the quantity of elements selected (22) is listed in the lower right.

> **WARNING:** *The "Select all instances > In Entire Project" command selected everything in the entire project, not just the current view! In this case, the current view contains all concrete columns in the project. So to be safe, you might have only selected the "Visible in View" option rather than "In Entire Project".*

26. With the concrete columns selected, note their *Instance Parameters* via the *Properties Palette.*

27. Set the *Top Offset* to **-8″**; be sure to add the minus symbol (see Figure 8-5.6).

    FYI: *When multiple elements are selected, you are changing them all at once here in the Instance Properties dialog.*

28. Click **Apply** to commit the changes.

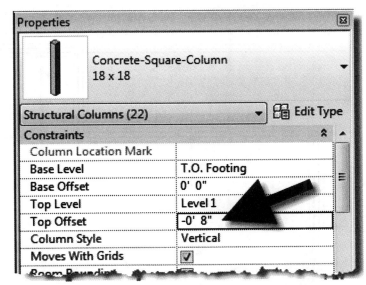

FIGURE 8-5.6
Changing top of concrete column elevation

Adding Footings (aka Foundations):

Now that you have all the below grade foundation walls and columns, you will add the footings, which spread out the load from the foundation walls on to the ground (aka, undisturbed or engineered soil). Revit provides a tool for this that nicely automates the process.

Wall Footings:

First you will add the continuous strip footing along the perimeter of the building, below the foundation wall. This footing will be 36″ wide and 12″ deep, centered on the 12″ foundation wall.

29. Select **Home → Foundation → Wall** from the *Ribbon* (see the image to the right).

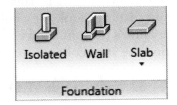

30. Make sure the *Type Selector* is set to **Bearing Footing – 36″ x 12″**.

31. Now simply click each foundation wall (Figure 8-5.7).

The footings have been added to the bottom of the foundation wall, at whatever depth it is, and centered on it. Later you will learn how to make the lines for the footings dashed.

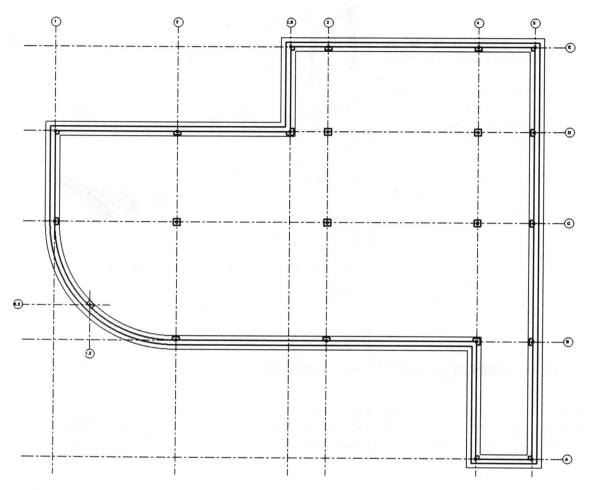

FIGURE 8-5.7 Level 1 slab and foundation plan; footings added

Isolated Footings:

Before placing the isolated footings you will switch to a different view. Revit will automatically look for a column at the point you pick and place the isolated foot at that column's bottom. However, in the **Level 1 Slab and Foundation Plan** view, it will only find the steel columns as they are the ones that pass though the Level 1 plane.

32. Switch to the **T.O. Footing** plan view.

    a. This is one of the architect's views (assuming you are the structural designer now); you can work in any view that is convenient and in your project.

Now you will add isolated footings below each column. These will be 9'-6" x 9'-6" x 1'-4". Notice the thickness varies from the strip footing. When you place isolated footings below the perimeter columns, you will want the tops to align so the bearing plane is consistent.

33. Select **Home → Foundation → Isolated** from the *Ribbon*.

Anytime the size or type you want is not listed, you need to duplicate an existing one and modify it to what you need. Next, you will make a new isolated footing type and adjust its size.

34. Click **Edit Type** via the *Properties Platte* to view the *Type Properties*.

35. Click **Duplicate**.

36. Type **9'-6" x 9'-6" x 1'-4"** and then click **OK**.

37. Adjust the *Width, Length* and *Thickness* parameters accordingly; make them match the new type name you just created. See Figure 8-5.8.

38. Click **OK**.

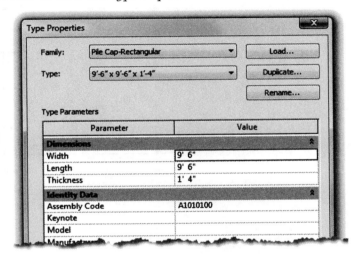

FIGURE 8-5.8 Isolated footing type properties

39. Click at the intersection of each grid line that has a concrete column.

   TIP: *Use the "At Column" option.*

40. Switch back to the **Level 1 – Structural Slab and Foundation Plan** view.

41. Make sure the *Model Graphics Style* is set to **Hidden,** via the *View Control Bar* or the *View Properties*.

The isolated footings are now shown (Figure 8-5.9). Notice how the two footings, *isolated* and *wall*, clean up automatically. Because the depth varies, a dashed line is added between them. Also, *Isolated* footings that touch each other are joined to properly represent a monolithic pour.

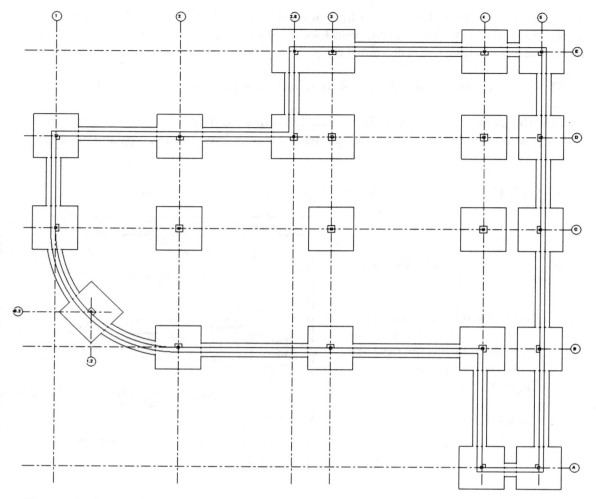

FIGURE 8-5.9 Isolated footings placed

View Range and View Depth Settings:

The final step in this exercise is to adjust the view so the footings are represented with dashed lines to distinguish them from the foundation walls. This is done with the *View Range* settings and the *Line Style* named <Beyond>.

First, you will be instructed to make the necessary changes and then an explanation will be given.

42. In the **Level 1 – Structural Slab and Foundation Plan** make sure nothing is selected and no commands are active.

43. Select **Edit** next to *View Range* in the *Properties Palette*.

44. Change the *Bottom* setting to **-1'-0"** (see Figure 8-5.10).

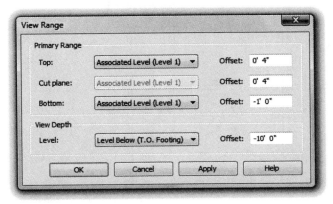

FIGURE 8-5.10 View Range settings

45. Click **OK** to close the open dialog box.

You should not yet notice any change to your view.

46. On the *Ribbon*, click **Manage → Settings → Additional Settings → Lines Styles**.

47. Expand the *Lines* row if needed, by clicking the plus symbol to the left.

48. Change the *Line Pattern* for <Beyond> to **Hidden 1/8"** (Figure 8-5.11).

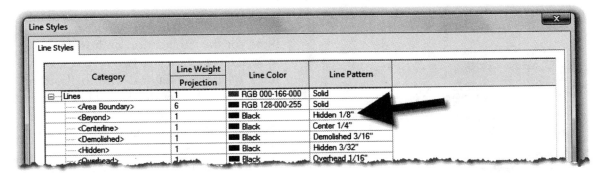

FIGURE 8-5.11 Line Style settings

49. Click **OK** to accept the changes.

Your plan should now look like Figure 8-5.12 below.

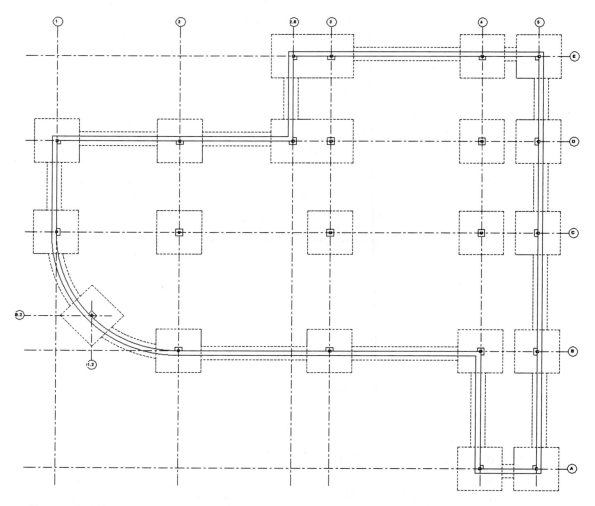

FIGURE 8-5.12 Level 1 – Structural Slab and Foundation Plan; footing now shown dashed

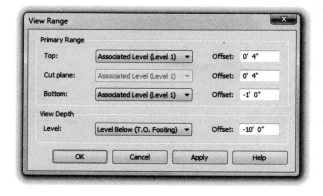

Now for the explanation on how this works. Every view has two settings, within the *View Range*, that deal with the bottom of the view: *Bottom* and *View Depth*. Often, they are both set to the same value, which is equal to the level. This is how Revit is able to show the 6th floor plan, for example, and not show everything else down to the basement, since it was told to stop looking at the level line.

Sometimes the Bottom setting is lowered to see beyond the level line in a plan view; for example, to show a recessed lobby or in the case of our example, to show the top of the concrete column.

Notice the image below which illustrates the two *View Range* items under consideration (Figure 8-5.13). The top of the concrete column is -8″ from Level 1 and the *Bottom* setting was set to -1'-0″. If the *Bottom* was set to 0'-0″ the concrete columns would not be visible in the plan view.

If the *View Depth* is set lower than the *Bottom*, in the *View Range*, the objects that occur between the bottom and the view depth, represented by the hatched area, have a special override applied to their linework. Revit has a special *Line Style* named "<beyond>" and its settings are applied to those lines.

The arrows in the image below point out the edges of elements, footings in this case, that will appear dashed due to them falling in the hatched area and the "<beyond>" line type being set to a dashed or hidden line pattern.

FYI: The *View Depth must be equal to or lower than the Bottom setting.*

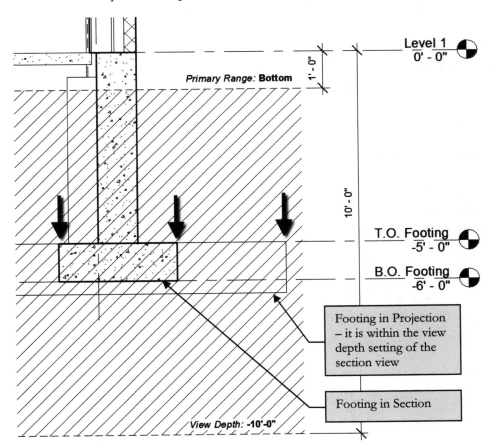

FIGURE 8-5.13 Section showing view range settings

Exercise 8-6:
Structural Annotation and Tags

In this last section specifically on Revit *Structure*, you will look at a few of the tools used to annotate the structural plans. Addition of text, dimensions and tags is an important part of the design process. Revit makes these tasks simple and efficient. All of the dimensions and tags you will add automatically display the correct information because the data is coming directly from the Revit elements being referenced.

Even though this is the only chapter specifically devoted to Revit *Structure*, it should be pointed out that many of the concepts covered in it also apply to Revit *Architecture*. For example, creating sections and elevations works the same way in all three flavors of Revit, as do the following:

- Elevations and Sections (Chapter 9)
- Placing stand-alone content (Chapter 10)
- Creating schedules (Chapter 11)
- Producing photo-realistic renderings (Chapter 14)
- Placing Views on Sheets (Chapter 15)
- Sheet index (Chapter 15)
- Creating custom Families (Chapter 16)

Dimensions:

Placing Dimensions is quick and simple in Revit; you select the *Aligned* dimension tool, select two elements you want to dimension between and click somewhere to position the dimension line and text. Anytime either of the elements move, Revit updates the dimension automatically. If either of the elements being dimensioned is deleted, the dimension is deleted. The dimension will be deleted even if the dimension is not visible in the current view. For example, if a grid is deleted in a section view, all of the dimensions to that grid will be deleted in the plan views.

Dimensions can be single or continuous; the image below shows one of each. The two 10'-0" dimensions on the bottom are one element, not two; therefore they move together and are quicker to place.

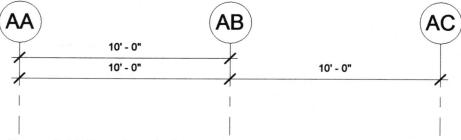

FIGURE 8-6.1 Dimensions; single or continuous

One more important thing to know about dimensions is that they are view specific; in fact, everything on the *Annotate* tab is view specific. This means the notes, dimensions and tags will only show up in the view they were created in, which makes sense; you do not want the structural beam tags showing up in the architect's floor plans or their door tags and notes about scribing a cabinet to a wall showing up in the structural plans. Only 3D elements show up in all views. Annotation is considered a 2D element.

Now you will dimension the grids in the **Level 2 – Structural Framing Plan** view.

1. **Open** your law office model using **Revit *Structure*.**

2. Switch to the **Level 2 – Structural Framing Plan** view.

3. Select **Annotate → Dimension → Aligned** from the *Ribbon*.

Aligned

4. Select Grid 1 and Grid 5 (first 2 of 3 picks required).

5. Select a spot just below the grid bubbles to locate the string of dimensions (pick 3 of 3). See Figure 8-6.2.

   a. The dimension should read **102'-0"**.

   FYI: The last pick cannot be near something that is dimensionable, as Revit will just place another witness line there rather than place the dimension. If you accidentally pick something, you pick it again to toggle that witness line off and then pick your final point away from it.

FIGURE 8-6.2 Overall dimension placed

Now you will add a second dimension line showing the major sections of the North side of the building.

6. Using the ***Aligned*** dimension tool again, pick Grid lines 1, 2.8 and 5 (first 3 of 4 picks). See Figure 8-6.3.

7. For your final pick, click near the previous dimension, but wait until you find the snap position where Revit indicates the standard distance between dimensions.

   a. The dimensions should read **50'-0"** and **52'-0"** respectively.

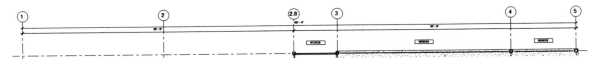

FIGURE 8-6.3 Second dimension placed

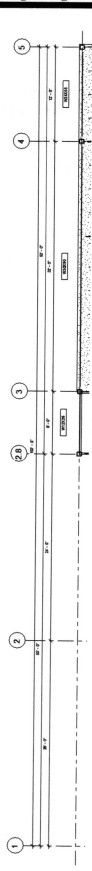

Next, you will create one more string of dimensions which locate each individual grid in the project.

8. Dimension each grid line as shown in Figure 8-6.4, placing the string at the standard spacing location.

    a. The dimensions should read, from left to right:
        i. 26'-0"
        ii. 24'-0"
        iii. 8'-0"
        iv. 32'-0"
        v. 12'-0"

If any of your dimensions do not work, you may go back and double check your previous work. However, if you are using the chapter starter files on the DVD that came with the book, you should not have any problems.

Now you will place dimensions along the East side of the building.

9. Place the dimensions as shown in Figure 8-6.5.

Note how the dimensions automatically rotate to align with the elements being dimensioned, grids in this case. You would need to use the *Linear* dimension tool if you want to force the dimension to be vertical or horizontal for angled elements.

Dimensions can be selected and deleted at any time; this has no effect on the elements being dimensioned. Dimensions can also be hidden in any view via the "VV" shortcut.

FIGURE 8-6.4 Third dimension placed - image rotated to increase size

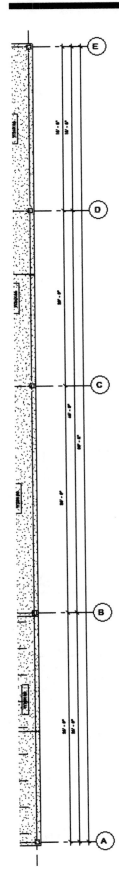

10. Add two dimensions to locate the grids near the curved beams as shown in Figure 8-6.6.

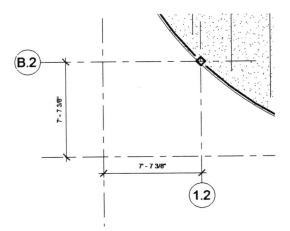

FIGURE 8-6.6 Dimension near curved beam

Even though the dimensions do not show up in the other plan views, you will want them in each of the structural plans. Next, you will learn how to quickly copy the dimensions from one view to another. This only works when there is something there for the Revit dimensions to latch onto. Your grids are, of course, consistent in each view so this method will work.

11. Select all the dimensions just placed in this exercise, by holding the Ctrl key and selecting them, use the *Filter* feature.

12. Select **Copy** in the *Clipboard* panel of the *Ribbon*, not the *Copy* icon on the *Modify* panel.

13. Switch to the **Level 1 – Structural Slab and Foundation Plan** view.

14. Select **Modify → Clipboard → Paste → Aligned to Current View**.

The dimensions are now placed in the current view; you did not have to place them manually!

15. Adjust the grid bubble location so no dimensions are overlapping the large spread footings.

FIGURE 8-6.5 Additional dimension placed

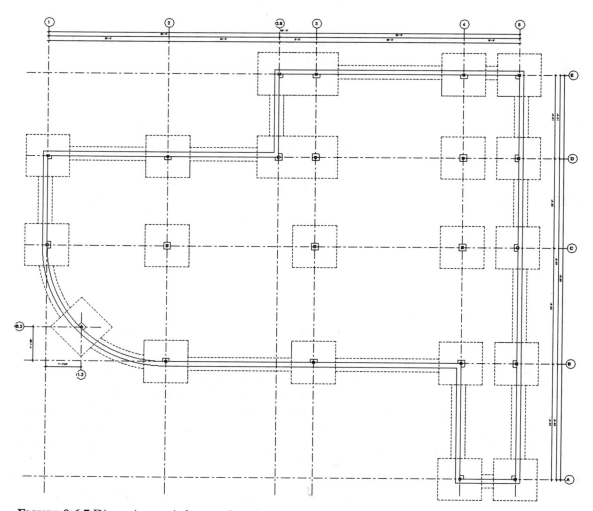

FIGURE 8-6.7 Dimension copied to another view

Placing Tags:

Most elements in Revit can be tagged. Each element category has its own tag family option, which means beams can have a different looking tag than footings; they can also display different information. Not all tags are loaded for every element. You may find that after trying to tag something, a tag for that type of element is not loaded and you have to use the *Load Family* tool to get one.

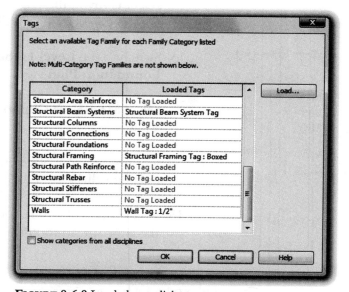

FIGURE 8-6.8 Loaded tags dialog

It is possible to have more than one tag for each element. You can use the *Loaded Tags* tool, in the *Tag* panel fly out, to specify which tag is the default; see Figure 8-6.8. Whenever a tag is selected you can swap it with other loaded tags within the tagged elements category. As an example, you may want most beam tags to simply list the beam size. However, some may want to list camber, studs, etc. You may have several tags loaded which can report this information in the tag.

Tags can be deleted at any time without losing information. All information displayed by a tag is coming from the element which it tags.

16. Switch to the **Level 2 – Structural Framing Plan** view.

17. Select **Annotate → Tag → Tag by Category** from the *Ribbon*.

18. **Uncheck Leader** on the *Options Bar*.

    a.   We do not want a line with an arrow from the tag to the element.

19. Pick one of the curved beams in the Southwestern corner of the building; be careful not to select the floor as it can be tagged as well.

The tag is automatically placed at the midpoint of the curved beam, and rotated to align with the beam at that point. The tag can be selected and repositioned to avoid overlapping of text and geometry (Figure 8-6.9).

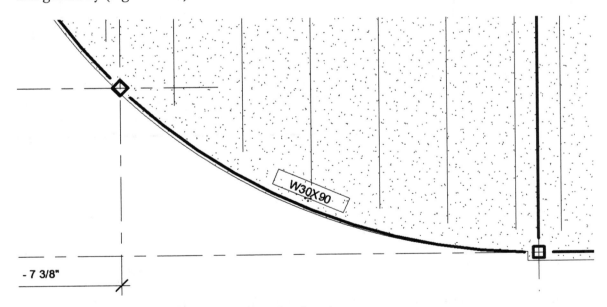

FIGURE 8-6.9 Beam tag placed; the tag is currently selected

20. Place a tag for the other curved beam.

Next you will place *Beam System* symbols. These will be added around the floor opening in the Northeastern corner of the plan.

21. Zoom into the area at Grids 3/4 and E/D.

22. Select **Annotate → Symbol → Beam** from the *Ribbon*.

Beam

23. Hover over the *Beam System* until it highlights with heavy dashed lines as in Figure 8-6.10, and then **click**.

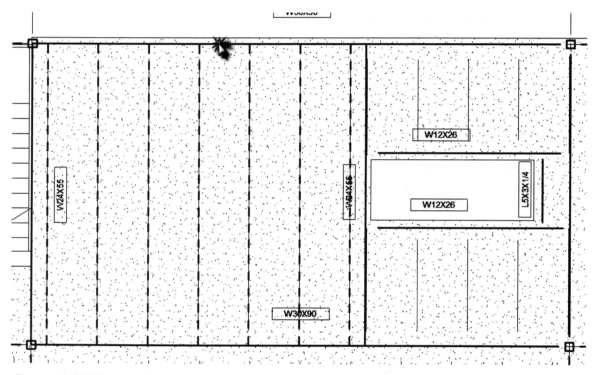

FIGURE 8-6.10 Placing a beam system symbol

24. Now click anywhere near the center of the *Beam System* to position the symbol; do not overlap the beam tags at the perimeter.

25. Repeat these steps for the two smaller beams to the right (if needed).

The Beam System symbol is now placed as shown in Figure 8-6.11.

Like tags, beam system symbols can also be selected and then moved or deleted. The size of the text and arrows for all tags, dimensions and symbols updates automatically whenever the view scale is changed.

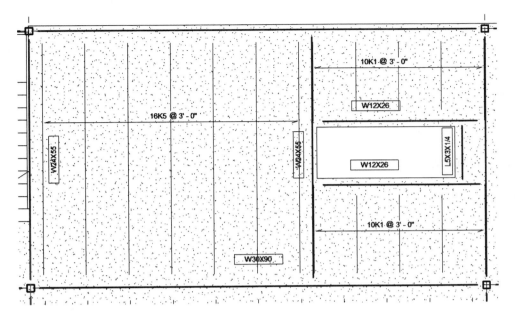

FIGURE 8-6.11 Beam system symbols placed

This is all the time that will be devoted to annotation specifically in Revit *Structure*. There are several other aspects that could be covered but fall outside of the scope of this textbook. For example, it is possible to set up a spot elevation that will report the elevation of the beam relative to the finished floor level. This information could be added directly to the beam tag.

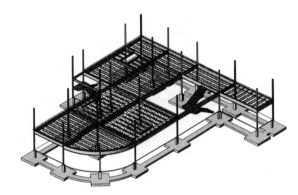

Setting Up a 3D Structural Model View:

It would be useful to set up a 3D view just for the structural portion of the model. Follow these steps if you would like to do so:

- Right-click and duplicate the ***Default 3D View***, named {3D}.
- Rename the view to **Structural 3D View**.
- Change the *Discipline* to **Structural** in the *Properties Palette*.
- Type **VV**.
- Turn off everything except the "structural" categories; make sure the "Show categories from all disciplines" option near the bottom is checked.
    - o Leave floors and stairs on as well.
    - o Check the *Transparent* option to the right of *Floors*.

That is it; you now have a permanent 3D view for the structural BIM.

26. **Save** and **backup** your work.

Self-Exam:

The following questions can be used as a way to check your knowledge of this lesson. The answers can be found at the bottom of this page.

1. *Revit 2011* cannot open *Revit 2012* projects. (T/F)

2. When you load a beam, every possible size is loaded. (T/F)

3. Tags can be automatically added when placing a beam. (T/F)

4. Use the _____ tool to narrow down the current selection.

5. The _____ _____ controls what part of the building a view is cutting through.

Review Questions:

The following questions may be assigned by your instructor as a way to assess your knowledge of this section. Your instructor has the answers to the review questions.

1. Revit *Structure* can add ceilings to the model. (T/F)

2. The Revit *Structure* user interface is very similar to Revit *Architecture*. (T/F)

3. The *Transfer Project Standards* feature can be used to import several structural settings into a project. (T/F)

4. Structural floor elements can show the profile of metal deck in sections. (T/F)

5. A *Type Catalog* allows you to select and load only the types you want from a family which contains a large number of types. (T/F)

6. Revit columns can only extend from one floor to the next. (T/F)

7. When a grid is selected, if the icon near it says 2D, it will only move the grid bubble location in the current view. (T/F)

8. Use a _____ _____ to quickly lay out the joists in a structural bay.

9. Beam elevations need to be changed to accommodate joist bearing conditions. (T/F)

10. It is not a good idea to delete tags as important information may be lost. (T/F)

Lesson 9
Law Office: ELEVATIONS, SECTIONS and DETAILS:

This lesson will cover interior and exterior elevations as well as sections. The default template you started with already has the four main exterior elevations set up for you. You will investigate how Revit generates elevations and the role the elevation tag plays in that process. Finally, you will learn how to link in AutoCAD drawings to reuse legacy details in Revit.

Exercise 9-1:
Exterior Elevations

Setting Up an Exterior Elevation:

Even though you already have the main exterior elevations established, you will go through the steps necessary to set one up. Many projects have more than four exterior elevations, so all exterior surfaces are elevated.

1. Using Revit *Architecture*, open the Chapter 9 starter file from the DVD to ensure you have the complete structural system in your project.

2. Switch to your **First Floor** plan view, aka, *Level 1*.

3. Select **View → Create → Elevation**.

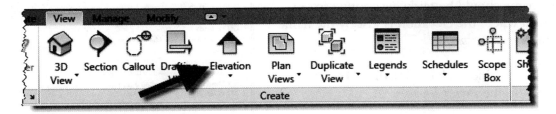

4. Make sure the *Type Selector* is set to *Elevation:* **Building Elevation** and then place the elevation tag in plan view as shown in Figure 9-1.1.

    NOTE: *As you move the cursor around the screen, the Elevation Tag automatically turns to point at the building.*

You now have an elevation added to the *Project Browser* in the *Elevations* category. **The first thing you should do after placing an elevation is rename it**; the default name is not very descriptive. These generic names would get very confusing on larger projects with dozens of views.

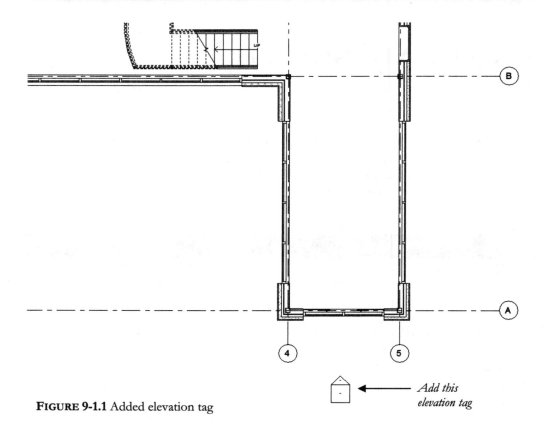

FIGURE 9-1.1 Added elevation tag

5. Right-click on the view name and select **Rename** (Figure 9-1.2).

6. Type: **South – Main Entry**.

The name should be fairly descriptive so you can tell where the elevation is just by the name in the *Project Browser*.

7. Double-click on **South – Main Entry** in the *Project Browser*.

The elevation may not look correct right away. You will adjust this in the next step. Notice though, that an elevation was created simply by placing an *Elevation Tag* in plan view.

8. Switch back to the **First Floor** plan view.

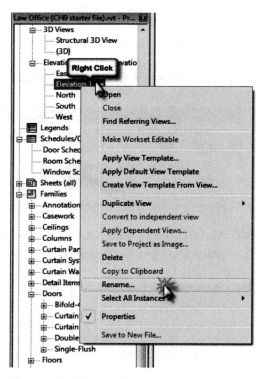

FIGURE 9-1.2 Renaming new view name

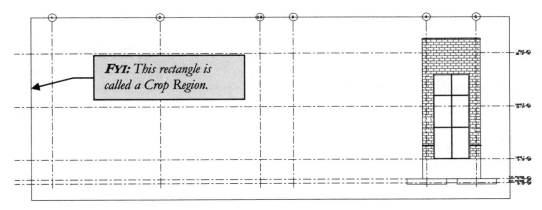

FIGURE 9-1.3 New exterior elevation view – initial state

Next you will study the options associated with the *Elevation Tag*. This, in part, controls what is seen in the elevation.

9.   The *Elevation Tag* has two parts: the pointing triangle and the square center. Each part will highlight as you move the cursor over it. **Select the square center part**.

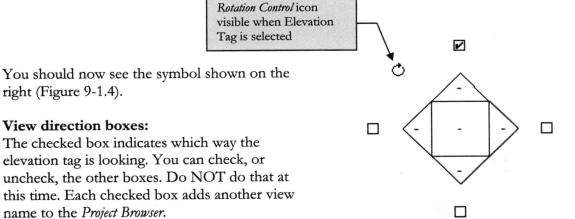

You should now see the symbol shown on the right (Figure 9-1.4).

View direction boxes:
The checked box indicates which way the elevation tag is looking. You can check, or uncheck, the other boxes. Do NOT do that at this time. Each checked box adds another view name to the *Project Browser*.

FIGURE 9-1.4 Selected elevation tag

Rotation control:
This control allows you to look perpendicular to an angled wall in plan, for example.

INTERIOR ELEVATIONS:

When adding the elevation tag to the floor plan you should select "Interior Elevation" from the *Type Selector*. This will use a different symbol to help distinguish the interior tags from the exterior tags in the plan views. Also, the interior and exterior views are separated in the *Project Browser*, making it easier to manage views as the project continues to develop. You will be looking at Interior Elevations in the next exercise.

10. Press the **ESC** key to unselect the elevation tag.

11. Select the pointed portion of the elevation tag.

Your elevation tag should look similar to Figure 9-1.5.

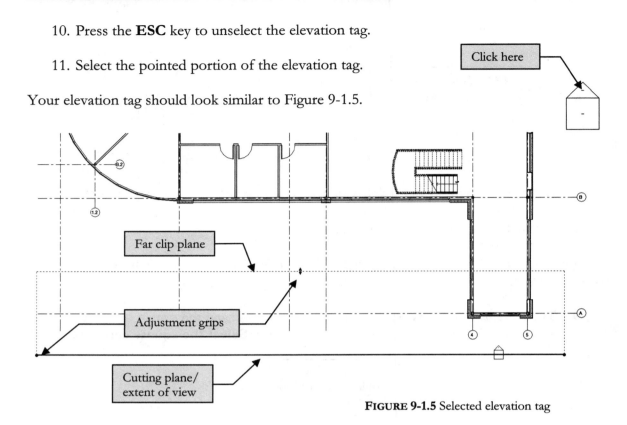

FIGURE 9-1.5 Selected elevation tag

The elevation tag, as selected in Figure 9-1.5, has several features for controlling how the elevation looks. Here is a quick explanation:

- **Cutting plane/extent of view line:** This controls how much of the 3D model is elevated from left to right (i.e., the width of the elevation). This list also acts like a section line in that nothing behind this line will show up.

- **Far clip plane:** This controls how far into the 3D model the elevation view can see. This can be turned off in the elevation's *View Properties*, not the plan's *View Properties*, making the view depth unlimited; the next page covers this more.

- **Adjustment grips:** You can drag these with the mouse to control the features mentioned above. These values can also be controlled in the elevation's *View Properties*.

Notice how the "extent of view" line was created to match the width of the building. You will be adjusting this later to only see the entry wall.

12. Select the view label **South – Main Entry** in the *Project Browser*; the *Properties Palette* now shows the selected view's *View Properties*.

You have several options in the *Properties* window (Figure 9-1.6). Notice the three options with a check box next to them; these control the following:

- **Crop View**: This crops the width and height of the view in elevation. *Adjusting the width of the cropping window in elevation also adjusts the "extent of view" control in plan view.*

- **Crop Region Visible**: This displays a rectangle in the elevation view indicating the extent of the cropping window, described above. *When selected in elevation view, the rectangle can be adjusted with the adjustment grips.* See Figure 9-1.3.

- **Far Clipping**: If this is turned off, Revit will draw everything visible in the 3D model, within the extent of view.

You will manipulate some of these controls next.

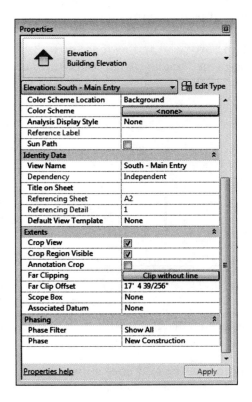

FIGURE 9-1.6 South – Main Entry view properties

13. With the elevation tag still selected; as in Figure 9-1.5, drag or move the "cutting plane/extent of view" line up **into** the main entry as shown in Figure 9-1.7. Do not move the tag itself.

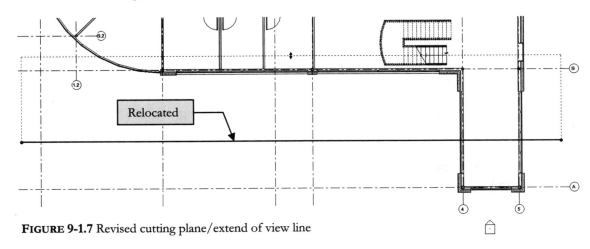

FIGURE 9-1.7 Revised cutting plane/extend of view line

14. Now switch to the *elevation view:* **South – Main Entry**.

Your elevation should look similar to Figure 9-1.8. If required, click on the cropping window and resize it to match this image.

The main entry wall and roof are now displayed in section because of the location of the "cutting plane" line in plan. Notice the steel beams and joists!

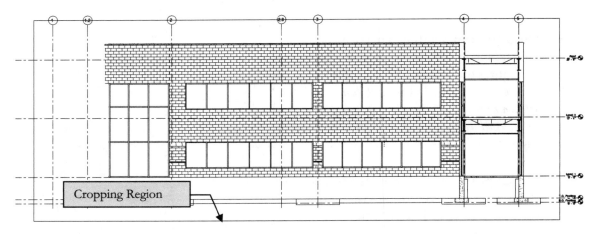

FIGURE 9-1.8 Elevation with cutting plane through main entry at Grids 4 and 5

As you can see, the grid lines appear automatically in the elevations, as do the level datums. Take a minute to observe how the far clip plane controls the visibility of Grid line **1.2** between Figures 9-1.3 and 9-1.8; it must be intersecting the grid lines in plan for it to show up in elevation; compare Figures 9-1.5 and 9-1.7. This is good as it just clutters the drawing to see grid lines that have nothing to do with this part of the drawing.

Notice that the curved wall near Grid **1** is not fully visible. This is not related to the cropping region shown in Figure 9-1.8. Rather, it is related to the "Far Clip Plane" set in the plan view, or in the view's properties.

15. Adjust the "Far Clip Plane" in the **Level 1 Architectural Plan** view so that the entire building shows in the **South – Main Entry** view.

> *TIP: Click on the grip and drag the "far clip plane" North until it is past the Grid line **C**, which is at the middle of the building.*

Now, when you switch back to the "South – Main Entry" elevation view, you should see the entire building.

> *DESIGN INTEGRATION TIP: When working on one model with multiple disciplines it is important to set the discipline parameters correctly in an elevation view's properties. This will prevent it from showing up in the structural floor plans, for example.*

Next, you will adjust the *Elevation Tag* to set up an enlarged elevation for the main entry area's South wall.

16. In the **Level 1 Architectural Plan** view, adjust the *Elevation Tag* to show only the main entry wall (Figure 9-1.9).

    • The *Cutting Plane/Extent of View* line is moved South so it is outside of the building footprint.

    • Use the left and right grips to shorten the same line.

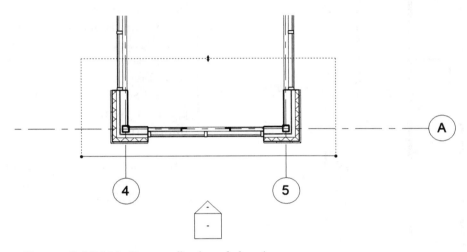

FIGURE 9-1.9 Main Entry wall enlarged elevation

17. Switch to **South – Main Entry** view to see the enlarged elevation you are setting up (Figure 9-1.10).

18. Make sure the **View Scale** is set to **½″ = 1′-0″** on the *View Control Bar* at the bottom of the screen.

Notice how the level datum symbols are now smaller; *Undo* and try it again if you missed it.

19. Click the ***Hide Crop Region*** icon on the *View Control Bar* to make the *Crop Region* disappear.

Once you modify the view constraints in plan view (Figure 9-1.9) and you switch to the new elevation view, you can click on the *Crop Region* and use the grips to make the view wider.

When you drag the *Crop Region* to the right, the *Grids* and *Level Datum* move so they do not overlap the elevation. This is another example of Revit taking the busy work out of designing a building!

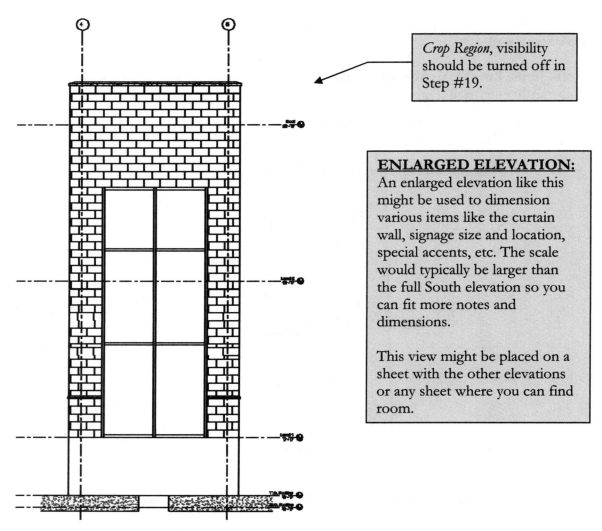

Crop Region, visibility should be turned off in Step #19.

ENLARGED ELEVATION:
An enlarged elevation like this might be used to dimension various items like the curtain wall, signage size and location, special accents, etc. The scale would typically be larger than the full South elevation so you can fit more notes and dimensions.

This view might be placed on a sheet with the other elevations or any sheet where you can find room.

FIGURE 9-1.10 Main Entry wall elevation

Modify an Exterior Elevation:

The purpose of the following steps is to demonstrate that changes can be made anywhere and all other drawings are automatically updated.

20. Open the **East** exterior elevation view.

21. Select the fixed window in the upper right, near Grid **D**.

You will copy the window to the right so the *Level 2* storage room in the Northeastern corner of the building has some natural daylight.

22. **Copy** the selected window **12'-8"** to the North, i.e., to the right in this view (Figure 9-1.11).

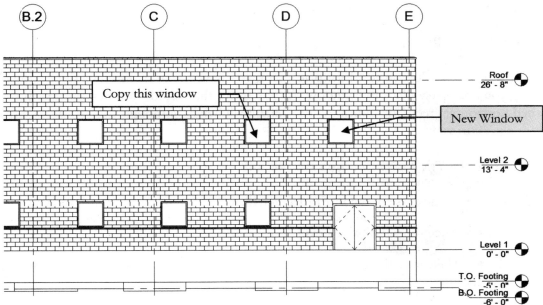

FIGURE 9-1.11 Modifying windows on the East elevation

Now you will switch to the **Level 2** plan view to see your changes.

23. Switch to the **Level 2 Architectural Plan** view and zoom in on the Northeastern area (Figure 9-1.12).

Notice how the windows in plan have changed to match the modifications you just made to the exterior elevations? This only makes sense, seeing as both the floor plan and the exterior elevation are projected 2D views of the same 3D model. Both views are directly manipulating the 3D model.

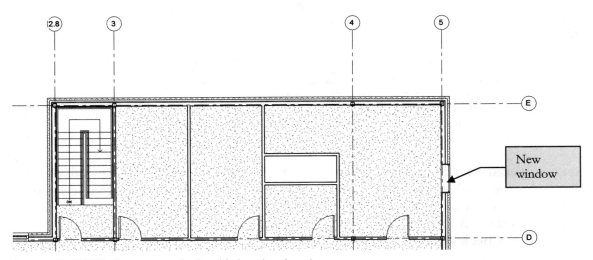

FIGURE 9-1.12 Window automatically added to the plan view

Next, you will insert a window in elevation using the *Window* command and look at a coordination issue with the structural design.

24. Switch to the **North** exterior elevation view.

25. Select the ***Window*** tool from the *Ribbon*.

Notice, with the window selected for placement, you have the usual listening dimensions helping you accurately place the window. As you move the window around, you should see a dashed horizontal green line indicating the default sill height, although you can deviate from this in elevation views.

26. From the *Type Selector* choose *Fixed:* **48"x48"**.

27. Place a window as shown in **Figure 9-1.13**:

- Place the window at Level 2.

- Make sure the bottom of the window snaps to the dashed, cyan colored, sill line.

- The window should be approximately centered on Grid 4.

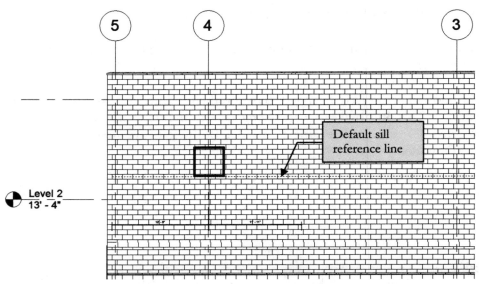

FIGURE 9-1.13 Placing a window on the North elevation

You now placed a window so that it conflicts with a column. Unfortunately, Revit does not tell you that the conflict exists; Revit will warn you if a newly placed window conflicts with a perpendicular interior wall. In this case you will visually be alerted to the conflict in both plan and elevation. Another way to discover this type of conflict is by running the **Interference Check** on the *Collaborate* tab, having Revit look for any windows which occupy the same space as any structural columns.

28. Zoom in on the new window and notice the structural column that is clearly visible (Figure 9-1.14).

29. Switch to the **Level 2 Architectural Plan** view to see the problem (Figure 9-1.15).

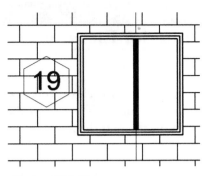

FIGURE 9-1.14
New window with column visible

Notice the column and window clearly conflict with each other. At this point you would need to move the window, delete the window or change the structural design, which is likely not practical for one window. In the next step you will delete the window from the floor plan view which, of course, will update the elevation.

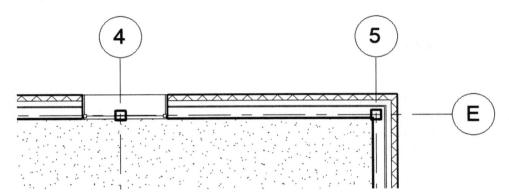

FIGURE 9-1.15 New window with column visible; plan view

30. While in plan view, select the new window and **Delete** it.

31. **Save** your BIM file.

> **TIP:** *Turning on shadows via the View Control Bar can make your 2D elevation view look more interesting; see image below. However, this makes working in the view very slow!*

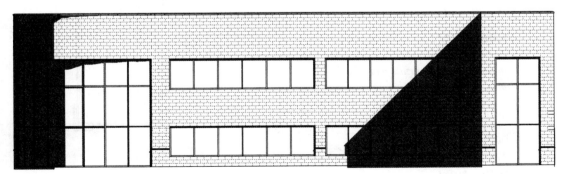

FIGURE 9-1.16 South elevation with shadows turned on

Exercise 9-2:
Interior Elevations

Creating interior elevations is very much like exterior elevations. In fact, you use the same tool. The main difference is that you are placing the elevation tag inside the building, rather than on the exterior.

Adding an Interior Elevation Tag:

1. Open your law office project using Revit *Architecture*.

2. Switch to the *Level 1 Architectural Plan* view, if necessary.

3. Select the *Elevation* tool.

In the next step you will place an elevation tag. Before clicking to place the tag, try moving it around to see how Revit automatically turns the tag to point at the closest wall.

4. Select *Elevation:* **Interior Elevation** and then place an elevation tag looking East (i.e., to the right), as shown (Figure 9-2.1).

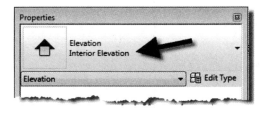

REMEMBER: *The first thing you should do after adding an Elevation Tag is to give it an appropriate name in the Project Browser list.*

5. Change the name of the elevation to **Lobby and Entry - East.**

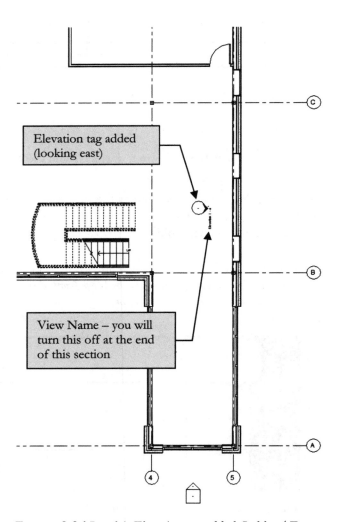

FIGURE 9-2.1 Level 1: Elevation tag added; Lobby / Entry

6. Switch to the **Lobby and Entry – East** view.

TIP: Try double-clicking on the elevation tag (the pointing portion).

Initially, your elevation should look something like Figure 9-2.2; if not, you will be adjusting it momentarily so do not worry. Next you will adjust this view. Notice how Revit automatically controls the lineweights of elements in section versus elements in elevations.

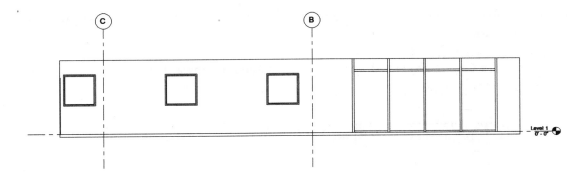

FIGURE 9-2.2 Lobby and Entry – East, initial view

7. Switch back to the **Level 1** plan view.

8. Pick the pointed portion of the *Elevation Tag* so you see the view options (Figure 9-2.3).

You should compare the two drawings on this page, Figures 9-2.2 and 9-2.3, to see how the control lines in the plan view dictate what is generated or visible in the elevation view, for both width and depth.

Revit automatically found the left and right walls, the floor and ceiling in the elevation view.

Notice the *Far Clip Plane* is also accessible. If you cannot see the windows in the elevation view that means the *Far Clip Plane* needs to be moved farther to the right.

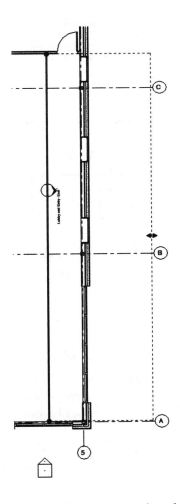

FIGURE 9-2.3 Elevation tag selected

FYI: The elevation tags are used to reference the sheet and drawing number so the client or contractor can find the desired elevation quickly while looking at the floor plans. It is interesting to know that Revit automatically fills in the elevation tag when the elevation is placed on a sheet, and will update it if the elevation moves or sheet number changes.

9. Switch back to the **Lobby and Entry - East** view.

Just to try adjusting the *Crop Region* to see various results, you will extend the top upward to see the second floor.

10. Select the *Crop Region* and drag the upper middle grip upwards to increase the view size vertically (Figure 9-2.4).

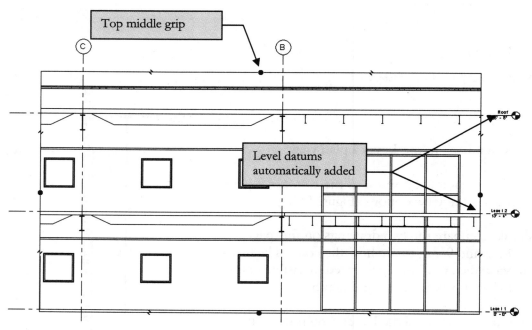

FIGURE 9-2.4 Lobby and Entry - East elevation; crop region selected and modified

Here you are getting a sneak peak ahead to the sections portion of this book. Notice the beams and joists. Notice that additional level datum lines where added automatically as the view grew to include more vertical information (i.e., Level 2, Roof). Notice the *Grids* automatically extended with the *Crop Region*. Also, the bar joists would have more detail if the *Detail Level* were set higher on the *View Control Bar*.

11. Now select **Undo** to return to the previous view (Figure 9-2.2).

The Level 1 level datum is not necessary in this view, so you will remove it from this view.

> **IMPORTANT:** *You cannot simply delete the Level datum because it will actually delete all associated views from the entire project (i.e., floor and ceiling plan views). This will delete any model elements that are hosted by that level and any tags, notes and dimensions in that view.*

To remove a level datum, you select it and tell Revit to hide it in the current view. You will do this next.

12. Click on the horizontal line portion of the **Level 1** level datum.

13. Right-click and select **Hide in View → Category** from the pop-up menu.

> **TIP:** *Selecting Element would make only the selected level datum disappear from the current view.*

14. Adjust the bottom of the **Crop Region** to align with the Level 1 top-of-slab (horizontal line).

15. On the *View Control Bar*, set:

    a.   *View Scale* to: **¼"=1'-0"**, if needed.

    b.   *Detail Level:* **Fine**

Your elevation should look like Figure 9-2.5.

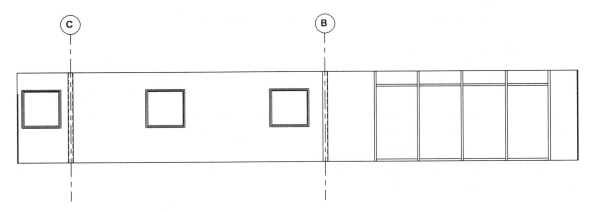

FIGURE 9-2.5 Lobby and Entry - East elevation

Notice in Figure 9-2.5 that the exterior columns are now showing. This has to do with changing the *Detail Level* from *Coarse* to *Fine*. In *Coarse* mode, Revit displays columns as stick figures and thus they were buried in the exterior wall. When the *Detail Level* was changed to *Fine* mode the actual 3D geometry of the selected steel shape is shown.

You can leave the crop window on to help define the perimeter of the elevation. You can also turn it off; however, some lines that are directly under the crop window might disappear.

> ***TIP:*** *If perimeter lines disappear when you print interior elevations, try unchecking "Hide Crop Regions" in the Print dialog and turn off the ones you do not want to see.*

Turning off the View Name on the Elevation Tag:

The interior elevation tag currently has the view name showing in plan view. You will turn this off as it is not required on the construction drawings.

16. Select **Manage** → **Settings** → **Additional Settings** (down-arrow)→ **Elevation Tags**.

17. Set the *Type* to **½" Circle** (Figure 9-2.6).

18. Select **Elevation Mark Body_Circle: Filled Arrow** from the *Elevation Mark* drop-down list (Figure 9-2.6).

19. Click **OK** to close the dialog box.

The view name should now be gone from the *Elevation Tags* in the floor plan view.

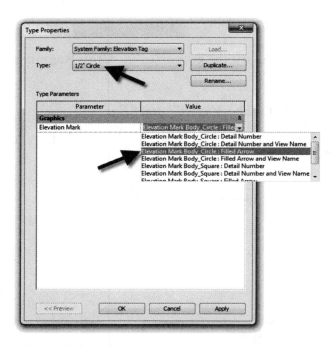

FIGURE 9-2.6 Adjusting the interior elevation tag

> ***FYI:*** *If you right-click on an elevation view name in the Project Browser, you will notice you can Duplicate the view (via Duplicate View → Duplicate). This is similar to how a floor plan is duplicated with one major variation: when an elevation view is duplicated, Revit actually just copies another elevation tag on top of the one being duplicated in the plan view. This is because each elevation view requires its own elevation tag. If two views could exist based on one elevation tag, then Revit would not know how to fill in the drawing number and sheet number if both views are placed on a sheet.*

Exercise 9-3:
Building Sections

Sections are one of the main communication tools in a set of architectural drawings. They help the builder understand vertical relationships. With traditional drafting techniques, architectural sections can occasionally contradict other drawings, such as mechanical or structural drawings. One example is a beam shown on the section is smaller than what the structural drawings call for; this creates a problem in the field when the duct does not fit in the ceiling space. The ceiling gets lowered and/or the duct gets smaller, ultimately compromising the design to a certain degree.

Revit takes great steps toward eliminating these types of conflicts. Sections, like plans and elevations, are generated from the 3D model. So it is virtually impossible to have a conflict between the various discipline's drawings. As many architects and structural, mechanical and electrical engineers are starting to share Revit models for even greater coordination, this is helping to eliminate conflicts and redundancy in drawing.

Similar to elevation tags, placing the section graphics in a plan view actually generates the section view. You will learn how to do this next.

Placing Section Marks:

1. Open your law office model.

2. Switch to **Level 1** plan view.

3. Select **View → Create → Section**.

Section

4. Draw a **Section** mark as shown in Figure 9-3.1. Start on the left side in this case. Use the *Move* tool if needed to accurately adjust the section tag after insertion.

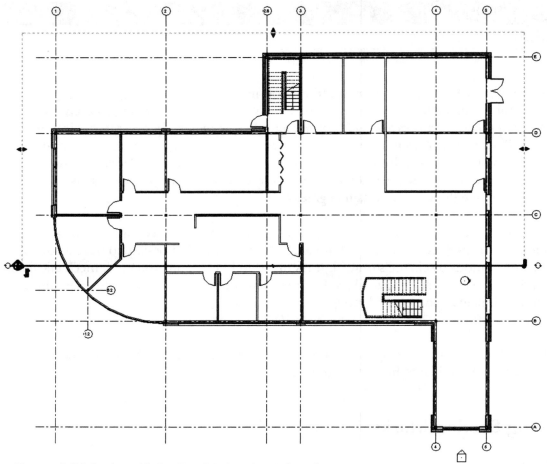

FIGURE 9-3.1 Section added to Level 1 plan view (selected)

You can see that the *Far Clip Plane* location in the plan view is out past the building perimeter; this means you will see everything (Figure 9-3.1). Anything passing through the section line is in section, everything else you see is in elevation; Revit calls it "projection". Everything behind the section is omitted from the view. Figure 9-3.2 also shows the *Crop Region.*

The image below lists the additional terms related to the *Section Mark* graphics in the plan view, as compared to *Elevation Tags.*

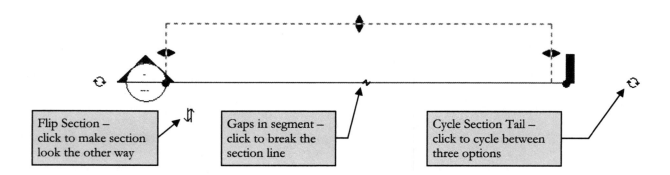

Flip Section –
click to make section
look the other way

Gaps in segment –
click to break the
section line

Cycle Section Tail –
click to cycle between
three options

The *Section* tool is almost exactly like the *Elevation* tool. The only differences are the graphics in plan and the location in the *Project Browser*. Other than that they both function the same; they can show things in elevation or projection, and in section.

Notice, in the *Project Browser*, that a new category has been created; <u>Sections (building Section)</u>. If you expand this category, you will see the new section view listed; it is called *Section 1*. You should always rename any new view right after creating it. This will help with navigation and when it comes time to place views on sheets for printing.

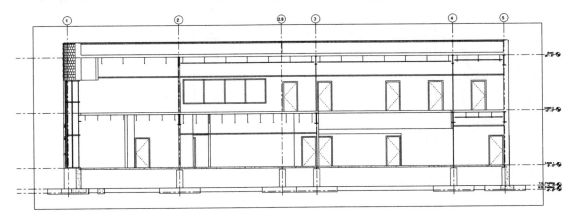

FIGURE 9-3.2 Initial Longitudinal section view

5. Rename section view *Section 1* to **Longitudinal Section**.

6. Switch to the new section view, **Longitudinal Section**.

   TIP: *Double-click on the section bubble head to open that view. The section needs to be unselected first; double-click on the blue part.*

7. On the *View Control Bar* change:

   a. *Detail Level* is set to **Medium**.

   b. **Hide Crop Region**

8. Zoom in to the upper right corner to see the detail available in this section view, near the intersection of the Roof level datum and grid line 5. (See Figure 9-3.3.)

Notice the steel beams and bar joists in section. The metal roof decking extends into the wall but the layers above it do not; this related to the roof's core material and the "extend to wall core" option you selected when creating the roof. You can also see the ceiling in the section; they are at the specified height and are the correct thickness. Finally, notice the elements in elevation (or projection): doors, beams and the parapet at the North exterior wall.

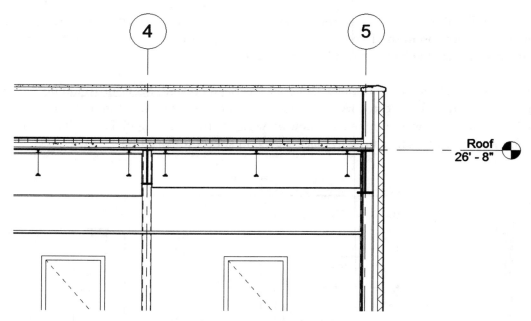

FIGURE 9-3.3 Longitudinal section view enlarged to show detail

9. Create another **Section** as shown in **Figure 9-3.4**.

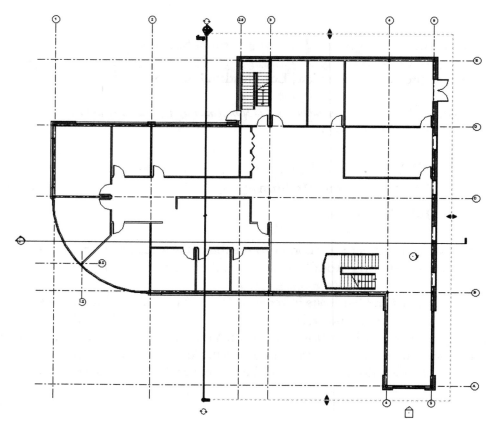

FIGURE 9-3.4 Cross section added looking East

10. Rename the new section view to **Cross Section 1** in the *Project Browser.*

11. Switch to the **Cross Section 1** view.

12. Set the *Detail Level* to **Medium** and turn off the **Crop Region** visibility via the *View Control Bar* (Figure 9-3.5).

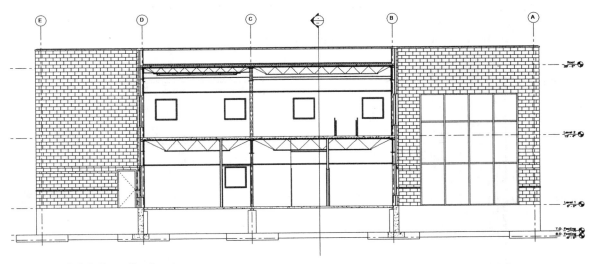

FIGURE 9-3.5 Cross Section 1

Revit automatically displays heavier lines for objects that are in section than for objects beyond the cutting plane and shown in elevation.

Also, with the *Detail Level* set to **Medium**, the walls and floors are hatched to represent the material in section.

Notice that the *Longitudinal Section* mark is automatically displayed in the *Cross Section 1* view. If you switch to the *Longitudinal Section* view you will see the *Cross Section 1* mark. Keeping with Revit's philosophy of change anything anywhere, you can select the section mark in the other section view and adjust its various properties, like the *Far Clip Plane.*

> **FYI:** *In any view that has a Section Mark in it, you can double-click on the round reference bubble to quickly switch to that section view. However, the section cannot be selected; the section head is dark blue when not selected.*

Making Modifications in the Model:

At this point you will take a look at making changes to the *Building Information Model* within your newly created *Cross Section* view. Currently, you will add the double doors to the main entry area, within the curtain wall.

13. Zoom into the curtain wall shown in elevation, between Grids A and B.

14. Select the vertical mullion shown in Figure 9-3.6.

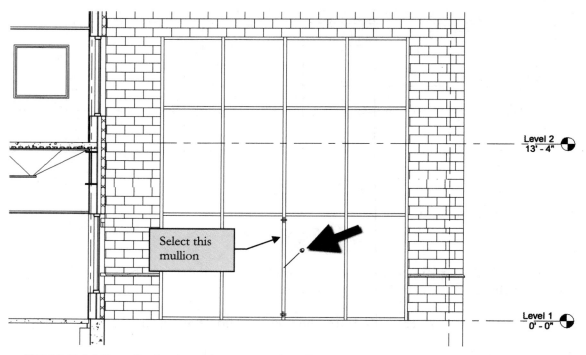

FIGURE 9-3.6 Cross Section 1 – main entry curtain wall area

This curtain wall was previously created using a wall type with rules that automatically added the vertical and horizontal mullions. If the width or height of the curtain wall were to be changed, the rules would automatically add or remove mullions and change their spacing. Because of this, all the mullions are pinned to prevent accidental changes.

In this case, we want to delete the vertical mullion and the two horizontal mullions below it on the ground. This is making room for the double doors about to be added.

> *FYI: Mullions start and stop automatically at each cell, or area of glass. That is why you are able to select just one as in the figure above.*

15. Click the **Pinned** symbol pointed out in Figure 9-3.6 to unpin the selected mullion.

16. Press the **Delete** key on the keyboard to delete the selected mullion.

17. **Delete** the two horizontal mullions, at the floor, as shown in Figure 9-3.7 below, per the previous steps.

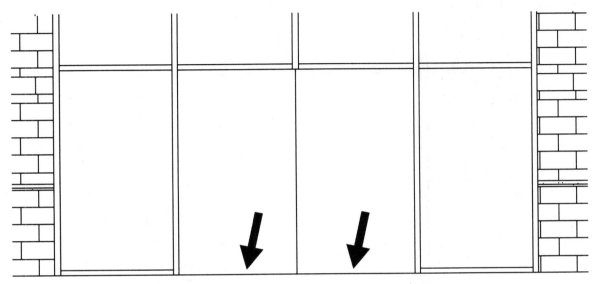

FIGURE 9-3.7 Cross Section 1 – main entry curtain wall area; three mullions deleted

Next you will need to remove a portion of the *Curtain Grid* to create one large *Curtain Panel* where the double door will go.

18. Select the vertical ***Curtain Grid***; hover your cursor until the heavy dashed line appears and then click on it. See Figure 9-3.8.

19. **Unpin** the *Curtain Grid* and then, with the *Curtain Grid* selected, click **Add/Remove Segments** from the *Ribbon*.

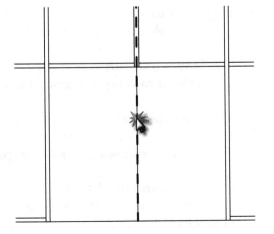

FIGURE 9-3.8 Selecting the curtain grid

You can now remove the selected portion of the *Curtain Grid*. When a portion of grid is removed, the *Curtain Panel* changes from two to one.

20. Click the same location again, shown in Figure 9-3.8.

21. Click **Modify** to finish the current operation.

Your double door opening should now look like Figure 9-3.9.

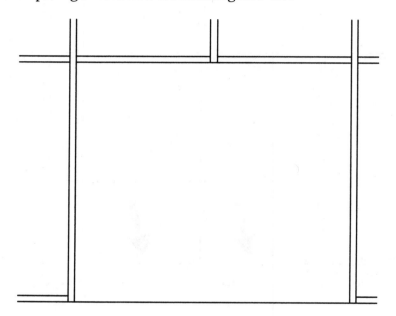

FIGURE 9-3.9 Mullions and curtain grid removed for double doors

Now you will add the double doors. To do this you select the *Curtain Panel*. This may require tapping the **Tab** button to cycle through the various elements below your cursor. Then select the double door family from the *Type Selector*.

22. Hover your cursor over the perimeter of the *Curtain Panel* and "tap" the **Tab** key, without moving the cursor, until the *Curtain Panel* highlights as in Figure 9-3.10.

23. Once the *Curtain Panel* is highlighted, click to select it.

24. Click the **pinned** symbol to **unpin** it.

You will now select the double door family you previously loaded from the *Element Type Selector*. Notice, you can also swap out the current panel for any of the standard Revit wall types as well.

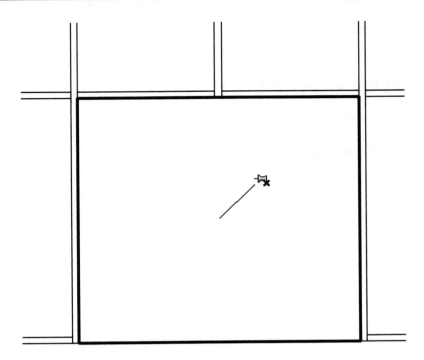

FIGURE 9-3.10 Curtain panel selected and un-pinned

25. With the *Curtain Panel* selected, pick **Store Front Double Door** from the *Type Selector*.

Your curtain wall should now look like the image below. The only thing you have to do now is verify the door swing in the plan view.

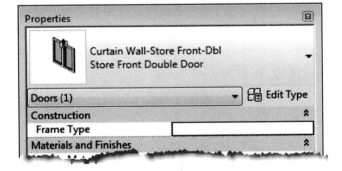

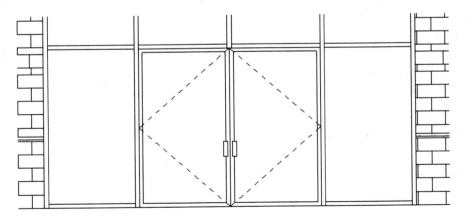

FIGURE 9-3.11 Double door added

The double door automatically stretches to fill the area contained by the *Curtain Panel*. This means the door may be too big or too small. Also, the double door is actually a special type of family for curtain walls, so it does not show up when using the *Door* tool. However, this door will show up in the *Door Schedule*.

26. Switch to the **Level 1 Architectural Floor Plan** view.

27. Zoom into the main entry area.

28. Verify the door swings in; if it does not:

    a. Select the door, using the **Tab** key if necessary.

    b. Click the *flip control* arrows to change the door swing.

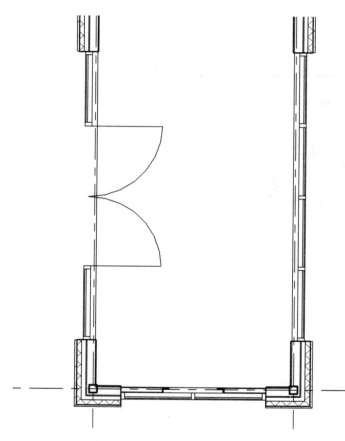

Obviously codes vary on minimum door sizes and the direction in which the doors must swing in relation to building type and occupant load. We will leave things as they are for this tutorial.

If the door width needed to change, you would select the *Curtain Grid* on one side of the door and move it; this would automatically cause the mullions and panels to update, including the double door.

If the door swung out and the project was in a frost susceptible area, the structural engineers would need to add a concrete stoop.

FIGURE 9-3.12 Double door shown in plan

29. **Save** your project.

Exercise 9-4:
Wall Sections

So far, in the previous exercise, you have drawn building sections. Building sections are typically ⅛″ or ¼″ scale and light on detail and notes. Wall sections are drawn at a larger scale and have much more detail and annotations. You will look at setting up wall sections next.

Setting up the Wall Section View:

1. Open your law office file; do not forget to make backups.

2. Switch to the **Cross Section 1** view.

3. From the *View* tab on the *Ribbon*, click the **Callout** tool and then select *Section:* **Wall Section** from the *Type Selector*.

4. Place a **Callout** tag as shown in Figure 9-4.1.

   Callout

   TIP: *Pick in the upper left and then in the lower right (do not drag) to place the Callout tag.*

   TIP: *You can use the control grips for the Callout tag to move the reference bubble, if desired, to move it away from notes/dimensions.*

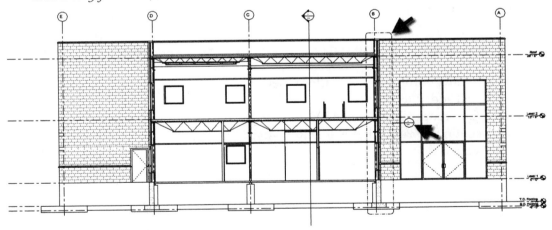

FIGURE 9-4.1 Cross Section 1 view with Callout added

5. Rename <u>Callout of Cross Section1</u> to **Typical Wall Section**.

Notice that a view was added in the *Sections (Wall Section)* category of the *Project Browser*. Because *Callouts* are detail references of a section view, it is a good idea to keep the new callout view name similar to the name of the section.

It is possible to create a wall section using the same *Section* tool used in the previous exercise. However, *Callouts* differ from section views in that the callout is not referenced in every related view. This example is typical, in that the building sections are referenced from the plans and wall sections are referenced from the building sections. The floor plans can get pretty messy if you try to add too much information to them.

6. Double-click on the reference bubble portion of the *Callout* tag to open the **Typical Wall Section** view.

7. In the *Properties Palette* adjust the ***View Properties*** as follows:

   a. *Far clip settings:* **Independent**

   b. *Far clip offset:* **2'-0"**

Notice, down on the *View Control Bar*, that the scale is set to ½" = 1'-0". This affects the *Level* datum and any annotation you add.

8. On the *View Control Bar*, set the *View Scale* to ¾" = 1'-0" and the *Detail Level* to **Fine**.

Notice the level datum's size changed.

If you zoom in on a portion of the **Callout** view, you can see the detail added to the view. The wall's interior lines (i.e., veneer lines) are added and the materials in section are hatched. (See Figure 9-4.4; this is at the second floor line.)

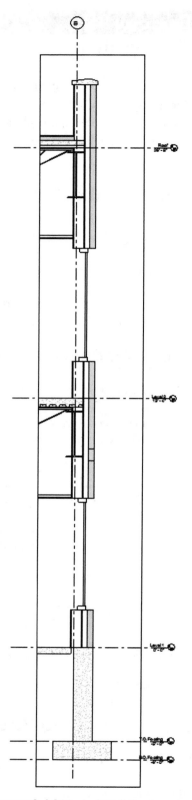

FIGURE 9-4.2 Typical Wall Section view

As before, you can turn off and adjust the *Crop Region*.

9. On the *View Control Bar*, turn off the **Crop Region Visibility**; do not turn off cropping all together. Also, set the *Detail Level* to **Fine**.

If you set the *Detail Level* to *Coarse*, you get just an outline of your structure. The *Coarse* setting is more appropriate for building sections than wall sections. Figure 9-4.3 is an example of the *Coarse* setting.

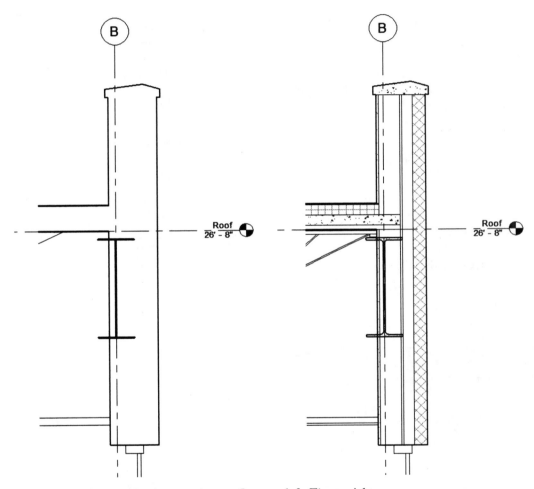

FIGURE 9-4.3 Detail level comparison – *Coarse* on left, *Fine* on right

Notice the steel beams and bar joists are shown as single-line representations in the *Coarse* detail level and the *Fine* view shows the true profile.

Add Notes and Dimensions:

Now you will add dimensions and text to the wall section. This process is the same for any view in Revit.

10. Add the dimension string as shown in **Figure 9-4.4**.

These dimensions are primarily for the masons laying up the CMU wall. Typically, when a window opening is dimensioned in a masonry wall, the dimension has the suffix M.O. This stands for Masonry Opening, clearly representing that the dimension identifies an opening in the wall. You will add the suffix next.

11. Select the dimension at the window opening.

12. Click directly on the blue dimension text (i.e., 6'-0").

13. Type **M.O.** in the *Suffix* field and then click **OK** (Figure 9-4.5).

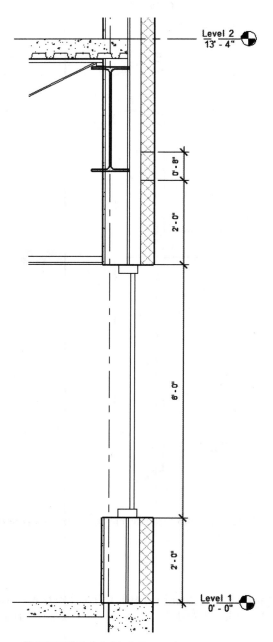

FIGURE 9-4.4 Added dimensions

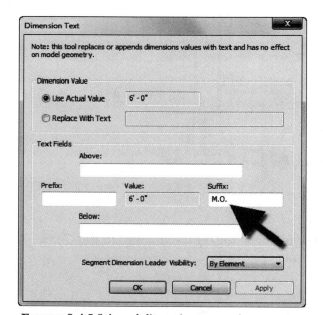

FIGURE 9-4.5 Selected dimension properties

Turn the *Crop Region* back on for a moment.

14. Select the **Crop Region**.

Notice the dashed line that shows around the *Crop Region*? It has its own set of positioning grips. This dashed lined area allows you to control the visibility of various elements in the current view, such as text. You will adjust the right-hand side so it will accommodate more text or notes. This can be toggled on or off in *View Properties* with the *Annotation Crop* option.

15. Drag the control grips for the vertical dashed line on the right as per **Figure 9-4.6**.

16. Turn the *Crop Region* off again.

17. Add the notes with leaders shown in Figure 9-4.7.

    a. The text style should be set to **3/32" Arial** via the *Type Selector* on the *Ribbon*, once in the *Text* command.

    TIP: Select the Text tool and then one of the "Two Segments" Leader options on the Ribbon.

18. Select the text and use the grips and the justification buttons to make the text look like **Figure 9-4.7**.

Text will not automatically update like dimensions will. The leaders and arrows do not really know what they are pointing at. This needs to be manually adjusted if something moves.

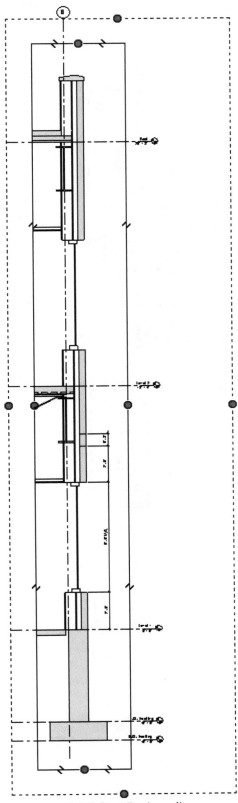

FIGURE 9-4.6 Crop Region edits

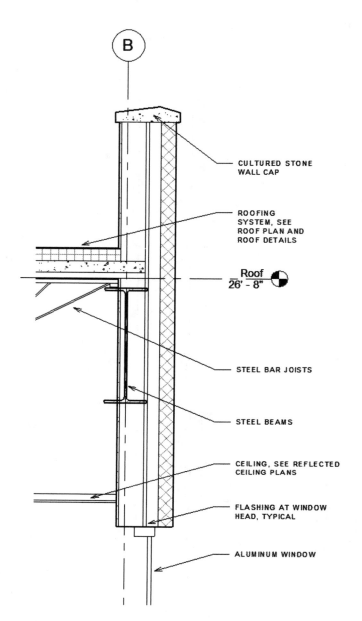

Notes on **Notes**...

When placing the text with the *Two Segments* option, you should be able to snap to points on the screen that will make the notes align vertically within the drawing. The drawings look neater and more professional when the notes align.

It is not always possible, but when the arrow is generally perpendicular to the element it is pointing at, the drawing is easier to read.

All text in a set of construction documents (CD's) is typically uppercase. Some lowercase fonts can become hard to read, especially when the drawings are printed half-size, which is the preferred size for easy reference at one's desk.

Detail Lines are added to show things like the flashing above a window. Operating Revit would become too slow to use if every little thing was modeled.

TIP: *Adjust the Far Clip Plane if the bar joist is not visible – i.e., increase the value.*

FIGURE 9-4.7 Notes added to wall section

Adding Detail Components:

Revit provides a way in which you can quickly add common 2D detail elements such as metal studs, dimensional lumber in section, anchor bolts, and wall base profiles to embellish your sections.

Next you will add just a few *Detail Components* so you have a basic understanding of how this feature is used.

You will add a metal stud runner track and batt insulation to the parapet wall.

19. Select **Annotate → Detail → Component → Detail Component**.

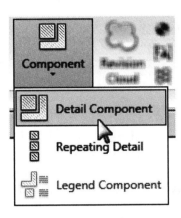

20. From the *Type Selector* pick *Light Gauge Metal - Channel:* **5 1/2" x 1 3/8** (Figure 9-4.8).

As you move the cursor around the screen, you will notice the *Detail Component* attached to your cursor will disappear whenever your cursor is outside of the *Crop Region*.

> **FYI:** *The light gauge channels are used in section and the studs are used in plan views. The channels (aka, runner tracks) receive the studs at the top and bottom of the wall where they are screwed together.*

21. Add the channels as shown in Figure 9-4.9.

> **TIP:** *When placing the metal stud or channel, you will need to press the spacebar to rotate and then move to properly position the element.*

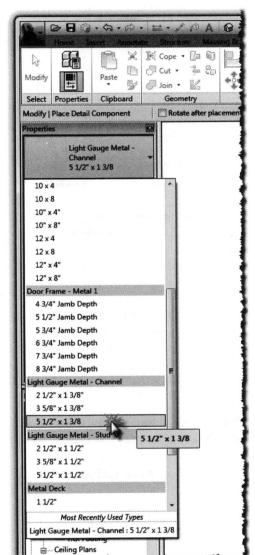

FIGURE 9-4.8 Detail Components

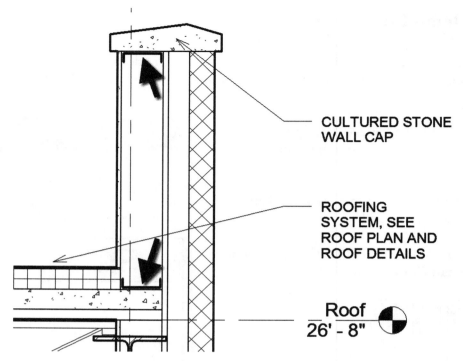

FIGURE 9-4.9 Typical Wall Section view; metal channels added

Detail Components can be copied once you have placed one in the view. Keep in mind that *Detail Components* are view specific and will not show up in any other view. You would have to repeat these steps in any other view in which they need to appear. Also, if the height of the parapet changes, the top channel you just placed will NOT automatically reposition itself unless you use the align and lock technique.

Next you will add the batt insulation (aka, fiberglass insulation), which occurs within the metal stud cavity.

22. Select **Annotation** → **Detail** → **Insulation**.

23. Enter **5 ½″** for the *Width* on the *Options Bar*.

24. Pick the midpoint of the sill plate and the top plate to draw a line that represents the center of the insulation symbol; you can pick in either direction (Figure 9-4.10).

These techniques can be used to add batt insulation to the rest of the wall in this section, as well as runner tracks and window headers. A *Detail Component* would be used to represent rigid insulation if not already accounted for within the wall type.

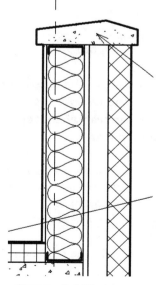

FIGURE 9-4.10
Insulation added

These tools just used are on the *Annotate* tab of the *Ribbon* because they are 2D graphics and only show up in the current view.

Drawing some elements like this, rather than modeling them three- dimensionally, can save time and system resources. A file could get very large if you tried to model everything. Of course, every time you skip drawing in 3D, you increase the chance of error. It takes a little experience to know when to model and when not to model.

Loading Additional Detail Components:

In addition to the *Detail Components* that are preloaded with the template file you started with, you can load more from the *Revit* content folder on your hard drive.

25. Select **Component → Detail Component** from the *Annotate* tab.

26. Click the **Load Family** button from the *Ribbon*.

27. Double-click on the **Detail Components** folder and then the following sub-folders: *Div 06-Wood* and *Plastic\064000-Architectural Woodwork\064600-Wood Trim*.

28. Double-click the file named **Crown Molding-Section.rfa** (Figure 9-4.11).

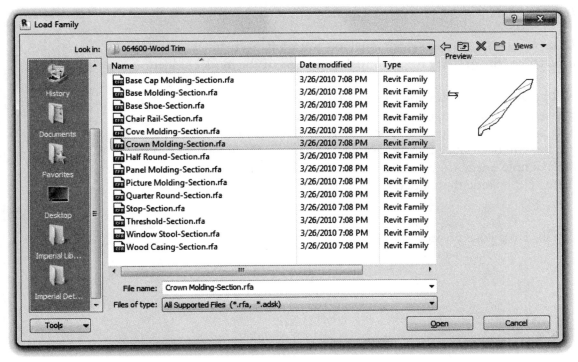

FIGURE 9-4.11 Load Detail Component dialog

You now have access to the newly imported crown molding. Take a minute to observe some of the other *Detail Components* that may be loaded into the project.

29. Place the **3/4″ x 5 7/8″** crown molding at the Level 2 ceiling as shown in Figure 9-4.12; press the *spacebar* to rotate before placing.

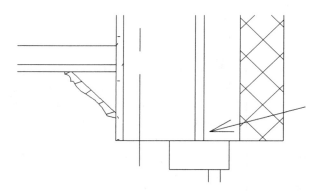

FIGURE 9-4.12 Crown molding placed at Level 2 ceiling

In addition to dimensions, text and detail components, you may also embellish your sections and elevations using *Detail Lines* and *Repeating Details*.

Detail Lines allow you to sketch anything you want. Sometimes you need to use the *Masking Region* to make portions of the model hidden.

A *Repeating Detail* allows you to pick two points on the screen and Revit will array a detail component between your two picks. For example, you can set up a Concrete Block (CMU) repeating detail and then pick the top and bottom of a section of wall to have CMU show up, as in the example image to the right. These have *Masking Regions* built into them so they hide the model linework below.

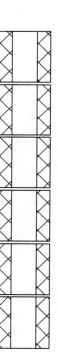

30. **Save** your project.

Exercise 9-5:
Details

This exercise shows you how to develop 2D details which are not tied to the 3D model in any way. Why would you want to do this, you might ask? Many design firms have developed detail libraries over the years for typical conditions. These details contain a significant amount of embodied knowledge of the firm as a whole. Many notes and dimensions have been added which cover certain situations that have come up and created problems or cost the firm money. For example, a window head detail might show flashing, which directs any moisture in the wall out, rather than into, the window or inside the building. Well, a note might have been added to instruct the contractor to turn the flashing up at each side of the window to ensure the moisture does not just run off the end of the flashing and stay in the wall.

If every detail were a live cut through the model, the designer would have to spend the time adding all these notes and dimensions, and more importantly try not to forget any. Even if typing them from a printed reference page, similar to what you are doing with this book. (Have you missed anything yet, and had to go back and make a correct?). Furthermore, if the part of the model changes, the detail could be messed up. Or, the item being details from the live model, might change and not be the typical condition anymore.

So, as you can see, there are a number of reasons a design firm maintains and utilizes static 2D details. *NOTE: Sometimes these details are used as starting points for similar details. This saves time not having to start from scratch.*

It should also be pointed out that standard details should always be reviewed before "dumping" them into a project. If a note says, for example "Apply fireproofing to underside of metal roof deck" and your building has precast concrete plank, you need to change the note and the drawing. All other parts of the detail may perfectly match the project design you are working on.

Linking an AutoCAD Drawing

This first exercise will explore linking AutoCAD drawings into Revit when the need to use legacy details arises.

It is better to recreate these details in native Revit format rather than linking an AutoCAD drawing. Any external files linked in have the potential to slow your BIM experience and introduce corruption. This is especially true with site plans created in AutoCAD or AutoCAD Civil 3D. Site plans are often a great distance from the origin (i.e., 0,0,0 coordinate in an AutoCAD drawing) and this creates several issues.

In general, it is best to avoid AutoCAD DWG files within Revit. However, when it is required, they should always be *Linked* in and not *Imported* and never *Exploded*. Importing DWG files makes them difficult to manage and exploding them creates lots of extra text styles, fill patterns and other items that clutter the BIM database.

1. Open ex9-4.rvt and **Save As ex9-5.rvt**.

AutoCAD DWG files can be linked directly into a plan view and be used as an underlay to sketch walls and place doors and windows, when modeling an existing building in Revit that has been drawn in a traditional CAD program.

In our example, we have a DWG file which contains a detail we want to reference and place on a sheet for our office building project. To do this, you create a *Drafting View* and link the CAD file into the drafting view. A *Drafting View* is a 2D drawing within the BIM project that has no direct relationship to the 3D model.

2. Click **View → Create → Drafting View** from the *Ribbon*.

Drafting View

Now you are prompted for a name and scale for the new drafting view; this can be changed later if needed.

3. Enter the following (Figure 9-5.1):

   a. *Name:* **Typical Roof Drain Detail**

   b. *Scale:* **1½" = 1'-0"**

4. Click **OK** to create the new *Drafting View*.

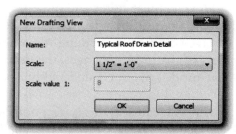

FIGURE 9-5.1 Creating a drafting view

You now have a new section, under *Views* in the *Project Browser*, called *Drafting Views* (Detail). Within this section is your new *Drafting View* – <u>Typical Roof Drain Detail</u>.

Within this new drafting view you could begin sketching a detail from scratch using the various tools on the *Annotate* and *Modify* tabs. Or, in this example, you may link in a DWG file.

This roof drain detail is a good example of why 2D details are still useful in Revit, either DWG or native Revit. As previously mentioned, many firms spend years developing standard details. These details have notes that have been added to and edited as building materials change and problems occur. It would take a lot of time to cut a section at a 3D roof drain in the model and then add all the notes, if one can even remember what all the notes are. Now, repeat this for 20 to 50 other items throughout the building project.

Now you will link in the DWG file from the DVD that came with this textbook.

5. While in the newly created drafting view, select **Insert → Link → Link CAD** from the *Ribbon*.

6. Browse to the **DWG Files** folder on the DVD.

7.   Select the file **Typical Roof Drain Detail.DWG**.

8.   Set the *Colors* options to **Black and White** (Figure 9-5.2).

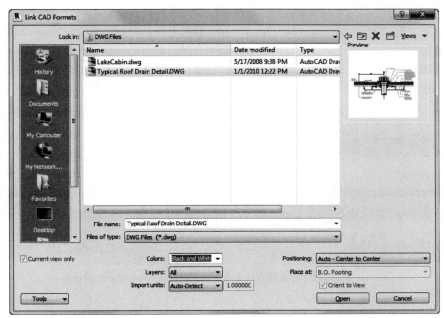

FIGURE 9-5.2 Linking an AutoCAD detail file

9.   Click **Open** to place the linked AutoCAD DWG file.

10. Type **ZF** (for **Zoom Fit**) on the keyboard; do **not** press **Enter**.

You should now see the roof drain detail, with line weights.

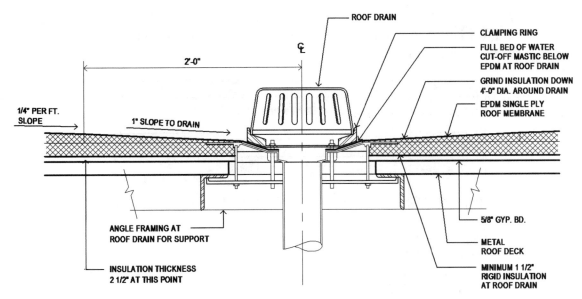

FIGURE 9-5.3 DWG file linked into drafting view

The drawing can be selected and moved around within the drafting view, but it cannot be edited. If you need to make changes to this drawing, you would have to do it in AutoCAD. Revit will automatically update any linked files when the project file is opened. It can also be done manually using the *Manage Links* tool.

When DWG files are linked into Revit, a specific set of line weights are used. These settings can be seen by clicking the small arrow (i.e., the dialog launcher) in the lower right corner of the *Import* panel on the *Insert* tab.

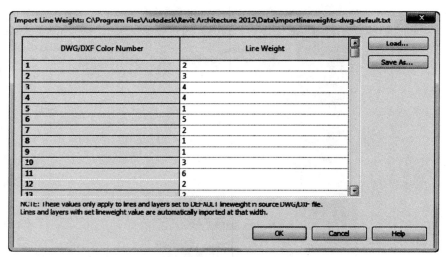

FIGURE 9-5.4 DWG color to Revit line weight conversion

Applying line weights is a onetime conversion process when the DWG file is linked in. Changing the line weight setting after a DWG has been linked in has no effect on it (only on new DWG files to be linked in).

> **TIP:** *Go to* **Manage → Settings → Additional Settings → Line Weights** *to see what each line weight number is equal to.*

If you type **VV** in the drafting view and then select the *Imported Categories* tab, you can see the AutoCAD *Layers* that exist in the imported DWG file (Figure 9-5.5). Un-checking a *Layer* will hide that information within the drafting view. You can also control the color and line weight of the lines on each *Layer*.

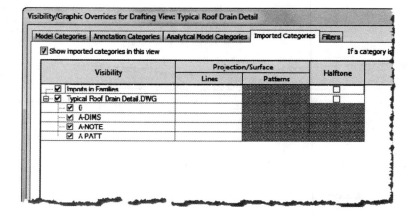

FIGURE 9-5.5 Controlling DWG layer visibility in Revit

Creating 2D Details:

Autodesk Revit Architecture has a large array of 2D detail components that can be used to create 2D details. These components allow for efficient detail drafting and design. Not every detail in Revit is generated from the 3D model; the amount of modeling required to make this happen is restricted by time, file size and computing power. The following is an outline of the overall process; this will be followed by a few exercises for practice:

11. To create a 2D detail, one would create a **Drafting View** via *View > Create > Drafting View*; providing a name and selecting a scale.

12. Once the *Drafting View* has been created, **Detail Lines** and **Filled Regions** (via the *Annotate* tab) can be added.

13. In addition to *Detail Lines* and *Filled Regions*, one can insert pre-drawn items from the <u>Detail Library</u>.

    a. Select *Component > Detail Components* from the *Annotate* tab.

    b. Select **Load Family** from the *Ribbon*.

    c. Click **Imperial Detail Library** from the shortcut bar on the left of the *Open* dialog.

    d. **Browse** to the specific "CSI organized" folder; for example, *Div 5-Metals→052100- Steel Joists Framing → K-Series Bar Joist-Side.rfa.*

    e. Click **Open** to place the component.

14. Add notes and dimensions to complete the 2D detail.

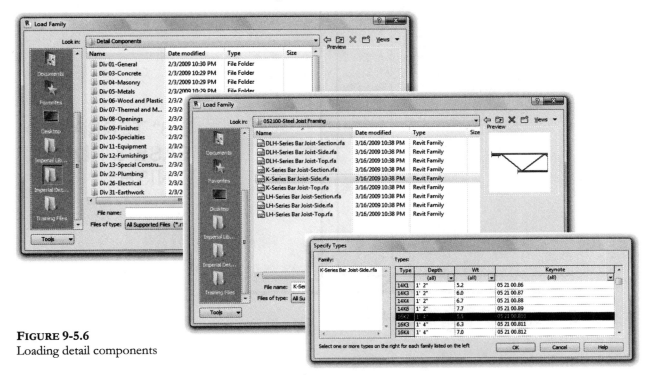

FIGURE 9-5.6
Loading detail components

Flooring Details

The first two details you will draw are simple details consisting of *Detail Lines*, *Filled Regions*, *Text* and *Dimensions*.

You will draw a high-end floor and wall base detail known as terrazzo. This finish is poured in a liquid state, allowed to dry and then polished to a smooth finish. The colors and aggregate options are virtually unlimited (for example, you could use a clear epoxy resin and place leaves within the flooring).

15. Per the steps previously covered in this section, create a new *Drafting View*.
    a. *Name*: Terrazzo Base Detail
    b. *Scale*: 3"=1'-0"

You will now draw the detail shown below. See the next page for specific steps.

Terrazzo floor example with brass inlay

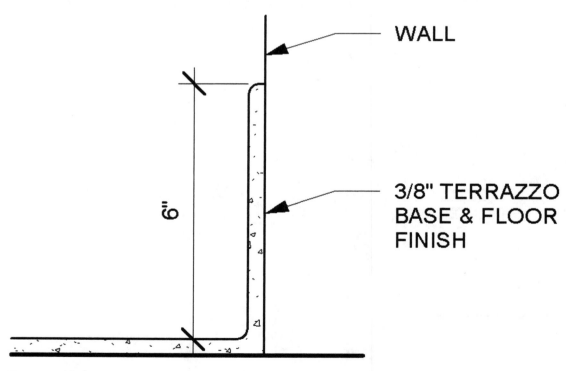

WALL

3/8" TERRAZZO BASE & FLOOR FINISH

6"

FIGURE 9-5.7 Terrazzo floor and wall base detail

16. Using the **Detail Lines** tool from the *Annotate* tab, draw the floor line **8″** long using **Wide Lines**. *FYI: The eight inch dimension is random, and does not represent anything other than a portion of the floor surface.*

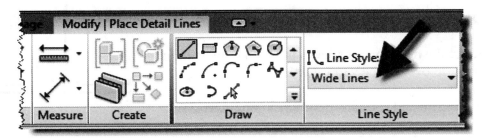

17. Draw a vertical line, also **8″** long, using the **Medium Lines** style. This line should be about 2″ from the right edge of the floor line (just so your detail is generally proportional to the one presented in the book).

Next, you will offset the two lines just drawn to quickly create the terrazzo floor and base.

18. Select **Modify → Offset** on the *Ribbon*.

19. On the *Options Bar*, enter an *Offset* value of **3/8″**.

20. Pick the floor line when the preview line appears above the horizontal line.

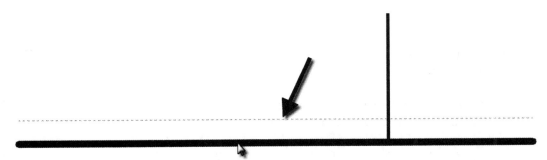

21. Now **Offset** the vertical line **3/8″** to the left.

Your drawing should now look like the image to the right (less the arrows). Next you will change the top horizontal line to a lighter line weight, offset it up 6″ to create the top of the wall base, and then use the *Fillet Arc* feature to round off the corners.

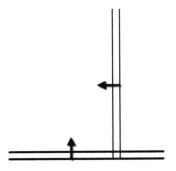

22. Select the top horizontal line and change the *Line Style* from *Wide Lines* to **Medium Lines** via the *Ribbon*.

23. **Offset** the top horizontal line upward **6"** inches.

24. Select the new horizontal line and then drag its right end grip over to the vertical line.

Next you will trim and round the corners in one step.

25. Select the ***Detail Line*** tool from the *Annotate* tab.

    a. Select **Fillet Arc** from the *Draw* panel.
    b. Set the *Line Style* to **Medium Lines**.
    c. Check and set the *Radius* to ¼".

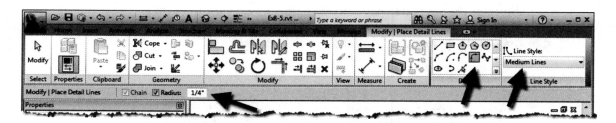

26. Click on the portion of the two lines you want to remain (see the two numbered clicks in the image to the right).

The line is now trimmed and an arc has been added.

27. Repeat these steps to round off the top edge of the wall base.

Next you will add a *Filled Region* to represent the terrazzo material with a pattern when viewed in a section. When creating the perimeter of a *Filled Region* you also specify a *Line Style* (similar to the *Detail Line* tool). In this case you will use *Thin Lines* for all but the left edge of the floor thickness. There you will change the *Line Style* to be an invisible line so as not to suggest a joint or the end of the flooring, but rather that the flooring material continues.

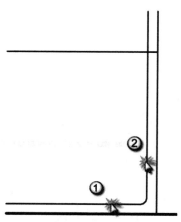

28. Select **Annotate → Detail → Region → Filled Region** from the *Ribbon*.

    a.   Select the **Pick Lines** option from the *Draw* panel.

    b.   Select **Thin Lines** from the *Lines Style* panel.

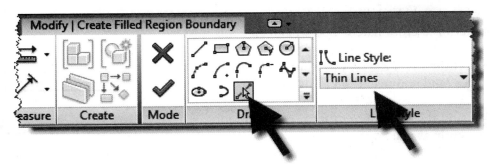

Selecting *Pick Lines* will allow you to quickly create the boundary of your *Filled Region* based on lines already drawn. So you simply click on a line rather than pick two points to define the start and endpoints of each edge. However, with the *Line* and *Arc* options you could also snap to the endpoints of the previously drawn line work. The one drawback to using the *Pick Lines* option is you will have to trim a few corners, because the *Filled Region* tool requires a clean perimeter be defined (similar to the *Floor* and *Roof* tools).

29. Pick the five lines and two arcs which define the edges of the floor and wall base.

30. Switch to the **Line** option in the *Draw* panel and then set the *Line Style* to **<Invisible Lines>**.

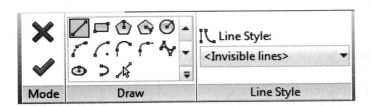

While in *Sketch* mode (i.e., the green check mark and red X are visible), for the *Filled Region* tool, the invisible lines are not actually invisible. This allows you to select and modify them as needed.

31. Draw a line to close off the open edge of the flooring on the left hand side.

32. Use the **_Trim_** tool to clean up the two corners where the lines run past.

33. Click the **green check mark** to finish the _Filled Region_.

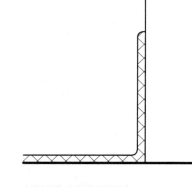

Your drawing should look like the one shown to the right. The default pattern is a cross hatch. You will change this next.

34. Select the _Filled Region_; you must click on one of the edges (and you may need to use Tab).

35. Expand the **_Type Selector_** to see the options currently available.

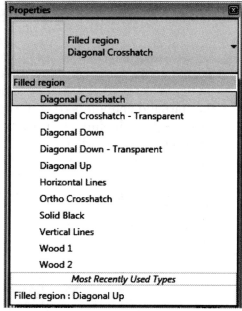

Looking at the list, we notice an option for concrete is not listed (which is what we decided we want). Next, you will learn how to add this.

36. Press **Esc** to close the _Type Selector._

37. Click **Edit Type**.

38. Click **Duplicate**.

39. Enter **Concrete** for the name.

40. Click in the _Fill Pattern_ field and then **click the icon** that appears to the right.

41. Select **Concrete** from the list and click **OK**.

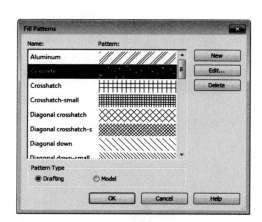

Notice the option to match the fill background opaque or transparent and the line weight setting.

42. Click **OK** to close the _Type Properties_.

Your terrazzo now has a concrete pattern. You can import additional fill patterns (using any AutoCAD hatch pattern file) or create custom ones with specific line spacing. This _Filled Region_ tool can be used in floor plans as well; maybe you want to highlight the corridors or private office areas. When a _Filled Region_ is selected, the square foot area is listed in the _Properties Pallet_. Thus, you could quickly create a _Filled Region_ just to list the area and then delete the _Filled Region_.

The last thing you will do is add the notes and dimensions. These will be the correct scale based on the *View Scale* setting (which should be 3″ = 1′-0″). Once you place the dimension, you will learn how to adjust the dimension style so the 0′ does not show up.

43. Add the dimension and two notes as shown.

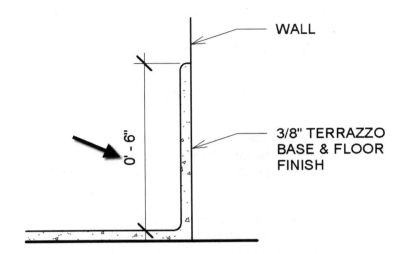

44. Select the dimension.

45. Select **Edit Type**.

46. Click the button to the right of **Units Format**.

47. Un-check **Use Project Units**.

48. Check **Suppress 0 feet**.

49. Click **OK** twice, to close both open dialog boxes.

Your dimension should now only say 6″ rather than 0′-6″. Because you changed this in the *Type Properties*, all dimensions will have this change applied (both previously saved and new). If you want to have both options, you would first need to *Duplicate* the dimension type, which is similar to creating new wall, door and window types!

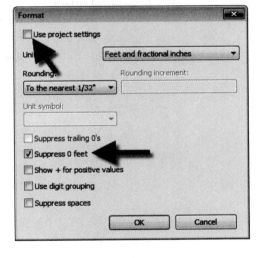

The last thing you will look at is adjusting the arrow style for the notes.

50. Select one of the notes.

51. Click **Edit Type**.

52. Change the *Leader Arrowhead* to **Arrow Filled 30 Degree**.

53. Click **OK**.

Your detail should now look similar to the one presented at the beginning of this exercise. This detail can now be placed on a sheet (covered in Chapter 15). You can also export this detail and save it in a detail library that you and others in your firm can utilize. To export the detail, simply right-click on the view name in the *Project Browser* and select *Save to new File*. Place the file on a server so everyone can get at it. To load this file into another project: select Insert → Insert from File → Insert Views from File.

Now you will draw another detail using the same tools and techniques. Keep in mind, every detail needs to go in its own *Drafting View*. This is required for Revit to manage the reference bubbles on the sheets.

54. Create a new **Drafting View**:
    a. *Name*: Floor Transition Detail
    b. *Scale*: $3'' = 1'-0''$

55. Draw the detail per the following guidelines:
    a. The detail will be plotted at $3''=1'-0''$ (this determines the text and leader size).
    b. Tile pattern is **Diagonal Up–Small**; this requires a new *Fill Region* style (see the previous exercise for more information).
    c. The grout (i.e., area under tile) is to be hatched with **Sand – Dense**; this also requires a new *Fill Region* style.
    d. Draw the tile ¼″ thick and 4″ wide.
    e. The grout is ¼″ thick.
    f. The resilient flooring is shown ⅛″ thick.
    g. The solid surface (i.e., Corian) threshold is set to 1⅞″ wide; draw an arc between the two floor thicknesses.
    h. Hatch the threshold with the solid hatch
        i. **Duplicate** the **Solid Black** *Filled Region* style.
        ii. Name the new style: **Solid Gray**.
        iii. Set the hatch's color to a light gray (RGB color 192).
    i. The bottom concrete floor line is to be the heaviest line.

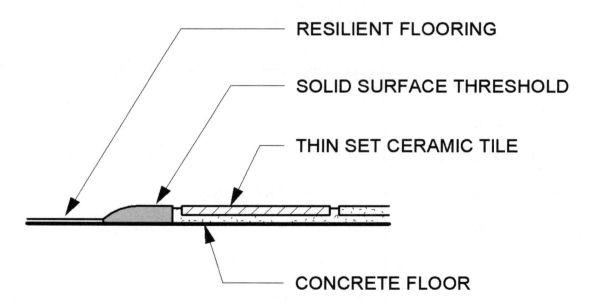

FIGURE 9-5.8 Floor transition detail: ceramic tile to resilient flooring

The previous drawing would typically occur in a door opening and the location of the door would also be shown in the detail. This lets the contractor know that the threshold is to occur directly below the door slab.

Base Cabinet with Drawers:

This section will dive right into drawing cabinet details. These are often based on industry standard dimensions so many of the dimensions and material thicknesses can be omitted (assuming the project manual/specification covers this).

> 56. Create a **Drafting View**:
>   a. *Name*: Base Cabinet Detail – Drawers
>   b. *Scale*: 1" = 1'-0"

Revit provides many *Detail Components* which aid in creating 2D details. Things such as side views of bar joists, section views of steel beams and angles, and more are available in the Detail Component library. The details below take advantage of three Detail Components which ship with Revit: particle board, lumber and the counter top. The only things drawn with the *Detail Line* tool are the tops of the drawers, the drawer pulls (i.e., handles) and the heavy wall/floor lines.

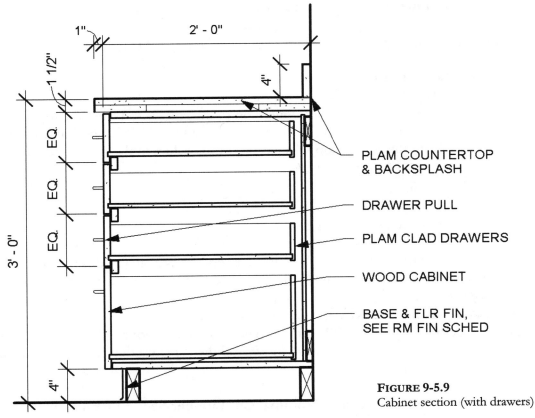

FIGURE 9-5.9
Cabinet section (with drawers)

57. Using the *Detail Line* tool, draw the floor and wall lines, shown in the image to the right, using the **Wide Lines** style. (Do not add the dimensions.)

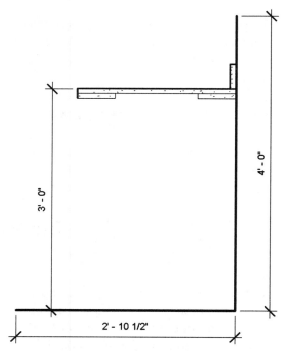

Next, you will load the counter top *Family* from the *Detail Component Library*.

58. Select **Annotate → Detail → Component → Detail Component** from the *Ribbon*.

59. Click **Load Family** from the *Ribbon*.

60. Click the **Imperial Detail Library** shortcut on the left (or just open the *Detail Components* folder).

61. Now, browse to: *Div 12-Furnishings → 123000-Casework → 123600-Countertops*.

62. Select **Countertop-Section.rfa** and then click **Open**.

Countertop-Section with type *24" Depth* is current in the *Type Selector*, and ready to be placed.

63. Place the countertop as shown:
    a. Aligned with wall;
    b. 3'-0" above the floor (Dimension to the line second from the top; the open heavy line is an exaggeration to highlight the added plastic laminate surface.)
    c. With the countertop selected, adjust the values in the *Properties Palette*:
        i. *Backsplash Depth*:   0' 1"
        ii. *Counter Depth*:   2'-1"
        iii. *Thickness*:   0' 1 5/8"
    d. Do not add dimensions yet.

Be careful not to click on the grips when the countertop is selected as this will adjust its dimensions. This is because the values are associated with an instance parameter rather than a type parameter.

Next, you will load and place the 2x lumber. The two on the floor are 4" high, which are cut down from a 2x6. So you will load a 2x4 *Family* and then create a duplicate and adjust the height from 3 ½" to 4".

64. Per steps just covered, load **Nominal Cut Lumber-Section.RFA** from the following location: *Detail Components → Div 06-Wood and Plastic → 061100-Wood Framing*.

To minimize the number of *Types* for the lumber *Family*, you are presented with the *Specify Types* dialog. This lets you pick just the sizes you want; more can be added later.

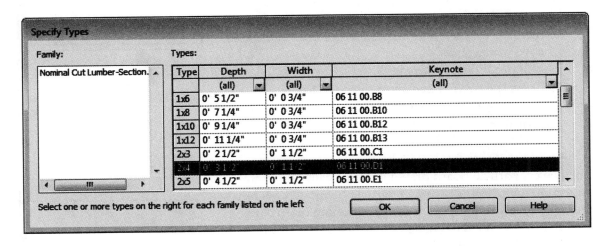

65. Hold the **Ctrl** key and select **1x4** and **2x4** and then pick **OK**.

66. Select **2x4** in the *Type Selector*.

67. Click **Edit Type**.

68. Click **Duplicate**.

69. Enter **2x4 Base Cabinets** for the name.

70. Change the *Height* from 3 ½″ to **4″**.

71. Click **OK** to close the *Type Properties*.

72. Place the two **2x4 Base Cabinet** *Detail Components* on the floor as shown in the image to the right. (Do not add the dimension.)

73. Place the two 1x4 components as shown.

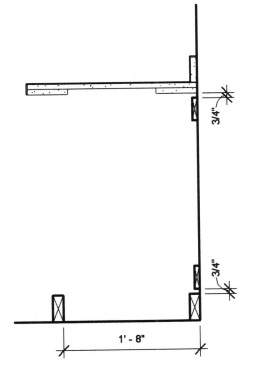

Next, you will load the detail component used to draw particle board. This *Family* is somewhat like the *Wall* tool. You pick two points and two lines and a fill pattern is generated. The *Type Selector* also has a number of standard thicknesses ready to use.

74. Per steps just covered, load **Particleboard-Section.rfa** from the following location: *Detail Components → Div 06-Wood and Plastic → 061600-Sheathing*.

75. Select the **3/4″** type from the *Type Selector.*

76. Draw the two pieces of particle board shown in the image to the right; these are the top and bottom of the base cabinet. *TIP: Use the space bar to flip the thickness while drawing, if needed.*

77. Draw the cabinet back; use the **3/8″** thickness option and extend it **1/4″** into the top and bottom boards. See image below. *TIP: Draw temporary detail lines so you have a place to pick if needed. Delete them when done.*

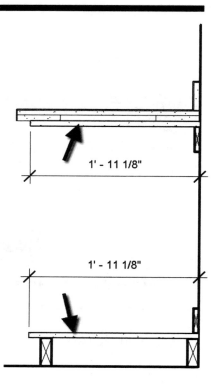

The newest particle board drawn automatically shows up on top of any previously drawn particle board. This is how the notice is created. There was not trimming or erasing required. If you need to change the order of the overlap, simply select the component and use the *Arrange* options on the *Ribbon.*

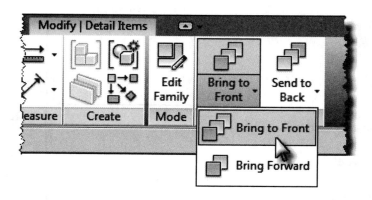

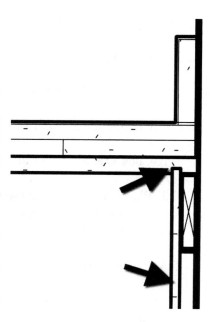

78. Draw the rest of the base cabinet using the techniques previously covered and the following information:

    a. The "EQ" dimensions are 6″.

    b. The drawer bottoms and backs are all ½″ particle board; everything else is ¾″.

    c. Use **Thin Lines** for the pulls and the top edge of the side drawer panel (seen in elevation in Figure 9-5.9). Use **Medium Lines** for the rubber base.

    d. Any dimensions not provided can be approximated; make it look like the image in the book as much as possible.

    e. Add all the notes and dimensions shown on the first image only.

Some things you should know about detailing:

In the previous steps you drew a typical detail showing a standard base cabinet with drawers. Interior designers occasionally draw these details, but more often they simply review them for finishes.

The countertop material needs to match that which is specified in the **Project Manual** and intended for the project. A PLAM (i.e., Plastic Laminate) countertop would not be appropriate in a laboratory where chemicals would be used.

The base of the cabinet typically has the same wall base as the adjacent walls. For example, if the walls have a rubber base (also referred to as resilient base), the toe-kick area of the base cabinet would also receive a rubber base; this is the type of base shown in the previous detail. If the project only had a ceramic tile wall base, you would show that.

The **notes for details** (or any drawing) should be simple, generic and to the point. Notice in previous detail drawn that the note for the base does not indicate whether the base is rubber, tile or wood. This helps avoid contradictions with the room finish schedule. The note simply says the cabinet and floor are to receive a finish and instructs the contractor to go to the *Room Finish Schedule* to see what the finish is. This is particularly important in buildings that have several variations of floor and base finishes.

Notes should not have any **proprietary or manufacturers' names** in them either. For example, you should not say "Sheetrock" in a note because this is the brand name; rather, you should use the generic term "gypsum board". Similarly, you use the term "solid plastic" rather than "Corian" when referring to countertops or toilet partitions. In any event, whatever term you use on the drawings should be the same term used in the Project Manual!

One last comment: the *Construction Documents* set should never have **abbreviations** within the drawings that are not covered in the *Abbreviations* list, usually located on the title sheet. *Construction Documents* are legal, binding documents, which the contractor must follow to a "T." They should not have to guess as to what the designers meant in various notes all over the set of drawings. It is better to spell out every word, if possible, only abbreviating when space does not permit. You would not want a bunch of abbreviations in your bank loan or mortgage papers you were about to sign! Plus, non-documented abbreviations would probably not have much merit before a judge or arbitrator in the case of a legal dispute!

79. Using the same steps just covered, draw the base cabinet shown below. Name the *Drafting View*: **Base Cabinet Detail**. The *Scale* is also **1″ = 1′-0″**.

TIP: Duplicate the Base Cabinet Detail – Drawer view and modify it to be this detail; much of this detail is exactly the same.

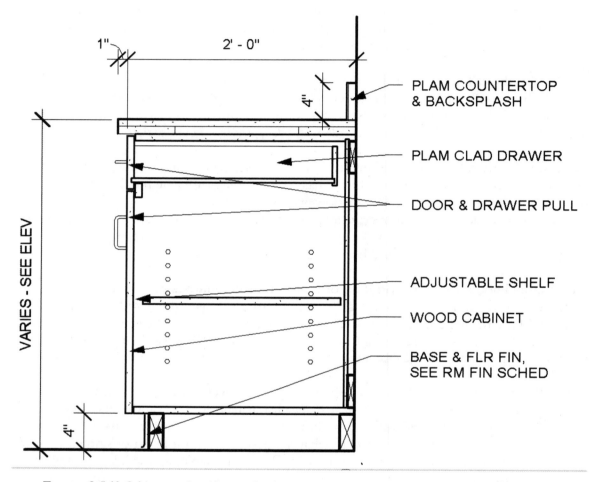

FIGURE 9-5.10 Cabinet section (door + drawer)

Cabinet details do not need to have every nook-and-cranny dimensioned because they are very much a standard item in the construction industry. Furthermore, the Project Manual usually references an industry standard that the contractor can refer to for typical dimensions, thicknesses and grades of wood.

The vertical dimension shown in the cabinet detail above says "VARIES - SEE ELEV". This notation, rather than an actual number, allows the detail to represent more than one condition. The interior elevations are required to have these dimensions, which may be the standard 36″ or the lower handicap accessible height.

Ceiling Detail:

Next, you will draw a typical recessed light trough detail at the ceiling. This is used often in commercial/public toilet rooms.

80. Create a new Drafting View:
    a. *Name*: Toilet Room Ceiling Detail
    b. *Scale*: 1½" = 1'-0"
    c. *See the next page for additional notes.*

81. Load the following *Detail Components* into your project:
    a. Div 09-Finishes → 092000-Plaster and Gypsum Board → 092200-Supports → 092216-Non-Structural Metal Framing
        iv. **Interior Metal Runner Channels-Section.rfa**
        v. **Interior Metal Studs-Side.rfa**
    b. Div 09-Finishes → 092000-Plaster and Gypsum Board → 092900-Gypsum Board → **Gypsum Wallboard-Section.rfa**
    c. Div 09-Finishes → 095000-Ceilings → 095100-Acoustical Ceilings
        vi. **Suspension Wall Angle-Section.rfa**
        vii. **Suspended Acoustic Ceiling-Square Edge-Section.rfa**

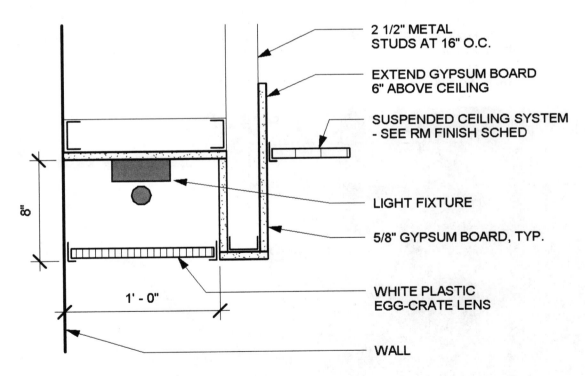

FIGURE 9-5.11 Ceiling detail

> ***TIP:*** *The notes in details should align on one edge as shown. Additionally, the leaders should not cross dimensions or other leaders unless it is totally unavoidable.*

When using the *Detail Components* you will occasionally run into a few challenges getting things to look exactly the way you want them. For example, many firms have traditionally shown the gypsum board as if it were continuous – not indicating the joints. Most contractors understand this and the designer usually does not want to imply the gypsum board be installed in a specific way or order. However, the *Detail Component* feature forces these edge lines to appear. Unfortunately, we **cannot** use the *Linework* tool to set some of the lines in a *Detail Component* to be invisible.

Another problem you will run into, when using *Detail Components*, is the fact that everything is drawn true to life size. You may think, isn't that a good thing? Usually it is, but some things often need to be exaggerated so they are legible on the printed page. Take the metal stud runner, for example; when placed next to the *Gypsum Board Detail Component* it is totally hidden because the gypsum line weight is heavier than the runner stud. The best thing to do is to edit the *Family* so the runner stud has a heavier line weight and its thickness is exaggerated inward (you don't want to change the overall width. However, this type of change is outside the scope of this exercise, so you will do the following:

82. Erase the runner stud *Detail Components* and draw **Detail Lines** using **Medium Lines** – inbound from the gypsum board.

83. Make the light fixture **4½″ x 1¾″** with a 1″ circle for the light. Use the **Solid Gray** *Fill Region* previously created.

84. Sketch the egg-crate lens using **Detail Lines**. Create a new *Fill Region* using the **Vertical-Small** fill pattern.

85. Add the notes and dimensions shown.

Photo of an installation based on ceiling detail.

Fixed Student Desk at Raised Seating Classroom:

This detail would work nicely for the fixed desks in a Lecture Classroom. However, assuming this detail came from a standard detail library, you would have to coordinate with what you have previously drawn in the floor plan. For example, the overall depth shown in the detail below is about 1'-5", and the depth drawn in plan might have preliminarily been drawn at 2'-0". They would need to match, changing the detail of the plan (or both, depending on what is needed for the given project).

86. Create a new **Drafting View**:
    a. *Name:* Fixed Student Desk
    b. *Scale:* 1½" = 1'-0"
    c. *See the next page for additional comments*

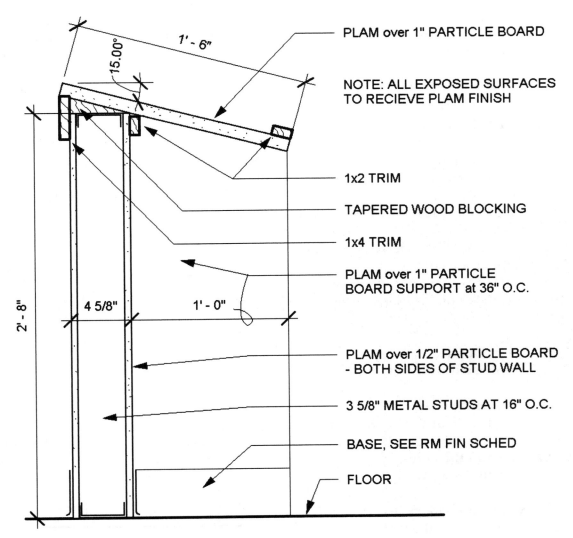

FIGURE 9-5.12 Fixed desk detail

87. Load the following detail component:
   a. Div 06-Wood and Plastic\062200-Millwork\Standard Millwork-Section.rfa
      i. Load the **1x2** and **1x4** sizes.

88. Develop the fixed student desk following these guidelines:
   a. All particle board and trim to be Detail Components.
   b. Tapered wood blocking to have **Wood 2** *Fill Pattern*.
   c. The curvy line pointing to the 1'-0" dimension should be drawn like this:
      i. First add the "PLAM" note using a regular leader;
      ii. Use the **Detail Line** tool;
      iii. Select the **Spline** *Draw* option;
      iv. Set the *Line Style* to **Thin**;
      v. Sketch the curvy line starting at the corner of the leader.
   d. Add a horizontal Detail Line at the top of the sloped work surface so you have something to pick when adding the angle dimension.

As you can see, some of the *Detail Components* have odd line weights when placed side-by-side. Both the wood trim and particle board are in section so they should be the same line weight. You would have to edit the family to make this change, which will not be covered at this time.

Using the Keynotes Feature:

The content that ships with Revit, both 2D and 3D, has a default keynote value assigned to it. Keynotes are used to save room and make details look neater; it is a reference number rather than a full note, and then an adjacent legend lists what each number means. This legend is for all the details on a sheet. You will lean how this works next. You will make a copy of the *Fixed Student Desk*, add keynotes and then create a keynote legend.

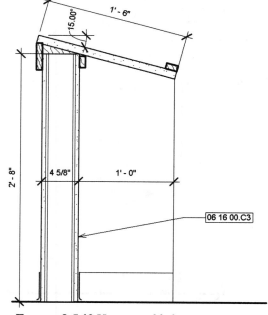

89. Right-click on the **Fixed Student Desk** item in the *Project Browser*.

90. Select **Duplicate →
   Duplicated with Detailing**.

91. Rename the new view:
   Fixed Student Desk – Keynotes

92. **Erase all the notes**, but leave the dimensions.

93. Select **Annotate → Tag →
   Keynote** from the *Ribbon*.

Keynote

FIGURE 9-5.13 Keynote added

94. With the *Keynote* tool active, click the ½″ particle board shown in Figure 9-5.13; you will see it highlight just before selecting it.

95. Click two additional points to define a leader and text location, just like placing text with a leader.

You now have a keyed note placed in your drawing. This only works for *Detail Components* (in drafting views) and not *Detail Lines* as they are too generic. Next, you will see where this keynote notation is coming from.

96. Select the ½″ particle board; go to its *Type Properties*.

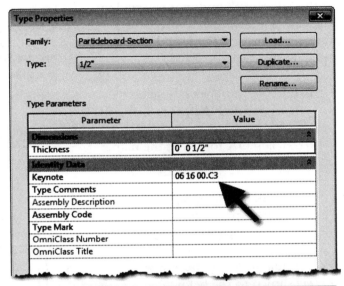

Notice the *Keynote* value listed. This was defined in the *Family* you loaded.

Now you will view the *keynote text file* so you can see how a family could be changed to "mean" something else. You might change a family directly or create a duplicate *Type* first.

97. Click in the cell listing the *Keynote*.

98. Click the small **icon** that appears to the right.

You now see a rather extensive listing of keyed notes. Take a minute to explore the various sections and descriptions for the keynote references.

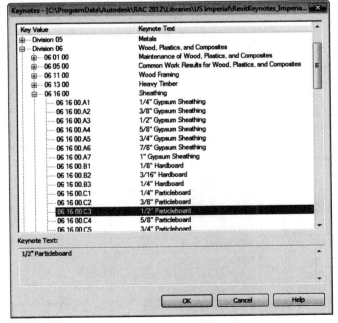

Notice the path listed at the top. This is the location of the text file being used for the keynotes. The path to this file is set via the *Keynoting Settings* icon located in the *Tag* panel expanded area on the *Annotate* tab.

99. After reviewing the keynote text file, click **Cancel**.

100. Click **OK** to close the *Type Properties* dialog.

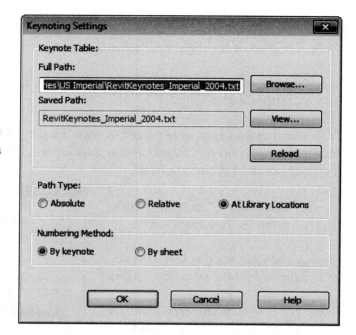

The last thing to learn is how to create the **Keynote Legend**. This legend can be added to any sheet with keynotes. If the "By sheet" option is selected in the dialog box shown to the right, only keynotes actually found on that specific sheet will be listed.

101. From the *View* tab, select **Legend → Keynote Legend**.

102. Click **OK** to accept the name: **Keynote Legend**.

103. Click **OK** to accept the default properties and to create the legend.

You should now see the *Keynote Legend* shown to the below.

> **FYI:** *Make sure the* numbering method *is still set to* By keynote *in order to see all the keynotes at this time.*

Later, in Chapter 15, you will learn how to place views on sheets.

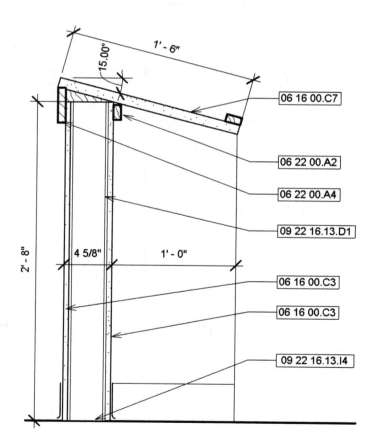

Keynote Legend	
Key Value	**Keynote Text**
06 16 00.	1/2" Particleboard
06 16 00.	1" Particleboard
06 22 00.	1x2 Wood Trim
06 22 00.	1x4 Wood Trim
09 22 16.	3 5/8" Metal Stud Framing
09 22 16.	3 5/8" Metal Runner
09 29 00.	5/8" Gypsum Wallboard

104. Add the remaining keynotes and then **Save**.

Finally, you can create elevations and sections that reference a drafting view rather than a true view of the model. This is another one of those places where you are breaking the intelligence of *Revit's* drawing sheet and number coordination.

To do this, you select the *Elevation* or *Section* tool, and rather than picking points in the drawing right away, you select a view that already exists in the project from the *Options Bar*. Even though you have not placed any roof drains, you could switch to the **Roof** plan view and add a section mark that references the roof drain detail.

The following steps do not need to be performed at this time:

105. Switch to the **Roof** floor plan view.

106. Select the **Section** tool on the *View* tab (or from the QAT).

107. On the *Ribbon/Options Bar* settings (Figure 9-5.14):

    a. *Type Selector:*   Detail View: Detail

    b. *Reference other view:*   check

    c. *Reference other view drop-down list:*   Typical Roof Drain Detail

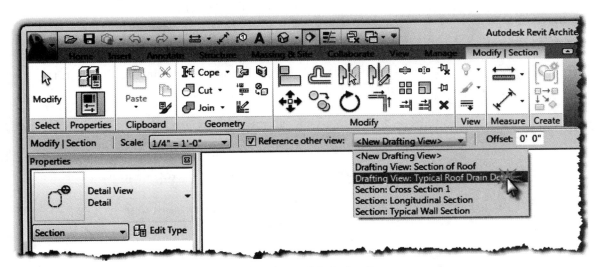

FIGURE 9-5.14 Placing a section that references the roof drain detail

108. Pick two points, roughly as shown in the image to the right

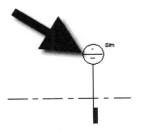

Try double-clicking on the blue bubble head; it should bring you to the roof drain detail. Once the detail is placed on a sheet, the bubble head will be automatically filled out!

109. Save as **9-5.rvt**.

Self-Exam:

The following questions can be used as a way to check your knowledge of this lesson. The answers can be found at the bottom of the page.

1. The plan is updated automatically when an elevation is modified, but not the other way around. (T/F)

2. You can use the *Elevation* tool to place both interior and exterior elevations. (T/F)

3. You can rename elevation views to better manage them. (T/F)

4. You have to resize the Level datum and annotations after changing a view's scale. (T/F)

5. The controls for the section mark (when selected) are similar to the controls for the elevation tag. (T/F)

Review Questions:

The following questions may be assigned by your instructor as a way to assess your knowledge of this section. Your instructor has the answers to the review questions.

1. The visibility of the crop window can be controlled. (T/F)

2. You have to manually adjust the lineweights in the elevations. (T/F)

3. As you move the cursor around the building, during placement, the elevation tag turns to point at the building. (T/F)

4. When a section mark is added to a view, all the other related views automatically get a section mark added to them. (T/F)

5. You cannot adjust the "extent of view" (width) using the crop window. (T/F)

6. What is the first thing you should do after placing an elevation tag?

    _____

7. Although they make the drawing look very interesting, using

    the _____ feature can cause Revit to run extremely slow.

8. It is possible to modify objects (like doors, windows and ceilings) in section views. (T/F)

9. You need to adjust the _____ to see objects, in elevation, that are a distance back from the main elevation.

10. AutoCAD DWG files should never be exploded. (T/F)

Lesson 10
Law Office: INTERIOR DESIGN:

This lesson explores the various interior developments of a floor plan, such as toilet room layouts, cabinets, casework and furniture design. Additionally, you will look at adding a guardrail and furring at the exposed structural steel columns. The rendered image below shows how Revit can be used to create an attractive, easy to understand presentation drawing of the building's interior design.

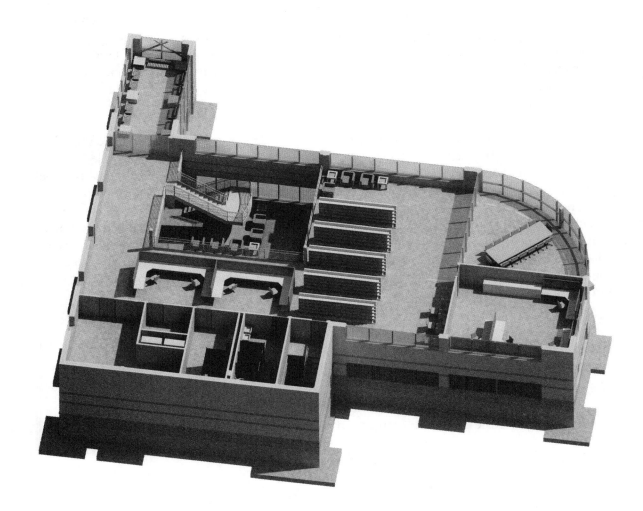

Exercise 10-1:
Toilet Room Layouts

There are several important factors in laying out a toilet room. The primary consideration typically is accessibility; that is, complying with local, state and federal accessibility codes so that people with various handicaps can easily access and use the toilet room facilities and the entire building in general.

Another consideration includes designed sight-lines. It is undesirable for a person in the hallway to see any of the toilet fixtures when the door is being opened by someone entering that restroom space. It should be obvious that privacy, especially between males and females, should be expected in a toilet room design. Seeing the sinks, or people washing their hands is not unacceptable but the designer needs to make sure the sight-lines are not extended by the mirror above the sink. The design techniques employed to impede improper sight-lines often takes up a fair amount of floor space.

Another consideration has to do with the plumbing fixtures. It is important to have the correct type of fixture drawn and have it drawn at the correct size. Some of the code requirements are based on the clear space in front of the fixture; thus, the fixture needs to be the correct size in order to verify compliance. Also, whether the fixture is wall-hung or a floor mounted tank-type fixture is important; the mechanical engineer needs to know as they specify the fixture in the Project Manual. If the toilet is wall-hung, the wall needs to be thick enough to conceal the support bracket and the plumbing; the wall is even thicker when two toilets are back-to-back. From a designer standpoint, wall-hung toilets are often desirable in commercial buildings because they are easy to clean under and can be equipped with automatic flushing to help ensure a better experience for everyone!

Placing Plumbing Fixtures:

You will start this exercise by loading several components to be placed into your project. You can use either Revit *MEP* or Revit *Architecture* to place the plumbing fixtures. Often the architectural team places them as they are doing the initial toilet room design. However, the content between the *MEP* software and the architectural software is, unfortunately, not the same. The *MEP* content has special connectors on them that allow the *MEP* designers to connect water and sanitary piping to the element. Given this information, we will save a step and load our plumbing fixtures from the *MEP* content folders. You will do this using Revit *Architecture*, seeing as we have not covered Revit *MEP* yet.

Placing Plumbing fixtures

Image credit:
Stabs, Wingate

1. Open Revit *Architecture*.

2. Open the **Law Office (CH10 starter file).rvt** file from the DVD; save this file to your working folder.

3. Select **Insert → Load from Library → Load Family**.

    NOTE: Revit MEP 2012 *must be installed on your computer for this step to work properly.*

    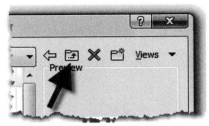

    FIGURE 10-1.1 Up one level icon

    a. Click the ***up one level*** icon in the upper right three times (Figure 10-1.1).

    b. Double-click the **RME 2012** folder.

    c. Double-click the **Libraries\US Imperial** folder.

    d. If you are having trouble finding the *MEP* content, you can also browse to the following folder:
        i. Windows Vista/Windows 7:
           C:\ProgramData\Autodesk\RME 2012\Libraries\US Imperial
        ii. Windows XP:
           C:\Documents and Settings\All Users\Application Data\Autodesk\RME 2012\Libraries\US Imperial

    FYI: *The Application Data folder is a* **hidden** *folder. In Windows Explorer: go to Tools →* *Folder Options → View tab and then select "Show hidden files and folders."*

4. Load the following Revit *MEP Families* into your law office project:

    Plumbing Components\Fixtures folder…
    a. Water Closets**Water Closet - Flush Valve - Wall Mounted.rfa**

    b. Urinals**Urinal - Wall Hung.rfa**

    c. Lavatories**Lavatory – Wall Mounted.rfa**

5. Load the following *Families* into your law office project:

    Families folder on the DVD… (or search Autodesk Seek via the Insert tab)
    a. **Grab Bar-3D.rfa**

    b. **Toilet Stall-Accessible-Front-Braced-3D.rfa**

    c. **Toilet Stall-Braced-3D.rfa**

    d. **Urinal Screen-3D.rfa**

Autodesk SEEK (http://seek.autodesk.com) is meant to mainly be for the actual manufacturer's Revit *Families*.

> **TIP:** *All Families that are required for the law office project are located in the Families folder on the DVD. This is helpful if the content was not installed with Revit.*

The files you just loaded into your project represent various predefined *Families* that will be used to design the toilet room. It is also possible to create custom families for unusual conditions (see Chapter 16 on the DVD).

6.   Switch to the **Level 1 Architectural** view.

Adding the Toilet Partitions

The toilet partitions offer privacy for toilets and urinals. They come in a few styles and materials. Styles range from floor-mounted to ceiling-hung; the latter offers better access to cleaning the floors, much like wall-hung toilets. Materials range from prefinished metal to solid phenolic core (i.e., plastic) to stainless steel.

The divider panels, pilasters and doors come in various thicknesses. However, each is typically drawn 1″ thick and is dimensioned to the center of the panel, so the thickness is not too important.

The example to the left shows a floor-mounted, overhead-braced toilet partition system.

Also, notice the urinal screen at the end of the countertop.

Floor drains are usually positioned beneath a toilet partition so users do not have to walk over the slightly uneven surface.

Notice the accent floor tile that also takes into consideration the location of the toilet partitions.

If you want to see images and more information on toilet partitions, you can visit the *Bradley Corporation* website listed below.

Select Tech data sheet PDF:
http://www.bradleycorp.com/products/mills/floor/viewproduct.jsp?pgid=673

Accessibility codes offer several layout options for toilet partitions. For example, if the door swings into the stall, more room is required in the stall to maintain the required clear floor space for the toilet fixture. Having a cheat sheet of several different layout options is a big help. Consult your local code for specifics.

The preceding image is very similar to the men's toilet room you are currently working on.

7. With the ***Component*** tool selected, pick **Toilet Stall-Accessible-Front-Braced-3D: 60″ x 60″ Clear** from the *Type Selector*.

8. Zoom in to the toilet room (east of the northern stair).

9. **Place** the toilet stall as shown and then move it into place using the ***Move*** (or *Align*) tool and your snaps (Figure 10-1.2).

   a. This is a *wall hosted* family, so it must be placed on a wall to exist in the project.

   b. Notice, when the toilet partition is selected, you have two flip controls which can be used to quickly change the orientation of the stall.

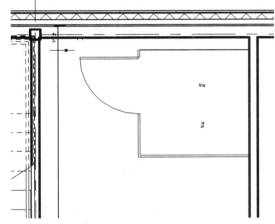

Once you move the toilet stall North, you will have your first stall in place.

FIGURE 10-1.2 Accessible Toilet stall

Next, you will place two standard size toilet stalls.

10. Place two toilet stalls (**Toilet Stall-Braced-3D: 36″ x 60″ Clear**) as shown in Figure 10-1.3.

As with most projects, you will need to modify the model as you develop the design. In this case, we notice that toilets that are back-to-back and stacked on each floor will require a thicker wall to accommodate the fixture brackets as toilets are not supported by light gauge metal studs, and larger piping. You will make this adjustment next.

For information on wall thicknesses behind double-hung toilets visit: **www.pdionline.org** and review the publication: *Minimum Space Requirements for Enclosed Plumbing Fixture Supports.*

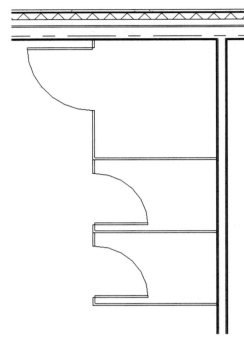

FIGURE 10-1.3 Std. Toilet stalls added

11. Select the middle wall and **Move** it **6″** to the West.

Notice how the toilet partitions moved with the wall because they are wall-hosted *Families*. The ceilings also adjusted.

12. Add an additional **4⅞″** gyp. bd. wall as shown in **Figure 10-1.4**.

In this case, you would not want to delete the original central wall and add two new walls. If you deleted the center wall, the wall-hosted content would also be deleted and the ceilings would no longer update.

Next, you will adjust the *Location Line* of the two "wet walls" (i.e., walls that have plumbing behind them). This will help keep the finished face of the wall in the proper location when you adjust its thickness in the next few steps.

13. Select the two wet-walls centered on the two toilet rooms and set the *Location Line* to **Finished Face: Exterior** via *Properties*.

14. Adjust the flip-control for each wall so they are positioned, in relation to the wall, as shown in Figure 10-1.4.

   FYI: You only see the flip-control when a single wall is selected.

15. Reposition the walls, if needed, so they match the dimensions shown in Figure 10-1.4; use the *Measure* and *Move* tools plus the temporary dimensions.

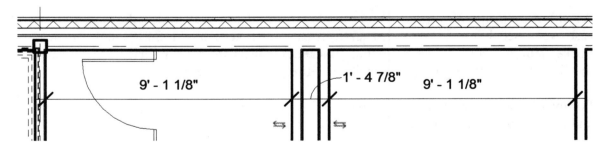

FIGURE 10-1.4 Toilet room wet-wall locations

Creating a Custom Wall Type

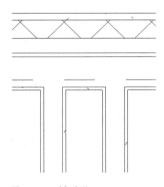

Now you will create a new wall type within your BIM project. The new wall type will be similar to the 4⅞″ stud wall, but it will only have gypsum board on one side of the wall.

Looking at Figure 10-1.5, you see the wall has gypsum board in the plumbing cavity, which is not appropriate. This would never be constructed this way, and if the BIM were used for quantity takeoff you would have too much gypsum board in the total.

FIGURE 10-1.5
Toilet room wet-wall

16. Select one of the two center toilet room wet-walls.

17. Select **Edit Type** from the *Properties Palette*.

18. Click **Duplicate**.

19. Type: **Interior - 4 1/4″ Furring Partition**.

20. Click **OK**.

21. Click the **Edit** button next to the *Structure* parameter.

22. Click on Row 5 to select it, the gypsum board *Layer* on the *Interior Side*.

23. Click the **Delete** button to remove the selected *Layer*.

Your *Edit Assembly* dialog should now look like Figure 10-1.6.

24. Click **OK** twice to close the open dialog boxes.

25. Select the other wet wall and change it to **Interior - 4 1/4″ Furring Partition** via the *Type Selector*.

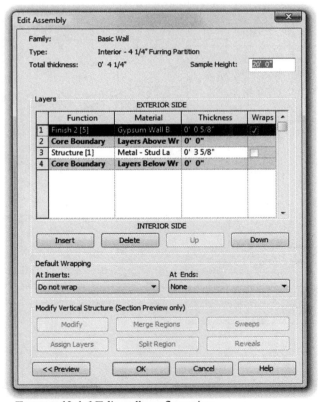

FIGURE 10-1.6 Edit wall configuration

Your two furring walls should now look like Figure 10-1.7. If the Location Line was not set properly, or the exterior side identified properly, the wall would have moved out of its proper position when you changed to a wall with a different thickness.

26. Use the *Measure* tool to ensure the walls are in the proper position; see Figure 10-1.4.

The exterior wall may have continuous gypsum board as shown. We will not modify that.

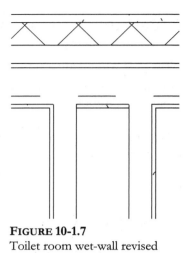

FIGURE 10-1.7
Toilet room wet-wall revised

27. Add the additional components as shown in **Figure 10-1.8**.

a. Note the family *name* is listed first and then the *Type*.

b. The height (hgt) can be changed via the *Instance Properties*.

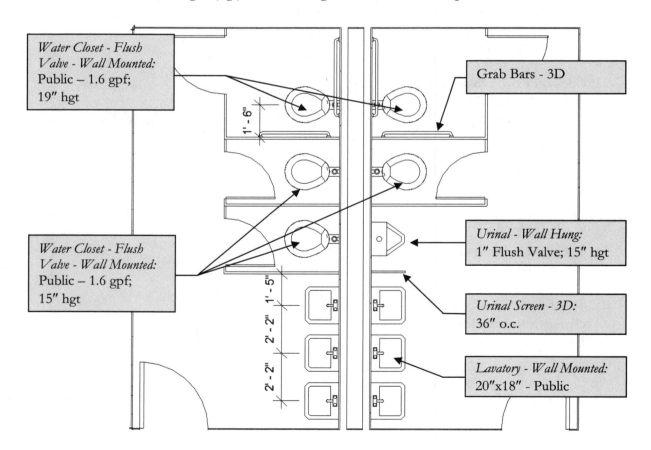

FIGURE 10-1.8 Toilet room layout

As mentioned previously, building codes vary by location. The toilets in the accessible stall area are usually mounted higher than the typical fixtures. When a room has more than one urinal, one is usually required to be mounted lower for accessibility and young children. Another example is that Minnesota requires a separate vertical grab bar above the horizontal grab bar on the wall next to the toilet; see Figure 10-1.9.

FIGURE 10-1.9 Grab bars

Creating a Group

Whenever you have a repeating arrangement of elements, you can create a **Group** and then copy the named *Group* around. When a change needs to be made to the *Group*, you change it in one place and all the others automatically update.

You will select the entire toilet room layout and turn it into a *Group*. Then you will place a copy of that *Group* on Level 2.

28. Select the entire toilet room layout:

   a. 2 Wet walls   e. 1 Urinal

   b. 5 Toilets   f. 1 Urinal partition

   c. 5 Toilet partitions   g. 2 Grab bars

   d. 6 Lavatories

29. With 22 elements selected, listed on the *Status Bar*, click the **Create Group** tool on the *Ribbon*.

FIGURE 10-1.10 Naming a group

30. For the *Group Name* type: **Toilet Room Layout** (Figure 10-1.10).

31. Click **OK**.

You now have a *Group* which can be inserted on Level 2. However, you must do one more thing before doing that. You need to define the insertion point of the *Group*. By default, the insertion point for new groups is the center point of all the elements within the *Group*. This is fine for furniture groupings, but not for our toilet room layout where we do not want to have to move it around to find the correct location once placed.

32. Click to select the <u>Toilet Room Layout</u> group in the **Level 1 Architectural Floor Plan** view.

33. Click on the *Origin* icon and drag it to the upper-right corner of the men's toilet room as shown in Figure 10-1.11.

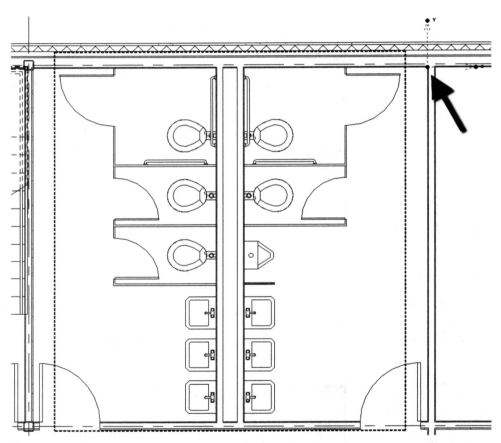

FIGURE 10-1.11 Repositioning the group's origin icon

Placing a Group

Now you will place a copy of your new Group on Level 2.

34. Switch to **Level 2** and zoom in to the toilet room area.

35. Delete the original center wall between the two toilet rooms.

36. On the *Ribbon*, select **Home → Model → Model Group → Place Model Group** (Figure 10-1.12).

37. With your *Group* selected in the *Type Selector*, click the upper-right corner of the men's toilet room area to place the *Group*.

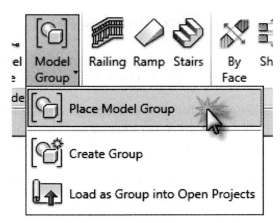

FIGURE 10-1.12 Place Model Group tool

You should now have a copy of your toilet room layout on Level 2! *Groups* can save a lot of time. See Figure 10-1.13.

To edit a *Group* you select it, and then click *Edit Group* on the *Options Bar*. When in *Edit Group* mode, the main model is grayed out so you can easily see what is in the *Group*. Once the changes are made, simply click *Finish Group* on the *Ribbon* and all instances of the *Group* are updated.

You will not make any changes to the *Group* at this time. If you decide to experiment, just *Undo* your changes before moving on.

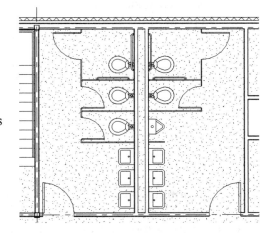

FIGURE 10-1.13 Group placed on Level 2

There are a few challenges to using groups:

- You cannot put a hosted element, such as a door or window, in a *Group* without the host (e.g., the wall).

- The height of the walls cannot vary, so the floor-to-floor height must be the same if you have walls in the group.

Near the bottom of the *Project Browser*, you will see a heading for *Groups*. You can find your *Group* listed there. If you right-click on the Group in the *Project Browser*, you can select *Save Group* to save a copy of the *Group* to its own file. This could be helpful if you needed to use this same layout in a multi-building project.

Interior Elevation View:

Next, you will set up an interior elevation view for the *Men's Toilet Room* using skills learned in previous chapters. You will also add a mirror above the sinks in elevation view.

38. Switch to **Level 1** and place an [interior] **Elevation** tag looking towards the wet wall, the wall with fixtures on it (Figure 10-1.14).

Notice again, how Revit automatically found the extents of the room when the elevation tag was placed in the plan view.

39. Rename the new view to: **Men's Toilet – Typical** in the *Project Browser*.

40. Switch to the new view. Adjust the *Crop Region* so the concrete slab is not visible. Your view should look like Figure 10-1.15.

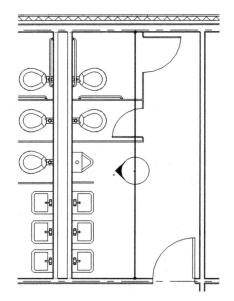

FIGURE 10-1.14 Elevation tag added

Your view should look like Figure 10-1.14. Notice how the lavatories (i.e., sinks) do not have faucets shown? This is because the *Detail Level* is not set to *Fine*. *Families* have the ability to be set up to show more or less detail as needed. The lower detail settings can make Revit run faster, but often the detail is needed to properly coordinate and annotate the drawings.

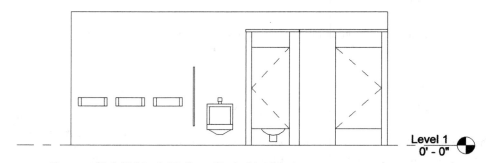

FIGURE 10-1.15 Men's Toilet – Typical initial view

41. Set the *Detail Level* to **Fine** and the *View Scale* to ½" = 1'-0" on the *View Control Bar.*

You should now see the faucets. Next, you will edit the *Group* to add mirrors above the sinks. This will automatically update Level 2.

42. Load the component **Mirror.rfa** from the DVD (or via SEEK).

43. While in the interior elevation view, select any of the elements that are in the *Group*.

Edit
Group

44. Select **Edit Group** from the *Ribbon*.

45. While still in the interior elevation view, place a **72″ x 48″ Mirror** on the wall above the sinks. Use the *Align* tool to align the mirror with the middle sink (Figure 10-1.16).

The mirror could only be added to the group because the wall it is to be placed on is in the same group.

46. Click **Finish** on the floating *Edit Group* panel (see image to right).

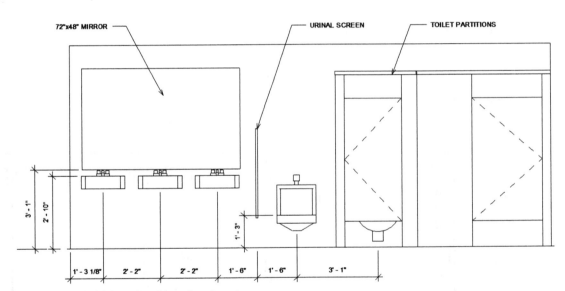

FIGURE 10-1.16 Updated interior elevation

47. Add the notes and dimensions per Figure 10-1.16. Adjust the heights and locations of the fixtures and components as required.

> *FYI: Keep in mind that many of the symbols that come with Revit, or any program for that matter, are not necessarily drawn or reviewed by an architect. The point is that the default values, such as mounting heights, may not meet ADA, national, state or local codes. Items like the mirror have a maximum height from the floor to the reflective surface that Revit's standard components may not comply with. However, as you apply local codes to these families, you can reuse them in the future.*

Adjusting the Reflected Ceiling Plan:

Because you added a wall in the East toilet room, the definition of the room that the reflected ceiling plan uses is incorrect. You will adjust that next. You will have similar problems on Level 2 because you deleted a wall and then placed a *Group*.

48. Switch to the **Level 1** ceiling plan (Figure 10-1.17).

49. **Hide** the interior elevation tag from this view. Select the two components; right-click and select **Hide in View → Elements**.

50. Select the ceiling in the *Men's Toilet Room*, and then click **Edit Boundary** on the *Ribbon*.

    a. You may have to tap the **Tab** key to select the ceiling.

51. **Adjust** the left side of the ceiling to align with the new wall; when finished, click **Finish Ceiling** on the *Ribbon* (Figure 10-1.18).

Remember, deleting an element and then replacing it can cause problems!

52. Correct the ceilings on Level 2.

53. **Save** your project.

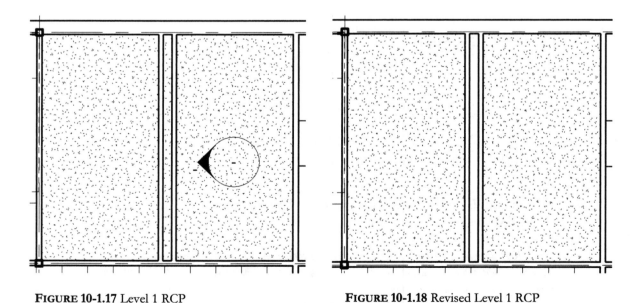

FIGURE 10-1.17 Level 1 RCP   **FIGURE 10-1.18** Revised Level 1 RCP

Exercise 10-2:
Cabinets

Introduction

This exercise covers the basic techniques used to add casework to your model. Casework is typically any built-in cabinets, countertops, desks, bars, etc., and is usually installed by a carpenter. This does not include systems furniture, or cubicles, which are sometimes attached to the wall.

The architectural floor plans typically show the built-in items (i.e., casework) and the FFE Plan (furniture, fixtures and equipment) typically shows the moveable items. Furniture placement is covered in the next exercise.

Cabinets rendered in Revit

The words "typical" and "usually" are used a lot because there is no exact science to how a set of drawings are put together. They can vary by country, state, city and even office.

Break Room Cabinets

Cabinets in a break room can vary quite a bit. The photo on the next page is similar to what you will be drawing next. The **base cabinets** are on the floor and are typically 24″ deep, but come in a variety of depths. The **wall cabinets** are attached to the wall and also come in various depths, 12″ and 14″ being the most common.

As you can see, the **electrical outlets** need to be coordinated with the electrical engineer; they need to be installed above the countertop and below the wall cabinets. When preparing the program, the designer should get a list of all the equipment required in each area. This will determine the number of outlets and locations. Often, items are overlooked or added later, creating an unsafe strain on the electrical system or requiring extension cords. For example, it is possible that the microwave shown in the photo was added by the users long after the design of the building; if the electrical system did not have enough capacity, it could make for an unsafe condition. If that were the case, a new outlet on another circuit would need to be added.

Notice two things about the wall cabinets: **1)** The cabinets have **under-counter lights** across the entire length. If this is desired by the client or designer, the electrical drawings need to be coordinated and the bottom of the cabinet recessed so the light fixture is not directly seen. **2)** The space between the top of the cabinet and the ceiling is filled in with studs and gypsum board for a clean, dust free finish, which is not always in the budget.

The cabinets in the break room often have plumbing to coordinate as well, for example, a sink or dishwasher. When drawing plans, these items are roughly placed and then more refined later with interior elevations. With Revit both are automatically updated at the same time.

Example of typical work room cabinets; see comments on previous page

Placing Cabinets:

You will add base and wall cabinets in a break room on Level 1.

1. Open your law office *BIM* file, using Revit *Architecture*.

2. Switch to **Level 1** view and zoom in to the area shown in Figure 10-2.1.

   TIP: Notice how the grids in the image below help locate what part of the plan is under consideration without the need to show the entire plan.

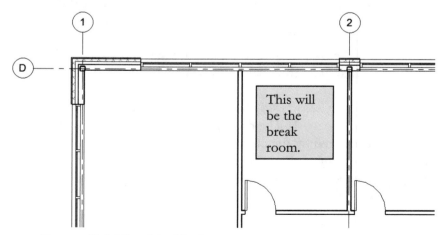

This will be the break room.

FIGURE 10-2.1 Level 1 – Northwestern corner

3. Load the following components into the project:

   (sub-folder: Casework\Domestic Kitchen):
   a. **Base Cabinet-4 Drawers**

   b. **Base Cabinet-Double Door Sink Unit**

   c. **Base Cabinet-Single Door**

   d. **Upper Cabinet-Double Door-Wall**

   > *TIP: You can load all four cabinets at once; just hold down the Ctrl key while you select them, and then click Open.*

   (sub-folder: Specialty Equipment\Domestic):
   e. **Refrigerator**

   (load from DVD Families folder):
   f. **Law Office Counter Top w Sink Hole**

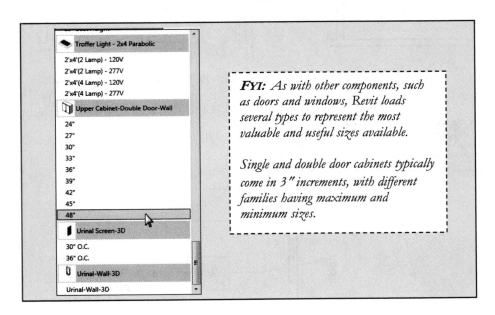

> *FYI: As with other components, such as doors and windows, Revit loads several types to represent the most valuable and useful sizes available.*
>
> *Single and double door cabinets typically come in 3" increments, with different families having maximum and minimum sizes.*

You are now ready to place the cabinets into your floor plan.

4. Select **Home → Component → Place a Component**, and then pick *Base Cabinet-4 Drawers*: **24"** from the *Type Selector*.

5. Place the cabinet as shown in **Figure 10-2.2**.

   > *TIP: The control arrows are on the front side of the cabinet; the cursor is on the back. Press the spacebar to rotate before clicking to placing the element.*

6. Place the other two base cabinets as shown in **Figure 10-2.3**, with a 24″ single door base cabinet in the middle and a 48″ sink base to the Northern end.

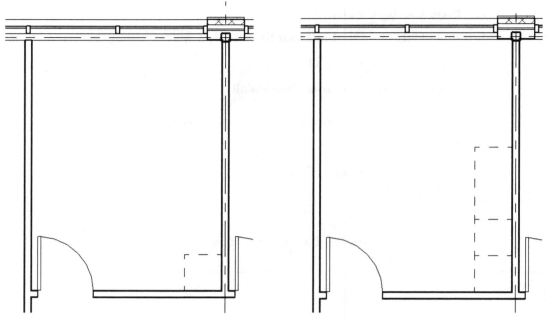

FIGURE 10-2.2 First base cabinet placed   **FIGURE 10-2.3** Three base cabinets placed

7. Add the four items as shown in Figure 10-2.4.

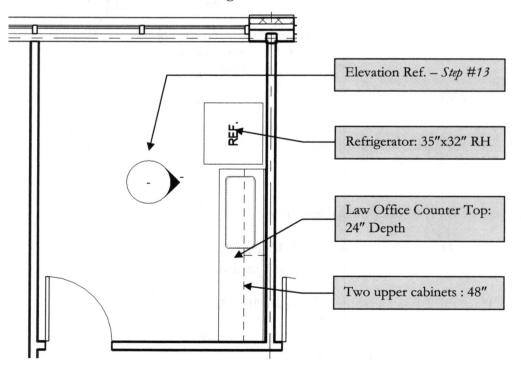

Elevation Ref. – *Step #13*

Refrigerator: 35″x32″ RH

Law Office Counter Top: 24″ Depth

Two upper cabinets : 48″

FIGURE 10-2.4 Break room plan view

> *FYI:* *The refrigerator has a hidden* Reference Line, *visible when the* Family *is selected, to help position the item the standard distance from the wall.*

Base cabinets are not hosted, which means they can be placed anywhere in the plan: against a wall or in the middle of a room as an island or peninsula. Uppers (wall) cabinets *are* wall hosted. Because wall cabinets are supported by walls, with rare exception, it makes sense that they be wall hosted similar to doors. When the wall moves, the upper cabinets will move with it; if the wall is deleted, the uppers will also be deleted. The base cabinets will not be moved if a wall is moved. This requires manual edits to the model. Both situations have pros and cons; for example, a group of wall cabinets cannot be easily moved to another wall, but a wall cabinet can be placed in an elevation view.

Placing the Sink:

Next you will be adding the sink. Similar to the previous exercise, you will be adding a sink from the Revit *MEP* content so it has the proper "connections" for the piping. None of the architectural content has these "connections" so we will not use them here.

The sink you are about to place is a **face** hosted component, which means it can be placed on any 3D face within the model. Much of the *MEP* content is *face* hosted, because the other hosted types, e.g. walls, floor, and ceiling, do not work when linked models are used. Revit cannot find a wall through a link, but it can find a face.

The reason you loaded a custom countertop, and not one from the standard Revit library, is that it has been set up to properly work with *face based* families. The version that comes with Revit has the 3D geometry hidden in plan views, so a *face based* family cannot find a face.

When you placed the countertop and wall cabinets, they were located at a default height above the floor, which is set in the family. The nice thing about *face based* families is that they automatically stick to the face, no matter at what elevation it is. Therefore, you do not need to know the height of the countertop when placing the sink. And, of course, if the height of the countertop is adjusted later in the design, the sink will move with it.

8. Load the sink. See page 10-3 on loading *MEP* content.
    a. *MEP content folder:* **Plumbing Components\Fixtures\Sinks**
    b. *Family/File name:* **Sink - Kitchen - Double.rfa**

9. With the *Component* tool selected, pick:
    a. *Family:* **Sink – Kitchen – Double**
    b. *Type:* **42"x21" - Public**

10. On the *Ribbon*, select **Place on Face**; see image below.

> *FYI: The default option for face based family placement is "place on vertical face," which would be the side of the countertop.*

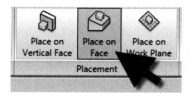

11. Click anywhere on the countertop to place the sink.

12. Move the sink into position, centered on the hole in the countertop (Figure 10-2.5).

It is not really necessary to have a hole in the countertop at sink locations. This would only be required when cutting a section through it at the sink or when creating a rendering. Notice that the faucet is added separately, even though the *Family* has a hot and cold water connection built in.

Creating an Interior Elevation:

13. Add an interior elevation tag to set up the interior elevation view (Figure 10-2.4).

14. Rename the new elevation view to **Break Room (east)**.

15. Switch to the new view, **Break Room (east)**.

16. Adjust the **Crop Region** so the slab on grade is not visible.

17. Set the view scale to ½″ = 1′-0″.

18. Set the *Detail Level* to **Fine** so the sink faucet is showing, via the *View Control Bar*.

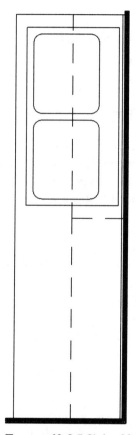

FIGURE 10-2.5 Sink added

Your drawing should look like **Figure 10-2.6**.

> *FYI: The wall cabinets are shown with dashed linework in plan because they occur above the floor plan cut plane. This helps to differentiate between wall and base cabinets.*

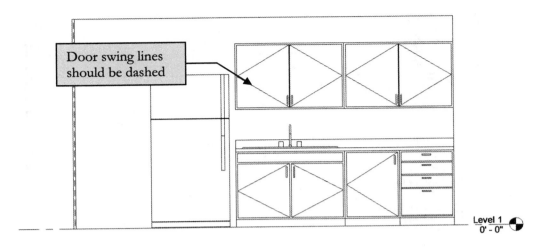

FIGURE 10-2.6 Interior elevation

Object Styles:

Next you will change the line type for the angled lines. These lines indicate the direction the cabinet doors open; they should be dashed. You could type "VV" and make the change for this view only. However, you will make the change from the *Manage* tab, on the *Ribbon*, and change this setting for every view!

19. Select **Manage → Settings → Object Styles**.

Any changes made in the *Object Styles* dialog box automatically update all views in the project.

20. On the *Model* tab, expand the **Casework** section (Figure 10-2.8).

21. Change the *Line Pattern* for Elevation Swing (sub-category) to **Hidden 1/8″** (Figure 10-2.8).

22. Click **OK** to apply the changes.

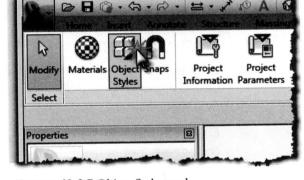

FIGURE 10-2.7 Object Styles tool

Your angled lines should now be dashed (Figure 10-2.8). Setting up line weights and patterns in the *Object Styles* dialog is an important step in setting up an office template. Do not forget about the "Show categories from all disciplines" check box to see everything when needed.

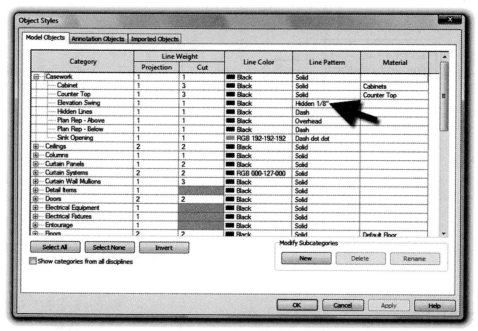

FIGURE 10-2.8 Object Styles dialog; Casework → Elevation Swing → Line Pattern changed

You will add notes and dimensions to the elevation. You can also add 2D linework to the elevation.

23. Add the notes and dimensions per Figure 10-2.9:

    a. All notes should be **3/32″ Arial** text style.
       i. Use the proper justification and leader option to make the notes look like those shown.

    b. Dimensions should be **Linear - 3/32″ Arial** and each string should be continuous, not individual dimensions.

    c. Use the ***Detail Line*** tool, on the *Annotate* tab, to draw the line on the wall behind the refrigerator indicating the vinyl base.

Detail Line

       i. Select the line and in the *Type Selector*, change the *Line Style* to **Thin Lines**.
       ii. Draw the line; snap to the endpoint of the base cabinet toe kick.

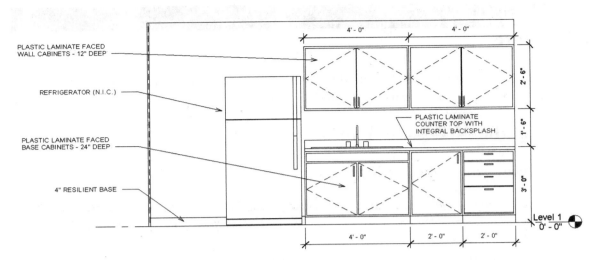

FIGURE 10-2.9 Interior elevation of Break Room with notes and dimensions added

> **FYI:** *The main difference between the* Model Line *tool on the Home tab and the* Detail Line *tool on the Annotate tab is this: Any linework drawn with the Model Line tool will show up on other views which see that surface. On the other hand, any linework drawn with the Detail Line tool will only show up in the view in which it was created.*
>
> *In other words, a Model Line is a 3D line and a Detail Line is a 2D line which is view specific. When drawing a Model Line you have to specify which plane you want to be sketching on, whereas the Detail Line does not care.*

It is possible to select a base or wall cabinet and swap it out with another cabinet via the *Type Selector*. When beginning to design a row of cabinets, it may be easier to place one base cabinet in plan and then switch to the elevation, copy the cabinet and swap it with the next cabinet needed; repeating these steps until done.

Notice how the countertop and wall cabinets were placed at the correct height. This was predefined in the family. If this same countertop was needed as a work surface at 30″, you could place it in plan and change the height via the element's *Instance Properties*, or simply move it in an elevation of section view.

Keep in mind these notes and dimensions may need to be manually adjusted if the cabinets are changed in another view, or this view.

Rather than dimensioning the width of the cabinets, it is also possible to tag them by category.

   24. **Save** your project.

Exercise 10-3:
Furniture

This lesson will cover the steps required to lay out office furniture. The processes are identical to those previously covered for toilets and cabinets.

Loading the Necessary Families:

1. **Open** your law office project.

2. Select the *Component* tool and load the following items into the current project. ***TIP:*** *All content needed in this book is located on the DVD. You can speed up this step by loading everything from the DVD as you can select multiple items and once when they are in the same folder.*

   Local Files *(i.e., Revit content on your hard drive)*
   a. Furniture System folder
       i. Work Station Cubicle
       ii. Storage Pedestal

   b. Furniture folder
       i. Cabinet-File 5 Drawer   vi. Chair-Task
       ii. Chair-Breuer   vii. Credenza
       iii. Chair-Desk   viii. Desk
       iv. Chair-Executive   ix. Table-Coffee
       v. Chair-Task Arms   x. Table-Dining Round w Chairs

   c. Specialty Equipment\Classroom-Library folder
       i. Single Carrel
       ii. Stack Shelving

   DVD Files *(the DVD that came with this book)*
   a. FN - Admin Reception Desk (custom family)

   b. FN – Reception Desk (custom family)

   c. Table-Conference2 w Chairs (can also be found on SEEK)

   Haworth Files *(from www.Haworth.com or DVD)*
   a. SLMS-FD01-8P (seating)

   b. SLMS-FD02-8P (seating)

   c. SLSE-SQ01-8P (lounge seating)

   d. SLSE-SQ02-8P (lounge seating)

   e. TOSE-SQW-BP (table)

These files represent various predefined families that will be used to design the offices.

> ***TIP:*** *You can set the View mode for the Open dialog box which is displayed when you click Load Family. One option is Thumbnail mode; this displays a small thumbnail image for each file in the current folder. This makes it easier to see the many symbols and drawings that are available for insertion.*

View set to Details mode   View set to Thumbnail mode

Designing the Office Furniture Layout:

3. The next two images of Level 1 and Level 2, Figures 10-3.1 and 10-3.2, show the furniture layout. Place the furniture as shown.

   TIP: *Use snaps to assure accuracy; use Rotate and Mirror as required.*

The two custom reception desks are examples of unique project related items that need to be created specifically for this project. You could not expect Autodesk to be able to create the infinite possibilities for you when it comes to content. Therefore, someone on the design team needs to be trained in creating content. In Chapter 16 of this book (on the DVD), an introduction to creating content is covered, but it just skims the surface. Chapter 5 covered a few basic concepts related to creating 2D families as well.

Custom Revit family

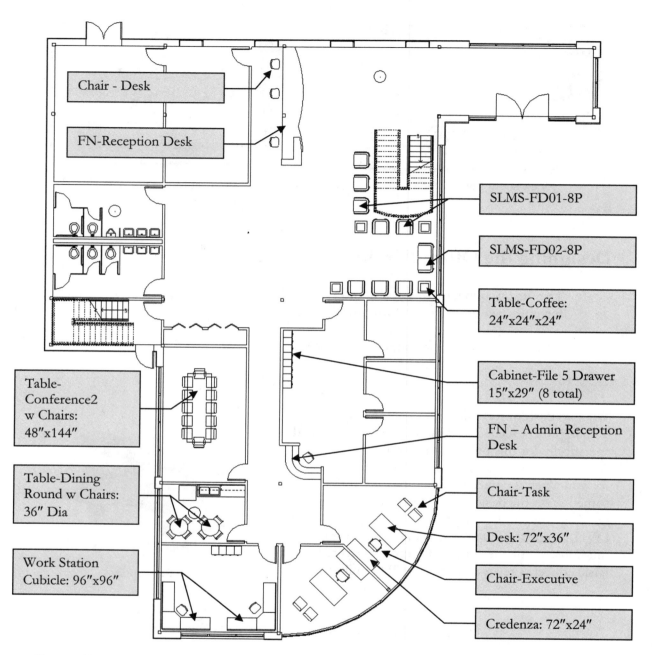

Figure 10-3.1 Level 1 furniture layout

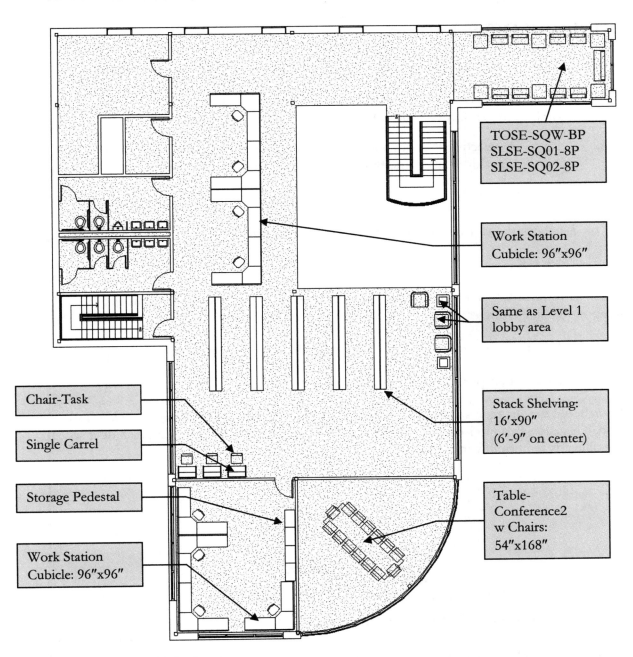

TOSE-SQW-BP
SLSE-SQ01-8P
SLSE-SQ02-8P

Work Station
Cubicle: 96″x96″

Same as Level 1
lobby area

Chair-Task

Single Carrel

Stack Shelving:
16′x90″
(6′-9″ on center)

Storage Pedestal

Table-
Conference2
w Chairs:
54″x168″

Work Station
Cubicle: 96″x96″

FIGURE 10-3.2 Level 2 furniture layout

3D view of Office Layout:

Next you will look at a 3D view of your office area. This involves adjusting the visibility of the roof.

4. Switch to the **Default 3D** view.

  a. Try selecting the roof and notice it becomes transparent. This is a quick way to quickly verify something hidden behind another element.

5. Type **VV**.

6. Uncheck the *Ceiling, Roof* and *Structural Framing* categories.

7. Click **OK**.

Now the roof, ceilings and steel beams and joists should not be visible. You can also temporarily hide entire categories of individual elements in a view.

8. Select the East exterior wall. (Again, notice the selected item becomes transparent.)

9. Click the **Temporary Hide/Isolate** from the *View Control Bar*.

You should see the menu shown in Figure 10-3.3 show up next to the *Temporary Hide/Isolate* icon. This allows you to isolate an object so it is the only thing on the screen, or hide it so the object is temporarily invisible.

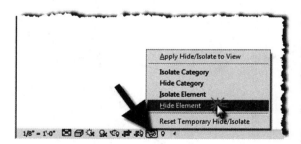

FIGURE 10-3.3 Hide/Isolate popup menu

10. Click **Hide Element** in the menu (Figure 10-3.3).

    FYI: This makes just the selected wall hidden; if you selected Hide Category, all the walls would be hidden.

Notice, while a *Temporary Hide/Isolate* is applied to a view, the perimeter of the view is highlighted with a heavy cyan line.

11. Adjust your **3D** view to look similar to **Figure 10-3.4** by clicking and dragging your mouse on the *ViewCube*.

You will now restore the original visibility settings for the **3D** view.

12. Click the *Hide/Isolate* icon and then select **Reset Temporary Hide/Isolate** from the popup up menu. (See Figure 10-3.3.)

> *NOTE: The* Temporary Hide/Isolate *feature is just meant to be a temporary control of element visibility while you are working on the model. If you want permanent results, you can click the "Apply Hide/Isolate to View" option. Also, to the right of the Hide/Isolate icon is the Reveal Hidden Elements icon, the light bulb icon, which will clearly show any elements that have been previously hidden.*

13. Reset the **3D** view's visibility settings so the roof, ceiling and structural framing are visible, via the *VV* shortcut.

14. **Save** your project.

> *Notice the furniture and toilet rooms are represented in 3D.*

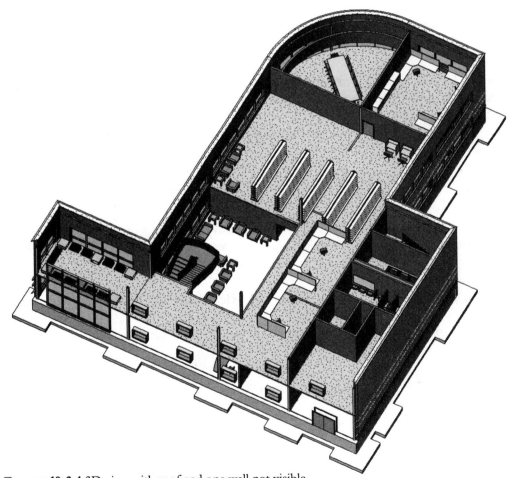

FIGURE 10-3.4 3D view with roof and one wall not visible

It is possible to save a copy of your **3D** view so you may leave it as shown in the image above. This would make it easy to refer back to this view. The view could also be placed on a sheet for presentation purposes.

Exercise 10-4:
Column Furring, Guardrails and Interior Curtain Wall

This lesson will cover the steps required to layout guardrails at the second floor opening, add a finish at the columns and add three additional doors into the interior curtain wall.

Adding Column Furring:

First you will add *Architectural Columns* at each of the structural column locations. These columns will automatically take on the properties of the wall they are placed on; thus they will show the gypsum board wrapping around the column. Structural columns do not take on the properties of elements they are joined to like architectural columns.

1. Open your law office project file using Revit *Architecture*; remember to make backups!

2. Switch to the **Level 1 Architectural** view.

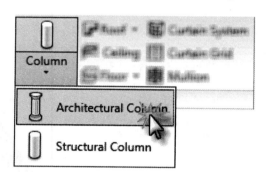

3. Select **Home → Build → Column → Architectural Column** from the *Ribbon*.

Looking at the *Type Selector*, you see there are three sizes available:
- 18"x18"
- 18"x24"
- 24"x24"

You will create a new type within the *Rectangular Column* family that is 8"x8", which is the size we want to wrap around and conceal the columns.

4. While still in the *Architectural Column* tool, select **Edit Type** from the *Properties Palette*.

5. Click **Duplicate** in the upper right to create a new *Type*.

6. Enter **8" x 8"** for the *Type* name (Figure 10-4.1).

FIGURE 10-4.1 Enter type name

You now have a new *Type* within the *Rectangular Column* family, but you still need to adjust the new *Type's* parameters to be the correct size.

7. Change the *Width* and *Depth* parameters to **8″** (Figure 10-4.2).

8. Click **OK** to save the changes.

Now you are ready to place one of the columns.

9. **Zoom** in to the Northeastern corner of Level 1.

10. Click at the intersection of Grids 5 and E.

As you can see (Figure 10-4.3), the outline of the column is not really visible. Is has blended in with the adjacent walls and now you have gypsum board that continues from the walls around the column.

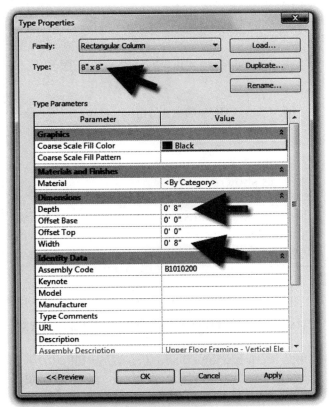

FIGURE 10-4.2 New type properties

In reality, this column may need to be a little larger to accommodate the metal furring which can range from ⅝″ channels to full 3⅝″, or larger, metal studs.

Now you will repeat this process at every column location on each floor. You will not be given images to follow as the concept is straight forward.

11. Add the same *Architectural Column* at every column location on **both** levels.

Some of the architectural columns in the middle of the building, not near a wall, do not have gypsum board showing. You will use the *Join* tool to tell Revit that the column should take on the properties of the adjacent wall.

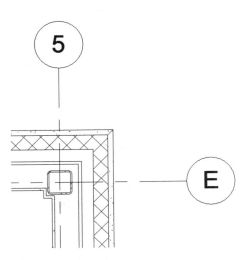

FIGURE 10-4.3 Architectural column added

12. On the *Ribbon*, select **Modify → Geometry → Join**.

13. **Select** one of the columns without gypsum board (e.g., Level 2 at Grids 4/C).

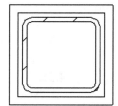

14. Now **select** any adjacent wall with gypsum board (to take on its properties).

15. Click **OK** to the warning about the joined elements not touching.

16. Repeat the previous steps as required so all the isolated columns have gypsum board as shown.

All your steel columns are now hidden by a finish. The architectural columns go from the floor, of the view you placed them in, to the level above by default. Sometimes this furring stops just above the ceiling; in this case you adjust the height via the column's *Instance Properties*.

Interior Curtain Walls with Doors:

In this section you will add a curtain wall with a door at the main entry vestibule and directly above it, in what will be a meeting lounge. Finally, you will change an interior wall, in the Level 2 large conference room, from a stud wall to a curtain wall and add a door.

17. Zoom in to the Level 1 main entry area in the Southeastern corner of the building.

18. Select the *Wall* tool.

19. Set the *Type Selector* to *Curtain Wall:* **Storefront**.

20. With nothing selected, note the *Instance Properties* via the *Properties Palette*.

You will adjust the height of the curtain wall to stop at the ceiling.

21. Set the *Unconnected Height* to **9'-6"**.

22. Click **Apply**.

23. Draw the curtain wall from right to left, directly on Grid line B, stopping short of the column furring on the west (see Figure 10-4.4).

The curtain wall wants to join to the exterior walls in a funny way at the corner condition on the West. Therefore, you will set the left side of the curtain wall so it does not join with other walls.

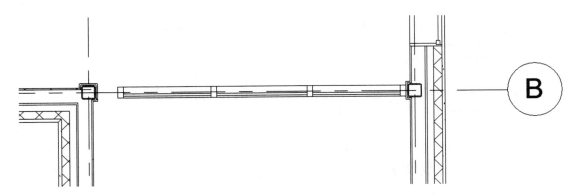

FIGURE 10-4.4 Interior curtain wall added; the West side is held back from the column furring

24. Click **Modify** or press **Esc** to end the *Wall* tool.

25. Select the interior curtain wall you just added; be sure to select the centerline which will appear when you cursor over it.

26. Right click on the blue dot on the West side of the wall.

27. Select **Disallow Join** from the pop-up menu (Figure 10-4.5).

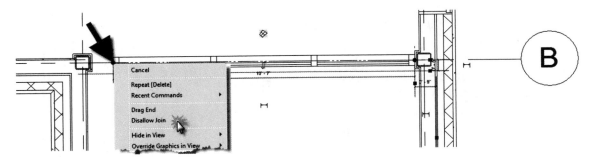

FIGURE 10-4.5 Wall selected; right-click on blue grip on the left to reveal menu

Now the wall will only go where you tell it. It will not try to join with the exterior wall and run past the column furring.

28. Drag the blue dot West to the column furring (Figure 10-4.6).

FIGURE 10-4.6 Interior curtain wall placed

Now you will place a door in the center position of the curtain wall. This can be done in plan or in elevation. You made edits in the building section view in a previous chapter; you will try it in the floor plan view this time.

First, you will delete the center mullion on the floor. You are only seeing the mullion on the floor because that is the only horizontal mullion below the cut plane of the current view.

29. Select the **center mullion** on the floor, and then click the *pin* icon to unpin it.

30. With the center mullion selected and unpinned, press the **Delete** key on the keyboard.

You are now ready to swap the glass panel out with a door.

31. Select the glass *Curtain Panel* (press **Tab** if required).

32. Click the *pin* icon to unpin it.

33. Select **Curtain Wall Sgl Glass** from the *Type Selector*.

34. With the door selected, again press **Tab** if required to select it, use the flip-controls to adjust the door's swing and hand as shown in Figure 10-4.7.

Now you will do the same thing in the same location on Level 2.

35. Following the steps just covered, place an 8'-6" tall curtain wall along Grid B on Level 2 (Figure 10-4.8).

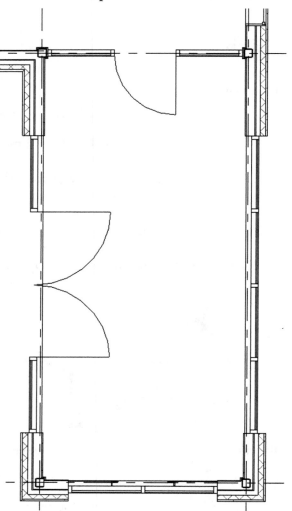

FIGURE 10-4.7 Interior door added

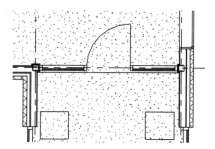

FIGURE 10-4.8 Level 2

Next, you will modify the East wall of the Level 2 *Conference Room* to be a curtain wall. This will let more light into the library area and make the space more dramatic.

The first thing you will need to do is split the wall so the East wall of the adjacent office space does not change from a stud wall. This process is typical anytime a change in wall construction occurs; you would not need to do this for a change in finish, such as paint or wall covering, unless you were tagging those materials directly off the wall. As you will see in the next chapter on schedules, you have to manually enter the finishes for each room. Unfortunately, they do not come from the wall types.

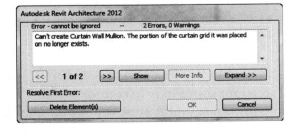

36. On Level 2, zoom in to the *Conference Room* with the curved wall.

37. Select **Modify → Edit → Split** from the *Ribbon*.

38. Click at the intersection of Grid 2/C with the wall highlighted, the wall that runs long Grid line 2, which is the one you will split.

You now have two walls where there was one. Next, you will select a wall of the *Conference Room* and swap it out with a curtain wall via the *Type Selector*.

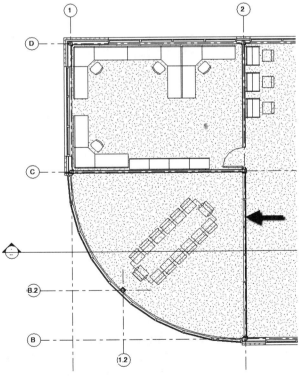

39. Select the East wall of the Level 2 *Conference Room*.

40. Pick *Curtain Wall:* **Storefront** from the *Type Selector* (Figure 10-4.9).

Now you may get an error related to the end conditions, similar to the other two just placed.

41. Select **Delete Element(s)** if you get this warning.

FIGURE 10-4.9 Wall changed to curtain wall

42. Select the curtain wall; right-click on each end grip and select **Disallow Join.**

43. **Drag** the end grips so they align with the column furring (Figure 10-4.10).

44. Add a door as shown in Figure 10-4.11 following techniques already covered.

You now have a glass wall and a door into the Level 2 *Conference Room.*

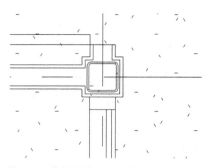

FIGURE 10-4.10
Curtain wall end condition

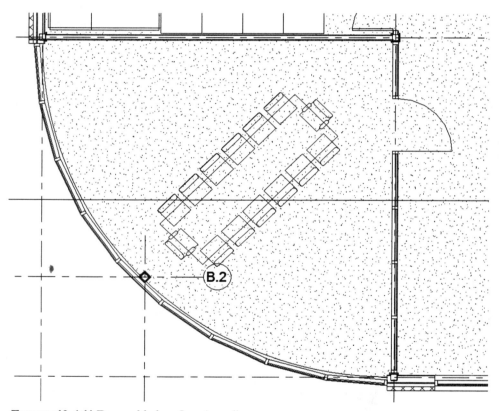

FIGURE 10-4.11 Door added to Curtain wall

The *Conference Room* wall would likely extend to the structure above to help control sound. Therefore, you would have to model a stud wall from the ceiling to the structure above. This can be drawn in the plan view if you know the dimensions above the floor; but you will not see it as it will be completely above the cut plane. You will not do this for our project, unless instructed to do so in a classroom setting.

Adding a Guardrail:

45. Switch to the **Level 2 Architectural Floor Plan** view.

46. Select **Home → Circulation → Railing**.

47. **Zoom** in to the open stair area.

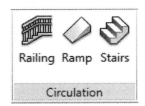

At this point, you will draw a line representing the path of the guardrail. The railing is offset to one side of the line, similar to walls. However, you do not have the *Location Line* option as you do with the *Wall* tool, so you have to draw the railing in a certain direction to get the railing to be on the floor and not hovering in space just beyond the floor edge.

48. Draw a line, in a clockwise direction, along the edge of the floor as shown in Figure 10-4.12.

> *TIP: Select Chain from the Options Bar to draw the railing with fewer picks.*

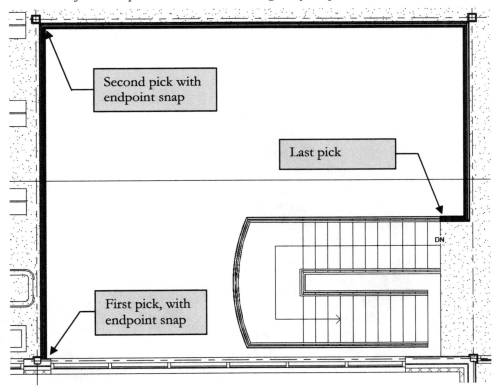

FIGURE 10-4.12 Adding guardrail – Level 2

49. Click **Finish Edit Mode** on the *Ribbon*.

50. Similar to the previous steps, draw a railing between the open stair and the exterior wall (Figure 10-4.13).

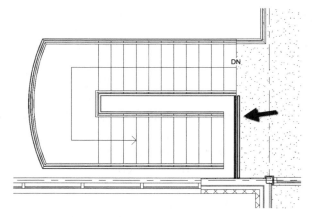

The railing has now been drawn. In the next step, you will switch to a **3D** view and see how to quickly change the railing style. This will also involve changing the height of the railing. Most building codes require the railing height be 42″ when the drop to the adjacent surface is more than 30″; this is called a guardrail.

FIGURE 10-4.13 Adding guardrail – Level 2

51. Switch to the **Default 3D View**.

52. Using the technique covered earlier in this chapter, hide the roof, ceilings and structural framing via the "V V" shortcut; notice the railing style in Figure 10-4.14.

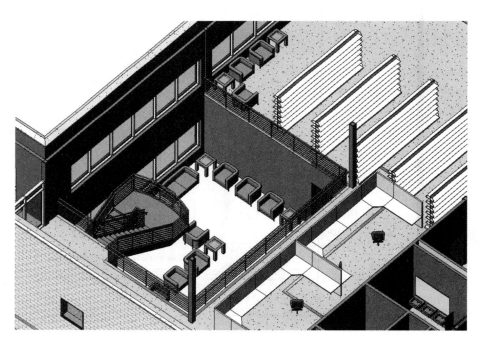

FIGURE 10-4.14 Added railing – 3D view

53. Select the railing. You may have to use the **Tab** key to cycle through the various selection options.

54. With the railing selected, select the various railing types available in the *Type Selector* on the *Properties Palette*. When finished, make sure **Railing: Guardrail – Pipe** is selected (Figure 10-4.15).

55. **Save** your project.

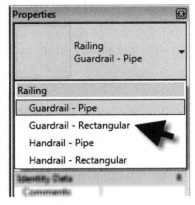

FIGURE 10-4.15
Options for selected railing

Sample Railing File:

Make sure to examine the railing sample file available on Revit's online content library (seek.autodesk.com – search for "Revit samples" and select the railing option). You can download this file, open it, select a railing and view its properties to see how it works.

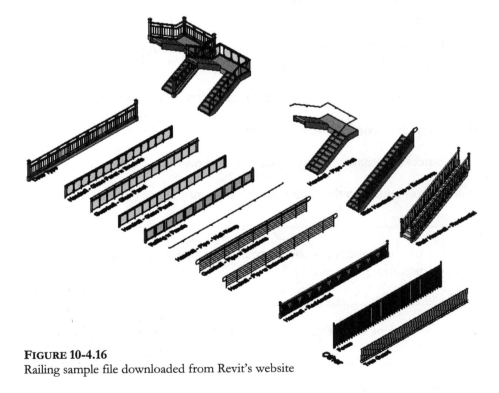

FIGURE 10-4.16
Railing sample file downloaded from Revit's website

You can Copy/Paste a railing style from this file into one of your project files. Then you select your railing and pick the newly imported one from the *Type Selector*.

Self-Exam:
The following questions can be used as a way to check your knowledge of this lesson. The answers can be found at the bottom of this page.

1. The toilet room fixtures are preloaded in the template file. (T/F)

2. Doors can be added to an interior curtain wall while in plan view. (T/F)

3. Revit content is not guaranteed to be in compliance with codes. (T/F)

4. You can draw 2D lines on the wall in an interior elevation view. (T/F)

5. Use the _____ tool to copy the entire *Toilet Room* layout to another floor in the building; this will also allow for easy updates of all instances.

Review Questions:
The following questions may be assigned by your instructor as a way to assess your knowledge of this section. Your instructor has the answers to the review questions.

1. Revit *Architecture* content does not have the *MEP* "connections" for piping/plumbing needed by the *MEP* "flavor" of Revit. (T/F)

2. Most of the time, Revit automatically updates the ceiling when walls are moved, but occasionally you have to manually make revisions. (T/F)

3. It is not possible to draw dimensions on an interior elevation view. (T/F)

4. Cabinets typically come in 4″ increments. (T/F)

5. Base cabinets automatically have a countertop on them. (T/F)

6. What can you adjust so the concrete slab does not show in elevation?

   _____

7. What type of component do you place around structural columns when you want the adjacent finish to wrap around it?

   _____

8. What is the current size of your Revit project?

   _____

9. What is the option you selected, when right-clicking on a selected wall's end-grip, so you could better control its endpoint location?

   _____

10. You use the _____ tool to make various components temporarily invisible.

Lesson 11
Law Office: SCHEDULES:

You will continue to learn the powerful features available in Revit. This includes the ability to create live schedules; you can delete a door number on a schedule and Revit will delete the corresponding door from the plan.

Exercise 11-1:
Rooms, Room Tags & Door Tags

This exercise will look at adding rooms, room tags and door tags to your plans. As you insert doors, Revit adds tags to them automatically. However, if you copy or mirror a door, you can lose the tag and have to add it manually.

Adding Rooms and Room Tags:

Revit has an element that can expand out in all directions and find the extents of a space: the floor, walls, ceiling, or roof. The element is called a **Room**. This element is used to hold information about each space within your building. For example, the *Room* element contains the square footage of a room as well as the column if "calculate volumes" is turned on.

The *Room* element also holds information like the room name and number, as well as finishes. Custom *Parameters* can be created, which would allow you to track virtually anything you want about each space.

Later in this chapter you will learn how to create a schedule listing the information contained in the *Room* object.

Rooms have to be manually added to each space. It is one of the few 3D elements you have to create in Revit that does not actually get built by the contractor. You only have to add a *Room* to a space once, and it does not matter which view you do it in; by default, the view you are in will also automatically get a *Room Tag*. Other views of that same space, like the electrical power plan, may need a *Room Tag* added, but not another *Room* element.

Be sure to read the appendix on Revit's Rooms and Spaces, an article written by the author for *AUGI AEC|Edge Magazine* (http://www.augiaecedge.com/).

You will be adding a *Room* and a *Room Tag* to each room on your Level 1 and Level 2 floor plans.

1. Open your law office file using Revit *Architecture*; or use the Chapter 11 starter file from the DVD.

The first thing you will do is make sure "Calculate Volumes" is turned on so the *Room* elements will extend up to the ceiling and not just use a default height.

2. Click the **Room & Area** panel fly-out on the *Home* tab of the *Ribbon* (Figure 11-1.1).

3. Select **Area and Volume Computations** as shown in Figure 11-1.2.

You are now ready to place your first *Room*.

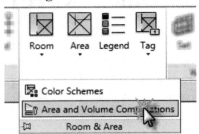

4. Select **Home → Room & Area → Room**.

FIGURE 11-1.1 Panel fly-out

Placing a *Room* is similar to placing a *Ceiling* in the reflected ceiling plan; as you move your cursor over a room, the room perimeter highlights. When the room you want to place a *Room* element in is highlighted, you click to place it.

5. Click your cursor within the *Mechanical Room* (in the Northeastern corner) to place a **Room**, which will also automatically place a *Room Tag* (Figure 11-1.3).

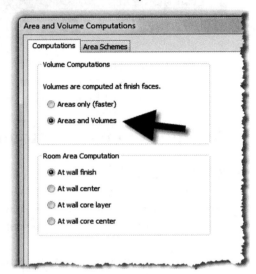

FIGURE 11-1.2 Setting Areas & volume

Notice, as you move your cursor around, an "X" appears within the space. This can help you determine if a space is properly enclosed by walls. Also, the intersection of the "X" is where *Room Tags* are initially located in other views.

While placing a *Room*, any spaces that already have *Rooms* will be indicated by the "X" and a light blue shade. This makes it easy to see which spaces still do not have *Rooms* placed in them.

Once the *Room* tool is ended, via **Modify** or **Esc**, the "X" and shade disappear.

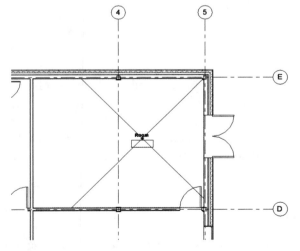

FIGURE 11-1.3 Room added to level 1 view

By default, Revit will simply label the space "Room" and number it "1"; you will change this to something different. Most commercial projects have a three digit room number where the first digit equals the level; for example, the rooms on Level 1 will begin at number 100 and on Level 2 will begin at 200. Larger projects might have four digit room numbers.

Room

| 1 |

6. Press **Esc** or select **Modify** to cancel the *Room* command.

Next, you will change the room name and number. When you change the room number to 100, Revit will automatically make the next room placed "101". So it is a good idea to place one room and then change the number so the remaining rooms do not need to be manually renumbered.

7. Click on the *Room Tag* you just placed to select it.

8. Now click on the room name label to change it; enter **MECH & ELEC ROOM**.
   TIP: Press Enter *or click away to finish typing.*

9. Now click on the room number to change it; enter **100**.

Adding Room Separation Lines:

Sometimes you need to identify an area that is not totally enclosed by walls. For example, the Level 1 hallway would typically have its own room tag, separate from the main lobby area. However, if you place a *Room*, it would fill both spaces. Revit has a special line you can draw, called a *Room Separation Line*, that will act like a wall, similar to a *Room Bounding* element.

10. **Zoom** in to the East end of the Level 1 hallway near Grids 3/C.

11. Select **Home → Room & Area → Room** (drop-down) **→ Room Separation line**.

12. Draw a line as shown in Figure 11-1.5.

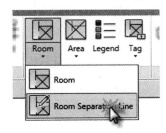

FIGURE 11-1.4
Room Separation Line

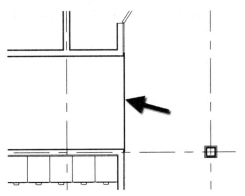

A *Room Separation Line* acts like a wall when it comes to placing *Rooms*. This will not have any effect on ceilings.

These lines can be turned off via the "VV" shortcut: *Model Categories* tab → *Lines* → *<Room Separation>*.

FIGURE 11-1.5 Room Separation Line added

Next, you will add *Room Separation Lines* at the reception desk and the two interior curtain walls along Grid B. The two curtain walls are a problem because we used the *Disallow Join* option to have better control over the curtain wall end conditions; this made a break in the *Room* boundary.

13. Add the **Room Separation Lines** shown in Figure 11-1.6.

    a. Do not add the dimension.

    b. Add the line just South of the interior curtain wall and the architectural columns to avoid any cleanup problems.

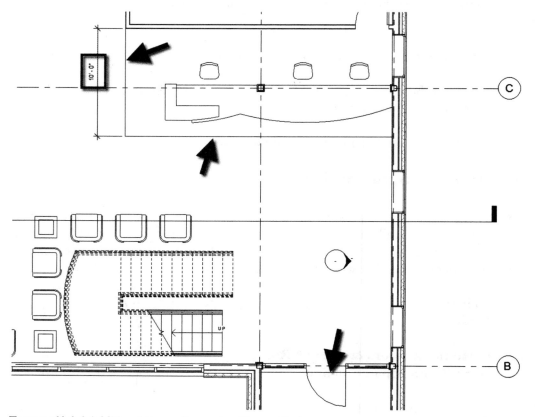

FIGURE 11-1.6 Additional Room Separation Lines added

14. Add two more **Room Separation Lines**, on Level 1, at the <u>Admin Asst. Receptionist</u> area (Figure 11-1.7).

    a. Click from the face of the wall to the center of the structural column.

15. Switch to the **Level 2 Architectural Plan** view.

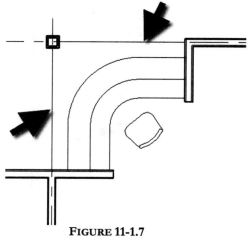

FIGURE 11-1.7
Two more lines added

11-4

16. Add the **four** *Room Separation Lines* shown in Figure 11-1.8.

    a. In this image, the lines are shown exaggerated because they overlap other linework.

    b. Pick at the center of the structural columns for the three lines around the opening in the floor.

    c. Draw the line just South of the interior curtain wall, just like on Level 1.

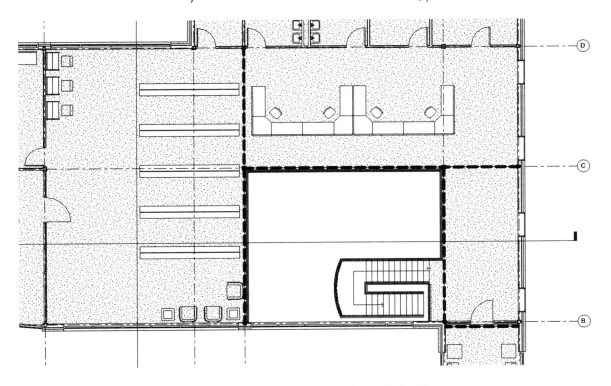

FIGURE 11-1.8 Level 2 Room Separation Lines added, shown as heavy dashed line

17. Using the **Room** tool, add *Rooms* for each space on Level 1 and Level 2; change the room name, and number if required, to match Figures 11-1.9 and 11-1.10.

    a. Where you click to place the *Room* is where the *Room Tag* is placed, so click where the *Room Tag* will not overlap other lines.

    b. <u>North Stair</u>: Place a *Room* on Level 1 and then skip Level 2 until Step #18.

    c. <u>Coat Closet</u>: Select the *Room Tag*, check "leader" on the *Options Bar*, and then drag the *Room Tag* out of the room.

The view scale has been adjusted in the next two images to make it easier to read the room names and numbers. Also, several categories have been temporarily turned off for clarity. You should not do this because you need to make sure the room tags do not overlap anything.

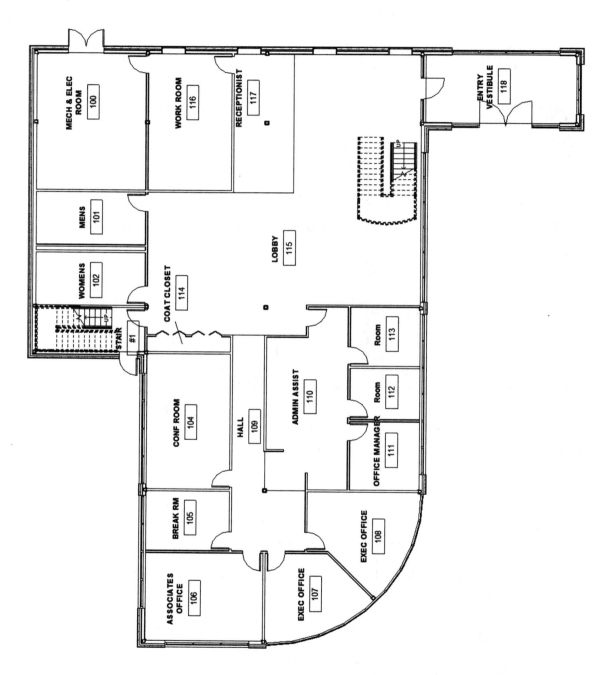

FIGURE 11-1.9 Level 1 room names and numbers; *image rotated on page to increase size*

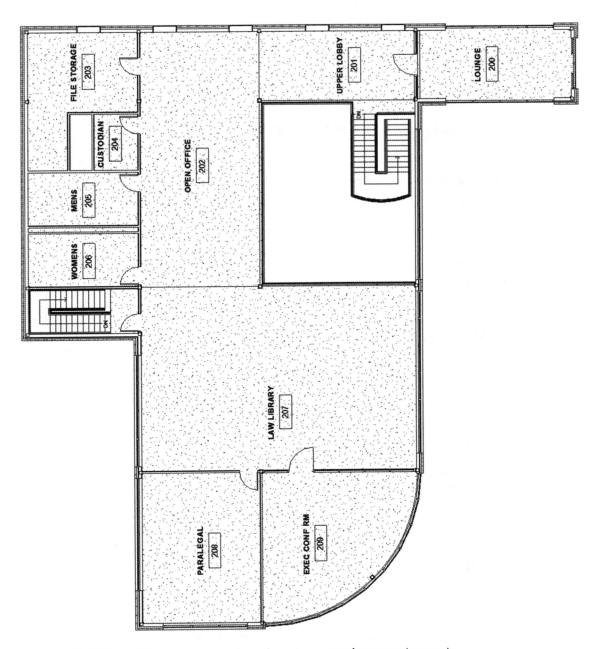

FIGURE 11-1.10 Level 2 room names and numbers; *image rotated on page to increase size*

Next, you will select the *Room* element on Level 1 and adjust its height. Then you can tag the same *Room* in the Level 2 view.

18. In the Level 1 view, select the *Room* element in *Stair #1*.

> **TIP:** *To select a Room, you need to move your cursor around the Room Tag until you see an "X" highlight, and then click to select it.*

19. Change the room's *Limit Offset* to **26'-8"** in its *Instance Properties (Properties Palette).*

20. Click **Apply** to accept the change.

21. Switch to Level 2 and zoom in to the North stair area.

22. Select **Home → Room & Area → Tag** from the *Ribbon.*

23. Click within the stair shaft; see Figure 11-1.11.

Notice how the room name and number fill out automatically. This is how you will add room tags in other plan views that do not already have them. As they are placed, they take on the properties of the previously placed rooms: room name and number in this case.

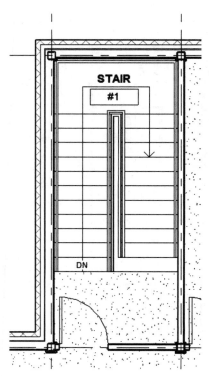

FIGURE 11-1.11
Level 2 with room tag added to stair

A *Room Tag* can display various information stored within the *Room* element. For example, if you select a *Room Tag*, not the *Room*, you can select a different tag *Type* from the *Type Selector.* The example below (Figure 11-1.12) shows a tag that reports the square footage of the space being tagged. Also, the tag *Type* can vary from view to view and even room to room. Try changing one and then change it back before continuing.

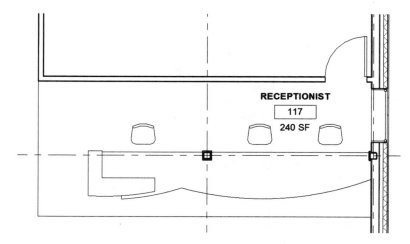

FIGURE 11-1.12 Room tag type that shows the area of a space

Adding Door Tags:

Next you will add *Door Tags* to any doors that are missing them. Additionally, you will adjust the door numbers to correspond to the room numbers.

Revit numbers the doors in the order they are placed into the drawing. This would make it difficult to locate a door by its door number if door number 1 was on Level 1 and door number 2 was on Level 3, etc.

Typically, a door number is the same as the room the door swings into. For example, if a door swung into an office numbered 304, the door number would also be 304. If the office has two doors into it, the doors would be numbered 304A and 304B.

24. Switch to **Level 1** view.

25. Select the **Annotate → Tag → Tag by Category** button on the *Ribbon* (Figure 11-1.13).

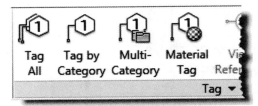

FIGURE 11-1.13 Annotate tab, Tag panel

Notice, as you move your cursor around the screen, Revit displays a tag, for items that can have tags, when the cursor is over it. When you click the mouse is when Revit actually places a tag.

26. **Uncheck** the **Leader** option on the *Options Bar*.

27. Place a *Door Tag* for each door that does not have a tag; do this for each level.

> **TIP: TAG ALL...**
> *This tool allows you to quickly tag all the objects of a selected type (e.g., doors) at one time.*
>
> *After selecting the tool, you select the type of object from a list and specify whether or not you want a leader. When you click OK, Revit tags all the untagged doors in that view.*

28. Renumber all the *Door Tags* to correspond to the room they open into; do this for each level. See Figures 11-1.14 and 11-1.15.

> **REMEMBER:** *Click Modify, select the Tag and then click on the number to edit it.*

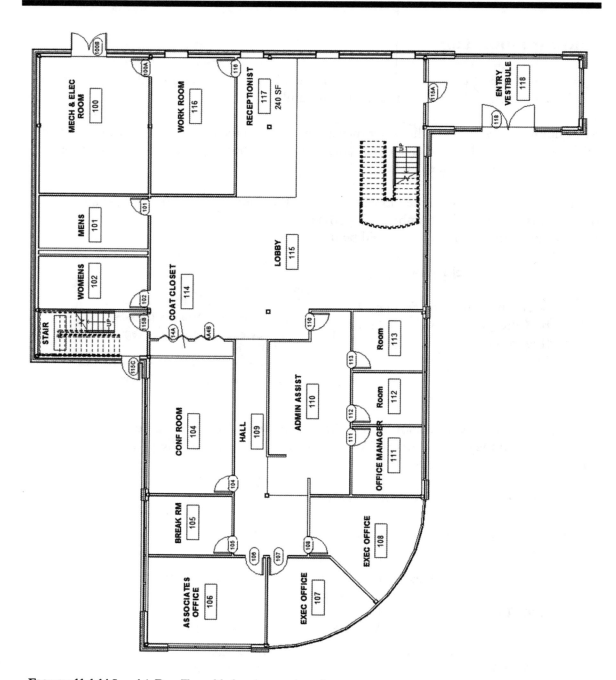

FIGURE 11-1.14 Level 1 *Door Tags* added and renumbered

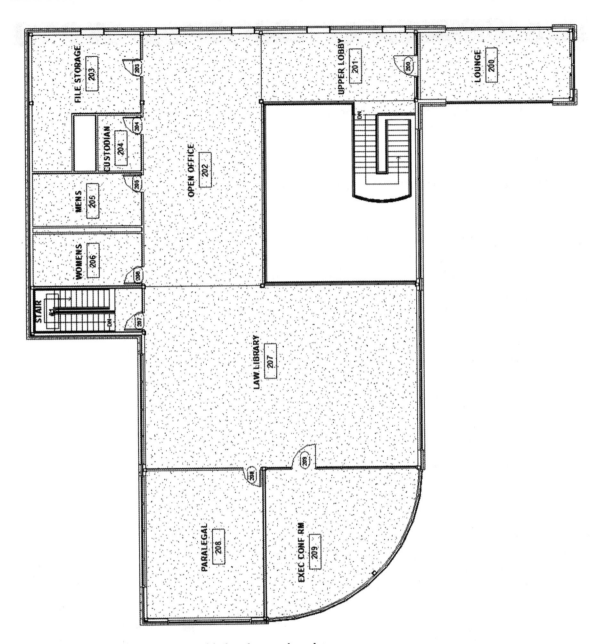

FIGURE 11-1.15 Level 2 *Door Tags* added and renumbered

29. **Save** your project.

Exercise 11-2:
Generate a Door Schedule

This exercise will look at creating a door schedule based on the information currently available in the building model.

Create a Door Schedule View:

A Door Schedule is simply another view of the building model. However, this view displays text/numerical data rather than graphical data. Just like a graphical view, if you change a Schedule view, it changes all the other related views. For example, if you delete a door number from the Schedule, the door is deleted from the plans and elevations.

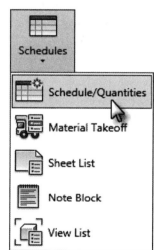

1. Open your law office *BIM* file.

2. Select **View → Create → Schedules →Schedule/ Quantities** button from the *Ribbon*.

3. Select **Doors** under *Category*.

4. Type **Law Office Door Schedule** for the *Name*.

5. Set the *Phase* to **New Construction**.

6. Click **OK** to create the schedule (Figure 11-2.1).

Your project already has a door schedule in it because it was pre-defined in the template. Thus, it would not really be necessary to create a door schedule. However, you need to understand how they are created to effectively modify and edit them.

You should now be in the *Schedule Properties* dialog where you specify what information is displayed in the schedule, how it is sorted and the text format.

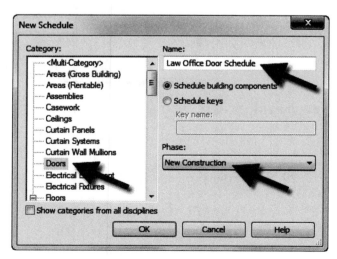

FIGURE 11-2.1 New Schedule dialog

7. On the ***Fields*** tab, add the information you want displayed in the Schedule. Select the following (Figure 11-2.2):

   a. Mark   ***TIP:*** *Click the Add* ➔ *button each time.*

   b. Width

   c. Height

   d. Frame Material

   e. Frame Type

   f. Fire Rating

As noted in the dialog box, the fields added to the list on the right are in the order they will be in the **Schedule** view. Use the *Move Up* and *Move Down* buttons to adjust the order.

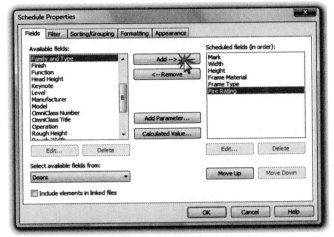

FIGURE 11-2.2 Schedule Properties – Fields

TIP: *If you accidentally clicked* OK *after the previous step, click one of the Edit buttons in the Properties Palette while the schedule view is active.*

8. On the ***Sorting/Grouping*** tab, set the schedule to be sorted by the **Mark** (i.e., door number) in ascending order (Figure 11-2.3).

FYI: *The* **Formatting** *and* **Appearance tabs** *allow you to adjust how the schedule looks. The formatting is not displayed until the schedule is placed on a plot sheet.*

Also, you cannot print a schedule unless it is on a sheet. Only views and sheets can be printed, not schedules or legends.

9. Click the **OK** button to generate the schedule view.

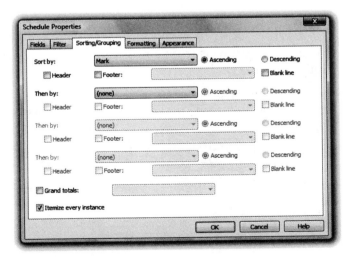

FIGURE 11-2.3 Schedule Properties – Sorting

You should now have a schedule similar to Figure 11-2.4.

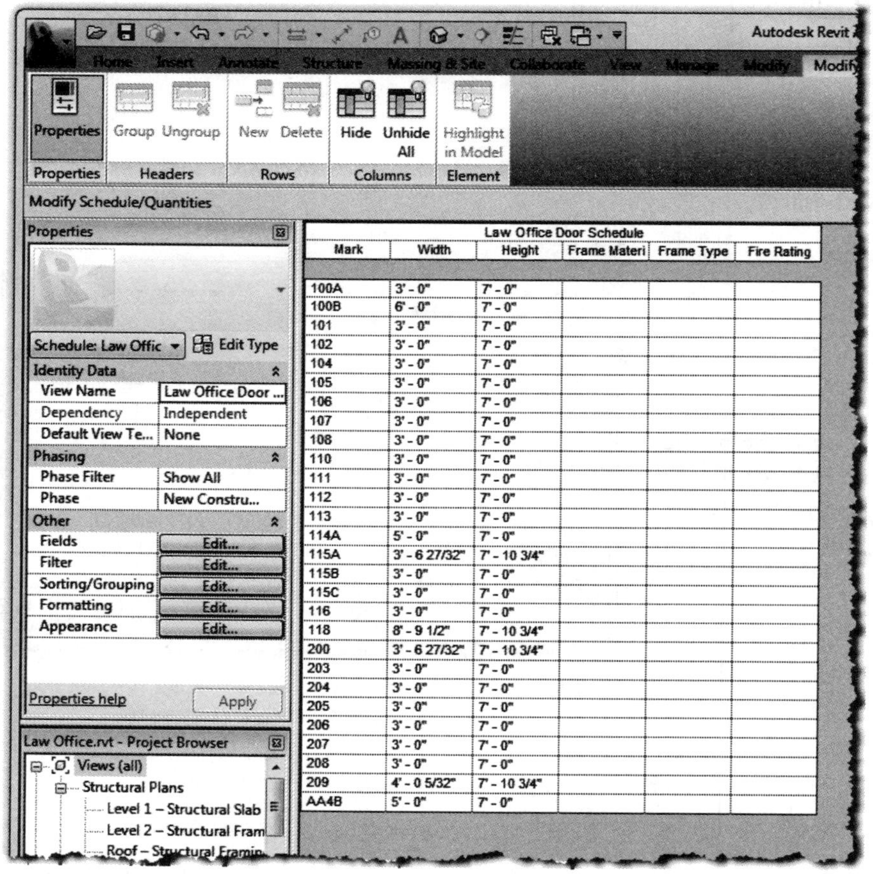

FIGURE 11-2.4 Door Schedule view

> **TIP:** *While in a schedule view, you can select* **Application Menu** → **Export** → **Reports** → **Schedule** *to create a text file (*.txt) that can be used in other programs like MS Excel.*

The example below is from a real Revit project; notice the detailed header information (i.e., grouped headers).

DOOR AND FRAME SCHEDULE												
DOOR NUMBER	**DOOR**				**FRAME**		**DETAIL**				**FIRE RATING**	**HDWR GROUP**	
	WIDTH	HEIGHT	MATL	TYPE	MATL	TYPE	HEAD	JAMB	SILL	GLAZING			
1000A	3' - 8"	7' - 2"	WD		HM		11/A8.01	11/A8.01					
1046	3' - 0"	7' - 2"	WD	D10	HM	F10	11/A8.01	11/A8.01 SIM				34	
1047A	6' - 0"	7' - 10"	ALUM	D15	ALUM	SF4	6/A8.01	6/A8.01	1/A8.01 SIM	1" INSUL		2	CARD READER N. LEAF
1047B	6' - 0"	7' - 2"	WD	D10	HM	F13	12/A8.01	11/A8.01 SIM			60 MIN	85	MAG HOLD OPENS
1050	3' - 0"	7' - 2"	WD	D10	HM	F21	8/A8.01	11/A8.01		1/4" TEMP		33	
1051	3' - 0"	7' - 2"	WD	D10	HM	F21	8/A8.01	11/A8.01		1/4" TEMP		33	
1052	3' - 0"	7' - 2"	WD	D10	HM	F21	8/A8.01	11/A8.01		1/4" TEMP		33	
1053	3' - 0"	7' - 2"	WD	D10	HM	F21	8/A8.01	11/A8.01		1/4" TEMP		33	
1054A	3' - 0"	7' - 2"	WD	D10	HM	F10	8/A8.01	11/A8.01		1/4" TEMP	-	34	
1054B	3' - 0"	7' - 2"	WD	D10	HM	F21	8/A8.01	11/A8.01		1/4" TEMP	-	33	
1055	3' - 0"	7' - 2"	WD	D10	HM	F21	8/A8.01	11/A8.01		1/4" TEMP	-	33	
1056A	3' - 0"	7' - 2"	WD	D10	HM	F10	9/A8.01	9/A8.01			20 MIN	33	
1056B	3' - 0"	7' - 2"	WD	D10	HM	F10	11/A8.01	11/A8.01			20 MIN	34	
1056C	3' - 0"	7' - 2"	WD	D10	HM	F10	20/A8.01	20/A8.01			20 MIN	33	
1057A	3' - 0"	7' - 2"	WD	D10	HM	F10	8/A8.01	11/A8.01			20 MIN	34	
1057B	3' - 0"	7' - 2"	WD	D10	HM	F30	9/A8.01	9/A8.01		1/4" TEMP	20 MIN	33	
1058A	3' - 0"	7' - 2"	WD	D10	HM	F10	9/A8.01	9/A8.01			-	33	

Image courtesy LHB (www.LHBcorp.com)

Next, you will see how adding a door to the plan automatically updates the door schedule. Likewise, deleting a door number from the schedule deletes the door from the plan.

10. Switch to the **Level 1** view.

11. Add a door as shown in **Figure 11-2.5**; number the door **104B**.

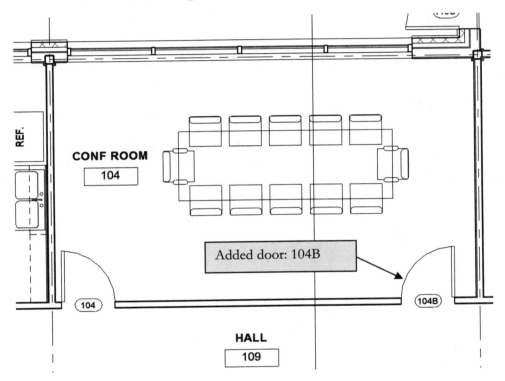

FIGURE 11-2.5 Level 1 – door added

12. Switch to the **Law Office Door Schedule** view, under *Schedules/ Quantities* in the *Project Browser*. Notice door *104B* was added (Figure 11-2.6).

If you select the door (i.e., the row) in the schedule and then click *Highlight in model* on the *Ribbon* (Figure 11-2.7), Revit will switch to a plan view and zoom in on that door. This makes it easy to find a door that does not have a number or any door you are not sure where it is.

| | Law Office D |
Mark	Width	Height
100A	3' - 0"	7' - 0"
100B	6' - 0"	7' - 0"
101	3' - 0"	7' - 0"
102	3' - 0"	7' - 0"
104	3' - 0"	7' - 0"
104B	3' - 0"	7' - 0"
105	3' - 0"	7' - 0"
106	3' - 0"	7' - 0"
107	3' - 0"	7' - 0"
108	3' - 0"	7' - 0"
110	3' - 0"	7' - 0"
111	3' - 0"	7' - 0"
112	3' - 0"	7' - 0"

FIGURE 11-2.6 Updated door schedule

Next, you will delete door *104B* from the door schedule view.

13. Click in the cell with the number **104B**.

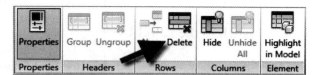

14. Now click the **Delete** button from the *Ribbon* (Figure 11-2.7).

FIGURE 11-2.7 *Ribbon* for the door schedule view

You will get an alert. Revit is telling you that the actual door will be deleted from the project model (Figure 11-2.8).

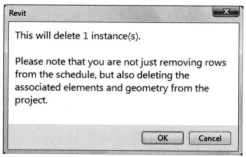

FIGURE 11-2.8 Revit alert message

15. Click **OK** to delete the door (Figure 11-2.8).

16. Switch back to the **Level 1** view and notice that door *104B* has been deleted from the project model.

17. **Save** your project.

> **TIP:** *The schedule view can be used to enter the information about each door. For example, you can enter the fire rating, the frame material, etc. This information is actually added to the Door object. If you switch to a plan view, select a door and view its properties, you will see all the information entered in the schedule for that door. You can also change the door number in the schedule.*

The image below shows a real Revit project with several doors; notice the door numbers match the room numbers. Also, the shaded walls are existing; Revit can manage phases very well.

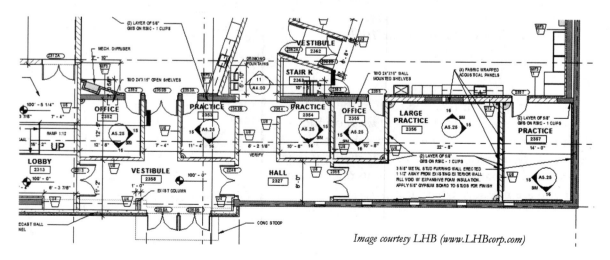

Image courtesy LHB (www.LHBcorp.com)

Exercise 11-3:
Generate a Room Finish Schedule

In this exercise you will create a room finish schedule. The process is similar to the previous exercise. You will also create a color coded plan based on information associated with the *Room* element.

Create a Room Finish Schedule:

1. Open your Revit project.

2. Select **View → Create →** Schedule **→ Schedule/Quantities** button from the *Ribbon*.

3. Select **Rooms** under *Category*.

4. Type **Law Office Room Schedule** for the *Name*.

5. Set the *Phase* to **New Construction**.

6. Click **OK** to create the schedule (Figure 11-3.1).

7. In the *Fields* tab of the *Schedule Properties* dialog, add the following fields to be scheduled (Figure 11-3.2):

   a. Number
   b. Name
   c. Base Finish
   d. Floor Finish
   e. Wall Finish
   f. Ceiling Finish
   g. Area

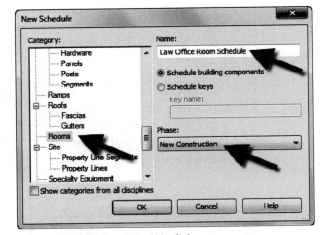

FIGURE 11-3.1 New Schedule dialog

Area is not typically listed on a Room Finish Schedule. However, you will add it to your schedule to see the various options Revit allows. It is possible to have multiple "room" schedules that list various things about the room.

8. On the *Sorting/Grouping* tab, set the schedule to be sorted by the *Number* field.

9. On the **_Appearance_** tab, check **_Bold_** for the header text (Figure 11-3.3).

10. Select **OK** to generate the Room Schedule.

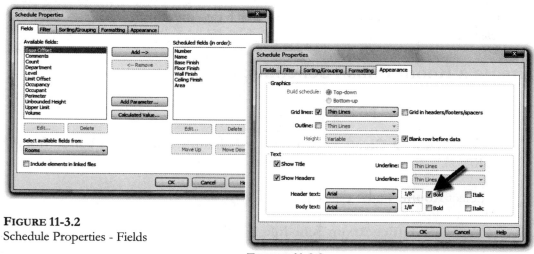

FIGURE 11-3.2
Schedule Properties - Fields

FIGURE 11-3.3
Schedule Properties - Appearance

Your schedule should look similar to the one to the right (Figure 11-3.4).

11. Resize the **_Name_** column so all the room names are visible. Place the cursor between _Name_ and _Base Finish_ and drag to the right until all the names are visible (Figure 11-3.4).

The formatting (i.e., _Bold_ header text) will not show up until the schedule is placed on a plot sheet.

It is easy to add custom parameters that track something about the element being scheduled (rooms in this case). Simply click the Add Parameter button seen in Figure 11-3.2.

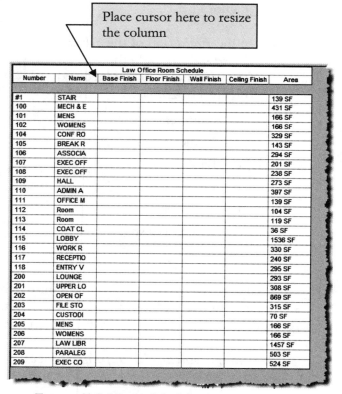

| Law Office Room Schedule | | | | | | |
Number	Name	Base Finish	Floor Finish	Wall Finish	Ceiling Finish	Area
#1	STAIR					139 SF
100	MECH & E					431 SF
101	MENS					166 SF
102	WOMENS					166 SF
104	CONF RO					329 SF
105	BREAK R					143 SF
106	ASSOCIA					294 SF
107	EXEC OFF					201 SF
108	EXEC OFF					238 SF
109	HALL					273 SF
110	ADMIN A					397 SF
111	OFFICE M					139 SF
112	Room					104 SF
113	Room					119 SF
114	COAT CL					36 SF
115	LOBBY					1536 SF
116	WORK R					330 SF
117	RECEPTIO					240 SF
118	ENTRY V					295 SF
200	LOUNGE					293 SF
201	UPPER LO					308 SF
202	OPEN OF					869 SF
203	FILE STO					315 SF
204	CUSTODI					70 SF
205	MENS					166 SF
206	WOMENS					166 SF
207	LAW LIBR					1457 SF
208	PARALEG					503 SF
209	EXEC CO					524 SF

Place cursor here to resize the column

FIGURE 11-3.4 Room Schedule view

Modifying and Populating a Room Schedule:

Like the Door Schedule, the Room Schedule is a tabular view of the building model. So you can change the room name or number on the schedule or in the plans.

12. In the **Law Office Room Schedule** view, change the name for room *209* (currently called *EXEC CONF RM*) to ***UPPER CONF ROOM***.

> **TIP:** *Click on the current room name and then click on the down-arrow that appears. This gives you a list of all the existing names in the current schedule; otherwise you can type a new name.*

13. Switch to the **Level 2** view to see the updated *Room Tag*.

You can quickly enter *Finish* information for several rooms at one time. You will do this next.

14. In the **Level 1** plan view, select the *Rooms* (not the *Room Tags*) for the offices shown – 4 total (Figure 11-3.5).

> **REMEMBER:** *Hold the Ctrl key down to select multiple objects.*

> **TIP:** *Move the cursor near the Room Tag but not over it to select the room; the large "X" will appear when the Room is selectable (see image below).*

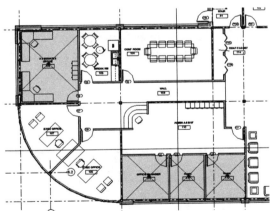

FIGURE 11-3.5 Level 1 rooms selected

15. Notice the parameters listed in the ***Properties Palette*** (aka, *Instance Properties*).

The *Parameters* listed here are the same as the *Fields* available for display in the Room Schedule. When more than one tag is displayed and a parameter is not the same, that value field is left blank. Otherwise, the values are displayed for the selected *Room*. Next you will enter values for the finishes.

16. Enter the following for the finishes (Figure 11-3.6):

    a. *Base Finish:*   **WOOD**

    b. *Ceiling Finish:*   **ACT-1** *(ACT = acoustic ceiling tile)*

    c. *Wall Finish:*   **VWC-1***(VWC = vinyl wall covering)*

    d. *Floor Finish:*   **CPT-1** *(CPT = carpet)*

17. Click **Apply**.

18. Switch back to the **Law Office Room Schedule** view to see the automatic updates (Figure 11-3.7).

You can also enter data directly into the **Room Schedule** view.

19. Enter the following data for the *Men's* and *Women's Toilet Rooms*:

    a. *Base:*   **COVED CT**

    b. *Ceiling:*   **GYP BD**

    c. *Wall:*   **CT-2**

    d. *Floor:*   **CT-1**

Hopefully, in the near future, Revit will be able to enter the finishes based on the wall, floor and ceiling types previously created!

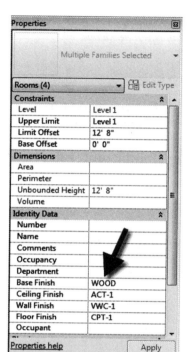

FIGURE 11-3.6 Element Properties – Room

TIP: You can add fields and adjust formatting anytime by right-clicking on the schedule view and selecting View Properties. This gives you the same options that were available when you created the schedule.

Law Office Room Schedule						
Number	Name	Base Finish	Floor Finish	Wall Finish	Ceiling Finish	Area
#1	STAIR					139 SF
100	MECH & ELEC ROOM					431 SF
101	MENS					166 SF
102	WOMENS					166 SF
104	CONF ROOM					329 SF
105	BREAK RM					143 SF
106	ASSOCIATES OFFICE	WOOD	CPT-1	VWC-1	ACT-1	294 SF
107	EXEC OFFICE					201 SF
108	EXEC OFFICE					238 SF
109	HALL					273 SF
110	ADMIN ASSIST					397 SF
111	OFFICE MANAGER	WOOD	CPT-1	VWC-1	ACT-1	139 SF
112	Room	WOOD	CPT-1	VWC-1	ACT-1	104 SF
113	Room	WOOD	CPT-1	VWC-1	ACT-1	119 SF
114	COAT CLOSET					36 SF
115	LOBBY					1536 SF

FIGURE 11-3.7 New data added to schedule

Setting Up a Color-Coded Floor Plan:

With the *Rooms* in place you can quickly set up color-coded floor plans. These are plans that indicate, with color, which rooms are *Offices, Circulation, Public,* etc., based the room name in our example.

20. Right-click on the **Level 1 Architectural** view in the *Project Browser*.

21. Select **Duplicate View → Duplicate** (without detail) from the pop-up menu.

22. Rename the new view (*Copy of Level 1*) to **Level 1 – Color.**

23. Select **Annotate → Tag → Tag All.**

24. Select *Room Tags:* **Room Tag** from the list.

25. Click **OK.**

Now, all the rooms have a *Room Tag* in them!

26. In the *New* view, select **Home → Room & Area → Legend.**

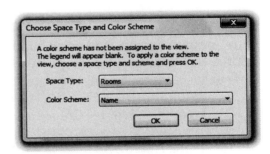

27. Click just to the right side of the plan to place the *Legend Key*.

28. Select **Name** and then **OK** to the following prompt (Figure 11-3.8).

You now have a color-coded plan where the colors are assigned by room *Name*; e.g., all the rooms named *"Office"* have the same color (Figure 11-3.9).

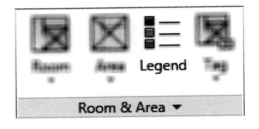

FIGURE 11-3.8 Color fill prompt

It is possible to sort by other parameters other than *Name*. For example, you could sort by *Department*. However, you would need to enter department names first (e.g., *Partner, Associate, Staff, Public,* etc.).

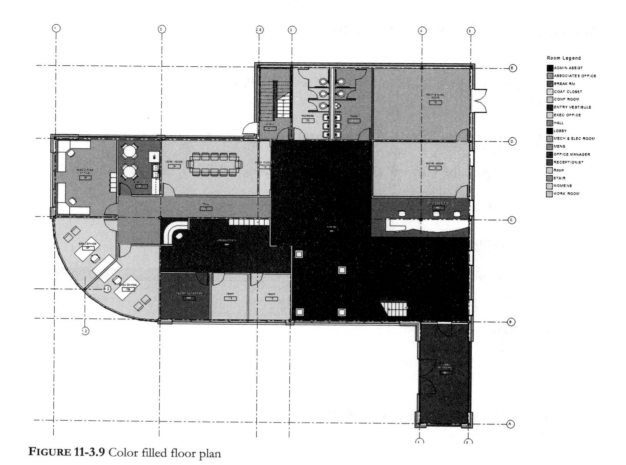

FIGURE 11-3.9 Color filled floor plan

> *TIP: Notice how the color coincides with the perimeter of the Room element previously placed. The room Separation Lines also control the room/color.*

Some furniture is white and other furniture is filled with the "fill" color of the room. The colored elements have the 3D geometry turned off in the plan view for increased performance. You will adjust this next.

29. Go to the **Level 1 – Color** view's *Properties (Properties Palette)*.

30. Set the *Color Scheme Location* to **Foreground** and click **Apply**.

The colors are now consistent; the only drawback is the colors go to the center of the walls now.

31. Select the *Room Legend* shown in **Figure 11-3.9**.

32. Click **Edit Scheme** on the *Ribbon* (Figure 11-3.10).

Edit
Scheme

FIGURE 11-3.10
Edit Scheme button

Each unique room name will get a different color. Before you finish, you will change one *Color* and one *Fill Pattern*.

33. Click on the *Color* for the **Lobby** (or the darkest color, which makes things within those rooms hard to see).

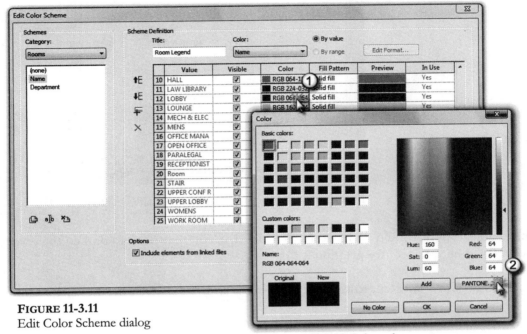

FIGURE 11-3.11
Edit Color Scheme dialog

FIGURE 11-3.12 Color selector

34. Click the **PANTONE...** button to select a standard Pantone color (Figure 11-3.12).

35. Pick any color you like (Figure 11-3.13).

36. Click **OK** to accept.

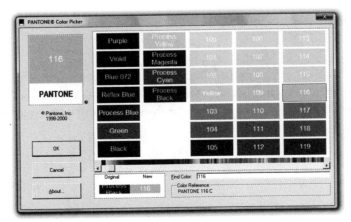

FIGURE 11-3.13 PANTONE Color Picker

37. Now click on the *Fill Pattern* for the **MECH & ELEC ROOM**.

38. Click the down-arrow and select **Vertical-small** from the list.

39. Click **OK**.

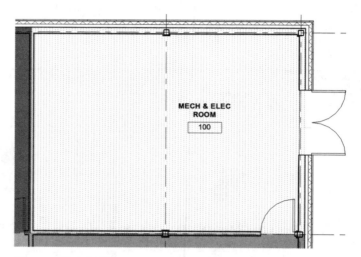

FIGURE 11-3.14 Fill pattern added to *MECH & ELEC ROOM*

Your mechanical room should look like Figure 11-3.14. You may need to darken the color if the lines are too hard to see (try printing it first).

40. Use the "VV" shortcut to turn off the *Sections* and *Elevations* in the **Level 1 – Color** view.

41. Follows the steps just covered to set up a **Level 2 – Color** view.

Your plan should now have the new color you selected for the *Lobby* and a hatch pattern in the *Mechanical Room*. Interior designers can create a color-filled plan based on the floor finishes. For example, all the rooms with *CPT-1* get one color and rooms with *CT-1* flooring get another color.

42. **Save** your project.

With the new "color" views set up, you can leave them in the project and refer back to them as needed. If you set up the colors in your main design views, you would likely need to remove the colors (*View Properties* → *Color Scheme* → *None*), making extra work when you needed the color view again.

Exercise 11-4:
Creating a Graphical Column Schedule

In this exercise you will create a Column Schedule using Revit *Structure*. Revit can create a Column Schedule similar to the Door and Room Schedules just covered; most elements can be scheduled like this. However, Revit *Structure* can create a graphical schedule of columns and their related grids. This type of schedule is typical industry practice for structural engineers on a set of Construction Documents (CD's).

Create a Column Schedule:

1. Open your Revit project using **Revit *Structure*.**

2. Select **View → Create → Schedules → Graphical Column Schedule** from the *Ribbon* (Figure 11-4.1).

You now have a Graphical Column Schedule (Figure 11-4.2) which can be placed on a sheet (to be covered in Chapter 15). Notice the grid intersections listed along the bottom. Also, each level is identified by horizontal lines within the schedules. The concrete foundation is shown, and then the steel. Some of the concrete columns look odd because they are missing the thickness for the foundation wall which passes by it. If you recall, you set the columns to start 8″ below the Level 1 floor slab; this can be seen and double-checked in this view.

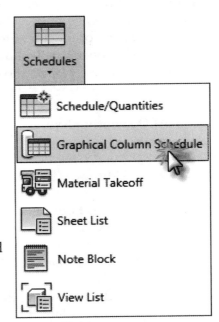

FIGURE 11-4.1
Create a graphical column schedule

The *Project Browser* now has a new category called *Graphical Column Schedules*. It is nice that the various categories only show up when something exists in that section; otherwise the browser list would be unmanageable.

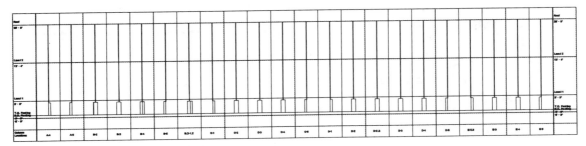

FIGURE 11-4.2 Graphical Column Schedule created

Next, you will look at a few ways in which you can control the graphics of the *Column Schedule*.

3. With the *Column Schedule* current, draw your attention to the *Properties Palette*.

4. Change both the *View Name* and the *Title* to **LAW OFFICE COLUMN SCHEDULE**.

Revit allows you to hide levels that are not needed in the *Column Schedule*, for example, if someone on the design team added a level to manage the height of the top of masonry walls or window openings. It should be pointed out that *Level Datums* should only be used to define surfaces you walk on to avoid unintended issues. In this case, you will turn off the **B.O. Footing** level as it is not needed in this schedule.

5. Click **Edit** for *Hidden Levels*.

6. Check **B.O. Footing** and click **OK** Figure 11-4.3).

7. Click **Edit** for *Material Types*.

If you unchecked *Concrete* here, Revit would remove the concrete columns from the schedule (Figure 11-4.4). You will not make any changes at this time.

8. Click **OK** to close the *Structural Material* dialog without making any changes.

9. Click **Edit** for *Text Appearance*.

10. Set the *Title Text* to **Bold** (Figure 11-4.5).

11. Click **OK**.

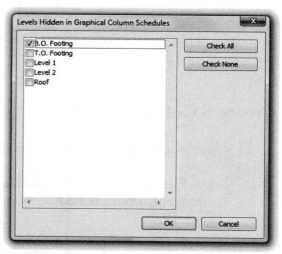

FIGURE 11-4.3 Hiding Levels

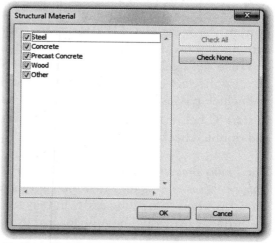

FIGURE 11-4.4 Structural materials

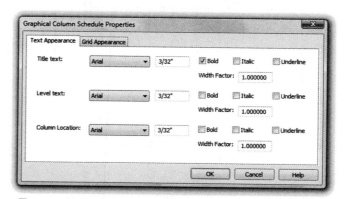

FIGURE 11-4.5 Text Appearance settings

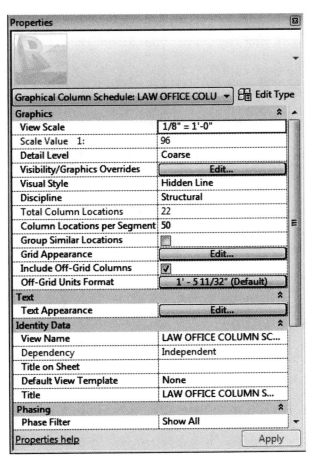

FIGURE 11-4.6 Graphical Column Schedule properties

Notice a few more things about the Column Schedule's *Properties* before closing it (Figure 11-4.6).

The total number of columns considered in the schedule is listed (22 in our example).

Also, *Include Off-Grid Columns* is checked. This will include columns that do not fall on any grid lines; most columns fall on grid lines as that is the main purpose of grid lines.

The *Group Similar Locations* option will show one graphical column for each column size and then list all the grid intersections below it. This makes the schedule smaller, but your project only has one column size so the schedule would actually be too small.

12. Click **Apply** to accept all the changes to the *Column Schedule*.

This completes the topic on *Graphical Column Schedules*.

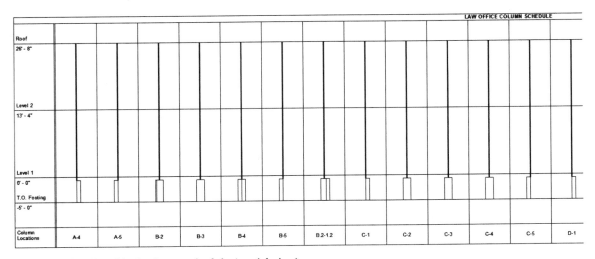

FIGURE 11-4.7 Graphical column schedule (partial view)

Self-Exam:

The following questions can be used as a way to check your knowledge of this lesson. The answers can be found at the bottom of this page.

1. Revit is referred to as a *Building Information Modeler (BIM)*. (T/F)

2. The area for a room is calculated when a *Room* element is placed. (T/F)

3. Revit can tag all the doors not currently tagged on a given level with the *Tag All* tool. (T/F)

4. You can add or remove various fields in a Door or Room Schedule. (T/F)

5. Use the _____ tool to add color to the rooms in a plan view.

Review Questions:

The following questions may be assigned by your instructor as a way to assess your knowledge of this section. Your instructor has the answers to the review questions.

1. The schedule formatting only shows up when you place the schedule on a plot sheet. (T/F)

2. You can export your schedule to a file that can be used in MS Excel. (T/F)

3. A door can be deleted from the Door Schedule. (T/F)

4. A *Room Tag* can have a leader. (T/F)

5. It is not possible to add the finish information (i.e., base finish, wall finish) to multiple rooms at one time. (T/F)

6. When setting up a color scheme, you can adjust the color and the

   _____ pattern in the *Edit Scheme* dialog.

7. Use the _____ _____ to adjust the various fields associated with each *Room Tag* in a plan view.

8. Most door schedules are sorted by the _____ field.

9. What tool must you use to define a room boundary in an open area where the boundary you want is not completely defined by walls?

   _____ _____

10. Revit automatically increments the room _____ as you place *Rooms*.

Lesson 12
Law Office: MECHANICAL SYSTEM:

This chapter will introduce you to Autodesk Revit *MEP 2012*. You will study the User Interface and learn how it is different from Revit *Architecture* and Revit *Structure*. You will also develop the ductwork and plumbing models for the law office, placing air terminals, ductwork, VAV's, water piping, waste piping and more.

Exercise 12-1:
Introduction to Revit MEP – Mechanical & Plumbing

What is Revit MEP 2012 used for?

Revit *MEP 2012* is the companion product to Revit *Architecture 2012* and Revit *Structure 2012*. Revit *MEP* is a specialized version of Revit for designing the Heating Ventilating and Air Conditioning (HVAC), Plumbing and Electrical systems in a building.

The image below shows the mechanical elements you will be adding in this chapter; you will actually just model a fraction of this. However, the next chapter's starter file will have all of this in it. Keeping in line with the overall intent of this textbook, you will really just be skimming the surface of what Revit *MEP* can do. For example, Revit *MEP* can size the ducts and do a total building heating and cooling loads calculation!

> ***WARNING:*** *This is strictly a fictitious project. Although some effort has been made to make the sizes of ducts and piping components realistic, this system has not been designed by a mechanical engineer. There are many codes and design considerations that need to be made on a case by case basis.*

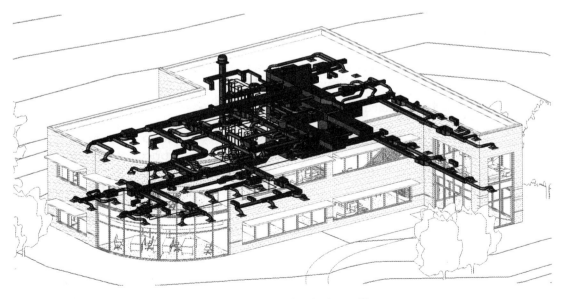

FIGURE 12-1.1 The completed mechanical model for the law office

Listed below are a few of the highlights of using Revit MEP:

- 3D modeling of the entire mechanical system
- Multi-user environment
  - Several people can be working on the same model when "worksharing" has been enabled (though not covered in this book).
- Coordination with Architectural and Structural
  - Visually via 2D and 3D views
  - Interference Check feature
- 2D construction drawings generated in real-time from the 3D model
  - Construction Drawings (CD's phase)
    - Views can show true 3D geometry or single line representation.
      - Ducts are typically shown actual size.
      - Piping is often single line for clarity.
  - Construction Administration (CA phase)
    - Addendum
    - Architectural Supplemental Information (ASI)
    - Proposal Request (PR)
    - Change Order (CO)
- Schedules
  - Schedules are "live" lists of elements in the *BIM* file.
- Design Options
  - Used to try different ideas for a mechanical design in the same area of a project (e.g., exposed ductwork; round duct vs. rectangular duct)
  - Also used to manage bid alternates during CD's
    - A bid alternate might be an extra 25'-0" added to the wing of a building. The contractor provides a separate price for what it would cost to do that work.
- Phasing
  - Manage existing, new and future construction
- Several options to export to analysis programs
  - Export model to external program (e.g., Autodesk Ecotect, IES Virtual Environment, etc.)

Many of the highlights listed on the previous page are things that can be done in Revit *Architecture* as well. The list was generated with the mechanical engineer and technician in mind relative to current software and processes used.

The Revit Platform

All three "flavors" of Revit are built on the same basic Revit platform. Much of the programming code is common between the three "flavors" which is why the design team can all view each other's models and even share the same *BIM* file if desired (which is what we are doing in this tutorial).

Whenever a project involves all three "flavors" of Revit, the same version <u>must</u> be used. Because Revit is not backwards compatible, it is not possible for the mechanical design team to use Revit *MEP 2011* and the architects and structural engineers use Revit *Architecture* and Revit *Structure 2012*. The mechanical design team would have no way to link or view the architectural or structural files; an older version of Revit has no way to read a newer file format.

Furthermore, it is not possible to "Save-As" to an older version of Revit as can be done with other programs such as AutoCAD or Microsoft Word.

It is perfectly possible to have more than one version of Revit installed on your computer. You just need to make sure you are using the correct version for the project you are working on. If you accidentally open a project in the wrong version you will get one of two clues:

- **Opening a *2011* file with *Revit 2012*:** You will see an upgrade message while the file is opened, which will also take longer to open due to the upgrade process. If you see this and did not intend to upgrade the file, simply close the file without saving. The upgraded file is only in your computer's RAM and is not committed to the hard drive until you save.

- **Opening a *2012* file with *Revit 2011*:** This is an easy one as it is not possible. Revit will present you with a message indicating the file was created in a later version of Revit and cannot be opened.

Many firms will start new projects in the new version of Revit and finish any existing projects in the version it is currently in, which helps to avoid any potential upgrade issues. Sometimes a project that is still in its early phases will be upgraded to a new version of Revit.

It should be pointed out that Autodesk releases about one Service Pack (SP) per quarter. This means each version of Revit (i.e., 2011 or 2012) will have approximately 3 SP's. It is best if everyone on the design team is using the same "build" (e.g., 2012 + SP3) but is not absolutely required.

The Revit MEP User Interface:

This section will mainly cover the differences between Revit *MEP* and Revit *Architecture*. You should note that about 90 percent of the material covered in Exercise 2-2, *Overview of the Revit User Interface*, applies to Revit *MEP* as well.

Looking at the image below (Figure 12-1.2) you see the Revit *MEP* User Interface (UI) is very similar to Revit *Architecture*. Both have a *Ribbon*, *Project Browser*, *Quick Access Toolbar*, *View Control Bar* and a drawing window (compare to Figure 2-2.1).

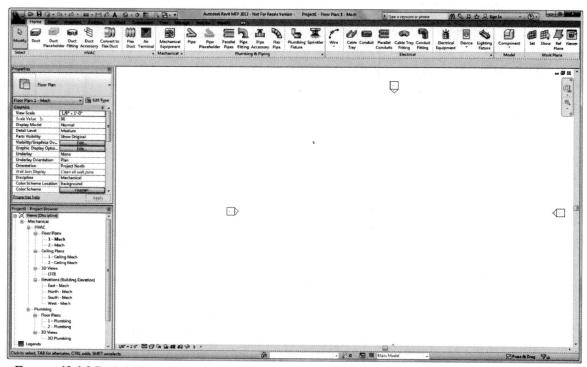

FIGURE 12-1.2 Revit MEP user interface

Many of the tabs on the *Ribbon* are nearly identical to the same named tabs in Revit *Architecture*. The following are identical to Revit *Architecture (RAC)*:

- Insert   (*exception:* 1 icon added to MEP)
- Annotate   (*exception:* 2 added icons on the RAC and 1 added on RME)
- Collaborate   (*exception:* 1 icon added to MEP)
- View   (*exception:* 2 additional icons on the RAC Graphics panel)
- Manage   (*exception:* 2 additional icons on the MEP Settings panel)

Ribbon – Home Tab:

As can be seen from the image above, the *Home* tab is laid out with the mechanical and electrical engineer or technician in mind. The very first tool is *Duct* (*Wall* is the first tool for Revit *Architecture*). Also notice the panel names: *HVAC*, *Mechanical* and *Electrical* are all MEP discipline oriented.

Many tools are duplicates from those found in Revit *Architecture*; they even have the same icon. Duplicate tools, such as *Stairs*, are the exact same programming code and create the same element, which would then be editable by either "flavor" of Revit.

The small down-arrow to the right of each panel title is what is called a ***dialog launcher***. On the *Home* tab, they open either the *Electrical* or *Mechanical Settings* dialog.

Ribbon – Analyze Tab:

The *Analyze* tab reveals several tools which allow the mechanical and electrical designer to specify various loads on their designs once it has been modeled.

Ribbon – Architect Tab:

The *Architect* tab provides several tools that are not typically required to be drawn by the MEP engineer. However, some "MEP only" firms may occasionally have a project that does not involve an architect and need to show existing walls, doors and windows. That is what this tab is for.

The *Conceptual Mass* tools can be used to create unusual shapes. These shapes should never be used directly as part of a project. Revit provides *Model by Face* tools which allow walls, curtain walls, floors and roofs to be created based on the surface of a *Conceptual Mass*. This allows certain elements to be created that could not otherwise be done in Revit.

Mechanical Settings Dialog Box:

From the *Manage* tab, select *MEP Settings* → *Mechanical Settings* to reveal the *Mechanical Settings* dialog box; see Figure 12-1.3 below.

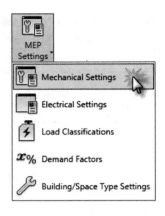

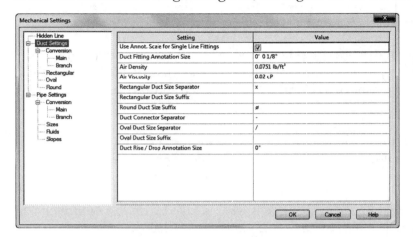

FIGURE 12-1.3 Revit MEP Mechanical Settings dialog

Revit *MEP* provides a *Mechanical Settings* dialog box that allows changes to be made in how the program works and displays things; a related *Electrical Settings* dialog will be mentioned in the next chapter. These settings only apply to the current project, but apply across the board to that project.

For this tutorial, do not make any changes in this dialog unless instructed to do so. This will help to ensure your drawings match those presented in the book.

MEP Content:

A large array of industry standard ducts, air terminals or diffusers, mechanical equipment, pipes, plumbing fixtures and more are provided! What is not provided can typically be modeled in Revit or the *Family Editor* as needed.

MEP Templates:

Revit *MEP* provides three templates from which a new MEP project can be started from. One is specifically for mechanical (**Mechanical-Default.rte**), another is specifically for electrical (**Electrical-default.rte**) and the third is for both in the same model (**Systems-Default.rte**). Three additional templates are provided, which are copies from the Revit *Architecture* offering.

The ideal setup is with both mechanical and electrical in the same model. However, due to software and hardware limitations, in the realm of speed and performance, the two disciplines are often split into separate models. Unfortunately, when the model is split some functionality is lost as the electrical design team cannot connect to mechanical equipment, which requires electrical, when it is in a linked file.

Because you will be starting the MEP model within the architectural model, you will not automatically have several important components ready to go. Not to worry, however, as the first thing you will do in the next exercise will be to import several settings from another project file, which will be based on the MEP mechanical template.

Autodesk Revit MEP Resources:

Autodesk's Revit MEP Resource Center:
resources.autodesk.com/adsk/servlet/Revit-MEP

Autodesk's Revit MEP Blog:
inside-the-system.typepad.com

Autodesk's Revit MEP Discussion Group:
forums.autodesk.com (also check out **Revitforum.org** and **AUGI.com**)
(and then click the links to *Autodesk Revit* → *Autodesk Revit MEP*)

Autodesk's Subscription Website (for members only):
subscription.autodesk.com

> **FYI:** *The subscription website provides several bonuses for those who are on subscription with Autodesk including tutorials and product "advantage packs". Subscription is basically what firms do to be able to budget their yearly design software expenses; which is a yearly payment with access to all new software the moment is becomes available. The subscription route also saves money.*

The image below is a *Camera* view, at eye-level, looking at the reception desk in the Level 1 *Lobby*. Revit *MEP* automatically makes the architectural and structural elements light gray and transparent so the MEP elements are highlighted. You will learn how to create *Camera* views in Chapter 14!

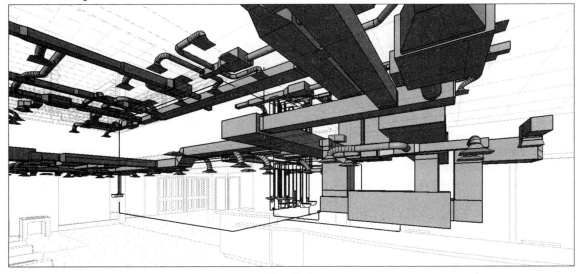

FIGURE 12-1.4 Camera view near the from reception desk

Exercise 12-2:
Creating Views and Loading Content

In this lesson you will begin to prepare your *BIM* file for the mechanical modeling tasks. One of the challenges with modeling everything in one model (versus separate models linked together) is that Autodesk does not provide a template specifically for this. A good starting template is provided for each discipline (or "flavor" of Revit) but not for a multi-discipline project.

The first steps in this lesson, therefore, will walk the reader through the process of importing *Project Standards* from another file into your law office project. Once that has been done, you can then set up views in which to model and annotate the mechanical aspects of the building. These views will be similar to the floor plan views that currently exist for the architectural and structural plans; they are defined by a horizontal slice through the building. The main difference is that various *Categories* will be turned off that are not directly relevant to the mechanical systems of the building.

Transfer Project Standards:

Revit provides a tool which allows various settings to be copied from one project to another; it is called *Transfer Project Standards*. This was first covered in Chapter 8. In order to use this feature, two Revit project files need to be open. One is your law office project file and the other is a file that contains the settings you wish to import. You will start a new Revit *MEP* project from a template file and use this file as the "standards" file; this file will not be used after this step is complete. The only reason this step is required is because the project was started from an architectural template, rather than one of the MEP templates.

1. **Open** Revit *MEP*.

   a. If you do not have this "flavor" of Revit, you may download it from Autodesk.com and use it in a 30-day trial mode for this chapter, which should be plenty of time to complete the tutorials. The free trial version is a fully functional version of the software. Also, students with a valid ".edu" email address may download the free 13-month version from students.autodesk.com.

   FYI: All three "flavors" of Revit can be installed on the same computer and even running at the same time. However, you cannot have the same file open unless "Worksharing" has been enabled. Your law office project does not have this feature enabled; it is beyond the scope of this textbook.

2. Create a new file from the **System-Default.rte** template. Select **Application menu → New → Project**; click **Browse**.

3. Click **OK** to create a new project.

   a. *The file should be* C:\ProgramData\Autodesk\RME 2012\Templates\ US Imperial**Systems-default.rte**

You now have a new Revit project with is temporarily named "Project1.rvt". This will be the project from which you import various MEP settings and families into your law office project. Take a moment to notice the template is rather lean; it has no sheets and several views set up. An MEP engineering department would take the time to set up an office standard template with sheets, families and views all ready to go for their most typical project to save time in the initial setup process.

4. **Open** your law office Revit project file using Revit *MEP*.

    a. You may wish to start this lesson from the data file provided on the DVD that accompanied this book.

With both files open, you will use the *Transfer Project Standards* tool to import several important things into the law office project file.

5. With the law office project file current (i.e., visible in the maximized drawing window), select **Manage → Settings → Transfer Project Standards**.

6. Make sure *Copy from* is set to **Project1** (the file you just created).

Transfer
Project Standards

7. Click the **Check None** button to clear all the checked boxes.

8. Check only the boxes for the items listed (Figure 12-2.1):

    a. Annotation Family Label Types

    b. [3 items starting with] "**Cable Tray**"

    c. [4 items starting with] "**Conduit**"

    d. Distribution System

    e. [6 items starting with] "**Duct**"

    f. [4 items starting with] "**Electrical**"

    g. Filters

    h. Flex Duct Types

    i. Flex Pipe Types

    j. Fluid Types

    k. Heating and Cooling Constructions

    l. [3 items starting with] "**Panel Schedule**"

    m. Physical material parameter set

    n. [*8 items that start with*] "**Pipe**" or "**Piping**"

    o. Space Type Settings

    p. View Templates

    q. Voltage Types

    r. [6 items that start with] "**Wire**"

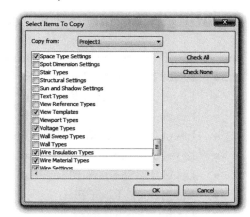

FIGURE 12-2.1 Transfer project settings

9. Click **OK** to import the selected items.

Because some items overlap, Revit prompts you about *Duplicate Types*; you can *Overwrite* or select *New Only*. Selecting *New Only* is safer if you are not sure what will be brought in by the template, or project file in this case. For the law office, you will use *Overwrite* to make sure you get all the MEP settings and parameters needed.

10. Scroll down to see all the "duplicate types" so you have an idea what overlap there is; click **Overwrite** (see Figure 12-2.2).

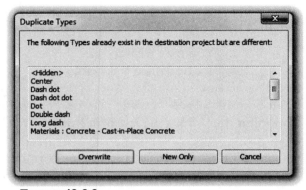

At this point you have many of the key settings loaded into your *BIM* file (e.g., *View Templates* and *Duct and Pipe Settings*). The settings you just brought into the model will accommodate both the mechanical chapter (this chapter) and the electrical chapter (the next chapter).

FIGURE 12-2.2
Transfer project settings; duplicate types warning

At this time you may close the temporary Project1 file without saving.

Creating Mechanical Plan Views:

Next you will create the following floor plan views *(Level; View Template to use listed on right)*:
- Level 1 – HVAC Floor Plan   *(Level 1; Mechanical Plan)*
- Level 2 – HVAC Floor Plan   *(Level 2; Mechanical Plan)*
- Level 1 – Domestic Water Floor Plan   *(Level 1; Plumbing Plan)*
- Level 2 – Domestic Water Floor Plan   *(Level 2; Plumbing Plan)*
- Level 1 – Sanitary Floor Plan   *(Level 1; Plumbing Plan)*
- Level 2 – Sanitary Floor Plan   *(Level 2; Plumbing Plan)*
- Mechanical Roof Plan   *(Roof; Mechanical Plan)*
- Under Slab Sanitary Plan   *(Level 1; Plumbing Plan)*

> **FYI:** *Adjust the* **View Range** *for the* <u>*Under Slab Sanitary Plan*</u> *view as follows:*
> Bottom = *Level 1 @ 0'-0"* and View Depth = *Unlimited (rather than Level 1).*

Next you will create the follow ceiling plan views *(use View Template listed)*:
- Level 1 – HVAC Ceiling Plan   *(Level 1; Mechanical Ceiling)*
- Level 2 – HVAC Ceiling Plan   *(Level 2; Mechanical Ceiling)*

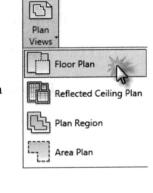

After creating each of these views, you will apply a **View Template**; which is a way to quickly adjust all the view-related parameters to a saved standard (i.e., a *View Template*).

11. While in the law office project, select **View → Create → Plan Views → Floor Plan**.

12. **Uncheck** *Do not duplicate existing views.*

13. In the *New Plan* dialog box, select:

    a. *Floor Plan Views:*   **Level 1**

    b. *Scale:*   **1/4" = 1'-0"**

14. Click **OK** (see Figure 12-2.3).

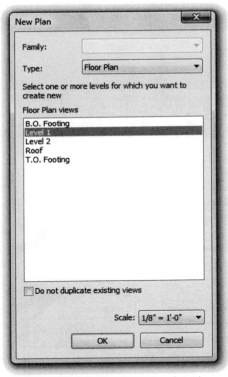

FIGURE 12-2.3 Creating new plan view

At this point you have a new *View* created in the *Project Browser*. This view is in the *Floor Plans* section, under *Views (all)*; see Figure 12-2.4). When you change the *Discipline* and *Sub-Discipline*, and then adjust the *Project Browser* to sort by *Discipline*, the view will move to a new section in the *Project Browser*. This will make things more organized, especially when you have so many floor plan views.

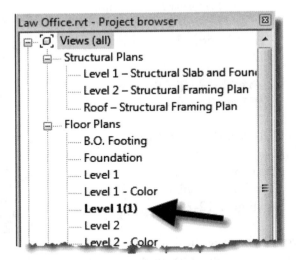

FIGURE 12-2.4 New plan view created

Next you will rename the *View* and apply a *View Template*.

15. In the *Project Browser*, right-click on **Floor Plans\Level 1(1)**.

16. Select **Rename** from the pop-up menu.

17. Enter: **Level 1 – HVAC Floor Plan**.

> *FYI: This is the name that will appear below the drawing when it is placed on a sheet.*

18. Click **OK**.

19. Click **No** to the *Rename corresponding level and views* prompt, if you get it.

View Templates:

Next, you will apply a *View Template* to your view so it is closer to what is needed for the design and documentation of an HVAC plan. First you will look at the current settings and how they will be changed by applying a *View Template*.

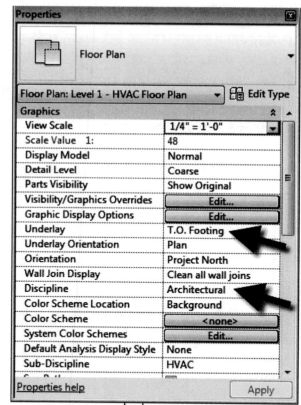

20. In the *Properties Palette*, adjust the *View Properties* so *Discipline* is set to **Architectural** and clear the *Sub-Discipline*.

> *FYI: You are doing this so you can see that the* View Template *fixes this mistake.*

Notice, in the *Properties Palette*, that *Discipline* is now set to *Architectural*, the *Sub-Discipline* is blank and an *Underlay* is active. The *View Template* will quickly correct these settings (Figure 12-2.5).

If you do not see the *Sub-Discipline* parameter you need to revisit the steps on *Transfer Project Standards*.

The **View Range** dialog has a significant role in what shows up in a plan view and what does not. In Revit *MEP*, things only show up in a view when they fall below the *Top View Range*, and are above the *View Depth*. This is different from the architectural discipline setting where only things at or below the *Cut Plane* are shown. This is because most of the ductwork is above the ceiling; but the *Cut Plane* is similar to the architectural views so the doors and windows show up in the plan. The *Cut Plane* will have the same settings as the current architectural view you just copied; it is just the discipline setting that effects how the ductwork is shown.

The **Visibility/Graphics Overrides** dialog also has a significant role in what shows up and what does not in a view. The main thing to understand here is that the visibility of the items on these various categories can be controlled here for the current view, and only the current view. Unchecking *Casework* hides all the items that exist within that category, such as base and wall cabinets and custom casework such as reception desks (assuming they have been created with the correct *Category* setting). The *View Template* you are about to apply to this view will uncheck a few of these *Categories*. However, the HVAC plans need to see much of the architectural elements so they can design for them or around them, unlike the structural lesson in Chapter 8, where much of the architectural content was hidden because it does not typically have a direct effect on the structural design (e.g. casework, furniture, specialty equipment, etc.).

Now you will apply the *View Template* and then review what it changes.

21. Once again, right-click on **Level 1 – HVAC Floor Plan** in the *Project Browser*.

22. Click **Apply View Template** from the pop-up menu.

23. On the left, select **Mechanical Plan**.

You are now in the *Apply View Template* dialog (Figure 12-2.6). Take a moment to observe all the settings it has stored and which are about to be applied to the selected view (i.e., the one you right-clicked on).

Notice the *View Scale* is set to ⅛″-1′-0″. You know the scale needs to be ¼″ = 1′-0″ and you have already set that. So you will uncheck the *View Scale* so it is not included when the template is applied.

24. **Uncheck** *View Scale* (Figure 12-2.6).

25. Click **OK** to apply the *View Template*.

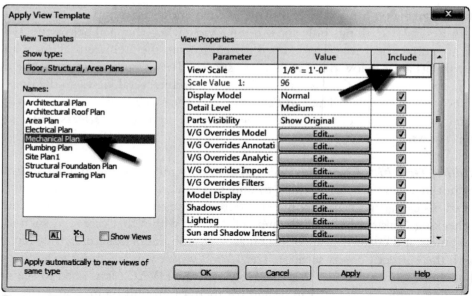

FIGURE 12-2.6 Apply View Template dialog – HVAC Level 1

The model visibility has now changed slightly (Figure 12-2.7). Notice how the architectural elements (i.e., walls, doors, furniture, etc.) are a light gray, and the plumbing fixtures are a medium black line so they stand out. Also, each discipline has its own set of section and elevation tags, so the architectural section marks and elevation tags have been hidden from this view.

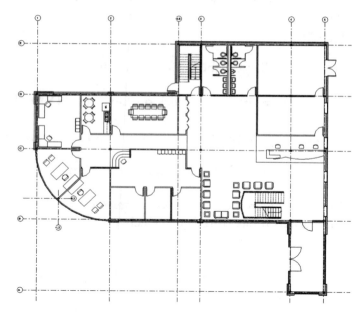

FIGURE 12-2.7 Result of applying view template

Sort the Project Browser by Discipline:

The various views will be easier to manage if they are sorted by discipline and not just stored in the same section. You will change the *Project Browser* to accommodate this.

26. Click on the ***Views (all)*** heading at the top of the *Project Browser* to select it (Figure 12-2.8).

27. Select the *Type* named ***Discipline*** from the drop-down list (Figure 12-2.8).

The *Project Browser* has now been changed to sort the views by its discipline setting (Figure 12-2.10). A MEP-only model would also sort by *Sub-Discipline* so the HVAC, Sanitary, etc., are in separate groups under the *Mechanical* heading.

In the following chapter, when you create the electrical views, a new *Electrical* heading will appear in the *Project Browser*.

Next, you will set up the remaining views. It is expected that you will refer back to the previous steps if you need a review of the process.

28. Create the remaining mechanical views, listed on page 12-10:

    a. Each to be ¼" = 1'-0"

    b. The *View Template* to be used is listed to the right, in parentheses, on page 12-10.

    c. Be sure to select *Reflected Ceiling Plan* when creating the ceiling plan views (compare to Step #11).

29. Adjust the *View Properties* for each of the reflected ceiling plans so the *Underlay Orientation* is set to **Reflected Ceiling Plan**.

The previous step is important in making the view look correct. The ceilings will only show up if the *Underlay Orientation* is set correctly in a ceiling plan view.

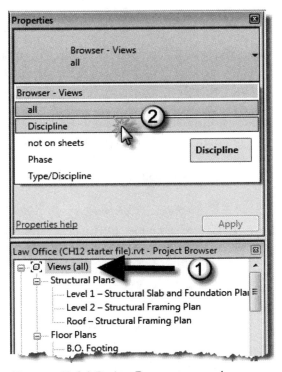

FIGURE 12-2.8 Project Browser properties

FIGURE 12-2.9 Project Browser by discipline

Loading Content:

Now that the mechanical views are set up and ready to go, you will load some MEP content into the project. The process is identical to how content is loaded using Revit *Architecture* and *Revit Structure*.

This section will just show you how to load a few elements; as you work through the rest of this chapter you will have to load additional content, referencing this information if needed.

30. Load the following content from the Revit *MEP* library:

Mechanical Components\Air-Side Components\Air Terminals:
- Exhaust Diffuser – Hosted
- Louver – Extruded
- Return Diffuser
- Supply Diffuser

Mechanical Components\Air-Side Components\Fans and Blowers:
- Centrifugal Fan - Rooftop - Upblast

Mechanical Components\Air-Side Components\Terminal Units:
- VAV Unit - Fan Powered - Series Flow

Plumbing Components\Fixtures\Drinking Fountains:
- Drinking Fountain - Handicap

Plumbing Components\Fixtures\Sinks:
- Sink - Mop

From DVD provided with this book:
- AHU-1 *(custom content)*
- Water Heater *(standard Revit family; modified to be in correct category)*

You now have the content loaded that will be used to model the mechanical system, both ductwork and plumbing. You should only load content that you need, when you need it. Each family takes up space in the project, making the file on your hard drive larger. Additionally, once you start using those components in the project, the file gets larger. At this point in the book, your *BIM* file should be nearly 18MB.

31. **Save** your law office project.

Exercise 12-3:
Placing Air Terminals and the AHU

In this exercise you will start laying out ceiling **diffusers**, or air terminals. Just in case you are not sure what we are talking about, one is pointed out in the picture below (Figure 12-3.1). These can be either supply, return or exhaust diffusers. Some diffuser *Families* are hosted, meaning they attach to and move with the ceiling. Some diffusers are non-hosted and can be placed anywhere. Each has its pros and cons. A hosted diffuser will move with the ceiling, but this sudden relocation may wreak havoc on the ductwork layout. Also, the hosted diffusers cannot be placed until the ceilings have been placed. Non-hosted diffusers can be placed in rooms that are not intended to have a ceiling, and the solid ductwork is intended to support the diffuser. However, when placed in rooms with ceilings, you have to know the ceiling height. You will mainly be placing non-hosted diffusers (supply and return), but the exhaust air terminals will be hosted.

Finally, to close out this exercise, you will place a large piece of mechanical equipment called an **Air Handling Unit** (AHU). Sometimes these are placed on the roof, but you will be placing yours in the mechanical room on Level 1.

FIGURE 12-3.1 Diffuser (air terminal) example

Placing Non-Hosted Diffusers:

You will place supply diffusers in the *Associate's Office (106)*.

1. **Open** you law office file using Revit *MEP*.

2. Switch to your **Level 1 – HVAC <u>Ceiling</u> Plan** view.

3. **Zoom** in to the *Associate's Office (# 106)* on Level 1, in the Northwestern corner.

4. Click on the ceiling to select it.

5. Note the ceiling height is **8'-0"** as seen in the *Properties Palette*.

When working in the same model, it is possible to adjust the ceiling height by changing the ceiling height in the *Properties* dialog. But, if you are not involved in the architectural design, it is typically not acceptable for you, as a mechanical designer, to change the ceiling height. However, most mechanical designers work within the context of a linked architectural model so it is not possible to change the ceiling height.

6. Select **Home → HVAC → Air Terminal**.

Air Terminal

7. Set the *Type Selector* to **Supply Diffuser** (family): **24 x 24 Face 12 x 12 Connection** (type name).

8. Set the *Offset* to **8'-0"** via the *Properties Palette*.

If you did not change the offset, Revit would give you a warning that the created element cannot be seen in the current view (Figure 12-3.2). This is because the diffuser was placed at the floor level (i.e., it is sitting on the floor) and therefore outside the *View Range*.

This warning can also occur if the category is turned off for the element you are placing in the current view. You can check this by typing *VV*.

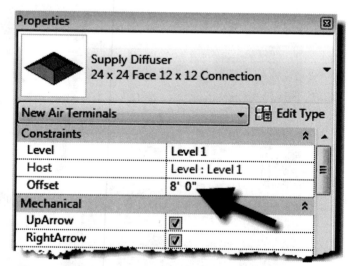

FIGURE 12-3.2 Diffuser offset from floor

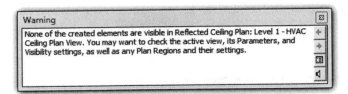

FIGURE 12-3.3 Not visible warning

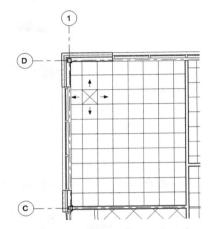

FIGURE 12-3.4 Diffuser placed

You should now be able to see the diffuser in the Ceiling Plan view. Notice the arrows, which indicate that air is leaving the diffuser (supply) and not entering it (return). These arrows can be turned off one-by-one, so a corner condition could show air supply on only two sides.

9. **Click** within the room to place the diffuser, and then use the ***Align*** command to reposition the diffuser as shown in Figure 12-3.4.

    a. Also reposition the ceiling grid if it does not match; simply select one of the ceiling grid lines and use the *Move* tool.

10. Now you can copy this diffuser to three other locations in the same room as shown in Figure 12-3.5.

    a. Select the diffuser, click *Copy* and then check *Multiple* on the *Options Bar*; click at the intersection of the ceiling grid lines.

You can now use this technique to populate the entire **Level 1 Ceiling Plan** view.

11. Copy the diffuser to all other locations on Level 1 per Figure 12-3.6. Be sure to verify the ceiling height for each room and adjust the *Offset* parameter accordingly.

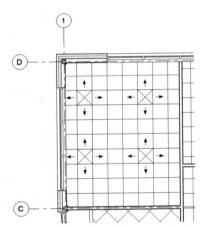

FIGURE 12-3.5 Diffuser copied

The image to the right shows what the diffuser looks like when selected. Notice the small icon to the right indicates the selected item has a *Duct Connector*. Specifically, it lets the user know it's a supply connection which is 12"x12". A similar, but different, icon appears for return and exhaust diffusers.

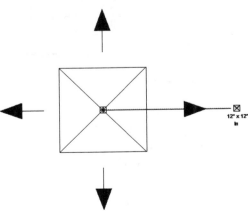

12. Select each diffuser and adjust the CFM value on the *Options Bar* to match that shown in Figure 12-3.6. The value shown is for each diffuser in the room.

> **TIP:** *Select all the diffusers in a room and then adjust the CFM.*

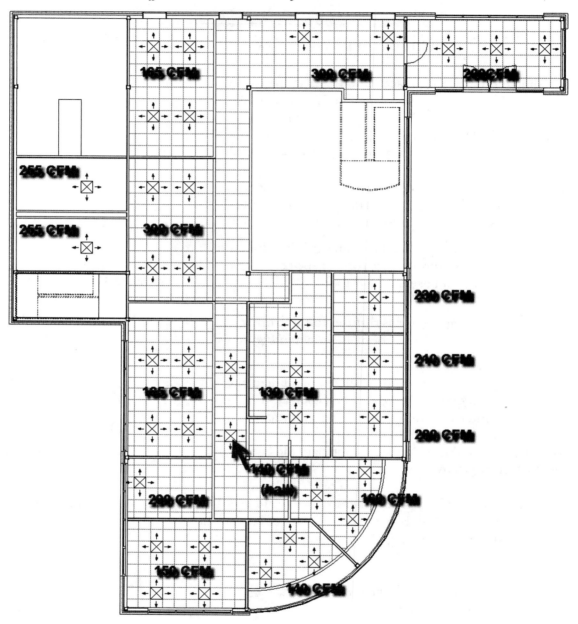

FIGURE 12-3.6 Level 1 supply diffuser layout

You may refer back to Chapter 7 to verify the ceiling heights in addition to selecting them and viewing their properties. Another option is to add *Spot Elevations* (dimensions) to each ceiling in the **HVAC Ceiling Plan** view.

> **TIP:** *This will not work when the view is set to wireframe.*

13. Add the Level 2 diffusers and CFM as shown in Figure 12-3.7.

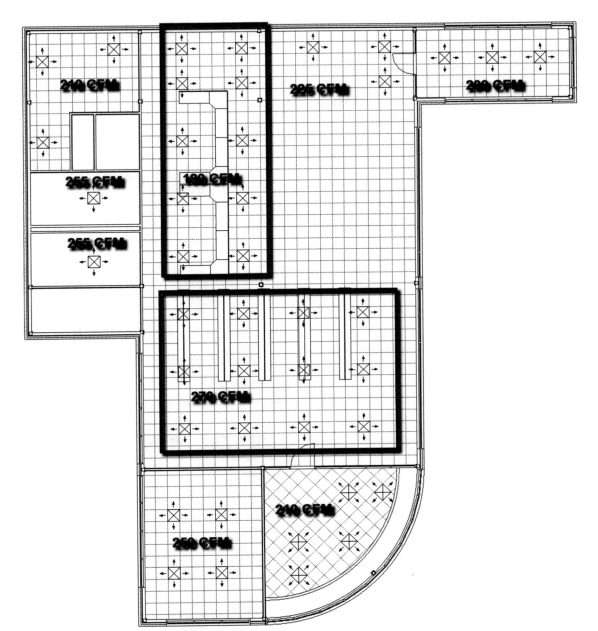

FIGURE 12-3.7 Level 2 supply diffuser layout

Diffusers are sized based on the number of them in a room and the size of the room. Having more at a lower CFM costs more due to the increased ductwork, but is quieter due to the lower air pressure.

Return diffusers are placed the same way. Next you will place a *face* based exhaust diffuser in one of the toilet rooms. An exhaust system is different from a return air system in that the air is blown out of the building, whereas the return air is filtered and reused.

Placing Hosted Diffusers:

14. **Zoom** in to any one of the *Toilet Rooms* (in one of the **HVAC Ceiling Plans**).

15. Select the *Air Terminal* tool.

16. Select **Exhaust Diffuser - Hosted** from the *Type Selector*.

17. Set the **Placement** type to **Place on Face**; *Place on Work Plane* is always the default. See image to the right.

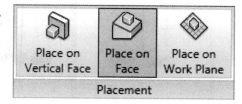

Next, you need to create a new *Type* for this family. It currently only has a 24″x24″ option; you need 12″x12″.

18. Click **Edit Type** from the *Properties Palette*.

19. Click **Duplicate**.

20. Type **12″ x 12″ Exhaust** and click **OK**.

21. Change the *Diffuser Width* to **1′-0″**.

22. Change the *Duct Width* to **10″**.

23. Click **OK** (Figure 12-3.8).

You now have a new exhaust diffuser size from which to choose. This was fast and easy due to the parametric nature of Revit's content.

24. Click within the Northern part of the *Toilet Room*.

    a. Notice the ceiling pre-highlights before you click to place the element.

25. Select the exhaust diffuser you just placed; view its *Instance Properties*.

26. **Uncheck** each of the four "arrow" options (Figure 12-3.9).

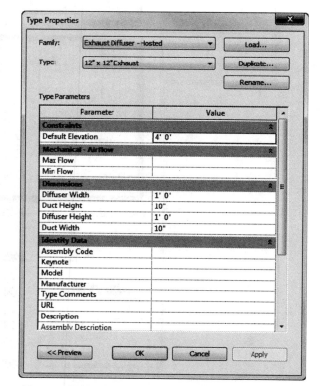

FIGURE 12-3.8 Exhaust diffuser properties

27. Set the exhaust *CFM* to **225**.

Your exhaust diffuser should look like Figure 12-3.10.

28. Place a 12"x12" exhaust diffuser in the other three *Toilet Rooms*.

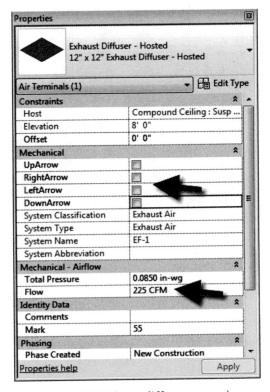

FIGURE 12-3.9 Exhaust diffuser properties

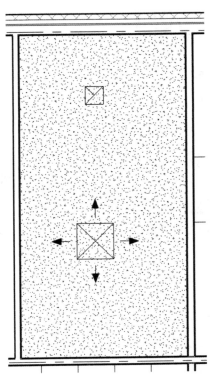

FIGURE 12-3.10 Exhaust diffuser placed

Placing the Air Handling Unit (AHU):

Now you will place the *AHU*, which is the same process for any *Mechanical Equipment* element (e.g., water heater, pump, etc.). The image on the following page (Figure 12-3.11) shows the item you will be placing. It is a simple 3D box which represents the size of the unit. It does not have to have all the minor bumps and recesses modeled, or the controls and such as this will make the file size unnecessarily large. In the image, the *AHU* is selected. Whenever a family is selected that has MEP connectors, those connectors are made visible, but only while the element is selected. Next to the connection icon is text that lists the duct/pipe size or voltage, depending on what type of connection it is: duct, plumbing or electrical. Right-clicking on one of these icons, and then selecting *Draw Duct (or Pipe/Wire/Cable Tray/Conduit)* starts the proper tools (i.e., *Duct/Pipe/Wire/Cable Tray/Conduit*) and sets it to the correct size to match the *Mechanical Equipment* to which you are connecting.

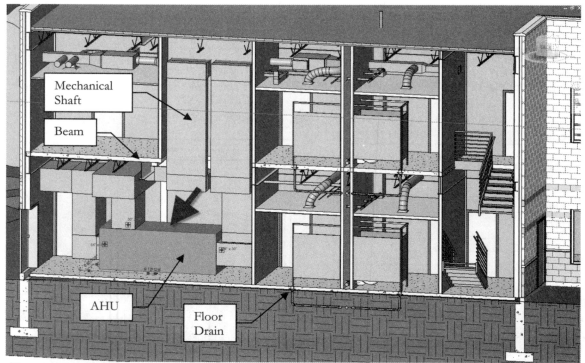

FIGURE 12-3.11 Air handling Unit (AHU); component is selected with connections visible

29. Zoom in to the *Mechanical Room* in the Northeastern corner of the **Level 1- HVAC Floor Plan**.

30. Select **Home → Mechanical → Mechanical Equipment** tool on the *Ribbon*.

    a. Click **No** when prompted to load a tag.

31. Select **AHU-1** from the *Type Selector*. This was loaded from the DVD in the previous exercise.

32. Click to place the AHU in the *Mechanical Room*; pick anywhere.

33. Adjust the location to match the dimensions shown in Figure 12-3.12. Do not add the dimensions.

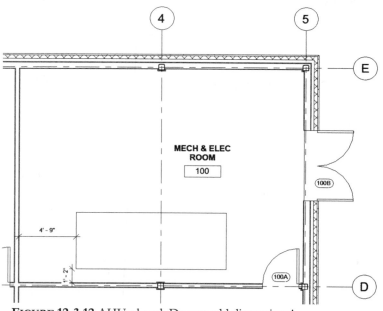

FIGURE 12-3.12 AHU placed. Do not add dimensions!

Finally, you will take a quick look at a few properties related to the AHU.

34. Click the AHU to select it in the **Level 1 – HVAC Floor Plan**.

As previously mentioned, when a family is selected that has MEP connections, they become visible. The square with the plus in it (⊞) represents a connection, and the text next to it indicates the size the ductwork needs to be when connecting to the equipment at that location.

The 30″x54″ connection is actually on the top of the AHU (Figure 12-3.13). A duct connects to the top at this location.

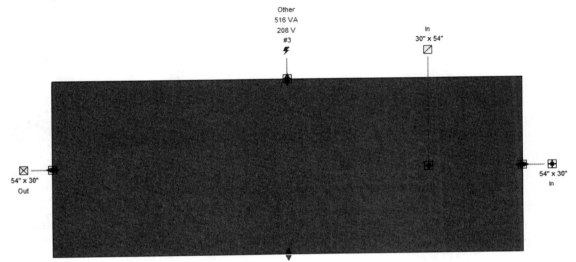

FIGURE 12-3.13 AHU selected in a plan view

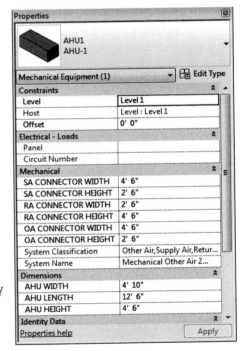

FIGURE 12-3.14
AHU instance properties

35. View the AHU's *Instance Properties*, via the *Properties Palette*.

Notice the AHU and connector dimensions are adjustable here. Also, notice the types of connections:

- SA = Supply Air
- RA = Return Air
- OA = Outside Air

36. **Save** your project.

> *FYI: It is possible to get more detailed families of mechanical equipment from some manufacturers. For an example, take a look at McQuay's website:*
> **mcquay.com/McQuay/BIM/Revit-BIMFiles**.

Exercise 12-4:
VAV Boxes, MEP Systems and Ductwork

With the diffusers in place, you will now look at placing *VAV* boxes and connect ductwork between the two. Due to the time involved in laying out the ductwork for the entire building, you will only do this to a few rooms so you understand how things work. The Chapter 13 starter file will have the ductwork for the entire building in it.

Placing a VAV Box:

A *Variable Air Volume* box (*VAV*) terminal unit allows the temperature to be efficiently controlled per room or per a group of rooms; each VAV box is connected to a thermostat, which lets it know what the heating/cooling need is. The AHU provides fresh air to the VAV boxes at a constant temperature, volume, humidity, etc. and the VAV box adjusts the air volume to meet the needs of the various spaces served. VAV boxes are typically hidden above the ceiling. You can do an internet search (type "VAV box") for more information on variable air volume terminal units.

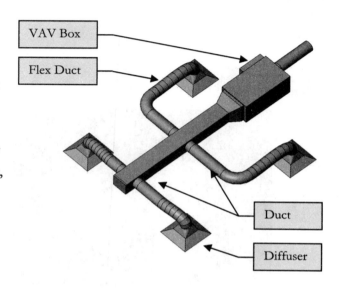

1. Switch to the **Level 1 – HVAC Floor Plan**.

Seeing as you know the VAV box will be placed on the floor and not visible in the Ceiling Plan view initially, you will work in the HVAC Floor Plan view. In fact, now that the diffusers are in the correct location relative to the ceiling grid, you can stay in the plan view to place mechanical equipment and draw ductwork.

2. **Zoom** in to the *Associate's Office*, Northwestern corner, again.

3. Select the ***Mechanical Equipment*** tool from the *Ribbon*.

    a. Click **No** if prompted to load a tag.

4. From the *Type Selector*, select *VAV Unit – Fan Powered – Series Flow:* **8"**.

5. Set the *Offset* parameter to **8'-6"** in the *Properties Palette*.

6. Press the spacebar as needed to rotate the VAV box.

7. Click to place the element as shown in Figure 12-4.1.

Your model should look similar to Figure 12-4.1; the exact location of the VAV box is not important.

8. **Select** the VAV box.

9. View its *Instance Properties*.

That is all there is to placing a VAV box. It will now show up in sections created by anyone on the design team. Next, you will place a few more units for more practice.

10. Use *Copy/Rotate* to place seven more VAV boxes as shown in Figure 12-4.2; move the two in the *Exec. Offices* up 1'-0"; you will have 8 total.

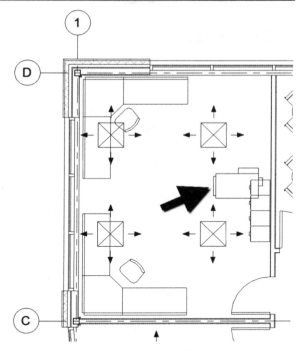

FIGURE 12-4.1 First VAV box placed

FYI: The view's Model Graphics Style has been set to Shading so the mechanical equipment is highlighted better.

TIP: Clicking and dragging an element while holding the Ctrl key is a quick way to make a copy. Also, selecting an element and pressing the spacebar rotates it after it has been placed.

REMEMBER: You can use the arrow keys to nudge selected elements.

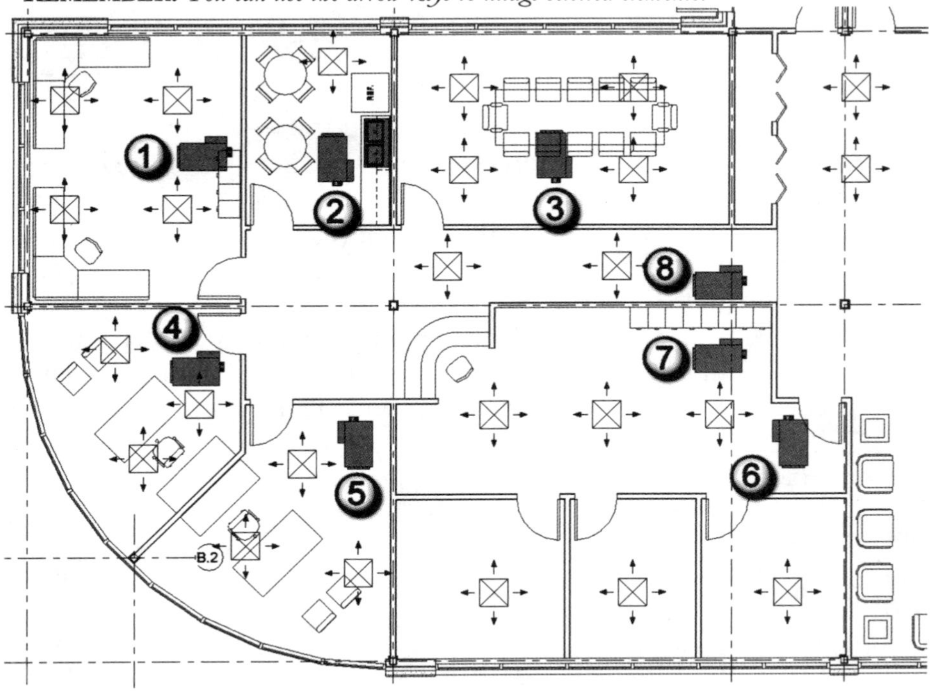

FIGURE 12-4.2 VAV box locations

Creating MEP Systems:

Now that you have the VAV boxes and diffusers placed, you can start to create *MEP Systems*. An *MEP System* is something Revit uses to understand the relationships between the various parts of an HVAC system. The term *MEP System* is specific to Revit and not used in the MEP construction industry.

Below are two examples of an *MEP System* and what they consist of:

- AHU-1 *(system name)*
  - AHU-1 *(Parent: Mechanical Equipment)*
  - One or more VAV boxes *(Child: elements served by parent)*

- VAV-1 *(system name)*
  - VAV-1 *(Parent: Mechanical Equipment)*
  - One or more Diffusers *(Child: elements served by parent)*

> ***FYI:*** *The terms "parent" and "child" are not Revit terms. They are just introduced here to better explain the concept.*

The process of creating a system is fairly simple. You select a "child" element in the project. From the *Ribbon*, you select the *Create Duct System* tool. Next, you give the *System* a name, and add additional child elements and pick the parent element. That is it.

11. Select one of the *diffusers* in the *Associate's Office*.

12. Select **Modify Air Terminals → Create System → Duct** from the *Ribbon*.

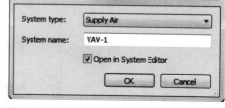

13. Make the following modifications to the *Create Duct System* dialog (Figure 12-4.3).

    a. *System Type:*   **Supply Air**
    b. *Name:*   **VAV-1**
    c. *Open in System Editor:*   **checked**

FIGURE 12-4.3 Create Duct System

Revit just created a system named VAV-1. The name is meant to match the name used to describe the "parent" element (the VAV box in this case) in the project. The system name should not be too generic, making it hard to find later once all the systems are created.

14. Notice the options on the *Ribbon* and *Options Bar* (see image below).

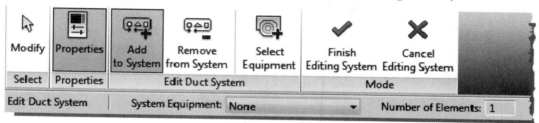

15. Click the **_Add to System_** button on the _Ribbon_ (which should already be the default selection).

Add
To System

You are now in the _Add to System_ mode. Thus, you can select the other diffusers in the room and add them to the _VAV-1_ system.

16. Click to select the other three diffusers in the room to add them to the _System_.

    a. The diffusers will turn from gray lines to black lines when they are selected and considered part of the _System_.

17. Pick **Select Equipment** from the _Ribbon_.

Select
Equipment

> **_FYI:_** _It is possible to select the equipment from the drop-down list on the Options Bar, but the list can become very long so it is usually easier to select the item graphically._

18. Select the VAV box in the same room as the diffusers.

19. Click **Finish Editing System** on the _Ribbon_.

Finish
Editing System

You have now created a _System_!

20. Create **seven** more _Systems_ using the same naming convention and the numbers provided in Figure 12-4.2.

    a. _VAV-6_ serves the three small offices to the South.

    b. _VAV-7_ serves the diffusers in the same room with it.

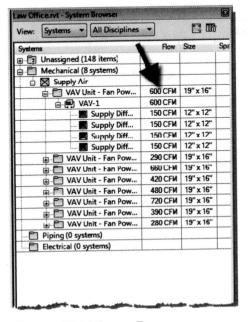

FIGURE 12-4.4 System Browser

Before moving on to the ductwork, you will look at a feature unique to Revit _MEP_ that allows you to see the various systems in a list similar to the _Project Browser_; it is called the _System Browser_.

21. Select _System Browser_ on the **_Analyze_** tab.

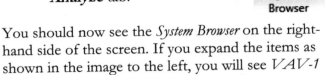

System
Browser

You should now see the _System Browser_ on the right-hand side of the screen. If you expand the items as shown in the image to the left, you will see _VAV-1_ and its total CFM, which is based on the values you entered into each diffuser (Figure 12-4.5).

Ultimately, you want the unassigned section to be empty so everything is on a _System_. If your numbers do not match the book, you should go back and double check your CFM values.

Adding Ductwork:

The following information will show how to draw the ductwork shown below. This will be an isolated example that has nothing to do with the law office project.

Duct

- After selecting the *Duct* tool, you specify the duct *Width*, *Height* and *Offset*, which is the distance off the floor to the center of the duct, on the *Options Bar*.

- Next, you pick your **first** and **second** points in the model (Figure 12-4.5).

- While still in the *Duct* tool, you change the *Options Bar* settings.

- Now pick the **third** point (Figure 12-4.5 again). Notice the duct transition is automatically added.

- To make the duct go vertical, simply change the *Offset* (move the cursor back into the drawing window momentarily) and click **Apply**. A duct will be drawn from the third point to the distance entered, above or below.

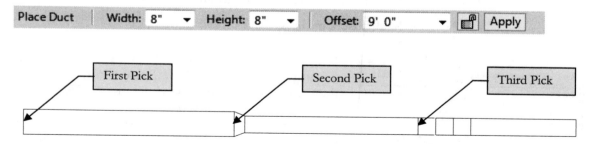

FIGURE 12-4.5A Modeling ductwork; plan view

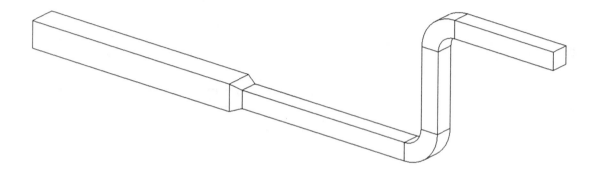

FIGURE 12-4.5B Modeling ductwork; 3D view

Now you will add some ductwork from the VAV box in the *Associate's Office* to the four diffusers.

22. In the **Level 1 – HVAC Floor Plan** view, zoom in to the *Associate's Office*.

23. Select the VAV box to reveal its connectors (Figure 12-4.6).

24. With the VAV selected, right-click on the 19″ x 16″ connector.

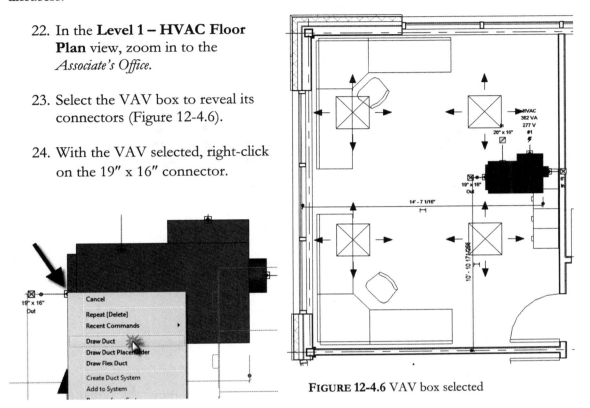

FIGURE 12-4.6 VAV box selected

FIGURE 12-4.7 Right-click on connector

25. Select **Draw Duct** from the pop-up menu (Figure 12-4.7).

The *Duct* tool is automatically started and the size and offset have been adjusted to match the connector size and elevation.

26. Set the *Type Selector* to *Rectangular* **Duct: Mitered Elbows / Taps**.

27. Change the duct *Width* to **12″** and the *Height* to **10″** on the *Options Bar*.

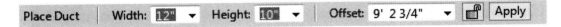

28. Click a point straight out from the connector, near the end of the diffuser (Figure 12-4.8).

29. Click **Modify** to finish the *Duct* tool.

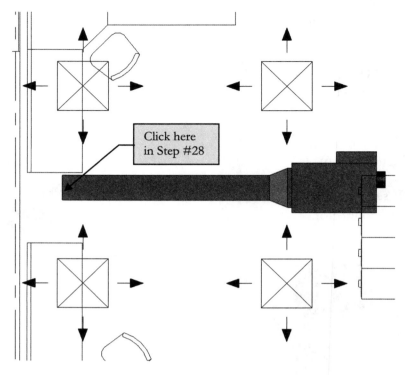

FIGURE 12-4.8 Drawing a duct off of the VAV

This is the main duct for this room/system. Next you will draw branch ducts that come off of the "main" duct and head towards the *diffusers*.

30. Select the ***Duct*** tool.

31. Set the *Type Selector* to **Round Duct: Taps**.

Notice the *Options Bar* changes to show a diameter in place of width and height.

32. Set the *Diameter* to **8″**; make sure the *Offset* is still **9′ 2 3/4″**.

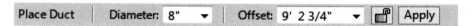

33. Click the two points shown in Figure 12-4.9.

34. Click **Modify** to end the *Duct* tool.

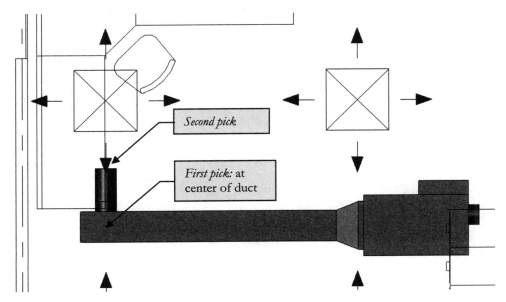

FIGURE 12-4.9 Drawing a branch duct

Next, you will draw another branch duct that turns the corner. Revit will automatically add an elbow at the corner, or duct fitting.

35. Similar to the previous steps, **Draw** an 8″ diameter branch duct by picking, approximately, the three points shown in Figure 12-4.10.

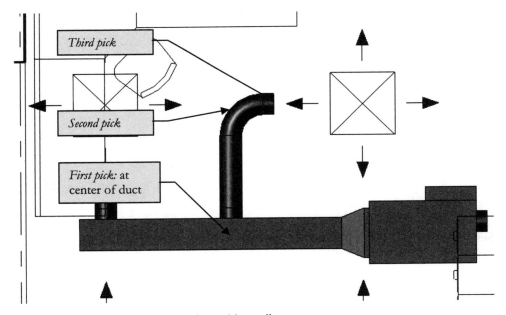

FIGURE 12-4.10 Drawing a branch duct with an elbow

Next, you will mirror the branch ductwork to the other side of the main duct.

36. **Select** the branch ductwork, including the round ducts, taps and fittings (Figure 12-4.11).

37. Use the ***Mirror*** tool to mirror the selected elements about the center of the VAV box.

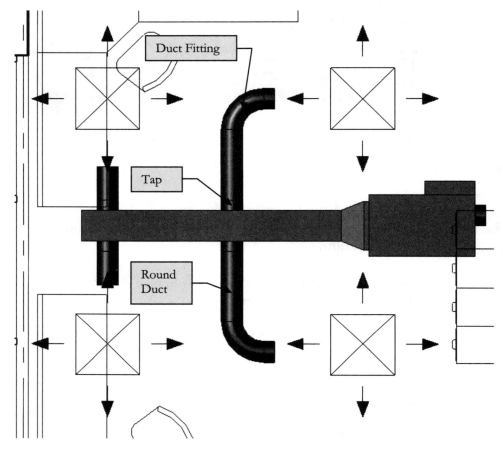

FIGURE 12-4.11 Mirrored "branch" ductwork about the VAV box

The next step will be to draw *Flex Duct* from the "solid" **duct** to the **diffuser**; things work best when drawn from in this order.

38. **Select** the "solid" round duct the upper-left corner (Figure 12-4.12).

39. With the duct selected, **right-click** on the *connector* icon at the open end.

40. Pick **Draw Flex Duct** from the pop-up menu.

41. Notice the *Diameter* is automatically set to **8″** on the *Options Bar.*

42. Pick at the <u>center</u> of the diffuser.

    a. Make sure you see the special "connector" snap before picking to ensure the flex duct gets connected to the duct "system" and is drawn at the right elevation.

FYI: The connector on the diffuser is 12″x12″, so when you connect an 8″ diameter flex duct (as in this example), Revit automatically adds a transition fitting between the diffuser and the flex duct.

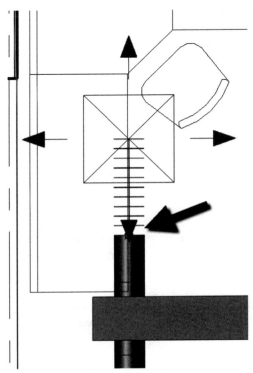

FIGURE 12-4.12 Modeling flex duct

43. Select **Modify**.

44. **Select** the flex duct.

45. View its *Instance Properties.*

46. Set the *Flex Pattern* to **Flex**.

47. **Repeat** the previous steps to add 8″ *Flex Duct* to the other three diffusers (Figure 12-4.13).

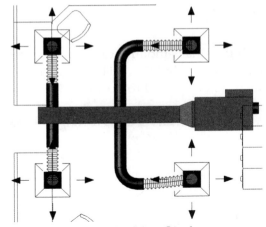

FIGURE 12-4.13 Modeling flex duct

The last thing you need to do to complete this system is to add an end cap to the open end of the main duct.

48. Load the following family:

    a. *Family name:* **Rectangular Endcap**

    b. *Folder:* Duct\Fittings\Rectangular\Caps

49. Select the ***Duct Fitting*** tool on the *Home* tab.

50. Set the *Type Selector* to **Rectangular Endcap**, click to place away from duct and then rotate and move into place.

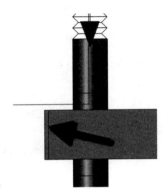

FIGURE 12-4.14 Endcap added

Now with the system complete, you can select the VAV box and see the total CFM (outlet airflow parameter), 600CFM in this case, in the *Instance Properties*. This is a handy way to verify the system is complete. Another good test is to hover your cursor over any part of the system and press **Tab** until the entire system highlights, if you then click, it will select everything highlighted. When the entire system never highlights, then something is not properly connected. In this case you need to select one of the ducts near the problem area, pull its end back and then drag it back to the proper area, looking for the "connection" snap; you may even have to delete and redraw some elements. This can be tricky but gets easier with experience.

Now you will repeat the previous steps in order complete the other ductwork systems.

51. Add the remaining ductwork at the other VAV box locations:

    a. Reference Figure 12-4.16.

    b. Make sure you use the duct with "taps" and not "tees".

    c. All "branch" ducts are 8″ diameter *Round Duct*.
        i. Exception: *Break Room* should be 10″ diameter.

    d. The "main" duct sizes vary; see image.

52. **Save** your project.

With the small amount of information covered in this chapter you can model the remaining portion of the building's HVAC system. However, due to space limitations in this book, you will not be expected to do so.

> **DESIGN INTEGRATION:** *If you switch to the cross section created earlier in the book, you will see the HVAC now added to the view (Figure 12-4.15). Here you can visually see there is enough space between the ceiling and the structure.*

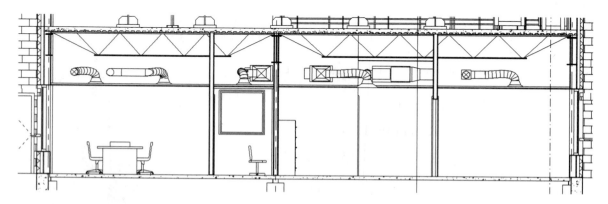

FIGURE 12-4.15 Ductwork now visible in the architectural cross section view

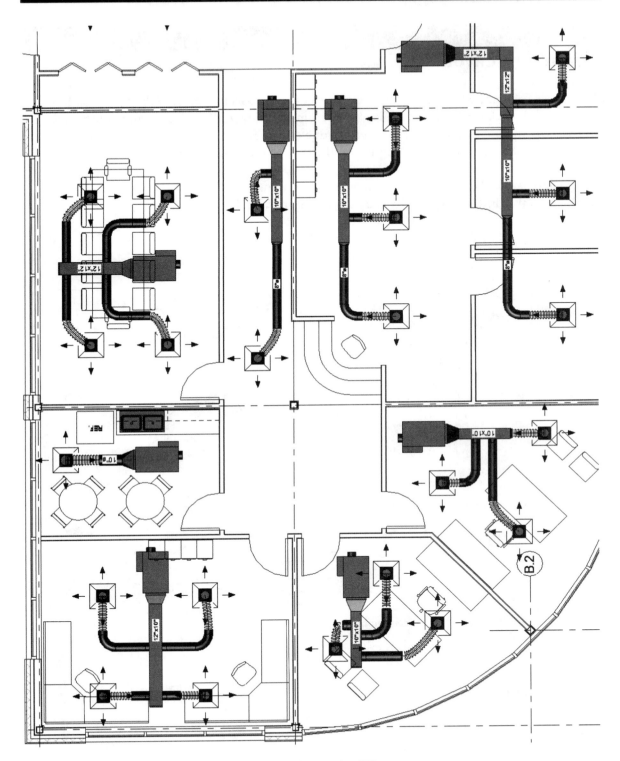

FIGURE 12-4.16 Ductwork added from each VAV box to the diffusers

Exercise 12-5:
Plumbing Layout

This short Exercise will review the *Plumbing* and *Piping* tools in Revit *MEP*. Autodesk has done a good job keeping steps similar between tasks. In fact, the steps to model piping are identical to laying out ductwork! Therefore, due to this fact and page limitations we will only place a water heater and connect piping to the sink in the *Break Room*.

The image below shows the entire piping and plumbing system for the law office. This data will be available in the Chapter 13 starter file (Figure 12-5.1).

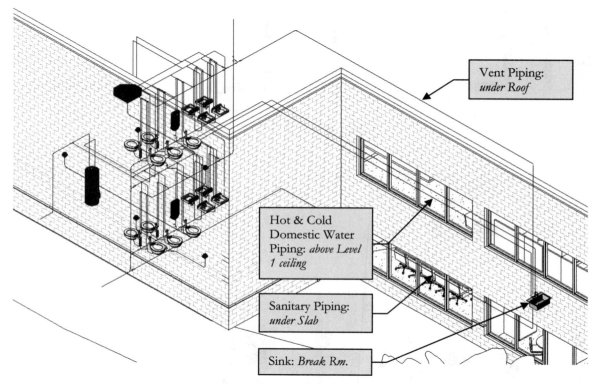

Vent Piping: *under Roof*

Hot & Cold Domestic Water Piping: *above Level 1 ceiling*

Sanitary Piping: *under Slab*

Sink: *Break Rm.*

FIGURE 12-5.1 3D view of law office plumbing system

Placing the Water Heater:

1. **Start** Revit *MEP*.

2. Switch to the **Level 1 – Domestic Water Floor Plan** view.

3. **Zoom** in to the *Mechanical and Electrical Room* in the Northeastern corner.

4. Select the **_Plumbing Fixture_** tool from the _Home_ tab on the _Ribbon_.

Plumbing Fixture

5. Select the **40 gallon** _Water Heater_ from the _Type Selector_.

6. **Click** approximately as shown in Figure 12-5.2 to place the element.

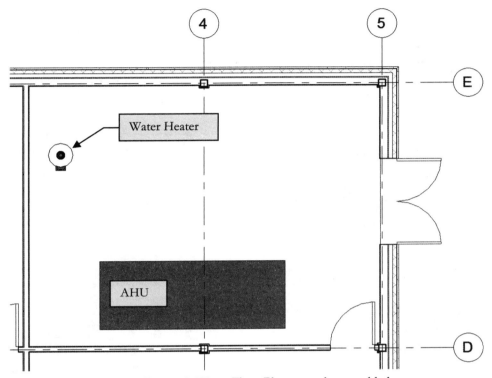

FIGURE 12-5.2 Level 1 – Domestic Water Floor Plan; water heater added

Immediately after the element is selected. Notice all the connectors available (Figure 12-5.3). This one family has the three major types of connectors: duct, pipe and power.

7. Click **Modify** to finish the _Plumbing Fixture_ tool.

The water heater that comes with Revit is set to be in the _Mechanical Equipment_ category. The one you loaded from the DVD has been changed to the _Plumbing Fixtures_ category so the water heater will show up if the _Mechanical Equipment_ is hidden from the domestic water plan views; you would not typically want to see all the VAV boxes in this view. Turn the _Mechanical Equipment_ category off if you want.

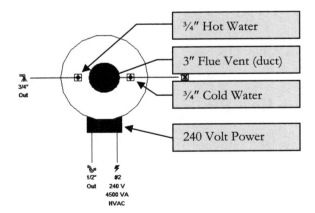

FIGURE 12-5.3 Water Heater connectors

HVAC Project Units:

Because you did not start from an MEP template, you need to change one setting so you are able to create pipes that are smaller than 1" in diameter.

8. Select **Manage → Settings → Project Units** from the *Ribbon*.

9. Set the *Discipline* to **Piping** (Figure 12-5.4).

10. Click the button to the right of **Pipe Size**.

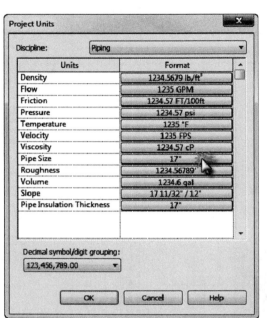

FIGURE 12-5.4 Project units; HVAC

FIGURE 12-5.5 Project units: Format

11. Set the *Rounding* to **To the nearest 1/4"**.

12. Click **OK** twice to close the open dialog boxes.

Modeling Piping:

Now you will run hot and cold water piping from the *Mechanical Room* to the sink in the *Break Room*. Piping views usually have the *Detail Level* set to *Medium*, as this will make the pipe single line (the pipe's centerline) and the ducts are still two line (actual thickness). *Detail Level* of *Coarse* makes both ductwork and piping single line and *Fine* makes them both two line. Small pipe drawn with two lines bleeds together into one fat line and this also decreases model performance.

13. In the **Level 1 – Domestic Water Floor Plan** view, select the water heater.

14. **Right-click** on the hot water connector (see Figure 12-5.3).

15. Select **Draw Pipe** from the pop-up menu.

16. Set the *Offset* to **9'-8"** on the *Options Bar*.

   a.   Notice the pipe diameter is automatically set to ¾" because you right-clicked on the MEP connector on the water heater to start the command.

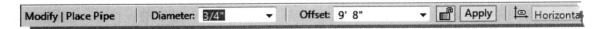

Notice, on the *Options Bar*, that you can specify a slope and Revit will automatically adjust the piping in the Z direction, that is, vertically, to maintain the required slope. This is used in sanitary and rain leader piping.

Now you need a vertical pipe up to 9'-8", which is the height the hot water piping will run above the ceiling. Revit will automatically draw this vertical pipe for you when clicking away from the water heater (i.e., "second pick" in Figure 12-5.6).

17. Pick points 2 and 3 as shown in Figure 12-5.6; make sure the *Diameter* is **3/4"** and the *Offset* is still **9'-8"** on the *Options Bar*.

You now have a vertical piece of pipe that goes from the water heater connector up to 9'-8" above the floor.

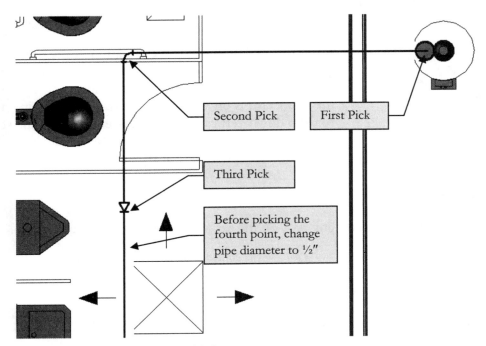

FIGURE 12-5.6 Hot water piping added

18. Set the *Diameter* to ½" and leave the *Offset* at **9'-8"**.

19. Pick points 4 and 5 as shown in Figure 12-5.7

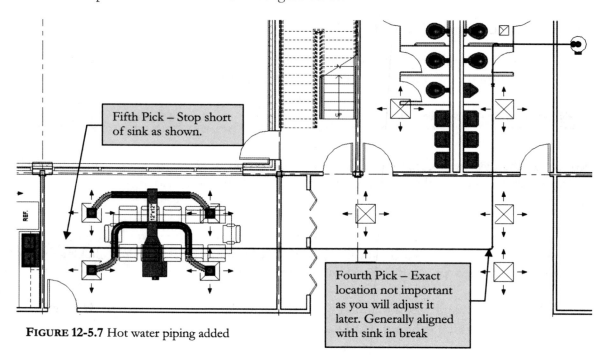

Fifth Pick – Stop short of sink as shown.

Fourth Pick – Exact location not important as you will adjust it later. Generally aligned with sink in break

FIGURE 12-5.7 Hot water piping added

If you run the *Interference Check* from the *Collaborate* tab, you will see that the pipe conflicts with the VAV box in the *Conference Room* (comparing *Mechanical Equipment* to *Piping*)!

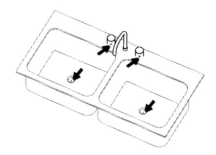

Because you do not know the elevation of the hot water connector, it is easier to draw pipe from the sink to the pipe you just drew nearby. Another thing to note is that the connector is on a horizontal surface, so the pipe needs to drop down vertically and then over into the wall; see image to the left from the *Family Editor*. Finally, two connectors are provided for the sink drains.

FIGURE 12-5.8 Sink family

20. Select the sink and then right-click on the hot water connector (Figure 12-5.9).

   TIP: *As you likely already know, the hot water is always on the left when you are facing the sink.*

21. Click **Draw Pipe** from the menu.

22. Change the *Offset* to **2'-0"** on the *Options Bar*.

23. *First Pick:* pick a point within the interior stud wall, directly to the east of the hot water connector. A vertical and horizontal pipe will be drawn.

24. Change the *Offset* to **9'-8"**. **REMEMBER:** *This is the same height as the pipe coming from the water heater.*

25. *Second Pick:* Click the endpoint of the pipe coming from the water heater. (If they do not align, follow the next step.)

26. If the pipe does not align with the pipe coming from the water heater (which it probably doesn't), your second pick should stop short of the previously drawn pipe so you can align it first. Use the *Align* tool to move the previously drawn pipe to align with the pipe coming from the sink. Finally, select one of the pipes and drag the endpoint over to the other (now aligned) pipe.

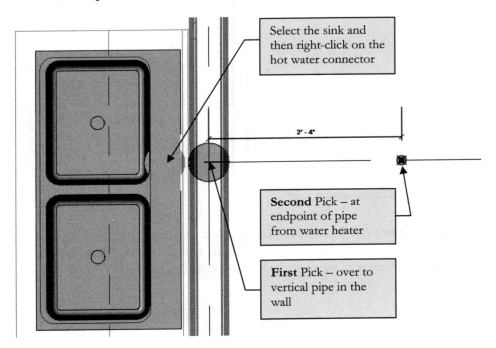

FIGURE 12-5.9 Sink piping

The two horizontal pipes at 9'-8" will automatically clean up, so there will be no joint; when a union is needed, it needs to be manually added. Now you will add the cold water piping.

27. Use the same process to draw the cold water piping (Figure 12-5.10).

    a. Draw cold water from the water heater towards the North exterior wall. This will be the entry point for the building's water; elevation at **10'-0"**.

    b. Off of the water line just drawn, draw a ¾" pipe as shown in Figure 12-5.10, heading towards the sink in the *Break Room*.

    c. Transition to a ½" pipe next to the hot water transition.

The cold water is drawn 4″ above the hot water to avoid conflicts when they cross each other. Notice, when they do cross, the lower one is graphically interrupted (Figure 12-5.10). You may have to select the *Tee* and change it to a *Generic Tee* via the *Type Selector*.

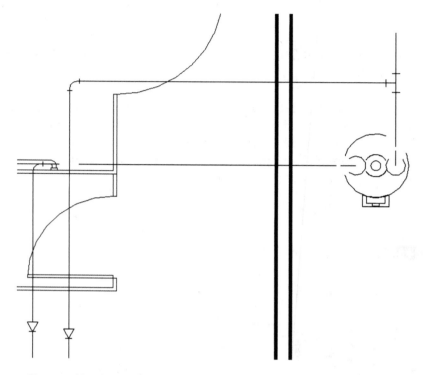

FIGURE 12-5.10 Cold water piping at 10′-0″

Below is a 3D view of the piping you have added to your law office project. You would continue this process to add drinking fountains, floor drains and the route piping to all connections. You should also create systems just like the examples in the HVAC exercise.

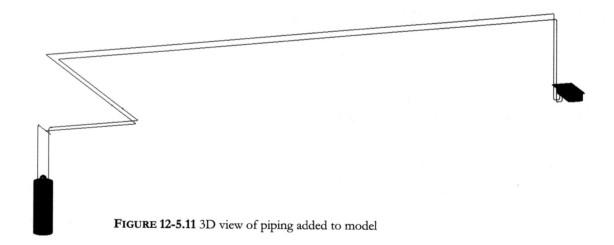

FIGURE 12-5.11 3D view of piping added to model

28. **Save** and **back up** your work to a flash drive or external hard drive.

Self-Exam:

The following questions can be used as a way to check your knowledge of this lesson. The answers can be found at the bottom of this page.

1. The User Interface (UI) is similar across the Revit "flavors". (T/F)

2. You can use *Transfer Project Settings* to import various settings from another project which is set up the right way. (T/F)

3. Modeling piping is very different from ductwork. (T/F)

4. In the ductwork view, set the _____ to *Mechanical* so the architectural walls turn gray.

5. Ducts will show up as long as they are within the _____ _____ .

Review Questions:

The following questions may be assigned by your instructor as a way to assess your knowledge of this section. Your instructor has the answers to the review questions.

1. Everyone on the design team must use the same release of Revit. (T/F)

2. You changed the *Project Browser* to sort by _____.

3. Air terminals (i.e., diffusers) can be either hosted or non-hosted. (T/F)

4. Selecting several diffusers allows you to change the CFM at once. (T/F)

5. Which family did you place that has all three major types of connectors:

    (i.e., pipe, duct and power) _____ _____ .

6. A *View Template* always changes the *View Scale*. (T/F)

7. Pressing the spacebar, while placing a component, mirrors it. (T/F)

8. A change in _____ _____ was required in order to draw pipe smaller than 1″ in diameter.

9. Duct and pipe elbows and transitions have to be added manually. (T/F)

10. Revit *MEP Systems* are used to understand the relationships between the various parts of an HVAC and plumbing system. (T/F)

Notes:

Lesson 13
Law Office: ELECTRICAL SYSTEM

This chapter will introduce the electrical documentation capabilities of Autodesk Revit *MEP*. You will develop the outlet and power panel layout as well as the lighting design.

Exercise 13-1:
Introduction to Revit MEP – Electrical

The previous chapter introduced the *User Interface* for Revit *MEP* and how it compares to Revit *Architecture* and Revit *Structure*. If you have not reviewed that information, you may want to do so know.

Mechanical, HVAC and plumbing, and electrical engineers work closely together and are often in the same office. Therefore, Autodesk created one product that meets each of these disciplines needs: Revit *MEP*.

In this chapter you will add the views, content and annotation required to document the electrical system. However, similar to the previous chapters, you will not be getting into any of the more advanced concepts such as wire sizing and balancing loads at a power panel.

Starting with Revit MEP 2011, the software can create code compliant panelboard schedules using the new *Demand Factors* and *Load Classifications* functionality. Most building electrical designs are based on the National Electric Code (NEC). There are still things Revit cannot do, however; for example, arc flash/short-circuit analysis and point-by-point lighting analysis. Other programs are still used for this, such as SKM Power Tools and AGI32.

> **WARNING:** *This is strictly a fictitious project. Although some effort has been made to make the electrical design realistic, this system has not been designed by an electrical engineer. There are many codes and design considerations that need to be made on a case by case basis.*

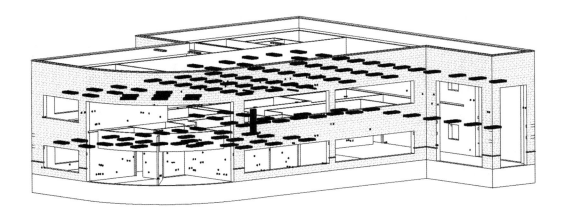

Exercise 13-2:
Creating Views and Loading Content

Most of the major MEP setup was done in the previous chapter with the *Transfer Project Standards* tool. If you did not do that yet, you should go to Chapter 12 and do so. You will set up views in which to model and annotate the electrical aspects of the building. These views will be similar to the floor plan views that currently exist for the architectural, mechanical and structural plans.

1. **Open** the Chapter 13 starter file from the **DVD**.

   a. The DVD starter file has a more complete mechanical system compared to what was covered in the previous chapter.

Creating Mechanical Plan Views:

Next you will create the following floor plan views *(using View Template listed to right)*:
- Level 1 – Power Floor Plan   *(Electrical Plan)*
- Level 2 – Power Floor Plan   *(Electrical Plan)*
- Level 1 – Systems Floor Plan   *(Electrical Plan)*
- Level 2 – Systems Floor Plan   *(Electrical Plan)*

Next you will create the following ceiling plan views *(using View Template listed)*:
- Level 1 – Lighting Plan   *(Electrical Ceiling)*
- Level 2 – Lighting Plan   *(Electrical Ceiling)*

After creating each of these views you will apply a **View Template**, which is a way to quickly adjust all the view-related parameters to a saved standard.

2. While in the law office project, select **View → Create → Plan Views → Floor Plan**.

3. **Uncheck** *Do not duplicate existing views.*

4. In the *New Plan* dialog box, select:
   a. *Floor Plan Views:*   **Level 1**
   b. *Scale:*   **1/4" = 1'-0"**

5. Click **OK**.

Next you will rename the *View* and apply a *View Template*.

6. In the *Project Browser*, right-click on <u>Mechanical\Floor Plans\</u>**Level 1(1)**.

7. Select **Rename** from the pop-up menu.

8. Enter: **Level 1 – Power Floor Plan**.

   FYI: This is the name that will appear below the drawing when it is placed on a sheet.

9. Click **OK**.

10. Click **No** to the *Rename corresponding level and views* prompt if you get it.

View Templates:

Next, you will apply a *View Template* to your view so it is closer to what is needed for the design and documentation of an electrical power plan.

11. Once again, right-click on **Level 1 – Power Floor Plan** in the *Project Browser*.

12. Click **Apply View Template** from the pop-up menu.

13. On the left, select **Electrical Plan**.

You are now in the *Apply View Template* dialog (compare to Figure 13-2.6). Take a moment to observe all the settings it has stored and are about to be applied to the selected view, the one you right-clicked on.

Notice the *View Scale* is set to ⅛"=1'-0". You know the scale needs to be ¼" = 1'-0" and you have already set that. You will uncheck the *View Scale* so it is not included when the template is applied.

14. **Uncheck** *View Scale*.

15. Click **OK** to apply the *View Template*.

Next, you will set up the remaining views. It is expected that you will refer back to the previous steps if you need a review of the process.

> *POWER USER TIP: A firm template file can have "placeholder" Revit Links loaded into it, one link for architectural and another for structural. This allows the View Templates to consider visibility settings for the linked files as well (e.g., hiding the architectural grid lines). When the actual architectural model is available, the placeholder link is swapped out using the* Manage Links *dialog and the* Reload From *tool therein.*

16. Create the remaining electrical views listed on page 13-2:

    a. Each should be **1/4″ = 1′-0″**.

    b. The *View Template* to be used is listed to the right, in parentheses, on page 13-2.

    c. Be sure to select *Reflected Ceiling Plan* when creating the ceiling plan views; compare step 11.

17. Adjust the reflected ceiling plans as follows:

    a. Set the *View Properties* so the *Underlay Orientation* is set to **Reflected Ceiling Plan**.

    b. Make sure the **Structural Faming** category is turned on.

The previous step is important in making the view look correct. The ceilings will only show up if the *Underlay Orientation* is set correctly in a ceiling plan view.

Loading Content:

Now that the electrical views are set up and ready to go, you will load some MEP electrical content (i.e., *Families*) into the project. The process is identical to how content is loaded using Revit *Architecture* and Revit *Structure*. This section will just show you how to load a few elements. As you work through the rest of this chapter, you will have to load additional content, referencing this information if needed.

18. Load the following content from the Revit *MEP* library:

    Annotation \ Electrical
    - Electrical Device Circuit.rfa
    - Electrical Equipment Tag.rfa

    Electrical Components \ Electrical Power \ Distribution
    - Lighting and Appliance Panelboard - 208V MCB - Surface.rfa
    - Combination Starter - Disconnect Switches.rfa

    Electrical Components \ Electric Power \ Terminals
    - Duplex Receptacle.rfa
    - Lighting Switches.rfa

You now have the content loaded that will be used to model the electrical system: power, systems and lighting. You should only load content that you need, when you need it. Again, each family takes up space in the project, making the file on your hard drive larger. Additionally, once you start using those components in the project, the file gets even larger.

At this point in the book, with all the mechanical modeled, your *BIM* file should be nearly 28-32MB.

19. **Save** your law office project.

Spaces versus Rooms:

Revit *MEP* is designed to use *Spaces* rather than *Rooms*. Both *Spaces* and *Rooms* work and behave exactly the same way in a project. The main reason to have two types of "room" elements has to do with the fact that most MEP models are in a separate file from the architectural model because of the size of the project and the engineers working in a different office and on a different server. Working over the internet is not an option with Revit.

In a Revit *MEP* model, the architectural model is linked in and the link's *Properties* are set to be "**room bounding**", which allows the *Spaces* to find the walls, floors and ceilings/roofs within the link. Then, when the *Space* has been placed in each room, the *Space* can automatically acquire several of the properties of the linked *Room*, such as room number, room name, area, and volume.

On the *Analyze* tab you will find the ***Space***, ***Space Separator*** and ***Space Tag*** tools. Revit *MEP* has a unique feature: once in the *Space* tool, the *Ribbon* has a **Place Spaces Automatically** option. This will add a *Space* to every enclosed area, even chases, which is required for doing heating and cooling load calculations. Any *Space* not touching another *Space* is assumed to be an exterior wall.

Once Spaces are placed, you can use the ***Zone*** tool, on the *Analyze* tab, to group *Spaces* together into MEP *Zones*. This is the same idea as a building being divided into heating and cooling zones, by thermostat or furnace. It is then possible to add color to a plan view, highlighting each zone for a presentation drawing.

If the architects rename or renumber a *Room*, the MEP model will automatically be updated when the file is reopened. However, if the architects change layout of an area, you may have to add new *Spaces* or move them around. When a room size changes, the center of the "X" for the *Space* is what determines which room the *Space* is in. So, if two *Rooms* are adjusted in size, it could be that both *Spaces* end up in the same *Room*.

One of the main reasons for using *Spaces* in an MEP project is to be able to add *Room Tags* (i.e., *Space Tags*) which can be moved around so they do not overlap lights and ductwork. *Spaces* also hold engineering data such as total heating and cooling loads and lighting levels.

> *TIP: Spaces/Space Tags can also be used by interior designers if they need to work in a separate model on an extremely large project, millions of square feet. This will give them a Room Tag they can move around and which is tied to the architect's names and numbers!*

See *Appendix D* for more information on *Rooms* and *Spaces* in Revit.

Exercise 13-3:
Panelboard, Power Devices and MEP Systems

In this exercise you will start laying out power devices (i.e., outlets) and panelboard (i.e., power panels with circuit breakers). The process is similar to the HVAC design; you place the components (e.g., outlets and light fixtures), create a system (i.e., a circuit), add components to the system, and select a panelboard for the circuit. Once finished, you can see the panel and its circuits nicely organized in the *System Browser*.

1.   **Open** your law office project using Revit *MEP*.

2.   Switch to the **Level 1 – Power Floor Plan**.

Placing the Panelboard:

First you will place the *panelboard*, or *power panel*, in the *Mechanical and Electrical Room*. This is a *face based* family that you will place on the wall.

3.   Select **Electrical Equipment** from the *Home* tab (no tag required).

Electrical Equipment

4.   Select the *Lighting and Appliance Panelboard - 208V MCB - Surface* - **400A** option from the *Type Selector*; make sure the placement option is **Place on Vertical Face**.

5.   Place the panel as shown in Figure 13-3.1.

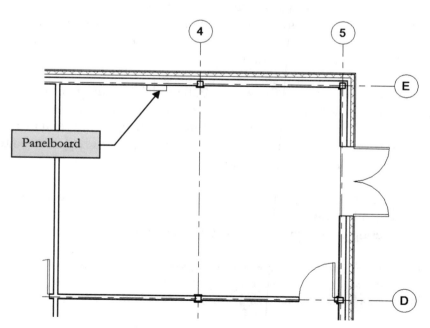

FIGURE 13-3.1 Panelboard placed in *Mechanical and Electrical Room*

Notice the *View Template* turned off all the ductwork and mechanical equipment to clean up the view so the electrical work is more easily read. However, this makes it hard to determine where the power panel should go. You cannot see the water heater, the AHU or the piping and ductwork. It might be better to leave that information on and make it all shaded gray like the architectural/structural. You can do this via the "VV" shortcut and check the halftone options to the right of any category. Do not do this now.

Distribution Systems:

The next thing you need to do is specify the power panel's *Distribution System*, which determines the types of things that can connect to this panel, such as outlets and lights versus high power industrial equipment.

In the *Electrical Settings* dialog you will see this is where the various *Distribution Systems* are defined (Figure 13-3.2). Notice the options: *Phase*, *Configuration*, number of *Wires* and *Voltage* information. The electrical settings also allow voltage definitions to be set up with max. and min. voltage. It is possible to *add* and *delete* systems as needed in this list, allowing a specialty firm to set things up correctly in their template for the kind of work they do.

The only thing you really need to know at this introductory level is that this feature does error checking by letting you know if you try to connect an electrical device to a circuit on a panel that is not compatible with it, meaning a sub-panel and transformer may be required which cost more time and money!

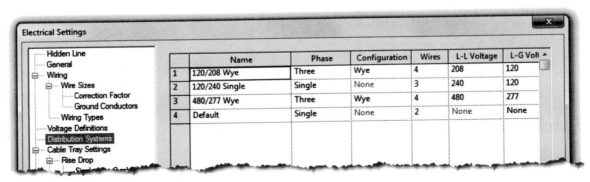

FIGURE 13-3.2 Electrical settings: Distribution Systems

6. **Select** the panelboard you just placed.

7. Note its *Instance Properties* via the *Properties Palette*.

In the next step you will give the panelboard a name, specify a *Distribution System* and specify the number of circuits in the panel.

8. Set the following parameters:

    a. *Panel Name:*   **Panel A**

    b. *Distribution System:*   **120/208 Wye** *(can also be set on the Options Bar)*

    c. *Max #1 Pole Breakers:*   **42**

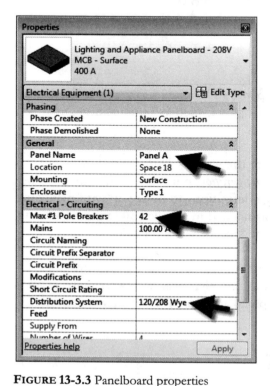

9. Click **Apply** to commit the changes to the panelboard.

Now that the panelboard is placed and set up properly, you can start placing outlets and light fixtures in the next *Exercise*. After the components are placed, you can then create the systems (i.e., circuits) and assign them to the panelboard.

It is generally possible to do the drafting part and not actually create the *MEP Systems* (i.e., circuits). However, this generates errors as the unassigned system has too many components on it. This warning is related to degraded model performance because Revit is constantly trying to cross-reference everything.

FIGURE 13-3.3 Panelboard properties

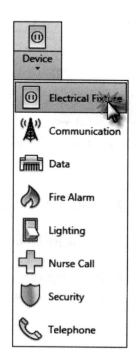

Placing Devices (i.e., Electrical Fixtures):

Now you will place several duplex outlets. The outlet families are *face based*, so they can go on any surface and then move with it. This will come in handy when you place the outlets on the *Reception Desk* for example, as it is a custom family.

10. From the *Home* tab, click the **Device** tool.

    a. Click the down arrow and select *Electrical Fixture*.

    b. Or, just click the upper part of the slip-button tool; notice the icon is the same.

    c. See image to the right.

    d. Uncheck **Tag on Placement** *(Ribbon)*.

11. Set the *Type Selector* to *Duplex Receptacle:* **Standard**.

12. On the *Ribbon,* the *Placement* options should be set to **Place on Vertical Face**.

Place on
Vertical Face

13. Click to place an outlet on the East wall, as shown in Figure 13-3.4.

14. Click **Modify** to end the current command.

Face based families have the ability to show both 2D and 3D geometry; which one you see depends on which view you are in. The plan views show the 2D geometry that is the industry standard symbol for an electrical receptacle (i.e., outlet) in plan. This symbol is shown on the face of the wall, rather than in the wall where it would become obscured by the lines and hatching of the wall. Elevations and 3D views show the actual face plate, which helps to coordinate with other things like windows and cabinets.

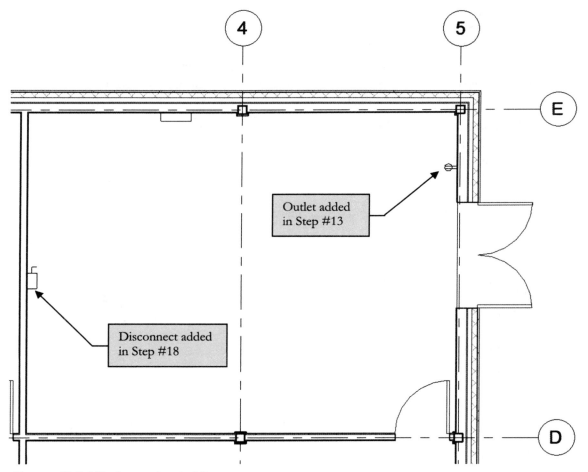

FIGURE 13-3.4 Placing an electrical fixture

Outlets are placed at a default height above the floor. The Revit-provided family has been set up to place the outlet at the standard 18″ above the floor (to the center of the face plate); this can be changed to comply with other codes and standards. In this case, we want 18″ and will manually change the few outlets that need to be at a different elevation.

The outlet you just placed needs to be 48″ *Above Finished Floor* (AFF) to comply with codes for outlets in mechanical and electrical rooms.

15. Select the outlet and **change** the *Elevation* to **48″** in the *Properties Palette*. Be sure to add the inch symbol so it does not get moved to forty-eight feet above the floor!

Next you will place the remaining outlets for Level 1, except at the *Reception Desk*.

16. Place the outlets approximately as shown in Figure 13-3.5.

    a. All outlets are *Type* **Standard** except in the *Toilet Rooms* and above the counter in the *Break Room*, which are to be *Type* **GFCI**.

    b. All outlets are to be the standard 18″ AFF unless noted otherwise.

    c. If another face is getting in the way when placing an outlet (e.g., *Mirror, Admin Reception Desk*), place the outlet farther down the wall and then use the arrow keys to nudge it into place.

    d. The outlet in the center of the *Conference Room* is in the floor.
       i. Placement needs to be set to **Place on Face**.
       ii. Place the outlet away from the table and then move it to the center of the table; this will ensure you do not place the outlet on the face of the table rather than the floor.
       iii. In this case, both the face plate and 2D symbol appear.

Looking at the architect's interior elevation at the *Break Room*, image to the right, you can see the power receptacle is now showing. You may have to move a note out of the way first. The outlet behind the refrigerator is not showing because the view *Discipline* is set to **Architectural** so the architectural elements are *not* transparent. This is design integration in action!

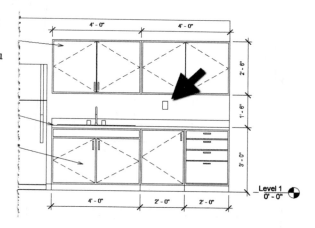

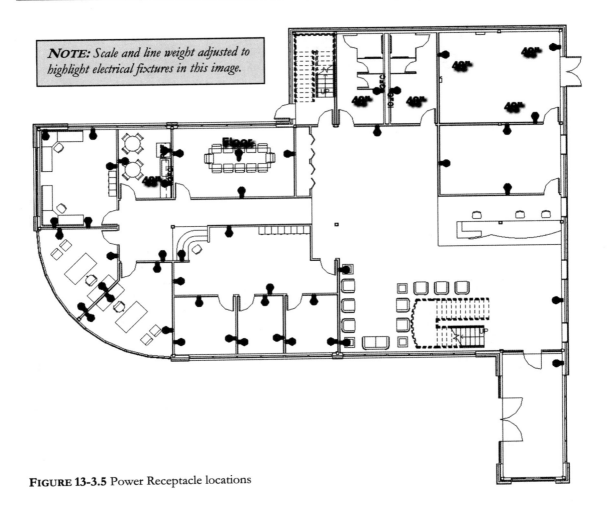

FIGURE 13-3.5 Power Receptacle locations

Placing the outlets at the *Reception Desk* is a little tricky because you cannot see the vertical surfaces that you will be placing them on; they are below the countertop. Therefore, you will create a temporary, or permanent if you wish, interior elevation looking at the back side of the *Reception Desk*. From here you can place the *face based* outlets easily, and then adjust the elevation via *Properties*.

17. Place the outlets at the *Reception Desk*. (See Figures 13-3.6 to 13-3.8).

    a. Create an interior elevation. *TIP: Point at column.*

    b. Place outlets in new elevation view.

    c. Adjust outlet elevation via *Properties Palette*.

    d. Delete the interior elevation tag, which will also delete the interior elevation view from the project. You can skip this step and leave the elevation tag in place if you wish.

    e. Make sure *Schedule Level* is set to **Level 1**.

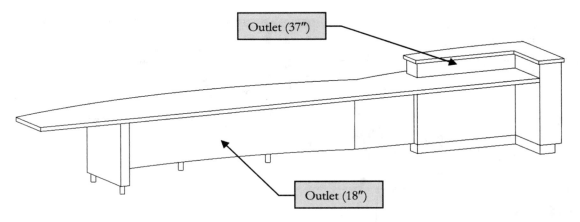

FIGURE 13-3.6 Outlets to be placed at reception desk

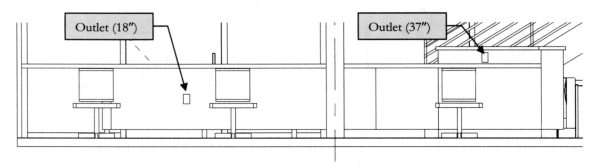

FIGURE 13-3.7 Outlets placed at *Reception Desk* (temporary interior elevation view created)

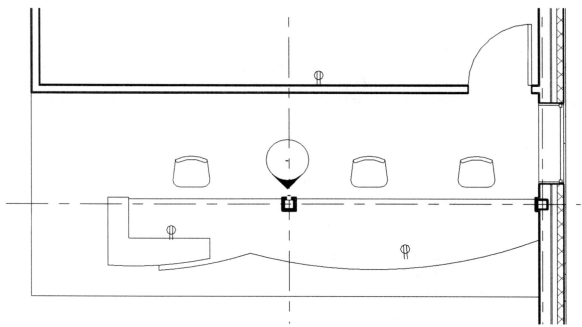

FIGURE 13-3.8 Level 1 Power Floor Plan view; outlets placed at *Reception Desk*

Notice how the outlets show up even though they are below the countertops (Figure 13-3.8). In the electrical and mechanical "disciplines," the architectural and structural elements are transparent.

Next, you will add a disconnect switch for the AHU. This allows the power to be shut off at the unit without the need to go to the panelboard.

18. Using the *Electrical Equipment* tool, place *Combination Starter - Disconnect Switches:* **208V – Size 1** family on the West wall of the Mechanical/Electrical Room (Figure 13-3.4).

   a. No tag is required.

You are now ready to place the Level 2 power devices.

19. Following the same instructions as Step 16, place the Level 2 outlets as shown in Figure 13-3.9.

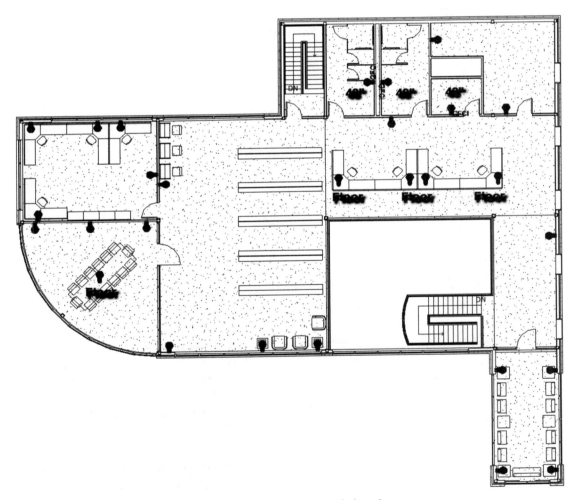

FIGURE 13-3.9 Level 2 power floor plan view; power receptacle locations

Next, you need to adjust the Level 1 Power Plan's *View Range* so the outlets in the floor above do not show up.

20. Switch to the **Level 1 Power Floor Plan** view.

21. With nothing selected and no commands active, Note the ***View Properties*** via the *Properties Palette*.

22. **Edit** the *View Range*.

23. Change the *Top Offset* to **-1'-0"**; do not miss the minus symbol.

The floor outlets on Level 2 are now out of the Level 1 *View Range* and are therefore no longer visible.

Creating MEP Systems (i.e., Power Circuit):

In the section you will create an MEP *System* which is very similar to the process used with the HVAC design in the previous chapter.

24. **Zoom** in to the *Mechanical/Electrical Room* on Level 1.

25. Select one of the outlets (i.e., electrical fixture) in the *Mechanical/ Electrical Room*.

26. With the outlet selected, click the ***Power*** tool, within the *Create System* panel, on the *Ribbon*.

Power

27. Click **Edit Circuit** on the *Ribbon*.

Edit
Circuit

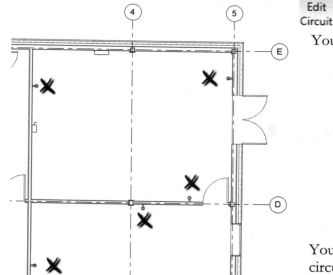

You are now in *Add to Circuit* mode.

28. Select the remaining four outlets shown in Figure 13-3.10.

29. Set the *Panel* drop-down, on the *Options Bar*, to **Panel A** (Figure 13-3.11).

30. Click **Finish Editing Circuit** on the *Ribbon* (i.e., green check mark).

You have just placed 5 outlets on the #1 circuit breaker in the power panel (Panel A).

FIGURE 13-3.10 Outlets for circuit #1

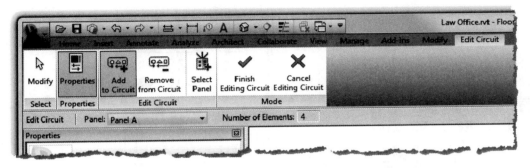

FIGURE 13-3.11 Power circuit; *Ribbon* and *Options Bar* settings

31. Select one of the outlets again and view its *Instance Properties (via the Properties Palette)*.

    a. Notice the *Panel* and *Circuit* are now listed.

You will now add the remaining outlets to circuits. In the next exercise, you will also add the light fixtures to *power circuits* (i.e., MEP *Systems*) as well.

32. Following the previous step, create circuits in the order of the numbers shown; see Figures 13-3.12 and 13-3.13.

    a. See Step #34 after creating the second *Power System*.

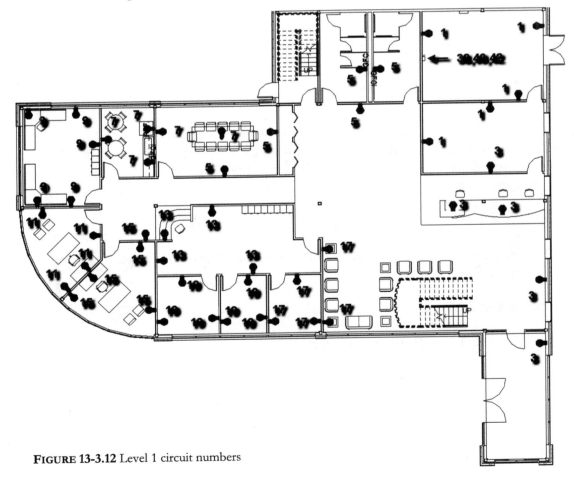

FIGURE 13-3.12 Level 1 circuit numbers

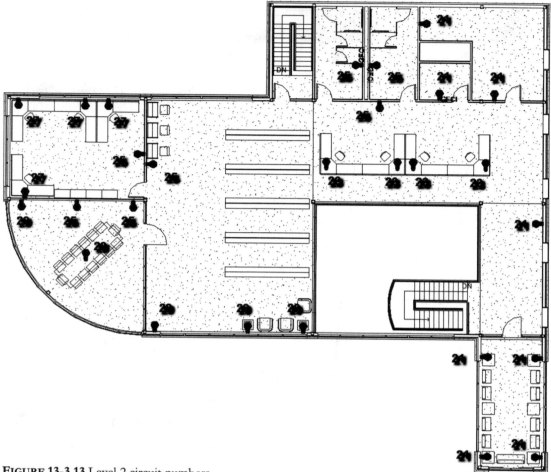

FIGURE 13-3.13 Level 2 circuit numbers

By default, Revit will select the next circuit available for you when creating a *Power System*. In our case we want to reserve all the even numbered circuits for the lighting system. So when you create the second *Power System* and Revit places it on *Circuit number 2* in *Panel A*, you will need to manually move it to *Circuit 3*. The following steps show how to do this.

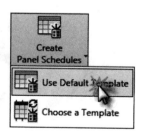

33. After creating the second *Power System*, select **Panel A**.

34. Click **Create Panel Schedules →Use Default Template** on the *Ribbon*.

35. Click in one of the "cells" for *Circuit 2*.

36. Click the ***Move Down*** button from the *Ribbon*.

37. Click the ***Move Across*** button.

38. Close the ***Panel Schedule*** view.

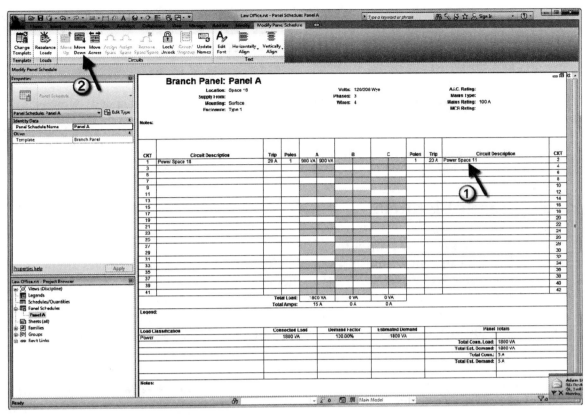

FIGURE 13-3.14 Editing circuits dialog for Panel A

The circuit is now moved from *2* to *3* (Figure 13-3.15). Notice the panel has 42 circuits, which you specified in the *Panel A Properties*.

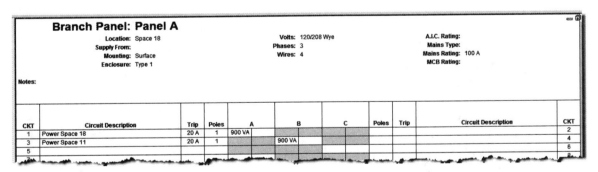

FIGURE 13-3.15 Circuit moved from 2 over to 3

The panel schedule can be accessed again via the *Project Browser*, under the *Panel Schedules* header, or by selecting the panel in the model and clicking the **Edit Panel Schedule** tool on the *Ribbon*.

Edit
Panel Schedule

This concludes the basic introduction to placing outlets, power panels and then creating circuits on the power panel for the outlets.

39. **Save** your project.

Exercise 13-4:
Light Fixture and Light Switch Layout

In this exercise you will place the light fixtures and create MEP *Systems* to specify which circuit specific lights are on.

1. Open your law office project using Revit *MEP*.

Placing Light Fixtures:

If you recall, you started your project from a Revit *Architecture* template. This template has 2x4 and a recessed can light fixtures preloaded in it. Unfortunately, these families are not the same as the ones that come with Revit *MEP*; the parameters are slightly different. Also, the Revit *Architecture* families are *ceiling hosted*, whereas the Revit *MEP* light fixtures are *face based* families; Revit *MEP* content is standardized on *face based* content because it is the only type of "hosted" family that works when the architect's model is linked in, not in the same model as in our case.

First, you will delete *families* not needed from the project and then load the correct ones from the Revit *MEP* content library.

2. Expand the **Families** section in the *Project Browser*.

3. Expand the **Lighting Fixtures** section (Figure 13-4.1).

4. Right-click on the *Downlight* and *Troffer* families (separately) and select **Delete** to remove them from the law office project.

The two families and their *Types* are now removed from the project. You may do this with any family that is not required in your project. This can reduce the project file size and reduce errors. Do not delete any other families at this time.

5. Load the following families from the Revit *MEP* content library:

    a. Electrical Components\Lighting\Internal:
        i. *Downlight – Recessed Can*
        ii. *Troffer Light – 2x4 Parabolic*

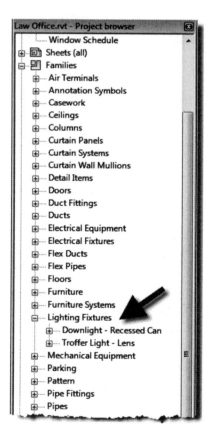

FIGURE 13-4.1
Project Browser;
Families\Lighting Fixture section

You are now ready to begin placing light fixtures. This will be done in the **Level 1 – Lighting Plans**. The 2x4 light fixture will actually snap to the ceiling grid, making it easier to place. The architectural light fixture does not snap to the ceiling grid.

6. **Open** the **Level 1 – Lighting Plan** view (which is a reflected ceiling plan view).

7. **Zoom** in to the *Associates Office* in the Northwestern corner.

8. In the view's *Properties*, double-check the following:

a. *Visual Graphics Style:*   Hidden Line (via *Graphic Display Options*)

b. *Underlay Orientation:*   Reflected Ceiling Plan

c. *View Range:*   Cut Plane = 7'-6"

Lighting
Fixture

9. Select the ***Lighting Fixture*** tool from the *Home* tab on the *Ribbon*.

10. Select *Troffer Light – 2x4 Parabolic:* **2'x4' (2 Lamp) – 120V** from the *Type Selector*.

11. Click **Place on Face** from the *Placement* panel on the *Ribbon* (no tag required).

12. Move your cursor within the office, and then press the **spacebar** (on the keyboard) to rotate the fixture 90 degrees.

13. Place the fixture as shown in Figure 13-4.2.

a. Make sure the fixture "snaps" to the grid before placing it; you may need to zoom in more.

14. Place the other three fixtures shown in Figure 13-4.2.

Next you will place the rest of the 2x4 fixtures on Level 1.

A nice thing about ***face based*** light fixtures, compared to *ceiling-hosted*, is that they can be placed on any face, not just a ceiling. In your back stair, you will be placing the fixture on the "face" of the underside of the floor above. Also, ceiling-hosted content does not work when the architectural model is linked in.

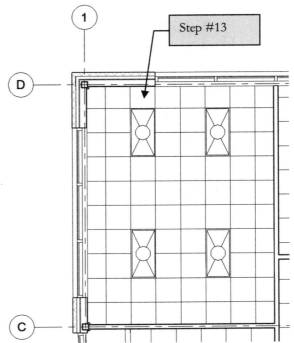

FIGURE 13-4.2 Light fixtures placed on Level 1

An important thing to know about *faced based* families is that you can **Copy** them from one room to another. If you do, the copied light fixture will become associated to the new ceiling if it is at the same height. If the light is copied to a location without a ceiling, or the ceiling is at a different height, it will become "not associated" meaning it has no Host. It is possible to select the light and use the *Pick New* tool and select a new host.

15. Place the remaining 2x4 light fixtures on Level 1 as shown in Figure 13-4.3.

   a. Load and use *Ceiling Light – Linear Box:* **1'x4'(1 Lamp) – 120V** in the North stairwell.

   b. Select each of the floor mounted outlets visible from Level 2 and then right-click and pick *Hide in View* → *Elements*.

   c. In the *Mechanical/Electrical Room*:
      i. Load and use the following family:
         Strip Lighting Fixtures: **4' 1 Lamp – 120**
      ii. Be sure to place the fixtures between the bar joists.

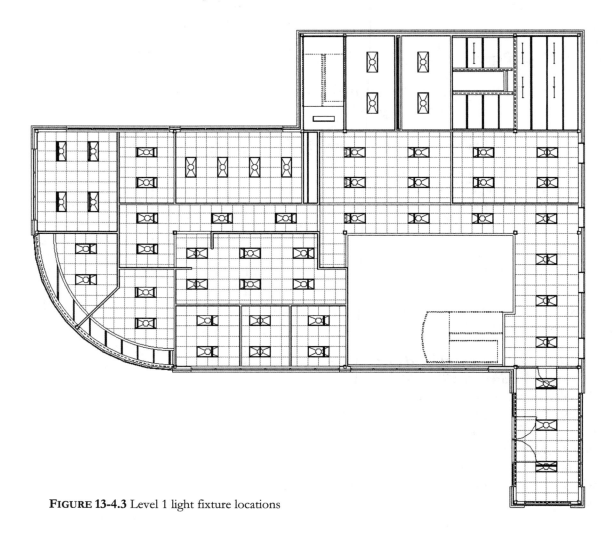

FIGURE 13-4.3 Level 1 light fixture locations

As you can see in the previous image, it is nice to have the bar joists visible when you can place the light fixtures so they will not conflict in rooms with no ceilings. It is rather odd that the bar joists are visible within the 2x4 light fixtures that are placed in ceilings (when a joist is directly above the fixture). This would be helpful if there was not enough space between the ceiling and the bar joist, but not in our case as we have plenty of room.

16. Place the Level 2 light fixtures as shown in Figure 13-4.4.

   a. Use *Ceiling Light – Linear Box:* **1′x4′ (1 Lamp) – 120V** in the North stairwell and the *Custodian's Room*.

   b. Turn off the *Visibility* for the *Furniture Systems* and *Specialty_Equipment* categories. ***REMINDER:*** *Check "show categories from all disciplines."*

   c. Adjust the *Top Offset* and *View Depth* to **1′-0″** in the *View Rage* to place the stairwell lights.

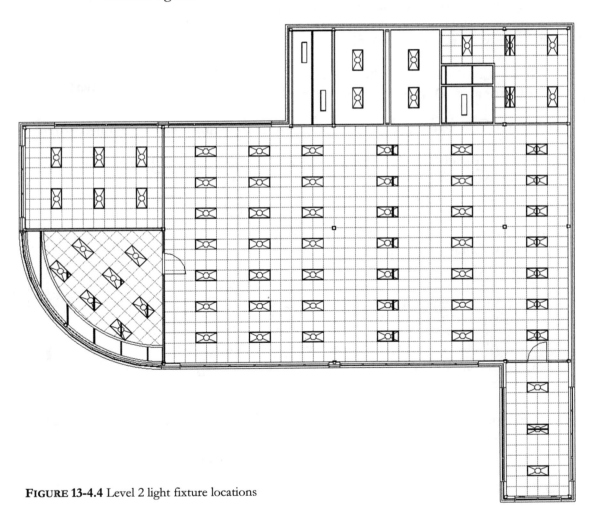

FIGURE 13-4.4 Level 2 light fixture locations

Now that you have all the light fixtures placed, you can connect them to circuits and light switches. First, you will place the light switches and then create the MEP *Systems*.

Placing Light Switches:

Now you will place the light switches. This is similar to placing the outlets. A rectangle will show up in the correct location in an elevation, but a symbol will show up in the plan view. If you recall, the *Cut Plane* for the ceiling plans is 7'-6", which is above the 7'-0" tall doors. Therefore, the doors do not appear in the Lighting Plan view. You will change this so the doors do show up as they are needed when placing light switches; they are typically on the latch side of the door. Additionally, if you want the light switches to show up in the Ceiling Plan view, the *Cut Plane* needs to be below the lowest light switch. The default light switch elevation is 4'-0". Therefore, you will change the *Cut Plane* to 3'-6".

17. Change the *Cut Plane* to **3'-6"** for both **Ceiling Lighting Plans**.

18. Turn off the *Casework, Furniture, Furniture Systems, Specialty Equipment* and *Structural Framing* categories to hide unnecessary information.

You should now be able to see the doors.

19. In the **Level 1 Lighting Plan** view, select **Home →
Electrical → Device (drop-down) → Lighting**

20. Set the *Type Selector* to *Lighting Switches:* **Single Pole** (load the family if needed).

21. Click on the wall (in the *Associate's Office*), near the door to place the light switch as shown in Figure 13-4.5.

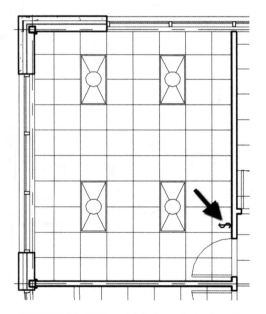

You now have a light switch at 4'-0" above the floor. Now you will place the remaining light switches on Level 1.

22. Place the remaining light switches on Level 1 per Figure 13-4.6.

    a. All are to be **Single Pole** at the default **4'-0"** AFF. *Exception:* The switch near the main entry and the two near the North stair (the back door) are to be **Three Way** type switches.

FIGURE 13-4.5 Level 1 light switch placed

23. Place the light switches on Level 2 per Figure 13-4.7.

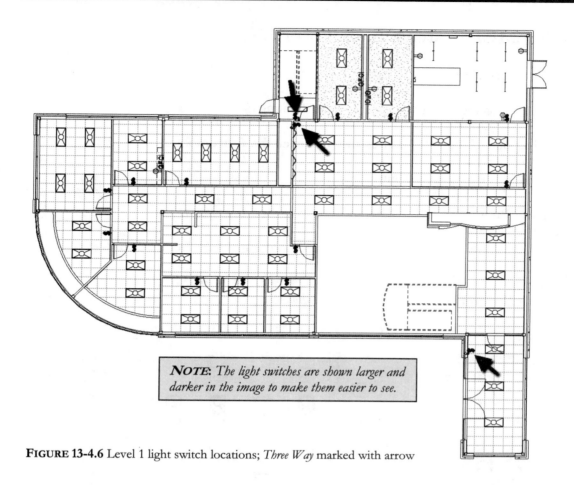

> **NOTE:** *The light switches are shown larger and darker in the image to make them easier to see.*

FIGURE 13-4.6 Level 1 light switch locations; *Three Way* marked with arrow

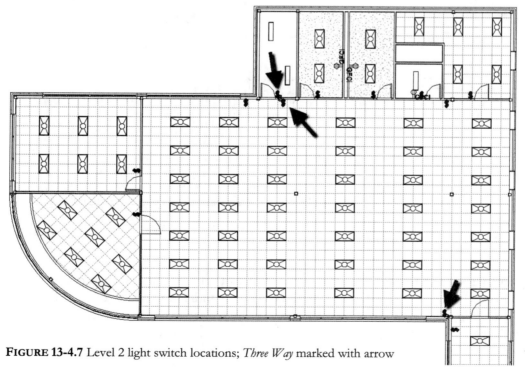

FIGURE 13-4.7 Level 2 light switch locations; *Three Way* marked with arrow

Creating MEP Systems (i.e., Power Circuit):

Now you will create the *power circuits* for the light fixtures.

24. Zoom into the Level 1 *Associate's Office* (lighting plan).

25. Select one of the light fixtures and then click the **Power** tool on the *Ribbon*.

26. Select the ***Edit Circuit*** button.

27. Select **Panel A** from the *Panel* drop-down list on the *Options Bar*.

28. With the **Add to Circuit** option selected on the *Ribbon*, select the light fixtures shown in Figure 13-4.8.

29. Click **Finish Editing Circuit** on the *Ribbon*.

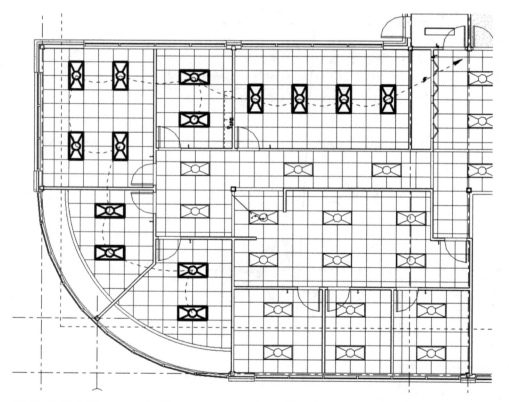

FIGURE 13-4.8 Level 1 light fixtures to go on circuit #6

If you hover over one of the light fixtures you just placed on a circuit and then press the **Tab** key on the keyboard, you will see several dashed arcs indicating which fixtures are on a circuit, as shown in Figure 13-4.8. If you then select the fixture, you can convert the temporary dashed arcs to *Wires*, which are lines that represent real wires the electrical contractor will install.

30. Per steps previous covered, move the new circuit to slot number *6* on *Panel A*.
   TIP: *Select the panel in plan and then click the* Edit Panel Schedule *tool on the* Ribbon.

31. Create the remaining circuits for Levels 1 and 2 based on the circuit numbers shown in Figures 13-4.9 and 13-4.10.

   a. **Circuiting fixtures on different levels:** The lights in the *Level 2* stair shaft are on the same circuit as a few fixtures on *Level 1*. While in *Edit Circuit* mode on *Level 1*, simply switch to *Level 2*, click the **Add to Circuit** button on the *Ribbon* and select the desired lights on *Level 2*.

   TIP: *If you need to edit a circuit again after it has been created: Select a light fixture already on the circuit and then, on the Electrical Circuits contextual tab on the Ribbon, select Edit Circuit.*

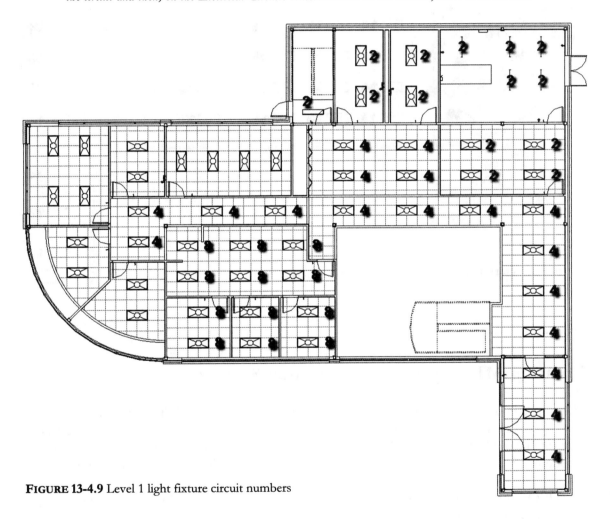

FIGURE 13-4.9 Level 1 light fixture circuit numbers

As you can see, many more light fixtures can go on a circuit than can outlets. This is, of course, due to the electrical load placed on each, plus the fact that lights are a *fixed load* that can be accurately anticipated, whereas outlets can have many variations in load, like an electrical pencil sharpener versus an air conditioner. Revit will give a warning when the load on a circuit reaches capacity; try adding all the lights on Level 2 until you get the warning, and then *Undo*.

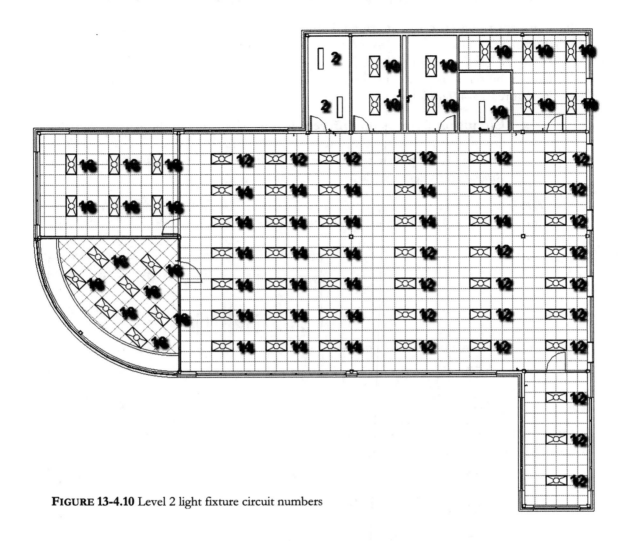

FIGURE 13-4.10 Level 2 light fixture circuit numbers

Creating MEP Systems (i.e., Switch System):

The final step in setting up the lighting system is to tell Revit which light fixtures are controlled by which light switches, or lighting device. The light fixtures on a circuit do not correlate to the lights controlled by a light switch. A circuit can support the operation of several rooms' worth of light fixtures, but each room typically has its own light switch.

32. On the **Level 1 Lighting Plan**, in the *Associate's Office* Northwestern corner), select one of the light fixtures.

33. Select the **Switch** button on the *Ribbon*.

Switch

34. Select **Edit Switch System** from the *Ribbon*.

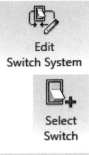

35. With **Add to System** highlighted on the *Ribbon*, pick the other three light fixtures in the room.

36. Click on the **Select Switch** button.

37. Select the light switch in the same room as the light fixtures.

38. Click **Finish Editing System**.

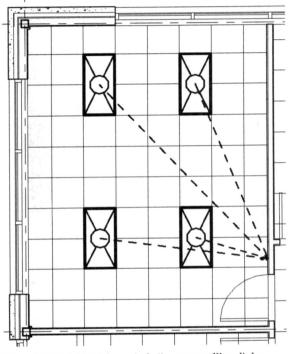

You have now told Revit which light switch controls the lights in the *Associate's Office*. If you hover over the light switch and then press the **Tab** key, you can see which lights are controlled by that switch (Figure 13-4.11).

Next, you will assign light switches to the remaining fixtures in the building.

FYI: Revit does not yet have the ability to manage multi switch systems such as three way or different bulbs within the same fixture. This must be managed manually with Shared Parameters (not covered in this text).

FIGURE 13-4.11 Light switch "connected" to lights

39. Create a *Switch System* for the remaining light fixtures in the building. Use your own judgment to decide which switches control which light fixtures.

Interference Check:

If you laid things out exactly as prescribed in the text, you will soon find there is a big problem. All the light fixtures were placed without coordinating the location of the HVAC diffusers. Many of the lights and diffusers overlap. It would have been best to have the diffuser *Visibility* turned on, but the *View Template* you used turns them off. You will use a Revit feature called *Interference Check* to reveal this hidden problem. This feature can be used to compare other categories as well, such as ducts and beams.

40. Select **Collaborate → Coordinate → Interference Check → Run Interference Check**.

Run Interference Check

41. Select **Lighting Fixtures** on the left and **Air Terminals** on the right (Figure 13-4.12).

42. Click **OK** to start the collision detection process.

Revit will show the results of the *Interference Check* (Figure 13-4.13). Each *air terminal* that conflicts with a *light fixture* is listed here. Expanding each will reveal the light fixture that is in conflict with it. With a listed light fixture or air terminal selected, you may click the **Show** button and Revit will switch to an appropriate view and zoom in on the element in question! Try it.

FIGURE 13-4.12 Interference Check dialog

43. Click the **Close** button.

Next, you will turn on the *Air Terminal* category and set it to be a halftone so the *light fixtures* remain prominent in the **Lighting Plan** view.

44. Type **VV** in the **Level 1 Lighting Plan** view.

45. Check the **Air Terminal** *Category*.

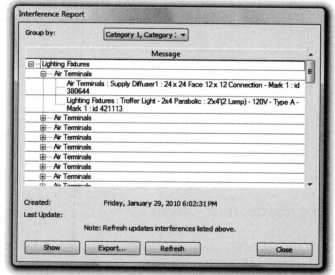

FIGURE 13-4.13 Interference Check results

46. Check the **Halftone** option to the right of the *Air Terminal* category.

47. Repeat these steps for the **Level 2 Lighting Plan** view.

48. Reposition any air terminals that are in conflict with the light fixtures.

The flex duct is forgiving when air terminals are repositioned. Setting the air terminals to be halftone allows the light fixtures to stand out in the lighting floor plan, but maintain coordination. The image below shows the corrected lighting plan. The light fixtures have a custom tag which lists the fixture's circuit number and type.

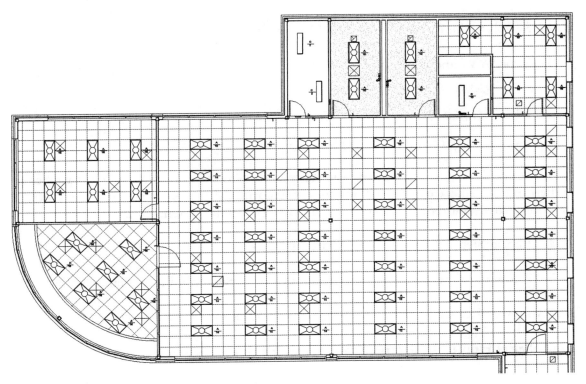

FIGURE 13-4.14 Corrected Level 2 lighting plan

That concludes the exercise on placing light fixtures, light switches and creating systems for them. The starter file for the next chapter will have tags added to each light fixture; it is a custom tag that lists the fixture *Type* and *Circuit* number.

49. **Save** your project!

Exercise 13-5:
Systems Layout

This short exercise will review the placement of system devices: data and phone in this case. Many phone systems are now VoIP (Voice over IP), which means they use the same connection as the computer network system. Therefore, in this case you will only place data devices. If you wanted to schedule the telephone system separately, you could load the telephone device families and place them and just consider the data type connections.

1. Open your law office project.

2. Switch to the **Level 1 – Systems Floor Plan** view.

3. Type "**VV**" and make the following changes:

    a. *Lighting Fixtures* category *Invisible*

    b. *Electrical Fixtures* set to *Halftone*

    c. *Lighting Devices* set to *Halftone*

The power devices, or outlets, are on the *Electrical Fixtures* category and the light switches are on the *Lighting Devices* category. Making these categories halftone allows them to be visible, and coordinated, but remain background information on the systems plans.

4. Repeat Step 3 for the **Level 2 Systems Floor Plan** view.

5. Zoom in to the *Associate's Office* in the **Level 1 – Systems Floor Plan** view.

Next, you will place a data device near each of the desks and on the East wall.

6. Select **Home → Electrical → Device → Data**. Data

7. Click **Yes** to load a *Data Device* family (Figure 13-5.1).

8. Load **Electrical Components\ Information and Communication\ Communication\Data Outlet.rfa**.

    a. Click **No** to load a tag

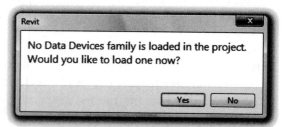

FIGURE 13-5.1 Prompt to load content

9. With **Place on Vertical Face** selected on the *Placement* panel, add the three *data outlets* as shown in Figure 13-5.2.

    TIP: *Be sure to zoom in and place the device on the wall and not on the face of the furniture.*

    a. Data devices are placed at a default 18″ above the floor like the power devices are; this can be changed via *Instance Properties*.

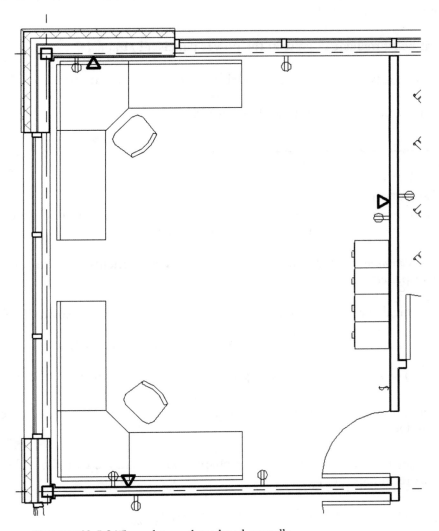

FIGURE 13-5.2 Three data outlets placed on walls

10. Using the process just covered, place outlets throughout the building in the **Systems Floor Plan** views.

11. You should open the **Power Floor Plan** views, make the *Data Devices* halftone and hide the light fixtures.

12. **Save** and **backup** your work.

Self-Exam:

The following questions can be used as a way to check your knowledge of this lesson. The answers can be found at the bottom of this page.

1. The electrical devices are *face based* in Revit *MEP*. (T/F)

2. Electrical devices placed in the electrical views will not automatically show up in the architect's views. (T/F)

3. Revit helps manage circuits in the power panels. (T/F)

4. The mechanical and electrical models have to be in separate files.

5. What feature allows you to look for conflicts in your model:

   _____ _____ .

Review Questions:

The following questions may be assigned by your instructor as a way to assess your knowledge of this section. Your instructor has the answers to the review questions.

1. The *Distribution System* is used to determine which elements can connect to which power panels. (T/F)

2. Mechanical and electrical engineers use the *MEP* "flavor" of Revit. (T/F)

3. *Face based* devices can only be placed on walls, not floors. (T/F)

4. Revit *Architecture* uses *Rooms* and Revit *MEP* uses *Spaces*. (T/F)

5. Deleting unneeded content from the project is recommended to keep file size down and reduce errors.

6. The light fixtures you placed in this chapter will not move with the ceiling, similar to the air terminals. (T/F)

7. The electrical *View Templates* are perfect as is. (T/F)

8. A Panelboard has several limitations related to code compliance. (T/F)

9. Revit *MEP* automatically places an outlet on a circuit when it is placed. (T/F)

10. The various MEP devices have a default elevation they are placed at when in a plan view. (T/F)

Lesson 14
Office Building: SITE AND RENDERING

In this chapter you will take a look at Revit's photorealistic rendering abilities as well as the basic site development tools. Rather than reinventing the wheel, Revit chose to use an established architectural rendering technology called Mental Ray. Autodesk offers several high-end rendering programs like *Autodesk 3DS Max, Autodesk Maya* and *Mental Ray,* which work with Revit models in various ways, and the integration options improve with each new release. You will use Revit *Architecture* for the rendering exercises, but the other two also support the rendering feature set.

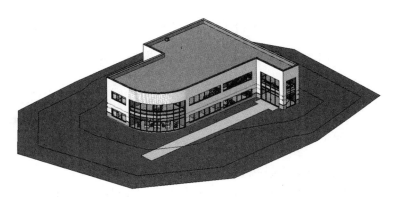

Exercise 14-1:
Site Tools

This lesson will give the reader a quick overview of the site tools available in Revit. The site tools are not intended to be an advanced site development package. Autodesk has other programs much more capable at developing complex sites, such as AutoCAD Civil 3D 2012. This program is used by professional Civil Engineers and Surveyors. The contours generated from these advanced civil CAD programs can be used to generate a topography object in Revit.

In this lesson, you will create a topography object from scratch; you will also add a sidewalk.

Once the topography object (the topography object, or element, is a 3D mass that represents part *or* all of the site) is created, the grade line will automatically show up in building and wall sections, exterior elevations and site plans. The sections even have the earth pattern filled in below the grade line.

As with other Revit elements, you can select the object after it is created and set various properties for it, such as *Surface Material, Phase,* etc. One can also return to *Sketch* mode to refine or correct the surface. This is done in the same way most other sketched objects are edited: by selecting the item and clicking *Edit* on the *Options Bar.*

Overview of Site Tools Located on the Ribbon:

Below is a brief description of what the site tools are used for. After this short review you will try a few of these tools on your law office project.

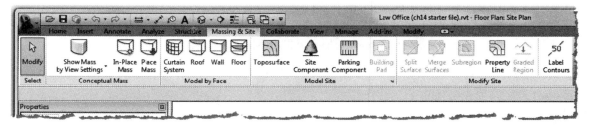

<u>Toposurface</u>: Creates a 3D surface by picking points (specifying the elevation of each point picked) or by using linework, within a linked AutoCAD drawing, that were created at the proper levels.

<u>Subregion</u>: Allows an area to be defined within a previously drawn *toposurface*. The result is an area within the *toposurface* that can have a different material than the *toposurface* itself. The *subregion* is still part of the *toposurface* and will move with it when relocated. If a *subregion* is selected and deleted, the original surface/properties for that area are revealed.

<u>Split Surface</u>: This tool is similar to the *Subregion* tool in every way except that the result is separate surfaces that can intentionally, or accidentally, be moved apart from each other. If a split surface is selected and deleted, it results in a subtraction or a void relative to the original *toposurface*.

<u>Merge Surfaces</u>: After a surface has been split into one or more separate surfaces, you can merge them back together. Only two surfaces can be merged together at a time. The two surfaces to be merged must share a common edge or overlap.

<u>Graded Region</u>: This tool is used to edit the grade of a *toposurface* that represents the existing site conditions and the designer wants to use Revit to design the new site conditions. This tool is generally only meant to be used once; when used it will copy the existing site conditions to a new *Phase* and set the existing site to be demolished in the *New Construction Phase*. The newly copied site object can then be modified for the new site conditions.

<u>Property Line</u>: Creates property lines (in plan views only).

<u>Building Pad</u>: Used to define a portion of site to be subtracted when created below grade (and added when created above grade). An example of how this might be used is to create a pad that coincides with a basement floor slab which would remove the ground in section above the basement floor slab (otherwise the basement would be filled with the earth fill pattern). Several pads can be imposed on the same *toposurface* element.

<u>Parking Component</u>: These are parking stall layouts that can be copied around to quickly lay out parking lots. Several types can be loaded which specify both size and angle.

<u>Site Component</u>: Items like benches, dumpsters, etc., that are placed directly on the *toposurface*, at the correct elevation at the point picked.

<u>Label Contours</u>: Adds an elevation label to the selected contours.

FYI: *Contours are automatically created based on the toposurface.*

Site Settings:

The *Site Settings* dialog controls a few key project-wide settings related to the site; below is a brief description of these settings.

The ***Site Settings*** dialog is accessed from the *arrow* link in the lower-right corner of the *Model Site* panel. You should note that various tools under the *Settings* menu affect the entire project, not just the current view.

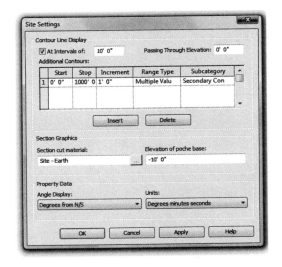

<u>Contour Line Display</u>: This controls if the contours are displayed when the *toposurface* is visible (via the check box) and at what interval. If the *Interval* is set to *1'-0"* you will see contour lines that follow the ground's surface and each line represents a vertical change of 1'-0" from the adjacent contour line (the contour lines alone do not tell you what direction the surface slopes in a plan view; this is where contour labels are important). The *Passing Through Elevation* setting allows control over where the contour intervals start from. This is useful because architects usually base the first floor of the building on elevation 0'-0" (or 100'-0") and the surveyors and civil engineers will use the distance above sea level (e.g., 1009.2'), so this feature allows the contours to be reconciled between the two systems. The *Additional Contours* section allows for more "contour" detail to be added within a particular area (vertically); on a very large site you might want 1'-0" contours only at the building and 10'-0" contours everywhere else. However, this only works if the building is in a distinctive set of vertical elevations. If the site is relatively level or an adjacent area shares the same set of contours, you will have undesirable results.

<u>Section Graphics</u>: This area controls how the earth appears when it is shown in section (e.g., exterior elevations, building sections, wall sections, etc.). Here is where the pattern is selected that appears in section; the pattern is selected from the project "materials" similar to the process for selecting the pattern to be displayed within a wall when viewed in section. The *Elevation of poche base* controls the depth of the pattern in section views relative to the grade line.

<u>Property Data</u>: This section controls how angles and lengths are displayed or information describing property lines.

Creating Topography in Revit

1. Open your law office project using Revit *Architecture*.

   a. Or use the Chapter 14 starter file on the DVD.

2. Switch to the **Site Plan** view.

   a. Adjust the category visibility so your view matches Figure 14-1.1. Also, set the *Detail Level* to *Fine*.

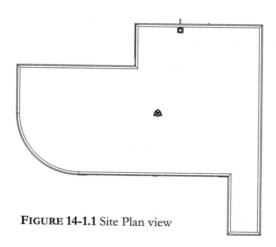

Here you will basically see what appears to be a roof plan view of your project (Figure 14-1.1). This view has the visibility set such that you see the project from above, and the various "site" categories are turned on so they are automatically visible once they are created. Next, you will take a quick look at the *View Range* for this view so you understand how things are set up.

FIGURE 14-1.1 Site Plan view

3. Click **Modify** to ensure nothing is selected in the model and no commands are active so the *View Properties* are showing in the *Properties Palette*.

4. In the *Properties Palette*, scroll down and select **Edit** next to *View Range*.

Here you can see the site is being viewed from 200' above the first floor level, so your building/roof would have to be taller than that before it would be "cut" like a floor plan. The *View Depth* could be a problem here: on a steep site, the entire site will be seen if part of it passes through the specified *View Range*. However, items completely below the *View Range* will not be visible.

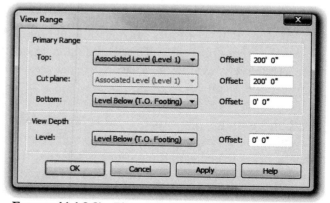

FIGURE 14-1.2 Site Plan view range settings

5. In the *View Depth* section, set the *Level* to **Unlimited**.

This change will ensure everything shows up on a steeper site.

6. Click **OK**.

You are now ready to create the site object. The element in Revit which represents the site is called *toposurface*.

> *TIP: Structural engineers can use the Toposurface tool to model ledge rock, which would aid in determining how deep foundations need to be.*

7. Select **Massing & Site** → **Model Site** → **Toposurface** from the *Ribbon*.

Toposurface

By default, the **Place Point** tool is selected on the *Ribbon*; you are now in *Sketch* mode. This tool allows you to specify points within the view at various elevations; Revit will generate a 3D surface based on those points, so the more points you provide, the more accurate the surface. Notice, on the *Options Bar* (Figure 14-1.3) that you can enter an *Elevation* for each point as you click to place them on the screen.

| Modify | Edit Surface | Elevation | 0' 0" | Absolute Elevation ▼ |

FIGURE 14-1.3 Options bar for Toposurface tool

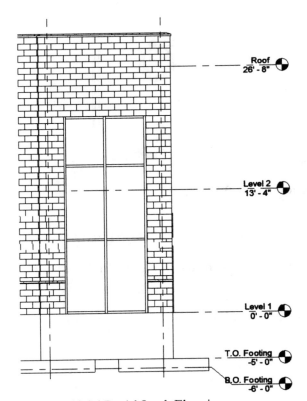

FIGURE 14-1.4 Partial South Elevation

What elevation should I enter on the Options Bar?

The elevation you enter for each point should relate to the *Level Datums* setup in your project; for example, look at your South exterior elevation (Figure 14-1.4). Recall that the *First Floor* is set to 0'-0" and the *Top of Footing* is set to -5'-0".

As you can see in the South elevation, the only place you would want to add points at an elevation of 0'-0" would be at the doors. Everywhere else should be at about -4" so the grade does not rise higher than the top of the foundation wall and come into contact with the brick, and possibly block the weeps and brick vents.

8. With the *Elevation* set to **0'-0"**, pick the six points shown in Figure 14-1.5; these points are at the exterior door locations.

   TIP: You can switch to the Level 1 Floor Plan view while in the Toposurface tool; just click the Place Point tool again on the Ribbon.

9. Change the **Elevation** to **-0'-4"** (don't forget the minus sign) on the *Options Bar* and then pick all the inside and outside corners along the perimeter of the building. Pick three points along the curved wall.

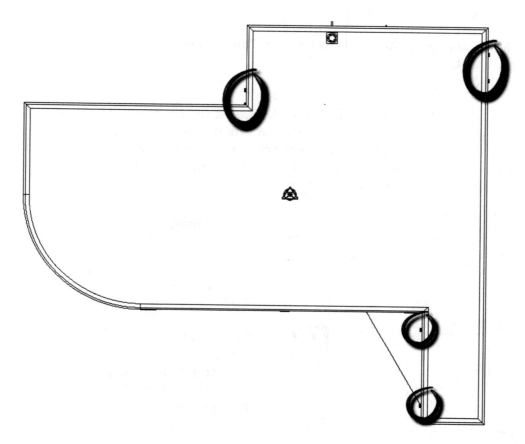

FIGURE 14-1.5 Site Plan view – 6 points to be selected (elev -0'-0")

10. Set the **Elevation** to **-2'-6"** and point to ten points shown in Figure 14-1.6 which define the extents of the toposurface.

    FYI: The elevations selected will generally provide a positive slope away from the building; this will be visible in elevations and sections.

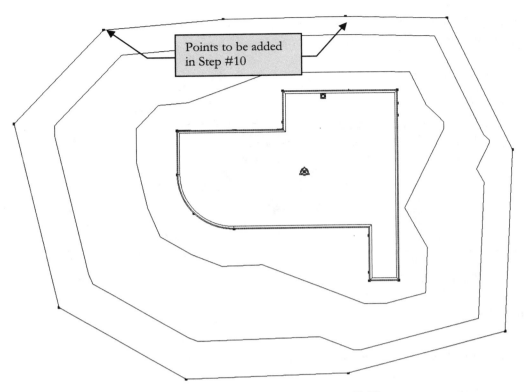

Points to be added
in Step #10

FIGURE 14-1.6 Site Plan view – 10 points to be selected (elev – 2'-6")

11. Select **Finish Surface** on the *Ribbon*.

Revit has now created the toposurface based on the points you specified. Again, the more points you add, the more refined and accurate the surface will be.

Ideally you would use the *Toposurface* tool to create a surface from a surveyors' points file or contour lines drawn in an AutoCAD file; Revit can automatically generate surfaces from these sources rather than you picking points. This process is beyond the scope of this tutorial.

12. Switch to the **3D** view to see your new ground surface (Figure 14-1.7).

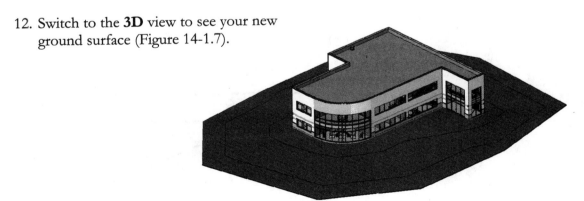

FIGURE 14-1.7 Toposurface seen in 3D view

The toposurface is automatically added in sections and elevations (Figure 14-1.8). It may need to be turned off in other views.

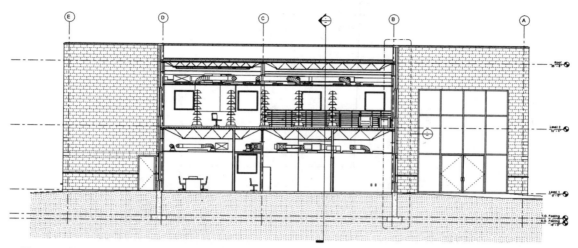

FIGURE 14-1.8 Section with ground pattern added

Next, you will quickly create a sidewalk to wrap up this Exercise.

You can use the *Subregion* tool or the *Split Surface* tool to create the driveway and sidewalks. The *Subregion* tool defines an area that is still part of the main site object; the *Split Surface* tool literally breaks the toposurface into separate elements. Splitting a surface can create problems when trying to move or edit the site, so you will use the *Subregion* tool.

13. Switch back to the **Site Plan** view.

14. Select the **Massing & Site → Modify Site → Subregion** tool and sketch the lines for the sidewalk (Figure 14-1.9).

15. Click **Finish Edit Mode** on the *Ribbon*.

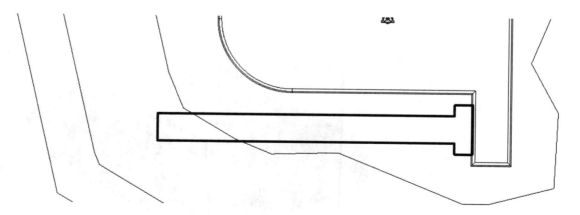

FIGURE 14-1.9 Partial site plan – closed sketch lines for subregion

16. Switch to **3D** view to see your sidewalk (Figure 14-1.10). Notice the 2D lines sketched in the **Site Plan** view have been projected down onto the surface of the 3D site object!

Notice also that the shade and render material is still the same as the main ground surface. You will learn how to change this in a moment.

When you select the toposurface and click **Edit Surface** on the *Ribbon*, you can select existing points and edit their elevation to refine the surface.

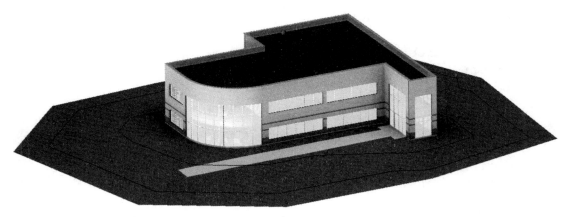

FIGURE 14-1.10 3D view with driveway and sidewalk added

17. In the **3D** view, select the sidewalk *subregion*.

18. Set the *Material* to **Concrete – Cast-in-place concrete** via the *Properties Palette*.

19. Set the main site element's *Material* to **Site – Grass**.

20. Make sure the *Visual Style* for your **3D** view is set to **Shaded** or **Consistent Colors** so you can see the "shaded" version of the materials. This can be set via the *View Control Bar*.

   TIP: *The image above has Visual Style set to Realistic and a feature called Ambient Shadows turned on.*

That concludes this overview of the site tools provided within Revit. You now have everything modeled in your project so you can start to develop rendered images of your project for presentations.

Exercise 14-2:
Creating an Exterior Rendering

The first thing you will do in terms of rendering is set up a view. You will use the *Camera* tool to do this. This becomes a saved view that can be opened at any time from the *Project Browser*.

Creating a Camera View:

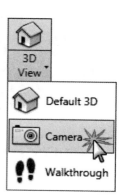

1. Open the **Level 1 Architectural** view using Revit *Architecture*, and **Zoom to Fit** so you can see the entire plan.

2. Select **View → Create → 3D Views → Camera**.

   a. This tool is also available on the *Quick Access Toolbar*.

3. Click the mouse in the lower left corner of the screen to indicate the camera eye location (Figure 14-2.1).

   NOTE: Before you click, Revit *tells you it wants the eye location first on the* Status Bar.

4. Next, click near the Northeastern corner; see Figure 14-2.1 to specify the direction you wish to look.

Revit will automatically open a view window for the new camera. Take a minute to look at the view and make a mental note of what you see and don't see in the view (Figure 14-2.2).

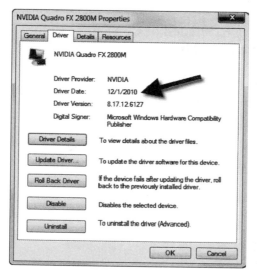

On large projects (100MB or more in size) it can take several minutes for the camera view to open. The speed of your computer can dramatically improve performance. The CPU speed, the amount of RAM and the quality of the graphics card is directly related to Revit's performance. Also, the graphics card's driver should be updated regularly to ensure optimal video performance. A new computer can come with a video driver that is one or two years old!

The image to the left shows the date of the video driver (i.e., Adapter) for a Windows 7 based computer. The driver is only a few months old, which is acceptable. The following should also be considered: **www.autodesk.com/ revitarchitecture-graphicscard**

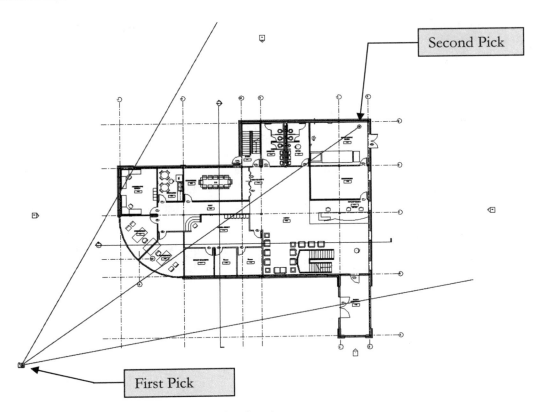

FIGURE 14-2.1 Placing a Camera in Level 1 plan view

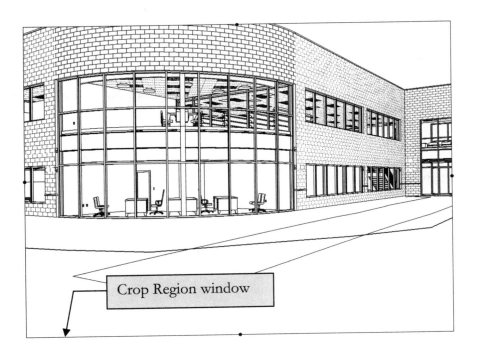

FIGURE 14-2.2 Initial Camera view

5. In **3D View 1** adjust the **Crop Region** to look similar to **Figure 14-2.3**.

This will be the view you render later in this exercise.

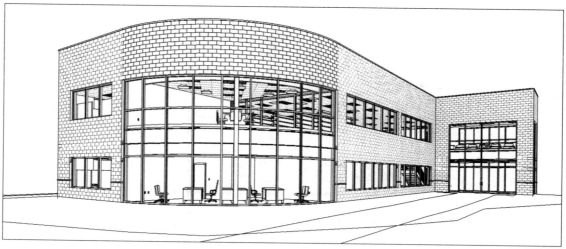

FIGURE 14-2.3 Revised camera – 3D View 1

Assigning Materials to Objects:

Materials are scanned images or computer generated representations of the materials from which your building will be constructed.

Typically, materials are added while the project is being modeled. For example, when you create a material (using the *Materials* tool on the *Manage* tab), you can assign the material at that time. Of course, you can go back and add or change it later. Next, you will see the material assigned for the exterior masonry wall.

6. Switch to **Level 1 Plan** view.

7. Select an exterior wall somewhere in plan view.

8. In the *Properties Palette*, click **Edit Type...** and then click **Edit** *structure*.

9. Notice the material selected for the exterior finish is **Masonry – Concrete Masonry Units**; click in that cell (Figure 14-2.4).

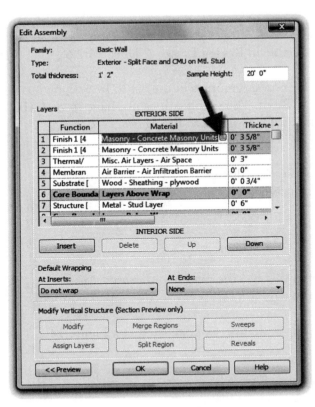

FIGURE 14-2.4 Exterior wall assembly

10. Click the "**...**" icon to the right of the label **Masonry – Concrete Masonry Units**.

Now you will take a look at the definition of the material

TIP: *You can also get here via:* Manage (tab) → Materials *once you know which material is being used.*

You are now in the *Materials* dialog (Figure 14-2.5). You should notice that a material is already selected on the *Appearance* tab (Figure 14-2.6).

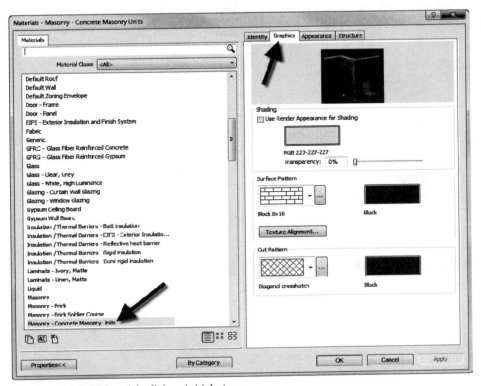

FIGURE 14-2.5 Materials dialog; initial view

11. Click the *Appearance* tab in the upper right.

You will now see all the masonry graphics available in Revit's *Library* (Figure 14-2.6).

You can browse through the list and select any render graphics in the list to be assigned to the *Masonry – Concrete Masonry Units* material in Revit. The graphic does not have to be CMU, but would be confusing if something like brick were assigned to the *Masonry – Concrete Masonry Units* material.

12. Click **Masonry** in the *Autodesk Library* section (lower left). Take a few minutes to look at the various render graphics available; click on a few of the categories to narrow the options.

13. **Cancel** all open dialog boxes.

When you render any object (wall, ceiling, etc.) that has the material *Masonry – Concrete Masonry Units* associated with it, it will have the light gray CMU imaged mapped on them.

If you need more than one CMU color, you duplicate the material listed in a Figure 14-2.5 and assign another render graphic.

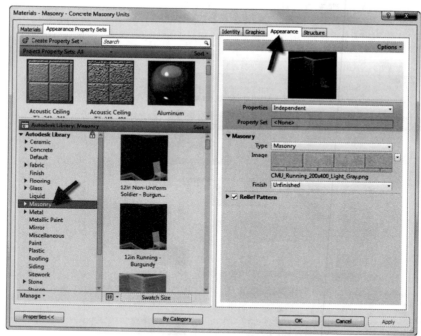

FIGURE 14-2.6 Revit's Render Appearance Library dialog

Next, you will look at the materials for the curtain wall. Both the mullions and the curtain panels, the glass in this case, have a material assigned to them.

14. Zoom in to one of the curtain wall elements.

15. Select one of the vertical mullions; hover and click only when the mullion highlights, pressing *Tab* if needed.

16. Open the **Type Properties** via the *Properties Palette*.

17. Notice the material for the mullion is set to **Metal – Aluminum** (Figure 14-2.7).

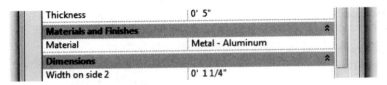

FIGURE 14-2.7 Mullion material

18. Click **OK** to close the open dialog.

Now you will look at the material for the *curtain panel*. To select the curtain panel, you will need to tap the *Tab* key in order to cycle through the options directly below the cursor.

19. Hover over the **curtain panel**, the glass, and tap the *Tab* key until it highlights; **click** to select it (Figure 14-2.8).

When the curtain panel is selected, you will see the lines change to the color blue and a push pin will appear indicating it is locked.

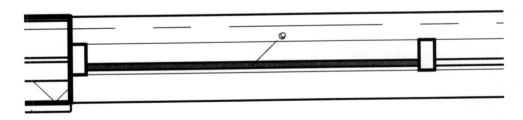

FIGURE 14-2.8 Select the Curtain Panel

20. View the curtain panel's **Type Properties**.

21. Notice the material is set to *Glass* (Figure 14-2.9).

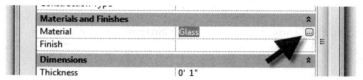

FIGURE 14-2.9 Curtain Panel material

22. Click on the material name **Glass**, to select the cell.

23. Click the small button that appears to the right (Figure 14-2.9).

Notice on the *Graphics* tab (see Figure 14-2.10) that the shading is set to a blue color with 75% transparency. This only relates to the shaded display styles and does not apply to rendered views. It is beneficial to check the *Use Render Appearance for Shading* option as the color will be automatically set to match the approximate color of the material that will be used for generating photorealistic renderings.

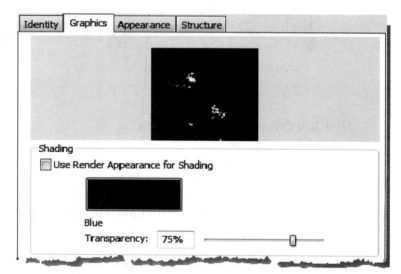

FIGURE 14-2.10 Editing material; Glass

24. Click the *Use Render Appearance for Shading* option.

25. Switch to the ***Appearance*** tab.

Notice the *Render Appearance* is set to the generic option (Figure 14-2.11). You will want to change this to a glazing material.

26. Click to expand **Glass** in the *Autodesk Library* pane (i.e., click the arrow on the left).

27. Click the ***Glazing*** category so the correct render graphics are displayed.

28. Select **Glazing Clear Reflective** from the options (Figure 14-4.12).

It is best to select one of the "glazing" *Rendering Appearances* for glass in windows and curtain walls. They are designed specifically for this situation and allow lighting calculations to work correctly if the model is exported to Autodesk *3DS Max Design*.

Notice, on the *Appearance* tab in the *Materials* dialog, that the number of sheets of glass is an option. Is your curtain wall double or triple glazed? Do not change this setting at this time. You should also notice the shading color changed on the *Graphics* tab to match the *Render Appearance* color.

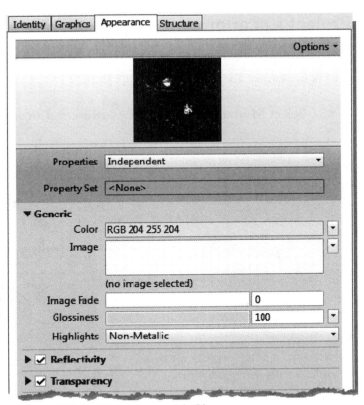

FIGURE 14-2.11 Editing material; Glass

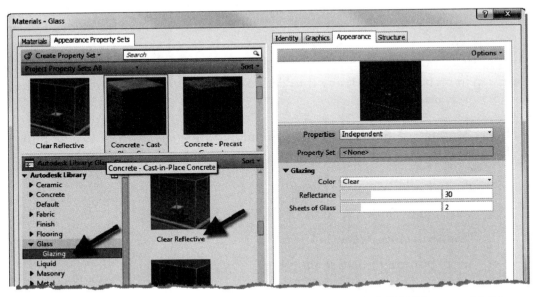

FIGURE 14-2.12 Editing material; Glass

29. Click **OK** to close all open dialog boxes.

The way in which you just changed materials is the same for most elements.

Project Location:

A first step in setting up a rendering is to specify the location of the project on the Earth. This is important for accurate daylight studies.

Location

30. Select **Manage → Project Location → Location**.

31. In the *Project Address* field, enter **Minneapolis, MN**.

    a. You may also enter your location if you wish.

    b. It is even possible to enter the actual street address.

32. Press **Enter**.

You should now see an internet based map of your project location, complete with longitude and latitude (Figure 14-2.13).

33. Click **OK**.

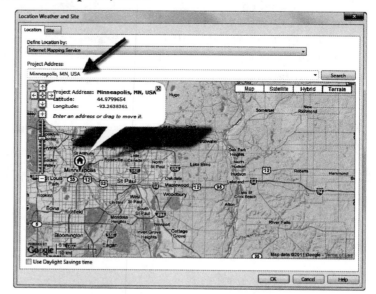

FIGURE 14-2.13 Location Weather and Site dialog

Sun Settings:

The next step in preparing a rendering is to define the sun settings. You will explore the various options available.

34. Select **Manage → Settings → Additional Settings** (*drop-down list icon*) **→ Sun Settings**.

35. Make the following changes (Figure 14-2.14)

    a. Solar Study: **Still**

    b. **Uncheck** *Ground Plane at Level*.

    c. Select **Summer Solstice** on the left.

    d. Click the ***Duplicate*** icon in the lower left.

    e. Enter the following name: **Law Office 6-30 at 3pm**.

    f. Adjust the Month, Day and Time to match the name just entered.

    g. Change the year to 2011.

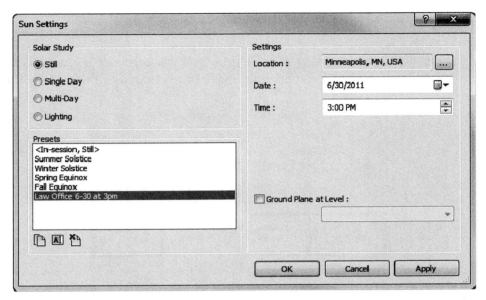

FIGURE 14-2.14 Sun Settings dialog

36. Click **OK** to close the dialog

The previous sun settings apply to the entire project, not just the current view, which is the intent of the *Manage* tab.

Specifying True North:

Another important step in rendering sunlight is telling Revit what true north is. All architectural drawings assume a project north being straight up for convenience of design and drafting. To set True North, you do the following (but do not make any changes now):

- Switch to the **Site Plan** view.
- Set the *Orientation* to *True North* in the *View Properties*.
- Select **Position → Rotate True North** on the *Manage* tab.
- Rotate the model accordingly.

Properly setting True North will make the renderings more realistic and daylighting studies valid.

All views set to *Project North* will not be rotated. Do not modify *True North* at this time.

Placing Trees:

Next, you will place a few trees into your rendering. You will adjust their exact location so they are near the edge of the framed rendering so as not to cover too much of the building.

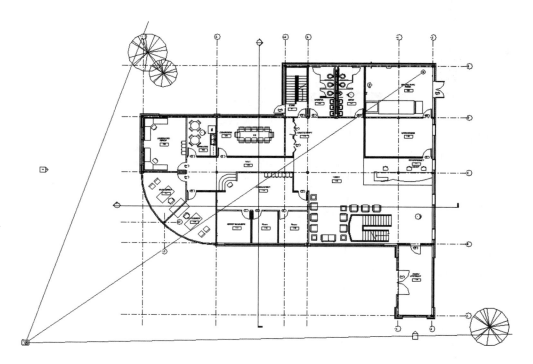

FIGURE 14-2.15 Level 1 with trees added

37. While still in the **Level 1 Plan** view, select **Home → Build → Component → Place a Component** from the *Ribbon*. **FYI:** *Click no for any tag prompt.*

38. Pick *RPC Tree – Deciduous:* **Largetooth Aspen 25'** from the *Type Selector* on the *Properties Palette*.

   FYI: *If the tree is not listed in the* Type Selector, *click Load Family and load the Deciduous tree family from the Plantings folder.*

39. Place three trees as shown in **Figure 14-2.14**. One tree will be made smaller starting in Step #41.

   FYI: *While in the Level 1 Plan view, right-click on the 3D View 1 label in the Project Browser and select **Show Camera** to see the field of view.*

40. Adjust the trees in the plan view, reviewing the effects in the **3D View 1** view, so your 3D view is similar to Figure 14-2.16.

41. In the Level 1 Plan view, select the tree that is shown smaller in **Figure 14-2.15**.

42. Click **Edit Type** on the *Properties Palette,* and then click **Duplicate** and enter the name: **Largetooth Aspen 18′**.

43. Change the *Plant Height* to **18′** (from 25′) and then click **OK** to close the open dialog boxes.

The previous three steps allow you to have a little more variety in the trees being placed. Otherwise, they would all be the same height, which is not very natural.

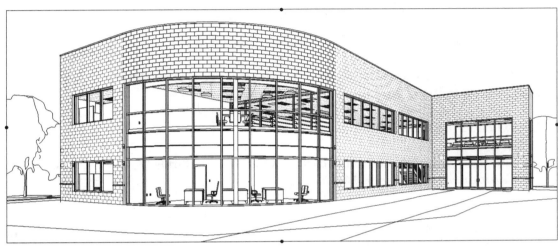

FIGURE 14-2.16 3D View 1 – with trees

Revit renderings can show a high level of detail if set up correctly. The images below show custom content created for use in projects. The content is accurate dimensionally and has materials assigned. The materials provided by Revit are high quality and help to create realistic renderings. Notice the transparent glass and reflections.

Images courtesy of LHB (www.LHBcorp.com)

Adding Exterior Sun Shades:

Controlling how the sunlight enters the building is an important part of an architectural design. In the next few steps you will add exterior sun shades to a few windows. This will block the hot sunlight during the summer months when it is high in the sky and allow it in during the winter months when the sun is low. This design technique can be validated in Revit by doing multiple renderings with various times and dates plugged in. Revit allows you to create animated sun studies as well!

44. Load the following two families from the DVD:

    a. Renderings**Exterior Sun Shade**

    b. Renderings**Exterior Sun Shade – Curved Wall**

Exterior Sun Shade is a custom *face based* family. You will add it in an elevation view. The length can be adjusted via grips or element properties.

45. Switch to the West Elevation view.

46. Add the two sun shades to the curtain walls between Grids D and C via the ***Component*** tool (Figure 14-2.17).

47. Add five more sun shades, including one curved, at the windows shown in Figure 14-2.24. Placed the curved shade in plan view and then move it to the correct vertical position via an elevation view.

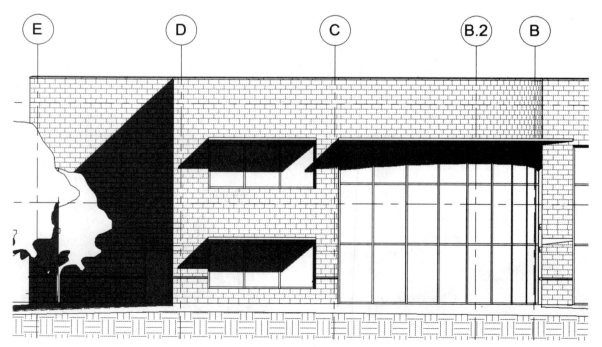

FIGURE 14-2.17 Sun shades added. Shades turned on in 2D view

Setting up the Environment:

You have limited options for setting up the building's environment. If you need more control than what is provided directly in Revit, you will need to use another program such as Autodesk *3DS Max Design 2012* which is designed to work with Revit and can create extremely high quality renderings and animations; it even has day lighting functionality that helps to validate LEED® (Leadership in Environmental and Energy Design) requirements.

48. Switch to your camera view: **3D View 1**.

49. Select the ***Show Rendering Dialog*** icon on the *View Control Bar*, it looks like a teapot (Figure 14-2.18).

   > **FYI:** *This icon is only visible when you are in a 3D view; the same is true for the SteeringWheel and ViewCube.*

The *Rendering* dialog box is now open (Figure 14-2.19). This dialog box allows you to control the environmental settings you are about to explore and actually create the rendering.

FIGURE 14-2.18 Scene Selection dialog

FIGURE 14-2.19 Rendering dialog

50. In the *Lighting* section, click the down arrow next to *Scheme* to see the options. Select **Exterior: Sun and Artificial** when finished (Figure 14-2.20).

The lighting options are very simple choices: Is your rendering an interior or exterior rendering, and is the light source *Sun*, *Artificial* or both? You may have artificial lights, light fixtures like the ones you placed in the office, but still only desire a rendering solely based on the light provided by the sun. *Sun only* will be faster.

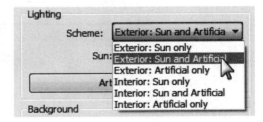

FIGURE 14-2.20 Lighting options

51. In the *Lighting* section, set the *Sun Setting* to <Still> **Law Office 6-30 at 3pm**. (This relates to the Figure 14-2.14 settings.)

> *FYI: In the Sun and Shadow Settings dialog box, Revit lets you set up various "scenes" which control time of day. Two examples would be:*
> - *Law Office Daytime, summer*
> - *Law Office Nighttime, window*
>
> *Looking back at Figure 14-2.14, you would click Duplicate again and provide additional names. The names would then be available from the Sun drop-down list in the Render dialog box.*

52. Click on the **Artificial Lighting** button (Figure 14-2.20).

You will now see a dialog similar to the one shown to the right (Figure 14-2.21).

You will see several 2x4 light fixtures. The light fixtures relate to the fixtures you inserted in the reflected ceiling plans using Revit *MEP*. It is very convenient that you can place lights in the ceiling plan and have them ready to render whenever you need to (i.e., render and cast light into the scene!). Here you can group lights together so you can control which ones are on (e.g., exterior and interior lights).

FIGURE 14-2.21 Scene Lighting dialog

53. Click **Cancel** to close the *Artificial Lighting* dialog.

54. Click the down-arrow next to *Style* in the *Background* area (Figure 14-2.22).

55. Select **Sky: Few Clouds**.

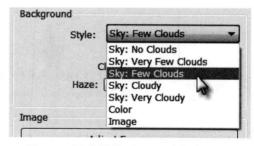

FIGURE 14-2.22 Background Style

Notice that for the background, one option is *Image*. This allows you to specify a photograph of the site, or one similar. It can prove difficult getting the perspective just right but the end results can look as if you took a picture of the completed building.

FIGURE 14-2.23 Rendering progress

56. Make sure the *Quality* is set to **Draft**.

> *FYI: The time to process the rendering increases significantly as the quality level is raised.*

57. Click **Render** from the *Rendering* dialog box.

You will see a progress bar while the rendering is processing (Figure 14-2.23).

After a few minutes, depending on the speed of your computer, you should have a low quality rendered image similar to Figure 14-2.24 below. You can increase the quality of the image by adjusting the quality and resolution settings in the *Render* dialog. However, these higher settings require substantially more time to generate the rendering. The last step before saving the Revit project file is to save the rendered image to a file.

> *FYI: Each time you make changes to the model that are visible from that view, you will have to re-render the view to get an updated image.*

Depending on exactly how your view was set up, you may be able to see light from one of the light figures. Also, notice the railing through the curtain wall; Revit has the glass in the windows set to be transparent!

FIGURE 14-2.24 Rendered view

58. From the *Rendering* dialog select **Export**.

> *FYI: The 'Save to Project' button saves the image within the Revit Project for placement on Sheets. This is convenient but does make the project size larger, so you should delete old ones from the Project Browser!*

59. Select a *location* and provide a *file name*.

60. Set the *Save As* type: to **JPEG**.

61. Click **Save**.

The image file you just saved can now be inserted into MS Word or Adobe Photoshop for editing.

The images below are examples of high quality renderings that can be produced by Revit. These images were part of a design competition submittal which took First Place. The award was given by the Minnesota Chapter of the United States Green Building Council (USGBC). The design team included Wesley Stabs (LHB) and Chris Wingate (UrbanWorks Architecture).

Realistic Display Setting:

In addition to *Shade* and *Hidden Line* display settings you can also select ***Realistic***. This will show the *Render Appearance* materials on your building without the need to do a full rendering. Although the shades and shadows are not nearly as realistic as a full rendering, turning on ***Ambient Shadows*** in the *Properties Palette > Graphic Display Options* comes pretty close. This is a great way to get an idea on how the materials look but you will find it best to minimize the use of this setting as Revit will run much slower.

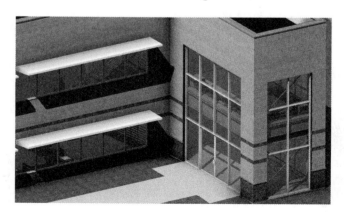
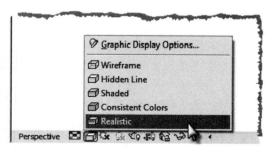

Exercise 14-3:
Rendering an Isometric in Section

This exercise will introduce you to a view tool called *Section Box*. This tool is not necessarily related to renderings, but the two features together can produce some interesting results.

Setting Up the 3D View:

1. Open your law office file.

2. Switch to the ***Default 3D View*** via the ***3D*** icon on the *QAT (not to the* 3D View 1 *from Exercise 14-2)*.

3. Make sure nothing is selected and note the ***View Properties*** in the *Properties Palette*.

4. Activate the **Section Box** parameter and then click **Apply**.

You should see a box appear around your building, similar to Figure 14-3.1. When selected, you can adjust the size of the box with its grips. Anything outside the box is not visible. This is a great way to study a particular area of your building while in an isometric view. You will experiment with this feature next.

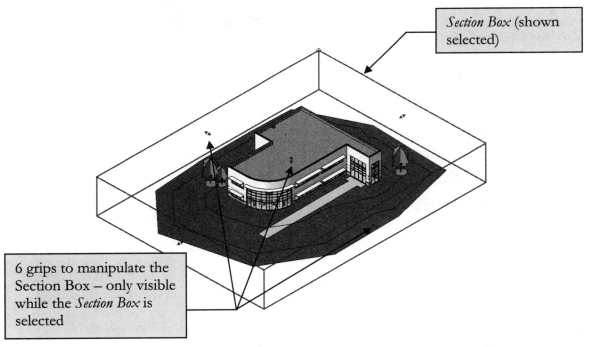

Section Box (shown selected)

6 grips to manipulate the Section Box – only visible while the *Section Box* is selected

FIGURE 14-3.1 3D view with Section Box activated

5. To practice using the **Section Box**, drag the grips around until your view looks similar to **Figure 14-3.2**. *FYI: Grips only show when section box is selected.*

    TIP: *This will require the ViewCube tool as well.*

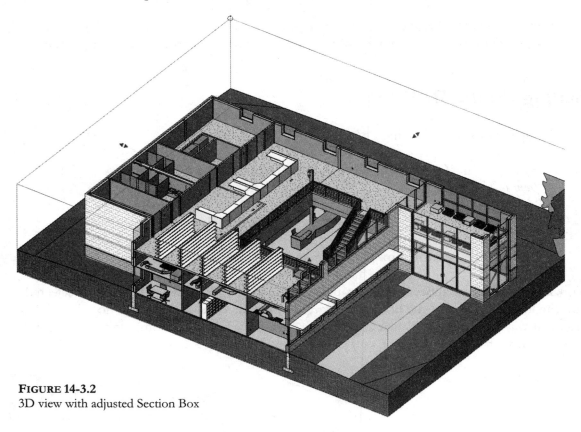

FIGURE 14-3.2
3D view with adjusted Section Box

This creates a very interesting view of the project. What client would have trouble understanding this drawing?

6. Select the ***Render*** icon.

    a. Select the *Scheme*: **Exterior: Sun only**.

    b. Set the *Sun Setting* to **Sunlight from Top Left**.

    c. Background *Style* to **Color** (set the color to white).

7. Leave all other settings as they are and **Render** the view.

After a few minutes, the view is rendered and can be saved to the project so the image can be placed on a sheet, or exported and used in other applications such as PowerPoint.

Notice how the ground is rendered in section. Also, the ductwork is showing above the ceiling. Much of the model is gray because the various elements have the default material selected. If you take the time to specify a material for everything, you can generate another rendered image that is much better looking.

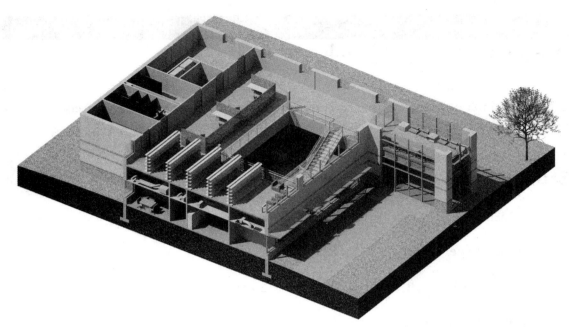

8. **Save** your project

The image below uses the technique described in this exercise. This is same award-winning design introduced in the previous exercise by Wesley Stabs (LHB) and Chris Wingate (UrbanWorks Architecture).

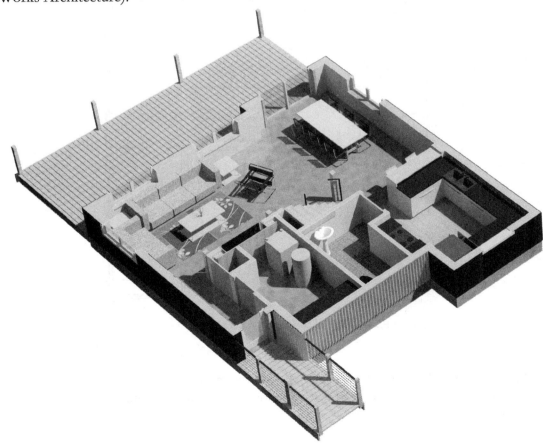

Exercise 14-4:
Creating an Interior Rendering

Creating an interior rendering is very similar to an exterior rendering. This exercise will walk you through the steps involved in creating a high quality interior rendering.

Setting up the Camera View:

1. Open your law office project.

2. Open **Level 1** view.

3. From the *View* tab, select **3D View → Camera**.

4. Place the *Camera* as shown in **Figure 14-4.1**.

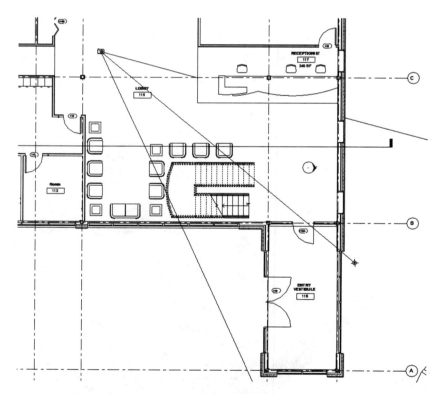

FIGURE 14-4.1 Camera placed – Level 1 view

Revit uses default heights for the camera and the target. These heights are based on the current level's floor elevation. These reference points can be edited via the camera properties.

Revit will automatically open the newly generated camera view. Your view should look similar to **Figure 14-4.2**.

FYI: Make sure you created the camera on Level 1 and picked the points in the correct order.

FIGURE 14-4.2 Initial interior camera view

5. Using the **Crop Region** rectangle, modify the view to look like **Figure 14-4.3**.

TIP: You will have to switch to plan view to adjust the camera's depth of view to see the tree.

REMINDER: If the camera does not show in plan view, right-click on the camera view label in the Project Browser and select Show Camera.

TIP: Turning on Consistent Colors on the View Control Bar is a great way to visualize your design while trying to setup a view to be rendered. It does not have dark, hard-to-see surfaces as the Shaded option has. Turning on Ambient Shadows adds a nice touch.

FIGURE 14-4.3 Modified interior camera; Hidden Line view with Ambient Shadows turned on

6. Switch back to **Level 1** to see the revised *camera* view settings.

Notice the field of view triangle is wider based on the changes to the *Crop Region* (Figure 14-4.4).

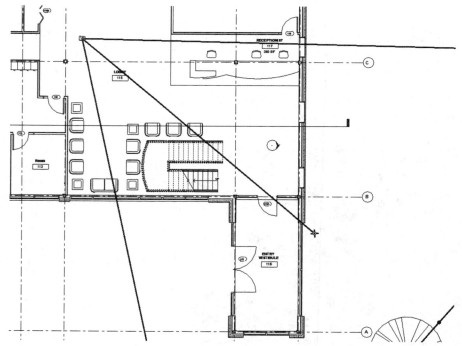

FIGURE 14-4.4 Modified camera – Level 1

Creating the Rendering:

Next you will render the view.

7. Switch back to your interior camera view, **3D View 2**.

8. Select **Show Render Dialog** from the *View Control Bar*.

9. Set the *Scheme* to **Interior: Sun and Artificial**.

    TIP: *Be sure to select the "interior" option.*

10. Set the *Sun* to **Law Office 6-30 at 3pm**.

11. Click **Render** to begin the rendering process.

This will take several minutes depending on the speed of your computer. When finished, the view should look similar to Figure 14-4.5.

12. Click **Export** from the *Rendering* dialog box to save the image to a file on your hard drive. Name the file **Lobby.jpg** (jpeg file format).

You can now open the *Lobby.jpg* file in Adobe Photoshop or insert into a MS Word type program to manipulate or print.

To toggle back to the normal hidden view, click **Show the Model** from the *Rendering* dialog box.

There are many things you can do to make the rendering look even better. You can add interior props (e.g., pictures on the wall, and items on the counter top). You can adjust the *Sun* setting to nighttime and then render a night scene.

> ***TIP:*** *Setting the output to Printer rather than Screen allows you to generate a higher resolution image. Thus, between the Quality setting and the Output setting, you can create an extremely high quality rendering, but it might take hours, if not days, to process!*

Revit also gives you the ability to set a material to be self-illuminating. This will allow you to make something look like it is lit up. You can also set a lamp shade to glow when a light source has been defined under it so it looks more realistic.

13. **Save** your project.

FIGURE 14-4.5 Rendered interior view

The image below shows a high quality interior rendering with materials thoughtfully added and plenty of lighting provided.

Image courtesy of LHB (www.LHBcorp.com)

Exercise 14-5:
Adding People to the Rendering

Revit provides a few RPC people to add to your renderings. These are files from a popular company that provides 3D photo content for use in renderings (http://www.archvision.com). You can buy this content in groupings (like college students) or per item. In addition to people, they offer items like cars, plants, trees, office equipment, etc.

Loading Content into the Current Project

1. Open your law office project.

2. Switch to **Level 1** view.

3. Select **Component → Place a Component**.

4. Click the **Load Family** button on the *Ribbon*.

5. Browse to the **Entourage** folder and select both the **RPC Male** and **RPC Female** files (using the Ctrl key to select both at once) and click **Open**.

6. Place two **Males** and one **Female** as shown in **Figure 14-5.1**.

   a. Change the Offset to 6'-4" for the person on the stair landing.

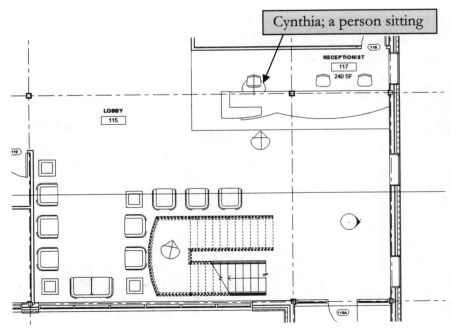

FIGURE 14-5.1 Level 1 – RPC people added

The line in the circle (Figure 14-5.1) represents the direction a person is looking. You simply rotate the object to make adjustments.

7. Select **Manage → Materials** from the *Ribbon*.

Next you will change the *Render Appearance* for the gypsum board so the walls are brighter. Any element in the building that uses the *Material* you are about to modify will be automatically updated.

8. Select **Gypsum Wall Board** from the *Materials* list.

9. Check the **Use Render Appearance for Shading** option.

10. Set the *Render Appearance* to **Paint Antique White Flat**.

11. **Close** the open dialog box.

12. Switch to your interior lobby camera view.

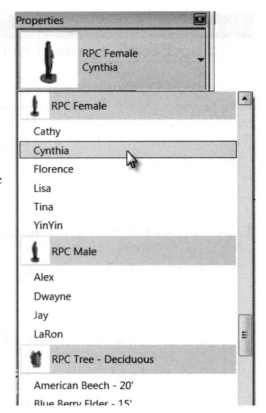

FIGURE 14-5.2 Type Selector

13. **Render** the lobby view with the settings previously used.

Your rendering should now have people in it and look similar to Figure 14-5.3.

FIGURE 14-5.3 Interior lobby view with people added

Adding people and other "props" gives your model a sense of scale and makes it look a little more realistic. After all, architecture is for people. These objects can be viewed from any angle. Try a new camera view from a different angle to see how the people adjust to match the view and perspective, maybe from the second floor looking down to Level 1.

14. **Save** your project.

> ***FYI:*** *As with other families and components, the more you add to your project, the bigger your project file becomes. It is a good idea to load only the items you need and delete the unused items via the Project Browser. Your project should be about 23MB at this point in the tutorial*

Sun Path

It is possible to turn on the feature called **Sun Path**. This shows the path of the sun over a day and a year. This is accessed from the *View Control Bar* while in a 3D view.

Once on, you can click and drag the sun along its daily or yearly path!

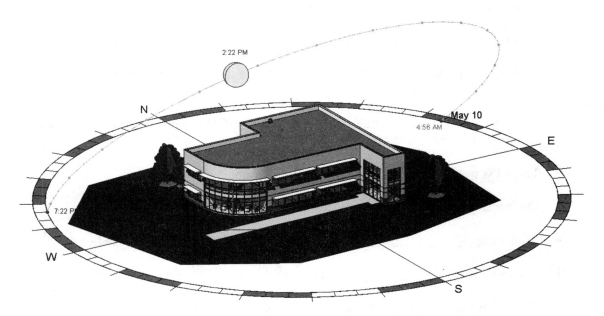

Self-Exam:

The following questions can be used as a way to check your knowledge of this lesson. The answers can be found at the bottom of this page.

1. Creating a camera adds a view to the *Project Browser* list. (T/F)

2. Materials are defined in Revit's *Materials* dialog box. (T/F)

3. After inserting a light fixture, you need to adjust several settings before rendering and getting light from the fixture. (T/F)

4. The *Site* element shows up in section and elevation automatically. (T/F)

5. Use the _____ _____ tool to hide a large portion of the model.

Review Questions:

The following questions may be assigned by your instructor as a way to assess your knowledge of this section. Your instructor has the answers to the review questions.

1. You cannot "point" the people in a specific direction. (T/F)

2. You cannot get accurate lighting based on day/month/location. (T/F)

3. Adding components and families to your project does not make the project file bigger. (T/F)

4. Creating photo-realistic renderings can take a significant amount of time for your computer to process. (T/F)

5. The RPC people can only be viewed from one angle. (T/F)

6. Once a site element is created, it cannot be modified (T/F).

7. Adjust the _____ _____ to make more of a camera view visible.

8. You use the _____ tool to load and insert RPC people.

9. You can adjust the *Eye Elevation* of the camera via the camera's

   _____.

10. What is the file size of (completed) Exercise 14-5? _____ MB

Lesson 15
Law Office: CONSTRUCTION DOCUMENTS SET

This lesson will look at bringing everything you have drawn thus far together onto sheets. The sheets, once set up, are ready for plotting. Basically, you place the various views you have created on sheets. The scale for each view is based on the scale you set while drawing that view, which is important to have set correctly because it affects the text and symbol sizes. When finished setting up the sheets, you will have a set of drawings ready to print, individually or all at once.

Exercise 15-1:
Setting Up a Sheet

Creating a Sheet View:

Sheet

1. Open your law office project with Revit *Architecture*.

The template you started with already has several sheets set up and ready to use. A few of them even have views placed on them. You will learn how to create new sheets, place views on them and modify the existing sheets to create a set of construction documents.

2. Select **View → Sheet Composition → Sheet**.

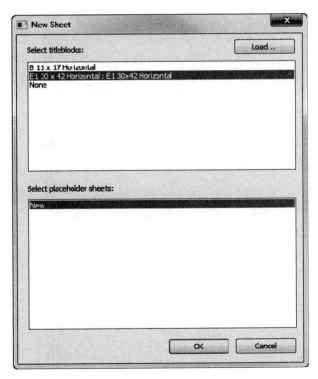

FIGURE 15-1.1 Select a Titleblock

Next, Revit will prompt you for a *Titleblock* to use. The template file you started with has two (Figure 15-1.1).

3. Select the **E1 30x42 Horizontal** titleblock and click **OK**.

That's it; you have created a new sheet that is ready to have views and/or schedules placed on it!

NOTE: *A new view shows up in the Project Browser under the heading: Sheets. Once you get an entire CD set ready, this list can be very long.*

Revit also lets you create placeholder sheets which allow you to add sheets to the sheet index without the need to have a sheet show up in the *Project Browser*. This is helpful if a consultant, such as a food service designer, is not using Revit. This feature allows you to add those sheets to the sheet index. Placeholder sheets can also be added in the sheet list schedule by using the *New Row* tool on the *Ribbon*. Once a placeholder sheet exists, it can be turned into a real sheet by selecting from the lower list in the dialog (Figure 15-1.1).

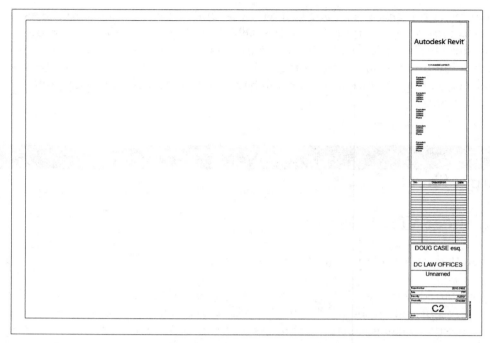

FIGURE 15-1.2 Initial Titleblock view

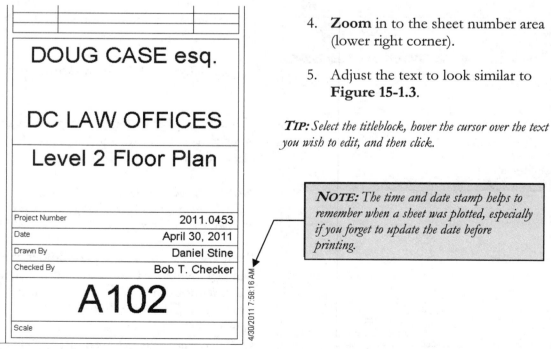

FIGURE 15-1.3 Revised Titleblock data

4. **Zoom** in to the sheet number area (lower right corner).

5. Adjust the text to look similar to **Figure 15-1.3**.

TIP: Select the titleblock, hover the cursor over the text you wish to edit, and then click.

NOTE: *The time and date stamp helps to remember when a sheet was plotted, especially if you forget to update the date before printing.*

You cannot have one view on two sheets. The Level 2 view is currently on the roof plan sheet. You will delete it so the Level 2 view can be placed on the proper sheet.

6. Switch to sheet **A3 – Roof Plan**, select the floor plan on the sheet and press the **Delete** key to remove it from the sheet.

7. Switch back to sheet **A102** and **Zoom out** so you can see the entire sheet.

8. With the sheet fully visible, click and drag the architectural **Level 2** view (under floor plans) from the *Project Browser* onto the sheet view (Figure 15-1.4).

You will see a box that represents the extents of the view you are placing on the current sheet. Because the trees are visible and the elevation tags may be a distance away from your floor plan, the extents may be larger than the sheet. For now you will center the drawing on the sheet so the plan fits.

9. Move the cursor around until the box is somewhat centered on the sheet (this can be adjusted later at any time).

Your view should look similar to **Figure 15-1.4**.

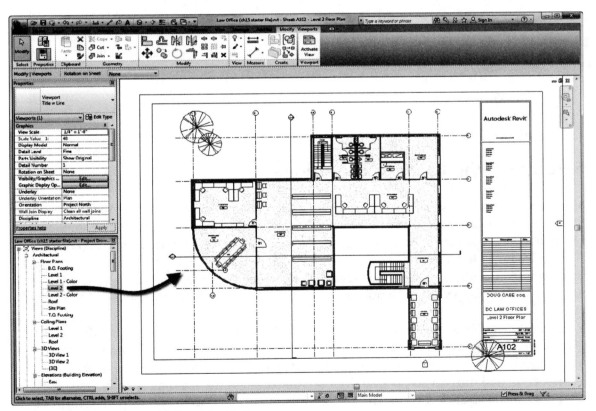

FIGURE 15-1.4 Sheet view with Level 2 added

10. Click the mouse in a "white" area (not on any lines) to deselect the Level 1 view. Notice the box goes away.

11. **Zoom In** on the lower left corner to view the drawing identification symbol that Revit automatically added (Figure 15-1.5).

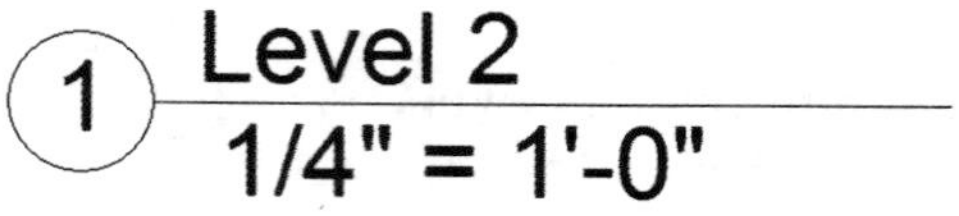

NOTE: *The drawing number for this sheet is added. The next drawing you add to this sheet will be number 2.*

(1) **Level 2**
1/4" = 1'-0"

The view name is listed. This is another reason to rename the views as you create them.

FIGURE 15-1.5 Drawing title

Also notice that the drawing scale is listed. Again, this comes from the scale setting for the Level 2 view.

12. **Zoom out** to see entire sheet again.

13. Move the drawing title below the floor plan. You need to click *Modify* first, so the floor plan is not selected.

FYI: *The title can only be moved when it is the only thing selected. The length of the title line can only be adjusted when the drawing is selected.*

14. Switch back to the Level 2 view and turn off the *Planting* category via the **VV** shortcut.

TIP: *You can also right-click on the drawing in the sheet view and select Activate View to edit the view.*

Setting Up the Exterior Elevations:

The project already has two sheets set up for the exterior elevations: sheets A4 and A5. These sheets already have the exterior elevations placed on them. This is done compliments of the template you started with. Looking at one of the sheets, you will notice two things (Figure 15-1.6). First, the drawings should be as large as possible to make them easier to read when printed. Ideally the plans and elevations would be the same scale. Secondly, the views will need to be cropped to the grade line so it does not extend off the page.

You will also notice in Figure 15-1.6 that the South elevation line cuts through the *Main Entry* area, creating a section view at that part of the building. If you did not want this, you would need to switch back to one of the plan views and select the point part of the South elevation tag and move it south so it does not cut through the building. In this case, you have a detailed elevation view of the portion missing, so you will not change it.

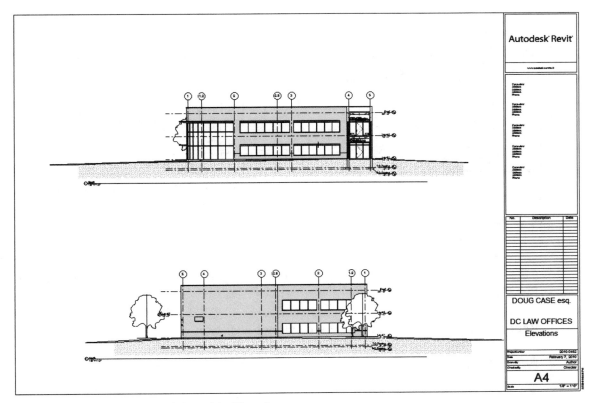

FIGURE 15-1.6 Initial layout of sheet A4 - Elevations

15. Switch to the **North elevation** view, not the sheet.

16. Change the scale to **1/4″ = 1′-0″**.

17. Hide the *Planting* category via "**VV**".

18. Toggle **on** *Crop Region* and *Crop Region Visibility* via the *View Control Bar*.

19. Adjust the *Crop Region* to be close to the building, as shown in Figure 15-1.7.

Notice how the levels for the footings are hidden when outside the *Crop Region*. Also, the levels and grids will move with the *Crop Region* when smaller than their extents. The *Crop Region* will print unless its visibility is turned off. You will do that next.

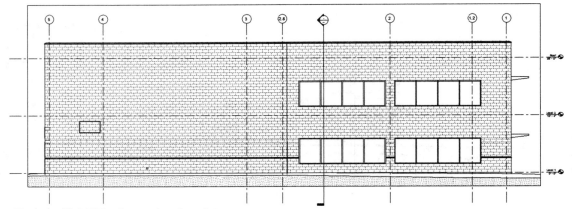

FIGURE 15-1.7 North exterior elevations

20. Click the *Crop Region Visibility* toggle, on the *View Control Bar*, to hide the *Crop Region*. But leave the view cropped.

21. Repeat these steps for the other three exterior elevation views.

22. Adjust the location of the elevations on sheets A4 and A5 as shown in Figure 15-1.8.

> **TIP:** *Sometimes it is easier to delete the view off the sheet and drag it back on from the Project Browser. This aligns the drawing title with the rescaled view. The entire view needs to be selected to adjust the length of the drawing title line. Select the drawing title to move it.*

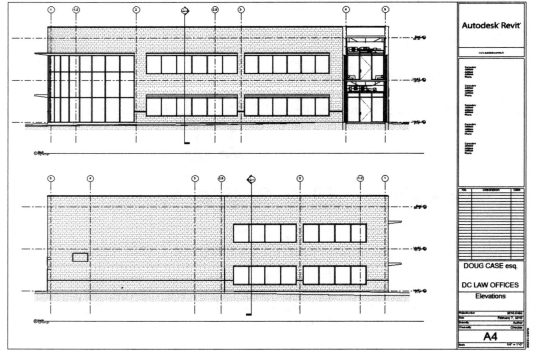

FIGURE 15-1.8 North exterior elevations

Now you will stop for a moment and notice that Revit is automatically referencing the drawings as you place them on sheets.

23. Switch to **Level 1** (see Figure 15-1.9).

Notice in Figure 15-1.9 that the number A5 represents the sheet number that the drawing can be found on. The number 1 (one) is the drawing number to look for on sheet A5.

Setting Up Sections:

24. Switch to sheet **A9 - Building Sections**.

25. Add the two building sections as shown in **Figure 15-1.10**.

26. Switch to **Level 1 Plan** view and zoom in to the area shown in Figure 15-1.11.

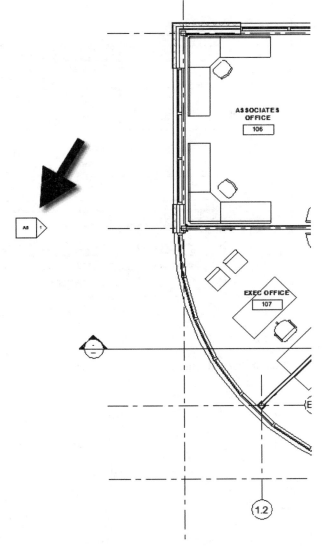

FIGURE 15-1.9
Level 1 – elevation Reference tag filled-in

Notice, again, that the reference bubbles are automatically filled in when the referenced view is placed on a sheet. If the drawing is moved to another sheet, the reference bubbles are automatically updated.

You can also see in Figure 15-1.9 that the reference bubbles on the building sections are filled in.

Because Revit keeps track of references automatically, a view in the *Project Browser* can only be placed on one sheet. The only exception is that *Legend* views can exist on multiple sheets. But they do not contain any elements from the 3D model and cannot be referenced. *Legend* views are for typical notes and 2D graphics that need to appear on multiple sheets.

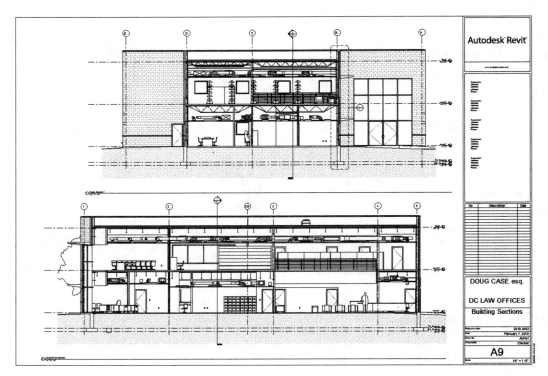

FIGURE 15-1.10 Sheet A9 - Building Sections

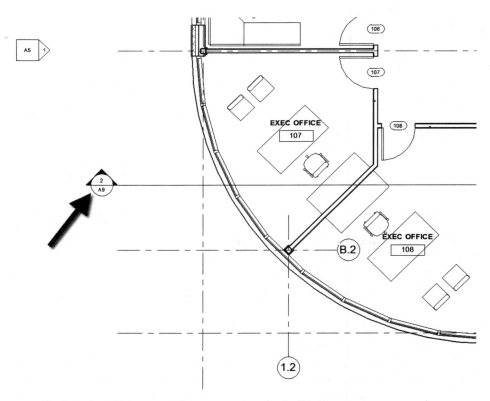

FIGURE 15-1.11 Section references automatically filled in

Set Up the Remaining Sheets:

Next you set up sheets for the remaining views that have yet to be placed on a sheet. You will also renumber sheets as required.

27. Create the following sheets **and** place the appropriate views on them; the view name will generally match the sheet name:

    FYI: Renumber any sheets as necessary; open the sheet and edit the sheet number, or edit via the sheet's properties.

    FYI: Sheets marked with an asterisk will not have a view to place on it; they are mainly to fill out the sheet index in the next exercise.

    Architectural Sheets
    - A101   Level 1 Floor Plan
    - A102   Level 2 Floor Plan
    - A103   Level 1 Reflected Ceiling Plan
    - A104   Level 2 Reflected Ceiling Plan
    - A105   Roof Plan
    - A200   Exterior Elevations
    - A201   Exterior Elevations
    - A300   Building Sections
    - A301   Building Sections*
    - A400   Wall Sections
    - A500   Interior Elevations
    - A600   Details*
    - A800   Schedules

    Structural Sheets
    - S101   Level 1 Slab and Foundation Plan
    - S102   Level 2 Framing Plan
    - S103   Roof Framing Plan
    - S200   Structural Details*
    - S201   Structural Schedules

    Mechanical Sheets
    - M100   Under Slab Sanitary Plan
    - M101   Level 1 Sanitary Plan
    - M102   Level 2 Sanitary Plan
    - M201   Level 1 Domestic Water Plan
    - M202   Level 2 Domestic Water Plan
    - M301   Level 1 Ventilation Plan
    - M302   Level 2 Ventilation Plan

- M400   Mechanical Roof Plan*
- M500   Mechanical Schedules*
- M600   Domestic Water Riser Diagrams*
- M700   Sanitary Riser Diagrams*

Electrical Sheets
- E100   Electrical Site Plan*
- E101   Level 1 Lighting Plan
- E102   Level 2 Lighting Plan
- E201   Level 1 Power Plan
- E202   Level 2 Power Plan
- E301   Level 1 Systems Plan
- E302   Level 2 Systems Plan
- E400   Electrical Details*
- E500   Electrical Schedules
- E600   Single Line Diagrams*

> **TIP:** *Two sheets cannot have the same number.*
>
> *Sheets with views placed on them will have a plus sign next to the sheet name in the Project Browser.*

Question: On a large project with hundreds of views, how do I know for sure if I have placed every view on a sheet?

Answer: Revit has a feature called *Browser Organization* that can hide all the views that have been placed on a sheet. You will try this next.

28. Take a general look at the *Project Browser* to see how many views are listed. (See Figure 15-1.13 on page 15-11.)

29. Select **Views (Discipline)** at the top of the *Project Browser* (Figure 15-1.12).

30. Select **Not on sheets** from the *Type Selector*.

31. Click **Apply**.

32. Notice the list in the *Project Browser* is now smaller. (See Figure 15-1.14 on page 15-11.)

FIGURE 15-1.12 Project Browser and Properties Palette

The *Project Browser* now only shows drawing views that have not been placed onto a sheet. Of course, you could have a few views that do not need to be placed on a sheet, but this feature will help eliminate errors.

Next you will reset the *Project Browser*.

33. Switch the *Browser Organization* back to **Discipline** and click **Apply**.

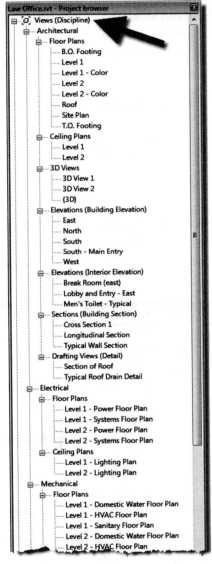

FIGURE 15-1.13
Project Browser; Views (Discipline)

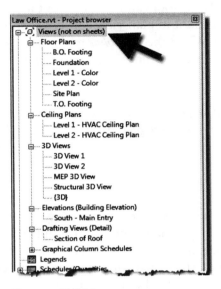

FIGURE 15-1.14
Project Browser; Views (not on sheets)

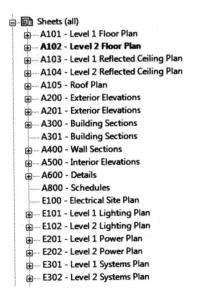

FIGURE 15-1.15
Project Browser; Sheets (All)

It is possible to customize the *Browser Organization* to sort views and sheets as needed.

34. **Save** your project.

Large Buildings – Matchlines and Dependent Views:

When the building floor plan is too large to fit on a single sheet you need to use the *Matchline* tool and the **Dependent Views** feature. Each can be used exclusive of the other but they generally are used together. You will not do this for the book project but the information is good to know.

The *Matchline* tool can be found on the *View* tab. It is similar to the *Grid* tool in that you add it in plan view and it will show up in other plan views because it has a height. When the *Matchline* tool is selected, you enter *Sketch* mode. Here you can draw multiple lines which do not have to form a loop or even touch each other.

Matchline

A *dependent view* is a view which is controlled by (i.e., dependent on) a main overall view, but has its own *Crop Region*. A main view can have several *dependent views*. Any change made in *Visibility/Graphics Overrides* is made to the main view and each dependent view. The dependent view's *Crop Regions* generally coincide with the *Matchlines*. However, the *Crop Regions* can overlap.

Additionally, if *a dependent view's Crop Region* is rotated, the model actually rotates so the *Crop Window* stays square with the computer screen. However, the other dependent views and the main view are unaffected. This is great when a wing of the building is at an angle. Having that wing orthogonal with the computer screen makes it easier to work in that portion of the building and it fits better on the sheet in most cases.

To create a dependent view, you right-click on a floor plan view and select **Duplicate View > Duplicate as Dependent**. The image to the right shows the result in the *Project Browser*, the **dependent views** are indented.

Once the *Matchline* is added and the dependent views are set up, you can add **View References** (from the *Annotate* tab) which indicate the sheet to flip to in order to see the drawing beyond the *Matchline*.

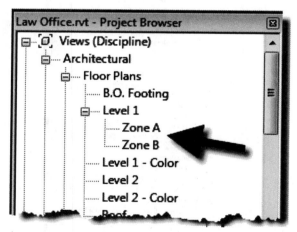

Finally, on large projects with multiple levels and floor plan views, you only have to set up the dependent views once (i.e., number and crop regions). With one plan set up, you right-click on the main view and select **Apply Dependent Views**. You will be prompted to select all the floor plan views for which you would like to have the dependent views created.

Exercise 15-2:
Sheet Index

Revit has the ability to create a sheet index automatically. You will study this now.

Creating a Drawing List Schedule

1. Open your project.

2. Select **View → Create → Schedule → Sheet List**.  Sheet List

You are now in the *Sheet List* dialog box. This process is identical to creating schedules. Here you specify which fields you want in the sheet index and how to sort the list (Figure 15-2.1).

3. Add **Sheet Number** and **Sheet Name** to the right:

    a. Select the available field on the left.

    b. Click the **Add →** button in the center.

4. Click **OK**.

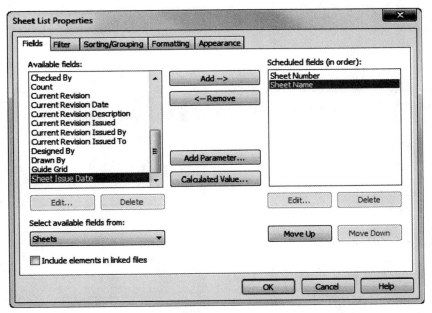

FIGURE 15-2.1
Drawing List Properties dialog; sheet number and name "added"

Now you should notice that the *Sheet Names* are cut off because the column is not wide enough. You will adjust this next.

5. Move your cursor over the right edge of the *Sheet List* schedule and click-and-drag to the right until you can see the entire name (Figure 15-2.2).

6. Edit **Sorting / Grouping** via the *Properties Palette* and sort the list by sheet number.

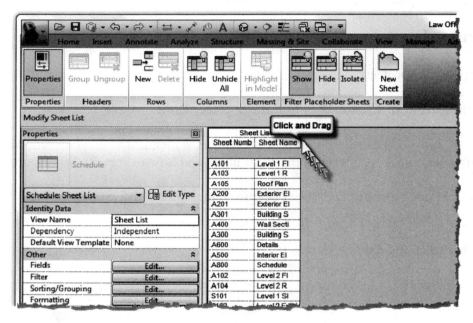

FIGURE 15-2.2
Sheet List view; notice sheet names are cut off in the right column

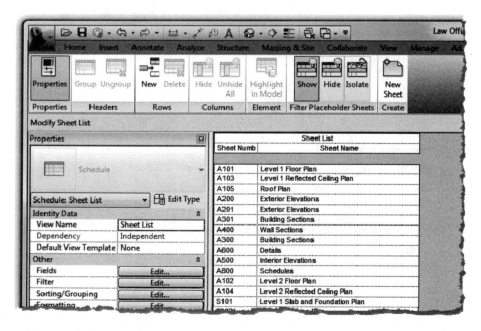

FIGURE 15-2.3
Sheet List view; sheet names are now visible

Setting Up a Title Sheet

Now you will create a title sheet to place your sheet index on.

7. Create a new Sheet:
    a. Number: **T001**
    b. Name: **Title Sheet**

8. From the *Schedules/Quantities* category of the *Project Browser*, place the schedule named **Sheet List** on the *Title Sheet*. Once on the sheet, drag the "triangle" grip to adjust the column width.

Next you will place one of your rendered images that you saved to file (raster image). If you have not created a raster image, you should refer back to Lesson 14 and create one now (otherwise you can use any BMP or JPG file on your hard drive if necessary).

9. Select **Insert → Import → Image.**

10. Browse to your raster image file, select it and click **Open** to place the Image.

11. Click on your Title Sheet to locate the image.

Your sheet should look similar to Figure 15-2.4.

   FYI: The text is added in the next step.

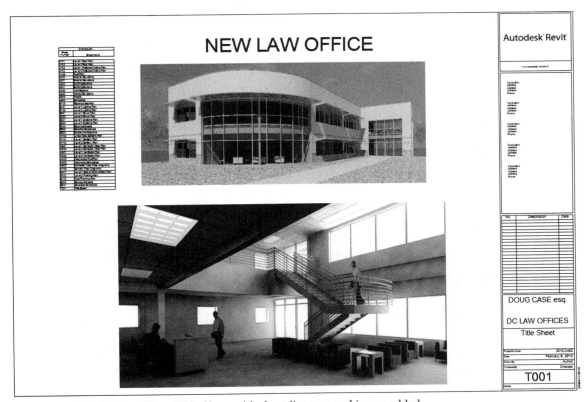

FIGURE 15-2.4 Sheet View: Title Sheet with sheet list, text and image added

12. Use the *Text* command to add the title shown in Figure 15-2.4.

   a. You will need to create a new text style and set the height to 1″.

When you have raster images in your project, you can manage them via the *Raster Images* dialog.

13. Select **Insert → Import → Manage Images**.

Manage
Images

You are now in the *Raster Image* dialog which gives you a little information about the image and allows you to delete it from the project (Figure 15-2.5).

Manage Images

Raster Image	Name	Count
	Hi Res Interior Rendering.jpg	1
	Rendering - Figure 14-2_22.jpg	1

Delete   OK

FIGURE 15-2.5 Raster Image dialog

TIP: You can create a custom parameter (via the Add Parameter button; see Figure 15-2.1) and then sort the schedule by that parameter. This allows you to force the "T" sheet to the top and the "E" sheets to the bottom.

14. Click **OK** to close the *Raster Images* dialog.

15. **Save** your project.

Exercise 15-3:
Printing a Set of Drawings

Revit has the ability to print an entire set of drawings, in addition to printing individual sheets.

Printing a Set of Drawings

1. **Open** your project.

2. Select **Application Menu → Print**.

3. In the *Print Range* area, click the option **Selected views/sheets** (Figure 15-3.1).

4. Click the **Select...** button within the *Print Range* area.

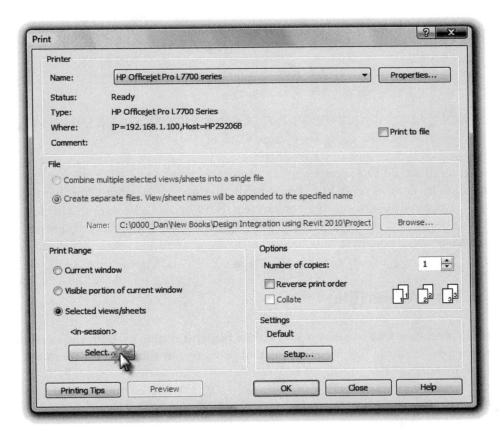

FIGURE 15-3.1 Print dialog box

You should now see a listing of all views and sheets (Figure 15-3.2).

Notice at the bottom you can **Show** both **Sheets** and **Views**, or each separately. Because you are printing a set of drawings, you will want to see only the sheets.

5. **Uncheck** the **Views** option.

The list is now limited to just sheets set up in your project.

6. Select all the *Sheets*.

7. Click **OK** to close the **View/Sheet Set** dialog.

FIGURE 15-3.2 Selecting tool for printing

> *FYI: Once you have selected the sheets to be plotted, you can click Save. This will save the list of selected drawings to a name you choose. Then, the next time you need to print those sheets, you can select the name from the drop-down list at the top (Figure 15-3.2).*
>
> *On very large projects (e.g., with 20 floor plan sheets), you could have a* Plans *list saved, a* Laboratory Interior Elevations *list saved, etc.*

8. IF YOU ACTUALLY WANT TO PRINT A FULL SET OF DRAWINGS, you can do so now by clicking OK. Otherwise, click **Cancel**.

The steps required to create a PDF file are similar. However, you need a PDF printer driver which is not provided by Autodesk. A PDF printer driver comes with Adobe Acrobat (not the free reader) or you can download a free version (e.g. pdf995.com). Be sure to check the "combine multiple sheets... into a single file" option (Figure 15-3.1) if you want to create a single PDF file with all the sheets in it.

Exporting a 3D DWFx File:

The *3D DWFx* file is an easy way to share your project file with others without the need to give them your editable Revit file (i.e., your intellectual property) or the need for them to actually have Revit installed.

> *NOTE: You can download Revit, from Autodesk's website, and run it in viewer mode (full Revit with no Save functionality) for free.*

The *3D DWFx* file is much smaller in file size than the original Revit file. Also, Autodesk Design Review is a *Viewer* that can be downloaded for free from www.autodesk.com/DWF.

9. Switch to your **Default 3D** view.

   a. You may need to go into *View Properties* and turn off the *Section Box* feature to see the entire model.

You must be in a 3D view for the *3D DWF* feature to work. If you are not in a 3D view, you will get *2D DWF* files:

10. Select **Application Menu → Export →DWF/DWFx**.

   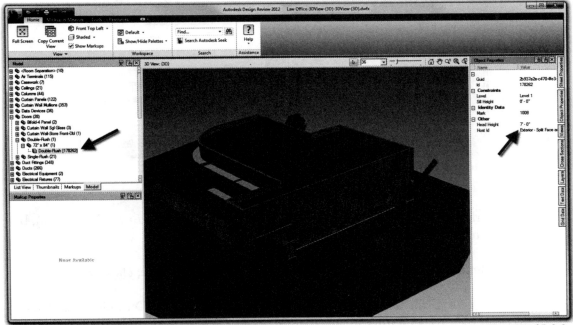

   DWF/DWFx
   Creates DWF or DWFx files.

11. Click **Next...**: Specify a file name and location for the DWF file; click **OK**.

That's all you need to do to create the file. Now you can email it to the client or a product representative to get a more accurate cost estimate.

The *3D DWF* file is a meager 1MB, whereas the Revit *Project* file is 24MB. (Your file sizes will vary slightly based on factors like the number of families loaded, etc.) In most cases, an individual's networks and servers are set up so they cannot receive large files via email, so the 3D DWF is very useful.

The *DWF Viewer* should have been installed with Revit. You can access it from *Start → All Programs → Autodesk → Autodesk Design Review 2012*. You can zoom, orbit and select objects. Notice the information displayed on the left when the front door is selected (see image below). Also notice, under the *Windows* heading, the sizes and quantities are listed.

> *TIP: Autodesk Design Review 2012 is a free download from Autodesk. This is their full-featured DWF viewer and markup utility!*

FIGURE 15-3.3
3D DWF in Autodesk Design Review

Exporting the sheets to a DWFx File:

It is also possible to create a DWFx file which represents some, or all, of the sheets in your project. This file is similar to a PDF file, but is in Autodesk's proprietary format. However, as just mentioned, the view can be downloaded for free and includes markup tools which allow someone to add notes and revision clouds. The PDF format can have markups but requires Adobe Standard (or Professional), rather than just the viewer. The viewer is free but Adobe Standard (or Professional) is not.

The following steps cover how to create a set of drawings in DWFx format.

12. Select **Application Menu → Export → DWF/DWFx**.

13. Do the following on the *Views/Sheets* tab (Figure 15-3.4):

    a. *Export:*   **<In session view/sheet set>**

    b. *Show in list:*   **Sheets in the model**

    c. Click the **Check All button**.

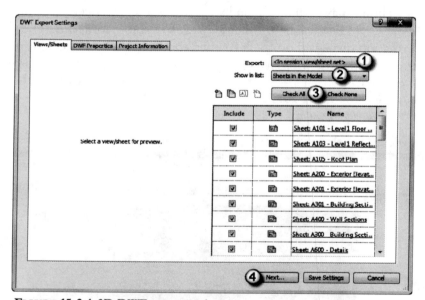

FIGURE 15-3.4 3D DWF export options

14. Review the options on the other two tabs (*DWF Properties* and *Project Information*), but do not make any additional changes at this time.

15. Click **Next**: Specify a file name and location for the DWFx file; click **OK**.

You now have a DWFx file with all the 2D sheets in it rather than a 3D model. This file can be used to print the project (either in an office/school or sent to a print shop). The file can also be an archive record of exactly what was sent out at each submittal point.

Next, you will take a quick look at the markup options in Autodesk *Design Review*.

16. Browse to the DWFx file just created and double click on it to open it.

   a. Or open *Design Review* and then use the **Open** command from the *Application* menu.

Notice, in Figure 15-3.5, the *Thumbnail* tab is selected on the left, which shows a small preview for each sheet in the file. Clicking on one of these previews opens that sheet in the larger viewing area.

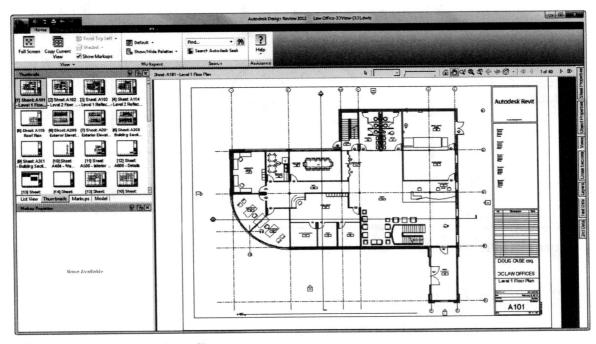

FIGURE 15-3.5 3D DWF sheets file

17. Make sure the *Level 1 Floor Plan*, **Sheet A101**, is selected.

18. Click the **Markup and Measure** tab on the *Ribbon*.

19. Use the **Cloud**, **Text** and **Line** tools from the *Draw* panel to add the markups shown in Figure 15-3.6.

20. **Save** the DWFx file (via the *Quick Access Toolbar*).

One unique feature about doing markups in DWFx format, rather than PDF, is that the markups can be referenced back into Revit. This workflow is useful when a senior designer does not use Revit, or a client or contractor is providing feedback on the design and emailing the DWFx file back to you. You will see how this works next.

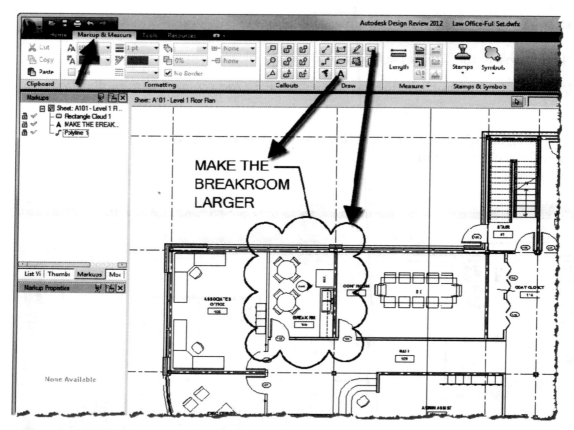

FIGURE 15-3.6 3D DWF sheets file with markups added

21. Open your Law Office file using Revit Architecture (or Structure or MEP).

22. From the *Insert* tab, select **DWF Markup**.

23. Browse to your DWF sheet file with the markups.

24. Select the file, and click **Open**.

25. Click **OK** (Figure 15-3.7).

26. Open **Sheet A101**.

Notice the markups added in *Design Review* are now in your Revit model (Figure 15-3.8).

27. Select the *Revision* cloud in the sheet view (Figure 15-3.8).

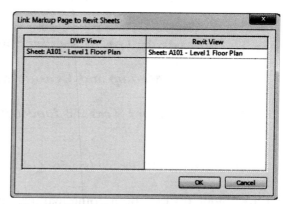

FIGURE 15-3.7 Import markup prompt

Notice the *Properties Pallet* provides information about the origin of the markup and its current status (i.e., *None*, *Question*, *For Review* and *Done*).

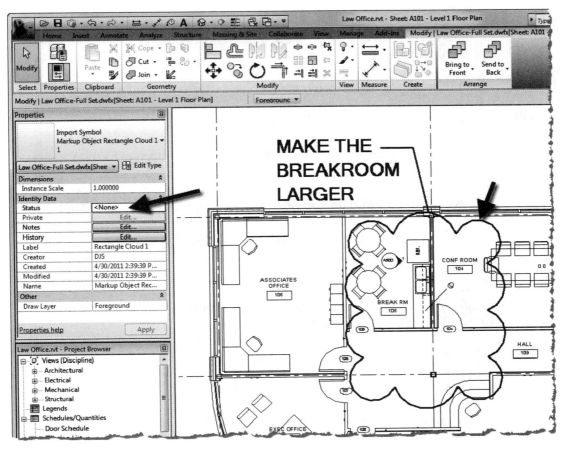

FIGURE 15-3.8 Markup overlay – revision cloud selected with properties shown

Follow these steps when you want to remove a *DWF Markup* link:

- **Manage → Manage Links**
- On the **DWG Markup** tab (Figure 15-3.9) select the markup and then click **Remove**.

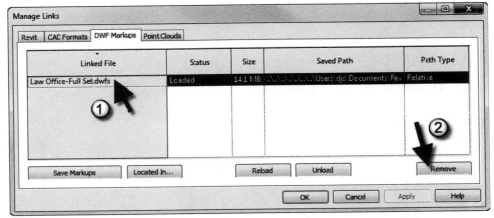

FIGURE 15-3.9 Markup overlay – revision cloud selected with properties shown

Self-Exam:

The following questions can be used as a way to check your knowledge of this lesson. The answers can be found at the bottom of this page.

1. You have to manually fill in the reference bubbles after setting up the sheets. (T/F)

2. *DWF* files are much larger than the Revit file. (T/F)

3. It is possible to see a listing of only the views that have not been placed on a sheet via the *Project Browser*. (T/F)

4. You only have to enter your name on one titleblock, not all. (T/F)

5. Use the _____ tool to create another drawing sheet.

Review Questions:

The following questions may be assigned by your instructor as a way to assess your knowledge of this section. Your instructor has the answers to the review questions.

1. You need to use a special command to edit text in the titleblock. (T/F)

2. The template you started with has only one Titleblock to choose from. (T/F)

3. You only have to enter the project name on one sheet, not all. (T/F)

4. The scale of a drawing placed on a sheet is determined by the scale set in that view's properties. (T/F)

5. You can save a list of drawing sheets to be plotted. (T/F)

6. You can be in any view when creating a *3D DWF* file. (T/F)

7. The reference bubbles will not automatically update if a drawing is moved to another sheet. (T/F)

8. On new sheets, the sheet number on the titleblock will increase by one from the previous sheet number. (T/F)

9. Image files cannot be placed on sheets. (T/F)

10. The *Sheet List* schedule never hides data. (T/F)

Appendix A
Autodesk® Revit® Architecture Certification Exam:

This appendix will cover the certification exam that is offered by Autodesk to help users prove their level of knowledge. This can be helpful when seeking an increase in salary from your current employer or to be listed on your resume.

Appendix A-1:
Introduction and Overview

In the competitive world in which we live it is important to stand out to potential employers and prove your capabilities. One way to do this is by passing the Autodesk Certification Exam. A candidate who passes this exam has credentials from the makers of the software that you know how to use their software. This can help employers narrow down the list of potential interviewees when looking for candidates.

When the exam is successfully passed a certificate signed by the CEO of Autodesk, Carl Bass, can be printed out and displayed at your desk or included with your resume; see example below. You also have access to an Autodesk logo for use on business cards or on flyers promoting your work; two examples are shown below as well. This author uses the professional logo in the front of books and in presentations.

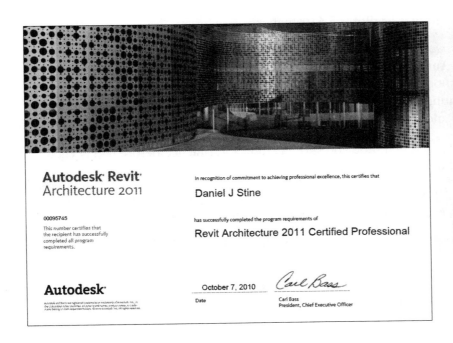

Autodesk offers two exams for Autodesk Revit Architecture; Certified Associate and Certified Professional.

- *Certified Associate*: This is an entry level exam to verify you have a basic understanding of the Revit user interface and functionality. The exam consists of 30 questions, many of which are multiple choice and some are matching or point and click (hotspot). The test is taken on a computer at any Autodesk Certification Center. The test must be completed in less than 60 minutes. You can check the required passing score at http://www.autodesk.com/certification and opening the document "Summary of Test Information". At the time of this printing, the cost for this exam is $75 (students: $25).

- *Certified Professional*: This is an intermediate level exam to prove you have a firm understanding of Revit Architecture's features. Before taking this exam, the associate exam must have been taken and successfully passed. Not only is this exam computer based, but it is also a hands-on Revit test. That is, you actually use the Revit Architecture software. There are twenty questions which have to be answered in 90 minutes. You can check the required passing score at http://www.autodesk.com/certification and opening the document "Summary of Test Information". At the time of this printing, the cost for this exam is $125 (students: $50).

Before taking the associate exam, you can prepare by working through this textbook and taking the assessment test online from home, work or school. One single assessment is available covering both exams. Note the following:

- *Associate Assessment Test*: This is a 67 question test. A time limit of 90 minutes is given but you can pause the test and restart it as often as you wish. At the time of this printing, the cost for this test is $20. Your computer must be Microsoft Windows based and have Internet Explorer 5.5 or higher.

- *Professional Assessment Test*: This test has 20 questions and a time limit of 90 minutes. You must have Autodesk Revit Architecture 2012 installed on your computer to answer the questions on the test; you can download the trial version if needed. At the time of this printing, the cost for this test is $30. Your computer must be Microsoft Windows based and have Internet Explorer 5.5 or higher.

Autodesk recommends how much time you should study and practice before taking each exam, the following highlights their recommendations:

- *Associate Exam*: A training session, plus 100 hours of hands on experience. Much of this requirement can be achieved by working through this book.

- *Professional Exam*: A training session such as this book, plus 400 hours of hands on experience.

  FYI: *This textbook may not cover every Revit concept or feature that could be asked on the exam. See the exam objectives on the next page.*

Be sure to manage your time while taking the test. Quickly go through the test and answer the questions that are easy to you, skipping the ones you are not immediately sure of. The exam software allows you to view a list of questions you have not answered or have marked. Once you have answered all the easy questions you can, then go back and think through those which remain. Do not exit the exam until you are completely finished, as you will not be able to re-enter the exam after that point.

Once the exam is finished you will immediately see your score. If you failed, you should note the objective areas where you missed questions and study those areas more before taking the test again. Be sure to print your score report and take it with you to study.

The following table shows you which chapter in this textbook you can study to gain knowledge that relates to the Associates certification exam.

Exam Section	Exam Objective	Chapter in this book
Revit Architecture Basics	- Describe the different types of building elements. - Describe project templates.	Chapters 2 and 6
Starting a Design	- Create a floor plan view and place building elements in it. - Describe levels and their uses.	Chapters 3 and 6
The Basics of the Building Model	- Describe wall properties. - Describe compound walls.	Chapters 3, 6 and 7
Loading Additional Building components	- Load component families and add components in a project.	Chapters 8, 10, 12 and 13
Viewing the Building Model	- Describe view properties. - Describe object visibility settings. - Describe the characteristics of a section view. - Describe 3D view types.	Chapter 2, 9 and 14
Using Dimensions and Constraints	- Describe permanent dimensions. - Describe constraints and the types of constraints.	Chapters 3, 6, 8 and 9
Developing the Building Model	- Describe floors. - Add and modify ceilings in a building model. - Describe roofs. * Create and modify curtain walls. - Create stairs and railings.	Chapters 2, 3, 6, and 7
Detailing and Drafting	- Describe callouts. - Describe text. - Describe tags. - Create detail views. - Describe drafting views.	Chapters 9 and 15
Construction Documentation	- Describe the properties of schedules. - Describe rooms. * Describe legends.	Chapters 9, 11 and 15
Presenting the Building Model	- Describe drawing sheets. - Describe titleblocks. * Describe revision clouds. - Describe renderings.	Chapters 14 and 15

* Topics not covered in this text due to the introductory focus. Refer to the Revit *Help System* for more information on these topics.

Resources:
- Autodesk Certification Site: www.autodesk.com/certification
- Autodesk Authorized Training Center (ATC): www.autodesk.com/atc
- Online Testing Service: http://autodesk.starttest.com

Exercise A-2:
Certification Exam Sample Test

This section is provided to help you test your Revit knowledge before paying to take the associates assessment test or the certification exam. The answers to the questions will be on the last page. Keep in mind these questions are meant to aid in preparing to take the associates exam and not the professional exam, as the latter is a hands-on software exam.

The questions are made up by the author and should not be memorized, thinking the same questions might be asked on the exam. These questions are similar in that they relate to the exam objectives listed on the previous page and are in the format described on the Autodesk website; multiple choice. You are provided 30 questions, equal to the actual exam. It is recommended that you time yourself so that you only have one hour.

It is recommended that you wait to take this sample test until you have completed all the tutorials in this book and on the DVD.

Directions: Answer the following questions in 60 minutes or less:

> *TIP:* The software helps you answer the question in the correct way. That is, if you are expected to select only one answer you can only select one; this looks like a circle. If you are expected to select all that apply, you select one or more square boxes:
>
> O = Select only one answer
> □ = Select all that apply

1. Which of the following is NOT a valid *Model Graphics Style*?
    - □ Shading with Edges
    - □ Realistic
    - □ Cartoon
    - □ Consistent Colors

2. How do you sort a schedule?
    - o Cut and Paste the rows
    - o Fields tab > Add Parameter
    - o Sorting/Grouping tab > Sort By
    - o Appearance tab > Sorting

3. What can you send a client or contractor that does not require them to have Revit and is a much smaller file; but only requires a free download to view?
    - o DXF file
    - o Word file (DOCx)
    - o DWF or DWFx file
    - o Excel file (XLSx)

4. Which are TRUE about a titleblock in Revit?
    ☐ "Sheet number" must be unique
    ☐ Are found on sheets
    ☐ Project title automatically appears on all sheets
    ☐ "Drawn by" field must be unique

5. Which TWO things are true about renderings
    ☐ Renderings never take more than 5 minutes
    ☐ Shadows are always created
    ☐ The sun always casts light
    ☐ The final rendering is not saved automatically

6. A *Room* has to be created in each level 1 plan you which to see a room tag in. For example: Level 1 Floor Plan, Level 1 Ceiling Plan, Level 1 Finish Plan.
    o   True
    o   False

7. What is NOT possible with the *Text* tool?
    o   Add a leader with no text
    o   Center justify the text
    o   Change the style
    o   Add multiple leaders

8. Which are true about *Detail Views*?
    ☐ The *View Scale* can be adjusted
    ☐ They update geometry when the model updates
    ☐ They are 2D drawings
    ☐ A different text tool is needed to add notes, compared to a model view

9. While sketching a stair, you can
    o   not adjust the stair width
    o   stop the sketch short of the specific level
    o   end up with various size risers
    o   not use snaps

10. Which are true about railings?
    ☐ Added automatically with stairs
    ☐ Can adjust height on options bar while sketching path
    ☐ Automatically added to edge of interior floor openings
    ☐ style can be changed, when selected, via the *Type Selector*

11. Select the item that can be loaded into the project from a file
    o   Wall
    o   Door
    o   Floor
    o   Roof

12. Which TWO views are automatically created when a level is added to a project
    - ☐ Floor plan
    - ☐ Detail view
    - ☐ 3D view
    - ☐ Ceiling plan

13. It is not possible to adjust the location of a ceiling grid once it is placed in the model.
    - ☐ True
    - ☐ False

14. Rows can be manually added to a schedule for items not found in the model.
    - o True
    - o False

15. Curtain walls can only have a consistent grid pattern.
    - o True
    - o False

16. Which are true statements about walls?
    - ☐ Tops can conform to underside of roof above
    - ☐ Corners and intersections automatically clean up with others of same type
    - ☐ Most detail shown while in *Coarse* detail level setting
    - ☐ Show heaver when they pass through the cut plane

17. Select the statements that are true about doors.
    - ☐ Doors may be placed in an elevation view
    - ☐ Doors can only be deleted in plan views
    - ☐ Doors are floor hosted
    - ☐ Doors can be deleted from the schedule

18. When a ceiling is added, the top of the ceiling is placed a distance from the floor that is specified in the *Properties Palette*.
    - o True
    - o False

19. Select the various constraints
    - ☐ Equality
    - ☐ Alignment
    - ☐ Pin
    - ☐ Length
    - ☐ Shared Parameter
    - ☐ Locked Dimension

20. Which statement is true about camera views?
    - ☐ The eye elevation cannot be adjusted
    - ☐ The target elevation can be adjusted
    - ☐ You cannot adjust how far into the model you see
    - ☐ Camera views can only be created form the *Ribbon*

21. If you delete a locked dimension you have the option to keep the constraint.
    - o True
    - o False

22. Which key do you use to be able to select elements which are overlapped?
    - ☐ Caps Lock
    - ☐ Alt
    - ☐ Tab
    - ☐ F6

23. Which are window family *Type Parameters*?
    - ☐ Window Sill
    - ☐ Width
    - ☐ Height
    - ☐ Type Mark

24. Where are newly created views listed?
    - o Options Bar
    - o Application Menu
    - o Ribbon
    - o Project Browser

25. You need to change the *Type Selector* to get different line options while using the *Detail Line* tool.
    - o True
    - o False

26. Which are components of the User Interface?
    - ☐ Options Bar
    - ☐ Application Menu
    - ☐ View Control Bar
    - ☐ Project Browser
    - ☐ Door Family

27. Which Statements are true about grid lines?
    - ☐ Two grids can have the same number
    - ☐ Show up automatically in elevation and section views
    - ☐ Start and end points will automatically align if drawn correctly
    - ☐ Grid heads and display on either end or both

28. Which statements are true about the rendering dialog?
    - ☐ The quality can be adjusted
    - ☐ Render time and quality are directly proportional
    - ☐ An image can be selected for the background
    - ☐ You can specify the season, summer, sprint, winter or fall.

29. A callout can be added in a plan, elevation or section view.
- ☐ True
- ☐ False

30. The default template is the preferred starting point for most projects.
- ☐ True
- ☐ False

ANSWERS:

1. Which of the following is NOT a valid *Model Graphics Style*?
   - o   Shading with Edges
   - o   Realistic
   - o   Cartoon
   - o   Consistent Colors

2. How do you sort a schedule?
   - o   Cut and Paste the rows
   - o   Fields tab > Add Parameter
   - o   Sorting/Grouping tab > Sort By
   - o   Appearance tab > Sorting

3. What can you send a client or contractor that does not require them to have Revit and is a much smaller file; but only requires a free download to view?
   - o   DXF file
   - o   Word file (DOCx)
   - o   DWF or DWFx file
   - o   Excel file (XLSx)

4. Which are TRUE about a titleblock in Revit?
   - ☐   "Sheet number" must be unique
   - ☐   Are found on sheets
   - ☐   Project title automatically appears on all sheets
   - ☐   "Drawn by" field must be unique

5. Which TWO things are true about renderings
   - o   Renderings never take more than 5 minutes
   - o   Shadows are always created
   - o   The sun always casts light
   - o   The final rendering is not saved automatically

6. A *Room* has to be created in each level 1 plan you which to see a room tag in. For example: Level 1 Floor Plan, Level 1 Ceiling Plan, Level 1 Finish Plan.
   - o   True
   - o   False

7. What is NOT possible with the *Text* tool?
   - o   Add a leader with no text
   - o   Center justify the text
   - o   Change the style
   - o   Add multiple leaders

8. Which are true about *Detail Views*?
   - ☐   The View Scale can be adjusted
   - ☐   They update geometry when the model updates
   - ☐   They are 2D drawings
   - ☐   A different text tool is needed to add notes, compared to a model view

9. While sketching a stair, you can
   - o   not adjust the stair width
   - o   stop the sketch short of the specific level
   - o   end up with various size risers
   - o   not use snaps

10. Which are true about railings?
    - o   Added automatically with stairs
    - o   Can adjust height on options bar while sketching path
    - o   Automatically added to edge of interior floor openings
    - o   style can be changed, when selected, via the *Type Selector*

11. Select the item that can be loaded into the project from a file
    - o   Wall
    - o   Door
    - o   Floor
    - o   Roof

12. Which TWO views are automatically created when a level is added to a project
    - ☐   Floor plan
    - ☐   Detail view
    - ☐   3D view
    - ☐   Ceiling plan

13. It is not possible to adjust the location of a ceiling grid once it is placed in the model.
    - o   True
    - o   False

14. Rows can be manually added to a schedule for items not found in the model.
    - o   True
    - o   False

15. Curtain walls can only have a consistent grid pattern.
    - o   True
    - o   False

16. Which are true statements about walls?
    - ☐   Tops can conform to underside of roof above
    - ☐   Corners and intersections automatically clean up with others of same type
    - ☐   Most detail shown while in *Course* detail level setting
    - ☐   Show heaver when they pass through the cut plane

17. Select the statements that are true about doors.
    - ☐ Doors may be placed in an elevation view
    - ☐ Doors can only be deleted in plan views
    - ☐ Doors are floor hosted
    - ☐ Doors can be deleted from the schedule

18. When a ceiling is added, the top of the ceiling is placed a distance from the floor that is specified in the *Properties Palette*.
    - ○ True
    - ○ False

19. Select the various constraints
    - ☐ Equality
    - ☐ Alignment
    - ☐ Pin
    - ☐ Length
    - ☐ Shared Parameter
    - ☐ Locked Dimension

20. Which statement is true about camera views?
    - ○ The eye elevation cannot be adjusted
    - ○ The target elevation can be adjusted
    - ○ You cannot adjust how far into the model you see
    - ○ Camera views can only be created form the *Ribbon*

21. If you delete a locked dimension you have the option to keep the constraint.
    - ○ True
    - ○ False

22. Which key do you use to be able to select elements which are overlapped?
    - ○ Caps Lock
    - ○ Alt
    - ○ Tab
    - ○ F6

23. Which are window family *Type Parameters*?
    - ☐ Window Sill
    - ☐ Width
    - ☐ Height
    - ☐ Type Mark

24. Where are newly created views listed?
    - ○ Options Bar
    - ○ Application Menu
    - ○ Ribbon
    - ○ Project Browser

25. You need to change the *Type Selector* to get different line options while using the *Detail Line* tool.
    - ○ True
    - ○ False

26. Which are components of the User Interface?
    - ☐ Options Bar
    - ☐ Application Menu
    - ☐ View Control Bar
    - ☐ Project Browser
    - ☐ Door Family

27. Which statements are true about grid lines?
    - ☐ Two grids can have the same number
    - ☐ Show up automatically in elevation and section views
    - ☐ Start and end points will automatically align if drawn correctly
    - ☐ Grid heads and display on either end or both

28. Which statements are true about the rendering dialog?
    - ☐ The quality can be adjusted
    - ☐ Render time and quality are directly proportional
    - ☐ An image can be selected for the background
    - ☐ You can specify the season, summer, sprint, winter or fall.

29. A callout can be added in a plan, elevation or section view.
    - ○ True
    - ○ False

30. The default template is the preferred starting point for most projects.
    - ○ True
    - ○ False

Index

Image below shows structural model created in Chapter 8.

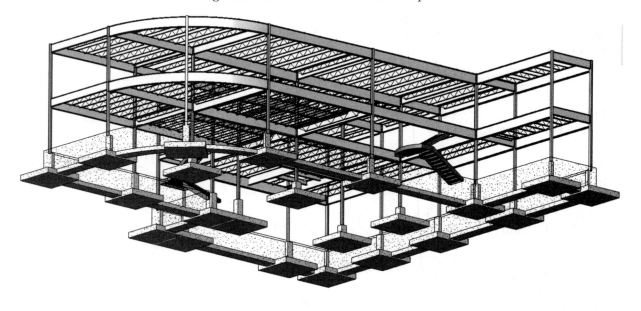